Chaucerian Polity

Absolutist Lineages and Associational Forms in England and Italy

Figurae

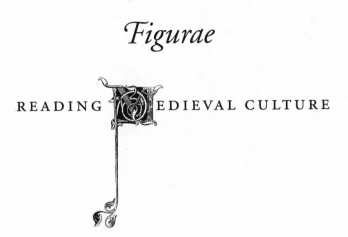

READING MEDIEVAL CULTURE

Chaucerian Polity

Absolutist Lineages and

Associational Forms

in England and Italy

David Wallace

Stanford University Press, Stanford, California, 1997

Stanford University Press
Stanford, California
© 1997 by the Board of Trustees of the
Leland Stanford Junior University
Printed in the United States of America

CIP data appear at the end of the book

Stanford University Press publications are distributed exclusively by
Stanford University Press within the United States, Canada, Mexico, and
Central America; they are distributed exclusively by Cambridge
University Press throughout the rest of the world.

FOR

Lilian Beryl Lucetta
and
Sidney John Wallace

PART OF THIS STORY

Contents

Plates

Preface

Experiences of time and space change and so challenge relations of diachronic
to synchronic emphasis within models of historical understanding. Those of
us living in the United States, plus others elsewhere tuning into its network
channels, are now offered limitless prospects for lateral imagining: global cov-
erage, around the clock. And yet the images on offer speak first to, and of,
an American public (as interpellated by American networks); whole regions,
almost whole continents, fail to figure in this picture. England (chiefly southern England, not necessarily including Scotland and Wales) now experiences
unprecedented connections with continental Europe: three hours by train
from London to Flanders or France. Yet this new sense of connectedness is
often voiced through reinvigorated assertions of cultural and political (economic is more difficult) insularity, yearnings for time-honored Englishness.
This forces, in turn, a new relationship to the past—conceived now as Heritage, fit for selective recycling. In the United States, the past is desired and
pursued with less urgency. When there is small encouragement to imagine
back fifty years, five hundred seems out of reach and tough to teach.

Bottled up in time and space, historicist criticism seems largely unre-
sponsive to such new contingencies, new disorientations. Under the impress
of New Historicism, English studies became more rather than less insular:
rather than developing a comparative historicism, critics have often settled for
national and monolingual frames of reference, even while calling for multicul-
tural approaches. Renaissance critics, with some exceptions, have expanded
their horizons westward (hence reinforcing rather than critiquing myths of
Anglocentric teleology) while ignoring continental Europe.[1] And the study of
Chaucer, to a surprising extent, still works within the foundational, nationalist parameters established by Victorian England.[2] The historical Chaucer
spoke many languages, encountered many dialects, and traveled extensively
throughout western Europe. Names such as Florence, Lombardy, Avignon,
Paris, Hainault, Flanders, Bohemia, and Tartary come charged with precisely evocative powers that still await full critical recuperation. Other areas of
Middle English studies could also profit from an expansion of horizons: 1381,

for example, can be understood as part of a European pattern of rebellion; and Margery Kempe may be studied in her movement through Europe and the world, rather than simply as a wife of Lynn and a subject of Lancastrian England.[3]

The insularity of historicist criticism in its renditions of space is complemented by the inertness of its temporal imaginings.[4] Hence we have been confronted with the paradoxical spectacle of synchronic historicism: attempts to generate historical explanation by making time, and hence history, stand still. Such crablike criticism, moving sideways from archival fragment to contemporary text, has served to reinforce traditional boundaries of literary periodization. This has particularly severe consequences for the period denoted as the Middle Ages. Renaissance critics are still generally content to locate the *medium aevum* as the far side of a paradigm shift that is never adequately explained and rarely even addressed but has always already happened. Although this has met spirited resistance from medievalists of late, the general effect of such *reactive* protests is to reinforce the primacy of the Renaissance paradigm in setting the period-making agenda. Such protests also tend to exaggerate the importance of such professional boundary wars. The disciplinary struggles that matter today are not those between medieval and Renaissance, but increasingly those between the culture of the historical present and *any* place and moment in the past.

In struggling to resist the deforming and constraining power of an aggressive and privileged paradigm, medievalists have much to learn from gender theory. Rather than engaging in forms of epistemic counteraggression—waging war on masculinist universalism—gender theorists have rather sought to develop "a different set of terms."[5] One particularly powerful set of terms has issued from the positive embrace of that which is framed pejoratively by the dominant culture (as, most famously, "queer").[6] Lower-case "medieval," continually redefined as that which must be expelled from upper-case "Renaissance," might similarly find cause for celebration precisely in the terms of its own supposed abjection. One of the most famous dicta of Jacob Burckhardt, the most influential of all Renaissance paradigm makers, proposes that in the Middle Ages, "man was conscious of himself only as a member of a race, people, party, family, or corporation—only through some general category."[7] Medievalists have countered this accusation by collecting and discussing an impressive range of medieval selfhoods.[8] But the reproof of "only as" may be adopted as proof of historical genius: in the Middle Ages, we might propose, people were conscious of themselves *as* members of a race, people, party, family, corporation, guild, craft, university, fraternity, sorority, nunnery, body of believers (conjoining the living and the dead), parish, household, and/or neighborhood. Medieval people, in short, experienced themselves as political subjects through the making and maintenance of associational forms. It may be that a coming to consciousness *through* such forms proves to be of more compelling interest (at our own particular political moment) than an individualism that would define itself by setting itself *against* every such "general category."

In speaking of medieval associational forms, however, we must continually guard against sentimental essentializing and atemporalizing of social structures. A particular collective body that proves expansive and welcoming during periods of economic boom may later prove hostile and exclusionary; acts of folly, viciousness, and stupidity may be achieved through collective action as well as by individual or despotic *diktat*.

Burckhardt, and Renaissance critics after him, take little interest in the particular forms and dynamics of medieval polity (or even in the process, foundational to their period-governed assumptions, of epochal transition). The terms "medieval" and "Renaissance," each suggestive of a free-standing finality, are themselves generally resistant to thoughts of historical transition. Attempts have been made to map and narrate putative spaces between them by, *inter alia*, religious polemicists, historians of state forms, historians of art, historians of religion, and Weberian sociologists. The most detailed account of this passage, however, has been generated by a Marxist historiography that would trace lines of development from the decline of feudalism, or bastard feudalism, to the rise of the absolutist state.[9] It is important to remember that absolutism, like feudalism or communism, is an abstract, teleological term that cannot be exactly applied to any particular historical regime. As a theoretical term, absolutism helps articulate something of the political transitions that occur, for example, between Richard II and Henry VIII. At the same time, we must acknowledge that absolutist lineages are plotted differently from one country to the next.[10] England, even during the massive and destructive centralization of power that occurs under Henry VIII, fits the absolutist model less perfectly than most European states. Richard II, who styled himself "entier Emperour de son roiaulme d'Engleterre" in 1397, might be described as a monarch with *entieriste*, if not absolutist, pretensions: but such claims were repudiated just two years later. Sir John Fortescue (c. 1394–c. 1476), in differentiating between absolute and limited monarchy, *dominium regale* and *dominium politicum et regale*, finds the political axiom *quod principi placuit, legis habet vigorem* (accepted in France) unacceptable to "the felowshippe that came in to this lande with Brute."[11] And some sixty years later, according to a remarkable passage of John Foxe's *Acts and Monuments*, a further attempt to adopt this same principle (by Thomas Cromwell, on behalf of Henry VIII) is firmly rejected.[12]

But rather than seeking to qualify further the terms of a political historiography, we might pause to ask: Whence this nervousness in the articulation of a broadly historiographical (rather than narrowly historicist) approach? During and immediately after the heyday of deconstruction, which coincides roughly with the rise of New Historicism, *grand récit* fell under suspicion and out of favor.[13] Few people today would tie themselves to a model of history envisaging, in Jean Baechler's words, "a linear and necessary evolution," one positing that "the only possible history is the one that in fact resulted."[14] Faith in "linear and necessary evolution" has led to historical disaster; accounts of one "possible history" have empathized with history's victors.[15] There is now heightened awareness of simultaneous historiographical trajectories, often running in different directions. The history of the Iberian peninsula, for example, is written differently for Jews, for Muslims, and for Christians, with different denotations of advance and retreat, conquest and Golden Age. Historians of medieval women (some perceiving a Golden Age, others not) trace trajectories different from those followed by historians of medieval men (as universal subjects) or by historians of medieval men *qua* men.

Disavowal of *grand récit* has typically been accompanied by a rejection of *longue durée*. This then fails to question the unfortunate academic habit of territorializing the past, dividing it into discrete professional fiefdoms (vigorously patroled and defended) through divisions of academic labor—medieval, Renaissance, Enlightenment, Victorian, modern, postmodern, and so on. Such carving up of the past, one senses uneasily, is distantly but distinctly complicit with (and is hence ill-qualified to critique) carving up of the world, the grandest European *récit* of all.[16]

Another factor that may weigh heavily in dissuading literary critics from enlarging their spatial, temporal, and historiographical parameters is fear of ridicule—the deepest and darkest of academic fears. When Fredric Jameson, for example, proclaims that "the human adventure is one," Geoff Bennington pops up to sneer at "the great 'human adventure' naiveties of Jameson."[17] But there are elements of wit and self-reflexive humor in Jameson's barefaced assertions, quite lost on Bennington, that are symptomatic of all intelligent historiography.[18] Jameson's *Political Unconscious*, it seems to me, is written in much the same style and spirit as those extraordinary sections of *Kapital* in which, in about thirty pages, Marx sets out to write the entire history of expropriated agrarian labor from late feudal times to his historical present. Working without the kind of archival resources that Weber had to draw upon, Marx strikes out with whatever weapons lie to hand: he begins with Adam biting the apple in the garden of Eden; he quotes historical data from the tenth edition of Macaulay's *History of England* while acknowledging Macaulay as "a systematic falsifier of history"; he tells an anecdote of how "the present Duchess of Sutherland entertained Mrs. Beecher Stowe, authoress of *Uncle Tom's Cabin*."[19]

The exuberant energy with which Marx strings out his argument bespeaks an awareness of its limitations: for although he can boast of letters fired off to newspapers and the odd "nice polemic," he can do nothing for the thousands of people who are, as he writes, being evicted from their landholdings.[20] Although it is nowhere so poignant as in these pages of *Kapital*, there is in all self-reflexive historiography a comparable sense of the gap between the all-inclusive pretensions of the project and what the writing of it can actually deliver. Engels's *Peasant War in Germany* acknowledges this gap straightforwardly and with disarming humor.[21] Raymond Williams, at the opening of his *Country and the City*, situates himself as a man in a muddy village gazing through the window at a horse (p. 3). And in the writings of Perry Anderson, this gap may be detected between the confidence of the seamless, undialogized prose and the tentative titles, which speak of "passages," "lineages," and "tracks."

The chief aspiration of a literary-historiographical criticism is to make visible, through an expansion of temporal and spatial parameters, relations and developments that would otherwise remain obscured or unconnected. It would also aim to repair one of the egregious defects of traditional historiography: blindness to gender and neglect of the historical experience of women.[22] This is achieved, in part, through the simple recognition that *all* historical criticism, consciously or not, takes place within the confining frame of grand historiographical metaphors; such metaphors, value-laden and gender-inflected, are thereby subjected to critical examination. Medieval political theory in particular can hardly complete a sentence without employing metaphors of marriage and union, passion and reason, bodies and body parts, male and female. Associational polities tend to deemphasize differences of gender (and class), whereas despotism intensifies them: but all such usages are always *about* the gendering of social relations.[23]

Exercise of the skills thought peculiar to literary critics, then, should facilitate collaborative rather than contestatory relations with professional historians. And all this should prove teachable, encouraging readings of paired and multiple texts that cross, and so examine, the boundaries of traditional periodization. The aim here is not to create a vantage point above the text from which the text—and the struggles of its protagonists—can be explained, or explained away. The aspiration is, rather, to restore the text to the movement of history; to recognize its own sense of precariousness in occupying a time and place that shifts even at the instant of its own articulation (which speaks, at least for me, to our own unsettled experience as historical subjects).[24]

It has been my privilege and pleasure to develop, discuss, and revise this book through my teaching at the University of Minnesota, Twin Cities. Particular thanks are due to the undergraduates who have read Chaucer with me and to the graduate students, in and around the Center for Medieval Studies, who have continually inspired me with their energy, dedication, sass, and brains. Shirley Garner, chair of the English Department, has both shared and enjoyed her responsibilities and so been the best chair I have known. Unanswerable questions, posed at various campuses, have stayed with me for months and years: thanks then to audiences at the University of Texas at Austin, Cambridge University (departments of English and Italian), Charles University (Prague), Dartmouth, Duke, Harvard, Loyola (Chicago), North Carolina (Chapel Hill), North Carolina State, Perugia, Queen Mary and Westfield College (London), Reiners Stiftung (Bad Homburg), Rochester, Stanford, Texas A&M, Trinity (San Antonio), Wisconsin (Madison and Milwaukee), and Yale. Thanks also to Wendy Steiner and new colleagues at Penn.

Seth Lerer and Karla Taylor returned deeply engaged, detailed, and extremely helpful readings of a long manuscript for Stanford; thanks, too, to an anonymous historian. My editor, Helen Tartar, has sustained me from start to finish with her vision, intelligence, confidence, and good humor. Ann Klefstad has made copy-editing a pleasurable and instructive *agon*. Particular debts are owed to the following people: David Aers, Jan Čermak, Helen Cooper, Barbara A. Hanawalt, Bruce Holsinger, Robin Kirkpatrick, Leah Marcus and her Texas Renaissance *cenacolo*, William P. Marvin, Anne Middleton, Lee Patterson, Derek Pearsall, Miri Rubin, Stephen B. Partridge, and James I. Wimsatt. Harvey Jackins and Susal Stebbins have encouraged me to think beyond academia; the late Elizabeth Salter, my first teacher of Chaucer, first taught me to think beyond national boundaries. Andrew Elfenbein and John Watkins, nonmedievalist colleagues and indispensable friends at Minnesota, read the entire manuscript to excellent effect "with knyf in hond." My intellectual debts to Rita Copeland, particularly in matters of rhetoric, hermeneutics, and translation, will become evident to anyone who persists with this book; debts personal and domestic cannot be counted. Paul Strohm, my *primo amico americano*, has read everything at least twice, in fragments and *seriatim*. I owe more than I can say to his peerless knowledge of archival sources, his openness to diverse theoretical approaches, our unending disagreements over synchronic/diachronic emphases, his ruthless editorial eye, and his perennial appetite for life.

Support from the National Endowment for the Humanities, the National Humanities Center, and the Paul W. Frenzel Chair has afforded me time and opportunity to research, write, and rewrite this book. Such a lengthy volume owes much to those who catalogue, advise, fetch, and manage in libraries. Hard-pressed staff at the Wilson Library, University of Minnesota, and the Perry-Castenada Library, University of Texas at Austin, have been extraordinarily and persistently helpful. More particular debts are owed to the British Library, the Corporation of London Records Office, the Guildhall Library, the Institute of Historical Research, the Public Record Office, and the Warburg Institute (London); Newbery Library (Chicago); Biblioteca Nazionale Centrale and Kunsthistorisches Institut in Florenz (Florence); Castello Sforzesco (Milan); and the Strahov Monastery (Prague). I owe much to the continuing hospitality of St. Edmund's College, Cambridge. I owe most to the Cambridge UL, ugliest and best of libraries.

Some paragraphs of Chapter 5 were first essayed in *Exemplaria* 2.1. Earlier versions of Chapters 6 and 8 appeared, respectively, in *Chaucer's England*, ed. Barbara Hanawalt (Minneapolis: University of Minnesota Press, 1992), 59–90; *Literary Practice and Social Change*, ed. Lee Patterson (Berkeley: University of California Press, 1990), 156–215. Sections of Chapter 11 first appeared in *Poetics: Theory and Practice in Medieval English Literature*, ed. Anna Torti (Cambridge: Boydell and Brewer, 1991), 117–30. Thanks are due to these editors for their input and to publishers for permission to reprint material. Grateful acknowledgment for the reproduction of visual material is also extended to the following: Art Resource (New York); Biblioteca Nazionale Centrale, Florence; George Braziller, Inc.; The British Library; St. George's Basilica, Prague; Shrewsbury Museums; Dean and Chapter of Westminster.

My parents, whose extraordinary lives bring together urban and agrarian experiences that stretch back for centuries, provide the surest ground and inspiration for my writing. To them this book is dedicated.

Chaucerian Polity

*Absolutist Lineages and Associational Forms
in England and Italy*

Introduction

Vers un nouvel humanisme . . .
— Frantz Fanon, *Peau noire, masques blancs*

Chaucer's encounters with the great Trecento authors offer extraordinary opportunities for the reading, testing, and dismantling of time-honored terms such as "medieval," "Renaissance," and "humanism." No magic curtain separated "medieval" London and Westminster from "Renaissance" Florence and Milan; all sites were interlinked for Chaucer (and, indeed, through Chaucer) as part of a transnational nexus of capital, cultural, mercantile, and military exchange. In 1373 Chaucer traveled to Florence on a trade mission. Between 1374 and 1386 he served as controller of the wool custom and wool subsidy in the port of London, a position that brought him into frequent contact with dozens of Italians. In 1378 he traveled to Lombardy, seeking to enlist the aid of Bernabò Visconti, the Milanese despot, and Sir John Hawkwood, a mercenary captain, in England's interminable war with France.[1] In visiting Florence and Lombardy, Chaucer was exposed to the most crucial material and ideological conflict of the Italian Trecento: the conflict between republican *libertas* and dynastic despotism. Physical warfare broke out periodically as Florence fought to keep the Visconti out of Tuscany; but ideological warfare raged continuously, as poets, propagandists, and political theorists strove to expose and deride the weaknesses of the opposing regime. Chaucer, I shall argue, read and interpreted the works of Dante, Boccaccio, and Petrarch within (and as part of) the framework of this conflict: Dante and Boccaccio he associated with Florentine polity, and Petrarch with Lombardy.

Trecento Florence affords the most celebrated example of what Marx hails as "the most brilliant achievement of the Middle Ages, the existence of independent city-states."[2] Trecento Lombardy represents the force that will ultimately destroy or subsume this achievement and comparable achievements of associative polity across Europe: Milan under Bernabò and Gian Galeazzo Visconti is the first, prototypically imperfect, absolutist state of modern times. In the Florentine-Milanese framework, then, we have the extraordinary prospect of a conflict fought out between earlier and later phases of a single historical paradigm: "Their dates are the same: their times are separate."[3] This paradigm also offers an interpretive framework spanning fourteenth-century and sixteenth-century England; the passage from Edward III to Elizabeth I, Chaucer to Shakespeare, may be plotted and tested beneath this Italian apex.

Florence typically celebrated its own sense of republican *libertas* by developing what we might term an associational ideology, suggesting that all inhabitants of the city-state share equal footing on a lateral plane. Such communal ideology may be developed in cell-like local structures (such as parish guilds) and reproduced through larger ones, such as city-oligarchies, city-states, and (ultimately) nations. Such communities are always to some extent imagined, exclusionary, and (between one group and the next) hierarchical; such contradictions are recognized by their very need for an ideological gloss. They contain many features that survive, or may be generalized, over space and time: the English guilds described in the returns of 1389 have much in common with those recorded by the certificates of 1546 and 1548. But they are also subjected to differing historical pressures: the guilds of 1389 survive, whereas in the 1540s thousands of guilds and chantries are despoiled and abolished. The mechanisms of Tudor statecraft that prompted and gave teeth to the 1547 Chantries Act may be traced back to forms and procedures pioneered under northern Italian despotisms of the late Trecento. The chief ideological vector here is vertical, one-way, and downward-descending: the king or duke unifies, through the power of his rule, a nation of individual *subditi domini*. The vertical subordination of subject to monarch generates ideological forms that, like their associational counterparts, are reproduced at both local and national levels. This process is well underway in Chaucer's lifetime. The statute 25 Edward III st. 5, c. 2 (1352) likens violence of subject against king to that of servant against master, layman or religious against prelate, and wife against husband; all of these acts of violence up the vertical axis are redefined as treason, a political crime.[4]

The most powerful instantiation of associational ideology in Chaucer comes through the formation of the pilgrim *compagnye* at the opening of the *Canterbury Tales*. This process of group formation, where the right to exist *as a group* is simply assumed from within rather than conferred from without, represents a singular moment of political confidence that will not be repeated on English territory. Nothing like this is conceivable on the Shakespearean stage; indeed, associational forms in Shakespeare (particularly those featuring a promiscuous mix of genders and social classes) are always subjected to pressure by an exterior, hierarchical gaze. The vertical vectors of the *Clerk's Tale*, however, find countless analogues in later centuries. This fable of despotic husband and lord and concessive wife and subject arrives ahead of its time, to judge from Chaucer's critique of the neohumanist Walter, but it is a tale that looks forward to a prosperous and more accepting future. The *Clerk's Tale* and the *General Prologue* may be taken to represent the political axes of Chaucerian fiction; his other fictions may be plotted within their vertical and horizontal planes. But even these two limit texts attest to the secret of all such ideological axes: their mutual dependence. Even the *Man of Law's Tale*, a narrative that seems perfect in its realization of hierarchical and hierocratic order, cannot even begin until such order is crossed by an archetypal associative form: a guild of merchants.

By this point, I hope it is clear that although my subject is "Chaucerian polity," my method does not entail the construction of a theoretical paradigm from the categories of medieval political thought that will then be carried to the text of Chaucer.[5] Most attempts of this kind have not been convincing. Their general effect is the mechanical subjection of Chaucer's text to a pre-fashioned theoretical gridwork, thereby squeezing the life, the spontaneous intelligence, from the poetry. The very act of constructing such a gridwork signals a basic failure to understand the nature of politics. Terms such as "the common good" and "common profit" resist stabilization, varying their meaning with each instance of deployment.[6] To read a history of medieval political thought *seriatim* is to be struck by how medieval political treatises are typically concerned to produce not a timeless statement but one of circumstantial value, to intervene in the specific struggle of a specific secular or religious ruler against a specific enemy at a particular moment.[7] The lexicon of political thought is of fundamental importance in providing tropes, motifs, and building blocks for such interventions. But each intervention is peculiarly a product of its own moment; it would be foolish, for example, to derive a general theory of papal power from the writings of Augustinus Triumphalis (who argues that a pope assumes an angelic body at the moment of his consecration).[8] The most skilled narrators of the history of political thought, like the best historiographers, possess the skills and techniques of gifted literary critics.[9] And this should encourage us, as literary critics, not to carry political schemata to the literary text but rather to read the text as if it were its own politics (developed through its specific envisioning of possible social relations). The chief subject of "Chaucerian polity," then, is the poetry and prose of Chaucer.

~

The opening chapter of this book establishes Chaucer within a continuous, much-traveled nexus of mercantile, military, mercenary, and artistic exchange. It follows him first to Florence—which struggled to integrate an associative polity of quite extraordinary inclusiveness—and then to Milan and Pavia, home to the despots or tyrants who imbue the name of "Lumbardye," in Chaucer, with such sinister potency. The writings and authorial legends of Boccaccio and Petrarch are considered in conjunction with other forms of cultural production—street poetry, *poesia d'arte*, manuscript illumination, deployments of public space, forms of devotion—that helped articulate the Florentine-Lombard divide in the late Trecento. Historiographies subsequently erected upon the structuring tensions of this divide, so crucial to our own working definitions of "medieval," "Renaissance," and "humanist," may thus be subjected to informed interrogation. Does humanism represent, as in Hans Baron's account, a heroic rearguard defense of communal liberties against the historical inevitability of despotism? Or, as Jacob Burckhardt long ago insisted, does humanist culture first evolve as an attempt, deliberately nurtured by despots, to ornament new faces of princely power with mystifying suggestions of legitimacy?[10] Chaucerians should no longer think themselves extraneous to such discussions; indeed, since the historical Chaucer encountered Italian texts within the structuring confines of the Florentine-Lombard struggle, the texts of Chaucer should become required reading for any future theorists of medieval/Renaissance periodization.

The next two chapters examine the act of political imagining with which the *Canterbury Tales* begins: the deliberate and painstaking formation of an associational form, a *compagnye* or *felaweshipe*. The first of a series of authorial signatures is articulated in this process, one that sustains the artistic confidence of *Troilus and Criseyde*, suggests anxiety and unease in operating within a complex division of labor, and glimpses the saving power of wifely eloquence. English guilds, which make themselves visible to central authority at a moment of heightened political tension (1388–89), are considered as a source of schooling in associative behavior. The distinctiveness of such schooling, it is argued, helps account for some salient differences between Chaucerian and Boccaccian realizations of collective behavior. Finally, in the first of a series of sight lines to the English sixteenth century, we note how the supposed obsolescence of Chaucerian fiction coincides with Tudor spoliations of guild and chantry cultures.

Although no claims are pressed for strict or programmatic sequencing, subsequent chapters situate themselves along this trajectory leading from associational to absolutist forms. Chapter 4, however, departs egregiously from this sequence, recognizing that Chaucer, in his very first Fragment, stages an egregious act of political rupture. Although the Miller's determination to speak after the Knight is generally considered as the defining rebellious act of Fragment 1, it is in fact the *Knight's Tale* that effects the decisive break: for, having constructed an associational form with such painstaking care in his *General Prologue*, Chaucer then moves abruptly to consider the unpicking or unraveling of associational bonds under a ruler who refuses to countenance any form of political *felaweshipe*. One particularly problematic aspect of Thesian polity is the absence of wifely counsel. In attempting to assess the costs and consequences of silencing Hippolita, we turn to Shakespeare: a brilliantly perceptive reader who provides informative glossing of Chaucer's enterprise even while attempting to push him back into the artisanal, guild-based culture from which—in the *General Prologue*—he has just precariously emerged.

The next two chapters address the country and the city, interconnected sites of prime importance for historiographical narrative. Reference both to the Italian Trecento and to the English sixteenth century—different times, different places, same story—confirms the strangeness of Chaucerian representation. We discover, in Chaucer, a countryside empowered and enchanted and a city that, as an imaginative or ideological construct, fails to cohere even as it is called into existence. Chapter 7, on the Constance story, finds in the complex notion of *creauncing*, in the internal spaces of cathedral and chapter house, in Dominican dialectic and in English legal discourse, continuous interplay between the rationalizations and promises of theological schemata and mercantile wealth. Boccaccio's Constance *novella* takes us far in the future direction of European expansionism while never quite losing sight of Chaucer's *Tale*. Both narratives recognize a crucial role, within a newly restless and productive world, for the invention and transmission of narratives, *novelle* and *tidynges*.

When Chaucer elects to authorize himself as a practiced producer of *tidynges* and tales, he chooses a Man of Law to frame the identification (2. 45–96). And when he decides to speak seriously *in propria persona*, he turns again to a lawyer, the Italian *causidicus* Albertano of Brescia. Albertano was an urban professional, dedicated to nurturing a fragile city-state culture in his native Lombardy while protecting it from the ruinous effects of magnate violence. This noble attempt met with an unhappy—one might say Boethian— ending, succumbing to the violence that by Chaucer's time had become synonymous with "Lumbardye." [11] It is, nonetheless, from the *Liber consolationis et consilii* of Albertano that the most powerful and distinctive aspect—or tool, or weapon—of Chaucerian polity develops: wifely eloquence. Chaucer envisions wifely rhetoric as uniquely capable of moving individual bodies, and hence social ones, to good or bad ends. His *Melibee* demonstrates how, through the timely exercise of *ars tacendi* and *ars dicendi*—that is, silence and speech—the wife in the household may prevent masculine violence from disrupting the public domain. His *Manciple's Tale*, paired with the *Melibee* through common debts to Albertano, explores the fate of wife and household once the same *artes* have been misapplied. This tale, told by the minor law court official with whom the pilgrim Chaucer shares half a line (1.544), represents the last poetic word of the *Canterbury Tales*.

Whereas the *Manciple's Tale* (Chapter 9) sees a godlike ruler bring on disaster by stepping momentarily into tyranny, the *Clerk's Tale* (Chapter 10) imagines tyranny sustained as a form of state. Rhetoric, under such a regime, is arrogated to the control of a masculine authority—a masculine way of looking—that takes the female body (with which rhetoric is traditionally associated) as its object. Such strange, counterintuitive procedures may be imaged and dramatized through an intimate collaboration of legend-hungry despot and legend-laden rhetor; each sustains the other in the myth that some men—great poets, great rulers—possess powers of sight and insight denied to the rest of humanity. Such claims, explored through the "Lumbardye" of Chaucer's *Clerk's Tale*, come dramatically unraveled in the "Lumbardye" of his Merchant.

It is evident from Fragment 4 that Chaucer recognizes the ambition and allure of Petrarchan *Latinitas*, its aspiration to save textuality from the vagaries and erosions of place and time, even as he elects to return the Griselde story to its vernacular origins. My last two chapters intensify this exploration of humanism, or *humanisms*: for the writings of Boccaccio and Petrarch advance very different political agendas. Petrarch, in his *De viris illustribus*, allures great men with the promise of textual immortality. Boccaccio, in his *De casibus virorum illustrium*, repudiates this promise (and this cult of great men) by using his *exempla* to pressurize, hence destabilize, the political present that such men would dominate. Chaucer, in his *Monk's Tale*, first recognizes the alluring promise of a "myghty man" (as his Host falls for his Monk) before revealing the inability of such men to sustain such fantasies, especially in the face of death. The *Monk's Tale* articulates a powerful and conscious affirmation of the Boccaccian paradigm; the *Legend of Good Women*, however, parts company with the gender politics of its Boccaccian source. Women are represented in Boccaccio's *De mulieribus claris* as creatures fit for recreational contemplation once the security of public life has been assured; women such as Alceste, in Chaucer's *Legend*, prove vital to the business of public life.

In attempting to live within the pressured ambit of absolute power, within the immediate gaze of a godlike (but emotionally fallible) masculine monarch, Chaucer prompts comparisons with Petrarchan rather than Boccaccian poetics. There is, in fact, a Petrarchan precedent for Chaucer's *Legend of Good Women*: a short treatise *de laudibus feminarum* written by Petrarch for an Anne of Bohemia. The Anne of Bohemia who married Richard II, I shall argue, proves to be a historical surrogate—by which I do not mean patron—of unparalleled importance within the imaginative economy of Chaucerian poetics. Her death in 1394 thus comes as a shattering blow to such poetics, precipitating the rewriting of the F *Prologue*, which had evoked so brilliantly a sense of current occasion, into the bookish pastness and finality of G. Here, then, we see the courtly Chaucer opting for the Petrarchan option of a text saved from time, but only at the point at which the most vital force of Chaucerian polity—wifely eloquence—disappears.

This final chapter widens spatial parameters further, moving from England and Italy to Bohemia and Prague. This allows us to consider how the Prague connection may have served as a conduit bringing Italian culture to England; it also suggests how and why the internationalist dimensions of Chaucer's poetics might have proved welcome to Bohemians entering a foreign land. Such expansion of the spatial frame forms the necessary complement to a longer diachronic view; both perspectives need to be brought to the analysis of texts and sources as well as to the movement of people. The *Filostrato* used to be studied as an immigrant text that washed up on English shores carrying no cultural or political baggage; Anne of Bohemia, similarly, has been regarded as "only" a sixteen-year-old girl (albeit the daughter of an emperor and empress) who brought nothing with her. Source studies have often tended, myopically, to study only the most recent avatar of a textual tradition rather than the tradition itself. Chaucer's *Melibee* needs to be considerd not only as a translation of its immediate antecedent, the French version of Renauld of Loens, but also as part of an extraordinary shape-shifting tradition involving hundreds of manuscripts. Chaucer's *Monk's Tale* must be read not only with reference to Boccaccian *De casibus* but also in conjunction with Petrarchan *De viris*, the project against which, within a shared frame of cultural reference, Boccaccio stages his political struggle.

The fact that there was such a struggle—one that the texts of Chaucer read with brilliant fluency—is soon forgotten in standard evocations of the Renaissance. These soon lose all purchase on specific time and place, locating themselves only in the singular personhood of Petrarch, a Petrarch-without-Boccaccio. Here is a typical example:

The Renaissance discovered itself with a new, intense consciousness of rupture and loss. Antiquity was far in the past, cut off from it by all the obscurity of the *medium aevum* between them, yet far in advance of the crude barbarism which had prevailed throughout the supervening centuries. Petrarch's passionate call, at the threshold of the new age, proclaimed the vocation of the future: "This slumber of forgetfulness will not last forever: after the darkness has been dispelled, our grandsons will be able to walk back into the pure radiance of the past." [12]

This, *mirabile dictu*, is Perry Anderson; vigilant attention to the particularities of historical struggle—a vigilance we look for, above all, in a materialist criticism—seems to fly out of the window the moment Petrarch enters the room. Anderson, remarkably, does not think to connect Petrarchan sensations of rupture, loss, and being cut off, with the form of polity for which Petrarch labored throughout his mature working life. This book, then, explores that connection as part of a project that would suspend belief in cultural partitions such as "medieval," "Renaissance," and "humanist." There is nothing going on in Petrarch and Boccaccio that cannot, with profit, be brought into intelligible relation with Chaucer; and there are, in Chaucer, vast resources for articulating what happens within and between Italian men.

Chapter **I**

Chaucer in Florence and Lombardy

Chaucer's encounter with Italy has long been romanticized as the crossing of an invisible but magical boundary (one that inevitably, if not explicitly, evokes the imaginary medieval/Renaissance divide). Here, for example, Donald Howard imagines how Chaucer's crossing of the Alps late in 1372 brings him to a new year, fresh territory, and a new state of mind:

So, as he arrived in the north of Italy at about New Year's, Chaucer must have felt a kind of joy he had scarcely known before. The travail at a certain point was behind him. Descending slowly through the foothills of Savoy, the party at last came down into temperate lowlands where there was no snow, where the days would have seemed longer than in England.[1]

The attitude conventionally evoked for Chaucer's first encounter with Florence is one of open-mouthed stupor; like an overheated academic tourist or a freshly arrived immigrant, Chaucer is imagined gazing in astonishment at a dazzling succession of buildings, paintings, and piazzas.[2] But it is illogical at once to celebrate Chaucer as an informed reader of Italian texts while representing him as a bedazzled voyeur in the face of all other aspects of Italian cultural production.[3] Since Chaucer was chosen to travel to Italy for his ability to read political signs and to help facilitate political negotiations, he was surely primed to read all cultural and civic forms (buildings, paintings, piazzas, and literary texts) as particular expressions of and clues to specific political communities. And he had not, of course, crossed any magical dividing line that would befuddle a "medieval" imagination with "Renaissance" cultural forms. He was operating within a familiar international framework of magnate militarism and merchant exchange: capital, warfare, and wool.

Chaucer's understanding of how literary activity might form part of greater cultural projects was not developed only by his encounters on Italian territory. On his diplomatic mission to Paris in 1377, for example, he had ample opportunity to observe how court-sponsored translations into French were furthering the nationalist ambitions of Charles V.[4] But Chaucer's visits to Italy in the 1370s are of particular importance for three good reasons. First, they allowed him not only to discover the texts of Dante, Boccaccio, and

Petrarch but also to situate them within the cultural and political contexts that they were designed to affirm or critique; he was thus able to imagine them *at work*, as cultural forces, before translating them to England as written or remembered texts.

Second, Florence and Milan offered stabilized and thus clarifying visions of basic political options glimpsed more fleetingly in London and West-minster. Florence practiced government through a regime that celebrated merchant capital, banned magnates from office, and justified itself through an ideology of *libertas* and all-inclusive association. Milan subordinated all aspects of commercial, cultural, and religious life to the will of a single, military-minded ruler who sought to invest himself with a mysterious, even godlike, authority. Chaucer, famously, attempted to inhabit two such worlds at once: as the son of a merchant who worked with merchant capitalists; and as a royal appointee, a member of the king's affinity, and poet at the fringe of court.[5] Florence and Milan, then, presented Chaucer with visions of pos-sible and alternative English futures. The Florentine option was realized most impressively during the early years of Richard's reign, when the London mer-chant capitalists made considerable efforts to share in central government.[6] They succeeded in outperforming the magnates not only in financing the war with France but also in fighting it.[7] They soon fell victim, however, to re-sentment by magnates (who saw war and government as their business) and a rapacious Crown. In June 1392, Richard resorted to the extreme measure (not seen since the time of Edward II) of imprisoning the mayor and sheriffs and taking the government of London into his own hands. Richard subsequently demanded "blank charters," sealed confessions of guilt, that subordinated London, certain counties, and hundreds of individuals to his own will and pleasure.[8] Such tyrannical tendencies were memorably imaged by the body-guard of 311 Cheshire archers that attended the king in seven *vigilia*, day and night.[9] The spectral possibilities of Lombardy, a territory explored in some detail in Chaucerian fiction, grew more topically alarming as Chaucer grew older. The values of association, despite the vigor of their initial exemplifica-tion in the *Canterbury Tales*, come tinged with suggestions of nostalgia, loss, and betrayal.

Third, the physical and ideological conflict played out between Florence and Milan during Chaucer's lifetime has proved to be the most crucial site for the construction of medieval/Renaissance paradigms in subsequent historiog-raphy (and, by extension, in literary periodization). For Burckhardt, the most influential of all theorists of the Renaissance, it is the Visconti who first exem-plify the new and ruthless individualism that will overwhelm the corporate and collective structures of the Middle Ages (most famously exemplified by the Florentine regime of 1343–78). Since it has not been considered appropri-ate to apply this new individualist paradigm to England before the sixteenth century, Chaucer has conventionally been defined as always already a medi-eval poet, walled off within a *hortus inclusus* of insular, medieval culture.[10]

And yet Chaucer, we have noted, traveled to both Florence and Lombardy and continued to work within the wider international nexus (capital, warfare, and wool) within which each of these polities was situated. By following Chaucer into the historical and political contexts of late Trecento Italy, then, we come to interrogate all a priori claims made for those mystifying, freefloating cultural markers, "medieval" and "Renaissance." Perhaps no magical divide (or Alpine peak) actually stands between Chaucer and Shakespeare; perhaps the terms "medieval" and "Renaissance" might be assigned to the trash can of historiography (and hence of literary history).

Chaucer in London: Capital, Warfare, and Wool

The 494 items that make up the *Chaucer Life-Records* suggest that Chaucer was schooled in social mobility from an early age, and that he became a skilled reader of political signs. As a teenager he moved from a family of London vintners (immigrants from Ipswich) to service in a Lancastrian household and thence to the royal household in 1367. He remained on good terms with John of Gaunt, the implacable enemy of the London victualing trades, despite his own victualing background. He avoided being lynched in 1381 (by peasants or Londoners) as an associate of Gaunt. When factional politics became perilous in the early 1380s (and his fellow author Thomas Usk grew ambitious), Chaucer withdrew to Kent to wait out the political storm. Usk was beheaded at Tyburn; Chaucer survived to represent the commons of Kent as "knight of the shire" in the turbulent parliament of 1386. He avoided prosecution by the Appellants in 1388 when three men he had worked with—Brembre, Burley, and Tresilian—were executed.[11] He was granted funds for the purchase of "unius goune de scarleta longa" by Henry of Derby in 1395–96; on May 4, 1398, he was issued a grant of royal protection as he went about "divers parts of England on the king's arduous and pressing business."[12]

Chaucer's adroit movement between groups differs markedly from that of those Elizabethans considered by Richard Helgerson as "writers of England" (authors of various kinds of nationalist discourse, including Spenser, Camden, Hooker, Hakluyt, Speed, and Shakespeare). Such "transitional men," Helgerson argues, were "uprooted by education and ambition from familiar associations and local structures"; they were hence "free—and compelled by their freedom—to imagine a new identity based on the kingdom or nation."[13] Chaucer's skilled mobility suggests the historical possibility of movement between particular social groups that need not require the final repudiation of any one of them. Chaucer moves within and between constituent parts of a (less coherently defined) national totality rather than deriving an identity from "the nation"; he remains "free" to reassume a place (as he does through the imaginative project of the *Canterbury Tales*) within "familiar associations and local structures."

The most onerous and prestigious public position Chaucer ever held was

Clerk of the King's Works: from July 1389 until June 1391, he was responsible for construction and repair at the Tower of London, Westminster Palace, the mews at Charing Cross, and at seven royal manors, including Eltham and Sheen. This required him to hire craftsmen, purchase and store supplies, pay honest workmen, and pursue and imprison delinquents. But the most formative and extensive period of Chaucer's public career was his twelve-year stint at the London customhouse (1374–85). Chaucer's mercantile background obviously helped qualify him for the job: both his father and grandfather had held minor offices in the customs service; one of his father's former business associates, Adam de Bury (now mayor of London), leased him the dwelling over Aldgate rent-free for life on May 10, 1374. As controller of the export tax, or customs, on wool, sheepskins, and leather, Chaucer occupied a position of considerable power and importance that held him poised most delicately between the interests of city and court. It was the responsibility of the controller, a royal appointee, to monitor the activities of the collectors who recorded each day's shipments from the port of London and the customs or subsidy that was charged on them. These collectors, drawn from the powerful merchant capitalist class, used customs revenue as security on the large loans they made to the king. Nicholas Brembre, John Philpot, and William Walworth all served as collector-creditors while Chaucer was in office. All three were Members of Parliament; all three accompanied Richard II to Smithfield for his confrontation with Wat Tyler in 1381 and were knighted for their valor. All three, incidentally, were neighbors of the Chaucer family in Vintry Ward. Controller and collectors met for a thorough "view" or audit each Michaelmas.[14]

The period of Chaucer's tenure as customs controller was especially sensitive. Although the economy was contracting, the early years of Richard II saw the highest (inflation-adjusted) volume of revenue exaction recorded by the English state in the three hundred years between Henry II and Henry VI.[15] Customs provided the chief source of revenue, and the wool export tax provided the state with its most remunerative and dependable source of income.[16] Chaucer's tenure of the controllership, which lasted longer than that of any of his contemporaries, placed him at a vital intersection of the economic and political powers of city and Crown (with magnate and monkish wool-growers as interested observers). Chaucer was bound up in a nexus of capital, warfare, and wool, merchants, magnates, and Crown: the capital generated on taxation levied on wool grown by magnates (and monks) and exported by merchants was channeled by the Crown to the magnates who would fight the war and the merchants who would furnish supplies for it. This profitable arrangement formed part of a greater international network in which Italians played the most significant role (apart from the French, of course, who showed a willingness to fight and so prolong the war). Chaucer's work brought him into contact with the king's Florentine financiers, Matthew Cheyne (Cennini) and Walter de Bardes, a member of the Bardi (the company that Boccaccio and his father had once worked for). The Bardi of Florence had warehouses and offices in ten Italian cities, as well as in London, Avignon, Barcelona, Bruges, Cyprus, Constantinople, Jerusalem, Majorca, Marseilles, Paris, Rhodes, Seville, and Tunis. Italian companies had financed English wars against the French, conducted money exchanges, and collected taxes in English counties for many generations.[17] By the time Chaucer took office, Italians were the only group to take part in the export of English wool. This brought Chaucer into daily contact with Italians, since the controller was obliged to be personally present on the quay whenever wool was weighed, and to keep his records in his own hand.[18]

The year before Chaucer became controller of customs, he traveled to Genoa with two Italians, John de Mari and Sir James de Provan, in order to negotiate the designation of a special seaport for the use of Genoese merchants. Chaucer then went on to Florence to conduct the king's "secrees busoignes": he may have been briefed to negotiate with the Bardi or with other Italian banking houses; he might possibly have been concerned with the procurement of eight or ten seagoing vessels for Edward III, who was soon to launch a new invasion of France.[19] Five years later, in 1378, Chaucer was granted a deputy at the wool quay and payment from the War Funds to enable him to accompany Sir Edward de Berkeley on a mission to Lombardy "pur ascunes busoignes touchantes lexploit de nostre guerre;"[20] Treasurers Walworth and Philpot were informed that the young King Richard required Chaucer and Berkeley to travel "en nostre message sibien au sire de Melan Barnabo come a nostre cher et foial Johan Haukwode."[21] Chaucer's encounters with Italian literary cultures, then, were made within a familiar international nexus of capital, mercantile activity, and warfare. In Florence and Lombardy, Chaucer found the most powerful socioeconomic forces of English society—merchant capital and magnate militarism—distinctly exemplified in separate forms of polity and set in a framework of permanent antagonism. Florence defined its liberties by referring to their absence in Lombardy; the Visconti argued for the necessity of absolutism by pointing to the chaotic state of politics in Florence. Physical warfare broke out periodically; ideological warfare ran continuously, produced and sustained through all aspects of civic life. Our analysis of this conflict begins with the Florentine regime, which was founded after all social classes united to overthrow the short-lived despotism of Walter of Brienne, duke of Athens, in 1343.

Chaucer in Florence, 1373: Guild Culture (and Female Slaves)

The notion that newcomers to Florence found themselves bedazzled by art and beauty was one that Florentines were anxious to accentuate, especially since Milan, by contrast, was large, dirty, and noisy. Dino Compagni, writing some sixty years before Chaucer's visit, asserted that many visitors came from

distant countries just to gaze in wonder upon Florence, rather than to trans-
act any business.[22] Chaucer, who arrived to do business, would have found
Florentine men as willing as ever to promote the beauties and excellencies of
their civic organization, their architecture, their economic dynamism, their
women: in fact, the compulsion to celebrate and mythologize Florence grew
more intense as the fourteenth century advanced and the threat from the
papacy and the Visconti grew ever more intimidating. The Florentine Republic is the best-documented state in medieval Europe. It has bequeathed
us not only official records and chronicles, but a vast repository of literary
ephemera from various social levels.[23] It has even provided us with a versified guidebook from 1373, the year of Chaucer's visit.[24] This was written by
Antonio Pucci, who had served as Florentine town crier (*banditore*) from 1349
to 1369. Pucci composed a number of *cantari* (the popular verse form adapted
by Boccaccio's *Filostrato*, *Teseida*, and *Ninfale Fiesolano*), many detailed descriptions of Florentine life, and numerous other pieces designed for public
recitation.[25] Pucci, who admired Boccaccio as his cultural superior, employs
Dantean *terza rima* in his 1373 description of Florence. By 1373, *terza rima*
had become a popular verse form that a semi-educated *canterino* like Pucci
found serviceable for a whole range of purposes.

Pucci begins his 300-line (100-tercet) account with an inventory of the
bridges, walls, gates, towers, and churches of Florence. He measures out the
dimensions of the city by describing walking itineraries between different
gates; this leads us through important reference points, such as the Mercato
Vecchio and the Arte della Lana. He experiences the city as a well-ordered
organic unity, and proclaims his admiration for the citizen who conceived
of such a natural-seeming disposition of space (23). He dedicates 24 tercets
to listing the most famous houses of Florence, beginning with the Bardi,
Rossi, and Frescobaldi (32–55), before embarking on a detailed account of the
political structures of Florence:

> Firenze governa oggi sua grandizia
>   Per otto Popolan, che son Priori,
>   Ed un Gonfalonier della Giustizia.   (56)

> Florence today governs its great affairs of state
>   Through eight *popolani*, who are Priors,
>   Plus one Standard-bearer of Justice.

The Signoria, as Pucci here describes it, represented the supreme executive
body of Florence, although ultimate authority lay (in theory at least) on the
far side of the Alps with the emperor. Pucci goes on to describe the constitution of the Sixteen and the Twelve, two colleges that gave counsel and advice
to the Signoria. The lower levels of communal administration were comprised
of a number of posts and commissions, including two commissions responsible for grain supply, two for mercenary troops (Boccaccio had served on one

of them), and one for the city's prison, the Stinche.[26] All of these appointments were short term: priors served for just two months, members of the Twelve and Sixteen for three and four months respectively.[27] This meant, of course, that the six hundred to seven hundred professional civil servants or notaries who provided administrative continuity were very powerful and, as Dante dramatizes so memorably in *Inferno* 21–22, well-situated for promoting barratry and graft. Pucci next describes the commune's two legislative bodies: the Council of the Popolo (300 members) and the Council of the Commune (200 members, including 40 magnates). These councils could not initiate legislation, but they brought the initiatives of the Signoria and colleges into contact with a broader range of public opinion.

The complexity of this governmental machinery, the end product of several centuries of civic evolution, was supposed to ensure that no single family, professional, or civic group could achieve a permanent monopoly of power. Similar anxieties ensured that the administration and execution of justice was entrusted not to Florentines but to professional outsiders on short-term contracts, the *podestà* (who brought 100 men with him) and the *capitano del popolo* (who brought 75).[28] Florence was a congenitally unruly city. Prominent families, still moved by feudal mores, habitually resorted to violence in regulating their affairs. The ideal of organic, amicable, self-regulating civic unity promoted by Florentine writers worked to conceal such endemic violence and the structural flaws under which the regime labored. Pucci was exceptionally patriotic even by Florentine standards, but some of these flaws, or restrictive conditions, are evident in the cloud of negatives that momentarily passes over his discussion:

> E niuno Grande può esser Priore,
> > Dodici ancora, nè Gonfaloniere,
> > D'ogni altro ufficio han parte dell' onore.
> Nè Ghibellino alcun, nè forestiere,
> > (Secondochè per legge par, che sia)
> > Cittadinesco uficio puote avere.
> Firenze è terra di mercatanzia,
> > Ed ecci ogni Arte . . .   (64–66)

> And no Magnate may be Prior,
> > Or a member of the Twelve, or Standard-bearer;
> > They may share in the honor of every other office.
> Nor may any Ghibelline, or foreigner
> > (Or anyone regarded as such by the law)
> > Hold any civic office.
> Florence is a homeland of merchant enterprise,
> > And every Guild is found here . . .

In the first two tercets here, Pucci captures the conflict of interest that posed the most continuously disruptive threat to the regime. The Florentine patriciate was divided into two legally defined categories: the *magnati* (magnates) and the *popolani*. Although distinctions had blurred considerably by 1373, magnates claimed descent from the Tuscan feudal nobility; several magnate families (such as the Ricasoli and Buondelmonti) still had large holdings in the *contado* and made no concessions to the mercantile ethos.[29] Magnates were seen as a threat to the peace and stability of Florence; since 1293 they had been effectively banned from most areas of communal government. Individual magnates were allowed to sever all family ties and become *popolani*; and *popolani* who proved violent or unruly were proclaimed magnates, which effectively cut them off from political life. This inversion of the traditional European hierarchy of aristocratic rank made trade or diplomatic dealings with northern Europeans particularly difficult for Florentines, since the operative lexicon of honor, trust, and prestige was deeply rooted in the international language of class hierarchy: nobles had noble principles, and villeins acted villainously.

Pucci's second tercet alludes to the mechanism by which some magnates and conservative patricians managed to influence political affairs from outside the communal structure: *ammonizione*, or admonition.[30] By the mid-fourteenth century, the pro-papal ideology of Guelfism was entirely victorious over its old pro-imperial enemy, Ghibellinism: all Florentines in Florence were Guelfs. The Florentine Parte Guelfa, realizing that the old battle could no longer be fought, created a new one by demanding that all Ghibellines be excluded from office as potential traitors. An individual could now be defined as a Ghibelline because of the politics of his ancestors, or because he was an immigrant from a Ghibelline city. Citizens were considered *ammoniti* (admonished, or dissuaded from participating in political life) if four of the six Guelf captains declared them to be Ghibellines. No public trials were necessary to enforce this mechanism of social control, which fed upon fear and insecurity. No writer would wish to lay himself open to the charge of Ghibellinism; it is interesting to note that very few *novelle* in Boccaccio's *Decameron* are set in Ghibelline cities. The Florentine chronicler Giovanni Villani was the most ardent of Guelfs, but his son Matteo, who continued his chronicle, was proscribed as a Ghibelline in 1362 through an imputation of Ghibelline ancestry. The accusation of Ghibellinism, which had no objective basis in social realities, tapped long historical roots in the Florentine psyche. In 1378, when the continuous and reckless employment of *ammonizione* had helped bring the regime to within days of terminal collapse, communal representatives could not steel themselves to dismantle the *ammonizione* apparatus and finally lay the ghost of an internal Ghibelline threat. It is not, I believe, irresponsible to compare the psychological and social power of *ammonizione* with the workings of McCarthyism.

Pucci's sweeping characterization of Florence as "a" (perhaps "the") "homeland of merchant enterprise" is an accurate one. All levels of society shared in the profit or labor of mercantile trade. The office-holding class was predominantly made up of capitalist entrepreneurs who promoted the interests of the industrialists, bankers, money-changers, and international merchants; their guiding axiom was that what was good for Florentine business interests was good for all Florentines. The guilds that Pucci goes on to enumerate formed a two-tier structure with antithetical interests. The upper guilds represented the merchants and capitalists who dominated communal government and favored a free market and open competition for local guildsmen; the artisans and shopkeepers of the lower guilds preferred a protected market and regulation of prices, wages, and production levels. They did not look kindly upon foreign immigrant labor, which flooded the market and dragged down prices.[31] This conflict of interests has a great deal in common with the struggle between the London merchant capitalists and the small masters. Indeed, each struggle passed through some similar phases, as artisans and shopkeepers allied with elements of a factionalized patriciate for short-term advantage. Lower guildsmen did serve in the Signoria. Between 1343 and 1378, three lower guildsmen (a swordmaker, a butcher, and a wine merchant) shared the record with one upper guildsman (a banker) by serving seven times.[32] The increasing influx of *gente nuova*, or "new men," from the lower guilds into the Signoria, which was especially marked between 1351 and 1371, was greatly resented by the upper echelons. Dante had complained of the stink of peasants and immigrants from Certaldo; Ceffo degli Agli refers to "these shitty artisans"; Boccaccio (himself from Certaldo) complains of country bumpkins abandoning the trowel and the plow to take up office in the Signoria.[33]

The lowest recognized level of Florentine society was known as the *popolo minuto*, a mass of unorganized, unenfranchised, and propertyless laborers. The largest component of this group worked under the control of the Lana guild as weavers, cutters, fullers, and wool carders. The capital-intensive cloth and wool industries were of vital importance to the economies of both Lombardy and Tuscany. Lombardy had hosted such industries since Roman times, but their intensive expansion and industrialization in Tuscany was a purely medieval phenomenon.[34] The Florentine proletariat was fluid and volatile: thousands of workers were killed off by the plagues of 1348 and 1363, to be replaced by immigrant labor from Germany and Lombardy. The Florentine obsession with blood pedigree was of little account to members of the supposedly subpolitical *popolo minuto*. Their political and economic masters, like their English counterparts, were anxious to prevent them from developing any organized forms of association. It followed (as in England) that at moments of political crisis the *popolo minuto* felt free to act like a class that had nothing to lose.[35]

Having analyzed the constituent political parts of Florence, Pucci rounds out his micro-*Commedia* of one hundred tercets with praise of the city considered as an organic unity. Florence is richly endowed with goods, persons, wisdom and tolerance (81), but makes surrounding cities tremble when she ("ella") exercises her power (82). Florence was devastated by the great flood (of 1333), but has now recovered, thanks to heavy capital expenditure channeled through the Monte (90–91), the funded communal debt established in 1345. Pucci's linkage of the Monte with Florentine patriotism is both appropriate and prophetic, since the commune's deepening dependence on a funded debt was steadily contributing to the erosion of the political and economic structures of the medieval commune and to the formation of state capitalism:

New allegiances and bonds would be created; private interests would diminish in the face of a mounting concern with state affairs. In communal society, the church, nobility, confraternities, *Parte Guelfa*, and great guilds with their affluent burghers had provided capital and credit; until then money and credit had been almost exclusively in the hands of these orders and medieval corporations, for the commune had little wealth. By the fifteenth century, however, the state had become the largest consumer of capital with a rentier class investing heavily in the interest-bearing public debt.[36]

This long-term shift of fiscal dependency away from corporations within the state to the state itself finds a discursive counterpart in the gradual mythologization of Florence (by successive generations of Florentine historiographers) as the transcendent focus of loyalty for all its inhabitants. One of the most important of these historiographers, Matteo Villani, was himself an official of the Monte. The superimposition of fiscal metaphors upon the traditional lexicon of moral approbation can already be read in Pucci's text:

> E il nostro Comune è, di pregio adorno,
>   Nella sua libertà rimaso al fine,
>   Ed è per sormontar di giorno in giorno.   (92)

> And our Commune, adorned with credit,
>   Has remained in liberty to the end,
>   And is set to rise from day to day.

The term "pregio" here has the double valence that the term "credit" retains today: it associates praiseworthiness with eligibility to receive a financial loan. The term "acquistare," as Pucci employs it three tercets later, is similarly bivalent: the territories that Florence has conquered or confirmed its domination over (96–99) are complacently represented as properties acquired in a commercial transaction:

> laond'io
> Poco mi curo omai, perch'io mi muoia,
> Poich' acquistato è tanto al tempo mio.   (100)

> and therefore I
> Am little concerned now if I should die
> Since so much in my time has been acquired.

Between these two tercets, Pucci struggles to find a language, or a conceptual scheme, to describe the sheer volume of wealth that flowed from the Monte (three million florins of public debt by 1400).[37] He resorts to the traditional European association of noble pedigree with value, but the image he appropriates is commodified and reproduced in the Florentine commercial spirit. If the women of Florence could bring their jewels here, Pucci says, we would amass a fortune:

> E dico, se le donne Fiorentine
>   Portar potesser qui le gioie loro,
>   Che in Firenze averie mille Reine
> Incoronate d'ariento, e d'oro,
>   Con tante perle, e con tanto ornamento,
>   Che veramente vagliono un tesoro.   (93–94)

And I declare that if Florentine women
    were able to bring their jewels here,
    there would be a thousand Queens in Florence
crowned with silver, and with gold,
    with so many pearls, and with so much ornament,
    that they really would be worth a fortune.

Pucci's brief fantasy of Florentine women publicly divesting themselves of their jewels forms a political equation: that Florentine polity is a thousand times more successful than any monarchy. But the terms of this equation also tell us something about the new image of women constructed within the Florentine commercial economy. Women are figured as signs through which any man can read the wealth and prestige of Florence: the fact that women are adorned with wealth is a sign that the Florentine commune is "di pregio adorno." Women are here commodified as voiceless figures within a new symbolic order. But there is always the risk that women will come to conscious recognition of their new symbolic importance: the masculine compulsion to adorn women may furnish women with working capital. The abundance of new sumptuary legislation, plus a chorus of misogynistic complaint from male authors such as Giovanni Villani and Boccaccio, suggests that women were quick to exploit the possibilities of their new public role.[38] Such possibilities are explored most memorably by Chaucer's *Shipman's Tale*, the most Boccaccian or Florentine-spirited of all Chaucerian narratives.[39]

The ways in which individual Florentines chose to spend or bequeath their capital both underline and undermine commitment to associational ideology as promulgated by official civic and religious authorities. Perhaps the most striking example of this is the extraordinary history surrounding Or San Michele, one of the busiest piazzas of the city. A Cistercian church on this site was knocked down in 1249 to make room for a grain market. In 1284 a *loggia* was built to provide shelter for the grain merchants. In 1292 "grandi e aperti miracoli" were reported before an image of the Virgin that hung on one of its pillars. A popular cult soon developed and large donations rolled in, exciting both the interest and envy of the friars (who exercised a dominating influence over the city's fraternities) and the communal authorities. In the early fourteenth century, the charitable company formed at Or San Michele attracted thousands of adherents and performed splendid work in assisting the poor and famine relief. When the fraternity became richly endowed after the Black Death of 1348, the city authorities passed a series of laws to bind it closer to the Signoria and attempted to channel the company's cash into officially sponsored projects. Or San Michele was officially declared a sacred space by the city authorities in 1357 and the grain market was moved elsewhere; pipers and trumpeters were hired to attract devotees to the newly constructed oratory. But the more the state authorities attempted to bring the site under official control, the less interest the public showed in supporting it: by the late Trecento, according to Sacchetti, the populace had gone in search of other Madonnas.[40] In Italy as in England, the formation and desuetude of particular guilds manifests the ebb and flow of social and economic energies that defy or escape precise official regulation. The broad outlines of their histories offer instructive parallels.

This survey of Florentine polity in 1373 must conclude by acknowledging the existence of a social class that finds no place in Pucci's versified guidebook. Our guide here is Iris Origo:

Beneath the cooperative associations of the guilds—the *arti maggiori e minori*—beneath even the oppressed, hungry rabble of the *popolo minuto*, the Tuscan cities held another class—made up of men and women without human or legal rights, without families of their own, without any recognized ties between them, without even a name, save that given to them by their master: the slaves.[41]

The shipping of slaves into Tuscany expanded dramatically after the Black Death of 1348 (which created a massive labor shortage). A decree of March 2, 1363, by the priors of Florence permitted unlimited importation of foreign slaves. The great majority of slaves sold in Florence were women; the women that commanded the highest price were those who had just passed puberty.[42] As female slaves were bought and valued for their sexual appeal, whole new taxonomies of female description grew up in new literary genres (the Register and deeds of sale).[43] The presence of so many young women in the household clearly undermined, and was designed to undermine, the newfound symbolic importance accorded to Florentine women of the merchant class. Antonio Pucci, although disinclined to include slaves in his survey of Florentine polity, was pleased to write a sonnet impersonating a Florentine lady who complains of female slaves.[44] Such a slave, "she" argues, enjoys every advantage ("vantaggio"): she's already bought and paid for, and needs no dowry; she satisfies the master's appetite better than his wife can, hence checkmating her ("dà scacco matto"). The latter part of the sonnet addresses the closely related topics of food and sex:

Ver è ch'in casa dura più fatica,
    com'è mestier da sera e da mattina
    ma di vantaggio sua bocca nutrica.

E se talvolta fa danno in cucina,
    quasi non par ch'a lei si disdica
    come farebbe a una fiorentina.

While it's true that she works hard in the house,
    as needed, evening and morning,
    she is well-placed to fill her mouth.

And if sometimes she messes things up in the kitchen,
    it's almost as if she's not to be told off
    as a Florentine woman would be.

Domestic troubles often began with a visit by the master of the house to the kitchens. Many of the children subsequently produced—who belonged to the master "only . . . as a calf belongs to the man who also owns the cow"[45]—were offloaded onto the foundling hospitals for which Florence is still famous.[46] Some female slaves were offered their freedom by the master on his deathbed (an action that could further enmity between female slaves and surviving wives). When Boccaccio wishes to stage a rebellion of the lower orders in the course of his *Decameron*, he sends to the kitchen, bringing forth (as we shall shortly see) a voluble female servant who argues for the realistic acceptance of rampant sexual promiscuity. For men of a certain social class, the kitchen is a site that promises good humor, good food, and an escape from serious concerns. For women of the same class it threatens control over the household, the one area of political life that they might aspire to rule, and draws them into endless same-sex rivalries and suspicions.[47] Florentine women readers of the *Decameron* might well understand, then, why Elissa feels moved to repress this female-headed kitchen rebellion with the kind of physical intimidation to which any female slave—or any *fiorentina*—could legally be subjected.

Disenfranchised workers, slavery, and the systematic exploitation of women do not find much space in guidebooks on Trecento Florence, medieval or modern. But such things and such people formed part of Chaucer's experience of Florence in 1373 even as part of the not-seen, or not consciously registered. On the quays at Genoa, where he was briefed to negotiate with shipping interests, Chaucer must have encountered, or tried not to encounter, "whole shiploads of bewildered, half-naked men, women and children . . . being prodded and paraded like cattle at a fair." The Genoese had long been "perhaps the boldest, most resourceful and most persistent" slave traders in the Levant.[48] At the time of Chaucer's visit, when the Genoese slave trade was at its peak, the slave population of Genoa was approximately 5,000 (as much as 10 percent of the population).[49] We do not know the point or the social level at which Chaucer's political intelligence began to work, the point at which something amenable to political understanding could be acknowledged as happening. Before proceeding to consider Chaucer's reading of Florentine polity, however, we should at least recognize such aspects of social organization, supposedly situated beneath or beyond the political. These, too, pressure his writing.[50]

Chaucer's stay at Florence in 1373 lasted from late February until just after Easter, time enough to grasp how the ideal of free discussion within associational forms of polity was jealously championed at all recognized social levels.[51] Even the Parte Guelfa, the most serious organized threat to the Commune, organized itself through structures of governance that were modeled on those of the Commune.[52] But the strains of balancing the conflicting interests of so many diverse groups, and of reconciling them with the unifying discourse of civic liberty that prevailed in political debate, were becoming intolerable. Since the Black Death, patrician politics had been riven with factional conflicts that polarized around two families, the Ricci and the Albizzi.[53] By the 1370s the Florentine economy had reached its lowest point since 1348; there was a rash of bankruptcies and serious layoffs in the cloth and wool industries. In 1372, the Albizzi bribed leading members of the Ricci, who were financially hard-pressed, to abandon their faction for the Albizzi. The *gente nuova* now feared that this patrician alliance presaged an aristocratic coup. On April 5, 1372, the Commune passed a decree stating that all sects were to be dissolved and eradicated. There were riots in the streets; one of the Strozzi (of the Albizzi faction) allegedly killed an artisan with a stone outside the Ricci palace. In January 1373, the Albizzi and Ricci families were banned from all communal offices for ten years. A popular party, built from the wreckage of the Ricci faction, led an attack on the economic privileges the patrician oligarchs had wrung from the Commune. In April 1373, the first of a series of oligarchs had magnate status forced upon him, and was thereby rendered ineligible for public office.[54]

Endgame: Florentine Polity Disintegrates, 1373–78

While Chaucer was in Florence, during the worst phase of an economic recession, Florentine polity was entering an endgame of terminal decline. The Florentine patriciate (like the English magnates in this period) could not reconcile itself to the idea that the *gente nuova* should be permitted to translate its newfound economic dynamism into political power. The *gente nuova* (much like the London merchant capitalists) could not cooperate with a patriciate that persisted in behaving as if it stood above or outside communal law. Popular resentment at patrician behavior is expressed most vividly in a charge against one of the Medici, who allegedly assaulted a poor widow in the *contado* and attempted to seize her inheritance: "He has never engaged in mercantile activity nor does he practice any trade. He has never earned an honest penny." [55]

In the winter of 1372–73, Florence's relations with the papacy were extremely poor. The pope was at war with the Ghibelline Bernabò Visconti, and expected material assistance from Florence, his traditional Guelf ally. Since the Parte Guelfa was causing such disruption within Florence, the Florentine government did not feel inclined to support papal battles outside its own walls. By 1375 the Florentines feared that Sir John Hawkwood, the English mercenary currently in the pay of the papacy, was intent on invading Tuscany once peace had been made with the Visconti. Having lost faith in papal diplomacy, the Florentines bought Hawkwood off (for five years at a cost of 130,000 florins) and signed a pact with Bernabò against the pope and the emperor. After a century of loyalty to the Holy See, Florence went to war with the papacy. The chief weapons of war were ideological rather than military. The new Florentine chancellor, Coluccio Salutati, wrote to governments across Europe justifying Florentine actions. In writing to Italian states, Salutati represented the struggle as a fight to preserve liberty against barbarian (French) invasion. In insisting upon *libertas* as the transcendent value, which could stand against all papal propaganda, Salutati was forced to insist that "perfect concord" reigned in Florence: "Believe me, when one fights for liberty, all civic discord will cease." [56] To prove the point, Florentines organized a tournament on the piazza in front of Santa Croce, where they jousted for the favors of Madonna Libertà. [57]

Pope Gregory's Breton mercenaries showed little inclination to fight; they settled in Romagna, looted the countryside, and avoided pitched battles. But in ideological warfare the papacy owned the ultimate weapon: on March 31, 1376, Florence was placed under interdict. All religious services in Florence were suspended. As outlaws of Christendom, Florentines were to be expelled forthwith from every state; their property could be confiscated, and their persons imprisoned or enslaved. [58] Florentine merchants and bankers all over Europe were suddenly rendered vulnerable to the depredations of local secular powers.

On October 6, 1377, a parliament of the *magno consilio* (the entire Florentine electorate) overwhelmingly rejected papal demands with the cry "Death to the rapacious wolf and cruel tyrant!" [59] The Signoria committed the city to disobeying the papal interdict: mass was to be celebrated on October 8, by order of the Signoria. This order proved an abject failure, since both priests and people refused to obey it. But on October 18, the Feast of the Virginity of Mary, the government organized a procession through the streets, featuring some of the most sacred relics from city and *contado*; Mass was celebrated on a platform erected in front of the city hall. [60] The Florentine Parte Guelfa now unleashed a Guelf Terror of *ammonizioni*: nearly one hundred Florentines were proscribed during the winter and spring of 1377–78, including a dozen *gente nuova* from the Lana guild. In March 1378 Bernabò Visconti oversaw negotiations between Florentine and papal representatives. Just as agreement was being reached, Gregory XI died. Florentines were ecstatic when an Italian, Bartolomeo Prignano, was elected Pope Urban VI. Although the position of the Florentine Parte Guelfa was obviously severely weakened, it foolishly persisted with proscription. A clothier and a tanner were proscribed on June 14. On June 22 violence erupted, as shopkeepers, artisans, and Ciompi burned oligarch houses and opened the Stinche. Last-ditch efforts were made to save the regime. The Ciompi, fearing they would be severely punished for their part in the June riots, made their own demands: they wished to form their own guild, free from control by the Lana guild; to choose their own consuls; and to participate in government. Faced with social revolution, the Signoria summoned troops from outlying districts, but few showed up. Thousands of artisans and laborers were on the streets. The government finally fell on July 22, 1378.[61]

Boccaccio's *Decameron*: Associational Ideology; Licisca's Rebellion

The Florentine regime of 1343–78 started out as one of the broadest based regimes in Italian medieval history: shopkeepers, artisans, and tradesmen shared in the business of government with patrician merchants, bankers, and rentiers. Ferdinand Schevill, writing in 1936, described this regime as a "democratic episode" that was "bound to end in failure," a preemptive formulation that sides with the view taken of Florence in contemporary Avignon, Milan, and Pavia.[62] The papacy and the Visconti, although rarely reconciled with one another, shared a vertical, downward-descending vision of power. Florence was moved by the internal and external threat of such hierarchic and hierocratic visions to develop an associative, laterally extending ideal of *libertas*. The task for Florentine political theory was to reverse the transfer, or alienation, of ethical (hegemonic) power from state to Church effected by Christian Aristotelianism. In Aristotle, the *polis* refers specifically to the Greek city-state; in Aquinas, it stands for political association in general, whether in a city-state or feudal monarchy or something in between. By making the state or *polis* a more abstract and generalizable term, Aquinas "lost Aristotle's notion of a specific and rather intimate cultural milieu in which participation in collective provision for the common good promotes the development of human virtue. For Aquinas, moral teaching and spiritual formation are the Church's province."[63] For Florentines, it was imperative that civic values be realized through the organic processes of their own city-state, rather than through an agency (the Parte Guelfa) representing a power external to the state. In fighting the papacy they needed to convince themselves that they could "win without sight of the body of Christ."[64] In fighting the Visconti, they would need to believe that the Florentine city-state had become a transcendent category: Visconti states would pass away with the despots who ruled them, but "the Commune cannot die."[65]

Nicolai Rubenstein has written that the principles of Florentine political ideology must be deduced from works which are not strictly political theory.[66] Quentin Skinner has offered a fine, detailed decoding of the famous Sienese fresco cycle of 1337–40, in which Ambrogio Lorenzetti celebrates republican city-state government by finding visual equivalents for political metaphors from Cicero and Seneca. One memorable representation of the horizontal exercise of power is formed by Lorenzetti's imaging of *aequitas*. This features 24 citizens of exactly uniform height: they are on "level terms" with each other in just the way Cicero's analysis of *aequitas* prescribes.[67] But although such an ideal might be achieved within (or across) the lowest and the highest political forms of a commune, from the parish guild to the Signoria, the space *between* such constituent forms was itself hierarchized. There was still a need for some form of cultural production that would both challenge ideologies that were hostile to associative polity and conceal the divisions within such polity by reconciling hierarchized relations along a single horizontal plane of *aequitas*, of *unitas civium*. Such complex ideological maneuvers, which defeat the strict logic of political theory, are adeptly performed by imaginative texts that conceal their own ideological character through the techniques of novelistic realism. The most famous of these, of course, is Boccaccio's *Decameron*, which was completed just as the concept of *unitas civium* was first beginning to appear in Florentine city records.[68]

Boccaccio's *Decameron* begins, famously, by describing the Black Death of 1348 which killed off approximately half of the population of Florence. Since the dead included his father and stepmother, Boccaccio had suddenly found himself (at 35, the midlife age at which Dante stages the journey of his *Commedia*) head of his own household in a city where the familiar forms of civic life had completely disintegrated. His account of plague-ravaged Florence bears comparison with Lorenzetti's vision of bad government at Siena: communal and cooperative structures break down; individuals grow excessively reclusive or wildly gregarious; strange new groupings, like the ad hoc entrepreneurial gravedigging fraternity of the *becchini*, rise like buboes on the body politic. The communal spirit that had formerly guided the city seems only to have secured or accelerated its ruin. In 1347, the ovens operated day and night by the charitable company of Or San Michele to alleviate the effects of famine had succeeded in drawing in thousands of starving peasants from the countryside; the presence of so many homeless and debilitated people at Florence in 1348 had allowed the plague to spread all the more rapidly.[69] The death of Boccaccio's father could only have been hastened by his performance of duties as an officer of the Commune responsible for rationing and hygiene.

Municipal authorities under the Visconti at Milan were more efficient and less compassionate: any house containing a plague victim was bricked up, leaving the living to die with the dead.[70]

As a plague survivor and fully enfranchised householder (participation in political life being restricted to males over 30), Boccaccio had immediately taken a full part in Florentine political life. When Florence went to war with the Visconti in 1351 he was dispatched on a series of important diplomatic missions; in 1354 he was Florentine ambassador to Pope Innocent VI at Avignon.[71] The writing of the *Decameron* is clearly to be seen as a part of, rather than a respite from, this period of intensive commitment to the Florentine body politic. The hygienic and therapeutic powers of literature were widely recognized in this period; songs and stories, because they alleviated the pain and depression of adversity, were endorsed by medical authorities as valued antidotes to both medical and social crises.[72] And Boccaccio's impulse to write of the Florentine response to moments of danger or catastrophe was shared by a strong, well-established tradition of historiographical prose written by men who shared his mercantile origins. The *Decameron*'s first creative gesture in representing Florentine resistance to the plague and its devastating social consequences is very much in spirit with this tradition: the formation of a cell-like social group, or *brigata*, that will keep the spirit of associative polity alive until such time as it can rule again throughout the city. In the church of Santa Maria Novella, which had lost 83 of its 130 Dominican friars, an ideal associational grouping forms, ostensibly untroubled by traditional hierarchizing factors such as age, sex, and class.[73] Ten young Florentines, seven women and three men of noble breeding ("di sangue nobile," 1. *Intro.* 49), will share the burdens and pleasures "associated with sovereign power" (1. *Intro.* 96; p. 65) as they move from city to countryside and pass the time through storytelling.

The tales told in the *Decameron* maintain a distinctively Florentine perspective even in covering an extraordinary range of geographic locales and political structures: for the Florentine mercantile economy, we have noted, extended itself to the furthest limits of the known world (and fantasized about what lay beyond). The very first *novella* begins by constructing a complex chain of dependencies connecting the French royal court, moneylenders in Burgundy, an Italian merchant, the pope, and Cepperello da Prato, "perhaps the worst man ever born" (1.1.15; p. 71). It is only through the ingenuity of Cepperello that this complex arrangement can achieve a seamless, mutually advantageous circulation of mercantile and religious capital.[74] Spatial limits are pushed out still further in the Second Day, which situates itself between two distant locales that were (for Florentines) both strange and exotic: Araby (Arab territories) in the south, and Britain in the north. Britain, as represented by 2.3 and 2.8, is governed by an archaic feudal polity that presents unlimited opportunities for Florentines to get rich by (for example) mortgaging barons' castles (1.3.13; p. 129). There seems to be no limit to what young Alessandro, the hero of 2.3, might achieve: by the end of the *novella* he has been seduced by an abbot (a princess in disguise), reconciled Henry II with Henry III, been created earl of Cornwall, and, finally, made himself king of Scotland by right of conquest. Araby, which lies beyond the bounds of Christendom, becomes the site for even more exotic, fantastic, and exploitative projections (invariably involving women). In 2.7 an Arab woman completes the journey to the man for whom she was originally intended only after having traveled thousands of miles and made love to eight different men perhaps ten thousand times (2.7.121; p. 191). In 2.9 a disgraced Christian woman must travel to Acre, site of a Christian-Saracen trade fair, to contemplate the worldwide circulation of commodities and so secure her own rehabilitation into Christendom.

Many *Decameron* narratives suggest, in overt or occulted ways, a wild and restless energy associated with the urge to get rich by traversing large tracts of land and sea; the impulse to acquire wealth descends as suddenly and mysteriously upon male protagonists as the impulse to love.[75] Sexual energy itself, however, may prove similarly wild and voracious (particularly, according to Boccaccio, in women): the Third Day frames itself between the enterprising nuns who wear out their convent gardener and the young Arab girl, Alibech, who wears out Christian hermits (3.1 and 3.10). Boccaccio develops various strategies to stabilize and utilize such potent energies. His favorite strategy for containing female sexuality is to keep women indoors: the Seventh Day stages a series of battles for control of domestic space (in which women learn that their power lies in being locked in the house, rather than shut outside); the whole strategy of his *Decameron*, of course, is to keep women indoors reading his book while men go about their public business.[76] The Tenth Day counterbalances the impulse to accumulate and retain wealth by offering models for generous and civilized disbursement, *magnificenzia*. (It also offers Dioneo's perverse antimodel, which sees Walter, a Lombard tyrant, making a gift to his wife of her own abducted children: 10.10.) But Boccaccio's chief hope for social stability patently lies in the associative habits and regulatory structures of cities. Urban structures in the *Decameron* show an almost mystical ability to expose and expel charlatans, fools, and swindlers. Their weapon of choice is human language; the most brilliant exponent of this urban art is, of course, Florence (which was, to judge from its voluminous archives, Europe's most talkative city).

Although the whole of the *Decameron* may be seen as an effort to keep the art of Florentine talking alive, the Sixth Day pays particular attention to those who, "on being provoked by some verbal pleasantry, have returned like for like, or who, by a prompt retort or shrewd maneuver, have avoided danger, discomfort, or ridicule" ("perdita o pericolo o scorno," 5. *Concl.* 3; p. 479). It is not surprising, then, that the Sixth Day should feature more Florentine protagonists and Florentine settings than any other *giornata*. The first *novella* opens with a group of knights and ladies (much like the *Decameron*'s own *brigata*) walking through the Florentine *contado* or countryside; it demonstrates how a woman may interrupt an incompetent male talker without cutting at his manhood. The seventh story features a brilliant courtroom defense by a Tuscan wife taken in adultery. Developing arguments shared by the Wife of Bath, the wife from Prato shifts the grounds of interrogation from legal precedent to laws of commerce and sexuality: if her husband has always taken "as much of me as he needed," then (she asks the *podestà*) "what am I to do with the surplus?" (6.7.17; p. 500). The statute that condemns her is amended on the spot by popular acclaim; the wife escapes burning and the citizens have a new story to tell.

Boccaccio's most optimistic fable of associational ideology is *Decameron* 6.2, which tells how a Florentine baker forges a momentary alliance with a Florentine aristocrat as their city approaches a moment of acute political danger. The exploits of Boccaccio's heroic baker will be compared with those of Chaucer's Cook (and with attempts to generate equivalent forms of associational ideology across Chaucer's London) in a later chapter.[77] The final story of the Sixth Day stars Frate Cipolla (Brother Onion, a man of many linguistic layers and a close relative of Chaucer's Pardoner).[78] Cipolla visits Certaldo, a small country town near Florence, to collect dues from a confraternity and fleece the rural population further by showing them a relic (a feather dropped by Gabriel at the Annunciation). His plans are thwarted, temporarily, by two young men identified not with the rural confraternity but rather with Cipolla's own (urban) *brigata* ("di sua brigata," 6.10.13; p. 502). The rural world, here as elsewhere in Boccaccio, is shown to be defenseless against those (like friars) who come schooled in urban tricks. Certaldo is Boccaccio's *patria*, but his own predilection for verbal trickery clearly places him with Cipolla's *brigata* rather than with those who, in rural Certaldo, still follow "the honest precepts of an earlier age": one that knows nothing of the "luxuries of Egypt" that have now flooded the market, "to the ruination of the whole of Italy" (6.10.27; p. 509).

The Cipolla story does suggest Boccaccio's willingness to recognize that the practices of an associational group, such as Cipolla's *brigata*, may be used to exploit those who lie beyond its limits. He is also willing to contemplate some of the internal limits and weaknesses of such structures. The eighth *novella* is both too brief and incompetently told; the teller, Emilia, admits that her attention is not really here ("qui," 6.8.4); the other storytellers will have to work the harder to keep their communal project alive. The next *novella* celebrates the Florentine habit of men clubbing together in *brigate* to entertain one another (and to welcome distinguished foreign visitors: 6.9.5; p. 503). At the same time, it upholds the right of individuals to resist the social pressures of co-optation exerted by such groups. The independent-minded protagonist here is Guido Cavalcanti, first seen walking through the ancient Roman sarcophagi surrounding the famous Florentine baptistry of San Giovanni (6.9.10; p. 504). The pleasure Cavalcanti takes in his own company is much resented by the Florentine *brigata* that he will not join: but Boccaccio clearly endorses the great poet's right to walk alone. Harassed by men on horseback, Cavalcanti vaults a tomb and escapes the *brigata*, leaving them with only an enigmatic utterance to ponder.

The most significant challenge to the culture and politics of Boccaccian *brigate* comes, however, at the very beginning of the Sixth Day. As Boccaccio's ten young storytellers are convening themselves for the first *novella* of the day, they are suddenly distracted by a "gran romore": a "great commotion, issuing from the kitchen, among the maids and menservants" (6., *Intr.*, 4; p. 481). The steward is summoned; the noisy culprits, Licisca and Tindaro, are brought before the aristocratic circle. This maid and manservant, it transpires, have been arguing over whether or not Sicofante's wife was a virgin on her wedding night. Tindaro tries to speak, but Licisca cuts him short: "You ignorant lout ('bestia d'uom'), how can you dare to speak first, when I am present? Hold your tongue and let me tell the story ('Lascia dir me')" (6., *Intr.*, 7; p. 482). She then boldly denounces the foolishness of men who imagine that young girls will be sexually inactive as they wait for their brothers and fathers to marry them off. Her torrent of graphic scabrous abuse cannot be halted by Elissa, queen for the day; the other women are helpless with laughter ("you could have pulled all their teeth out," 6., *Intr.*, 11; p. 482). When Licisca has come to the end of her speech, Elissa asks Dioneo to adjudicate. When Dioneo pronounces the maidservant to be right and the manservant to be a fool, Licisca gloats and starts speaking again. The queen then decides that the time has come to assert her authority, on behalf of her *brigata*, by putting a definitive end to this "romor":

E, se non fosse che la reina con un mal viso le 'mpose silenzio e comandolle che più parola né romor facesse se esser non volesse scopata e lei e Tindaro mandò via, niuna altra cosa avrebbero avuta a fare in tutto quel giorno che attendere a lei. (6., *Intr.*, 15)

But for the fact that the queen sternly commanded her to be silent, told her not to shout or argue any more unless she wanted to be whipped, and sent her back to the kitchen with Tindaro, there would have been nothing else to do for the rest of the day but listen to her prattle. (p. 483)

Although this downstairs rebellion is brief, it has important long-term effects upon the *Decameron*'s storytelling. In speaking of married women, Licisca asserts: "I could tell you a thing or two about the tricks they play on their husbands" (6., *Intr.*, 10; p. 482). This suggestion is taken up by Dioneo at the end of the Sixth Day and is adopted as the Seventh Day's theme. But there is no question of Licisca's returning to tell her a "thing or two": she is not heard from again. The manservant Tindaro is summoned at the end of the day, but only to play his bagpipe as an accompaniment to the *brigata*'s dancing. The *brigata* will draw much of its storytelling material from the lower orders of society in the second half of the *Decameron*, but the lower orders will not be called upon to speak for themselves. And yet, from the beginning of the work, Boccaccio's text has acknowledged the existence of what we might term a shadow-*brigata*: a group of four female and three male servants that marks the limits of Florentine associational ideology. Separated from the main *brigata* by a considerable social distance, this group is also denied an internal equality at its own social level. Pampinea, the *Decameron*'s first queen and the main *brigata*'s moving spirit, assigns the women more menial tasks than the men and puts them under masculine authority (1., *Intr.* 98–101; p. 66); there is no mention of authority here being shared or rotated. The ideal prescribed for this shadow-*brigata* is silence and invisibility; tables are found ready-laid and meals are served without a sound. And yet there is always the possibility, realized at the work's midpoint, that such arrangements may be disrupted by a "gran romore" issuing from the kitchen. The term "romore" is, of course, cognate with the term habitually used by English chroniclers to represent the voice of rebellion in 1381.[79]

The constant dread of Boccaccio's Florence was that the delicate arrangements of a complex polity, glossed by an associational ideology that purported to speak for all but in fact excluded the *popolo minuto*, might be brought crashing down by a rising of the lower orders. Boccaccio's *Decameron*, despite its enthusiastic exemplification of Florentine associational ideology, cannot shake the shadow of this historical possibility. The Florentine regime was under pressure when Chaucer left Florence in 1373; when he returned to Italy five years later it was overrun. Chaucer viewed the collapse of the regime in which Boccaccio had invested his life from the far side of the Florentine-Milanese divide. The Visconti would certainly have encouraged him to reflect on the inherent weaknesses of associational form that led to the collapse of 1378. These reflections no doubt stayed with him during the popular rebellion of 1381 and during the bitter struggles between London guild factions that went on throughout the 1380s.

The possibility of a lower-order rebellion that might disturb the prescribed order of storytelling in the *Decameron* is entertained only by way of dramatizing its containment. The rebel voice, here female and domestic, is soon subdued by the threat of physical violence and then rendered invisible; Licisca remains only as an inspiration to future storytelling, not as the teller of her own stories. The equivalent moment in Chaucer is, of course, the Miller's rebellion of Fragment 1. Chaucer's decision to give voice to the Miller, and later to the female and rebellious Wife of Bath, has also been evaluated as (ultimately) as a strategy of containment.[80] Chaucer's *compagnye* will prove to be much more socially inclusive, and much more flexible in its procedures, than Boccaccio's *brigata*. Yet it, too, will come to perpetuate the contradiction

inherent in all such constructions of associational form: the call to *felaweshipe* may also be heard (from the historical outside) as a call to suppression
and exclusion. The insurrections of 1378 and 1381, which formed part of a
Europe-wide pattern of rebellion,[81] nurtured an anxious apprehension in the
minds of the literate and enfranchised: namely, that associative structures
might (at any time) be turned to the purposes of peasants and journeymen,
millers and wool-workers,[82] and (later) unlearned readers, male and female,
of religious texts.

Chaucer in Lombardy, 1378

When Chaucer returned to London in 1373 the political travails of Florence
remained, from the vantage point of the customhouse, plainly visible. News
of the papal-Florentine conflict made Florentine merchants uneasy and vulnerable throughout Europe. When Florence was placed under interdict in
1376, Florentines who prided themselves in a tradition of *libertas* were suddenly reduced to the status of slaves. Chaucer's sometime neighbors in the
Vintry, the merchant capitalists he worked with at the customhouse, were
eager to exploit this sudden disenfranchisement of the Florentine merchants.
Florentines in London enjoyed royal protection until the opening of the Good
Parliament in April 1376, when the English merchant class moved against
the Florentine "covyne." Merchant and city opposition to the royal government was led after this parliament by William Courtenay, bishop of London;
Courtenay's publication of the papal interdict in January 1377, against royal
wishes, was seen as an act of municipal defiance. Wyclif sided with Gaunt and
opposed Courtenay and the pope for licensing civil powers to curtail the liberties of individual Florentines. Under the threat of violence, the Florentine
merchants persuaded the king to place them in the Tower of London, along
with their goods. Released a few weeks later, they were allowed to remain in
England as legal chattels (serfs) of the king. This extraordinary arrangement
brought letters of thanks to Gaunt and Edward from the Florentine Commune; duke and king were eulogized as wise princes who could perceive the
innocence of Florentines and the iniquity of the pope. But the Florentines
never recovered their position in the English wool market, since monastic
houses (unwilling to cross the pope) were the chief suppliers of export wool.
Florentine importing of English wool (some 6,000 sacks in 1372) shrank to
nothing, thereby exacerbating the serious underemployment of the Florentine wool-workers, the Ciompi.[83] In the summer of 1378, when the Florentine
regime was finally overthrown by the Ciompi revolution, Chaucer was again
in Italy, this time in Lombardy.[84]

Chaucer arrived in Milan as the Visconti state was entering its most
powerful economic and political phase.[85] The demise and collapse of Florentine republican polity, viewed from the perspective of Lombard despotism,

was historically inevitable. Florence would recover, of course: but, when the guild regime established by the Ciompi finally collapsed after three years and five months, Florence returned to the oligarchic form of government that Schevill takes to be the norm of Florentine polity.[86] But although Florence did not return to the broad-based associative polity of 1343–78, the intensity and volume of Florentine propaganda grew steadily as native *libertas* was repeatedly threatened by the expansionist designs of Lombard despotism. By the summer of 1402 Florence, without allies or friends, was isolated and surrounded: Bologna, Cortona, Lucca, Perugia, Pisa, and Siena had all been taken.[87] Florence would have fallen had not Gian Galeazzo Visconti suddenly died. This fortunate accident, which led to the liquidation of the Visconti empire, inspired some rapid retrospective myth-making by Florentine historiographers. Their efforts, as mediated by modern historians, have come to condition our understanding of the genesis of Renaissance civic humanism.[88] It is important to recall that when Chaucer died in 1400, however, the republican *reggimento* of Florence (already more narrowly based than the regime he did business with in 1373) still appeared fragile and vulnerable. In late fourteenth-century England, the destructive power of Lombard tyranny was more real, more apparent and intelligible as a political phenomenon, than the incipient promise of Florentine humanism.

The Florentine-Milanese struggle was more complex than the categories of political ideology can suggest: and yet, of course, this struggle was waged in part *through* such categories, as the associative, mercantile-based *libertas* of Florence contended with the downward-descending princely power of the Visconti state. "What else is the whole of history," asked Petrarch in 1373, "but the praise of Rome?"[89] *Romana laus*, however, was in 1373 also an ideological battleground, in which Florentines chose to praise the republic and Visconti supporters the empire. Rome could not be both republican and imperial at the same time: Viscontian propagandists insisted that the republic must yield to the empire. Nineteenth-century historiographers were inclined to believe that despotic regimes—*signorie*—came to power by infiltrating and controlling the judicial offices of republican regimes. Later studies have shifted from the internal workings of the city to the *contado*, or countryside, where ambitious families established a power base before attempting to enter city government. There then followed a protracted struggle between two family clans or groupings, which ended with the extinction of one party and the establishment of an absolutist regime by the other. This is what happened at Milan, where the Visconti, a family of feudal extraction, concluded a long and bloody struggle with the feudal della Torre at the Battle of Dessio in 1277.[90]

Florentine republican polity, we have noted, was forced to live with many feudal mores that were perpetuated through the lives of magnates and *popolani*. When the Visconti left their feudal estates for Milan and Pavia they established control of city and *contado* not by renouncing the political forms of feudalism but by a selective intensification of them. As imperial vicars, the Visconti had exercised powers of *infeudazione* for some time by the late fourteenth century. They were keen to weaken local feudal ties and to develop new bonds in which feudatories were entirely and directly dependent upon the lords of Milan and Pavia. In 1378, the powerful mercenary captain Iacomo dal Verme was infeuded, or enfeoffed, by Galeazzo Visconti with the "Castrum et Villi Olxerii" near Piacenza; more feuds were bestowed upon dal Verme by Gian Galeazzo Visconti in 1380 and 1383. Some *feudi* brought no land at all, but simply a grant of money; sometimes the term *feudum* was applied to what was no more than a stipend or pension.[91] These new feudal bonds were established as a means of binding individuals closer to the state — an objective belatedly and ineffectively pursued by the frantic retaining policy of Richard II's later years.[92] Those infeuded to the Visconti (rather than to the emperor or other lords) knew that if the Visconti fell, their goods and privileges fell with them. This made their loyalty to Viscontian polity as naturally self-interested as that of most Florentines to Florence and the Monte, its interest-paying public debt.

The fundamental political differences between the Florentine and Milanese regimes were, we have noted, intelligible to Chaucer: the struggle between merchant capitalist oligarchy and centralizing feudal monarchy was contested in England with exceptional bitterness after the death of Edward III in 1377. But such clean lines of demarcation between the prerogatives of traditional estates disguised more complex historical practices in both England and Italy: namely, the interdependence of magnate militarism and merchant capital. For a while in England it seemed that merchants were more adept at managing national affairs, and even at waging war, than magnates. When Chaucer left London for Lombardy on May 28, 1378, Gaunt was *gubernator* of the realm, but Walworth and Philpot were its appointed treasurers: Gaunt had to write to the London merchants to secure payment for Chaucer's journey out of the War Funds.[93] The interconnected realities of commercial and military power, which often ran contrary to the ideological fictions of mercantile-based or magnate-directed regimes, were powerfully personified in the Englishman Chaucer was briefed to negotiate with in Lombardy: the mercenary captain Sir John Hawkwood. In following a self-interested, commercial logic in switching his personal loyalties and military forces between Florence and Lombardy, Hawkwood provides a sobering and mundane subtext to this much-vaunted ideological conflict. And it is the framework of this conflict that provides the context for Chaucer's first encounter with Boccaccio's *Teseida*, the source of his *Knight's Tale*. Terry Jones may weaken his case by claiming that Chaucer's Knight *is* a mercenary, but his work should at least prompt us to consider the possibilities of Chaucer's reading Boccaccio's Italian martial epic within Italian and Anglo-Italian, as well as English, military and mercantile contexts.[94] Indeed, the strange mix of pessimism,

commercialism, and dark nostalgia that is so characteristic of Chaucer's *Tale*
may be more readily found in the culture and politics of contemporary Italy
than in the youthful, prepandemic *ottave* of Boccaccio's *Teseida*. In 1378 and
thereafter, Chaucer had occasion to contemplate these forces as embodied in
the life and legends of the mercenary captain Sir John Hawkwood, England's
most famous export to the Italy of Boccaccio and Petrarch.

Entrepreneur de Guerre: An English Mercenary in Italy

The *condottiere* Sir John Hawkwood, known in Italy as Giovanni Acuto, operated with extraordinary success and acclaim within the international political,
commercial, and military framework we have delineated.[95] The son of a tanner from the Essex village of Sible Hedingham and (legend has it) a one-time
tailor's apprentice, Hawkwood learned his military tactics by fighting in the
Hundred Years' War.[96] The Treaty of Brétigny, signed between England and
France in 1360, stranded thousands of landless and penniless troops—English, Welsh, Irish, Scots, French, Gascon, Breton, and Flemish—who formed
themselves into free companies, ravaged the French countryside, and looked
for fresh employment. Hawkwood joined many thousands of others who
traveled down the Rhône to visit the pope in Avignon. Innocent VI granted
them plenary indulgences and large sums of money to move on to fresh
wars in Italy, Spain, and the Rhineland. In January 1364 Hawkwood became
captain-general of the White Company, the Compagnia Bianca. He served
the Republic (and later the Doge) of Pisa. In 1368, Hawkwood moved to
Milan and frustrated the descent of the Emperor Charles IV into Italy.[97]
This ensured that the marriage of Violante, daughter of Bernabò Visconti, to
Lionel, Duke of Clarence, could go ahead without imperial interference. In
September 1372, on the pretext of delayed payments, Hawkwood left Bernabò
for the pope; within a few weeks he was fighting against Milan. In May 1375
he was briefed to invade Tuscany, but was bought off by the Florentines for
130,000 gold florins. He was awarded a stipend of 1,200 florins for life by the
Florentines and became a papal feudatory with estates in Romagna. In 1377,
Cardinal Legate Robert of Geneva persuaded the people of Cesena, who had
resisted the looting of his Breton mercenaries, to hand in their weapons. He
then sent Hawkwood to join the Bretons in the systematic massacre of the
city. Five thousand men, women, and children were murdered in three days.[98]
A few months later, in May 1377, Hawkwood left papal service and married
Donnina Visconti, illegitimate daughter of Bernabò Visconti. In 1378 Cardinal Robert of Geneva became the French antipope Clement VII; his Breton
mercenaries were retained to fight the Italian Urban VI.

No figure more perfectly embodied the contradictions that inspired the
coining of the term "bastard feudalism" than the late medieval mercenary,
defined by Georges Peyronnet as an "entrepreneur de guerre."[99] In shuttling

between the service of republics, despots, and popes, Hawkwood lived by the commercial contract rather than through forms of feudal vassalage. But he was still able to satisfy a widely felt nostalgia for the idealism and romance of ancient chivalry. His company, much feared and admired, was called the Compagnia Bianca because of its highly polished armor. The core of this company was formed by Hawkwood's *casa*, which, like a royal household, contained his most experienced and trustworthy men-at-arms as well as his personal attendants. When Hawkwood died in 1394, having spent most of his later years contracted to the Florentines, he was treated to a great funeral procession at Florence that featured the entire body politic, including the Signoria. But he was buried not at Florence but at Sible Hedingham, following an appeal from Richard II for the return of his bones to England.[100] Forty years later Uccello was commissioned to paint the equestrian portrait of Hawkwood that still hangs in the Duomo at Florence (plate 1). A century later Hawkwood was cited as a knight of noble and exemplary chivalry, worthy of imitation by moderns, in Caxton's *Ordre of Chyvalry*.[101]

Such romanticizing of the chivalric prowess of a knight who ran his company like a commercial venture, switching his allegiances for greater personal profit, may seem odd, hypocritical, even (to some) unmedieval.[102] But we should remember that mercenaries had long formed an important part of European armies, especially Italian ones: even at Campaldino in 1289, almost half of the one thousand Florentine cavalry that the youthful Dante fought with were foreign mercenaries.[103] Men captured in battle, who ranged in significance from the youthful Chaucer to the king of France, knew that the laws of ransom envisaged the relationship of prisoner to captor as analogous to that of vassal to lord. But they also knew that the word of honor they gave on the battlefield would soon be augmented by a written contract. The rights their captor enjoyed over them were as complete as rights over a freehold, which would be sold for the highest price possible. In 1360 the king of France was ransomed for three million gold crowns, and Chaucer for £16.[104]

The *condottiere* phenomenon is to be seen, then, not as a perversion of chivalric mores, but as a more overt recognition of the contractual character of late medieval military relations. The *condottiere* took his name from the *condotta*, or contract, that he signed with his employer. This arranged for the provision of a given number of troops for a given period in exchange for payment, chiefly in cash. *Condotte* had much in common with English indentures and French *lettres de retenue*. The main difference was that French and English contracts were usually issued to subjects of the king, whereas the Italians usually employed foreigners.[105] Florentines favored foreign *condottieri* for the same reason that they insisted on foreign *podestà*: outsiders on short-term contracts posed less of a threat to internal political order. But dependence upon mercenaries, undertaken as a short-term expedient, often had long-term costs, since the *condottiere* was in business not to win battles and restore peace

Plate 1. Paolo Uccello, *Memorial to Sir John Hawkwood*. Fresco transferred to canvas, Santa Maria del Fiore, Florence.

but to wage war. This point is wryly acknowledged by Franco Sacchetti, the Florentine politician and *novellatore*, in his account of a meeting between Sir John Hawkwood and two Franciscans. The friars greet Hawkwood politely, wishing him God's peace ("Dio vi dia pace"). Hawkwood grows angry; the friars grow alarmed. Since he lives by war, peace, Hawkwood explains, "would be my undoing" ("mi disfarebbe").[106]

When the friars return to their friary, Hawkwood's riposte is treasured there as a precious new verbal commodity ("una bella e buona novella"). But Sacchetti does not rest content with having added one more Hawkwood anecdote to the repertoire; he doubles the length of his *novella* by calculating the political cost of this cult of "messer Giovanni August":

And certainly, he himself lasted longer as a soldier of fortune in Italy than anyone else, for he lasted sixty years, and virtually every territory paid money for his protection; and he was gifted in business, so that there was very little peace in Italy in his time. And woe to those men and those peoples who trust too much in the likes of him, since peoples, and communes, and all cities live and flourish through peace; and his kind live and flourish through war, which brings cities destruction, waste, and decline. In his kind there is neither love, nor faith. They often inflict more harm on those who give them money than they do on soldiers of the opposing side. For although they make a show of wanting to fight and do battle with each other, they wish greater good for one another than they do for those who paid [condotti] them their money—it's as if they're saying: rob them over there, for I can rob them well here. . . . And why are so many cities in Italy, that once were free, now subjugated to despots? And why is Apulia in its present state; why Sicily? And what led Padua and Verona into war, and many other cities which today are reduced to ruined towns [triste ville]? (181.6–8)

Sacchetti's questions here are rhetorical, of course. It is the dependence upon mercenary captains that has led so many areas of Italy into ruin. It was as obvious to the Italian Trecento as it was to Machiavelli that only the formation of a citizens' militia would cure a city's dependence upon mercenaries. But the objection was always the same: permanently armed and organized insiders might present a greater threat to political stability than foreigners on short-term contracts. This argument was not altogether spurious. As John Larner notes, the armed insiders of fourteenth-century England, "a native, hereditary, but still paid military aristocracy," rose up to depose their king in 1327 and again in 1399.[107]

This lack of coordination between merchant capital, military force, and political governance represents one of the great weaknesses of medieval polity, one that makes the centralizing fusion of the absolutist state seem natural and inevitable. Merchant oligarchs in Florence and London were anxious to emphasize that they were ill-suited to participation in military affairs, and they instinctively resisted attempts to divert their capital into the public financing of military ventures (except when their own interests were under immediate

threat). Their very identity as merchants and financiers depended upon free
access to their own capital: "hir money is hir plogh," as Chaucer's "noble
marchant" says (7.281, 288). But much of this money was, of course, ploughed
back into the private contracting of military provisions for the endless wars.
In England, a commercial war party joined with aggressive elements of the
nobility in urging Richard II to keep the war going when things were going
badly in the field: beyond profits from contracting to the armies, these groups
could see that vast amounts were to be made from bringing Flanders within
the orbit of the English wool trade.[108] In Avignon, Tuscan merchants bought
up armor and weaponry from English and Breton soldiers who were made
idle by truces in the Hundred Years' War, and then sold them back to the
mercenary companies that were soon to descend on Italy. It was commonplace for the same merchant to supply troops on both sides of a conflict. In
1382, on hearing of the rout of a company of Free Lances in Liguria, a Tuscan
merchant immediately sent an agent to buy up all he could: "For, when peace
is made, they are wont to sell all their armor." [109]

   Chaucer dedicates four lines of his *Knight's Tale* to the looting of the battlefield after the defeat of Creon by Theseus. Although the *Riverside Chaucer* argues that "reasonable pillage" was permitted by the laws of medieval warfare,
the term *pilour* carries no positive connotations:[110]

> To ransake in the taas of bodyes dede,
> Hem for to strepe of harneys and of wede,
> The pilours diden bisynesse and cure
> After the bataille and disconfiture.   (1.1005–8)

The chief "bisynesse" here is clearly that of trading in surplus battle gear.
But without this profit-driven urge to trade, the *Knight's Tale* (like the *Man of
Law's Tale*) would be a very short story indeed. The "pilours," like the guild of
Syrian merchants in Fragment 2, form a vital linkage within a highly complex
narrative economy (one that renders the ways of Christian providence enig-
matic, if not inscrutable). Were it not for the Muslim merchants, Custance
may never have left Rome; were it not for the pagan "pilours," Palamoun and
Arcite would never have laid eyes on Emelye.

   Fourteenth-century merchants and mercenaries, who frequently had occasion to do business with one another, mythologized their own activities in very
similar ways. An army recruited by a *condottiere* was known as a *compagnia di
ventura*, a "company of fortune," just as if it were a commercial *compagnia*:
companies of merchants liked to think of themselves as merchant venturers,
as if they were a military band, perennially engaged on some perilous mission.[111] Such designations suggest a difficult, freewheeling, semiassimilated
relationship to the established structures of political power. Richard II, we
have noted, struggled long and hard (and with limited success) to strengthen
and regularize the relations of the state to the powerful resources of mag-

nate militarism and merchant capital. A comparable policy of drawing and binding commercial and military powers closer to the authority of the state was developed with exemplary efficiency by the Visconti in Lombardy. They willingly conceded *privilegium civilitatis Mediolani*, rights of citizenship, to foreign merchant houses that promised them financial support. As the Visconti state expanded, there was a high level of immigration into the *dominio*; by the end of the fourteenth century, a lot of talent and capital had been recruited from Tuscany (which had political as well as economic advantages). Merchants at Milan enjoyed little political power, but relied on the Visconti to ensure the safe passage of their goods and to deny all rights of association to the laboring poor.[112] *Condottieri* contracted for the expansion of the *dominio* were tied to the Visconti state through Bernabò's plentiful supply of illegitimate daughters; his illegitimate sons became *condottieri*.

Merchants and mercenaries were drawn together in Lombardy through the famous weapons industry that flourished at Milan: the Milanese dominated the international markets throughout the fourteenth century, exporting as far afield as Spain, France, and England. Milanese war-horses were also famous: it is quite plausible that the "M" branded on the flank of the Knight's horse in the Ellesmere manuscript would have been understood as a reference to Milan.[113] The volume of output was staggering: in 1380, for example, the Venetian ambassador to the Visconti sent Venice 2,228 basinets, 1,445 breastplates, 2,140 *libbre* (pounds weight) of saltpeter, and 180,000 lances in the space of nine months. Bernabò Visconti, who promoted the erection of an iron foundry at Brescia, was keen to harness the capital-intensive metalworking industry to the service of despotic regimes, chiefly his own.[114]

When the Tuscan merchant Datini wrote in 1378 that "Milan is a fine city and at the head of our trade," the trade he was thinking of was probably in weapons and armor.[115] Milan is "fine," not beautiful: even the Milanese had to concede that they could not compete with the beauty and elegance of Florence. But they did boast of the sheer size and wealth of their city (which was twice as big as Florence) and of the efficiency of the "urban machine" that governed its affairs.[116] This, then, was the city to which Chaucer came in 1378: not a *paradiso terrestre* of emergent humanism but a Dantean inferno of hundreds of noisy, dirty, metal-working suburban workshops surrounding an efficient civic administration that took its orders from a single lord.

The despatching of Chaucer to Milan in 1378 contains many historical ironies. Some of these must have become visible to Chaucer himself; some remained hidden. Sir John Hawkwood represented a new strain of commercialized military violence that had been engendered by the Hundred Years' War: Chaucer was now briefed to return such violence to its point of origin. He was expected to help his monarch by negotiating with Bernabò Visconti, but it was Richard's resemblance to despots such as Bernabò that would hasten his political and personal ruin. The Tudors would finally impose the kind of absolutist polity that was first established at Milan, but only after the country had replayed the protracted struggle between magnate groups that had brought the Visconti to power. Bernabò himself would come to a violent end; only four of the twelve Visconti despots died of natural causes.[117] The Visconti would finally be ousted by the Sforza, a dynasty that began as *condottieri* like Hawkwood.

The Visconti and the Formation of the Absolutist State

Although Viscontian and absolutist ideology worked to blur distinctions between the body of the ruler and the body of the state, Lombardy learned to live with the fall of princes. Most Viscontian despots died violently, but the Visconti state survived. The prototypically absolutist polity that had developed under the Visconti was inherited by the Sforza, who lasted for 85 years, and was replicated all over Renaissance Europe. When historians speak of the Duchy of Milan as "the first modern state in Europe," they assume that by modern state we mean the absolutist state.[118] Many of the lineaments of this modern state may be discerned in Milan of the late Trecento. What was achieved in Milan was aspired to elsewhere under monarchies, such as that of Richard II, which lacked the economic, military, and political power to develop and impose their own particular visions and variants of the absolutist paradigm.

One common feature of the development of absolutist polity is that the expropriation of the agricultural hinterland is rationalized and intensified. The city and the court, or the court in the city, become the focus of all cultural aspirations as the countryside becomes an invisible source of supply. This process of "precapitalist restructuring" was well enough advanced in Trecento Lombardy to enable the Visconti state to survive slumps in the urban economy or sudden demographic falls. Peasant holdings shrank or were swallowed up into much larger areas that were managed for the landowners by a *massaro*, or steward. The *massaro* was bound to his master by what purported to be a bond of enfeoffment, but was in fact a short-term commercial contract, signed before a notary. The conditions laid upon the *massaro* became ever more precise and demanding; he might be forced to pay for debts and damages by the direct confiscation of his personal goods, without right of public appeal. As holdings grew ever larger, and production became more intensive, the *massaro* and his family were joined by untenured migrant laborers. Before the rise of the Visconti most peasants owned or controlled the house they lived in and the lands they worked on; by the sixteenth century whole villages had been cleared and a new class of landless, deracinated laborers moved from one rural area to another, hounded by all kinds of hostile legal sanctions.[119]

These developments in Lombardy represent a precocious version of what was to happen elsewhere at a slower rate: in England, for example, between the fourteenth and seventeenth centuries.[120] And Milan was not alone in its ruthless subjugation and exploitation of its rural hinterland. Florence exerted unquestioned political and economic control over its *contado*;[121] it is evident throughout the *Decameron* that the rural poor of Trecento Tuscany are helpless in the face of the ingenuity and exploitativeness of city-dwellers.[122] Nonetheless, the mode of relationship contracted between peasant and proprietor was more quickly purged of any associative qualities—any sense of mutual obligation—in Lombardy than it was in Tuscany or elsewhere; the formation of the Visconti state facilitated and accelerated the destruction of the old agrarian structure.[123]

The Visconti were not interested in encouraging immigrants from the *contado* to embrace Milan as their new patriotic heartland: the focus of loyalty was to be the state, not the city. The population of Trecento Milan was of mixed origin, and it grew ever more mixed as merchants, notaries, and judges were recruited from other Lombard cities and then from other Italian regions.[124] Jewish bankers were allowed to settle in the city, and they soon became an essential pillar of support for Visconti finances. They were, inevitably, subjected to exceptionally heavy taxation and to occasional threats of execution, confiscation of property, or expulsion.[125] The Visconti, who were not themselves of Milanese origin, were pleased to enlist deracinated professionals who owed no patriotic allegiance to Milanese traditions: bankers, merchants, mercenaries, and even transient humanists such as Petrarch were drawn in from all over Italy and Europe. This policy of employing functionaries, *funzionarismo*, proved a useful means of excluding established Milanese families from participation in or identification with city government.[126]

The local, popular traditions of parish and *porta* (local district) at Milan had been established for many centuries, and the Visconti recognized that they were obliged to co-opt them rather than seek their abolition. They left many communal structures intact, transforming them through the infiltration of their own appointees from decision-making bodies into simple administrative and executive offices. Periodically they even allowed these civic bodies to exercise themselves by confirming the Visconti succession: this happened in 1339, 1349, 1354, 1377, and 1385.[127] Most aspects of communal life were controlled by the *vicario*, who served a two-month term. The *vicario* was directly answerable to the Signore from 1313 on; he continued to exercise his office in the Palazzo del Commune until the end of the eighteenth century. The office of *podestà* predictably lost much of its former meaning, whereas that of *referendario* (controller of finances) gained in importance. Membership of the Consiglio Generale, once the principal organ of communal government at Milan, lost its active political significance and became a badge of privilege to be worn by "the best, the richest, the most noble citizens."[128] Through the vagaries of patronage, encouraging first one house and then another, the Visconti ensured that no unified grouping could form itself from the leading noble or mercantile families, some of which traced their origins back to communal times.[129]

In 1288, the chronicler Bonvesin de la Riva argued that those with money ("sufficientem pecuniam") lived extremely well at Milan.[130] Fifty years later, Galvano Fiamma sings the praises of Milanese merchants for a long paragraph of his *Chronicon extravagans*.[131] Although the excessive destructive capacity of Bernabò led the Milanese economy into a stagnant period, Milanese merchants continued to prosper under Gian Galeazzo.[132] The historical understanding reached between the Visconti and the Milanese entrepreneurial class was, once again, indicative of what was to happen in sixteenth-century England: the merchant capitalists were to direct their own affairs and amass considerable wealth while, in exchange, surrendering significant participation in affairs of state.[133]

A further parallel between Tudor England and Visconti Milan is suggested by the employment of humanist-trained notaries and chancery clerks for the drafting and promulgation of princely decrees. In 1536, for example, Richard Morison left his humanistic studies at Padua to join Cromwell's staff. He was soon penning a set piece of humanist oratory against the Catholic rising known as the Pilgrimage of Grace, namely, "A Lamentation in Which Is Showed What Ruin and Destruction Cometh of Seditious Rebellion." The piece was demanded at short notice: "As for my *Lamentation*," Morison wrote, "I did it in my boots . . . in a[n] afternoon and a night."[134] Similar tasks were required of those who worked in the Visconti chancellery. All ducal letters and all internal and external decrees were transmitted through this office. Some important early humanists such as Pasquino Capelli and Antonio Loschi were put in charge of this operation, which sought to endow the will of the prince with the legitimating power of humanist rhetoric.[135] This task could be as perilous under the Visconti as it was under Wolsey and Cromwell. In August 1398, for example, Capelli was accused of having deceived the Viscontian mercenary Iacopo dal Verme with a false letter. He was found guilty and put to death.[136]

Notaries and jurists who labored in Bernabò's *curia* at Milan occupied a huge block of buildings known as the Broletto Nuovo, a site that formed the political and administrative center of Milan from its establishment in 1327 until the coming of Napoleon. Law was theorized and elaborated there at the Collegio dei Giureconsulti and enforced from the Casa del Podestà. The *vicario delle provvisioni* marshaled an army of notaries during his two-month tenure: every official act that entered or issued from his office had to be duplicated in its appropriate register. Close by, the nine hundred members of the Consiglio Generale met in a huge *salone*. Outside, a great crowd of lawyers and notaries served clients from tables set up in the piazza, and commercial life was organized from the Badia dei Mercatanti.[137]

The Broletto was an energetic, crowded place where all kinds of people could meet and do business. But, as a civic center, it was structured and designed to dramatize centralized control over the population rather than to accommodate the people themselves. Bernabò's famously intimidating equestrian statue, in the church of San Giovanni in Conca, was situated right next to his *curia*.[138] In 1396, Gian Galeazzo decreed that the porticoes beneath the Broletto should remain free of any encumbrance—except the perches provided for the falcons, goshawks, vultures, and other birds of prey that were kept beneath the vaults of the *palazzo centrale*. (The *podestà* of Milan was obliged to present the Signore with a hunting dog and a falcon every year as a sign of homage.) The main block of buildings was designed to function like a city within a city: if trouble threatened, a drawbridge was raised and the Broletto closed itself off, like a fortress.[139] This symbolic domination, or appropriation, of civic space was a familiar instrument of Visconti policy. At Parma, for example, the main piazza was closed off with chains from the general population between 1318 and 1326 and was later sealed off entirely by a crenellated wall; this space was renamed, as a warning to the people who once walked across it in communal days, "Sta in Pace" (Keep the Peace).[140]

Visconti Culture and the Ghost of Petrarch

The Visconti and those who chronicled them had a keen understanding of the political functions of architectural style:

Azzo Visconti . . . set his mind to making himself a glorious house, for the philosopher says in *Ethics* book four that the building of a house is a task befitting a great man. For the people, on seeing such astonishing dwelling places, remain mentally stupified through intense admiration [mente suspensus propter vehementem admirationem], just as *Politics* book six says. From this is derived the belief that the prince is so powerful that it is impossible to attack him.[141]

Galvano Fiamma, a Dominican at the Milanese monastery of Sant' Eustorgio, was a "farraginous compilator" who set out to glorify and defend Milan; Giovanni Visconti was apparently sufficiently impressed to make Fiamma his own *cappellanus et scriba* ("chaplain and scribe").[142] The Dominican makes much use of Aristotle, "the philosopher," in his attempt to justify the ways of the Visconti, but is often visibly struggling to reconcile their actions with the notion of *bonum commune* as filtered through medieval understandings of Aristotelian ethics and politics:

It befits a magnificent prince to make great expenditures on behalf of the entire community, as the philosopher says in the *Ethics*, for common goods [bona communia] somewhat resemble goods consecrated by God. For the divine good is weakly represented in a single person, or in a private or individual setting; but a divine cult or divine good shines more beautifully when set in the whole community. And so Azzone Visconti, lord of the political community [dominus civitatis], to whom the whole of the social body [totius universitatis] looks for its well-being, having seen to the construction of his private residence, turned his attention to public building in magnificent manner. (p. 20)

Fiamma's loyalty to Aristotle commits him to some tortuous maneuvers here as he attempts to show how a *dominus civitatis* acts for and expresses the will of an entire community. An apologist for such a *dominus* would be better advised to abandon Aristotle entirely and turn to Augustine, for whom the value of the "order of the state," *rei publicae*, is that "it controls the wicked within the bonds of a certain earthly peace."[143] The sin of Adam, for Augustine, means that fallen and corrupted human nature no longer instinctively seeks the common good. Some form of state is needed, "and even the worst tyranny has some justification."[144] Petrarch's reverence for Augustine, and his contempt for Aristotelians, proved to be excellent qualifications for an apologist of Viscontian and absolutist power.

In 1378, the Visconti completed work on the new facade of Santa Maria Maggiore, the ancient basilica of Milan. An effigy designed for this facade neatly illustrates the relationship between ancient and modern envisaged by this project: the Madonna della Misericordia, representing the new Duomo, towers above the old church and protects it beneath her outspread mantle.[145] Such a compromise, and such an image, suited the Visconti for less than ten years: in 1387, Gian Galeazzo announced plans for a comprehensive new building project. The ancient basilica, which had been the traditional focus of Milanese religious life for many centuries, was to be completely destroyed. The spectacle of destruction itself must have taken the best part of a year. The new Duomo was to break with the architectural and sculptural styles practiced by Pisans, Tusans, and Venetians at Milan in favor of a northern European postgothicism. This radical departure symbolized the Viscontian dream of establishing a European Ghibelline block uniting the powers of Austria, Bavaria, Burgundy, Hungary, and Milan.[146]

This new architectural language was also forced upon subject cities within the Visconti *dominio*. Through the employment of foreign professionals from north of the Alps, local traditions were erased in favor of the centralized model of the Milanese Duomo. Within the city itself, the financing and building of the Duomo was made the chief public concern of each district, or *porta*. Each *porta* was obliged to collect offerings for the building fund and then, once a year, parade through their own district and hand over the proceeds to the Duomo.[147] These processions included decorated wagons that became stages for the playing out of spectacles in the piazza before the Duomo. The first recorded list of expenses (December 22, 1389) includes materials needed to decorate the wagon or chariot of Jason, "to make it similar to the ship of the Argonauts."[148] Such spectacles form a point of transition between the earlier, dramatized religious processions recorded by Galvano Fiamma and the Renaissance *trionfi* (another Petrarchan mode) in which the Signore would pass through arches of triumph to make a dramatic entrance in his *carro trionfale*.[149] The real historical drama here is the gradual absorption of local, associative forms of *festa cittadina* into the staging of princely power, and the gradual merging of princely and religious authority. As early as 1404, the citizens of Milan could look upon the statue of San Giorgio in the Milanese Duomo and recognize the features of Gian Galeazzo Visconti.[150]

The Visconti were infatuated with Gothic style long before they began redesigning their Duomo. In attempting to construct an authentic court culture they looked, above all, to the model of the French Valois. In 1360, when the treaty of Brétigny obliged the captive King John to pay a huge ransom, the Visconti offered him 300,000 florins for the hand of his daughter, Isabelle, plus 300,000 florins for the purchase of a suitable dowry in France. The Florentine chronicler Matteo Villani insinuates that when Isabelle entered Milan on October 8, to marry the ten-year-old Gian Galeazzo, she lost her pedigree within the Viscontian bordello: "And from that point on, oblivious to her royal dignity and nobility of blood, she made reverence to messer Galeazzo and to messer Bernabò and to their women."[151] Gian Galeazzo was certainly keen to advertise his French pedigree, styling himself the "Conte di Virtù" after the tract of land in France in the county of Vertus (some eighteen miles from Châlons-sur-Marne) that his 300,000 florins had bought him. Although Florentine propagandists ridiculed this opportunistic word-play suggesting that Gian Galeazzo was "the Count of Virtue," he regularly used this title until he became duke in 1395.[152] Valentina, daughter of Isabelle and Gian Galeazzo, was married to Louis d'Orléans, younger brother of King Charles VI of France, in 1387. When Isabelle died, Gian Galeazzo appropriated her motto, "à bon droyt."[153]

There was a steady demand for French illuminated missals and books of hours in northern Italy throughout the Trecento. Toward the end of the century, however, Lombard illuminators developed styles and techniques of their own sufficiently distinctive and distinguished to attract notice in France as *ouvraige de Lombardie*: it is highly probable, for example, that the representation of December in the *Très riches Heures du duc de Berry* is influenced by the style of Giovannino de' Grassi.[154] Giovannino's lavish use of three kinds of gold, of silver, and of beautiful, rare, and extremely costly lapis lazuli in the famous *Visconti Hours* hardly squares with the kind of civic-spirited public munificence Galvano Fiamma applauds in his *Opusculum*. The *Visconti Hours* is designed for limited display within a small and privileged coterie. The political priorities suggested by this miniature, private, and capital-intensive form of artistic production (as opposed, for example, to the monumental art of Trecento Tuscany) are spelled out in detail on every page of the famous codex through a continuous overlapping, doubling, and confusion of Christian and Viscontian iconography.[155]

Gian Galeazzo is represented three times in the *Visconti Hours*.[156] Unlike his famous French counterpart, the duc de Berry, he never kneels before angels or saints in a religious posture; his head is depicted in a medallion. This lifelike head, with its receding hairline, sloping brow and forked beard, makes its first appearance on folio BR 105r. in a medallion beneath the illuminated D of *Dixit Domine*. This psalm (109) was associated with the anointing of kings, and there is some suggestion that Gian Galeazzo has achieved charismatic powers through his anointing because he is staring at the Annunciation depicted on the folio opposite. God beams his word down to Mary from the top left corner of the illumination on BR 104v., and the Count of Virtue looks along the same line of sight from the bottom of 105r. (plate 2a). Gian Galeazzo, in short, is looking in the face of God.

Gian Galeazzo next appears on BR 115r. in a medallion beneath the D of *Defecit in salutare tuum anima mea* (Psalm 118.81; plate 2b). "Why Gian-galeazzo's portrait appears in the midst of this Psalm," Kirsch comments, "is not apparent."[157] But this extraordinarily lengthy psalm is entirely concerned with *lex Domini*. It begins:

> Beati immaculati in via,
> Qui ambulant in lege Domini.
>
> Blessed are the undefiled in the way,
> who walk in the law of the Lord.

Within Giovannino's capital D, God dictates his law to an elderly King David, seated on a faldstool. But this scene is framed by the symbols of the earthly lord depicted beneath: the most infamous Visconti emblem, a viper swallowing a man whole and alive (waving his arms) appears on shields in all four corners; fleur-de-lys encircle the scene and the French motto (here contracted to "adroyt") is set above the biblical text in a sunburst (another Viscontian symbol). Gian Galeazzo's portrait in profile, which takes up the bottom third of the page, is framed by hunting dogs in pursuit of deer. Five folios later, King David (rejuvenated as a long-haired version of Gian Galeazzo) himself appears as a hunter (BR 120v.; plate 2c). The courtly life of Gian Galeazzo has now migrated from the margins to camp within the central religious space of the illuminated initial: framed by the L of *Letatus sum* (Psalm 121), the monarch sits on a throne, rests his feet on a cushion, and listens to three musicians playing upon a viol, a psaltery, and a portable organ. Two hunting dogs lie at his feet, and Temperance and Fortitude (two of the cardinal virtues employed as emblems of the Count of Virtue) appear as elegantly attired ladies of the court; a third lady plays chess with a male courtier within a draped pavilion that rises up to mark the toe of the L. Text and miniature are framed by a lavish border that repeats the "adroyt" motto twelve times in gold. The whole scene represents an outrageously literal and secular response to the invitation issued by the psalmic verse:

> Laetatus sum in his quae dicta sunt mihi:
> In domum Domini ibimus.

> I was glad when they said unto me,
> Let us go into the house of the Lord.

Just two folios later (122v.; plate 2d), another psalmic verse offers sentiments for illustration sure to please a Visconti lord: "Nisi Dominus aedificaverit domum" ("Unless the Lord build the house, they labor in vain that build it," Psalm 126). Within the N of "Nisi," a team of five men labors mightily in mixing and hauling mortar, in carrying bricks up a ladder, and in laying them with trowels. But the only man "building" here, according to the logic of the text, is the *dominus* looking out over the work site from his balcony. Lordly vision creates the building; in the margin below, a team of five angels supports a banderole proclaiming "adroyt" (Gian Galeazzo's motto).

The Viscontian *dominus* makes his last appearance on folio BR 128r. beneath a verse proclaiming "I will praise thee, O Lord, with my whole heart" (Psalm 137). He is set within a sun that blazes forth long golden rays, drawing attention away from the somewhat cramped scene within the initial. A smaller sun in the top border contains a dove, another Viscontian symbol that sometimes does double duty as the Holy Spirit. Left and right margins contain blazing mandorlas framing Viscontian helmets and shields. Such marginal motifs, which lead the eye away from the central scene of religious revelation toward Viscontian insignia, inspire a more dramatic setting later in this same book of hours (LF 4v.; plate 2e). Here God, with his left hand on a text and his right hand raised, directs his word of revelation down from the top half of an initial K (in *Kyrie*) to the upturned faces of a crowd of saints below. In the left and right margins, angels of greater physical dimensions appear from clouds to hand down Viscontian emblems (vipers swallowing men) into the upstretched arms of courtly ladies. These angels, in their blue clouds, are modeled on the figure in the left margin of BR 145r. (plate 2f), where God hands down to Moses the tablets of the law.

By associating Mosaic law with Viscontian law, the Lord with the Viscontian lord, the house of the Lord with the Visconti household, David the Hunter with Gian Galeazzo the hunter, then, the miniaturists of the *Visconti Hours* share in a cultural mission more commonly associated with court poets and notaries: the legitimation and mystification of Visconti power. Comparisons might be made with the aggrandisement of Richard II in the Wilton diptych (in which English *angeli* wear his personal livery badge).[158] But for an appropriation of religious motifs that rivals Viscontian boldness, one must await an English monarch whose personal style rivals Viscontian violence, namely, Henry VIII.[159]

A complementary aspect of book culture under the Visconti was represented by the libraries at Milan and Pavia. No records survive from Bernabò's library at Milan, which was set on fire during the riots that accompanied his downfall in 1385. The library founded at Pavia by Galeazzo and developed by Gian Galeazzo is recorded by an inventory of January 1426 that lists

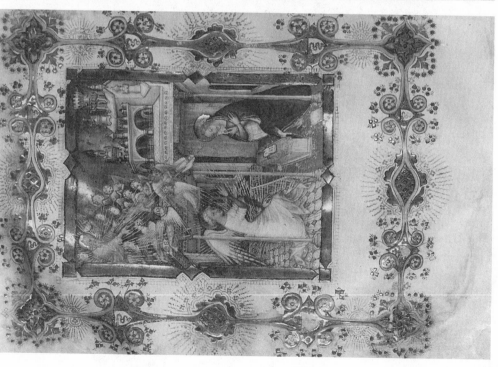

Plate 2. *Visconti Hours.* In 2 manuscripts, Biblioteca Nazionale, Florence: Banco Rari 397 (BR; illuminations by Giovannino dei Grassi and assistants); Landau-Finaly 22 (Belbello da Pavia and assistants).

(a) BR 104v, *Annunciation;* 105r., Psalm 109, "Dixir Dominus "

(b) BR 115r, Psalm 118.81, "Defecit in salutare . . ."

(c) BR 120v, Psalm 121, "Letatus sum . . ." (initial).

(d) BR 122v., Psalm 126, "Nisi Dominus . . ."

(f) BR 145r., *Canticle of the Three Hebrews (in the Fiery Furnace),* "Benedicite . . ." Detail, left margin.

(e) Landau-Finaly 4v., "Kyrie . . ."

988 volumes; about one hundred of these are housed today in Paris at the Bibliothèque Nationale.[160] The chief inspiration for this library was, once again, the example of the Valois. Despite Petrarch's long years of association with Milan and Pavia, the library reflects a preponderantly conservative taste and a deep attachment to cultural models for which Petrarch reserved his loftiest contempt: French romance and scholastic learning. No sign of Petrarch's vernacular verse survives, and the Petrarchan works in Latin found in the library were, for the most part, comfortably assimilated by conservative clerical culture.[161] Most of these were not, in any case, brought to Pavia until Gian Galeazzo's defeat of the Paduan *signore* Francesco Novello da Carrara in 1388.[162] But, as many critics have noted, a remarkably large number of Chaucerian source texts were to be found in Pavia.[163] It is quite possible, for example, that Chaucer first came across the *Filostrato* in Lombardy rather than Tuscany: item 800 in the Pavia inventory refers us to "Liber unus . . . in vulgari qui dicitur philostrato . . . incipit *Molte fiate già nobilissima donna* [which tells us that this exemplar came complete with Boccaccio's prose prologue] et finitur *domando vendeta cum.*" Item 859 refers to a work "vocatur *Amorosa Visio* domini Johannis bochacij Certaldo"; there were two copies of the *Decameron* (296, 870).

It is not surprising to find the *Filostrato* in the library of a Francophile Visconti prince because it was written under the spell of the French-derived court culture of Angevin Naples. No fewer than sixteen French romances were to be found at Pavia: three of these were dedicated to the *matière* of Charlemagne, seven to Arthur (including 916, "tractans de mortis regis Artusij,"), and six to classical matters. Five of these six classical romances deal with Troy. It seems likely that the Italian *Filostrato* was a popular work in Visconti court circles, since French romance was much in vogue. In 1371 Ambrogio Visconti, illegitimate son of Bernabò, wrote to his "Magnifice ac potens Domine et tanquam pater carissime" from the midst of a military campaign, requesting the loan of "quendam pulchrum *Aspremontem* tractantem de Karulo Magno."[164] Bernabò himself had a whimsical fondness for naming his illegitimate offspring after the heroes and heroines of French romance: Ginevra, Isotta, Lancellotto, Palamede, Sagromoro.[165]

Latin learning at Milan and Pavia was traditionally reserved for a narrowly defined clerical world; there are few signs to suggest that lay people succeeded in breaking into these closed circles of late medieval scholasticism. But the extraordinary range and number of French translations of Latin texts at Pavia suggests that there was a sustained and concerted attempt to mediate Latin culture to court circles: there were, for example, three manuscripts in French containing the Boethian *De consolatione* (841, 867, 936) and an "Albertanus in gallico, incipit *car le loer* et finitur *sans fin*" (238). There were also Tuscan and Florentine translations of Latin texts and prayers, saints' lives and prayers to saints that may have originated in these vernaculars; there were four copies of the *Commedia*, plus "Dantis Comentum satis magnum" (220). All four of the encyclopedic works written by Boccaccio to facilitate the reading of *auctores* were at hand: *De mulieribus claris* (381), *De montibus* (382), *De casibus virorum illustrium* (384), and *De genealogijs deorum antiquorum* (384). There are two works in Provençal (412, 890), but there is nothing that represents work of genuine Milanese provenance.[166] The Visconti, like the Neapolitan Angevins, showed no interest in promoting or encouraging the resources of their local vernaculars. Their apparent acceptance of Tuscan as the normative Italian tongue meshes with their general policy of alienating local populations from local traditions.

The figure who most powerfully embodies the deracination and self-alienation suggested by Viscontian culture is, of course, Petrarch. Gabrio de' Zamorei, a longtime servant of the Visconti, described Petrarch as "a Florentine, the chief of poets and my second father."[167] The position of a famous Florentine in Lombardy was certainly highly anomalous. Petrarch's Florentine correspondents could never accept that the leading light of an emergent literary culture, a movement that would later be termed humanism, had elected to serve despots. Petrarch's decision to settle at Milan and to work for the regime that posed the gravest threat to his own republican *patria* may be seen as a typically self-contradictory, self-alienating act expressive of a new, postmedieval individualism. It may also be seen as an astute and precise calculation of personal advantage that required some tortuous acts of self-justification.

Petrarch's power as an international cultural celebrity was without parallel or precedent in medieval Europe. The Visconti employed him frequently and to great effect during and after his years at Milan (1353–61). He was shipped up the Po to Pavia to lend luster to the famous "Visconti wedding" of May 25, 1368. He paid his last visit to Pavia in May 1369 and died during the night of July 18, 1374. Milan and Pavia still boasted many signs of Petrarch's presence in 1378 and contained many people who were professionally associated with him. Gabrio de' Zamorei, for example, who spoke of Petrarch as his "amicum dilectum," continued to serve the Visconti until Gian Galeazzo awarded him a house in Parma in 1386.[168] When Giovanni, Petrarch's first patron, died in 1354, Zamorei was asked to compose the metrical elegy that can still be read on his tomb. He chose a direct form of address, as if Giovanni were speaking for himself: "You, who pass by, read and learn . . ." Zamorei understood how a Viscontian image might be empowered even as it spoke as a *memento mori* renouncing such power: "I was a great and powerful tyrant when alive: our name was feared by heaven, land, and sea. Powerful cities were subject to my rule: the obedient city of Milan, the territory of Lodi . . ." (a long list of cities and territories follows).[169] Zamorei wrote a coronation address for Emperor Charles IV, Anne of Bohemia's father, who was crowned at Milan in 1355. He continued to compose orations and tomb inscriptions for many years to come; this was the kind of politico-literary piecework that Petrarch routinely performed for the emperor, the Visconti, and other despotic patrons.[170]

There were at least two pictorial representations of Petrarch in the Visconti castle at Pavia. One of these was a color portrait, and the other a painting of a famous scene that Galeazzo was keen to memorialize: the infant Gian Galeazzo, on being asked to identify the wisest man present at a banquet, chooses Petrarch.[171] The eclogues through which Petrarch sang the praises of Galeazzo provided a model for later poets, although the miserable *canzone* composed by Braccio Bracci on Galeazzo's death in 1378 shows little Petrarchan *gravitas*.[172] Court poets were keen to invoke the spirit of Petrarch in their continuing attempt to legitimate the political aims and ambitions of the Visconti. Francesco Vannozzo goes so far as to raise Petrarch from the dead. He imagines that Petrarch appears to him, commanding him to take a celestial gift to Gian Galeazzo. This gift might be characterized as political counsel, although it amounts to little more than the assurance of divine underwriting for despotic "desio": tell your "signor giocondo," the ghostly Petrarch says, "that God is on his side / and the heavens are disposed to accommodate his desire."[173]

The idea that Petrarch might speak from beyond the grave was perhaps prompted by his reputation as a necromancer. Petrarch himself attributed such "laughable nonsense" to his well-known devotion to Vergil.[174] Vergil's reputation as magus and necromancer had been reinforced in some semi-educated and clerical imaginations by his role in Dante's *Commedia*. When Petrarch died in 1374 he is said to have been found sitting at his desk, lying forward with his head resting on the text of Vergil. This story meets expectations generated by a lifelong personal regimen that was, for many of his contemporaries, notably eccentric and mysterious: his predilection for wild, woody, or deserted places; his habit of getting up in the middle of the night, or of studying until dawn; his fondness for "pagan" culture. Petrarch himself worked to promulgate rather than suppress knowledge of his extraordinary personal habits through the detailed self-analyses of his correspondence. This art of constructing a singular and eccentric personality, at once powerful and innocuous, centered and marginal, was tested and developed by Petrarch within the pressured ambit of despotic power.[175] The fund of stories, anecdotes, and personal observations cultivated through such art were doubtless still circulating in Viscontian circles in 1378. The Visconti were always keen to advertise their connections with Petrarch, since they clearly recognized that he was the most authoritative and successful apologist they had ever had.

Renaissance Historiography and the Origins of Civic Humanism

Dante, Boccaccio, and Petrarch were authors promoted as cultural legends within the political communities that claimed them; such legends were tailored to fit the particular needs of their sponsoring communities. Chaucer may have heard stories about Petrarch from the five hundred Englishmen who attended the Visconti wedding in 1368 and perhaps from the Bohemians who accompanied Anne of Bohemia to England in 1381.[176] In 1378, however, he had ample personal opportunity to situate the cult of Petrarch (and the tortuous self-interrogation of Petrarchan poetics, memorialized in Book 1 of *Troilus and Criseyde*)[177] within and as part of a form of polity designed to individuate and aggrandize the power of a single despotic ruler. Five years earlier, while Chaucer was in Florence, Florentine citizens with civic and literary interests were discussing the possibility of *lecturae Dantis*, a series of lectures that might continue the process of rehabilitating Dante as a Florentine author. The public petition seeking these lectures was approved by a majority of 167 votes; Boccaccio, who was looked to as the most distinguished exponent of literary culture in Florence, was the obvious choice as lecturer.[178] In visiting Florence and Milan, then, Chaucer was educated not only by his textual encounters with three preeminent writers but also by his sense of how such texts are actively shaped and posthumously mediated by the changing needs of distinctive political communities. Such reflections would encourage a writer to meditate not only on his next composition, but on the function and meaning of this composition in its textual afterlife.

In following Chaucer as he comes into relationship with the great Trecento poets, we have moved him into the framework of a historiographical narrative that finds closure only centuries later through the Europe-wide emergence of the absolutist state. But the incipient revolution in cultural awareness associated with this change of political forms has been held to be a national affair: the Italian, according to Burckhardt, was "the first-born among the sons of modern Europe."[179] The political and cultural space between Florence and Milan in the late Trecento has come to assume quite exceptional importance for western historiography, perhaps unparalleled importance. It has been represented as the cradle or crucible of Renaissance consciousness and of civic humanism, as the site of the great paradigm shift that shattered the narrow confines of medieval thinking by opening up Europe to the possibilities of New Worlds—first the world of classical antiquity, and later the Americas. In the course of this long chapter, we have acquired some detailed historical understanding of this Florentine-Milanese divide; we have also situated Chaucer's movements both within this space, and beyond it, in a greater, circumambient international nexus of merchant capital, mercenary enterprise, and magnate militarism. All this qualifies us and urges us to interrogate some of the claims made for medieval/Renaissance periodization that are supposedly founded in this particular Italian terrain. Although such claims are rarely interrogated, they continue to enforce limits on what the text of Chaucer— defined a priori as an insular, medieval text—can possibly mean.[180]

A preliminary, ground-clearing survey of modern historiography of the Renaissance might begin with Voltaire or Michelet, but Jacob Burckhardt's *Die Kultur der Renaissance in Italien* is a more appropriate starting point, since it continues to exert enormous influence over what Alberto Tenenti dryly delimits as "études anglo-saxonnes sur la renaissance florentine."[181] William Kerrigan and Gordon Braden, in their prize-winning *The Idea of the Renaissance*, make Burckhardt the acknowledged hero of their attempt "to mount a Hegelian history of the Renaissance": Burckhardt's story, they insist, is "the history of early modern individualism," "a story that still matters today."[182] Burckhardt, we have noted, connects the triumph of Renaissance individualism with the demise of the collective and associational forms of medieval times. "In the Middle Ages," Burckhardt writes, "man was conscious of himself only as a member of a race, people, party, family, or corporation—only through some general category."[183] According to Braden, the ambition to achieve "personal identity independent of 'some general category,' a desire and frequent ability to see oneself as something other than a 'member of a race, people, party, family, or corporation' is still for the most part the Renaissance we think and write about."[184]

For Braden, Burckhardt's work is exemplary "in the enterprise of reading a particular culture as a unified whole, of integrating political, social, and material history together with our continuing response to the art and literature of the time."[185] But the "whole" that Burckhardt seeks to evoke is essentially a Hegelian zeitgeist; he ignores economic matters and shows little interest in broader questions of causation.[186] He does examine many aspects of despotic and republican cultures, but the forms of contestation between such regimes are judged less significant than the "grosses geistiges Continuum" that envelops them both.[187] Burckhardt begins his account of this "new life" with the despotic regimes, because they represent "the completer and more clearly defined type" of Renaissance state (1.22; 13). Frederick II is identified as "the first ruler of the modern type" through his determination to effect "the complete destruction of the feudal state" (1.24; 13). The cruelty and ruthlessness required by all despots is supposedly imitated, at this originary moment, from political practices in the Islamic world.[188] (Those who "wasted their lives" in resisting incipient despotism are neatly isolated, by Burckhardt, from "the majority who were content with a strictly private station, like those of the urban population of the Byzantine Empire and the Mohammedan states.")[189] Despots such as the Visconti, working with "Mohammedan" ruthlessness,[190] discouraged organized political resistance and in so doing helped foster a new *Individualismus* by encouraging a turn to the private realm.[191] Petrarch, a vital figure in this transition, is brought forward early in Burckhardt's volume in the act of advising a despotic patron on the treatment and definition of "citizens":

Weapons, guards, and soldiers thou mayest employ against the enemy—with thy subjects goodwill is sufficient. By citizens, of course, I mean those who love the existing order; for those who daily desire change are rebels and traitors, and against such a stern justice may take its course.[192]

This epistle, dated November 28, 1373, was written for Francesco da Carrara, the Paduan despot who became Petrarch's chief patron after he left the Visconti. Francesco allowed the *signoria* of Padua to pass to his son Francesco Novello in 1388; Padua was swallowed up into the Visconti Empire in 1393, and the older Francesco (like Bernabò) died a prisoner in one of Gian Galeazzo's castles. Burckhardt is by no means embarrassed by the fact that Petrarch spent his mature years in the service of despots. Later historiographers, however, have gone to extraordinary lengths to conceal, ignore, or rationalize away this troubling phenomenon. Hans Baron shows a consistent tendency to segregate the poetical and humanist Petrarch from the political conditions in which he worked, and to divide the younger Petrarch ("who seems to be travelling straight toward the Quattrocento") from the mature Petrarch (whose vision is dimmed "by a recrudescence of Augustinian reservations, a prevailing attitude of pessimism, and, to some extent, seclusion from the world").[193] Rather than connecting this change in Petrarch with his choice of despotism, Baron locates Petrarch in a mythical limbo that escapes definitions of time and place: "Petrarch . . . was, as I see him, neither 'medieval' nor 'Renaissance,' but (if I may use the figure) rather a Moses, first to see a new land, but not granted to enter it."[194] This dehistoricized, mythical Petrarch, an odd hybrid of Dante's Vergil and an Old Testament prophet, continues to haunt the pages of Baron's admirers and disciples. Even Perry Anderson, we have noted, cannot resist Petrarch's vatic spell.[195] Anderson speaks eloquently of the Renaissance discovering itself "with a new, intense consciousness of rupture and loss"; and yet he does not think to associate such a consciousness with the self-alienating effects of living under despotism, where the rupture with communal liberties and the loss of meaningful political life are still (in the fourteenth century) keenly felt.

The subject of despotism in Burckhardt's account undergoes something akin to the classic romance motifeme of exile and return.[196] Recognizing his political impotence in the public sphere, such a subject retreats into fashioning himself as the new *Privatmensch*. If cultivated with sufficient discipline and intensity, this role may enable him to return to public life as an agent of the prince, for, according to Burckhardt, the prince, the mercenary captain, and the poet are united by their common pursuit of *Individualismus*:

Despotism . . . fostered in the highest degree the individuality not only of the tyrant or *condottiere* himself, but also of the men whom he protected or used as his tools—the secretary, minister, poet, and companion. These people were forced to know all the inward resources [innern Hilfsquellen] of their own nature, passing or permanent; and their enjoyment of life was enhanced or concentrated by the desire to obtain the greatest satisfaction from a possibly very brief period of power and influence.[197]

Burckhardt's last sentence here offers a political rationale for what might be termed the *de casibus* sensibility, the poet's or despot's newly heightened awareness of the brittle and contingent character of seigniory.[198] The essential task is to prevent the turn of the wheel, the fall from power. This, for Burckhardt, is achieved through the core quality of this new individualism, the exercise of will. Burckhardt, we should remember, was a friend and colleague of Nietzsche at Basel; both men were admirers of Schopenhauer, who insisted on the importance of will in history where Hegel had stressed reason.[199] Burckhardt's infatuation with *Willenskraft*, the power of will, enables him to experience Dante's *Commedia* as a hymn to the power of individualism. Dante's poem is severed from the communal and associational values that inform it from first to last; it is, in short, evacuated of social content and infused with the power of will:

Dante, who even in his lifetime was called by some a poet, by others a philosopher, by others a theologian, pours forth in all his writings a stream of personal force [persönlicher Macht], by which the reader, apart from the interest of the subject, feels himself carried away. What power of will [Willenskraft] must the steady, unbroken elaboration of the *Divine Comedy* have required![200]

It is difficult to recognize any aspect of Dantean poetics in this notion of a text written to no end but the exemplification of the willpower that writes it. For Dante all action is public action, and the possibilities of action conducive to the public good are powerfully constrained by the political circumstances within which they are performed. Even the best-intentioned individuals may fall short of salvation by attempting to live in a corrupted city such as contemporary Florence, which is mirrored by Dis, its infernal counterpart.[201] Dante fails to match the profile of the Burckhardtian *Privatmensch* because his writing does not admit the possibility of a private sphere, or of any sphere of activity that is discontinuous with the public values that the writing itself must exemplify. But whereas Dante is an exiled Florentine, Petrarch is a deracinated emigré who has negotiated a new *modus operandi* with despotic patronage. In exchange for the possibility of independent political action, Petrarch is granted access to a limitless realm of imaginative and artistic freedom. He may exercise his artistic will within this private literary world with as much vigor as his despotic patron employs to exercise his will on the public stage. Since the power of will is, for Burckhardt, the mark of greatness, both poet and patron may share in analogous forms of glory: the poet reflects, and is reflected in, the splendor of the prince.

In Hans Baron's *The Crisis of the Early Italian Renaissance*, the political differences between Florence and Milan, as articulated by early Renaissance humanists, assume a central importance. Baron declares himself loyal to Burckhardt's "fundamental discovery, that the Renaissance was a prototype of the modern world," and commits himself to the method "of interpreting great turning-points in the history of thought against their social or political background."[202] But whereas Burckhardt argues that fourteenth-century despots were the first to embody this new individualistic spirit of the Renaissance, Baron insists that the crucial shift in human consciousness took place within the walls of Florence between 1400 and 1402, generating the ethos of "civic humanism." Baron concedes that the constituent parts of this new ethos, or ideology, had been gestating for some time within the body politic of Trecento Florence. But it was not until Florence was faced with the imminent threat of annihilation by Gian Galeazzo that a Ciceronian ethos of public service fused with an acceptance of worldly wealth to form the new consciousness, this "prototype of the modern world."[203]

Baron's development of a crisis model of historical explanation was clearly influenced by the spreading threat of Nazism across Europe. In 1942 he argued that the failure of Italy to achieve national unity under the Visconti was not, as most historians since the Risorgimento had maintained, a disaster: on the contrary, "without Florence's survival in the decisive hour, there would not have been in the Quattrocento anything like the outburst of cultural energies that we call the Renaissance."[204] The saving of the Renaissance necessarily entailed the saving of Petrarch. So it is that Baron sees the "revolution in intellectual life" precipitated by the 1400–1402 crisis as an intellectual homecoming for Petrarch, whose "humanism was transplanted into civic surroundings—first and foremost into the civic world of Florence."[205] Petrarch's uncivic, or precivic, humanism was evidently not touched or compromised by the despotic soil or manure it lay buried in; on being transplanted to Florence, the Petrarchan seed, "unable to sprout during the Trecento, finally took root."[206] Suddenly, as the new century wipes the slate clean, humanism can assume its authentic social dimension:

Not until after 1400 did the climate change; then, in Florence, for the first time in medieval lay society, an entire group built its ideals on the conviction, whose influence on the practice of life is manifest, that every man, including the scholar and the man of culture, can discharge his full responsibilities as a human being only by living and working as a member of a political and social community.[207]

There are many oddities and anomalies here; I will comment on just four. First, it seems that Baron's Renaissance marks a return to Burckhardt's Middle Ages: to the time when "man was conscious of himself only as member of a race, people, party, family, or corporation" rather than as a "spiritual *individual*."[208] The commitment to communal values Baron insists upon belongs, for Burckhardt, to the time when "human consciousness . . . lay dreaming beneath a common veil . . . of faith, illusion, and childish prepossession." Burckhardt's Renaissance begins when the new "spiritual *individual*" recognizes his (always his) singularity, and hence becomes capable of "an *objective* treatment and consideration of the State and of all the things of this world" (1.143; 137). The self-discovery of Baron's Renaissance subject also precedes commitment to the state: having discovered himself as separate *from* the state, the subject commits himself to living and working *for* the state. There is no suggestion here of a dialectical definition of identity: the private subject lives and works for the political and social community not to discover or realize his own being but to "discharge his full responsibilities." Despite his insistence upon the "civic" dimensions of Renaissance consciousness, then, Baron is still working from a Burckhardtian model of *Individualismus*. This model better explains the consciousness of the nineteenth-century subject in capitalist society, who knows himself to be alienated from the state, than it does the mentality of 1400, in which the values of family and corporation are still of primary importance.[209]

The second dubious feature of Baron's civic humanism is the suggestion that it is in no way complicit with despotism, but actually forms a heroic rearguard action against "the triumphant progress of Tyranny in Renaissance Italy."[210] By its very nature, Latinate humanism tends to narrow rather than broaden the audience it speaks for: Lauro Martines has characterized it as "a program for ruling classes."[211] In rewriting the two volumes of his 1955 *Crisis* into the single-volume edition of 1966, Baron took pains to work against "the time-honored identification of the Volgare tradition with the medieval Commune, and of Humanism with the Tyranny of the Renaissance" (p. xxvii). But even when Florentine humanists resort to the vernacular, it often appears that, as a class, they have more in common with the Milanese humanists than they do with any other element of Florentine society. When Coluccio Salutati fired off the violent, accusatory sonnet "O scacciato dal ciel da Micael," for example, Antonio Loschi fired back "O Cleopatra, o madre d'Ismael." Fired back or mirrored back: the formal and rhetorical similarities of the two sonnets are as striking as the political differences (Florentine republicanism, Lombard despotism) they give voice to.[212] It is not surprising to learn that Salutati and Loschi were both students of the Cremonese humanist Pasquino Capelli. Loschi worked with his former teacher at the Milanese Chancellery until Capelli was put to death by Gian Galeazzo; he then took over his job. Salutati acceded to Gian Galeazzo's request for an epistle justifying tyrannicide following the death of Bernabò in 1385.[213]

Third, it should be observed that this small, élite group of Florentine humanists served and reflected the ideals not of Florentine society but of the small, élite group that controlled it. (Baron elides this difference by speaking of "an entire group," then "every man," then "political and social community.") The epoch of civic humanism did not see an increase in political involvement, but witnessed rather a progressive alienation of the citizenry from public life.[214] Citizens were transformed into more or less passive subjects as "an élitist regime . . . developed from the old corporate chrysalis."[215] The constitutional trappings of this time-honored corporate *integumentum* were retained, and the myth of a regime based upon the whole guild community was promulgated with renewed vigor. The chief mythmakers of this narrowed oligarchy were, of course, the humanists, who took a leading part in transforming the medieval commune into a modern bureaucratic state.

If Baron had been genuinely committed to looking for a crisis in the mind of the Florentine civic body, one directly experienced by more than an élite group within that body, he might well have considered the period when Florence went to war with the pope and was placed under interdict: there can hardly have been a more dramatic and symbolically suggestive conflict, acted out within the city walls, between associational and hierocratic claims to power. Or he might have traced the long revolution in civic consciousness that dawned in the mind of Giovanni Villani in 1300 and was developed by a succession of historiographers throughout the Trecento.[216] But these writers were all of merchant stock, and Baron subscribed to the view "that as far as the economic activities of the Italian merchant class are concerned, 'Renaissance individualism' had already reached its zenith by about 1300, if not earlier, and that during the period called by the cultural historian 'The Renaissance' . . . the merchant's enterprising spirit, as well as his public-mindedness, had become inferior to what they had been in the preceding centuries."[217] Ferguson notes that Baron did make one excursus (under the influence of Weber) to explore the influence of economic factors on the formation of humanist consciousness; here he does acknowledge the importance of the new class of merchant industrialists who came to power after the bankruptcy of the great Florentine banking houses in the 1340s.[218] But Baron later defended his neglect of economic factors as an "enforced limitation": one must "frankly admit that at this moment not every cultivated area of Renaissance research can receive an adequate share in a coherent interpretation of the civilization of the Renaissance."[219]

One suspects that the whole post-Renaissance history of humanism, the tradition within which Baron writes as a "cultural historian," would not encourage Baron to look for any significant revolution of consciousness in the minds, or in the vernacular manuscripts, of Trecento chroniclers from merchant stock.

The fourth and perhaps most widely experienced misgiving about Baron's work stems from his insistence that the crucial "climate change" lies bottled within the time capsule of 1400–1402. (It is worth noting that this supposedly epoch-making, all-Italian affair coincides with—and to some limited extent plays a part in—the English struggle that ended with Henry of Hereford's defeat of Richard II.)[220] Critics such as J. G. A. Pocock, Quentin Skinner, P. O. Kristeller, and Charles Trinkhaus have drawn attention to earlier phases of the Florence-Milan conflict and to earlier traditions of rhetoric and political theory that contributed to the evolving humanist mentality.[221] A remarkable number of social, economic, military, and demographic historians share Baron's own assessment of the singular importance of the 1340s, what Brucker has termed "the decade of disaster."[222] Without wishing to revive a simplistic base-and-superstructure model to explain how the collapse of banking houses, the tightening of tax structures, the surpassing of citizens' militias by mercenary companies, or the catastrophe of plague affects cultural production,[223] it seems plausible to nominate Boccaccio's *Decameron* as a text voicing the real crisis (if we must look for crisis) of Florentine civic consciousness. The powerful rhythms of Boccaccio's prose style, which many readers have experienced as naturalistic or realistic, lighten the ideological burden that weighs more heavily on the pages of his fellow Florentine mythmakers. These merchant historiographers, who shared Boccaccio's class origins, were keen to extoll, "both in fact and theory, the sway of communal law." [224] Boccaccio himself, no less civic-minded, found more subtle ways of celebrating the vigor, versatility, and self-regulating competence of Florentine polity. And yet the homogenizing effect of the *novella* form and the serene functioning of the official *brigata* cannot subdue the restless and unsynthesized energies that trouble the narrative surface. The *novella* contains within itself heterogeneous voices from a variety of genres of varying social provenance; the ten storytellers are shadowed by a lower-order, kitchen-dwelling *brigata*. The plague is not necessarily over when Boccaccio returns us to Florence. Recurrent disaster, natural or social, remains an active possibility.[225]

Before concluding this section, we should note that all these attempts to theorize a period or paradigm shift known as the Renaissance are silently influenced by a huge, all-enveloping gynecological metaphor. For Burckhardt the deployment of this metaphor was a matter of deliberate choice: "The Renaissance will be presented," he said in planning his *magnum opus*, "in so far as it has become the mother and home of modern man." [226] The Italians, we have noted, were to be celebrated as "the first-born among the sons of modern Europe." This first-born son, as despotic individualist, was responsible for bloody, cruel, and violent acts. Here Burckhardt is influenced by Goethe's notion of a new age "that brought forth men of rare passion, marked by gross sensuality and feverish, brutal vindictiveness, but also by higher yearnings." [227] The most famous of first-born sons is Cain: the suggestion here, then, is that the bloody excesses of the son are to be associated, but not too overtly, with the passion and sensuality of the mother. Trecento Italy is thus established as the Eva and Ave of modern consciousness.

Bastard Poetics: Chaucer in Florence and Lombardy

In following Chaucer to Florence and Lombardy, we have cut across (and hence come to question) the cultural categories and historiographical schemata that define and constrain medieval English poetics. We have considered the poetics of Trecento Italians within and as part of distinctive (but mutually defining) political systems. The narratives generated by the collaborative enterprise of Boccaccio's Florentine *brigata* exemplify and critique the associational ideology of Florentine polity; the deracinated individualism of Petrarchan poetics finds a home within the ambit of Visconti despotism. These polarized Italian options, I have argued, offered Chaucer (as poet and political subject) clarifying visions of possible English futures: the possibility of constructing and maintaining a *felaweshipe*, an associational form that is clearly inspired by the Boccaccian *brigata*; the tyrannical possibilities of "Lumbardye," explored in four different narratives (and found to be increasingly topical as Richard II's reign wore on).[228] But Chaucerian fiction does not, of course, consistently map itself along the lateral and vertical axes of associational and despotic polity best exemplified by the *General Prologue* and the *Clerk's Tale*. The discrete yet mutually defining paradigms of Florence and Lombardy serve not only to clarify the possibilities of English polity but also to reveal its extraordinary complexity. This point may readily be grasped by considering one last historiographical metaphor, one that speaks not of new birth nor of rebirth ("Renaissance") but of dubious political parentage.

In 1885, Charles Plummer spoke of "the period of pseudo-chivalry, which, under a garb of external splendour and a factitious code of honour, failed to conceal its ingrained lust and cruelty, and its reckless contempt for the rights and feelings of all who were not admitted within the charmed circle." This characterization seems tailor-made for the Visconti, but is in fact applied to "the reign of Edward III," the period that "saw the beginning of . . . bastard feudalism."[229] K. B. McFarlane, in a seminal essay, isolated this last phrase and suggested that if the negative connotations of bastardy were suspended, "bastard feudalism" might well prove a useful term in the attempt to characterize late medieval English polity. The "quintessence" of this "new order," according to McFarlane, "was payment for service."[230] Such a definition tends, once again, to suggest continuities rather than differences between English and Italian experience. The Visconti, we have noted, made extensive use of a thoroughly bastardized feudalism in order to secure loyalties to their territorial state. The merchants of Florence, who were forced to accommodate residual feudal elements within their associative polity, discovered that through the principle of "payment for service," mercantile wealth could be translated into the continuous exercise of political power. English annuitants and retainers discovered "greater freedom of choice at every stage," as traditional notions of liege homage yielded to various forms of contract service.[231]

The "bastard" aspect of all this might be crudely summarized as the incipient experience (if not the understanding) of what the movement of capital can do, what magic it can work, as it loosens traditional bonds, obligations, and metaphysical certainties. Boccaccio interprets this experience within, and on behalf of, the associative polity of Florence: the *Decameron* is the most subtle and complex expression of an emergent city-state ideology. Petrarch, through his unparalleled cultural celebrity or fame, creates an unprecedented "freedom of choice" for himself. He chooses to continue his cultural mission, subsequently characterized as the founding of humanism, within and as part of a despotic polity that promises physical security, privacy, and a new, wholly individualistic form of artistic freedom. Chaucer's experience in seeking to establish and stabilize a distinctive poetics is the most complex, the most bastardized of all, because his own political positioning is the most complex and conflicted. The historical Chaucer lived and worked at the intersection of royal, magnate, and mercantile worlds and witnessed a dizzying succession of polities, from the broadest-based associational model (peasant uprising) to the narrowest form of hierarchy (the tyranny of Richard II).

By situating Chaucer in Florence and Lombardy, then, we discover not only a context for his reading and interpretation of Boccaccio and Petrarch, but also a metaphor for the unparalleled complexity of his own positioning as an English poet. He functions within both associational and hierarchic forms; in responding to the exceptional complexity of fourteenth-century English polity, he is at once the poet of Florence and Lombardy. The heterogeneity of Chaucer's *Canterbury Tales* is unique. No other framed collection contrives to enable so many genres to follow their own laws of operation and hence achieve such a plurality of imaginative worlds. This does not happen in Trecento Italy. Nor does it happen in sixteenth-century England, which, finding itself dissatisfied with the diversified forms of Chaucer, turns to novella and sonnet, the homogenized generic forms of Boccaccio and Petrarch. As English polity comes closer to realizing the centralizing absolutist paradigm, and as traditional associational forms are abolished or constrained, Chaucer is found archaic and semi-intelligible, hence rustic and provincial. The terms of Chaucer's displacement by Elizabethan writers, ostensibly stylistic, are fundamentally political. For Sidney, the great champion of Italian-inspired humanist poetics, Chaucer is to be imagined as a rustic dung-spreader, one who manures the way for the high-flying wit of modern times.[232] For Puttenham, Chaucer (along with Langland, Gower, and Lydgate) is hindered by a language "now out of use with us."[233] He is in effect a northerner, since those north of the Trent are recognized as speaking "the purer English Saxon."[234] Despite or because of such a pedigree, such a language "is not so Courtly nor so currant as our Southerne English is." Even in declaring "the usuall speach of the Court, and that of London and the shires lying about London within lx. myles" as normative, Puttenham's dicta for humanist-inspired ornament effectively exile Chaucer from the capital.[235] Chaucer is now to be classed with the "rum ram ruf" artists that he himself—"a Southren man," always writing close to the center of power in London, Kent, and Westminster—had once defined provincial (10.42–43).

Chapter 2

The *General Prologue* and the
Anatomy of Associational Form

The *General Prologue* to the *Canterbury Tales* proposes that adults representing (almost) every profession, cultural level, age, and sexual orientation can come together under one roof, form themselves into a corporative unity and regulate their affairs without reference to external authority. Historically speaking, this is a remarkable proposition, one that is difficult to imagine by 1415 and impossible by 1600. And the ease with which Chaucer, as poet and first-person speaker, meets and enters into such a group finds no parallel in later English literature: in T. S. Eliot's *Waste Land*, for example, the social and linguistic divide between the London pub dwellers ("Goonight Lou") and the poet ("good night sweet ladies," echoing Shakespeare) is never closed; corporate integration is never an option.[1] Given the singularity of the *Prologue*'s achievement, then, it is remarkable that recent Chaucer criticism has concerned itself with that part of it which, since Jill Mann's *Chaucer and Medieval Estates Satire*, requires least exegesis: the descriptions of individual pilgrims. By dedicating so much space to the *Prologue*'s middle section, Chaucer criticism unconsciously evokes an institutional setting that has no contemporary relevance: the pilgrim *descriptiones* are figured as portraits hanging for leisurely scrutiny in a Tennysonian palace of art.[2] It is time to forget the master metaphor of the art gallery and focus attention on the cultural institution that is actually taking shape in the *Prologue*: the *felaweshipe* or *compagnye* of pilgrims.

The first half of this chapter will trace the process through which Chaucer's *compagnye* gradually brings itself into being. The self-constituting dynamics of associational form, analogous to processes that we have observed at work in Boccaccian Florence, form the chief subject of Chaucer's *Prologue*. In Southwark as in Florence, however, a *brigata* or *felaweshipe* must remain vigilant against the despotic proclivities of its own members (such as those of Herry Bailey, "Oure Hoost"). Having sought the resources in political theory and historical practice that enable Chaucer's *Prologue* to assert that humankind is by nature an associative animal, we will consider, briefly, the alternative vision put forward by Augustinian and Robertsonian readings. The medieval guilds, I shall argue, functioned as a schoolroom for teaching the basic grammar of group behavior exemplified by Chaucer's *felaweshipe*.[3] The perennial temptation to sentimentalize guild structures, a temptation that writers such as Baron, Durkheim, and Gierke have found difficult to resist, will be countered (in this chapter and the next) by detailed historicization. The possibility of idealizing the *Prologue* as an associational form is, I shall argue, denied by Chaucer himself: the *Prologue* contains an extraordinary number of subgroups that operate within and against the unifying structure of the *felaweshipe*; it also contains a number of extraordinary individuals (the Pardoner, the Wife) who remain unassimilable.

Émile Durkheim has argued that the social division of labor facilitates, rather than obviates, *solidarité organique*, a superior form of group solidarity. Chaucer's confidence in the possibility of constructing a functional associative polity (and a great work of fiction) from social elements that are so sharply diversified might seem to endorse a Durkheimian optimism concerning the social effects of the division of labor. Chaucer, I shall argue, tempers optimism with doubt. He begins, through the poem's first authorial signature, by recalling his allegiance to a great European tradition of writing even as, at the same moment, he doubts the value of the English text he is about to write. And yet finally, in figuring himself as a putative husband for the Wife of Bath, he proves willing to claim paternity, to own himself the *makere* of this pleasurable and instructive project of dilated narrative.[4]

Forming the *Felaweshipe*

In the opening period of the *Canterbury Tales*, according to Derek Pearsall, Chaucer "emphasises a scientific and philosophical perception of spring, not a human and social one."[5] But there is no hard opposition here between the human-social and the scientific-philosophical, as there is, say, in the *Knight's Tale* or *Troilus and Criseyde*, where (in certain passages) a protagonist seems especially vulnerable when isolated beneath the rotation of impersonal (scientific and philosophical) schemata. The disjunction between these two sets of discourses is bridged in this opening period by nature, or Nature,[6] which appears both as concept and (at work among birds, 1.11) personification. It is as if Chaucer has fused the opening of his *Parliament of Fowls* with its close: the impersonal cosmological dream of Scipio with the gathering of human voices and bird bodies surrounding Nature. The succession of the seasons, the blowing of the west wind, and the movement of the sun are described directly in terms of their effects on vegetable, animal, and human nature. The main verb of this extraordinary sentence, discovered in line 12, is "longen"; its grammatical subject, discovered immediately afterwards, is "folk," a collective noun. What folk are said to "longen" to do is surprising. The steady emphasis upon the promptings of nature (and the expectations engendered by count-less dream visions and romances) prepare us for a longing for love; instead we find a longing for pilgrimage. And this quickly, somewhat gratuitously, brings us to the dominant theme of the division of labor. Even pilgrimage has its professional specialists:

> And palmeres for to seken straunge strondes,
> To ferne halwes, kowthe in sondry londes.   (1.13–14)

Returning abruptly to England in the next line, we discover that this long-ing for pilgrimage is both natural and voluntary: pilgrims seek out Becket, the martyr, because he helped them recover from illness. This sense of obli-gation, which amounts to the honoring of a contract, is foreign to the animal and vegetable worlds. The period closes with the discovery of a uniquely human act.

The general effect of the opening period, to quote Pearsall again, is to situate Chaucer's "great poem . . . under the canopy of a wise and ami-able governance."[7] The emphasis upon natural amiability is maintained as the poem turns from divine to man-made governance. The second sentence brings us to a solitary individual—Chaucer—who is soon joined by 29 other individuals viewed as a preformed corporate entity, a *compagnye* or *felawe-shipe*. The impulse that moves the pilgrim Chaucer to communicate with this group is both entirely natural and peculiarly human. Man, Aquinas remarks in his commentary on Aristotle's *Politics*, "is more inclined than any other animal to communicate with others."[8] The facility with which Chaucer is received into the *felaweshipe* bespeaks a confidence in the natural sociability of human beings that is shared by Dante as he forms his own *compagnye*, his *Convivio*: "ciascuno uomo a ciascuno uomo naturalmente è amico."[9] And the single means of this incorporation accentuates the unique importance that language—more specifically, the human voice—must assume for Chaucer (as for Dante) as the source and sustenance of social and political life. Chaucer, quite simply, talks his way into the *felaweshipe*:

> And shortly, whan the sonne was to reste,
> So hadde I spoken with hem everichon
> That I was of hir felaweshipe anon.   (1.30–32)

The duration of Chaucer's speaking is measured by the movement of the sun. This serves to connect the making of *communitas* with the greater natural movements encountered in the opening period. This third period has a defi-nite air of closure about it; the next sentence initiates the lengthy description of individual pilgrims. This turn to individuals does not signal a temporary neglect of communal concerns: the individual pilgrims are described chiefly in terms of their work, and the need for specialized work skills can only attest to the necessity of organized society.[10] Work is as natural and unique to human beings as language; the necessity of work and language argues that humankind is a political animal, not an aggregate of atomized individuals.

Chaucer signals the end of his pilgrim descriptions, after some 672 lines, by referring to an agreement, or "forewarde," contracted with a community beyond the text: "Now have I toold you . . ." (1.715). This reference outward to a second community, the unstable and constantly varying "us" of his readership, accentuates the strangeness of the Chaucerian "I," which sometimes situates itself with "us" as readers, sometimes with "them" as pilgrims, and is sometimes an invisible third person. A significant shift takes place in the course of the pilgrim descriptions. The pronouns "hem" and "they" give way to "we" and "us";[11] the externalized perspective suggested by "ech of hem" and "whiche they weren" (1.39–40) yields to talk of "how . . . we baren us," "our viage," and "oure pilgrimage" (1.721–24). This new emphasis upon the first-person plural is hammered home with peculiar force (an "us" in every line) immediately before the last of the pilgrim *descriptiones*:

> Greet chiere made oure Hoost us everichon,
> And to the soper sette he us anon.
> He served us with vitaille at the beste;
> Strong was the wyn, and wel to drynke us leste.   (1.747–50)

The Host, of course, has not yet been received into the *felaweshipe*; he addresses it from the outside. His description is detached from the main body of pilgrim portraits, and it is different in kind. There are few professional tricks and traits here that are peculiar to tavern-keeping:

> A semely man OURE HOOSTE was withalle
> For to been a marchal in an halle.
> A large man he was with eyen stepe—
> A fairer burgeys was ther noon in Chepe—
> Boold of his speche, and wys, and wel ytaught,
> And of manhode hym lakkede right naught.
> Eek thereto he was right a myrie man.   (1.751–57)

It is striking that the two specific social and political identities applied to the Host describe him in terms of where and what he is not. He is not a citizen of Cheapside, London, but of Southwark (a crucial distinction explored in the next two chapters); nor is he "a marchal in an halle." The likening of the Host to a "marchal" is both suggestive and ominous for the process of group formation that is about to ensue. A marshal, according to the *Boke of Nurture* ascribed to one John Russell, needed to be expert in reading fine discriminations of social degree: he needs to know that a sergeant of law may sit with a former mayor of London (but not with a current one) and that a master of Chancery may sit with a "worshipfulle prechoure of pardoun."[12] In assigning such pairings, a marshal is concerned to establish social equivalencies, associative groupings of two. But his preeminent concern, of course, is with hierarchy: who sits above, who sits below. His aim is not to nurture general conversation but to prevent it:

> These worthy Estates a-foreseid / high of renowne,
> Vche Estate syngulerly in halle shall sit a-downe,
> *that none of hem se othure* / at mete tyme in feld nor in towne,
> but vche of þem self in Chambur or in pavilowne.   (1073–6; my italics)

The Host's marshallike proclivities will make themselves apparent through his first attempted pairing (1.3118–19) of storytellers, "sire Knyght" and "sir Monk."[13] These two pilgrims are what Bataille would term sovereign individuals: they are the preeminent representatives of a "feudal and priestly hierarchy." With their greyhounds and battle gear they practice "the consumption of wealth as against labor and servitude," and their "sovereign attitude is exemplified by use of the surplus [production] for nonproductive ends."[14] Such a pairing (and the hierarchical schema it portends) will, of course, be rejected by the Miller and hence by the collective project of the *felaweshipe*. The Host will, however, continue to be seduced by his personal fantasy of the "sovereign" or "myghty man" (7.1951); the *felaweshipe* will need to remain on its guard.[15]

The Host's initial approach to the *felaweshipe* promises "myrthe" and governance; the impulse to "doon a myrthe" comes first:

> "I saugh nat this yeer so myrie a compaignye
> Atones in this herberwe as is now.
> Fayn wolde I doon yow myrthe."   (1.764–66)

The Host no sooner thinks of an appropriate "myrthe" (767) than he discovers, like Aquinas before him, that there can be no *felaweshipe* without governance: "The Fellowship of society being thus natural and necessary to man, it follows with equal necessity that there must be some principle of government within the society."[16]

The Host's first thought, as he grasps the need for governance, is that he will embody it in his own person (a person, we should note, that remains as yet external to the *felaweshipe*). The pilgrims are to exercise themselves as a corporate entity only to vote away their own sovereignty and subject themselves, in silence, to the judgment of a single outsider.[17] This form of government seems set to strangle the *myrthe* to which it is struggling to give birth:

> "And therfore wol I maken yow disport,
> As I seyde erst, and doon yow som confort.
> And if yow liketh alle by oon assent
> For to stonden at my juggement,
> And for to werken as I shal yow seye,
> Tomorwe, whan ye riden by the weye,
> Now, by my fader soule that is deed,

> But ye be myrie, I wol yeve yow myn heed!
> Hoold up youre hondes, withouten moore speche."   (1.775–83)

The fact that the Host swears an oath is important since, "narrowly defined, a commune is an association on the basis of an oath"; "commune means
exactly the same as a common oath." [18] But the Host's oath can do nothing
for communal integrity because it is sworn outside the *felaweshipe* and binds
nobody but the Host himself (to his father's ghost). His proposals for regulating the *myrthe* envisage only complete success or absolute failure and leave no
space for flexibility or political maneuver. If he fails the pilgrim body can have
his head: the proposition both mocks and mirrors the form of governance he
is currently proposing—a corporate body ruled by a head to which it is not
actually attached.

The political tact and acumen lacking in the Host is generously supplied
by the *felaweshipe* itself. The pilgrims realize that the Host's desire to organize
a *myrthe* is ill-conceived but not malicious: "Us thoughte it was noght worth
to make it wys" (1.785). The Host gets himself into less of a political muddle
when he restricts himself to the practicalities of the tale-telling contest; in
speaking of himself as a fellow traveler and "gyde" (1.803–4) he no longer
sounds like a demented despot. His plans prove acceptable to the pilgrims,
who swear their oaths and make the Host swear his. It is at this point that
the *compagnye* is formally constituted as a *communitas*; its corporate aims are
immediately set down with admirable precision and economy:

> This thyng was graunted, and oure othes swore
> With ful glad herte, and preyden hym also
> That he wolde vouche sauf for to do so,
> And that he wolde been oure governour,
> And of oure tales juge and reportour,
> And sette a soper at a certyn pris,
> And we wol reuled been at his devys
> In heigh and lough; and thus by oon assent
> We been acorded to his juggement.
> And therupon the wyn was fet anon;
> We dronken, and to reste wente echon,
> Withouten any lenger taryynge.   (1.810–21)

This crucial passage, which is dense with the terminology and symbolic
action of political life, requires close attention. The first important thing to
notice, after the oath-taking, is what the *felaweshipe* asks the Host to be: "oure
governour." "Governour" is a title soon to be applied to Theseus (in the third
line of the *Knight's Tale*), but with an important qualification: Theseus is "lord
and governour," whereas the Host is plain "governour." A *governour* is not
necessarily a lord, enjoying absolute rights of power or ownership; he is simply
someone who directs affairs. When Chaucer wishes it to be understood that

a specific *governour* is also a lord (or a god), he makes the qualification with evident care.[19] When John of Gaunt served England as *gubernator* during the minority of Richard II, he helped govern the realm but was not lord of it.[20]

The term *governour* derives from the Latin *gubernator*, a helmsman or pilot of a ship.[21] Such connotations might encourage us, momentarily, to imagine the incorporated *felaweshipe* as a vessel about to leave harbor with the Host at the helm, especially since the Tabard has just been described as a "herberwe" (1.765).[22] This might please critics who have strained to see Chaucer's *felaweshipe* as expressive of a newly emergent nation-state consciousness. But such a metaphor is very difficult to sustain (the rest of the *Tales* offers us little encouragement), especially if we put this ghost ship up against a genuine literary vessel: the ship *Souveraine*, conceived by Philippe de Mézières just as Chaucer was writing his *General Prologue*.[23] The three-decked *Souveraine*, also called *Gracieuse*, represents the French ship of state sailing toward Jerusalem (with a weather eye open to its own commercial profit). Her three decks represent the three estates; her rudder is called *tymon barionsis*, her yard is the cross and her captain the king.[24] The French text here associates progress in sailing to Jerusalem (and in amassing great mercantile wealth en route) with the fortunes of the French state; pilgrimage here (as in both parts of Shakespeare's *Henry IV*) becomes a nationalist metaphor.[25] There is little of this in Chaucer, who is writing a different kind of vernacular pilgrimage text; his Canterbury *felaweshipe* is very unlike a ship of state.[26]

Having asked the Host to be its *governour*, Chaucer's *felaweshipe* at once (completing the couplet) adds a more specific duty: the Host is to be "of oure tales juge and reportour." This last term, "reportour," appears nowhere else in Chaucer (or, it would seem, in Ricardian England).[27] But Hoccleve offers an interesting gloss on it in a passage of his *Dialogue with a Friend* which is evidently influenced by this part of the *General Prologue*:

> Considereth ther-of / was I noon Auctour;
> I nas in þat cas / but a reportour
> Of folkes tales / as they seide / I wroot:
> I nat affermed it on hem / god woot!   (1.760–63)[28]

The opposition posited here between "auctour" and "reportour" suggests that a *reportour* is to be seen as the oral equivalent of a scribe, the lowest figure in the literary hierarchy.[29] As applied to the *Canterbury Tales*, this establishes a distinction between Chaucer as *auctor* outside the text and the Host (rather than Chaucer the pilgrim) as *reportour* within it. We find the Host performing his role as custodian of the *felaweshipe*'s oral text on the very next morning: "Ye woot youre foreward, and I it yow recorde" (1.829).

The legalistic precision of this utterance is accentuated by the verb *recorden*, which (as *recorder*) was applied to the process in Norman law of reciting or testifying "on recollection what had previously passed in court"; the task of recording "was the duty of the judges and other principal persons who presided at the *placitum*."[30] We should also note that the term *tale* (as in "of oure tales juge and reportour") is heavily freighted with legal connotations: a plaintiff's first pleading was known as a *narratio, count,* or *tale*;[31] and Skeat finds equivalents in French and Latin for the legalistic tag phrase "in heigh and lough."[32] By the time the pilgrims finally repeat the rhyme of 777–78, then ("by oon assent/juggement," 1.817–18), the *felaweshipe* is being described by a language highly suggestive of legal incorporation. Small modifications are still being made: the Host had proposed that the *felaweshipe* would "stonden to" his judgment, whereas the pilgrims agree to "been accorded" to it. The last modification of all (in the pilgrims' drinking habits) comes last and is the most important. Earlier on, the pilgrims had drunk just for pleasure: "Strong was the wyn, and wel to drynke us leste" (750). Now the drinking serves a purely symbolic function in seeking a common agreement: "And *thereupon* . . ." (1.819). Its symbolic status is preserved by insisting on the brevity of its duration: the pilgrims drink and then retire, "Withouten any lenger taryynge" (1.821).

As the next day dawns, the Host's newfound powers of governorship are celebrated in humorous vein. Where we expect to find sunrise and cockcrow, natural and traditional markers of temporality, we find, instead, the Host:

> Amorwe, whan that day bigan to sprynge,
> Up roos oure Hoost, and was oure aller cok,
> And gadrede us togidre alle in a flok . . .   (1.822–24)

These lines announce a new day with a rapidity and lack of ceremony that seem the very antithesis of the *Prologue*'s leisurely opening period. Such intensive usage of animal imagery in describing human governance wryly acknowledges that problems of political discourse are bound up with the limits of language. Corporate bodies tend to imagine their existence by shifting natural imagery (sun, cock, and flock) into metaphor. But choices of metaphor influence our assessment of specific corporations: if the *felaweshipe* is a "flok," and the Host is "gathering" it, is the Host to be situated within or outside the terms of the *felaweshipe*? Such questions remain with us as we see Chaucer put his flock on horseback and get on with the business of storytelling (1.824–25).

Sources and Vocabularies of Associational Form

The lexicon of medieval political thought is notoriously difficult to work with. Terms shift their meaning with each instance of deployment; the political theories they combine to construct tend to detach or abstract themselves from historical practice.[33] Single words often contain such a range of meanings and applications that they themselves require a whole dictionary of terms to accommodate their interpretive possibilities. A prime example of this is *felaweshipe*,[34] an ungendered collective noun that incorporates the singular and masculine *felawe*: "Lat every felawe telle his tale aboute . . ." (1.890).

The only pilgrim said to be skilled in *felaweshipe* is the Wife of Bath ("In felaweshipe wel koude she laughe and carpe," 1.474); the suggestion that this skill might extend to housing or incorporating *felawes* is developed later on: "I koude noght withdrawe / My chambre of Venus from a good felawe" (3.617–18). *Felaweshipe* is as old as Eden: God made woman from Adam's rib, the Parson says, "for womman sholde be felawe unto man" (10.927). But *felaweshipe* should not be confused with equality, nor (God forbid) with female superiority: "For ther as the womman hath the maistrie, she maketh to muche desray" (10.926). *Felaweshipe*, a political term, brings a gender politics (more or less visible) to each instance of deployment. It rarely suggests affective neutrality or indifference because it speaks from the condition of being bound up, or closed in, with other people. Recognition of such association, or *felaweshipe*, may in both modern and medieval usage be expressed in terms suggestive of approval, resentment, or something in between: "my fellow Americans," or "my good fellow."

The multiplicity of meanings, connotations, and inferences generated by the word *felaweshipe* is matched and multiplied by the lexicon of terms that brings the *General Prologue*'s *felaweshipe* into being. The fact that this vocabulary is drawn from so many sources (and thus that it grows in many different directions) might tempt us to despair. More usefully, however, we might recognize that this very abundance of terms attests to the immense importance of this process, namely, the construction of associational forms. The Middle Ages was (as Burckhardt acknowledges, albeit dismissively) more corporate-minded than any later period; allegiance to a specific *felaweshipe* or *universitas* could often outweigh loyalty to civic or state authorities.[35]

We best appreciate the power and pervasiveness of associational thinking when we find it in unexpected places: in the medieval papacy, for example, or in the governing structures of feudalism. It is not surprising to discover that medieval religious guilds have much in common with early Christian communities;[36] both emphasize group loyalty in the face of a hostile secular world.[37] The monarchical, absolutist, and sometimes fantastical pretensions of popes and their theorists from later periods (most famously, perhaps, Boniface VIII and Augustinus Triumphus)[38] might induce us to forget that many clerical writers continued to argue for the rights of chapters, monasteries, and other groups as self-regulating *universitates*. Innocent IV wrote to define and uphold the rights of men in any profession, whether grammarians or bakers, to incorporate and rule themselves "by their own authority if they wish"; his commentaries have been acclaimed as "a Magna Carta for the guilds."[39] During the Investiture Controversy, when the papacy contested the emperor's right to appoint his own aristocratic bishops, arguments for the liberty of towns and *libertas ecclesiae* could be seen as "related parts of the same movement for corporate self-determination."[40] And yet this new corporate consciousness of urban communes owed something to the sworn associations that bound country-dwelling feudal lords to their followers; the sense of mutual obligation in the feudal bond was later experienced as a hinderance to royal absolutism.[41]

Aristotelian terms, as adapted by Aquinas and others, have already figured in my analysis; the importance of Aristotle before and after William of Moerbeke's translation of the *Politics* (c. 1260) can hardly be exaggerated.[42] Moerbeke translates Aristotle's *koinonia* as *communitas*; *koinonia* (which Aristotle never defines) is created by a bond of friendship and involves "a plurality of participants, with a common aim pursued by common action, with full differentiation between its members but without any relations of subjection or domination on the basis of it."[43] Quillet is surely right to propose that "a society that by nature was corporative and associative could not fail to find reassurance for its aims in the Aristotelian model which made it intelligible in theoretical terms."[44] Prior knowledge of Cicero, we might add, helped prepare the way for Aristotle's teachings on the naturalness of political life.[45]

Such confidence in this natural, human impulse to self-government was not shared by Augustine, who is perpetually mindful that human nature, since the fall of Adam, is corrupt. Government can only function as *remedium peccati*: "it controls the wicked within the bounds of a certain earthly peace."[46] Rebellion against harsh or corrupt government is inexcusable and self-contradictory, since man is essentially helpless and corrupt through original sin. The best course of action is "a painful quietism of acceptance that evil conditions created by men perhaps ought not to be reversed because they were, after all, deserved."[47] It is no accident that when Petrarch decided to accept, and become an apologist for, absolutist polity his mind turned to Augustine.[48] It is no accident, either, that D. W. Robertson should home in on the wrestling miller ("the very picture of *discordia*")[49] as the leitmotiv of human governance in the *Canterbury Tales*; such an image serves admirably as preface to a mighty torrent of political Augustinianism:

It is appropriate that this character should thrust himself forward out of order at the conclusion to the *Knight's Tale*, offer to "quit" the knight, stir up a quarrel with the reeve, and tell a tale whose high point is the "revel and melodye" of the flesh. If the pilgrimage to Canterbury is a reflection of the manner in which the pilgrimage of life was generally carried out in Chaucer's England, the fact that it follows a drunken wrestler out of town to the tune of a bagpipe is an amusing if slightly bitter comment on contemporary society—a society which, Chaucer must have felt, was far from the amiable concord it should have developed in imitation of "Jerusalem celestial." (p. 243)

The "slightly bitter" flavor Robertson tastes in the text here is all of his own making; it is the inevitable effect of bringing Augustinian aesthetics to a reading of Chaucer. This reading is highly selective: the earlier, undeniably cheerful and optimistic parts of the *Prologue*, in which the pilgrims show a natural inclination to communicate with one another and form a *felaweshipe*, are flatly ignored.

Robertson's Augustinianism is usually maintained as an aesthetic critique.[50] Augustinian politics are usually kept out of sight. The aesthetics and politics are all of a piece, of course; their relevance to a reading of the *General Prologue* is, at best, highly questionable. I am not suggesting that the formation of the Southwark *felaweshipe* bespeaks straightforward allegiance to a neo-Aristotelian organicism. Chaucer, as we shall see, takes great pains (and pleasure) in testing the capacities of the corporate structure he chooses to invent. And in developing this structure, I shall argue, Chaucer was influenced not so much by his reading of Aristotle as by his daily acquaintance with a pattern of social practice that is drastically undertheorized: the Germanic tradition of the guilds.[51]

Guild Structures, *Conscience Commune*, and the Division of Labor

The term "guild" was applied in the Germanic languages to any group bound together by friendship, rite, or custom. In its first known usage (sometime before 400 A.D.), *gilda* refers to a sacrificial meal. Eating and drinking, which celebrated or enacted the solidarity of the group, remain important throughout guild history: guilds were sometimes known as *convivia* (Dante's *Convivio*, we may recall, is best translated as "the banquet"), and members met at appointed times to "drink their guild" (*potabunt gildam suam*).[52] Through such shows of group solidarity, which included the swearing of mutual oaths, the guilds played out their most distinctive political claim: that they owed their corporate existence to the free will and spontaneous action of their neighbors (and not to some external or delegated source of authority).[53] As the centuries passed, such claims to self-origination and self-governance met with increasing resistance from Roman and ecclesiastical law, but guild structures, while retaining certain essential features, proved highly adaptable to changing religious, economic, and political conditions. Handicraft guilds, parish confraternities, and merchant guilds formed "the first cells of many village and urban communes."[54] Guild membership was essentially incompatible with servile status; guild structures helped organize aspects of cultural, commercial, and industrial life in ways still visible in both (vestigial) socialist and capitalist modes of socioeconomic organization.

Reviews of late medieval guilds often observe or impose a simplistic distinction between craft guilds and religious confraternities. Such a distinction was evidently not so clear-cut in the fourteenth century. If it had been, secular authorities would not have expended so much time and trouble in determining exactly what a specific guild, *conventicle*, or *covyn* did and discussed at its meetings. This variety (or indeterminacy) of social purposes is reflected by the extraordinary range of names borrowed (from Roman, ecclesiastical, or common law sources) or invented to designate a specific guild: *unio, conjuratio* (suggesting an oath); *fraternitas, confraternitas, bruderschaft, frairie, fraternity* (brotherhood); *compagnie, felaweshipe* (suggesting fellowship).[55] Some guilds lasted for centuries (by evolving, say, from a merchant *fraternitas* into the city government); others lasted for the duration of a single business transaction; some were established in the course of a single perilous journey by land or sea.[56] The guild phenomenon may best be understood not as a specific institution but as a form of consciousness, a mentality.[57] This, I shall argue, is what generates and sustains the *felaweshipe* of the *Canterbury Tales*.

The argument that the associative tendencies exemplified in the *General Prologue* reflect a form of consciousness developed in the guilds requires some immediate qualifications. I am not suggesting that the "nyne and twenty in a compaignye" who join Chaucer at Southwark represent a particular guild (although there were parish guilds in this period that sponsored pilgrimages to St. Thomas à Beckett);[58] I am proposing that the fact that these "sondry folk" know something about collective, mixed-gender behavior suggests that each of them was schooled (more or less perfectly) in the guilds. It may prove tempting in a postwelfare, hyperindividualistic period like our own to fall into the trap, patented by Gierke, of sentimentalizing the epoch of guild collectivity.[59] Before returning to Chaucer, then, it will be salutary to establish the medieval guild as a shape-shifting phenomenon, forever responsive to and generative of new cultural and economic pressures, rather than as an ideal, hence ahistorical, form.

Gierke's enthusiasm for guilds expressed a yearning for an authentic and essential Germanness: the search for the perfect Ur-guild led him (as new and contradictory evidence became available) to push back ever deeper into history. Such a quest, Antony Black wittily observes, could only end in "the inpenetrable forests of Tacitus' *Germania*";[60] it certainly takes us a long way from the imperfect world of postpandemic England. Medieval guilds, we have noted, were both versatile and adaptable; their ethos and character, if not their operating procedures, underwent profound changes in the course of the fourteenth century. During the boom years of the medieval economy (commonly dated approximately 1100–1300),[61] guilds proliferated rapidly, spearheading political and cultural as well as economic growth throughout Europe. Commerce expanded; new religious orders (most significantly, the friars) sprang up to serve the spiritual needs of this dynamic market economy, and to extract the economic surplus from it. In this period it might conceivably have been possible to regard guilds as *milieux morales*, sites for the development of a professional ethics that would maintain high standards and so benefit the whole of society. The medieval guild, for Durkheim, prefigured an organic solidarity,[62] *solidarité organique*, that our own century should seek to replicate as the guarantor of moral life:

We may say that what is moral is everything that is a source of solidarity, everything that forces man to take account of other people, to regulate his actions by something other than the promptings of his own egoism, and the more numerous and strong these ties are, the more solid is the morality.[63]

For Durkheim, such *solidarité organique* was to be achieved through, not in spite of, the division of labor (a proposition that parts company with Marxist accounts of workers' alienation). Such solidarity evolved out of more primitive societies, where morality was determined by a *conscience commune*: individuals shared a common sense of obligation to an external (religious or seigneurial) authority. Since they were all moved by the same set of beliefs and sentiments, such individuals were poorly individuated; their collective experience was best described as *solidarité mécanique*.[64] As society grew more complex, however, the old *conscience commune* faded,[65] superseded by a new sense of social differentiation and mutual obligation: *solidarité organique*, guarantor of both a new individualism and a heightened corporate consciousness.

Durkheim pinned his hopes for the future on the reemergence of "secondary institutions": "institutions that were placed midway, so to speak, between the remote world of the state's powers and the concrete everyday world of the individual."[66] Chaucer's *felaweshipe* offers an interesting if imperfect correspondence with (and critique of) Durkheim's ideal. It is obviously guided by *conscience commune*: each pilgrim has the same thought of seeking out the martyr's shrine. Such association through collective devotion forms part of Durkheim's ideal of medieval corporate consciousness:

"The corporation," says Lavasseur, "united in close ties people of the same trade. Not infrequently it was instituted in the parish or in a special chapel, and placed itself under the invocation of a saint who became the patron of a whole community. . . . It was there they assembled, there that the confraternity attended solemn masses in great state, the members afterwards rounding off the day together in a joyous banquet."[67]

This passage evokes the kind of convivial jollity we associate with the beginning and end of Chaucer's *Prologue*, but it also highlights a peculiarity of the *Prologue*'s middle section, namely, the detailing of so many different trades, crafts, and callings. Each of Chaucer's pilgrims is described as a (the indefinite article is important) member of a specific social group. In forming one group from many groups, the *Prologue* subjects all arguments about the naturalness and desirability of associational form (from Aristotle to Durkheim) to the severest scrutiny: for each member of Chaucer's *compagnye* comes equipped with a set of assumptions about professional ethics and associative behavior that they have learned elsewhere. Can such "diverse folk," descriptively individuated in a way that accentuates the division of labor, raise themselves into a higher associative unity?[68] The stakes are high; Durkheim outlines the positive possibility in a final, optimistic footnote:

Because individuals form a society, new phenomena occur whose cause is association, and which, reacting upon the consciousness of individuals, for the most part shapes them. This is why, although society is nothing without individuals, each one of them is much more a product of society than he is the author.[69]

Some Chaucerians would argue that the *Canterbury Tales* finally achieves, through such a dialectical interchange between self and individual, *solidarité organique*, a collective consciousness that is more than the sum of its parts.[70] Others find that such a dialectic fails to happen; each individual (including the reader) remains essentially apart from all others. The ethical imperative in such a world is to negotiate, to live with or within, this abiding sense of isolation:

A world of specialized skills, experience, terminology, and interests confronts us; we see the world through the eyes of a lazy Monk or a successful Merchant, and simultaneously realize the latent tension between his view and our own. But the tension is latent, because the superficial agreement and approval offered in the ironic comment has this amount of reality—it really reflects the way in which we get on with our neighbours, by tacit approval of the things we really consider wrong, by admiring techniques more than the ends they work towards, by regarding unethical behaviour as amusing as long as the results are not directly unpleasant for us, by adopting, for social reasons, the viewpoint of the person with whom we are associating, and at the same time feeling that his way of life is "not our business."[71]

Jill Mann's concluding remarks on the *General Prologue* suggest a Marxian pessimism rather than Durkheimian optimism about the moral effects of the division of labor. The isolation of professional techniques from social ends brings great historical dangers: perhaps the greatest danger of all comes with complacent acceptance of this state of affairs, the fashioning of an adaptive, laissez-faire, makeshift morality that enables us to coexist with what is "not our business." The specialized business of others, of course, exerts a fascination that at certain moments in the *General Prologue* becomes almost mesmeric; such fascination, which holds our attention within particular divisions of the generalized division of labor, distracts us further from grasping general social effects. This can prove disastrous at any period of history. The worst consequences of such distraction in our own century have been brilliantly spelled out by Heinz Schirk in a film about a committee meeting, the kind of *compagnye* many of us keep, professionally.[72]

In Chaucer's lifetime, there was much in the character of associative polity to strain any optimism. Just as guild structures had risen and proliferated with the economic boom of 1100, so they declined or changed their character when the medieval economy reached its saturation point after 1300. Liberal policies turned protectionist; social solidarity, under negative economic pressures, evolved into collective self-interest. Towns became overregulated; city corporations, which had earlier encouraged the establishment of new guilds, attempted to fix or freeze the number of corporate bodies.[73] Associations higher up in the social hierarchy opposed the associational rights claimed by groupings down below; worker revolts eventually broke out all over Europe. Growth in population density, which according to Durkheim provides the motor of or chief inducement to *solidarité organique*, ran backwards in 1348 and showed scant signs of recovery.[74]

If we are to read the *Canterbury Tales* as an essay in associational form, then, we must acknowledge that it occupies a very difficult historical moment. It was already evident in the *Parliament of Fowls*, however, that Chaucer had little interest in adumbrating an ideal of associative polity; he sees associational governance as a difficult, precarious, practical affair. In the *General Prologue* he deliberately compounds such difficulties by including so many subgroups united by blood, bond, vow, or vocation, which precede and challenge the all-inclusive *compagnye*. We begin with a particularly powerful group: the actual military power (Knight), lineage (Squire), and territorial control (Yeoman) of landed aristocracy. Some pilgrims share a religious vocation; the Prioress and her attendants represent a specific religious community. Parson and Plowman exemplify a physical and spiritual kinship, *bretherhede*, that bridges two estates; the Sergeant and the Franklin (who "was in his compaignye," 1.331) meet at the intersection of centralized and localized justice (or legal administration). The simplest or most homogeneous group in the *Prologue* evidently proved the most difficult for the evolving *Tales* to assimilate: the liveried "fraternitee" of craft or parish guildsmen is not heard from again (except by association with its Cook). The dropping of the guildsmen was precipitated, I would suggest, by a twofold realization of political and artistic redundancy. Their individual crafts are matched (the Reeve is a carpenter) and surpassed by the more promiscuous and interesting group of six tacked onto the rear of the *compagnye*; and their group polity as *fraternitee* is replicated by the pilgrimage as *felaweshipe* (more on this shortly).

Not all subgroupings within the *felaweshipe* are stable or finalized; the Pardoner and the Wife of Bath suggest, through their own bodily presence, metaphors of bodily lack or excess that destabilize the body politic, the governing metaphor of corporate existence.[75] The Wife is introduced as the veteran of five marriages (1.460); her interest in a sixth (and her status as a widow) she will disclose herself, unbidden, in Fragment 3. The Pardoner is defined early on in terms of physical lack: "I trowe he were a geldyng or a mare" (1.691). The authorial logic that loses the Pardoner his *coillons* is akin to that which would put Brunetto Latini among the sodomites:[76] suggested physical aberration betokens perversion of the *impetus naturalis* that spurs man to communicate with his peers. The opposite of communication, according to Oresme's *Livre des Politiques*, is excommunication;[77] the physical "cutting off" Herry Bailly has in mind may betoken estrangement from corporate Christendom. And yet we sense that such physical and spiritual deficiencies are somehow integral to, generative of, the most powerful and captivating personality on the pilgrimage. For Duns Scotus, *personalitas* is defined as *negatio communicationis*, denial of communication with others, and requires "an ultimate solitude—the negation of any dependence, actual or potential, in regard to any person of another nature."[78] If such solitude is read as the negative effect of the division of labor in a period of economic stagnation, the Pardoner emerges as the perfect exemplar of a new, freshly atomized individualism. We cannot expect such individuals to merge themselves into corporate unity, *solidarité organique*; they remain as individuals within a *communitas aggregationis*, parts of a unity that (according to Scotus) is composite or aggregate, never an organic whole.[79]

"Welcome the Sixte": Authorial Signature and the Wife of Bath

The Pardoner appears in the *General Prologue* as part of a subset defined by parasitic individualism, "a rogue's gallery of miscellaneous predators, associated only in the skill with which they batten upon the society that has just been described."[80] The sixth and final portrait promised in this gallery is that of Chaucer himself:

> Ther was also a REVE, and a MILLERE,
> A SOMNOUR, and a PARDONER also,
> A MAUNCIPLE, and myself—ther were namo.   (1.542–44)

No portrait of the pilgrim Chaucer is offered in the *General Prologue*, of course; a few choice details are offered by the Host later on. Why, then, does Chaucer choose to name himself here, as the sixth and last member of a group of "miscellaneous predators"? In concluding *Troilus and Criseyde*, Chaucer had looked forward to the making of some future "comedye" before positioning himself after five classical *auctores* as the sixth in a tradition of six writers:

> Go, litel bok, go, litel myn tragedye,
> Ther God thi makere yet, er that he dye,
> So sende mygt to make in som comedye!
> But litel book, no makyng thow n'envie,
> But subgit be to alle poesye;
> and kis the steppes where as thow seest pace
> Virgile, Ovide, Omer, Lucan, and Stace.   (5.1786–92)

This sixth of six *topos*, previously taken up by Jean de Meun, Dante, and Boccaccio (but most famously by Dante, who among the virtuous pagans of *Inferno* 4 has himself nominated as "sesto tra cotanto senno," "sixth among such lofty intellects," 102) bespeaks the highest poetic ambition: a desire to complete a sequence of poetic activity conjoining pagan antiquity and the Christian present.[81] By the end of the *Troilus*, Chaucer has plainly earned the right to name himself as a sixth of six: but the evocation of the same *topos* at the beginning of the *Canterbury Tales*, which may be taken as the future "comedye" promised by the *Troilus*, is comically problematic. Instead of Vergil, Ovid, Homer, Lucan, and Statius we find Chaucer keeping company with a reeve, a miller, a summoner, a pardoner, and a manciple; he is identified not as an *auctor* bridging pagan and Christian epochs but as an imperfect witness to a recent event of scant historical significance.

What, then, are we to make of this strange self-identification, the first authorial signature of the *Canterbury Tales*?[82] It assures us, clearly enough, that Chaucer brings to his writing ambitions of European magnitude. It also suggests, in substituting social predators for illustrious poets, that Chaucer harbors misgivings about the ethical value of such writing. Such misgivings will not assume the proportions of full-blown Langlandian neurosis, but they will not be laid to rest before the drastic *rekenynge* of the "retracciouns" (10.1085). Chaucer's testing of the structures (substructures and antistructures) of associational governance plainly extends to authorial self-scrutiny. How, given the general division of labor, a phenomenon that questions the possibility of general or uniform morality, is a man who identifies himself as a vernacular author to equip himself, and to what end? The social imperative that Durkheim brings us to here is also, for Chaucer, a religious one. The social questioning conducted throughout the *Canterbury Tales*, however, seems remarkably prescient of concerns explored in *De la division du travail social* some five centuries later:

"The yardstick for our perfection is no longer to be found in satisfaction with ourselves, in the plaudits of the crowd or the approving smile of an affected dilettantism, but in the sum total of services rendered, and in our ability to render them." Thus the moral ideal, from being the sole one, simple and impersonal, has become increasingly diversified. We no longer think that the exclusive duty of man is to realize within himself the qualities of man in general, but we believe that he is no less obliged to have those qualities that relate to his employment. . . . In short, in one of its aspects the categorical imperative of the moral consciousness is coming to assume the following form: *Equip yourself to fulfil usefully a specific function.*[83]

It is imperative that Chaucer, if he is to assume the specific identity of *auctor* within the general division of labor, comes equipped with the technical skills of authorship. It is further imperative, however, that he should find—invent—a body of material about which to write. Through the business of finding the *felaweshipe*, then, Chaucer comes to employ his particular skills and hence to claim *his* specific, social function. Within the body of pilgrims, however, there is one body in particular that shows forth, in memorably intensified form, everything that Chaucer seeks; everything that he needs to fulfill his particular function as *auctor*. I speak, of course, of the Wife of Bath, "whose centrality to Chaucer's poetics is due," Carolyn Dinshaw has argued, "to her value as a representation of the letter, the body of the text."[84] Within the broad parameters of a literary tradition that genders literary text as feminine and the operations done to texts—inventing, glossing, compiling—as masculine,[85] the meeting of Chaucer and the Wife represents that union out of which the *Canterbury Tales* will come to fruition. When Chaucer positions himself as a sixth of six, then, he identifies himself as just the man that the Wife is looking for: "Welcome the sixte, whan that evere he shal" (3.45). What are the consequences of accepting this invitation to view Chaucer as, potentially, the Wife of Bath's sixth husband? First, the invention of the *Canterbury Tales* cannot be seen as a self-sufficient act of masculine, neohumanist, or individualistic genius: Chaucer remains utterly dependent upon that which the Wife embodies in her own person, upon her particular expertise within the division of labor (knowledge of the body; wifely eloquence; dealing in *textus*; *felaweshipe*, pilgrimage, and "wandrynge by the weye").[86] Against the (preeminently humanist) tradition of women figured as wax, awaiting the seal of poet, prince, or father,[87] the Wife cannot be read as raw material awaiting the shaping impress of a masculine hand. She is herself imbued with knowledge of the techniques of clerkly exegesis, knowledge that allows her to actively interrogate rather than passively receive the terms of clerkly and antifeminist critique. (In this regard, comparisons between the textual and fictional Wife of Bath and the textual and historical Margery Kempe are not extravagant.)[88]

Second, in presenting the Wife's many and particular talents as part of a general account of the division of labor, Chaucer establishes wifehood as an indispensable part of his social totality. Even when practiced behind closed doors, wifehood remains an art that is public and political, rather than private and individual. Third, Chaucer's impending union with the Wife espouses a commitment to the uses and pleasures of narrative dilation. Such a commitment in no way implies a forgetting of the acute professional and political questioning that this chapter has adumbrated. Fourth, and finally, the historical singularity of Chaucer's relation to the eloquent Wife, one of affectionate and fruitful interdependence,[89] might readily be grasped by comparison with our Italian *auctores*. Dante's Beatrice, in the *Vita nuova*, does not speak at all; Boccaccio's encounters between the scholar and the widow in *Decameron* 8.7 prove brutally (and unfinishably) savage; Petrarch's beloved Laura is glimpsed as female body parts scattered through the unpeopled landscapes of humanist introspection.[90] Chaucer's commitment to exemplifying the social and political efficacy of wifely eloquence—within associational groupings; within mercantile, magnate, royal, and despotic households—is, by contrast, phenomenal. It will prove to be the most distinctive feature of Chaucerian polity.

Chapter 3

"From Every Shires Ende":
English Guilds and
Chaucer's *Compagnye*

Chaucer's devising of his pilgrim *compagnye* coincides with a moment of unprecedented self-consciousness and self-scrutiny for associational forms in England. Following a demand from the Cambridge parliament of 1388, all English guilds were required to submit a written account of themselves to the authorities at Westminster. Thousands of guild brothers and sisters gathered in their guilds, or conferred with neighboring guilds, to strategize a response; their handiwork may be read in the remarkably heterogeneous bundles, booklets, and strips of parchment now known as the guild returns of 1389.[1] A reading of these documents suggests that guild culture, especially when read against the more static model of the parish, shows extraordinary dynamism in seeking out new pockets of social, political, and economic energy. Guild membership nurtures political intelligence through the internal workings of corporate procedures, and also through the imagining of local, national, and transnational structures of authority. It also gains strength by imagining a community that unites the living and the dead. The 1389 returns have inevitably become a contested point of origin for many and various accounts—religious, political, feminist—of a historical *longue durée* that ends with the parliamentary acts (37 Henry VIII. c.4; 1 Edward VI. c.14) that bring this characteristically English culture to a sudden and violent demise.

Many of the guilds represented by the 1389 returns take a general interest in pilgrimage; some show a particular interest in pilgrimage to the shrine of St. Thomas at Canterbury. But it is in their totality (as a grammar of governance, as a fund of collective culture, as a strange amalgam of worship and drink) that these guilds offer the most instructive analogies with what happens in Chaucer. The likeness of English guild and Chaucerian *compagnye* cultures may be readily grasped by turning, again, to Boccaccio's Florence. Both the Florentine guild-based regime and the *Decameron*'s *brigata*, despite their ostensible commitment to associational forms of governance, prove resistant to the notion of spontaneous, self-governing structures that would follow the logic of newly emergent socioeconomic energies. Florentine guilds are subject to tight internal and external controls; Boccaccio's *brigata* is the exclusive domain of a socially homogeneous group that can brook no challenge from below. Here again one sees why Boccaccio becomes the more acceptable model for imitation in sixteenth-century England; the Chaucerian *compagnye*, after 1547, becomes as culturally quaint and as politically irrelevant as a newly abolished guild.

Stasis and Dynamism; Guilds and the Parish

"The guild or fraternity," writes Gervase Rosser, "was a form of voluntary association bound by oath."[2] Such a definition is sufficiently broad to admit Chaucer's *compagnye*: but our argument is not that the voluntary, oath-bound group formed in the *General Prologue is* a guild, but that forms of associational behavior learned and practiced in the guilds facilitate its formation and regulation.[3] The peculiar relevance of guild structures to Chaucer's fictional group is more readily appreciated by comparing the guild to its chief competitor as a community organization: the parish. There is no need to assume that relations between these two structures were always antagonistic: every guild, after all, met in a parish (and so needed to maintain good relations with parochial clergy). But parish and guild are certainly different in kind. The parish was an all-inclusive structure that could demand the payment of tithes and attendance at church; the guild was both voluntary and exclusionary. Parishes were defined and confined by geographic limits; guilds were able to draw together members from many different areas. Parishes, after 1300, found it very difficult to subdivide themselves and so form new parishes, according to demographic pressure;[4] guilds were able to form, reform, expand, and abolish themselves with remarkable speed.

The guild, in short, is an altogether more dynamic, protean form than the parish. One source of its dynamism lies in the recognition that its members need, for many reasons, to cross parish lines in pursuing their religious, social, and economic objectives. For example, the Trinity Guild of Coventry, founded in 1364, drew its members from almost every part of England (and even from overseas).[5] Franklins, farmers, dealers, and craftworkers from neighboring towns and villages joined the guild as a means of maintaining relationships with the cloth-making industries centered on Coventry. Wool producers from other districts, plus merchants, shipmen, and manufacturers from London, Bristol, Chester, Newcastle, Boston, Calais and various Irish communities all found it expedient to join the Trinity Guild. So, too, did powerful magnates such as John of Gaunt and Thomas of Woodstock. Richard II never joined the guild, but Henry IV and his Lancastrian successors did, thereby ensuring that Coventry favored Lancastrian interests. Some important ecclesiastics joined the guild, in addition to a good number of chaplains and chantry priests. Margery Russell, a powerful merchant who obtained letters of marque in order to seize £800 worth of goods from Spanish traders (so recouping an earlier loss), was a sister of the guild.[6]

The modest Shepherd's Guild of Holbeach, Lincolnshire—dedicated, appropriately enough, to the Nativity of the Blessed Virgin Mary—would seem at first to have little in common with the mighty Trinity Guild of Coventry.[7] Two common characteristics are worth noting, however. Both guilds formed part of the international nexus of the wool industry; both found it necessary to imagine and develop forms of corporate identity that crossed or transcended parish lines, since the guild community could not (for practical reasons) assemble at will. The shepherds and herdsmen of Holbeach often found themselves, by the nature of their profession, far from their parish church. Unable to participate in the mass, they funded the burning of a candle before the image of the Virgin in the parish church and two torches at the elevation on festivals.[8] The experience of guild solidarity, for a single shepherd working far from home, was entirely imaginary. But such an appeal to the imaginary was not untypical of the guild experience, since all guilds envisaged an ideal solidarity between the living and the dead: deceased members were not struck from the register, but were numbered among the living.

The formation of a guild, then, always points (through the forms of religious practice) to developing forms of social, political, and economic energy. Such energies are readily discerned in the histories of the rise and fall of particular guilds; they are also abundantly evident in the formation of Chaucer's pilgrim *compagnye* and in the narratives that issue from it. The dynamism shown by Chaucer's group in working out its collective identity as it moves from parish to parish ("Lo Depeford . . . Lo Grenewych . . . Loo, Rouchestre . . .": 1.3906–7; 7.1926) is historically attuned to the energy with which guild structures crossed parish lines. Such freedom of movement, in which large-scale spatial movement betokens a measure of political independence, would not survive into Henrician and Elizabethan England: the abolition and spoliation of the guilds in 1547 was to be accompanied by an enforced return to the more stable and conservative norm of the parish. It is worth noting, however, that Chaucer's text, even as it picks its way between the highly particularized viewpoints of its social subgroups, holds out the prospect of a final return to the parish as the normative model of localized spirituality. The *General Prologue*'s portrait of the Wife, cloth-maker (hence guild member) and preeminent pilgrimage expert, is immediately followed by that of the "povre persoun of a toun." The keynote of this *descriptio* is the bond between the parson and "his parisshens," particularly "his povre parisshens" (1.482, 488). Chaucer labors hard to evoke the physical and moral energy of a man determined to work within, but not to cross, parish boundaries:

> Wyd was his parisshe, and houses fer asonder,
> But he ne lefte nat, for reyn ne thonder,
> In siknesse nor in meschief to visite
> The ferreste in his parisshe, much and lite,
> Upon his feet, and in his hand a staf. (1.491–95)

The rhetorical energy generated by this description issues, however, not so much from the dedicated pursuit of pastoral care within parochial limits as from vigorous denunciation of shitty shepherds (504) who abandon the parish:

> He sette nat his benefice to hyre
> And leet his sheep encombred in the myre
> And ran to Londoun unto Seint Poules
> To seken hym a chaunterie for soules,
> Or with a bretherhed to been withholde;
> But dwelte at hoom, and kepte wel his folde,
> So that the wolf ne made it nat myscarie;
> He was a shepherde and noght a mercenarie. (1.507–14)

This Parson, Chaucer assures us, will not be swallowed up by some rich fraternity, "a bretherhede," and thus rendered invisible to his "povre parisshens." Such an assertion does beg the question of why the Parson should have absented himself from his parish to ride as part of Chaucer's *felaweshipe*. The simple answer is that Chaucer needs him there (however unlikely it might seem) so that his complex exploration of social identities may be bracketed within a triad of idealized and exemplary portraits, forming the familiar three estates model: the Knight, the Parson, and the Parson's brother, the dung-laying, tithe-paying Plowman. The Plowman (at least before Thynne's edition of 1542) has no tale to tell; the Knight and Parson frame the storytelling, first and last, with the lengthiest narrative performances. But it is what happens between the Knight's verse and the Parson's prose, beginning with the Miller's *rebellyng*, that generates the distinctive energy of Chaucer's *compilatio*. Chaucer's Parson portrait, and the "vertuous mateere" of his *Tale* (10.38), figures or stands in for a journey that Chaucer's text never actually makes: the dispersal of the *compagnye* through a return to the fixed localities of parish and shire. The social groupings that clustered about St. Paul's (citizens and foreigns from every London parish; clerics and chaplains looking for a *bretherhede*; men of law waiting for briefs; scribes and copyists waiting for texts) are more generously represented in the *Canterbury Tales* than the "povre parisshens" that the Parson is beholden to. Chaucer's text, in short, is much more of a running to St. Paul's than it is a patrolling of parish boundaries.

"From Every Shires Ende": The Guild Returns of 1389

The Guild of St. Christopher, Norwich, founded in 1384, began each of its meetings with a prayer, structured on the traditional three estates model, that is remarkable both for the specificity of its details and for its universal inclusiveness. The men and women of the guild begin by praying "deuoutely for þe state of holy chirche, and for þe pees of þe londe"; they then pray for the pope of Rome and his cardinals, for the patriarch of Jerusalem, and for the reconquest of the holy land.[9] Moving down through "alle Erchebisshopes and bisshopes" (pausing to acknowledge their own "bisshope of Norwiche"), they come to pray for all parsons and priests, and for all those in religious orders; and they pray that all members of this first estate may perform their tasks "þat it be to goddes worshepe." Moving now from the bottom of the first estate to the top of the second, they pray for "oure lord þe kyng, for oure lady þe qwen, Duckes, Erles, Barouns, and Bachelers of þe londe"; God should save them, keep them "fro dedely synne," and give them grace to rule over the kingdom, "holy chirche," and their own souls. Prayers for the third estate take up most space because the composition of this estate (their own) is most complex and their needs and responsibilities most diverse. This third grouping is to live by the common ideal of "treuthe" (a word not heard before). The suggestion is made that five masculine subgroupings (from knight to franklin) and three feminine ones are inherently legitimate; other social identities, collective and individual, are to be respected only as they are found to be "trewe." The fraternity prays, then,

for alle knyghtes, squyers, citeȝenis and Burgeys, fraunkeleyns, and alle trewe tyliers and men of craft, wydoues, maydenes, wyfes, and for alle þe communalte and cristen peple, þat godd of his mercy saue hem and kepe hem þat in þis werld leuen wiþ treuthe, and ȝeue hem grace so to done þat it be worshepe to godd and saluacioun to here soules; for alle trewe shipmen, and trewe pilgrymes, þat godd for his grace ȝeue hem wederyng and passage, þat þei mowen sauely commen and gone; for þe fruyte of þe londe and of þe see and þe wederyng; for alle þe men þat bene in fals beleue, and wolde bene in goode beleue, godd ȝeue hem grace to comen to her desir; for oure faders soules, and moders, bretheren and sisteren, and for alle þe bretheren and sisteren of þis gilde, and for alle cristen soules: amen.

It would be difficult to find a historical document more richly suggestive of the spiritual, imaginative, and political consciousness mapped out by Chaucer's *General Prologue*. Both texts are structured by "what may be termed the two antagonistic tendencies in medieval political thought: the concern for universality on the one hand, and on the other, a profound awareness of subgroups as making up the web of human social existence."[10] Let us first consider their remarkable understanding of "universality." The striving for spatial inclusiveness in Chaucer's poem, in its opening period, takes us "to straunge strondes" and "ferne halwes . . . in sondry londes" (a movement that surprises us momentarily by moving beyond the immediate occasion of a pilgrimage to Canterbury). The men and women of St. Christopher's fraternity begin, similarly, with thoughts of the Patriarch of Jerusalem, the holy cross, and the winning back of the holy land. Like the readers of Chaucer's poem, they situate themselves within the rotation of the seasons and the rhythms of "þe wederynge"; and, as in Chaucer's poem, the guild return suggests how a specific community may transcend its own temporal bounds by imagining a seamless continuity between the living and the dead: "For oure faders soules, and moders, bretheren and sisteren." And yet, in establishing this all-inclusive framework, both texts recognize that the traditional three-estate structure is unsettled by complex divisions within the third estate. The group of six pilgrims described last in the *General Prologue* seems to grow *upon* the body politic, like fungus, rather than to grow within it, as part of it. Some subgroups have an assured place within the natural order envisioned by the fraternity's prayer; others must prove themselves "trewe." Tillers of the earth (and possibly "men of craft"), shipmen, and pilgrims are subject to this hermeneutic of suspicion. Guilds, as we shall see, took a particular interest in pilgrims: they felt obliged to support them, and yet recognized that the estate of pilgrim formed a challenge to their own corporate identity: pilgrim "bretheren" are absent; their *felaweshipe* lies elsewhere.

The document in which the guild of St. Christopher describes itself is just one of the many hundreds of returns that were sent from all over England to the Chancery at Westminster in the early months of 1389. This particular return shows a balance of religious and political understanding that invites comparison with Chaucer; other returns are less sophisticated.[11] We must remember that these guilds did not choose to describe themselves of their own free will. They are writing in response to a writ from central authority that threatens them with dire penalties for noncompliance.[12] Some returns are defensive, or defensively vague; others (particularly those written some distance from Westminster) are more forthcoming.[13] The guild returns of 1389, then, must be considered not just as individual documents but as part of a greater political complex that raises difficult interpretive problems. Taken as part of this totality, they assume great importance as a historical *monument* from the period when the guild movement in England was enjoying explosive growth.[14] Written at the very time when Chaucer was devising the fictional interactions of his Canterbury *felaweshipe*, these returns offer remarkable glimpses of how, "at every shires ende" (I.15), men and women were developing and living out their own understandings of associational behavior.

The 1389 Returns and English Historiography

The reading of poetic texts in association with specific historical documents may help open new historiographical perspectives, but may also slip into some well-worn tracks. Such possibilities, we have noted, are famously exemplified by accounts of the conflict between Florentine republicanism and Milanese despotism, in which the war years of 1400–1402 assume epochal importance.[15] The 1389 Chancery returns have long been employed as part of a historiographical narrative that might be summarized as an English variant of the Florentine-Milanese paradigm.[16] It has not proved possible to discuss, edit, or paraphrase the Ricardian returns without referring forward to their Tudor counterpart, their historical evil twin, the returns of 1546–47 made in response to the parliamentary act of 1545. In the 1389 returns the English fraternities describe themselves, their own associational habits and mechanisms, at the peak of their religious and political vigor; in 1546–47, the fraternities are described by agents of a royal authority intent on their wholesale spoliation and abolition. The difference between these documents invites comparison with the associational-absolutist conflict articulated in Italian historiography: it is, after all, covered by the same cultural signifiers of "medieval" and "Renaissance." But whereas Italian historiography finds convenient synchronic coordinates (two cities) for its narrative of cultural and political change, English historians work diachronically, measuring differences between two sets of documents set some one-and-a-half centuries apart. This accounts for a peculiar feature of English cultural history: the medieval-Renaissance transition is experienced less as a finite struggle between opposing historical forces than as a gap in historical time, a second *medium aevum*, dividing the England of Chaucer from the England of Wyatt and Shakespeare.

The 1389 guild returns have long been mediated to us by two volumes working from very different social and political agendas. Toulmin Smith's *English Gilds* (1870) was shaped by a lifelong dedication to the cause of self-improvement, local government reform, and national self-determination.[17] In his *Parish Gilds of Mediaeval England*, a work published by the Society for the Promotion of Christian Knowledge in 1919, H. F. Westlake accuses Smith of exaggerating the social, "self-help" aspects of medieval guilds and of underemphasizing their religious motivations.[18] Distinctions between craft and religious guilds, which are often very difficult to sustain, are often unhelpfully polarized between Smith and Westlake.[19] Both scholars found, however, that their work with the 1389 returns drew them into heated discussion of the merits, causes, and consequences of the Reformation.[20] Medieval guilds have also figured importantly in recent accounts of the Reformation by scholars such as J. J. Scarisbrick[21] and Eamon Duffy.[22] The general trend has been to represent the guilds as a lost Eden of associative polity, religious purity, or both.[23] For Lucy Toulmin Smith,[24] who was chiefly responsible for getting *English Gilds* into print, they formed part of a different historiographical trajectory: that of the social and political enfranchisement of women.[25]

The long *récit* of women's social and political history within which Lucy Toulmin Smith inscribes herself passes through 1547 but obviously extends far beyond the death of Henry VIII.[26] The 1389 returns, then, assume considerable importance in originating or instantiating many different cultural and historiographical trajectories. Before looking at them more closely, we might resist the forward pull of such grand narratives for a moment by considering the Cambridge parliament of 1388, their own point of historical origin.

Motives and Circumstances in 1388

At first sight, the command sent out from Westminster in November 1388 for every guild to disclose its traditions, oaths, forms of governance, goods, and chattels to central authority seems to crystallize the struggle between associational form and incipient absolutism that is the chief subject of this book:

Nov. 1   To the sheriff of Lincoln. Order, for particular causes declared in the
Westminster   parliament last holden at Cantebrigge, on sight etc. to cause proc-
lamation to be made, that all masters and wardens of gilds and fraternities shall before the Purification next certify in chancery the manner, form and authority for the foundation of such gilds, the continuance and ruling thereof, the oaths of the bretheren and sisters, their meetings, the liberties, privileges, statutes, customs etc. thereof, their lands, rents etc. mortified and not mortified, their goods and chattels, the value of their lands and price of their goods, and all circumstances relating to the same, under pain of forfeiture of their lands, goods, etc., bringing before the king and council any charters and letters patent of the king or any of his forefathers concerning the same under pain of revocation thereof, and annulment of the liberties, privileges and grants therein contained; and order to certify before the octaves of St. Hilary next the days and places where proclamation was made, and the names of those who made it.

The like to singular the sheriffs throughout England.

To the sheriff of Lincoln. Order to make proclamation ordering all masters, wardens and overseers of misteries and crafts likewise to bring charters etc. concerning the same.

The like to singular the sheriffs throughout England.[27]

Richard II showed an increasing fondness for centralized information gathering as a means of controlling, intimidating, and extracting money from his subjects.[28] Here the surveillance is to be carried out on a national scale. In November 1388, however, Richard did not have control of government apparatus in England: the Lords Appellant held sway until May 1389. The document also makes it clear that the demand that guilds should "certify" themselves originated not at Westminster but at the parliament which sat at Barnwell, Cambridge, from September 10 to October 17, 1388. Three main issues were argued out in this parliament: livery and maintenance, labor and wages, guilds and fraternities. The first of these saw the Commons arguing against the magnates; the second, advanced in at least thirteen separate petitions, pitted the many small landowners among the Commons against the landless and unrepresented poor.[29] The third issue was also introduced by a Commons petition. This asked not for an enquiry into, but rather for *the suppression of*, all guilds and fraternities.[30] The burgesses and knights of the shire who argued for this had doubtless been unsettled by the Rising of 1381;[31] those with commercial interests were also suspicious that any attempt to associate by their workers, albeit for ostensibly religious purposes, could pose a threat to business. Their proposal that the goods and chattels of the guilds should be sold off to pay for the war with France proved their loyalty to the Crown and promised to make their own business easier. This proposal was never accepted; the administration at Westminster took no significant action against the political independence of the guilds.[32] The 1389 returns were shelved in the Chancery and then forgotten.

The chief threat to the guilds in 1388, then, issued not from the king or magnates but from the Commons. This obviously vitiates any simplistic mapping of the laterally extending liberties of guild culture against the hierarchical prerogatives of royal and noble authority. The consequences of this will be fully addressed when we come to consider the *Cook's Tale* within and as part of the complex and contradictory structuring of London guild politics.[33]

Guild Governance, Discipline, and Culture

In surveying the 1389 returns, one is immediately struck by the fact that so many of the guilds are of recent foundation.[34] This means that many thousands of lay people in this period had experience participating in a guild or guilds, and also in forming a new one.[35] Drawn together by a perception of a common need (the need for professional solidarity, the need to repair a bridge, to reverence an image, or to go on pilgrimage), they assume their right to form themselves into a corporate body and then, perhaps, to hire a chaplain. The confidence of this gesture of self-incorporation is, from the long perspective of the historiography of political forms, truly remarkable. Our account here begins with questions of structure, organization, and discipline before considering some of the cultural activities sponsored by the guilds; this pattern corresponds, albeit loosely, to the order followed by the returns themselves. No single aspect of the 1389 guild returns can be considered in isolation, of course; political, religious, economic, social, and cultural categories are always waiting to offer competing or concurrent terms of analysis.

The 1389 returns proceed from the assumption (that is, they assume rather than argue) that a guild is fit and able to govern itself. Such emphasis on self-governance is typically expressed through a detailed account of rules, regulations, and expenses. The Shipmen's Guild of Lynn, for example, stipulates that there shall be three meetings ("morwespeches") per year, "and mo if it nede be." [36] Any guild brother who misses a meeting, without the alderman's permission, may be fined one pound of wax. Should the dean forget to summon a brother to a meeting, that member being "in toun," he will be fined three pence, "but if he haue grace." Any alderman found neglectful of his office will be fined, "to amendement of þe gild," three shillings. A negligent steward ("skeueyn") will be fined two shillings, a negligent dean one shilling. Newcomers to "thys fraternite" shall pay, on entering it, eight pence: four pence to the alderman, two to the clerk, and two to the dean. One London guild, dedicated to St. Katherine, specifies that new brothers and sisters shall kiss each member of their fraternity, on entering it, "in tokeynge of loue, charite, and pes."[37] Other guilds are keen to ensure that members do not litigate with one another: "noman ne no woman" of the Guild of St. Edmund, Bishop's Lynn, shall go to law with a fellow guild member until "þe aldirman and þe gilde breþere han assayed for to bringen hem at ones."[38] Members of the Guild of St. Margaret, Lincoln, are enjoined to stand by any brother or sister charged with crimes (such as theft or homicide at fairs or markets) "as if they were all children of the same father and mother."[39]

Such strong emphasis on group solidarity is reinforced by an insistence on secrecy: "who-so be-wreys þe counseyl of þis gilde to anny straunge man or woman," warn the statutes of the Guild of St. Mary, Lynn, "sal pay, to amendement of þe lyght, a pounde of wax."[40] Even after death, guild members could count on continuing solidarity with their guild. A member of the London carpenters' guild dying within London "or in þe subarbes" could expect the fraternity—"alle þe bretheren and sostren"—to convene itself around the member's dead body before moving it to church.[41] Members of an Aldersgate, London, guild who died "wiþoute þe citees ende" could envisage their bodies being brought back to London, so long as they died within ten miles of the city.[42] Drowning members of a Wiggenhall, Norfolk, guild could expect their bodies to be recovered, if found within six miles of the home church, "and the lyghte be broughte be-for hem to the kirke."[43] And guild members could also look forward, beyond their death, to a time when the prayers of their fraternity, functioning like "a cooperative chantry,"[44] would help them endure "the bitter payne of purgatore."[45] Their names would not be struck from the guild register: indeed, it was possible to become a guild member posthumously.[46] Death, for members of a London parish clerks' guild, meant a change of *estate* within the fraternity, not exclusion from it, since members prayed for five social categories: clerks, priests, secular brothers, secular sisters, and dead brothers and sisters.[47] Death, one notes, dispenses with gender distinctions.

It might seem wasteful, in social and political terms, for these associative groupings to invest so much in the afterlife. The 1540s acts (one might argue) were following a semiconscious economic logic in seeking to free up the capital invested, or buried, in the support of perpetual chantries. But the social power of a group solidarity extending beyond the grave should not be underestimated. Nor was it: a proclamation of 1383 shows government officials to be very nervous of any group determined "to live and die together."[48] The oaths sworn by members of guilds expressed loyalty to the guild rather than to any authority beyond it, and specifically to the letter of its statutes: "Also, þo þat comen here-after to þe bretherhede, as brethren oþer sustren, he shal swere on þe papir, to-fore þe wardeins þerof, for to kepe wel and trewely alle þe pointes of þis papir atte here power."[49] Some of the 1389 guild returns found it prudent to assert that they did not intend to flout or compete with common law: "Ande þis is here entent, to make non ordinaunce in prejudice ne lettyng of þe comoun lawe, but only in worshepe of godd and seynt cristofore, and norisshyng of loue and charitee."[50]

Guilds were at pains to emphasize that such "nourishing of love and charity" could only be conducive to the "comune profyt."[51] Members of the Guild of Garlikhithe, London, were moved to incorporate themselves in 1375, so the return tells us, "for amendement of her lyues and of her soules, and to noriche more loue bytwene þe bretheren and sustren of þe bretherhede."[52] This dual emphasis upon spiritual and social values typically manifested itself in the two most characteristic activities of guild members: worshipping and drinking. It would be a mistake to try and pry these two activities apart (to suggest that the drinking in the guildhall or tavern came as a relief from sitting in church), since they evidently form part of a continuous experience of corporate identity. Members of the modest Guild of St. Giles (Tydd St. Giles, Cambridgeshire) financed the maintenance of candles (three to be lit at the Elevation of the Host) by subscriptions paid in beer; the brothers and sisters of this guild, the return tells us, "are in perfect charity, good will and accord."[53] Enterprising people were sometimes inspired to redress the balance between conviviality and spirituality (when it grew lopsided) by forming a guild. People and pilgrims were attracted to the church of St. Benet's, Gracechurch Street, London, because of its good "hostellrie"; the Guild of Our Lady was set up to finance a chaplain so that people could hear mass before going about their business.[54]

The association of communal drinking with the feast day of a guild's patron was sufficiently strong for this meeting to be referred to as the *potatio* or "þe drynkyng" or the "tyme of drynk."[55] Drinking on these occasions amounted to more than a symbolic gesture. The Guild of Holy Cross, Hultoft, reckoned to get through thirty gallons of ale at its guild feast (the residue being given to the poor).[56] The alderman of the Guild of St. James, Lynn, was entitled to two gallons; every steward got a gallon, and "þe Clerk, a potel" (a half-gallon).[57] Brothers or sisters of this guild who were absent through sickness "in tyme of drynkyng" were likewise entitled to "a potel."[58] Sick brothers and sisters of the Guild of the Holy Cross, Bishop's Lynn, were entitled to a full gallon, as were "ony brother or sister . . . in pelgrimage."[59] Some guilds moved from the church to an inn for their guild-day meeting; some held their *drynkyng* at the house of a brother or sister.[60]

This emphasis on drinking no doubt accounts in part for the considerable space dedicated to group discipline in these guild regulations. No guild member shall call one of his bretheren thief or "scurra"; nobody shall be "rebel of his tounge," or fall asleep "in tyme of drynke," or refuse to pass the cup.[61] There shall be no "noyse or janglinge" at the meeting; any brother who resorts to physical violence at the *drynkyng* will be fined four pounds of wax.[62] One London guild states that "eny riotour, oþer contekour," shall be expelled from the guild until he amends his ways; all members "shul be helpynge aȝeins þe rebelle and vnboxhum." Guild members were enjoined not to fall "in debat" with one another; brothers and sisters "ne schal noght debat with oþer."[63] But *rebellynge*, loud-mouthing, and *janglynge* were obviously perennial problems for certain guilds (such as the Guild of St. John Baptist, Bishop's Lynn):

And also who-so is rebel ageyns þe alderman, or ageynes sistere or bretheren, in tyme of drynk, or of morunspeche holdun, he shal pay 1 lb wax vp grace to þe liȝt. And who-so discuretes þe counseil of þe gilde to ani straunge man or womman, he shal paye 1 lb wax to þe liȝt. And qwo-so jangle in time of drynk, or of morunspeche holdun, and þe Deen comaund hem to be stille, and he wilnouht, he shall pay ½ lb wax.[64]

Strong authority, preferably backed by a robust physical presence, was obviously required to maintain order at delicate moments of guild *drynkynges*. Many different strategies were pursued in channeling and coordinating the creative and physical energies of the bretheren. The most celebrated of these was, of course, the guild-sponsored drama that was ultimately to develop into the great English mystery cycles.[65] The Pater Noster Guild of York, founded to revive and maintain an old play urging the virtues of the Lord's Prayer, probably did not generate a great deal of dramatic excitement.[66] Other spectacles glimpsed through the 1389 returns promised better, or livelier: one thinks of the baiting and hunting of a guild-sponsored bull through Stamford, Lincolnshire, and of the dancing women of Baston (who performed in honor of their patron, John the Baptist).[67] But although the returns do afford some glimpses of local color, their choices of guild patron and expressions of religious devotion (in play, pageant, and narrative) are markedly conservative. They prefer virgin martyrs from antiquity to local and more recent saints;[68] they prefer, above all, the Virgin Mary (one-third of all guilds being named in her honor).[69] Two guilds from Beverley, Yorkshire, offer a more typical picture of guild culture than a single report, from Wiggenhall, Norfolk, of guild brothers wearing oak-leaf garlands in church at their annual meeting.[70] The Guild of St. Helen and St. Mary, Beverley, founded at a Franciscan church in 1378, celebrated the Feast Day of St. Helen with a procession (honoring her finding of the cross): a youth dressed as Queen Helen was preceded by two old men, one carrying a cross, the other a spade. The Guild of the Purification of the Blessed Virgin Mary moved in procession through Beverley with one of their number dressed as a queen (representing the Virgin) with the appearance of a son in her arms. Two other members (carrying a frame of twenty-four lights) played angels; two more played the parts of Simeon and Joseph. Having arrived at the church, the Virgin offered her son to Simeon at the high altar; the brothers and sisters offered one penny each and their lights.[71]

Guilds dedicated to the Virgin cater more often to a feeling for affective piety than to a taste for spectacle. A guild at Leverington, Cambridgeshire, was founded in 1386 to repair a picture of St. Mary, to hire a chaplain for regular worship, and to burn two torches daily at the singing of the *Salve Regina*.[72] This antiphon was obviously a favorite among guild members: it was sung at dusk every day at guilds dedicated to the Virgin at Louth, Lincolnshire, and at Northampton.[73] Marian devotion and popular affective piety—and their dark underside, anti-Semitism—combined in the devotions of the Peltiers' Guild of St. William at Norwich Cathedral. On one Sunday every year, this guild gathered in the cathedral to honor "God, the Virgin Mother and St. William." A young child played the part of the boy saint by carrying a candle and walking "betwyxen to gode men, tokenynge of þe gloryous marter."[74] The "knave chyld innocent"[75] commemorated by this performance was a twelve-year-old boy whose mutilated body had been found in a wood outside Norwich in 1144 (more than a century before the remains of nine-year-old Hugh were recovered from a well at Lincoln).[76] The suggestion that this William had been the victim of ritual murder by Jews was first recorded in 1149; the Norwich Guild of St. William was founded in 1376.

The taste for pathos, fantasy, and massive retribution excited by tales of the "knave chyld innocent" at Norwich was met elsewhere by stories of virgin (female) martyrs. Saints Agnes, Barbara, Faith, and Margaret each had their share of guild dedications; St. Katherine (patroness of the dying, of young girls, of students, and of people whose work depended on wheels) was exceptionally popular.[77] One guild dedicated to St. Katherine makes separate provision for the devotions expected of its "lettered" and "unlettered" members;[78] another offers us a rare instance of the kind of narrative that circulated through these guilds. The brothers and sisters of the Guild of St. Katherine in the church of St. Andrew, Cambridge, we are told,

have established, made, and ordained one gild, or fraternity, to the praise of God and in honor of the glorious virgin, our advocate, whose body was carried (by divine command) by angels to Mount Sinai for burial. In honor of this virgin, our Lord Jesus thought it fitting to perform countless miracles. In one of these, this most noble of virgins disputed with and triumphed over fifty orators [*rethores*] who, through the king's command, had come to tear down the Christian faith. These *rethores*, once their eyes were opened (which the devil had held closed) and their minds illuminated through this same virgin, converted to the Christian faith. The king, on hearing of this, commanded them all to be burned. Calling on the name of Christ, they suffered (for the palm of martyrdom) the burning of the fire (their clothing and hair remaining untouched and unharmed by any injury of the fire). These miracles and just as many others, which we must refrain from telling in this book on account of their great length, were performed by Almighty God for the love of this same glorious virgin.[79]

A guild return is no place to rehearse miracles, but the writer of this return makes it clear that many stories of the life and legend of St. Katherine of Egypt were known to the men and women of this "gilde." Katherine, a high-born, learned, and beautiful woman of Alexandria, protested to the Emperor Maxentius against the worship of idols. Having defeated the fifty *rhetores*, she refused to deny her faith and marry the emperor (who had her beaten for two hours and sent to prison). An attempt to break her on a spiked wheel failed when the wheel flew apart (killing some bystanders with splinters). Two hundred soldiers were sufficiently impressed to be converted (and immediately beheaded). When Katherine herself was beheaded, milk, rather than blood, flowed from her severed arteries.[80] Such "edifying romance,"[81] one imagines, was the most familiar form of religious narrative heard within these guilds.

Another guild patron, by far the most popular selected from more recent times, is celebrated in an opening to a 1389 return that has all the formulaic qualities of a popular romance:

In þe worchep and honor of Jhesu Crist, and of his mild modir seynt marye, and of alle þe holy Company of heuen, and specially of þe holy martir seynt Thomas of Cauntirburye, men and woman [sic], þorow a grete deuocioun to þe forseide martir seynt Thomas, hauend, in þe the toun of lenne, þis fraternite be-gonne.[82]

The town of Lynn—home to that much-traveled pilgrim, Margery Kempe—reported no fewer than five different guilds dedicated to St. Thomas of Canterbury in 1389. One of them was founded "lately" by six townsfolk returning from a pilgrimage to Canterbury; another, founded as far back as 1272, speaks of "the honor which so many townsfolk bear towards St. Thomas."[83] It is easy for us to forget the exceptional popularity of St. Thomas of Canterbury in the fourteenth century because signs of his cult have since been systematically erased. Henry VIII, in a proclamation of November 16, 1538, denounced Beckett as "a rebel and traitour to his prince." "Images and pictures, through the hole realm" (the proclamation continues), "shall be put down and avoided out of all churches, chappelles, and other places."[84] Many churches and gilds dedicated to St. Thomas of Canterbury found it prudent, after this, quietly to transfer their allegiance to St. Thomas the Apostle.

The association of guilds with pilgrimages extends beyond devotion to St. Thomas of Canterbury. Most guilds at Lincoln made special provision in their ordinances for members wishing to go on pilgrimage. Members of the Guild of St. Anne, Lincoln, proposing to go on pilgrimage to the holy land, Rome, or St. James, were led from their home parish of St. Peter's in the

Skinmarket to the cross at Lincoln Green; here they were given two pence by the Graceman (the master of guilds at Lincoln), one penny by the two wardens of their guild, and a halfpenny by every guild member.[85] Members of another Lincoln guild accompanied guild brothers and sisters intent on pilgrimage to the city gate and gave them each "a halfpenny at least."[86] The Guild of St. James, Burgh, Lincolnshire, was founded by five men returning from pilgrimage to Compostella who narrowly escaped (were miraculously saved from) drowning at sea.[87] A brother (or sister) of the Guild of the Virgin, Kingston-upon-Hull, who intended to make a pilgrimage to the holy land, was excused his yearly dues (until his return), "in order that all the guild may share in his pilgrimage"; another guild reportedly sent a single pilgrim to Canterbury every year.[88]

Guild Culture, Chaucer's *Compagnye*, and Boccaccio's *Brigata*

It is perhaps worth repeating at this point that I am not insisting that the *compagnye* formed by Chaucer's pilgrims *is* a guild; my argument is that many aspects of the associative behavior and cultural performance enacted in the *General Prologue* (and beyond) may be clarified by reference to guild phenomena. At its boldest, my argument claims that Chaucer's pilgrims behave as if they were schooled in the guilds. A further qualification might be made. They behave as if they were schooled in the *English* guilds, for although the guild movement was a Europe-wide phenomenon, some significant local and national variations are evident in matters of political organization and cultural expression.[89] To clarify this further, we will first summarize the relations of English guild culture to Chaucer's text and then proceed to a brief comparison of two associative forms: Chaucer's *compagnye* and Boccaccio's *brigata*.

Chaucer decides to bring his storytellers together not in a church (the site favored by the *Decameron*) but in a tavern. Church and tavern need not be thought of as invariably antithetical in their social aims; *potatio* and worship could form a continuous corporate experience. Chaucer's pilgrims, bound for Canterbury, drink together before forming themselves into a voluntary association, bound by oath; they drink again afterwards (in a more restrained and deliberately symbolic fashion). Herry Bailey provides the drink necessary to establish the *compagnye* and offers the social and physical authority required to keep it together. Some of his bretheren will grow "rebelle and unboxum"; some will drink to excess; some will be given to "janglynge" and fall "in debat" over professional rivalries. The integrity of the group (tested and confirmed by the sudden appearance of an outsider, the mysterious Canon) will remain the preeminent concern of his short-term rule.

The Chaucerian tales that have most in common with guild-generated narratives tell us least about guild structures (or any other aspect of fourteenth-century political form, for that matter). They are the two tales assigned to female religious: the *Prioress's Tale* and the *Second Nun's Tale*. The first of these, said to render "every man . . . sobre" (7.691–92), blends a highly affective Marian piety, perhaps the most typical form of devotion in the guilds, with the kind of archaeologizing anti-Semitism ("it is but a little while ago," 7.686) exemplified by the Norwich Guild of St. William. The evil genius of the *Prioress's Tale* lies in bringing two strains of sensibility (love for the Virgin and children; hatred of Jews) into a unified narrative sequence. The singing of the antiphon *Salve Regina* was, we have noted, a familiar and comforting feature of guilds dedicated to Mary; in the *Prioress's Tale* it is the very singing of a Marian antiphon by a young "innocent" that is said to plant murderous thoughts "in Jues herte" (7.559). The triumph of Cecelia, in the *Second Nun's Tale*, over the logic of Almachius, the Roman prefect, is obviously akin to that of Katherine over the fifty *rhetores*. Both narratives offer the momentary triumph of an enlightened female figure withstanding the tortures inflicted by unseeing paganism; both end with the murky pathos of a virginal, female body finally succumbing to such physical assaults, winning "the palm of martirdom" (8.274) and becoming a new site for pilgrimage and cultic devotion. Both narratives are indebted to the collections of saints' lives formalized in texts such as Jacobus de Voragine's *Legenda Aurea*.[90]

The anti-Semitism of the *Prioress's Tale* may also be glimpsed, briefly and chillingly, in a single line of the *Second Nun's Tale*: "Whoso that troweth nat this, a beest he is" (8.288). The speaker, Cecelia's brother-in-law Tiburce, has just seen the folly of pagan idol worship; "whoever refuses to see this," he says, "is a beast." His position here matches that of Peter the Venerable, Abbot of Cluny, author of *A Tractate Against the Longstanding Insensibility of the Jews*.[91] For Abbot Peter, Jeremy Cohen argues, "the Jews' refusal to submit to incontrovertible proofs and accept Christianity has placed them outside the realm of human reason, in the category of beasts."[92] The community that groups itself around Cecelia has often been admired as an attempted return to the apostolic simplicity of early Christianity, an attempt supposedly shared by the medieval guilds. But the proposition "Whoso that troweth nat this . . ." reminds us that any associational grouping may seek to secure internal solidarity through the outward-focused act, threat, or memorialization of exclusion: we come together through (and sometimes only through) our common recognition that we are not them. The exclusion of Jews, exemplified by Cecelia's Roman circle, is an unspoken, unifying force for Chaucer's *compagnye* (as for England itself after the expulsions of 1290).

One last aspect of guild culture might be mentioned, somewhat more tentatively, as sharing a peculiar quality of the *Canterbury Tales*: its propensity to bridge, and sometimes to float between, the realms of the living and the dead. This tendency is seen in Chaucer not only in the religious tales but also in some of the more comic or irreligious performances. One thinks of the *Pardoner's Tale*, which begins at a tavern in time of plague, and the *Friar's Tale*, which sees a devilish yeoman carry off a summoner. Fears of death and dying, major stimuli to guild activities, are boldly exploited by two figures with guild associations: the Pardoner (who is affiliated with the guild hospital of Roncesvalles, Charing Cross, an institution with a very troubled recent history)[93] and the friar in the *Summoner's Tale* (who pursues Thomas and his wife, members of his convent's lay fraternity, to their home village).[94] The relentless pursuit of piety in fraternities obviously generated some irresistible opportunities for impious, humorous, or scandalous behavior. The 1389 returns are not likely to advertise such goings-on, but one can occasionally deduce some possibilities for macabre humor and sexual license:

If any man wishes, as is common, to keep night-watches with the dead, this will be allowed, on the condition that he neither calls up ghosts, nor makes any mockeries of the body or its good name, nor does any other scandal of the kind; lest, by such scandals, the discipline of the church may be brought into contempt, and the great judge may be provoked to heavier vengeance, who ought rather, by reason of the sins of the people, to be asked for love and mercy. And never shall any woman, unless of the household of the dead, keep such a night-watch.[95]

The kind of "scandal" envisaged here is actually more strongly reminiscent of the *Decameron* than of Chaucer: one thinks especially of Boccaccio's opening description of the 1348 plague, in which the niceties of Christian burial are openly mocked and many women reportedly abandon all sense of bodily decorum. But such behavior is not in any way characteristic of Boccaccio's storytellers: indeed, their *brigata* forms itself precisely to reject the grotesque and libidinous actions that have engulfed the plague-stricken city. Boccaccio's group, unlike Chaucer's, is not representative of the greater public world (unless that world be conceived in very narrow terms). All ten storytellers are young, healthy, well-mannered, and of high social pedigree; they are further united by prior ties of friendship, neighborliness, kinship, or courtship.[96] Their associative grouping regulates itself through the mechanism of a rotating monarchy, a concept devised by the eldest woman, Pampinea, as she sits with six female companions in the Dominican church of Santa Maria Novella. Although this *compagnia* is formed under the pressure of acute social need, its authority as a group *does not* derive from its own act of self-incorporation: for the *brigata* remains incomplete, acephalous, until men arrive to take their place as head of it. "This company" ("questa compagnia"), Filomena suspects, "will soon break up without honor to any of us if we do not take a guide other than ourselves." Elissa agrees: "Men are truly the head of women" ("delle femine capo," *Intr.* 75–76).

Elsewhere in Boccaccio's *Introduzione*, the tendency of social groupings to form themselves according to need is seen as a sign not of social vigor but of social malaise. Particularly memorable (and repellent to the narrator) is the spontaneous emergence of a new craft or professional grouping, the *becchini*:

> Moreover it was rare for the bodies of the dead to be accompanied by more than ten or twelve neighbours to the church, nor were they borne on the shoulders of worthy and honest citizens, but by a kind of gravedigging fraternity [una maniera di beccamorti], newly come into being and drawn from the lower orders of society [di minuta gente]. These people assumed the office of sexton, and demanded a fat fee for their services, which consisted in taking up the coffin and hauling it swiftly away, not to the church specified by the dead man in his will, but usually to the nearest at hand. They would be preceded by a group of four or six clerics, who between them carried one or two candles at most, and sometimes none at all. Nor did the priests go to the trouble of pronouncing solemn and lengthy funeral rites, but, with the aid of these so-called sextons [becchini], they hastily lowered the body into the nearest empty grave they could find. (*Intr.* 35; p. 55)

Boccaccio plainly identifies with the "worthy and honest citizens" here, rather than with the "gravedigging fraternity" from the *minuta gente* that dumps the citizenry in mass graves. The plague's greatest horror for Boccaccio lies in losing the power to regulate terms of death and dying; part of this horror lies in the prospect of being delivered, dead or dying, into the hands of the lower orders.[97] Boccaccio's *brigata* avoids or at least defers this fate by leaving the city for the countryside. Of course, it must take the lower orders along. Its seven servants (four women, three men) will function as an ideal shadow-*brigata*, bidden to serve the needs of the ten storytellers and (for the most part) remain silent and invisible.

The shadow-*brigata* does, we have noted, make a single, violent irruption into the aristocratic circle at the beginning of the Sixth Day, when the storytellers are suddenly distracted by the "great commotion [romore] issuing from the kitchen."[98] The maidservant Licisca proves briefly entertaining, but is silenced at precisely the moment that she begins to realize and validate the worth of her own lived ("vivuta") experience: "Thanks be to God, I haven't lived for nothing" (6, *Intr.*, 15; p. 483). Narrative is brutally abbreviated here (by the Sixth-Day Queen, with a threat of whipping) at the point at which the Miller (and hence the distinctive dialogical discourse of the *Canterbury Tales*) begins. Boccaccio, unlike Chaucer, will not allow more than a momentary intersection between such distinct social spheres. The techniques for dispute resolution that are developed so carefully throughout the *Canterbury Tales* are not to be found in Boccaccio. Silence is simply imposed upon a lower-class speaker ("le 'mpose silenzio," 15); another word or another sound may be physically punished. If we are to find a political paradigm underlying the interaction between Elissa, Queen for the Sixth Day, and Licisca, we might look not to guild culture but rather to another Trecento Tuscan paradigm: slavery.[99]

The great framed collections of Chaucer and Boccaccio seem, on the face of it, to share a commitment to the exploration of associational form. On closer inspection, though, the two writers seem often to be traveling in opposite directions. In moving from the *Troilus* to the *Tales*, Chaucer has relinquished the exploration of courtly interiors, with their small, familial, and intimate circles of aristocratic lovers and fighters, in favor of a broader, looser, more inclusive social grouping that discovers a peculiar developmental logic within itself. Boccaccio, writing within the most broadly inclusive regime of medieval times, devotes his energies to a *brigata* of ten young aristocrats, defined against a shadow-*brigata* of seven servants, that is as tightly and narrowly defined as a court circle or humanist *cenacolo*.[100] When the core values of this grouping are threatened, Boccaccio moves abruptly from an associational ideology (celebrating equity across the group) to markedly authoritarian and hierarchical positions. Man may be a social animal, but when the organic logic of social needs creates the *becchini*, Man rounds up his servants and moves out of town. Servants are entertaining for a moment, but when they threaten to speak for themselves (and steal the show) they must be silenced.

Another way of articulating this same contrast between Chaucer and Boccaccio is to say that Chaucer, in evolving his broadly inclusive self-regulating Canterbury *compagnye*, follows a Germanic tradition in which a self-incorporated body assumes the right to exist without appealing to external authority.[101] Boccaccio, on the other hand, frequently appeals to external criteria: women, gravedigging fraternities, and servants must be called upon to recognize authority outside and above themselves. At certain pressured moments, Boccaccio speaks not like a champion of Florentine *libertas* but like an Augustinian: government is devised not to facilitate what happens naturally but to put a brake on nature by imposing authority from above. This slide to Augustinianism is associated with the erosion of communal liberties in the face of despotism; it is also linked to the revival of Roman law. It is worth remembering that Boccaccio maintained close connections with Augustinian friars. When he died, he left the *cenacolo agostiniano* of Santo Spirito, Florence, both his writings and his library.[102]

The peculiar tension between associative freedom and hierarchical constraint that is played out in Boccaccio's *brigata* is also evident in the Florentine religious guilds. In comparing these guilds with their English counterparts two major differences are immediately evident: the Italian guilds are kept much more tightly under clerical control, and they offer very little scope for female participation. Friars took a leading role in writing the statutes of these guilds, in directing their devotions, and in skimming their capital for services rendered.[103] Two major forms of religious guild flourished in Trecento Florence: the flagellants (*disciplinati*) and the lauds singers (*laudesi*). Flagellants (who were forbidden to enter taverns) practiced a bodily discipline that seems quite alien to the convivial, hymn-and-*potatio* spirit of the English guilds. Lauds singers, who were particularly devoted to the Virgin, were expected to be in church for services every evening of the week.[104] Both groups receive short shrift from Boccaccio: the Franciscan tertiary and (suspected) [105] flagellant of *Decameron* 3.4 is cuckolded as he follows the self-mortifying regimen prescribed by his spiritual director, a Franciscan friar; Gianni, the master weaver of 7.1, is kept so busy by his duties as leader of the lauds singers at Santa Maria Novella that his wife seeks entertainment elsewhere. Boccaccio's narrator, Emilia, is also contemptuous of the kind of literature that Gianni is supplied with by the friars as a member of this fraternity: "copies of the Paternoster in the vernacular and the song of Saint Alexis and the lament of Saint Bernard and the laud of Lady Matilda and a whole lot of other drivel." [106] Although Boccaccio's *brigata* assembles at Santa Maria Novella, its members would hardly think of interacting with the artisans from lower guilds who gathered there to sing *laude*.[107]

Florentine governments made concerted efforts in the fourteenth century to tap into the wealth of the confraternities; in the fifteenth century they strove to reduce their potential for political activity. Richer fifteenth-century *laudesi* in Florence paid professionals to do their singing for them; in Venice, members of the sixteenth-century "Scuole dei Battuti" (hoping for a vicarious spiritual benefit) hired self-flagellating outsiders to augment their festivals.[108] Official control in Florence was further strengthened by the census of 1524–27, a final stage of a policy aimed at keeping societies under tighter control.[109] This pattern of increasing state regulation is comparable, of course, with what happened in England. But it is important to note that even in Boccaccio's time, craft workers were forbidden to form any type of fraternity for worship, mutual aid, or burial. Members of the powerful guilds were fearful of their workers meeting *sub religionis pretextu* to organize protests against working conditions and political marginalization (a fear shared, as we shall see in Chapter 6, by powerful guild masters in Chaucer's London). The penalty for creating such a guild was death; the wool carder Ciuto Brandini was executed for forming a *fratellanza* in 1343.[110]

The court-and-humanist procedures and values of Boccaccio's *brigata* owe little, then, to the craft and religious guilds of Trecento Florence. Chaucer's *compagnye*, by contrast, shows important points of intersection with guild culture both in its personnel (English guilds, we should note, have been seen as representing, "predominantly, a middle class artisan movement") [111] and in its *modus operandi*. Sixteenth-century English writers, anxious to equate Chaucer with Boccaccio and Petrarch as founding fathers of vernacular eloquence, were evidently embarrassed by the company Chaucer keeps in the *Canterbury Tales*. Sidney's *Defence of Poesie* concedes that Chaucer "did excellently in his *Troilus and Creseid*," but has nothing to say about his *Canterbury Tales* and speaks enigmatically of his "great wants, fit to be forgiuen in so reuerent an Antiquitie." [112] Some thirty years earlier, Protestant monarchists had employed the term "Canterbury tale" as a term of opprobrium. Edmund Becke, addressing Edward VI through the Preface to his new Bible edition, opposes popular taste for "Cronicles & Canterbury Tales" to "the reading of this boke."[113] Thomas Cranmer, in his *Sermon concerning the time of Rebellion*, asks at a heated moment: "To what purpose tendeth such dissimulation and hypocrisy? If we take it for a Canterbury Tale, why do we not refuse it? Why do we not laugh it out of place, and whistle at it?"[114] Hugh Latimer, preaching before Edward VI, argues that "if good lyfe do not insue and folow upon our readynge to the example of other[s] we myghte as well spende that tyme in reading of prophane hystories, of cantorburye tales, or a fit of Roben Hode."[115]

Becke, Cranmer, and Latimer are all writing in 1549, just two years after the act of Parliament that led to the abolition of 2,374 fraternities, chantries, and guilds.[116] The spoliation of guild and monastic property was still in full swing: jewels, rings, and Beckett's "staff" (set with pearls and stones) had been delivered into Henry VIII's own hands by the treasurer of the Court of Augmentations; crown agents were now traveling to "every shires ende" in search of disposable assets.[117] Sixteenth-century readers must have seen quite clearly how Chaucer's *Tales* was invested in the medieval guild culture that was wiped away in midcentury; the familiar charges of "coarseness" and "obsolesence," ostensibly leveled as a purely literary critique, clearly have social and political resonance. Sixteenth-century writers were glad to follow the lead offered by John Leland, Henry VIII's historical researcher, in inventing a biography for Chaucer requisite for his fashioning a vernacular "of purity, of eloquence, of conciseness and beauty," a language that can "justly be reckoned among the thoroughly polished languages of the world."[118] This Chaucer, accordingly, was "a youth of noble birth" who enjoyed a brilliant career at Oxford, completed his education in France, and was held dear by "Richard of Bordeaux" and his successors; "in addition to this," we are told, "all the nobility of England looked upon him as the consummate example of high-wrought expression."[119]

The *Fabulae Cantianae* (as Leland terms them) do, of course, contain some fine examples of "high-wrought expression," but they also contain voices from many different social registers in many different genres. Such heterogeneity of genre and style caused post-humanist, post-Dissolution English writers to turn their back on Chaucer's *Tales* and look to Boccaccio.[120] The *Decameron* certainly contains a wide range of social voices, but all of its voices are mediated through the univocal narration of one social class and a single, homogenized literary form—the nobility and the *novella*. Chaucer's diversity of literary styles and social estates, contained within a single self-regulating *compagnye*, cannot find a historical or political correlative in post-Henrician England; such is its extralinguistic "coarseness" and "obsolesence." The multivoiced, localized cultures sustained by the guilds and celebrated by the *Tales* can now only be heard around the campfires of Shakespeare's *Henry V* at Agincourt, at the moment of their integration into a single national ideology.

Chapter 4

"No Felaweshipe": Thesian Polity

In moving from the *General Prologue* to the *Knight's Tale*, Chaucer travels backwards in time to revisit the locales of his earlier, court-centered *makyng*.[1] As the pilgrim *compagnye* begins its traversing of a contemporary English landscape, heading away from London and Westminster, Chaucer's rust-stained and battle-weary Knight tells a long tale of ducal power in ancient Athens. By the standards of his own courtly writing, Chaucer's account of the wooing of Emelye is exceptionally bleak, cheerless, and songless. His drastic cutting of the *Teseida*, and particularly of the humorous and leisurely sexual negotiations of the first Book, concentrates attention upon the business and mechanisms of political rule. Some readers have characterized the statecraft fashioned by Theseus as tyrannical. Although this charge is inaccurate, the urge to make such a claim (against the complacency of the Boethian and neo-Platonic idealists) is itself instructive.[2] By the political standards established by the greater corpus of Chaucerian fiction, something is indeed rotten in the Thesian regime. In fact, the *Knight's Tale*, which unpicks the process of collective determination articulated so carefully throughout the *General Prologue*, effects the first political rebellion of the *Canterbury Tales*—a reversal of political direction achieved so smoothly, so *noiselessly*, that it seems to have escaped our notice.

Gender politics, here as elsewhere, provide vital clues to problematic, disfunctional, or contradictory aspects of statecraft. It will be noticed, for example, that Theseus tends to view love, or Love, as a competitor; as a rival feudal lord. His strategy here, replicating that of his narrator, the Knight, is to save himself from subjection to Love by banishing Love to the past, as a thing of youth. Resistance to this strategy is offered by another tale of Theseus, found elsewhere within the Chaucerian corpus and linked, intertextually, to the *Knight's Tale* through mutual dependence on the *Teseida*: the *Legend of Ariadne*. Theseus's deliberate destruction of sisterhood in this *legenda* alerts us to one particular aspect of his war on Femenye, carried forward to the *Knight's Tale*: the silencing of Hippolita. In Chaucer a silent queen is unusual, almost unnatural. Hippolita, as a foreign warrior queen drawn by *raptus* or marriage into the body politic, represents an acute political embarrassment for Thesian polity, a form of one-man rule based upon the systematic refusal of *felaweshipe*.

Shakespeare, a politically astute reader of Chaucer, prepared for his own first representation of Thesian polity by meditating on the court and gender politics of the *Merchant's Tale*, the *Knight's Tale*, and select *legendae* from the *Legend of Good Women*.[3] *A Midsummer Night's Dream* replicates, even amplifies, the silence surrounding the unassimilable Hippolita, flushing out the political embarrassments that in Chaucer remain half-hidden. Shakespeare's belated restoration of a voice to Hippolita, for the commendation of his own poetic craft, represents a moment of exceptional sympathetic alignment with Chaucer (for whom the alliance of queenly voice with poetic craft is a matter of vital, even life-sustaining, importance). Finally, however, Shakespeare pushes Chaucer back into the past, identifying him with the archaic, guild-based dramatics of semi-educated, "hard-handed artisans." Shakespeare, in effect, deciphers the *General Prologue*'s authorial signature aright and takes Chaucer at his word. As the sixth of six in a guild-based social structure, Chaucer invites comparison not with Shakespeare but with Shakespeare's clown, Bottom the weaver.

"Fresca Rosa": Cutting the *Teseida*

Although the *Knight's Tale* is ostensibly a love story, it contains little of the poetry we might expect from a courtly poet of love. When Arcite rides into the fields "to doon his observaunce to May," we are told that he sings a "roundel" (1.1529), but we are allowed to hear just three lines of it (1.1510–12). Poetic energy is soon concentrated into the long and bloody fight between the mad, lionlike Palemon and the cruel, tigerlike Arcite. When this battle is expanded from an affair involving two magnates in the poem's second section to two hundred and two in its fourth, poetic energy is given over to inventories of weaponry and the nailing, filing, and hammering of armorers. The time that passes between these two moments ("fifty wykes," 1850) is a dead space. Nothing is earned and nothing learned. Merchants might make their capital grow in a year; the young knight in the *Wife of Bath's Tale*, under female tutelage, will be granted the chance to learn in the "twelf-month and a day" granted him by the Queen (3.909). But the young knights in the *Knight's Tale* will perform just one more circuit of a seemingly endless cycle of magnate violence. Arcite, "korven out of his harneys" in line 2696, has not made much progress since he was "torn . . . out of the taas" by "pilours," looters of battlefields, almost seventeen hundred lines earlier.

The lyrical possibilities of Boccaccio's *ottave*, exploited to fine effect in *Troilus and Criseyde*, are consciously refused by the *Knight's Tale*'s slow-moving couplets. This decision to develop a darker, more astringent mood accounts for the deliberate excising of the *Teseida*'s first Book. Here, as at the beginning of the *Clerk's Tale*, Chaucer takes pains to draw attention to his decision-making as he cuts and compresses an Italian source:

> And certes, if it nere to long to heere,
> I wolde have toold yow fully the manere
> How wonnen was the regne of Femenye
> By Theseus and by his chivalrye;
> And of the grete bataille for the nones
> Bitwixen Atthenes and Amazones;
> And how asseged was Ypolita,
> The faire, hardy queene of Scithia.   (1.875–82)

Such a passage prompts any audience to meditate for a moment on what they are losing through this particular telling of the story: *tydynges* of a kingdom, or queendom, of Womankind; battles between Greeks and Amazons; tales of a warrior queen who is both "hardy" and "fair." Recourse to the *Teseida* confirms that Chaucer is indeed sacrificing a great deal in bringing us this darkly masculinist *Knight's Tale*. Boccaccio's Hippolita is said to lead her troops as a "duchessa" (and is therefore to be seen as equivalent in rank to Duke Theseus, 1.72).[4] The Amazon women fight with arrows (as Boccaccio coins the extraordinary phrase "donne saettando," "arrowing women"), flamethrowers, catapults, pitch, oil, and soap (1.51–52). The latter phase of the Teseo-Ipolita conflict is conducted as an epistolary exchange (1.99–115). Boccaccio's Hippolita is not conquered in the field; she negotiates agreements ("patti") with Theseus only after explaining her motives to her women in a lengthy, six-stanza (48-line) speech (1.116–21).

Boccaccio's narrative reveals the beauty of Hippolita only after all wedding agreements have been patiently negotiated (and the laws established by the queen for her own territory have been reaffirmed, 1.125). The form of this revelation is unmistakably that of the *cantare*, the popular tradition of oral-derived narrative that bears direct comparison with English tail-rhyme romance:[5]

> Ipolita era a maraviglia bella
> e di valore accesa nel coraggio;
> ella sembrava matutina stella
> o fresca rosa del mese di maggio;
> giovine assai e ancora pulcella,
> ricca d'avere, e di real legnaggio,
> savia e ben costumata, e per natura
> nell'armi ardita e fiera oltre misura.   (1.125)

> Hippolita was marvellously beautiful
> and aflame with fearless courage;
> she was like a morning star

or a fresh rose in the month of May;
very young and still a maiden,
rich in possessions, and of royal lineage,
wise and well-mannered, and by nature
passionate in arms and fierce beyond measure.

The closest that Chaucer comes to this kind of cheerful, tag-laden verse is the parodic tail-rhyme of his own *Sir Thopas*. He does allow some of Boccaccio's generic, *cantare*-derived diction to color his description of Emelye in the garden (which mentions "May" four times in fourteen lines, 1.1034–47), but no such language is expended on Hippolita. His evocation of Emelye's beauty, which speaks of roses, lilies, and angelic song, achieves its effectiveness chiefly by contrast with what comes before and after; its language suggests an innocence of poetic register that, elsewhere in this grim and world-weary *Tale*, is lost, forgotten, or overshadowed.[6]

Chaucer's erasure of the Amazonian, pre-Athenian history of Hippolita, of her physical and psychological battles with Theseus, and of the "fresca rosa" diction that confirms her sisterhood with Emelye combines a darkening of poetic register with a narrowing of sexual and political possibilities. His demolition of *Teseida*, Book I, is as ruthless and calculated as Theseus's destruction of Thebes.[7] The *Knight's Tale's* uneasy mixing of nostalgia for past chivalric glories with revulsion at magnate vanity, instability, and violence ("Vomyt upward . . . downward laxatif," 2756) undoubtedly, as Patterson eloquently argues, speaks to Chaucer's involvement with English magnate politics.[8] It also bears the impress, I would add, of the Italian context within which Chaucer found his Italian text: a nexus both commercial and military, responsive to the triumphs and failures of celebrity mercenaries such as Hawkwood, to Florentine banking houses, to Lombard tyrants, and to the shifting fortunes of the Hundred Years' War.[9] The downgrading of "duchessa" Hippolita to a silent, subordinate, and alien bit player in the Athenian regime is dictated by Chaucer's decision to explore the possibilities and limitations of one-man rule within a context of magnate rivalry. His *Knight's Tale* thus sets out to imagine a world in which a masculine monarch—moderate rather than tyrannical—elects to rule without benefit of queenly or wifely counsel.[10]

"O Regne, That Wolt No Felawe Have with Thee!"

Although many readers have been moved to consider Thesian Athens as a case study in tyranny, it is technically inaccurate to describe Theseus as a tyrant.[11] The term "tyranny" has admittedly been employed extremely loosely by medieval as well as by modern readers. And by medieval fictional characters, too: when Arcite complains of "oure lynage" being "so lowe ybroght by tirannye" (1.1110–11), it is not at all clear whose tyranny he is speaking of.

Have he and Palemon been brought low for siding with "the tiraunt Creon" (961)? Or do they experience Theseus's military invasion of Thebes and his wholesale destruction of their *patria* as a tyrannical act? Or could it be that Palemon is speaking of no earthly figure at all, but of the gods (principally Juno) who seem determined to extirpate the Theban aristocracy? This last seems the more likely option; later on in the *prima pars*, we find Palemon (now alone in his cell) apostrophizing thus:

> Thanne seyde he, "O crueel goddes that governe
> This world with byndyng of youre word eterne,
> And writen in the table of atthamaunt
> Youre parlement and youre eterne graunt,
> What is mankynde moore unto you holde
> Than is the sheep that rouketh in the fold?"   (1.1303–8)

Religious and political vocabularies converge here, generating contradictions productive of a powerful, pessimistic effect. The gods presume to "governe," but they are "cruel" (an epithet habitually associated with tyranny).[12] The "word" that proceeds from these divinities is no life-giving *logos* but a word that binds and incapacitates. This word is written in stone ("atthamaunt"); "parlement" is reduced to the recitation of "eterne graunt," a text already scripted; human beings (inclined by nature to join together in discussion and debate) are reduced to cowering sheep. Such crossing of religious and political vocabularies is typical of this *Tale*. The importance of religion to medieval politics is axiomatic: the Bible has long been recognized as a major source of medieval political thought. Here, though, we see politics shaping a view of religion. Palemon writes his politics into the heavens in trying to read the behavior of the gods.

All this represents just one viewpoint expressed at one unfortunate moment in a particular man's life: Palemon does not accuse the gods of tyranny at the end of the poem when they grant him Emelye. Medieval political vocabularies, like their modern equivalents, were often employed in loose and idiosyncratic ways. Medieval Florence, we have noted, tended to characterize as tyrannical anything considered contrary to Florentine interests. Nonetheless, common medieval understanding of the meaning of tyranny may be established with some degree of precision. This will be addressed at some length in Chapter 10, on the *Clerk's Tale*, but a quick working definition may be offered here: a tyrant, in medieval terms, is a person in authority who gives free rein to his or her emotions rather than acting for the common good. By this definition, Theseus is no tyrant: indeed, I would argue, Chaucer goes to some lengths to suggest that Theseus is an un-tyrant, a ruler who is offered temptations to follow his emotions into tyranny but reins himself back for the *bonum commune*. When, for example, the Theban widows grab at his bridle, ruining the "feste" of his homecoming with Ypolita, Theseus's initial outrage moderates to become, quite quickly, an offer of assistance. He learns, by observing, questioning, and listening, that their emotion is *not about him*; they are, in their own emotional lives, mysterious, sovereign subjects:

> "What folk been ye, that at myn homcomynge
> Perturben so my feste with criynge?"
> Quod Theseus. "Have ye so greet envye
> Of myn honour, that thus compleyne and crye?
> Or who hath yow mysboden or offended?
> And telleth me if it may been amended,
> And why that ye been clothed thus in blak."   (1.905–11)

The intelligence of Theseus's looking and questioning here forms a powerful counterpart to the fixated tyrannical gazing that we are to encounter from many later protagonists: from Walter and January in Fragment IV; from Apius in the *Physician's Tale*; from "irous Cambises," taking target practice to prove the integrity of "myne eyen sight" [13] in the *Summoner's Tale*. Theseus, then, is no tyrant, yet his perennial tendency to stand alone, to try and work out everything for himself (as in the passage above) remains full of troubling potential. Men at the apex of power (the despot; the great householder; the magistrate) become socially destructive when their need to stand alone becomes obsessive and all-consuming. They refuse all forms of *felaweshipe*, and in this (as Palemon observes), they behave like jealous lovers:

> "O Cupide, out of alle charitee!
> O regne, that wolt no felawe have with thee!
> For sooth is seyd that *love ne lordshipe*
> Wol noght, his thankes, have no felaweshipe."   (1.1623–26; emphasis mine)

Palemon does more here than state the obvious: that a love-struck tyrant is a terrible thing, especially for a Griselde, May, or Virginia. He parallels, rather than collapses together, a structure of power ("regne") and a form of affect (single-minded cupidinous love), thereby suggesting that even a non-tyrannical ruler is as jealous as Cupid and therefore, by nature of his position, unable to share in fellowship. From the moment of their falling for Emelye, Palemon and Arcite feel compelled to unpick the *felaweshipe* that has hitherto bound them together. This lengthy and elaborate procedure, which begins by rehearsing the obligations of *bretherhede* and ends by renouncing them (1.1129–86), throws the entire *felaweshipe*-forming impetus of the *General Prologue* into reverse. By the end of this process, each knight is determined to follow his own individualistic "aventure" (1186). The natural terrain for such "aventure" is to be found not in some wild landscape, or on the battlefield, but at the royal court itself:

> "And therfore, at the kynges court, my brother,
> Ech man for himself, ther is noon oother."   (1.1181–82)

By becoming subjects of Cupid, the God of Love, Palemon and Arcite assimilate themselves to the wholly self-interested ethic said to prevail at "the kynges court." We must remember, of course, that such theorizing proceeds from the brains of love-crazed Thebans; it may prove possible to find some forms of *felaweshipe* in royal circles (although they will be more problematic than those worked out in the Tabard). One broader point, however, seems indisputable: that the political subjects of "regne," the political project of one-man rule, will always take a close interest in, feel themselves subject to, the emotional life of their ruler. And if such a lord has no "felawe," his emotions may run unchecked and rule his intellect (and hence his subjects). In *De monarchia*, Dante chooses to engage with this potential objection to one-man rule head-on; his syllogistic solution is elegant, but lacks all psychological plausibility.[14] The *Knight's Tale* both engages the problem (in analyzing Theseus's struggle to control his anger during present-time frustrations of his desire) and suppresses it (in distancing itself from Theseus's past history as a lover). The result of such selective remembering and forgetting is strange: a tale told by a Knight lacking a lady about a monarchical ruler who thinks of love only in retrospect; his newly won and wedded queen says nothing.

"Now Be We Duchesses, Bothe I and Ye"

The Knight of the *General Prologue* has no lady; amatory aspects of chivalry are assigned to his son, the Squire, who studies the arts of love with professional dedication. So too, in the *Knight's Tale*, the pursuit of love is seen as the province of a younger generation. Theseus has no lady love: he has Hippolita, a military adversary captured and wedded on a foreign campaign (1.866–69). Love, for Theseus, is a thing of retrospect, an abstract, personified power that he once was subjected to but now no longer serves. In deliberating on the fate of Palemon and Arcite in *pars secunda*, he is moved not by love for Hippolita but by the idea of love; or rather, by Love, a lord whose incontestable power mirrors his own:

> "The god of love, a benedicite!
> How myghty and how greet a lord is he!"   (1.1785–86)

Theseus, now a great and mighty lord himself, can no longer (as conqueror and governor) afford to be a fool for love. But he does recognize that he himself once served in Love's retinue:

> "A man moot ben a fool, or yong or oold—
> I woot it by myself ful yore agon,
> For in my tyme a servant was I oon."   (1.1812–14)

Theseus could (although he chooses not to) recall the follies of the time when he was 20—or, as the *Legend of Good Women* insists with dogmatic precision, 23:

> A semely knyght was Theseus to se,
> And yong, but of a twenty yer and thre.   (F 2074–75)

The *Legend*, of course, is written at the command of "the myghty god of Love" (F 226; G 158) by one who is attempting to win back the favor, or at least suspend the wrath, of this lord and his retinue. The sixth *legenda*, concerning "Adriane de Athenes," opens by resolving

> to clepe ageyn unto memorye
> Of Theseus the grete untrouth of love;
> For which the goddes of the heven above
> Ben wrothe, and wreche han take for thy synne.
> Be red for shame! Now I thy lyf begynne.   (F 1889–93)

Chaucer gives the impression that the "lyf" we are about to hear is not that of the "good woman Ariadne," but rather that of the treacherous Theseus (a man who should be the victim, rather than the self-appointed instrument, of god-sanctioned "wreche," or revenge). And indeed, a good deal of this legend is dedicated to the false oaths and hollow protestations of Theseus:

> "And if I profre yow in low manere
> To ben youre page and serven yow ryght here,
> But I yow serve as lowly in that place,
> I preye to Mars to yeve me swich a grace
> That shames deth on me ther mote falle,
> And deth and poverte to my frendes alle;
> And that my spirit by nyghte mote go,
> After my deth, and walke to and fro,
> That I mote of traytour have a name."   (F 2060–68)

Theseus here proposes that any future betrayal of Ariadne on his part be condemned as a political crime ("of *traytour* have a name"); the condemnation sounds loud and long in the *House of Fame*, where more lines are dedicated to Theseus as a betrayer of women than to all other faithless men combined.[15] All of this, of course, is forgotten by the *Knight's Tale* (and by all those critical studies of Theseus as nobility or *trouthe* incarnate). In Chaucer's other ancient and classical epic, however, Criseyde knows that her lavish oaths of loyalty to Troilus will be remembered, rewritten and retranscribed, "unto the worldes ende": "thise bokes wol me shende"; her story will be told "thoroughout the world" (5.1058–62). Theseus harbors no such fears: he conquers the world; he commissions the books and paintings; he has more than one "lyf." He controls, in short, the means and occasions of artistic production and the circulation of texts. Theseus's demeanor in the *Knight's Tale* adheres, for the most part, to the squeaky-clean script of Statius; the memory of the other Theseus, the Ovidian betrayer of women, is not called to mind.[16]

The traitor's name that Theseus wills upon himself in the *Legend of Ariadne* springs not from desperation in love but rather from desperate and immediate fear of being fed to the Minotaur. At this moment, facing death, Theseus (like the youthful and desperate Aurelius)[17] is willing to trade away his "herytage," toss his lineage to the winds, and live as a page or laborer:

> "Forsake I wol at hom myn herytage,
> And, as I seyde, ben of youre court a page . . .
>
>   . . .
>
> And for myn sustenaunce yit wol I swynke."   (F 2036–37, 41)

Such will to work is obviously reminiscent of Arcite's eagerness to "drugge and drawe" (1.1416) at the court of Theseus once he has been released from prison. The middle section of the *Legend of Ariadne* (lines 1960–2122) and the *Knight's Tale* are conjoined by a whole series of intertextual linkages that reflect their dependence on a common source, Boccaccio's *Teseida*.[18] These begin with the motif of imprisonment in a tower, although the *Legend* works a curious variation here by having a single male in a "tour" overlooked by "chaumbers" belonging to "doughtren tweyne" (1960–66). Rather than fighting over Theseus—as the Theban knights, "of sustren two yborn" (1.1019), fight over Emelye—the two sisters cooperate in planning to release him from prison and save him from death. Theseus, ever mindful of being "torn . . . by the Mynotaur" (F 2104), makes egregious (and patently false) professions of devotion to Ariadne. The duration of his putative *love-longynge*, one notes, matches the time that Palemon gazes at Emelye from his prison cell before escaping (1.1452):

> "Upon my trouthe I swere and yow assure,
> This sevene yer I have youre servaunt be.
> Now have I yow, and also have ye me,
> My dere herte, of Athenes duchesse!"   (F 2119–22)

Ariadne smiles at Theseus's "steadfastnesse," but is not tempted into fantasizing about her life as the duchess of Athens. Such a temptation, which would effectively isolate one sister from the other, is successfully resisted by Ariadne's decision to address herself to Phedra rather than to Theseus. They will *both* be duchesses:

> "Now, syster myn," quod she,
> "Now be we duchesses, both I and ye,
> And sekered to the regals of Athenes,
> And bothe hereafter likly to be quenes."   (F 2126–29)

The fantasy of becoming duchess of Athens is here supplanted by the greater fantasy of a sisterly solidarity that continues beyond marriage. Such a fantasy cannot be staged without some elaborate preparation. Phedra, Ariadne tells Theseus, will marry "youre sone" (F 2099). Since Theseus is just twenty-three years old, his son can hardly be more than six. Chaucer, it seems, goes to unlikely lengths to create this image of two duchesses of Athens, a fantasy made all the more poignant by our certain knowledge that Theseus will abandon Ariadne on Aegina and sail off with her sister.

Those wishing to hear more of the abandoned Ariadne's "compleynyng" are explicitly referred, at the end of this *legenda*, to the *Heroides* (F 2220). In the opening line of her epistle, Ovid's Ariadne claims that every race of wild beasts ("genus omne ferarum") has proved itself kinder to her than Theseus.[19] Comparisons to beastlike behavior are commonly employed in the lexicon of tyranny: Boccaccio applies the epithet *bestialità* to Walter (Griselde's husband) and Gower *feritas* to Richard II.[20] Those who wander further afield in the *Heroides* to find out what happens to Phedra ("Naso," Chaucer tells us, "telleth al," 2220) will find that she did indeed fall for Theseus's "sone," and that this "sone" is called Hippolitus.[21] Most medieval authorities followed the tradition that Hippolitus was the son of Theseus and Hippolita;[22] those who knew of no such tradition would surely assume such a mother-son (-a / -us) relationship. Chaucer's textual corpus (and the texts it gestures toward) clearly suggest, then, that the Theseus-Hippolita narrative *precedes* that of Theseus-Ariadne; the "older" Theseus of the *Knight's Tale* is actually younger than the youthful, feckless lover of the *Legend*.

It makes good political sense, of course, for the *Knight's Tale* to distance Theseus from his own erotic history by assigning such history to the distant past. Theseus is a lord and Love is a lord: Theseus could not have attained lordship without renouncing or betraying Love's service; nor could he remain a lord by subjecting himself to him. Love, according to Theseus, is a lord who shows scant respect for his own retainers. "Se how they blede!" he exclaims, pointing to the two young Thebans (while dropping into a bastard feudal register that speaks of livery, fees, and wages):

> "Be they noght wel arrayed?
> Thus hath hir lord, the god of love, ypayed
> Hir wages and hir fees for hir servyse!"   (1.1801–3)

Theseus is now, supposedly, a greater and more equitable lord than Love. This might make good sense to a medieval exegete: Theseus, the argument might run, has put *cupiditas* behind him and is now focused on the common good. But several problems arise here. First, it is not clear what understanding of a transcendent good Theseus, as a pagan ruler, is now guided by.[23] Second, he cannot have left Love's service without betraying his vows to the lovers he once served. Both Theseus and his narrator, the Knight, seek to distance themselves from past personal history by alienating love as a concern proper to a younger generation. This tactic forces the rescripting of history through a scrambling of chronology, a process that Chaucer, in reworking the *Teseida*, clearly expects us to spot. Even as Theseus rides out to avenge the women of Thebes against Creon, he displays the sign of his youth and his past (or future) infidelity in his golden *penoun*,

> in which ther was ybete
> The Mynotaur, which that he wan in Crete.
> Thus rit this duc, thus rit this conquerour.   (1.979–81)

The sign of the Minotaur, which Chaucer did not find in the *Teseida*, cannot help but "drawen to memorie" the story of Ariadne and thus implicate Theseus in the narratives of youthful love that he presumes to stand above and adjudicate upon. This invitation to read the Emelye, Palemon, and Arcite narrative against that of Theseus, Ariadne, and Phedra is reinforced elsewhere within the Chaucerian corpus by the *Legend of Ariadne*. Indeed, it might be argued that the *Knight's Tale* stands in relation to this particular *legenda* as the *Troilus* stands to the *Legend* as a whole: the *Legend* narratives work to dispute the viewpoint of official masculinist history. By diverting our attention to this earlier (or later) phase of Thesian history, we realize that the role of Duchess of Athens is perennially problematic and destructive for women, an ongoing defeat for "Femenye" that divides one sister from another. For just as he succeeds in defeating Ariadne's fantasy of creating two sister duchesses within the Athenian state, so Theseus succeeds in dividing Hippolita from her sister Emelye and subjugating them to his own statecraft. Emelye becomes the prize that both provokes and contains a long and bloody magnate rivalry; Hippolita, conquered, wedded, and "broghte . . . hoom" in the space of four lines (1.866–89), is veiled in silence.

The Silence of Hippolita

Some of the contradictions and shortcomings of Thesian polity that remain latent through this silencing of Hippolita are flushed into the open by *A Midsummer Night's Dream*. Shakespeare begins by acknowledging what the *Knight's Tale* elides: that there can be no smooth transition from war to wedding, from violent subjugation to assent to love:

> Hippolyta, I woo'd thee with my sword,
> And won thy love, doing thee injuries;
> But I will wed thee in another key,
> With pomp, with triumph, and with revelling.   (I.i.16–19)

Shakespeare allows Hippolita just one short, inconsequential speech in this opening act (and she is not heard from again until Act IV). But he does allow her one eloquent look that speaks to the frustration and humiliation of her plight in being forced to surrender her own political power and follow a foreign conqueror into exile. Just twenty lines into this opening scene, Theseus's plotting of his new campaign of nuptials is interrupted by the arrival of an irate father, plus a daughter and two rival masculine lovers (another *Knight's Tale* triangle). The father, Egeus, complains that Lysander has "bewitched" his daughter Hermia through the powers of poetry and song:

> Thou, thou, Lysander, thou hast given her rhymes,
> And interchang'd love-tokens with my child;
> Thou hast by moonlight at her window sung
> With feigning voice verses of feigning love,
> And stol'n the impression of her fantasy.   (I.i.28–32)

Such persuasions to love are just what Theseus has in mind for Hippolita, of course, as he sets out to woo her "in another key." The irony is lost on Theseus as he squeezes the wayward daughter, Hermia, with the most brutal of patriarchal metaphors:

> To you your father should be as a god;
> One that compos'd your beauties; yea, and one
> To whom you are but a form in wax,
> By him imprinted, and within his power
> To leave the figure, or disfigure it.   (I.i.47–51)

When Hermia inquires after her options should she refuse to follow her father's wishes, she is offered death, physical or civil: judicial execution, or "the livery of a nun," in which

> To live a barren sister all your life,
> Chaunting faint hymns to the cold fruitless moon.   (I.i.72–73)

Following Hermia's refusal "to give sovereignty" to "the unwished yoke" of a "lordship" that is not of her own choosing, Theseus addresses her one more time before sweeping from the stage with his retinue:

> For you fair Hermia, *look you arm yourself*
> To fit your fancies to your father's will;
> Or else the law of Athens yields you up
> (Which by no means we may extenuate)
> To death, or to a vow of single life.
> Come, my Hippolyta. What cheer, my love?
> Demetrius and Egeus, go along;
> I must employ you in some business
> Against our nuptial . . .   (I.i.117–24; emphasis mine)

The military metaphor with which Theseus addresses Hermia intrudes itself strangely here into his speaking: the daughter should "arm" herself for a battle that can only end with her defeat at the hands of her father. For Theseus, the Hermia-Egeus conflict is clearly analogous to the battle he has just won (and now seeks to celebrate) against the Amazon queen. The parallel is evidently not lost on Hippolita. As Theseus repeats his threat of death or inclaustration and then returns to organizing his nuptials, she gives him a midline look that provokes the question "What cheer, my love?" Hippolita's look can be as eloquent as an actor, actress, or director cares to make it. It can speak to the local and immediate business of "our nuptial" (the royal plural leaves it in doubt whether "our" includes "her nuptial"); it can speak against the whole system of ducal and patriarchal authority within which Hippolita finds herself entrapped. It offers us, at the very least, the opportunity to register the resistant personhood of Hippolita on the space of the stage. The *Knight's Tale* envisions no equivalent moment. By allowing his Hippolita no resistance to, or even apparent cognizance of, her own defeat and abduction, *raptus*, marriage, or enslavement, Chaucer accentuates both the political power and the personal isolation of his all-conquering duke. Such isolation is not normative either in Chaucerian narrative or in fourteenth-century English history: monarchs or household heads as diverse as Edward III, Richard II, Melibee, and King Arthur all employ the reasoned interventions of eloquent wives to save themselves from the rigidities of their own behavior.[24] The *Knight's Tale* does contain one such moment, although it can hardly be termed a *reasoned* intervention since it consists of tears after the declaration of a death sentence. Hippolita, one notes, here loses her name; her particular expression of grief is soon submerged within a collective, womanly weeping:

> "Ye shal be deed, by myghty Mars the rede!"
>   The queene anon, for verray wommanhede,
>   Gan for to wepe, and so dide Emelye,
>   and alle the ladyes in the compaignye.   (1.1748–51)

The female courtiers, recognizing that the court has suddenly shifted from *Hof* to *Gericht*, from play-space to law-space, collectively imagine themselves on the block with the two young knights:[25] "Have mercy, Lord, upon us women alle!" (1.1757). The women are represented as petitioners to Theseus in a way that images political subjection through physical abjection: they fall onto "hir bare knees"; they attempt to kiss his feet (1.1758–59). His reaction to them is, in turn, highly physical (as hard anger turns to trembling and shaking, 1.1762). His next move, however, turns inwards rather than outwards: he thinks things out "in his resoun" in an unvoiced monologue (1.1767–73) that modulates into a speech heard only by himself ("And softe unto hymself he seyde . . . ," 1.1773). Theseus, it seems, is moved by the bodily proximity of women, but not by their powers of language. He saves himself from stepping into tyranny, but he does not pass the privilege of decision-making to the queen (as does the Wife of Bath's King Arthur, 3.897). And he defeats the impulse to act out of "ire" (1762, 1765, 1782) not by seeking queenly or wifely counsel but by listening to his own sovereign reason. This, in Chaucerian terms, makes him something of an oddity—a hermaphrodite Melibee, embodying his own Prudence.

The assimilation of Hippolita into generic "wommanhede" is forced by political considerations. Theseus cannot rely on a former military enemy at moments of emotional disequilibrium (particularly an enemy who may bear a memorial sign of militarism upon her own body: the very word "Amazon," according to the *Teseida*, means "without breast").[26] Hippolita's lack, real or imagined, is disguised through her absorption into conventional, two-breasted "wommanhede." The net effect of this is further to accentuate the isolation and self-sufficiency of Theseus: here is a monarch who assumes personal control of all aspects of statecraft, including theology, philosophy, architecture, and artistic production. The apex of this development is reached just before the tournament, which follows rules devised by Theseus within a "noble theatre" designed, built, and decorated under his immediate supervision:

> Duc Theseus was at a wyndow set,
> Arrayed right as he were a god in trone.   (1.2528–29)

This momentary suggestion of absolute power, however, is also one of maximal vulnerability. "Arrayed right thus as [*if*] he were . . ." recalls Theseus's own, sarcastic "Be they nat wel arrayed?" (1801); Theseus's dressing up in god's clothes may prove as ludicrous (when viewed from a higher vantage point) as the young Thebans' dressing up in one another's blood.[27] And when the "real" gods above do indeed frustrate his plans, Theseus has nothing and nobody to blame or fall back on except his own masculine lineage, namely, his father, Egeus.[28] The eloquence and comfort that Egeus has to offer (1.2843–49) prove barren and feeble indeed when compared to the *copia verborum* of Chaucer's great wifely counselors.

Rather than assuming total responsibility for all aspects of statecraft, Theseus might have delegated some of that authority to professional apologists, especially those gifted with the rhetorical powers of poetry. It was from poets, after all (Boccaccio writes in his *Trattatello in laude di Dante*) that the earliest rulers learned how to hold their subjects in awe. Physical subjugation (enslavement) and a rhetoric of public display (*ornamenti*) were what brought the earliest men to power:

And they called themselves "kings," and appeared before the people with both slaves and ornaments, things unheard of among men before this time. And they commanded obedience and, ultimately, adoration. And provided that there was someone willing to make the attempt, all this was achieved without too much trouble: for to the commoners who observed them, such people seemed to be not men, but gods. Such people, unwilling to trust in their own innate powers, began to stoke up religious sentiment and to use the resultant faith to frighten their subjects, and to secure by oaths the obedience of those that they would not have been able to constrain by force. And in addition to this they took pains to deify their fathers, their grandfathers, and their ancestors so that they might be the more feared and revered by the populace. These things they could not accomplish without the collaboration of poets, who in order to amplify their own fame, to please the princes, to delight the princes' subjects, and to urge virtuous behavior on everyone . . . employed various and masterly fictions . . . thereby causing to be believed that which the princes wished to be believed.[29]

From the very beginning of *pars tercia*, it is evident that Theseus has recognized the powers of poets and their *ornamenti* by absorbing their functions into his all-encompassing polity of one-man rule. Chaucer takes pains to emphasize, three times, that every aspect of the construction and ornamentation of the "noble theatre" is conducted under the Duke's direct supervision. Theseus, having recently characterized love as a matter of wages and fees (1.1803), now conceives of artistic collaboration as a matter of "mete and wages" (1.1900), costing "largely of gold a fother" (1.1908), "many a floryn" (1.2088), done "at his grete coste" (1.2090). Artistic production under such a form of direct, all-seeing patronage is made to feel as claustrophobic as the space it is allotted to work in: the temples allow small room for artistic free play, since they are conceived of as encapsulating forms of foreknowledge handed down by a ruler "as god in trone." Similarly, Theseus's lengthy and definitive "First Moevere" monologue offers no space or opportunity, no *quando*, for dialogic engagement. Theseus the architect is evidently employing an architectural mnemonic (of the kind described by Mary Carruthers) [30] as he punctiliously eyeballs the preassigned *loci* of his monologic discourse:

> Whan they were set, and hust was al the place,
> And Theseus abiden hadde a space
> Er any word cam fram his wise brest,
> And with a sad visage he siked stille,
> *His eyen sette he ther as was his lest.*
> *And after that* right thus he seyde his wille.
>   "The Firste Moevere . . ."   (1.2981–87; emphasis mine)

Women cannot originate such discourse. They must wait at the margins of masculine-generated public speaking and then know just when (*quando*, in the terms of rhetorical treatises) to time the moment of intervention.[31] But when Theseus launches on his monologue he has all the time in the world: he cannot and will not be interrupted. No circumstance for female intervention is envisaged here, and so Hippolita remains silent even as Theseus proceeds to break the relationship between herself and her sister. There is no talk here of "duchesses, both I and ye"): the Amazon Emelye will marry the Theban Palemon.

The silence of Hippolita suggests that in the shadow of such a Thesian monologue, scripts for female speaking are rendered redundant: bad news for the poet of Prudence, Alceste, Griselde, May, Dorigen, and Alisoun of Bath. Chaucer's discomfiture here extends beyond artistic frustration to issues of personal safety. To work with any degree of independence, to follow *fantasye*, the poet needs an advocate who can both identify with and speak for him when he falls foul of the wrath of a masculine patron: duke, king, or god of Love.[32] But if Thesian polity imagines itself speaking a language of seamless sovereign reason, it will recognize no need for the protection, mediation, or counsel that an eloquent wife might offer a fallible *makere*. This supposition, advanced by the conclusion of Chaucer's first poetic fiction, will be rejected by his last. The *Manciple's Tale*, as egregiously short as the *Knight's Tale* is long, features another ancient and classical lord who is not merely godlike but a god; he too maintains a silent spouse. This Apollo, surprised by his own passions, will kill his own wife. His household will disintegrate and his caged songbird, clearly a figure of the courtly poet, will lose its livery and be flung out of doors.[33]

The *Manciple's Tale* and the *Knight's Tale*, which bookend Chaucer's Canterbury fiction, offer very different accounts of a husband of classical pedigree conducting himself "as he were a god in trone." The *Knight's Tale* is challenged not just by this distant and mirroring fiction, however, but by its own internal secrets. Within this narrative, and in narratives that surround it, are plentiful hints of a past or alternative Theseus: "acts of bestiality and incest, of parricide, uxoricide, filicide, and suicide; sexual fears and urges erupting in cycles of violent desire—from Pasiphae and the Minotaur to Phaedra and Hippolitus."[34] The silencing of Hippolita both conceals this other Theseus and, from the moment we become conscious of it, pushes him to the forefront of our attention. Given Chaucer's lifelong dedication to female eloquence, Hippolita's speechlessness seems strange and anomalous. The first and most celebrated *overt* rebellion of the *Canterbury Tales*, that of the Miller, has long been recognized as an artisanal rewriting of the Knight's magnate world. But the second, that of the Wife of Bath, effects a more radical repudiation of the *Knight's Tale* script. Whereas the Miller replicates the basic narrative structure of the Knight—two young men compete for one young woman—the Wife strikes out not for replication or translation, nor even "wreke" (revenge), but "redresse" (3.696). Through his silencing of Hippolita and hence of wifely conversation and counsel, the Knight has attempted to nourish the pilgrim body with unwholesome fare. The Wife, therefore, will talk this body back to health. Beginning by speaking of herself, she will end with a knight's tale of her own devising. The only knightly *aventure* allowed in this story will be a year-long quest, initiated by a queen, in search of female, and particularly wifely, eloquence.

Chaucer as Bottom the Weaver

Shakespeare, we have noted, focuses attention on the Hippolita problem (the difficulty of integrating a warrior from Femenye into the body politic through marriage) whereas the *Knight's Tale* hurries past it.[35] Louis Adrian Montrose has offered an excellent account of how Shakespeare's Theseus secures personal control of his state by systematically turning the screws of patriarchal authority, a process culminating in the triple marriage of Act V.[36] Montrose devotes less space, however, to class analysis: to how the magnates consolidate themselves (in the fifth act) by grouping themselves against urban artisans, "hard-handed men" (Philostrate explains to the Duke),

> that work in Athens here,
> Which never labor'd in their minds till now. (V.i.72–73)

The poetic language spoken by these manual laborers may be traced directly back, as Donaldson has shown, to Chaucer's *Tale of Sir Thopas*.[37] Such poetic archaism comes coupled with, is expressive of, a social archaism: for these Athenian artisans are guildsmen without a guild. They have a good deal in common with the guildsmen of Chaucer's *General Prologue* (the "solemn and greet fraternitee," consisting of a hatmaker, a carpenter, a dyer, an all-purpose weaver, and a weaver of carpets, 1.361–64).[38] Each of Shakespeare's group of six is named to identify him with his profession: Bottom the weaver is named after the skein on which yarn is wound; Quince the carpenter after quines, blocks of wood used for building; Flute the bellows-mender after fluted bellows. "Snout" (the tinker) suggests the spout of a kettle; Starveling is as thin as tailors are traditionally reputed to be, and Snug the joiner joins with a snug fit.[39] But this group wears no livery, nor does it constitute itself as a self-sufficient "company" (the first word used to designate the group, I.ii.1). This group exists only with reference to, at the sufferance of, the duke: it hopes for royal preferment, should the duke be pleased (Bottom, as chief actor, might hope for "sixpence a day during his life," IV.ii.20); it fears death, should it arouse his displeasure ("That would hang us, every mother's son," I.ii.78). Its chief political function is to allow the magnate group to constellate itself around Theseus by practicing the humanist art of literary criticism. The artisans are chosen as the objects of criticism *because of* the defects ("not one word apt, one player fitted," V.i.65) of their poetic performance, as Theseus makes clear ("Our sport shall be to take what they mistake," V.i.90).

Demetrius and Lysander, the two young male lovers, ingratiate themselves with Theseus by engaging him in quick-fire commentary on the artisan text. Hermia and Helena, the young female lovers, remain silent and have no part in this "sport." Hippolita at first flatly rejects the play ("This is the silliest stuff that ever I heard," V.i.210) but then, following a defense by Theseus of his ingenuous subjects (215–16), finds herself strangely affected by it: "Beshrew my heart," she says, contemplating Bottom-Pyramus, "but I pity the man" (290). The lines that move her pity are strongly reminiscent of the tail-rhyme of *Sir Thopas* (277–88). The last such speech, spoken by Thisbe over the body of Pyramus, recalls *Sir Thopas* not only in its rhyming but also by mixing masculine and feminine canons of physical description:[40]

> These lily lips,
> This cherry nose,
> These yellow cowslip cheeks,
> Are gone, are gone.
> Lovers, make moan.

His eyes were green as leeks.
   O Sisters Three,
   Come, come to me,
With hands as pale as milk;
   Lay them in gore,
   Since you have shore
With shears his thread of silk.   (V.i.332–43)

Shakespeare, the author of these lines, avoids identification as the poet of Bottom-Pyramus by a suggestive transfer of paternity (through his evocation of *Sir Thopas*) to Chaucer. This is a shrewd maneuver, since Chaucer, laboring at the infancy of the English poetic tradition, had volunteered for such a role as the author of tag-heavy tail-rhyme. Chaucer can be seen as the poet who writes for Bottom; more precisely, he can be seen *as* Bottom, the poet who wears the ass's head as he steps forward to speak his self-made doggerel and then acclaim it as "the beste rym I kan" (7.928). *Sir Thopas*, after all, is set in the countryside not of England or of ancient Greece, but of Flanders, a name synonymous with the craft of weaving, Bottom's profession.[41] The infantilization ascribed to Shakespeare's artisans ("every mother's son," I.ii.78; III.i.73) is innocently assumed by Chaucer in *Sir Thopas*.[42] And Chaucer, like Bottom, is a sixth of six: the one member whose particular talent, among a company from the lower reaches of society, is supposedly that of artistic representation itself. The singularity of Bottom's talent is dramatically underscored by the five Athenian artisans, about to perform "Pyramus" before the Duke, as they anxiously await the arrival of their sixth and most vital member:

Flute: If he come not, then the play is marr'd. It goes not forward, doth it?
Quince: It is not possible. You have not a man in all Athens able to discharge
    Pyramus but he.
Flute: No, he hath simply the best wit of any handicraft man in Athens.

                                (IV.ii.5–10)

The play that follows is Chaucerian not just in form but in content: the Pyramus and Thisbe story was evidently one of Chaucer's favorites. Shakespeare certainly knew the full-length *legenda* of "Tesbe Babilonie, martiris" from the *Legend of Good Women*. The possibilities of a compressed, doggerel-intensive version of this tragedy, however, were more likely glimpsed through his reading of the *Merchant's Tale* (which supplied Shakespeare with his prototypical king and queen of the fairies in Proserpine and Pluto, who "disporten hem and maken melodye," accompanied by "al hire fayerye," in January's garden, 4.2038–40). It is shortly after this that Chaucer's Merchant launches into his apostrophe to "noble Ovid" and his four-line version of Pyramus and Thisbe "rownynge thurgh a wal."[43] For Bottom's apostrophe to "wikkede wal," for the wall's constituent "lym" and "ston," and for the wording "with blody mouth" in the description of the lion, Shakespeare turned to the *Legend of Good Women*.[44] And the whole episode of a fairy queen's love-longing for

Bottom is, of course, the fulfillment of a dream once dreamed by Chaucer's Sir Thopas:

> Me dremed al this nyght, pardee,
> An elf-queene shal my lemman be. (7.787–88)

In refashioning Chaucer's *Knight's Tale*, then, Shakespeare undermines the medieval poet's pretensions to neoclassical seriousness by associating him with the neoclassical foolishness of Bottomian "Pyramus." He pins him to a tale—*Sir Thopas*—that Wyatt, half a century earlier, had recognized as the very antithesis of the Knight's "noble" story.[45] And he further associates Chaucer not just with archaic and déclassé forms of diction and poetic form, but also—through the labors of a weaver, a carpenter, a bellows-mender, a tinker, a tailor, and a joiner—with an archaic and socially degraded drama: that of the medieval guilds. At Coventry, just twenty miles from Stratford-upon-Avon, the weavers played a prominent part in the production of guild paegants. They also proved willing to allow men from other crafts to join their brotherhood (for acting and other purposes); these included a baker, a barber, a butcher, a draper, a hostler, a painter, a shoemaker, a tanner, a whittawer (dresser of whit-leather, John Shakespeare's craft), and the prior of Coventry.[46] According to the 1583 edition of Foxe's *Acts and Monuments*, the weaver John Careles, jailed at Coventry, "was let out to play in the Pageant about the City with other his companions"; having played his part, he returned voluntarily to prison, died, and (in 1556) "was buryed in the fieldes in a dounghill."[47] As late as 1579, before the earthquake of April 1580 furnished an excuse for the suppression of the Coventry pageants,[48] the Account Book of the Coventry Weavers records payments "to symeon," "to Iosephe," "to mary," and to various other biblical characters; incidental expenses include claims for singing, for gloves, for "bred and ale," and for nails, two beards, and a cape.[49] Other highlights of the weaver's guild year included the annual dinner (which prompted accusations of excessive drinking) and the boisterous, open-air celebrations of "Mydsomer even."[50]

In 1539, the pageant-playing and Midsummer Night's celebrations proved so rowdy as to attract the attention of Thomas Cromwell; the mayor of Coventry, "your assured bedeman," was moved to write Cromwell an anxious and defensive letter.[51] Such unruliness doubtless stirred memories of the conspiracy hatched by guild members in December 1523, which planned to assassinate the mayor and aldermen and then to raise men to take Kenilworth castle and hold it against the king. The chief source of resentment here was the crippling taxation laid on the city, and specifically on the Trinity and Corpus Christi guilds, by a royal authority anxious to pursue a foreign war.[52] In 1377 Coventry had been the third-largest provincial city in England and, according to Charles Phythian-Adams, "the nodal point of the provincial urban network."[53] The preeminence of late medieval Coventry was founded almost exclusively upon its status as a major textile-manufacturing center;

its products were exported as far afield as Portugal, the Baltic, and Iceland. Gradually weakened by competition from other cloth-producing regions, however, Coventry went into irremediable decline; the Henrician taxation of 1523 represented a final crippling blow.[54] By 1550, "the glittering prosperity of the city had not merely dulled; it had vanished."[55] The fellowship strength of the weavers, whose prosperity was directly tied to the health of the textile industry, dwindled (with a declining ratio of masters to journeymen); their dramatic activity became less ambitious.[56]

By choosing a weaver as the guiding spirit of a pseudomedieval, neo-Chaucerian guildsmen's drama, then, Shakespeare weds Chaucerian poetics to a craft culture that, despite recollections of ancient vigor, is currently in terminal decline. The degraded, archaic, and downwardly mobile craft of weaving is at one with the Flemish poetics of *Sir Thopas*.

Having contemplated Shakespeare's stitching up of Chaucer, it is fitting that we should reverse the lines of critique by offering a Chaucerian view of *A Midsummer Night's Dream*. Seen from the perspective of the *Canterbury Tales*, Shakespeare's play seems politically pusillanimous, an opportunistic floating with the tide of history. Writing on the occasion of an aristocratic wedding, one attended or fit to be attended by a queen,[57] Shakespeare stages a short artisanal drama that is viewed and ridiculed (and thus contained) by a circle of aristocrats wielding the linguistic weapons of humanist critique. Forgetting his own lineage as the son of an aletaster, unlicensed dunghill-builder, apprentice glovemaker, whittawer, wool-dealer, moneylender, burgess, petty constable (and later chamberlain, bailiff, and alderman),[58] Shakespeare slips from the company of artisans—leaving Chaucer and Bottom in his place—to view proceedings from the external perspective of a courtly circle.[59] (John Shakespeare, the poet's father, was in fact no more literate than Bottom: he witnessed corporation documents by making his mark, usually "a gracefully drawn pair of compasses, the instrument used for measuring and making ornamental cuttings in the backs of gloves.")[60] What might his play have looked like had Bottom, "the best wit of any handicraft man in Athens," IV.ii.9–10), performed it *after* Theseus and company had left the stage? Bottom's play, unlike the two performances that Theseus rejects, is no *Mousetrap* (*Hamlet* III.ii.237). It is difficult to read any aspect of Theseus's long and bloody career as lover, soldier, adventurer, and politician into Bottom's *Pyramus and Thisbe*.[61] But in the *absence* of Theseus and company, and without the critical commentary that continually interrogates and interrupts their performance, the artisans might have succeeded in suggesting (to an appropriate audience) a parody of magnate behavior. After all, Bottom, on first hearing of the play-to-be, had asked a question of Pyramus that had often been asked of Theseus (thereby recapitulating Palemon's twinning of "love" and "regne" as jealous lords, 1.1623–26): "What is Pyramus? A lover, or a tyrant?" (I.ii.22).

Shakespeare cannot allow Theseus to be measured against such a stereotypical understanding of magnate character. The magnates must be seen to define and integrate themselves by reconfirming the stereotypical traits of "hard-handed men." Chaucer, however, does give his urban and rural artisans the final word in Fragment 1. And in Fragment 3, he atones for the silence of Hippolita through the self-originating eloquence of the greatest weaver of them all: Alisoun of Bath, whose homegrown craft exceeds that of any foreign, specifically Flemish, pretender.[62] Such rebellions may not shake the social framework to its foundations, but they offer more than can be dreamed of in the postguild culture of Elizabethan England.

This inverse historiographical triumphalism might be tempered, however, by acknowledging that Shakespeare does, in the final act of his *Dream*, show an intuitive, even restorative, understanding of Chaucerian poetics. Act V opens with Theseus declaring his nonbelief in "antique fables" and "fairy toys"; he then reflects on the ways of lunatics, lovers,[63] and poets. His formal dividing of labor (between lunatic, lover, and poet) and his recourse to mundane explanation yield an analysis in the light of "cool reason" every bit as mechanical, as meat and wages, as that of Chaucer's Theseus: "How easy is a bush suppos'd a bear!" (V.i.22). It takes Hippolita, rescued from the silence to which Chaucer has exiled her, to intuit kinds of experience (such as that of the lovers on Midsummer Night) that amount to more than the physical elements from which they are constructed:

> "But all the story of the night told over,
> And all their minds transfigur'd so together,
> More witnesseth than fancy's images,
> And grows to something of great constancy;
> But howsoever, strange and admirable."   (V.i.23–27)

Hippolita speaks here, of course, not just to the story of the lovers, but to the greater project of the poet whose "images" they are. Through this late discovery of an intuitive, mutually sustaining bond of understanding between poet and queen, Shakespeare restores a vital aspect of Chaucerian polity to his post-Chaucerian drama; one that Chaucer elected to do without in exploring the possibilities and dangers of one-man (no-woman) Thesian rule. Shakespeare does not permit the artisans to walk the stage once Theseus and his court have left.[64] He does, however, allow one last visit from the singing and dancing King and Queen of the Fairies, representing a realm of the "strange and admirable" that the Wife of Bath once dreamed of (just before beginning her own knight's tale),[65] that Hippolita intuits, and that Theseus cannot comprehend.

Chapter 5

Powers of the Countryside

Under the lonely, hierocratic *regne* of Theseus, *felaweshipe* is exemplified chiefly through its undoing (between Palemon and Arcite), denial (between Theseus and anyone else), or absence (between Hippolita and her Amazon sisters). Although Chaucer may be meditating both on his own prior history of court-centered poetics and on the possibilities for one-man rule close to home (for which a distant paganism provides a convenient cover), his *Knight's Tale* leaves us far removed in time, space, and political orientation from the Tabard at Southwark. The Miller's intervention returns us closer to our point of origin: here, finally, we come to see how the dynamics of associational form, so punctiliously exemplified through the *felaweshipe* formation of the *General Prologue*, might play out as part of contemporary English urban life in Oxford, Cambridge, or London.

The need to generate some sense of common cause among city-dwellers in postpandemic England was (historians are agreed) particularly acute: high urban mortality rates invited successive waves of immigration from outlying districts; ecclesiastical establishments continued to jostle with artisan and mercantile businesses; the continuing dominance of the putting-out system of commercial production made for noisy and dirty neighbors, prone to fight with one another for scarce natural resources (such as water). The best hope for the development of such an associational ideology lay with the guilds.[1] Everyone, from the humblest parish guild member to the grandest oligarch, understood and felt invested in forms of cultural performance, vocabulary, and unifying mechanisms that were nurtured in the guilds. A successful associational ideology, such as that repeatedly exemplified in Boccaccio's *Decameron*, can persuade all the inhabitants of a given city that they have common cause with one another; better, it can begin to suggest that the city itself is possessed of mysterious powers of self-regulation and self-determination; that it can take on a life of its own and then hold its own against any intruder.

From the first, however, we cannot help but notice that Chaucer's representations of urban life involve openings to, consciousness of, the countryside.

Professional obligations draw John the carpenter out of Oxford; Soler Halle, in the *Reeve's Tale*, must dispatch two of its students to the countryside to seek out services not available in Cambridge. The dynamic and historically progressive character of medieval English rural society—home to some 95 percent of the population—has been asserted with increasing conviction by Weberian and Marxian critics in recent years.[2] Randall Collins, developing a Weberian line of inquiry, sees the institutional preconditions for capitalism largely fulfilled by the great monastic houses, whose monks "created the first dynamic, world-transforming capitalism, albeit in religious form."[3] Robert Brenner and his Marxian interlocutors have focused attention away from city-generated trade and onto a landowning class that concentrated its efforts on extracting surplus from the agrarian sector. The countryside powers the medieval economy; towns and cities function primarily as markets for goods generated outside their walls.[4]

This chapter investigates the ways in which the extraordinary imaginative energies invested in Chaucer's rural landscapes speak to the historical powers of the medieval English countryside. It is difficult for us to grasp or even to think to look for signs of power or intelligence in rural settings: we are all heirs to long traditions of political prejudice in which city-centered standards of *civilitas* are defined against the countryside. More insidiously, the brutishness of country life is asserted even as urbanites deliberately set about the business of subjecting country dwellers to brutal and degrading treatment. In Boccaccio's *Decameron* such degradation of the countryside by urbanites becomes thoroughly predictable; it is part of the glue that holds together the ideological claims of the Florentine city-state. The assault on the countryside is well under way in Chaucer, too: a whole sequence of city-dwellers make their way into rural landscapes in Fragments 1 and 3, intent on sexual *disparagement*, or on using various associational ideologies as stalking horses for exploitation of the rural population. But the countryside, as Chaucer tells it, bites back: it leaves its mark on the body of overweening city-dwellers; it finds forms of resistance in neo-Dantean metaphysics or in its own social mechanisms.

One problem to be acknowledged at the outset is that of terminology: the term *countryside* does not enter general English usage until the nineteenth century. Chaucer's use of the term *contree* has something of the flexibility that has always been found in the Italian term *paese*, a word that can be applied to a single village, a region, or a nation.[5] For the most part, though, *contree* contains political resonances in Chaucer; these tend to make themselves felt even when it seems, at first glance, that *contree* is a state of nature and not part of *regne*, a political state. In the *Legend of Dido*, for example, Aeneas comes across a single woman in a "wildernesse" and attempts to compliment her by assuming her to be Diana. He is rebuffed and given a quick lesson in local tradition and political geography:

"I n'am no goddesse, sothly," quod she tho;
"For maydens walken in this contre here,
  With arwes and with bowe, in this manere.
  This is the reyne of Libie ther ye ben,
  Of which that Dido lady is and queen."   (F 989–93)

Citee, *toun*, and *village* also prove to be tricky terms in Chaucer. In the *Knight's Tale*, *citee* is deployed thirteen times; it is applied twice to London in the *Cook's Tale*, but is not applied at all to Oxford or Cambridge by Miller or Reeve. *Toun* proves to be a useful swing term; Chaucer sometimes applies it to cities, sometimes to villages, and sometimes to what we would call towns. *Village* is employed more sparingly, and with greater precision: *toun* does well enough in the *Summoner's Tale* until the friar leaves Thomas's house in a rage to seek out the "lord of that village" (3.2165). Friar John complains to the lord of the "despit" he has just suffered "in youre village" (3.2177); he evidently employs the term in studied fashion to remind the lord of his political responsibilities as governor of the *vill*. The term *village*, which according to C. C. Dyer "was scarcely used in the Middle Ages,"[6] appears eleven times in Chaucer (and always with a distinctive political resonance): it is employed once by the Shipman, twice by the Summoner, and four times each by the Clerk and the Pardoner.

It would be unproductive, then, to try and establish rigid lines of demarcation between city and countryside in Chaucer (or between cities, towns, and villages).[7] Paul A. Olson has recently argued that Chaucer's *General Prologue* "moves from court to city to country in concentric circles."[8] This leaves him with some awkward explaining to do: What is the Franklin doing with the city crowd, or the Manciple with the country dwellers?[9] But while it remains a boundary line that is difficult to fix, the city-country divide remains a useful distinction in analyzing Chaucer. It is worth noting that the term *country* is itself founded upon, includes within itself, the recognition of difference: it derives from the medieval Latin feminine adjective *contrata*, as in the term *contrata terra*, land "lying opposite, over against or facing." *Country*, in its earliest separate meaning, denoted a tract of land laid out before an observer: "that which lies opposite or fronting the view, the landscape spread out before one."[10] This sense that the countryside, a landscape often found to contain women, is something to be constituted by the gaze of a (masculine) outsider is already operative in Chaucer (well exemplified, as we have just seen, by the *Legend of Dido*, in which Aeneas sets out "the cuntre for t'espie," F 966).

This chapter begins in the city or *toun* and then follows the gravitational pull of Fragments 1 and 3 as they move ever deeper into the countryside. The motif of urban betrayal introduced by the *Miller's Tale* will be explored both in this chapter (as it is carried to the countryside) and the next (as it pertains to London).

"But Stonde He Moste Unto His Owene Harme"

Readers have always been impressed by the detailed concreteness with which the urban, workaday milieu of the *Miller's Tale* realizes itself: Alisoun's shining forehead, washed clean after work (1.3311); an oath to a local saint ("Seinte Frydeswyde," 1.3451); the friars who sing lauds "in the chauncel" (1.3656). Such details add texture to the *Tale*, but they are not instrumental to its outcome. What makes this narrative work? The master tactician is Nicholas: he may be cast as a young lover, fighting for a lady, but he clearly aspires to the role of a Theseus. Nicholas is plainly attracted to Alisoun (he dedicates four lines to courting her), but he is entirely seduced by the idea of deceiving John the carpenter. Like Theseus, he goes to the most elaborate extremes to determine an outcome, situating his practical efforts within an entire imaginative world that takes in typology, cosmology, and an extraordinarily compelling vision of life afloat in barrels after the second coming of Noah's flood. His ability to conjure moving pictures out of nothing is rivaled only by the Pardoner and the friar in the *Summoner's Tale*. And yet (like Theseus again) he discovers the outcome of such elaborate staging to be quite unexpected. The final reckoning of the *Miller's Tale* is determined by successive acts of interpretation, or misinterpretation: the first by the carpenter and the second by Nicholas, Alisoun, and their neighbors.

The first misinterpretation is innocent; it comes when Nicholas, "scalded in the towte," lets out a great cry of "Water!" that convinces the old carpenter that Noah's flood has indeed returned. The second is deliberate, or malicious (at least where Nicholas and Alisoun are concerned); it is generated from within the circle of neighbors that forms around John the carpenter once he has hit the ground, knocked himself silly, and broken his arm. Lee Patterson has focused attention on the carpenter's humiliation by adopting a half-line from this final scene as the title for an article: "no man his reson herde" (1.3844).[11] While agreeing on the importance of this climactic scene, I would choose a different line to encapsulate the social process that it unfolds: "But stonde he moste unto his owene harm" (3830). This line has been somewhat timidly glossed by the *Riverside Chaucer* as "But he had to stand up, though it turned out badly for him" (p. 76). Kolve and Olson, in their edition of nine *Tales*, do better by abandoning such halting literalism in favor of unambiguous interpretation: "But he must accept responsibility for his own misfortune."[12] The judiciousness of the Kolve-Olson gloss is borne out both by the immediate context of the line and by reference to contemporary social history. First, the context:

> The neighebores, bothe smale and grete,
> In ronnen for to gauren on this man,
> That yet aswowne lay, bothe pale and wan,

For with the fal he brosten hadde his arm.
But stonde he moste unto his ownene harm;
For whan he spak, he was anon bore doun
With hende Nicholas and Alisoun.   (1.3826–32)

The neighbors here are not to be dismissed as idle bystanders: they take an active interest in establishing the details of the carpenter's misfortune; their findings will have an important bearing on his future. They would not have been surprised to hear of a carpenter breaking his arm; carpenters were expected to fall off houses:

Also is ordeined þat uche brother & soster of þis fraternite schal paie to þe helpyng & susteynyng of seke men which þat falle in dissese as by falling doun of an hous or hurtyng of an ey or oþer diuerse sekenesses twelfe penyes by þeȝer.[13]

This *gilda* "of þe brotherede of Carpenteres of London," as represented by its return of 1389, is just one of many guilds that were willing to compensate members unable to work due to loss of eyes, feet, or broken limbs.[14] The Guild of Corpus Christi, Northampton, was willing to pay a brother fallen in need £5 or more; but should it be determined that the brother's troubles came as the result of his own rashness or negligence, the guild would pay nothing.[15] The London carpenters were keen to emphasize that "onliche men & women of gode fame & of gode name" could join them; those who proved to be "of euel fame oþer of euel name" would be "put out of þe fraternite."[16] The rhyming of "brosten hadde his arm" / "unto his owene harm" suggests, then, a bleak future for Chaucer's old carpenter: not only has he lost his livelihood, he may also have forfeited (through his own rash behavior and wild "fantasye") the assurance of compensation from his guild.[17] The charge of madness that is spread against him "in al the toun" adumbrates his social death, his exile from the comforts of profession, guild, and neighborhood.

The fall of John the carpenter is, as I read it, a peculiarly urban phenomenon. Oxford certainly shrank in size and importance in the later fourteenth century; during the reign of Richard II (who took little interest in the city) it was little more than a small market town, containing perhaps some three thousand people. And yet, since appealing for their first royal charter in 1191, it is clear that the leading citizens of Oxford (who presumed to speak for "all the citizens") set great store by their city's independence.[18] Oxford's liberties were modeled on those of London, and this meant that its mayoral court could try certain cases (involving, for example, usury, slander, and the enrollment of wills) that were usually reserved for ecclesiastical jurisdiction.[19] Chaucer's London readers would certainly have recognized the crowding together of artisanal, clerical, and ecclesiastical forces (of bedroom, workplace, and chancel) that is represented in Chaucer's Oxford. The London letter-books are full of incidents that tell of, or hint at, the stressful consequences of crowding many vocations into one space. Fullers went to the river, intent on fulling (shrinking and thickening) their cloths in river water with the aid of urine. Hurers came to full their shaggy woollen caps (which tended to ruin more delicate cloth on contact). Dyers, objecting to too much urine, would attempt to ply their trade in the same stretch of water. When squires and pages led the horses of their lords to drink, then, they might find three crafts doing battle with one another and a river running yellow and blue.[20] Londoners living or working near St. Paul's (who might include men of law, fraternity chaplains, scribes, and copyists) were disturbed by an armorer's forge set up in the vicinity in 1377: mighty sledgehammers ("grossis malleis") beat away at great sheets of iron called "Osmond," turning out "brestplates," "quysers," "jambers," and other pieces of armour. Neighboring houses filled with the stench and smoke of sea-coal, used to fire the forge; houses shook to their foundations, which ruined the ale and wine in the cellars.[21] Others complained of the "nuisance, noise, and alarm" caused by blacksmiths who were too eager to ply their trade at ungodly hours.[22] Gerveys the blacksmith is already hard at work, sharpening "shaar and kultour," when Absolon knocks at his door in the *Miller's Tale*. The friars have just sung lauds (before daybreak); Gerveys asks Absolon a question that his own neighbors might ask of him: "Why rise ye so rathe?" Such are the tensions of urban life.

The city, as realized in the *Miller's Tale*, is a site of betrayal (for a "riche gnof," a most solid citizen). John the carpenter is betrayed by three of the fundamental elements of urban life: household, parish, and guild. His household, as personified by Alisoun and Nicholas, cuckolds him and proclaims him mad; the parish clerk (Absolon) vies for his wife and (with the hot coulter) elicits the cry that seals his ruin; the guild is likely to abandon him to his own folly. This theme of urban betrayal is to be repeated both by the *Canon's Yeoman's Prologue* (where an apprentice betrays a master) and its subsequent tale (where a master fleeces a London chantry priest). Chaucer seems, then, to have little good to say for the city; the associational ideals of *compagnye* and *felaweshipe* established in the *General Prologue* find little correspondence in his representations of urban life.

The Mark of the Countryside

Economic and social powers of the countryside—emphasized by revisionary English Marxism against traditional city-centered approaches—are acknowledged even in the *Miller's Tale*. John the carpenter leaves Oxford to do business with the Augustinian canons at Oseney, and (like many Oxford carpenters of the time) was evidently in the habit of traveling deeper into the countryside in search of timber, the raw material of his trade.[23] Nicholas's plot, elaborated during the carpenter's absence, hinges on fast-talking deceptiveness, a quality exemplified elsewhere in Chaucer by urbanites, particularly friars and pardoners. It seems fitting, then, that the instrument of chastisement applied to Nicholas should be a "kultour" (a coulter, a blade fixed to the front of a plough); the countryside, in the form of its most characteristic, down-to-earth implement, makes a searing critique on the rear end of an urban overreacher. Chaucer takes pains to suggest that the plough-blade will leave a lifelong impression on Nicholas; he too, like John the carpenter, experiences a kind of death:

> Of gooth the skyn an hande-brede aboute,
> The hoote kultour brende so his toute,
> And for the smert he wende for to dye.   (1.3811–13)

Violent opposition between city and countryside, little more than a painful hint in this *Tale*, is more fully developed in the narrative that follows, the *Reeve's Tale*. The outcome is the same: the countryside leaves its mark, permanently, on the body of the overingenious city-dweller. The interdependence of city and countryside, already imaged by John's quest for timber and Gerveys's work on ploughshares, is reestablished early on in this *Tale* as two students leave Cambridge in order to seek the services of a local miller. These young collegians are emphatically *not* native Cantabrigians: they come from somewhere way up north ("I kan nat telle where," 4015) and their language is heavily marked by dialect. Their very nonnative status, however, makes them particularly apt representatives of a medieval urban culture that forged its diverse forms of *felaweshipe* from aggregations of strangers.[24] Soler Halle, the "greet collegge" which houses these students, is forced to send them outside the city because of the "greet sokene" enjoyed by the miller, the exclusive (and therefore profitable) right to grind grain in a specific area (3987–89). It is worth noting that the narrative actually *begins* in the countryside, with an extended description of the miller and his household, before moving back to the city. Symkyn, the miller who lies in wait for the students, is distinguished by his professional versatility (3296–97), by the weaponry he carries about his person (sword-bladed cutlass, dagger, and knife), and by two distinguishing physical features: a bald head and a pug nose. The "camus" nose is obviously both a generic trait (shared by the bride in Peter Bruegel's *Peasant Wedding Feast* of 1568–69, plate 3)[25] and a family inheritance: Symkyn's daughter is also said to have a "kamus nose" (1.3934, 74). Such a nose lies in wait for Aleyn, the most ingenious of the clerks, as the plough-blade warmed for Nicholas.

The *Reeve's Tale* presents two sites in which to resolve its conflicts: the workplace and the bedroom. The workplace is imagined on a vertical plane: John proposes to stand at the top of the mill, by the hopper where "the corn gas in" (4037); Aleyn stands below, "where the mele falles doun" (4042). The short drop between hopper above and trough below (which the text dwells on for some ten lines) is of crucial importance, of course: for it is from this space that Symkyn derives his professional identity (and all the social pretensions,

Plate 3. Peter Bruegel the Elder, *Peasant Wedding Feast* (detail)

laid out at the beginning of the *Tale*, that go with it). This vertical plane, for Symkyn, has almost a metaphysical valence; he controls it more jealously (and more successfully) than Theseus does events at Athens. The students' attempt to oversee and so control the workplace is dismissed by Symkyn as mere foolishness, "nycetee" (4046); he soon has them rushing far out across a country landscape in pursuit of an errant male horse, itself in hot pursuit of "wilde mares" (4065).

The unreined, galloping horse introduces the theme of unbridled sexual energy and so leads us to the second major locale of the *Reeve's Tale*, the site of its resolution: the bedroom.[26] The two students attempt to ingratiate themselves with Symkyn by offering money and, at the same time, employing proverbs, the traditional cultural currency of the countryside: "With empty hand men may na haukes tulle," says John (4134).[27] The *Reeve's Tale* features the highest density of proverbs anywhere in Chaucer; John is their most prolific speaker.[28] Once granted permission to sleep with the miller and his family, however, the students revert to their own patois, the language of law and logic they are learning at Cambridge: "Som esement has lawe yshapen us" (1.4179).[29] In coupling with the miller's wife and daughter, the young clerics are both avenging the theft of corn and reuniting both women with the Church. Since the miller's wife is a parson's daughter, it is logical (as the Reeve argued earlier) that

> hooly chirches good moot been despended
> On hooly chirches blood, that is descended.   (1.3983–84)

The final outcome of this *Tale*, like the *Miller's Tale* before it, is precipitated by a crucial act of misinterpretation. When Symkyn's wife is awakened by Aleyn and Symkyn fighting and falling over her in the dark, she grabs a staff, intent on clubbing the student. She is unable to tell the two men apart, but then, seeing "a whit thyng in hir ye" (4301), she makes the extraordinary deduction that the student must be fighting in a nightcap. The "white thing" is, of course, the miller's bald head (a physical detail set in place early on in the narrative, along with the camus noses); her staff comes crashing down and lays out the miller, who cries "Harrow! I dye!" (4307). The students beat the miller, retrieve their corn, and return to the city.

The Reeve, in rendering accounts at the end of the *Tale*, is understandably keen to focus attention on the humiliation and degradation suffered by the miller and his family; his intent (he reminds us, in his final line) has been to "quyt the Millere in my tale" (4324). He spends no time on any injuries that the students might be carrying with them as they return to the city: for him, the students are simply instruments for getting at the miller. It is worth noting, however, that the boldest of the students pays a high price for meddling with the miller's daughter. "Who dorste be so bolde," Symkyn asks,

> "to disparage
> My doghter, that is come of swich lynage?"
> And by the throte-bolle he caughte Alayn,
> And he hente hym despitously again,
> And on the nose he smoot hym with his fest.
> Doun ran the bloody streem upon his brest;
> And in the floor, with nose and mouth tobroke,
> They walwe as doon two pigges in a poke.   (1.4271–78)

Miller and student, *walwynge* in the dark like sacked pigs, bring the discursive field of proverbs to life, Bruegel-fashion, at the high point of the *Tale*'s frantic drama.[30] But it is not clear, exactly, what proverb is brought to mind here, since two pigs in a poke seems one too many. We have the elements of proverbial wisdom (pigs, sacks) but lack a clear sense of what particular proverb they might add up to. The miller's wife, we might say, buys a pig in a poke (but lets the cat out of the bag); her confusion in wielding her staff mirrors our confusion in attempting to read these country signs.[31] The significant outcome of this confusing hermeneutic moment, however, may be gauged at the simple, literal level (as so often in Chaucer) through the fate of bodies. Symkyn is momentarily flattened, but Aleyn's nose is flattened for good: he returns to the city bearing the mark of the miller in the middle of his face. In flattening Aleyn's nose, Symkyn has (to borrow a term from the Wife of Bath) *paraged* Aleyn, made him his equal in birth and rank.[32] The camus nose shared by Symkyn and Malyne is, we have noted, a sign both of generic social rank (peasantry) and of a specific family lineage (father and daughter). In laying this sign upon the student, then, there is a suggestion that the miller is realizing his sexual dominance: the student's nose is as pliant as the feminine wax that, in countless masculine fantasies, is to be shaped to the master's liking.[33]

The extraordinary, bloody violence that marks the meeting of Symkyn's fist and Aleyn's nose finds no parallel in the analogues. In both versions of

Le Meunier et les deux clers, a French fabliau, the miller goes so far as to grab the offending student by the throat, but he goes no further (and is soundly beaten).[34] In *Decameron* 9.6, the outraged father, on being told by one of his young visitors that he has "been to the bower of bliss" with his daughter "half a dozen times at the very least" (p. 712) offers no violence at all: he accuses his guest of "villainy" ("la tua è stata una gran villania," 9.6.20), but allows the whole situation to be resolved, or to dissipate itself, through talking. It is worth noting exactly where Pinuccio, the male lover, thinks he has been in making love to his host's daughter: he has been "in villa" (9.6.19), a phrase rendered by McWilliam as "the bower of bliss" that may be more strictly translated as "the country house, the country-seat." It is quite appropriate, then, that he be accused of "villania." Like many urbanites before him in the *Decameron*, he has left the city to screw the countryside.

Although the *Decameron* analogue, like the *Reeve's Tale*, explores the relationship of city-dwellers to their rural hinterland, it allows no suggestion that city and countryside are interdependent. The young men in Chaucer head into the countryside because the city cannot provide a particular form of labor, milling, that is necessary for their sustenance. The young Florentines in Boccaccio visit the Mugnone Valley with the express, premeditated intention of bedding their host's daughter, Niccolosa.[35] Their self-sufficiency is so complete that they can avoid eating peasant fare: they eat only the food that they have brought with them (9.6.11; p. 711). Their host is bereft of economic and hence social independence because he makes his modest living from catering to wayfarers, *viandanti*, such as the two Florentines (9.6.4; p. 711); he naturally offers them the best bed available.[36] The *swyving* of his wife and daughter is the price he must pay, then, for laying open his household to city-dwellers. In the *Decameron*, such degradation or *disparagement* of the countryside by the city becomes routine. Each instance is sealed by the laughter of Boccaccio's Florentine storytellers.

The *Decameron's* most graphic and egregious example of the city screwing the countryside comes at the end of the Ninth Day. This *novella* is set in Barletta, a city some forty miles northwest of Bari up the Adriatic coast. This Apulian city is a long way removed from Florence: it was, however, much frequented by Florentine merchants and contained branch offices of both the Bardi and Peruzzi banking companies.[37] The action of the *novella* opens with Father Gianni, a priest from Barletta who augments his income by trading in the fairs of Apulia, riding his mare in the company of Compar ("Neighbor") Pietro. Compar Pietro practices the same trade as Father Gianni, but he rides an ass ("asino"). The priest offers Pietro a place to sleep at his church whenever he visits the city; Compar Pietro feels obliged to reciprocate, although his tiny house in the country is "hardly big enough to accommodate himself, his [ass], and his beautiful young wife" (9.10.8; p. 727). Father Gianni is obliged to sleep in the stable: he does not mind this, he says, because he can turn his mare into "una bella zitella," a beautiful young woman, whenever he feels like it (9.10.11; p. 728). Comar Gemmata, Pietro's wife, is intrigued by the possibilities of this: if *she* could be turned into a mare by day (turning back to a woman by night), she could help out with business. Father Gianni gets Gemmata to remove all her clothes "and to stand on all fours like a mare" (9.10.17; p. 729). Before working his priestly magic, Gianni instructs Pietro that he must not utter a word, whatever he sees, otherwise the magic will be broken. He fondles Gemmata, part by part, until

a certain uninvited guest was roused and stood erect. And he said:
"This be a fine mare's breast."
He then did the same to her back, her belly, her rump, her thighs and her legs: and finally, having nothing left to attend to except the tail, he lifted his shirt, took hold of the dibber [pivuolo] that he did his planting with, and stuck it straight in the appropriate furrow [solco], saying: "And this be a fine mare's tail."
Until this happened, Neighbor Pietro had been closely observing it all in silence, but he took a poor view of this last piece of business, and exclaimed:
"Oh, Father Gianni, no tail! I don't want a tail!" (9.10.18–19; p. 729)

Compar Pietro's cry, which comes after the priest has given up "the vital sap which all plants need to make them grow," enables the priest to declare that his magic has been ruined; the wife cannot now become a mare. Gemmata turns on her husband, berating him with what, in the *Decameron*, has become the iron law of the countryside: "You're as poor as a church mouse already, but you deserve to be a lot poorer" (9.10.23; p. 730). The *novella* closes, as it began, with Father Gianni and Neighbor Pietro riding side by side in search of trade. Nothing has changed; the inevitable order of things has been confirmed.

Italian city-states, both Tuscan republics and Lombard despotisms, exerted ruthless and exploitative control of their rural hinterlands.[38] In the *Decameron*, urbanites such as Father Gianni inevitably outwit country folk such as Compar Pietro and Comar Gemmata. "Outwit" is altogether too weak a term, of course, for what the city-priest does to the country couple: he exploits their awe of priestly magic to transform the wife into a beast, a mare, and then proves himself to be a better farmer than the husband by inseminating the wife as if she were a ploughed field. In the *Miller's Tale*, we have noted, it was the countryside that left its mark on the body of the urbanite; here that process is reversed. And in the *Reeve's Tale*, we encountered the galloping horse as a figure of unbridled sexuality; here, the priest assumes the position of one who rides and controls his own sexual impulses (which the wife is made to personify). This last inversion goes against a long iconographic tradition in which a man's sexual desires enslave him to a woman who rides, quite literally, on his back (the most famous example being Phyllis, mistress of Alexander the Great, who rides Aristotle).[39] In *Decameron* 9.10 the city-dweller is both rider and ridden. The country folk, obliterated as political subjects, function only as instruments of the urbanite's desires.

Powers of the Countryside: Fragment 3

The protagonist of *Decameron* 5.1, Cimone, has the powerful and attractive physique that noblemen were supposed to have without any of the concomitant mental prowess: he is "to all intents and purposes an imbecile" (5.1.4; p. 406). The clearest sign of his imbecility is his preference for living with farm workers in the countryside rather than with citizens in the city. The "refined sentiment" (p. 407) that Cimone's teachers try to beat into him is, in the Italian, "cittadinesco piacer" (5.1.8), literally, "citizenly pleasure." [40] Here, as elsewhere, Boccaccio's text assumes the viewpoint of the city-dweller in defining the countryside as the home and resort of the imbecilic and uncivilized. The countryside is the noncity, a place that can possess no powers or secrets of its own. Such a city-centered ideology was aggressively imposed by Florence on its *contado* in the fourteenth century. Economic and political dominance was underscored by a policy of desacralizing the countryside: local cults were suppressed; relics of local saints were confiscated and taken to Florence, and a calendar of saints (in step with the centralized Florentine model) was imposed on the local populace.[41] Country-dwellers were thereby encouraged to envision Florence not only as their political and economic master but also as their spiritual center, their *telos* of pilgrimage. The English countryside, as represented by the *Canterbury Tales*, retained much greater powers in this period: powers that are both mysteriously suggestive and politically concrete. When Chaucer wishes to explore urban despotism or urban commerce he goes abroad: to Italy in the *Clerk's Tale* and *Physician's Tale*; to France and Flanders with the Shipman. When exploring the countryside he prefers to stay at home: Fragment 3, which offers his most sustained analysis of country politics, goes no further afield than rural Yorkshire.

The Wife of Bath is not from Bath, but from "bisyde Bath," a phrase that might echo the term "juxta Bathon" that was applied to the parish of St. Michael-Without-the-Walls. The chief occupations of this parish (that had sprung up outside the north gate of Bath) were weaving and spinning; the phrase "biside Bath" could, however, as Robertson argues, be taken to refer to any village near Bath.[42] It is clear, at any event, that the Wife's considerable wealth and economic independence is rooted firmly in the rural economy.[43] It is interesting to note how, in her *Prologue*, she seems naturally to gravitate "into the feeldes" when she seeks "leyser for to pleye" (3.551–53); her plan to marry her fourth husband, Jankyn, is first evolved and disclosed "in the feeldes" (3.564). This translation to the countryside is carried further in her *Tale*, which opens with a female monarch celebrating, amid her compeers, her possession of a rural landscape:

> The elf-queene, with hir joly compaignye,
> Daunced ful ofte in many a greene mede.   (3.860–61)

This motif of women assuming physical possession of a country landscape recurs twice more in the course of the *Tale*: first in the person of the "mayde" who chooses to walk between the court and the river; second in the company of ladies dancing "under a forest syde" who disappear to reveal the old wife sitting "on the grene." These three images of elf-queen, maiden, and wife do more than represent women *in* the countryside; they suggest that women are *of* the countryside, that they somehow embody and articulate the spirit and wisdom of rural place. All three are first encountered in a rural setting: their male assailants (friars, a young knight-rapist) come from outside and embody particular claims *to* the countryside that are encoded as sexual violence. "Wherever there was a town," R. W. Southern remarks, "there were friars; and without a town there were no friars."[44] The mission of friars (at least as exemplified later in this Fragment by the *Summoner's Tale*) is to extract the maximum of surplus from the country economy and transfer it to the city. A friar will not impregnate women, but (according to the Wife's tortuous construction) "he ne wol doon hem but dishonour" (3.881). The knight-rapist is an aristocrat and a courtier: his rape of the maid is immediately preceded by hunting (3.884), the pursuit through which an aristocratic court celebrates and reaffirms its physical domination of the countryside. The *Tale* begins by conceding that the age of the elf-queen is over: friars now strive to turn all places into the same place by itemizing them as sites for expropriation: "Citees, burghes, castels, hye toures, / Thropes, bernes, shipnes, dayeryes" (3.870–71). The *Tale* insists, however, that the wisdom sought for at court will be found in the countryside. Even the learned, curial wisdom of Dante (the critique of nobility supplied by *Purgatorio* 7 and *Convivio* 4) must be imported from the countryside and then taught, patiently, at court (3.1125–58).

Powers of the Countryside: Metaphysics (the *Friar's Tale*)

The next two tales of Fragment 3 begin, as the *Wife of Bath's Tale* had begun, by establishing the motif of city-based ecclesiastical predators setting out to prey on country folk. Chaucer opens the *Friar's Tale* not with his protagonist but with a figure who will dominate the narrative for the first twenty lines and then play no further part in it: "Whilom ther was dwellynge in my contree / An archedeken . . ." (3.1301–2). By doing this Chaucer focuses attention away from his protagonist-to-be, the summoner, and onto the ecclesiastical system within which he will operate:

> He made the peple pitously to synge,
> For er the bisshop caughte hem with his hook,
> They weren in the erchedeknes book.   (3.1316–18)

The archdeacon is the middle term in this hierarchy, with the archbishop above him and the summoner, his executive arm, below: "He hadde a somonour redy to his hond . . ." (3.1321).

Actually, there is one lower link in this ecclesiastical chain, namely, the "wenches" that the summoner keeps in his "retinue" for purposes of sexual entrapment (3.1355–62). Chaucer's strategy here of connecting the top of a social hierarchy with scurrilous activities at lower levels is often pursued by Boccaccio (for comparable purposes of systemic rather than individual critique). The *Decameron*'s very first story also opens with a middleman, the merchant Musciatto Franzesi. Musciatto himself occupies two places on the social ladder, since he "has become a fine gentleman after acquiring enormous wealth and fame as a merchant in France" (1.1.7.; p. 69). Musciatto's new social prominence brings him into the service of Messer Carlo Senzaterra, Lord Charles Stateless (Charles of Valois, brother of King Philip the Fair of France); Musciatto and Lord Charles are then summoned to Tuscany by order of Pope Boniface VIII. But Musciatto can only maintain his newfound status of gentleman by pursuing his old profession of merchant business. On finding that he needs to recover some loans back in Burgundy he employs one Cepperello of Prato. Cepperello, Boccaccio's protagonist, is a murderer, blasphemer, drunkard, sodomite, robber, glutton, gambler, and card-sharper: "He was," says Boccaccio, "perhaps the worst man ever born" (1.1.15.; pp. 70–71). Cepperello expedites Musciatto's business but falls sick at the house of two Florentine moneylenders who imagine themselves characterized by the local townspeople as "Lombard dogs" (1.1.26.; p. 72). Having decided to help the moneylenders out, Cepperello makes a final confession of heartrending scrupulosity to a good-hearted and gullible "holy friar." On his death, Cepperello's body is carried in procession to the friars' church; the legend of his saintliness spreads and the local people tear the clothes from his back as sacred relics: "Those who succeeded in grabbing so much as a tiny fragment felt they were in Paradise itself" (1.1.86.; p. 80). Cepperello is then cycled into the religious economy as "Saint Ciappelletto" (1.1.88.; p. 81); the hierarchy that the pope rules over maintains its equilibrium and is infused with fresh capital, material and spiritual (see figure 1).

Boccaccio begins and ends *Decameron* 1.1 by proclaiming that his story celebrates the power and love of God; it should convince us that "our hopes will rest in Him as in something invisible" (1.1.2.; p. 69). There is obviously no perfect overlap here between the will of God in history and those institutions that profess to discern and execute it. The same holds for Chaucer's *Friar's Tale*, in which the power of God saves a Christian subject from the evil engendered within the ecclesiastical system that should be her protector. But there are important differences between the Italian and English narratives. Boccaccio's God floats above and beyond the whole system that links fine gentlemen with Florentine moneylenders, the pope with "the worst man ever

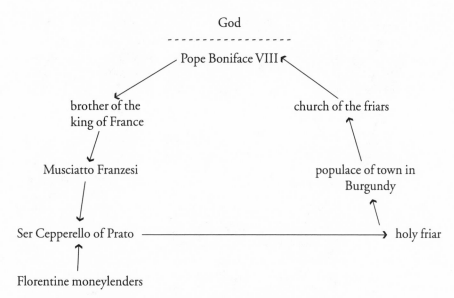

Figure 1. Scheme and sequence of dependencies in *Decameron* 1.1.

born"; Boccaccio's *novella* resolves its narrative crises by proposing a seamless circulation of capital through mercantile, financial, urban, and ecclesiastical worlds. Chaucer's narrative proposes that a single woman, alone in the countryside, can trust her safety to metaphysics.

Chaucer's narrative makes a wholly secular opening (even in describing an ecclesiastical hierarchy) but takes a metaphysical turn as soon as it leaves town and heads into the country. Such a turn might be figured as a movement from Boccaccian, city-centered narrative to a landscape of Dantean metaphysics. The countryside of the *Friar's Tale* is, metaphorically speaking, Dante country: the names of Dante and Vergil, "Dant" and "Virgile," are explicitly invoked by the figure that the summoner finds there (3.1519–20).

The key term in the latter part of the *Friar's Tale* is *entente*. Such a term shifts us from the *Tale*'s initial analysis of social institutions to the atomized self-analysis that each Canterbury pilgrim (including Chaucer, in his "retracciouns," 10.1084) will finally be delivered to. The drama of *entente*, and its problematic relationship to language, is played out most memorably (and most suggestively for Chaucer) in Dante's meeting with the damned friar Guido da Montefeltro in *Inferno* 27.

Dante and Vergil first encounter Guido da Montefeltro as a walking ball of flame. Guido's words must struggle to find a passage from their origin within the fire to the tip of the flame, where they become audible (4–18): the mediated character of language, the space between thought and speech, is painfully and graphically insisted on from the first. What follows accentuates the historical character of human language, its unfolding through time. At this point beyond time (in the *Inferno*) it might seem that this has ceased to matter: time is illusory; every moment that is, was, or will be is eternally present to the mind of God. But (to continue this Augustinian line of reasoning) the historical *present* is a means used by God to unfold his purposes to human understanding. To follow the logic of this unfolding it is essential for the individual to master the terms of language: to understand the difference between past, present, and future. Guido's failure to master these terms delivers him into the hands of the devil and secures his damnation.

Inferno 27 would seem to employ an extraordinary range of verbal tenses and moods: past, present, and future; active, passive, and subjunctive. Such an impression is perhaps determined by the studied attention to language, particularly to verbal sequence, that the canto makes such a crucial part of its own drama. Dante asks a simple question of Guido: "Now who are you . . . ?" ("Ora chi se' . . . ," 55). This is answered by a famous sequence of subjunctives in which Guido envisions as impossible that which Dante is actually undertaking:[45]

> "S' i' credesse che mia risposta fosse
> a persona che mai tornasse al mondo,
> questa fiamma staria sanza più scosse."   (27.61–63)

> "If I believed that my reply might be given
> to someone who might ever return to the world
> this flame would cease to shake."

In describing who he is Guido inevitably resorts to the preterite: present identity here can only be explained in terms of past history: "Io fui uom d'arme, e poi fui cordigliero . . ." ("I was a man of arms, and then a corded friar," 67). The use of parataxis here is typical of this canto, which features a high density of simple "e" ("and") conjunctions. This expresses history in its simplest terms: one thing and then another. Guido continues narrating his personal history. Having retired from public life to seek spiritual security within a religious order, he is summoned by the pope (Boniface VIII again) to give political advice. He is unnerved, but Boniface is reassuring:

> "finor t'assolvo, e tu m'insegna fare
> sì come Penestrino in terra getti."   (27.101–2)

> "right now I absolve you, and you teach me how
> Palestrina can be battered to the ground."

In accepting such reassurance Guido seals his own fate:

> "ch'assolver non si può chi non si pente,
> nè pentere e volere insieme puossi
> per la contradizion che nol consente."   (27.118–20)

> "for one can't absolve a man who does not repent,
> nor can a man repent and will at once,
> for the contradiction does not allow it."

The exegete here is the devil who drags Guido off to damnation. He mirrors the grammatical structuring of Boniface's promise ("t'assolvo, e tu m'insegna") and in so doing exposes its fallacious ordering of terms: as a good logician ("loico," 27.123), the devil knows that "to will" and "to repent" is a reasonable historical sequence, but the opposite—"pentere e volere"—is impossible.

The devil in the *Friar's Tale* pays similarly scrupulous attention to linguistic detail. This devil is looking for a damned soul to identify himself through a perfect matching of verbal signifiers with evil spiritual intent. The carter who curses his horses fails to qualify, but the summoner may talk himself into the position where the devil can take him. The two crucial terms here, as in Dante, are repentance and absolution. The summoner damns himself not by confusing their sequence but by cutting himself off from each of them in turn. By doing this he rejects any possibility of a future that differs from his present spiritual state, which is damnable. The summoner's present state is translated into an eternal one in two easy stages. He first abjures the sacrament that promises absolution: "I shrewe thise shrifte-fadres everychoon" (3.1442). At this point the yeoman feels free to smile (1446) and reveal himself as a devil. Finally the summoner declares "that is nat myn entente . . . / . . . for to repente me": the devil now takes possession of him "by right" (3.1630–35).

Dante's Guido and Chaucer's summoner are damned through the deficiencies of the language they have learned within religious institutions. The powers of discernment that the summoner has acquired in identifying "a sly lecchour, / Or an avowtier, or a paramour" (1371–72) prove useless in detecting or dealing with the presence of evil. Unlike the summoner, Guido does have a language for dealing with the metaphysical world. But he fails to grasp that "pentere e volere," the verbs that govern his actions, must find their rightful place on either side of the conjunction, the "e" that stands for historical sequence. But does this mean that history may be reduced (once again) to a sequence of linguistic terms? The conjunctions of *Inferno* 27 that open this possibility finally serve to close it as Dante and Vergil move away from Guido: "Noi passamm'oltre, e io e 'l duca mio" ("We passed on further, both [lit. 'and'] I and my leader," 27.133).

The two terms conjoined here through a double "e" are not verbs this time but substantives: Dante and Vergil. This suggests that the two linked terms, being nouns, can occupy one place. But the "e" that conjoins also represents a hiatus as language extends through time: Vergil is born before Christ, and Dante after. Christ, we might say, is the mysterious conjunction that enables Vergil to come to Dante without crossing the threshold of the incarnate word.[46] That which enables is that which divides. Divine power, in choosing to represent itself through human signifiers, retains the power of enigma: it is the devil-logicians in Dante and Chaucer, and not the authors, who insist that salvation history can be restricted to the analysis of linguistic terms.[47]

"Bretherhede" and the Widow's Curse

The *Friar's Tale* is no *de casibus* tragedy: it tells of a confrontation between a minor ecclesiastical functionary and a penniless country widow. And yet the seriousness of the issues unfolded in this unlikely place invites comparison, I have tried to suggest, with the most powerful and intricate of Dantean dramas.[48] What is at stake, socially and politically, in this remarkable *Tale*? The narrative is generated by a local conflict between two pilgrims, Summoner and Friar, that is symptomatic of a greater rivalry between secular clergy and religious orders. The Host is at first anxious to curb such a rivalry by employing the kind of language we have associated with the regulation of guilds: "In compaignye we wol have no debaat" (3.1288).

As the rivalry continues to simmer, however, the Host comes to realize that some entertaining narrative capital can be generated from such a conflict: "Now telleth forth," he instructs the Friar,

> "thogh that the Somonour gale;
> Ne spareth nat, myn owene maister deere."   (3.1336–37)

At this point the Host has plainly elected to leave in abeyance the standards necessary for the long-term survival of an associational form; "debaat" may now take on the form of narrative entertainment. Even as the Host abandons the discourse of *bretherhede*, however, it is taken up, in the *Friar's Tale*, by a new spokesman:

> "*Depardieux*," quod this yeman, "deere broother,
> "Thou art a bailly, and I am another.
> I am unknowen as in this contree;
> Of thyn aqueyntance I wolde praye thee,
> And eek of bretherhede, if that yow leste."   (3.1395–99)

This offer of *bretherhede*, extended by the mysterious yeoman, is readily accepted by the summoner; the two men formalize their union with the same deliberateness that Palemon and Arcite unpick theirs:[49]

> Everych in ootheres hand his trouthe leith,
> For to be sworne bretheren til they deye.   (3.1404–5)

Identities and professional secrets are gradually disclosed within this new framework of *bretherhede*; the term "brother" is exchanged sixteen times. This process of associative bonding, which in the *General Prologue* (as in the guilds) is not heavily gender inflected, here takes on suggestions of *Männerfreundschaft*, male bonding,[50] and erotic courtship: "Now lat us ryde blyve," says the yeoman to the summoner,

> "For I wole holde compaignye with thee
> Til it be so that thou forsake me."
> "Nay," quod this somonour, "that shal nat bityde!"   (3.1521–23)

Through this developing intimacy the fraternal viewing perspective gradually establishes itself as normative. When something or someone foreign
crosses its line of vision, it (she) can only be represented as wholly alienated
and objectified: "Brother," quod he, "heere woneth an olde rebekke" (3.1573).
The kind of associative discourse that we have observed in the formation of
the pilgrim *compagnye*, and in the constitution of guilds in cities, towns, and
villages, is here represented as a threat to a single female living in the countryside. We have, in effect, returned to the beginning of the *Wife of Bath's Tale*.
When the summoner first set out, he was figured as a hunter in search of a
preselected "pray," namely "an old widow, a ribibe" (3.1376–77). He has now
closed on his quarry. The widow who faces two intruders experiences them as
threats to her well-being, just as the Wife's maiden experienced the knight-
rapist as he rode toward her. The outcome cannot, within the unfolding
narrative, be known to her. How, then, can the countryside save her?

The old widow is saved both by the innate corruption of the *compagnye*
formed by the two males, and (as in the *Wife of Bath's Tale*) by a figure
that seems synonymous with the countryside itself. The *compagnye*, while
technically flawless in its self-constitution, is undermined from the start by
bad faith: rather than the sharing of professional secrets (as encouraged in
the guilds) we find a disguising of professional identities (or, in the summoner's case, outright lies: 3.1392–94). The "gay yeoman" who proves to be
the widow's protector is first glimpsed "under a forest syde" (3.1380), an exact
echo of the site where we found the Wife of Bath's old wife (3.990). Like the
old wife, the yeoman seems to merge with the countryside he inhabits: she
sits on the green, and he wears it (in the form of a "courtepy," 3.1382). The
yeoman wears the green, and he also manages it: he is a "bailly"; he rides
through the countryside "to reysen a rente" that is owing to his lord (3.1390–
92). He recognizes the summoner, the would-be hunter of old widows, as a
poacher on his lord's domain; he saves the widow by trapping the summoner
and claiming him as his lord's "duetee."

An elderly widow living in the countryside in fourteenth-century England, then, can rest assured of being saved from the rapacious assaults of
a corrupt ecclesiastical system by a metaphysical intervention played out
through the mechanisms of rural estate management. Such a scenario seems
fit for the political fairyland evoked by Alisoun of Bath earlier in this Fragment (one that she assigns, regretfully, to "th'olde days," 3.857). Historical
evidence suggests a different kind of landscape: "based on the everyday behavior of rural women of all marital statuses," Judith Bennett has argued, "a *bon
vieux temps* will not be found in the medieval countryside."[51] It is important,
however, that we register the continuing *desire* in Chaucer's text to represent
the countryside as endowed with and protected by immanent metaphysical
powers. We might also notice that the text yields a figure who, momentarily,
speaks with a passion that dissolves such metaphysical assurances and gives us

a glimpse of genuine historical contingencies. I speak of the old widow herself at her moment of greatest rage.

The widow in the *Friar's Tale* is not named, except by the devil in an epithet that must be generic: "Mabely, myn owene mooder deere" (3.1626). The summoner addresses her as "thou olde virytrate" and "olde stot," terms that recognize her reproductive and physical powers only through their absence. When the devil and the summoner go to hell, the narrative discards her; this is not her story. Her function within this institutional and metaphysical drama compares with that of the wenches employed by the summoner: it is accidental; she is used as bait for a man-trap. Her outrage at the imaginary crimes she is charged with has more, then, than a local and passing resonance. It challenges not just the summoner but the whole framing of the narrative, the positioning of the reader (who "discovers" her at the end of the *Tale*), and her own positioning in rural poverty and within the ecclesiastical-metaphysical system within which she is first threatened and then saved: "'Thou lixt,' quod she, 'by my savacioun . . .'" (3.1618). The female subject here first rejects masculine discourse and then reinscribes herself within it, since, through the sacramental system it presides over, it controls the language of "savacioun."[52] Such an articulation is best described not as self-contradictory but as antagonistic. Whereas logical contradiction implies an objective relation between two concepts—a relationship of difference—antagonism attests to the failure of difference. In Laclau's account, antagonism represents "the experience of the limits of any possible objectivity, the way in which any objectivity reveals the partial and arbitrary character of its own objectification." Antagonism denotes "the limit of the social, the witness of the ultimate impossibility of society, the moment at which the sense of precariousness reaches its highest level."[53]

We are to see many such antagonistic moments in the fifteenth century, inside and outside of the Lollard movement. Margery Baxter will claim that she carries a charter of salvation in her womb (that no friar can lay his hands on).[54] Margery Kempe will let out a cry that is both resistant to ecclesiastical authority ("thou lixt") and expressive of a wholly personal and subjective religious experience ("*my* savacioun"). The one-line accusation/affirmation of "Mabelye," then, may well be the most powerful historical force found hidden, immanent, in the depths of Chaucer's countryside.

Powers of the Countryside: Social Structure (the *Summoner's Tale*)

The *Friar's Tale* opens in a rural setting that, viewed from the perspective of London and Westminster, seems remote and inaccessible. Even here, however, we find a friar, one of those restless city-dwellers who, according to the Wife of Bath (3.867), leave town to "serchen every lond and every streem":

Lordynges, ther is in Yorkshire, as I gesse,
A mersshy contree called Holdernesse,
In which ther wente a lymytour aboute
To preche, and eek to begge, it is no doute.   (3.1709–12)

Holderness is not, as the *Riverside Chaucer* has it, "a town in Yorkshire"
(p. 129): it is rather (as Chaucer has it) "a mersshy contree," a *wapentake*,
a *libertas* (and a rural deanery). A *wapentake* is a subdivision of an English
shire, corresponding (as Trevisa points out) to a *hundred*.[55] The term derives
via Old English from the Old Norse *vápnatak* (a vote of consent expressed by
the waving of weapons); its survival reminds us of coastal Yorkshire's former
vulnerability to Danish invasion. Holderness is defined as a *libertas*, or liberty, in the rolls of the Yorkshire justices of the peace.[56] The country district
known as Holderness lies to the north of the mouth of the Humber and
is bordered to the west by the River Hull, to the north by the *wapentake*
of Dickering, and to the east by the North Sea. Holderness was certainly
"mersshy": many settlements had been reclaimed by drainage of woodland,
waste, and marsh before 1300, but the area fell back into "widespread decay
and regression" in the fourteenth and fifteenth centuries.[57] Rising sea levels
threatened settlers on newly colonized lands by making their soils heavy and
waterlogged; the Black Death of 1349 shrank certain villages out of existence.
As local populations fell, lords turned increasingly from the production of
corn (less profitable, with fewer mouths to feed) to sheep farming (lower labor
costs, therefore more profitable).[58] No friars were based in Holderness in the
Middle Ages; the closest friaries were to be found in Beverley and Kingston
(Hull).[59] In descending upon a village in Holderness, then, Chaucer's friar
is attempting to bleed a country district that is already in steady social and
economic decline. And yet this village, as Chaucer tells it, will find more than
adequate resources within itself to defeat and expel a rapacious urban invader.

"Nere Thou Oure Brother, Sholdestou Nat Thryve"

The central drama of the *Summoner's Tale* is fought out at a liminal site (the
sickbed) at the very heart of feudal society (a peasant house).[60] Friar John
has already preached in the church, and he is soon to visit the manor house.
The friar is able to infiltrate the peasant dwelling by advancing the claims of
bretherhede: both Thomas and his unnamed wife are members of a confraternity attached to Friar John's convent. Membership in such guilds, we have
noted, allowed people in far-flung country districts to find some form of collective identification with, or a *pied à terre* in, urban organizations. Here the
lines of communication are reversed: the friar pursues a guild member from
his sharing of collective identity in the town to the site of greatest intimacy
(his bed, his worldly goods, his body) in the village. Thomas can only be cured

of his sickness, the friar argues, by the round of prayers said at the convent, "day and nyght," on his behalf: "Nere thou oure brother, sholdestou nat thryve" (3.1944).

Friar John had earlier been distracted from pressing the claims and obligations of *bretherhede* by Thomas's wife, who had complained of the death of her child. With breathtaking speed (closing the couplet that the wife begins), the friar launches into a completely imaginary scenario that is rivaled only by Nicholas's evocation of the new Noah's flood:

> "Now, sire," quod she, "but o word er I go.
> My child is deed withinne thise wykes two,
> Soone after that ye wente out of this toun."
>   "His deeth saugh I by revelacioun,"
> Seide this frere, "at hoom in oure dortour.
> I dar wel seyn that, er that half an hour
> After his deeth, I saugh hym born to blisse
> In myn avision, so God me wisse!
> So dide oure sexteyn and oure fermerer,
> That han been trewe freres fifty yeer;
> They may now—God be thanked of his loone!—
> Maken hir jubilee and walke allone.
> And up I roos, and al oure covent eke,
> With many a teere trillyng on my cheke,
> Withouten noyse or claterynge of belles;
> *Te Deum* was oure song, and nothyng elles."   (3.1851–66)

Here, through this energetic evocation of convent life, Friar John skillfully markets the benefits of confraternity membership: brothers and sisters in remote places gain spiritual solace by thinking of the benefits accruing to them in the urban friary. In fact, in this instance, the villagers are relieved of the burden of imagining: Friar John brings his "avision" from town to village and does the imagining for them. This fantasy of communal life is interrupted only by the couplet given over to the two old friars who, after fifty years, have been granted the privilege of walking the countryside alone (rather than in pairs). This momentary distraction serves to remind us, of course, that the friar's true *bretherhede* lies not with the villagers but with his fellow friars. We first glimpsed Friar John working his way from house to house with "his felawe," another friar (3.1740). This second friar is not present during Friar John's colloquy on *bretherhede* with Thomas, but is picked up again as soon as John leaves the peasant domain (3.2159).

Friar John preaches the evils of anger to Thomas at the bidding of "oure dame" (1797), Thomas's wife: "Chideth him weel," she urges. "He is as angry as a pissemyre" ("ant," 3.1824–25). Domestic *chyding*, of course, is a wife's job; so too, in Chaucer's aristocratic households, is the crucial task of talking men out of their anger.[61] Friar John, then, is out of place both in gender and in social terms. It is quickly apparent that the sermon he preaches to the ailing Thomas has no relevance to the peasant world. His tales of "irous" potentates are addressed, rather, to the seigneurial strata: it is worth recalling that friars had been confessors to magnates and monarchs in England since the time of Henry III.[62] The effect of his preaching is to intensify, rather than diminish, the particular passion that the peasant is burdened with, namely, *ire*.[63] The bonds connecting peasant to friar are soon to be blown asunder. Just before this happens, Thomas pointedly reminds us just what these bonds are by rehearsing the terms that supposedly incorporate himself and his wife into the friar's confraternity. "Ye sey me thus," he asks Friar John,

> "how that I am youre brother?"
> "Ye, certes," quod the frere, "trusteth weel.
> I took oure dame oure lettre with oure seel."
> "Now wel," quod he, "and somwhat shal I yive
> Unto youre hooly covent . . ."   (3.2126–30)

The mighty, horselike (2150–51), rural fart that Thomas bestows upon Friar John blows him clean out of the peasant domain, annulling the ties of *bretherhede* that supposedly bind peasants to friars and their convents.[64] The particular implications of this crucial moment of expulsion may be more readily grasped by turning to a Boccaccian narrative, *Decameron* 6.10. This *novella* is set in Certaldo, a village some 25 miles to the southwest of Florence, famous only for its onions. Frate Cipolla (Friar Onion) visits once a year to collect dues from the members of the confraternity attached to his convent.[65] "It is precisely to collect these contributions of yours," he tells them, "that my superior, Master Abbot, has sent me among you" (6.10.10; p. 506). Having assured them that, for a share of their crops, St. Anthony of Padua "will protect your oxen, asses, pigs and sheep from harm" (6.10.9; p. 506), he promises them a special treat. Later that day, outside the church, he will show them "a sacred and most beautiful relic": "one of the feathers of the Angel Gabriel, which was left behind in the bedchamber of the Virgin Mary when he came to annunciate her in Nazareth" (6.10.11; p. 507). The country folk seem defenceless against such seamless rhetoric ("he was Cicero in person, or perhaps Quintillian," 6.10.7; p. 506), but two young men even the odds by exchanging his parrot's feather for some lumps of coal. Cipolla discovers this change in midsermon: at this point, it seems, the village just might get wise to him and expel him from its midst. But Brother Onion simply sheds one skin of sermonizing and presents another: these coals, he proclaims, were snatched from the fire over which St. Lawrence was griddled (6.10.49; p. 513); God made this substitution (he now realizes) since the day after tomorrow is the Feast of St. Lawrence. The villagers, mightily impressed, give bigger donations than usual and beg the friar to touch them with the coals: "So Friar Cipolla took the coals between his fingers and began to scrawl the biggest crosses he could manage to inscribe on their white smocks and on their doublets and on the shawls [veli] of the women" (6.10.54; p. 513).

Here, as Frate Cipolla smears his signs all over the confraternity members, we see a simple reinforcement of the Father Gianni narrative: the urban ecclesiastic will always dominate (by ploughing, inseminating, or besmirching) the body, singular or collective, of villagers. The two young men who substitute the coals for the feather (and who are delighted by Cipolla's performance) are not confraternity members, but are said to be of Cipolla's *brigata* (6.10.13; p. 507). The villagers are plainly not members of this *brigata*; here, as in the *Summoner's Tale*, it is plainly foolish to imagine that peasants and friars can operate within a single collective structure. Although Boccaccio himself happens to be a native of Certaldo, his *Decameron* plainly puts him in the same city-centered *brigata* as Frate Cipolla.

Village structures in the *Decameron*, then, prove wholly incapable of identifying and resisting rapacious outsiders. But city structures prove more than adequate in dealing with the canniest of newcomers (including friars). Representations of the city as a self-regulating, self-protecting social system occur with remarkable frequency in the *Decameron*. The most celebrated example is *Decameron* 4.2, featuring Berto della Massa, a "thief, pander, swindler, and murderer" who becomes so famous that his native city of Imola "no longer afforded any outlet for his roguery" (4.2.8; p. 344). So Berto moves to Venice, becomes Frate Alberto OFM, and convinces Monna Lisetta that the Archangel Gabriel wishes to make love to her through his body. On being disturbed in his lovemaking by Lisetta's relatives, this Archangel flies out of the window and swims off in a Venetian canal. On the far side of the water, the naked friar convinces a tenant, "an honest-looking fellow" (4.2.46; p. 350), to take him in. This "buono uomo" soon hears news of Frate Alberto's exploits at the Rialto, the center for mercantile exchange. He persuades Alberto that he can only escape by assuming a carnival disguise and parading through the streets; he smears his body with honey and covers him with feathers. Frate Alberto's final ceremonial unmasking occurs at the Piazza San Marco, the public space flanked by the city's most important ecclesiastical and civic buildings. He is saved from the mob by his fellow friars, who escort him back to the friary (see figure 2).

Gossip proves to be the vital mechanism in the uncovering of Frate Alberto: Lisetta boasts of her lover to a lady friend, and "within forty-eight hours the news was all over Venice" (4.2.44; p. 350). In Chaucer, too, the social body is cured as well as threatened by talking. The fast-talking friar at the end of the *Summoner's Tale* is effectively talked out of existence. When the talking stops, as it does in the *Physician's Tale* and threatens to do in the *Melibee*, violence may take its place.[66]

The Eighth Day of the *Decameron* features two more routine (and easily diagrammable) examples of urban self-regulation. Florence customarily em-

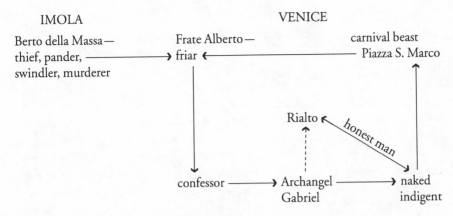

Figure 2. The identities of Berto della Massa: the movement through city space

Key: ——   physical movement
        - - -   gossip

ployed a *podestà* and his legal team from another city on six-month contracts in the hope of securing a judicial administration that was free of factional influence. Here, once again, the Florentine body politic needed to safeguard itself against foreign subjects in its midst. In 8.5 an outraged judge from the Marches, having been publicly humiliated by young practical jokers, "began to swear by the bowels of God that somebody should tell him whether it was the custom in Florence for a judge to have his breeches removed whilst sitting on the bench of justice" (8.5.19; p. 613). The short answer is yes: the *podestà* who imported this inept judge soon realizes "that this had only been done in order to show him that the Florentines knew that he had brought fools with him instead of judges so as to save money [per averne miglior mercato]" (8.5.20; p. 613). He thinks it best "to hold his tongue, and nothing more was said about the matter" (8.5.20; p. 613). In 8.9 the threat to Florence is posed by the fact that "fellow-citizens of ours [return] from Bologna as judges or physicians or lawyers, tricked out in long flowing robes of scarlet and vair, looking very grand and impressive" (8.9.4; p. 650). Two penniless Florentine painters convince one such lawyer that they belong to a secret society that enjoys sumptuous banqueting, music, and an endless supply of beautiful women. The physician, anxious to join this *brigata*, agrees to undergo an initiatory ordeal. He is picked up at the Piazza Santa Maria Novella by one of the painters (wearing a bearskin and a devil's mask), carried outside the city limits, and dumped into a cesspool used by farmers for manuring their fields.

This last expulsion narrative follows the logic of all such Boccaccian *novelle*: the hero is the city-state; the villain is a *villein*, a citizen of a foreign city, or (as in 8.9) a Florentine who has been abroad too long. In the *Summoner's Tale*, however, the crucial gesture of expulsion comes direct from a peasant body at the heart of the feudal village structure. This gesture is not conclusive, however: the friar is not blown clean out of the village, but is moved from the second to the third element of village society (from peasant hovel to seigneurial "court," 3.2162). The lord of the manor is evidently on first-name terms with the friar (3.2171); the outcome of the affair remains finely balanced as the lord acknowledges, in turn, the claims of "my confessour" and "my cherl" (3.2195, 2238). Closure, once again, can only be effected through a complex social hermeneutic. The action of the peasant Thomas is considered, renarrated, within three distinct discursive systems (convergent at the site of the "court"). The lady of the manor adopts a robust, circular logic suggestive of an Aristotelian viewpoint: "I seye a cherl hath doon a cherles dede" (3.2206). By this reasoning, it seems, Thomas's text may be taken to confirm the logic of existing social relations; it exerts a force that recognizes social difference (peasants and friars) while confirming social sameness. "God lat hym nevere thee!" exclaims the lady of the manor; a peasant can never "thee" (thrive), from the perspective of the manor hall, because he is always a peasant.

The second interpreter, the lord, is guided by abstract interpretative principles that might be associated with Roman law.[67] He subjects Thomas's text, and the conditions for transmission and division that Thomas has attached to it, to an abstract and general form of philosophical inquiry. Such analysis finds itself utterly defeated. Thomas has proposed an *impossibilium*; there is no precedent for what he has just proposed:

> "Who evere herde of swich a thyng er now?
> To every man ylike? Tell me how.
> It is an inpossible . . ."   (3.2229–31)

The third speaker, the squire Jankyn, first appears in the guise of *puer ad mensam*; he stands at his lord's table, carving his meat. Jankyn, so pictured, obviously represents the values of *Hof* rather than *Gericht*. But although he speaks *in game*, Jankyn makes a fine show of observing scientific and philosophical principles, and his discourse is dignified by an impressive-looking rubric. Jankyn can vouch for the appropriateness and commentative efficiency of Thomas's text since he has himself employed such a language earlier in the day; he glossed the friar's church sermon with "fartes thre" (3.2284). His prize-winning interpretation exemplifies an ingenuity that is typical of a certain strain of canon law: rather than losing itself in abstractions, it deals directly with the nitty-gritty details of the case in hand.[68] Rather than embodying any particular principle of law, though, the triumph of Jankyn attests to the capacity of village society to solve problems internally, without setting them down on paper or calling on outside authorities. Jankyn shows admirable professional sense in securing terms of payment before providing the lord with his interpretation. Thomas's fart (like the dead body of Ciappelletto in *Decameron* 1.1) is translated into fresh cultural capital, achieving lasting memorialization in the new gown that Jankyn will wear upon his back. The friar must retain his anger, or let it disperse; he must, at any event, leave the village.

The trajectory of Friar John through the *Tale* is easy to represent:

———————→ parish church ———————→ peasant hovel ———————→ lord's court ———————→

Figure 3. The movement of Friar John through the three domains of the feudal village

In the *Summoner's Tale*, the feudal village operates as efficiently as a Boccaccian city-state in marking and expelling a rapacious intruder. The lord and lady exercise their authority only *through* their attempts to follow principles of law, thereby upholding the dictum of the English jurist Bracton: "Car la dame ne le sire n'en est seigneur se non dou dreit."[69] They maintain credibility by recognizing the limits of their capacities (and of their legal thinking); they turn the matter over to Jankyn and accept his opinion. Boccaccio's country-dwellers, we have noted, are entirely defenseless against the fast talk of urban clerics. What, then, is at stake in Chaucer's championing of the traditional tripartite structure of village society? We might suspect Chaucer of sentimentality, but not of nostalgia: the *Tale* is not assigned to a distant past, and the ethic of commercial calculation practiced by Jankyn, who knows how interpretative knowledge might best be commodified, would do credit to any Boccaccian merchant.[70] The central gesture of the *Tale*—the expulsion of the friar from the peasant body—proves definitive, but only once it has been examined and ratified by the lord's "court"; Thomas is *not* granted the authority to expel the friar, only to shift him from the second to the third domain of village society.[71] This powerful but qualified gesture seems in keeping with the historical practices of the late fourteenth-century English village.[72] Lords looked to peasant labor as their chief source of income. They were obliged to interest themselves in peasants in order to extract rents and services from them, but their chief interests lay elsewhere. Without full-time officials or police, they were obliged to enlist the peasantry to extract surplus from the peasantry, delegating powers to peasant reeves, bailiffs, aletasters, pledges, jurors, affeerers, and so on. Even when freed from the mutual obligations of feudalism, lords served their own interests best by respecting the complex internal mechanisms of traditional village society. Since the peasantry was already paying dues to the other constituent elements of feudalism (the parson and the lord of the manor), plus a third level of taxation to Westminster, it made little sense for local lords to encourage ties of *bretherhede* between friars and peasants.

One question remains: why, in representing a feudal community that shows exemplary strength in repelling rapacious outsiders, does Chaucer choose the remote location of Holderness? Perhaps because true *dominium* over this region was held not by the lord of the *Summoner's Tale* but by Queen Anne of Bohemia, "ad terminum vitae suae."[73] The ultimate power appealed to in the *Summoner's Tale* turns out, after all, to be both political and metaphysical: the evocation of that mysterious bond between peasant and royalty that was to prove so crucial to the course of events in 1381.

After 1381: Listening for the Countryside

Chaucer's few references to the Peasants' Revolt, or English Rising, of 1381 tend to register the collective action of peasants as *sound*: wide-orbiting Saturn claims to hear "the murmure and the cherles rebellyng" in the *Knight's Tale* (1.2459); the *Nun's Priest's Tale* evokes a village barnyard scene that puts the narrator in mind of the sound of murderous and rebellious peasants:

> So hydous was the noyse—a, benedicitee!—
> Certes, he Jakke Straw and his meynee
> Ne made nevere shoutes half so shrille
> Whan that they wolden any Flemyng kille.   (7.3393–97)

This "noyse," of course, is nothing more than the pursuit of a fox that has run off with a cockerel. It is, one should note, an organized pursuit and a noise with a purpose: the widow has raised the hue and cry, the most important mechanism for immediate judicial redress in both rural and urban areas.[74] Her cry is soon taken up by other village dwellers, wielding staves:

> And cryden, "Out! Harrow and weylaway!
> Ha, ha! The fox!" and after hym they ran,
> And eek with staves many another man.   (7.3380–82)

Such representations of peasant collectivities as sound, heard at a distance or kept at a distance through farcical, mock-epic framing, are consistent with contemporary representations of 1381 as an accident of nature, comparable to a plague or an earthquake.[75] The "shoutes . . . shrille" attributed to the rebel Fleming-killers in Chaucer's text are also heard in a range of contemporary chronicles. According to the Benedictine chronicler Walsingham, the execution of Archbishop Sudbury was accompanied by a *clamor horrendissimus*: as Sudbury was dragged to Tower Hill, "a most horrible shouting broke out, not like the clamor normally produced by men, but of a sort which enormously exceeded all human noise and which could only be compared to the wailings of the inhabitants of hell." Walsingham finds this nightmarish memory of inhuman peasant noise difficult to shake, once broached. "Such shouts," he continues, "used to be heard whenever the rebels beheaded anyone or destroyed houses, for as long as God permitted their iniquity to be unpunished. Words could not be heard among their horrible shrieks but rather their throats sounded with the bleating of sheep, or, to be more accurate, with the devilish voices of peacocks."[76] This barnyard nightmare came home to haunt Walsingham when a group of rebels under William Grindcobbe besieged his monastery at St. Albans and then beheaded a prisoner: "With a devilish shouting which they had learnt in London at the time of the archbishop's execution, they carried off his head and fixed it to the top of the pillory."[77] In Yorkshire, this shout had a name: "hountays," shouted as the rebels dragged a citizen of Scarborough from his home to imprisonment and decapitation, is set into the Latin deposition as an alien, mysterious term: "cum maxima voce vocata *hountays*, usque ad prisonam ibidem duxerunt."[78]

The ears of certain Chaucerian narrators (such as the Knight and the Nun's Priest) are primed, it seems, to detect similar signs of trouble, "sounds" or *noyse*, from the English countryside. Many hints of such sounds can be heard by listening attentively to rural England as represented in the *Canterbury Tales*. Boccaccio, we have noted, respects the power of the city-state and derides the countryside; the Florentine regime he had served was finally toppled from within the city-state by unemployed wool-workers in 1378. Chaucer, by contrast, respects the powers of the English countryside; the great rebellion of 1381 that captured the Tower of London, burned the Savoy, massacred Flemings, and beheaded the Archbishop of Canterbury began (so tradition and the *Anonimalle Chronicle* have it) in three villages in the "marshee contree" of southern Essex.[79] What happened in 1381 could (like the plague) break out again. It is not surprising, then, that the deep countryside is not a place where Chaucer's nerve-racked courtiers and urbanites go to ease their minds: they seek out, rather, dream visions and allegorical gardens (which remain tightly annexed to the court).[80]

Despite Spenser's best efforts to reconfigure him as "Tityrus," Chaucer (unlike his Italian contemporaries) took little interest in pastoral.[81] His neo-Boethian *Former Age* envisages a drastic regimen for its "lambish peple" that is, if anything, prepastoral: "paleis-chaumbres" and the "swety bysinesse" of mining had not been invented then, but neither had the mill, the handmill, or the plough.[82] Unlike most postmedieval pastoral, Chaucer's representations of country scenes resist receding into the evocation of an earlier and better rural past. It is strange to observe later English writers harking back to a Chaucerian England that finds no counterpart in Chaucer's writings (except, perhaps, in the Lombard village lorded over by Walter); they evoke "an idealization of feudal and immediately post-feudal values . . . an order based on settled and reciprocal social and economic relations of an avowedly total kind."[83] Such an idealizing vision could only be dreamed after the historical infrastructure of "feudal and immediately post-feudal England" had been swept away: Sidney's *Arcadia*, Raymond Williams reminds us, "was written in a park which had been made by enclosing a whole village and evicting the tenants."[84] The earl of Leicester, patron of letters, similarly depopulated whole villages through acts of enclosure: "I am like the ogre in the old tale," he observed, "and have eaten up all my neighbors."[85]

In 1549, just two years after the abolition of guilds and fraternities, Parliament made it treason for forty or more persons to assemble for two hours or more with the intention of destroying enclosures, parks, fishponds, burning hayricks, or killing game. Elizabethan statutes reduced rights of association in the countryside still further by making it a capital felony for twelve persons to remain assembled for one hour once a magistrate had read the order to disperse.[86] Resistance to the engrossment of farms and the enclosure of land continued long after Sydney's *Arcadia* had been written, of course. In the eighteenth century (in a famous formulation of Marx) "the law itself now becomes the instrument by which the people's land is stolen";[87] enclosure by then, according to E. P. Thompson, "was a plain enough case of class robbery, played according to fair rules of property and law laid down by a parliament of property-owners and lawyers."[88] All this helps further explain why, after the fifteenth century, Boccaccio's *Decameron* (where urbane wit is often proved and sharpened by degrading the countryside) seems more in step with the times than the archaic landscapes of Chaucer.

What might pass as archaism for Chaucer's sixteenth-century readers might, to his contemporaries, have seemed like a reasonable historical assessment: that urbanites who fool with country matters will not survive unscathed. Fragment 1 leaves Nicholas and Aleyn with marks of the countryside, respectively, on rump and nose. In Fragment 3, attempts to carry to the countryside the ideological baggage of urban organizations—*bretherhede, confraternitas*—are repudiated; whether by metaphysical intervention or social regulation, the countryside proves capable of saving itself. The attempt of Friar John to sell the benefits of guild membership to villagers seems particularly misguided, since (according to Holt and Rosser) "the guild evidently provided, within the rootless and shifting world of the town, a substitute for the natural supportive strength of the extended family which was more characteristic of the countryside."[89]

Chaucer's recognition of the powers of the countryside—the work site of nine-tenths of his English contemporaries—takes the form not of fabliau realism or fairyland fantasy but of a peculiar combination of the two. Three of his most enigmatic figures (each charged with mysterious metaphysical powers) are first encountered at liminal rural sites: both the Wife of Bath's old wife and the *Friar's Tale*'s yeoman are first glimpsed "under a forest syde" (3.990, 1380); the rioters in the *Pardoner's Tale* who set out for "that village" where Death is to be found encounter the old man "Right as they wolde han troden over a stile" (6.706, 712).[90] Part of the power of these figures comes from the suggestion that they are both in and of the countryside; their individual charisma seems continuous with something greater immanent in the folds of the landscape. Such mystery (a term which, by the fourteenth century, blended or confused theological with vocational terms of reference)[91] seems even to surround figures who out of their rural contexts might seem more prosaic. The rural landscapes that the Wife of Bath evokes serve to compound, perhaps even stand in for, the "mystery" of female sexuality; the "cote and hood of grene" worn by the weapon-laden Yeoman in the *General Prologue* (1.103) have for some readers bestowed mysterious charm upon the most basic and brutal of rural functions, protection of the lord's domain.[92] Perhaps the most complex and unlikely exemplification of this two-way tension is the Reeve, as characterized by the *General Prologue*. There seems little that is mysterious (in the modern sense) about the Reeve, who runs his life by "rekenynge" and thinks of crop yields, inventories of pigs, horse, and poultry, and new ways to swindle his underage master. And yet even the Reeve, this most prosaic of characters, is enfolded by the mysterious color of the countryside. He does not sit upon the green like the old wife; he does not wear it like the Yeoman; but he lives in its shadow:

> His wonynge was ful faire upon an heeth;
> With grene trees yshadwed was his place.   (1.606–67)

Much has been made of the Miller's leading the pilgrims out of town with his bagpipe,[93] but it is worth noticing that it is the Reeve who brings up the rear: "And evere he rood the hyndreste of oure route" (1.622). One of the Reeve's notable skills is the sniffing out of "covyne" (1.604), factional treachery, a term much on the mind of London authorities in the late fourteenth century.[94] It seems fitting, then, that a rural watchdog should ride with everyone before him as the pilgrimage moves away from the city and into the countryside. It is a testimony to the powers of the English countryside that the Reeve, a figure who would be accorded no respect whatever in an Italian setting, should occupy such a place in the *Canterbury Tales*; even a Reeve, in Chaucer, comes charged with some hint of the mystery and authority of the rural landscape he inhabits.

Chapter 6

Absent City

Sweet Thames, run softly till I end my song

Whereas the countryside in Chaucer is both mysterious and powerful, the city is notable chiefly by its absence. *Troilus and Criseyde* manages to suggest something of the experience of a walled medieval city, and in 1381 London, often termed "New Troy," bore a resemblance to its ancient namesake in being walled, besieged, and finally overrun.[1] But although the possibilities of such historical repetition plainly unsettled Gower, driving him to some of his most vivid poetic imaginings,[2] the Troy of the *Troilus* plainly differs from Chaucer's London. Whereas the court, religious, and judicial lives of the fictional Trojans—from the singing of Antigone to the long parliament of Book 4—all transpire within a unified walled space, the lives of Chaucer and his compeers were conducted *between* such spaces: between, that is, London and Westminster. One of Chaucer's most problematic figures, the Pardoner, actually splits the physical space between these two distinct sites (he is "of Rouncivale," the guild hospital at Charing Cross).[3] And the pilgrimage itself does not actually begin in London. It begins south of the Thames in Southwark and moves us steadily away from the city walls. The projected return journey, which might encourage us to consider London as a *telos* fit to benefit from the socially regenerative effects of completed pilgrimage, is never made.[4] And Chaucer's solitary attempt at pure London fiction comes to an abrupt end after just 58 lines: "Of this cokes tale," writes the Hengwrt scribe, "maked Chaucer na moore."[5]

The London in which Chaucer lived and worked for much of his life yielded countless narratives of peculiarly urban forms of trickery, verbal dexterity, imaginative extravagance, and low deceit: material that, given the precedent of Boccaccio's city-centered narratives, surely offered tempting fictional possibilities for Chaucer. The English poet, however, refuses them. And whereas Boccaccio brilliantly imagines a unifying urban ideology developed through the agency of a humble Florentine baker (*Decameron* 6.2), the *Tale* of Chaucer's London Cook lapses quickly into silence. Even in its short span, Chaucer's London *Tale* comes to suggest suspicion of associational forms rather than celebration of them. How does Chaucer's city come to be so evasive, so difficult to imagine, when the Chaucerian countryside is so powerful?

London and Southwark

London's absence from Chaucer is rendered particularly striking when the *Canterbury Tales* is read against its Italian twin, Boccaccio's *Decameron*. Boccaccio's text begins and ends in Florence. The form of governance that orders its storytelling is established in the church of Santa Maria Novella, a key site in both the religious and political history of the city. The rhetorical skills that the ten young Florentines take to the countryside will prove indispensable for the governance of the city once the plague has abated and civic life can be reestablished. Their tales feature dozens of historical Florentine protagonists and Florentine locales; the Sixth Day is entirely devoted to stories set in Florence.[6] The only figures in Chaucer's text that may be paired with historical personages are Chaucer himself and "Herry Bailey" (1.4358), who is presumably to be associated with the "Henricus Bayliff, Ostlyer" recorded by the Southwark Subsidy Rolls in 1380–81.[7] The "Cook of London" (1.4325) who names Herry Bailey identifies himself as " 'Hogge of Ware' " (1.4336). The Cook is himself addressed with facetious reverence by the Host as " 'gentil Roger' " (1.4353); he may be associated with the "Roger of Ware of London, Cook," a convicted nightwalker who figures twice in pleas of debt.[8]

The choice of a Southwark tavern, named after an ale tank,[9] as the gathering place for Chaucer's pilgrimage is at once plausible and arrestingly eccentric. Pilgrims from London to Canterbury often spent the night in Southwark so that they could begin their journey before the city gates were opened for the day: Chaucer's pilgrims, we should note, "made forward erly for to rise" (1.33). But there was nothing to prevent Chaucer from assembling his pilgrimage at a familiar London landmark: the cross at St. Paul's, for example. The effect of assembling at Southwark is to emphasize the randomness of this encounter between Chaucer and the "compaignie" (which is itself a random grouping, "by aventure yfalle / In felaweshipe," 1.26). And the business of establishing a form of governance in Southwark under the tutelage of an innkeeper must have seemed (to a London readership) comically misguided. Southwark functioned as a dumping ground and exclusion zone for early modern London: messy or marginal trades such as lime-burning, tanning, dyeing, brewing, inn-keeping, and prostitution flourished; criminals fleeing London courts and aliens working around London trade regulations found a home there. Southwark was a suburb of London but also an independent parliamentary borough (albeit a borough lacking a charter of incorporation). The "tangled and disharmonious snarl of jurisdictions"[10] overlapping in Southwark is a historian's nightmare. Southwark recognized no single authority but was divided between five manorial jurisdictions (four in ecclesiastical hands; one owned first by the Crown and later by the city); each had its own set of courts. Southwark's parishes were only partially coterminous with these manorial jurisdictions, and the boundaries of the aggregate term "Southwark" vary from document to document. The Crown controlled the courts and prisons of the Marshalsea and King's Bench and exercised its authority through permanent county officers such as sheriffs, escheators, coroners, and justices. The city of London struggled tirelessly to swallow up (sometimes by legal tactics, sometimes by simple encroachment) the unchartered community on its south bank that continually undermined the monopolies and privileges of its trade and craft guilds. The charter of 1444 confirming the city's rights in the Guildable manor speaks of the "diverse doubts, opinions, differences, ambiguities, controversies, and dissensions" [11] that had characterized relations between London and Southwark since time immemorial. This is the site at which Chaucer's pilgrim body recognizes Herry Bailey as "oure governour" (1.813).

The *Canterbury Tales'* relationship to London at its opening differs markedly, then, from that of the *Decameron* to Florence. Whereas Boccaccio establishes a form of associational governance within the city that is then carried to the countryside, Chaucer establishes no form of governance until his pilgrimage has left the city; his order of storytelling is then established at a place experienced by fourteenth-century London as a challenge to its own integrity, as "a perpetual jurisdictional affront." [12] Southwark defined itself against London politically but, economically, found London indispensable. The name of Southwark, in short, identifies governance as a problematic issue, takes this issue out of the city, and yet cannot quite leave the city behind.

Having emphasized the centrifugal impulse of Chaucer's Canterbury pilgrimage—its quick self-distancing from London as a point of origin—we should also recognize that there was much movement in the opposite direction in late fourteenth-century England. Religious and secular magnates continued to maintain residences in the capital and to buy up and rent out properties. The royal household moved in a tighter circle around London and more of its administrative apparatus was permanently housed at Westminster. [13] Foreigners, *uplondish*, and *outlandish* men sought out the royal court, the law courts, the Inns of Court and the international markets; young men and women from every part of Britain came to serve their time as apprentices, find work, or contract marriages. Both modern historians and medieval Londoners tend to speak of London as a fluid entity, a place to which people come and go, rather than as a permanent, sharply delimited site. [14] And yet, at the same time, London authorities were keen to represent London as "the capital city and the watch-tower of the whole realm," and to insist "that from the government thereof other cities and places do take example." [15]

Narrative and Governance in Fourteenth-Century London

Chaucer's London was, by postpandemic standards, a metropolis: the poll tax returns of 1377 indicate a population more than three times greater than that of York or Bristol, its nearest English rivals. And although Chaucer wrote little of the city he lived, worked, and wrote in, there are many contemporary texts that speak in detail to the specifically *urban* character of London life. Many of them feature the kind of tricksters and impersonators that flourish as the urban division of labor grows ever more complex. One such character, a Welshman called John Haselwode (alias John Harehull) goes on a tour of London breweries with a white staff in his hand, purporting to be "a taker of ale for our Lord the King." [16] Another, Roger Clerk of Wandlesworth (Wandsworth), offers to exercise his skill as a physician to cure the bodily infirmities of Johanna, wife of Roger atte Hacche. Having received a down payment of 12 pence, Roger Clerk hangs a scroll (*cedulam*) around Johanna's neck upon which, he says, "was written a good charm for fevers." Later, on being asked what the words of this charm of his were, Roger replies:

"*Anima Christi, sanctifica me; corpus Christi, salva me; in isanguis Christi, nebria me; cum bonus Christus tu, lava me.*" And the parchment being then examined, not one of those words was found written thereon. And he was then further told by the Court, that a straw beneath his foot [sub pede suo] would be of just as much avail for fevers, as this charm [carmen] of his was; whereupon, he fully granted that it would be so.[17]

The court in question is that composed of the mayor and aldermen who sat in the Chamber of the London Guildhall. The letter-books which record their proceedings usually employ Latin, but often switch to Anglo-Norman or Middle English when noting proclamations and ordinances. *Letter-Book H*, the volume that most concerns this chapter, is a work of impressive dimensions (12 inches by 17 inches) and, with some noteworthy exceptions, unhurried execution.[18] Its narratives of crimes and misdemeanors often detail some quite spectacular examples of native wit and inventiveness. In 1380, for example, John Warde and Richard Lyneham, two men considered "stout enough to work for their food and raiment," came before the court accused of impersonating mutes through an elaborate pantomime employing pincers, an iron hook, two ell measures, and (so the Latin entry tells us)

a piece of leather, in shape like part of a tongue, edged with silver, and with writing around it, to this effect, —"*this is the tonge of John Warde*"; with which instruments, and by means of diverse signs, they gave many persons to understand that they were traders [mercatores], in token whereof they carried the said ell measures; and that they had been plundered by robbers of their goods; and that their tongues had been drawn out with the said hook, and then cut off with the pincers; they making a horrible noise, like unto a roaring, and opening their mouths; where it seemed to all who examined the same, that their tongues had been cut off: to the defrauding of other poor and infirm persons, and in manifest deceit of the whole of the people, etc.[19]

This piece of street theater, which seems no great crime by modern standards, evidently shocked and scandalized the mayoral court. The "evil intent
and falsity" of the malefactors are denounced at some length and the punishment meted out to them is exceptionally severe. On the Monday, Wednesday,
and Friday before the Feast of St. Simon and St. Jude they are to be placed
upon the pillory, with their pincers, hook, leather tongue, and ell measures
hanging around their necks; they are then to be jailed in Newgate until further notice. The Guildhall was evidently determined to stage some theater of
its own (a one-week run) "to the end that other persons might beware of such
and the like evil intent, falsity, and deceit." What accounts for this severe
reaction by the London authorities? The reference to "other poor and infirm
persons" offers one line of explanation: both secular and religious authorities
in this period showed a new and determined resolve to discriminate between
"genuine" paupers (who had a right to beg because of physical infirmity) and
sturdy beggars (who could work but were too idle to do so).[20] A second line of
explanation, a complementary rather than alternative one, concerns the false
signifier of the text-inscribed severed tongue. This scandalous tongue is isolated by the *Letter-Book* through a momentary switch from Latin to Middle
English; its strange objectification puts us in mind of the celebrated tongue
of Chaucer's Pardoner.[21] City authorities needed to uphold respect for the
integrity of symbolic representation within the city, since their own precarious authority could often itself only be imaged through the suggestive power
of symbolic drama. One such histrionic high point occurred in 1387, when
the right hand of William Hughlot was laid upon the block in the Guildhall
Court, ready to be chopped off by an axe held by one of the sheriff's officers.[22]
The right hand that Hughlot was about to lose had earlier stabbed a barber in
his house in Fleet Street, assaulted an alderman, and wounded one of the Fleet
Street constables. But Hughlot's hand was never amputated because at the
last minute John Rote, the alderman he had attacked, asked "that execution
of the judgment aforesaid might be remitted unto him." Hughlot was then
sentenced to imprisonment for a year and a day and "condemned to suffer the
disgraceful punishment of the pillory." But he never went to the pillory and
was released from prison just nine days later. Such leniency is soon explained.
It is exercised, the *Letter-Book* tells us, "in reverence for our said Lord the
King, whose servant the said William then was." The mayor and aldermen are
at pains to emphasize, throughout the document, that they too are officers of
the king. But even as officers of the king they were not bold enough to strike
off the right hand of someone in royal service: they settled for a lesser drama,
in which Hughlot was obliged, on the day of his release from prison, to carry
a lighted wax candle from the Guildhall to the Church of St. Dunstan, the
parish in which he had committed his crime.[23]

The light sentencing of William Hughlot is in sharp contrast to the fate
of two men convicted of breaking into the house of a "citizen and mercer

of London" in 1390.[24] The brief entry devoted to their trial concludes as follows: "the said John Prentys and John Markyngtone are guilty of the felony aforesaid. Therefore they are to be hanged. Chattels of the same felons there are none etc." The fact that the two men have no possessions, that they are men of no substance, means that they have nothing with which to pay for their crimes except their miserable lives. This ideal of commutative justice is dramatized in the punishment of the pillory (which is generally reserved for people of lower degree): the malefactor is reunited with his crime as he stands with the symbols or instruments of his transgression around his neck. John Haselwode the would-be ale-taker stood with his white wand at his side; Roger Clerk the quack physician, having been led through the city with trumpets and pipes on a saddleless horse, stood with his magic spell and a whetstone around his neck and urinals hanging before and behind him.[25] Such imaging of justice, which freezes malefactors in time at the moment of their crime, is most perfectly represented by Dante's *Inferno*: we think, for example, of the Florentine usurers sitting in the seventh circle with their purses hanging around their necks, each one decorated by their family coat of arms.[26] The lower reaches of the *Inferno* are encompassed by the walls of a city; Dante's Hell is a subterranean version of Dante's Florence.

But although the narratives in the London letter-books terminate with a Dantean imaging of justice—an hour in the pillory prefigures and warns of an eternity of punishment—the narrative energy preceding such closure is more strongly reminiscent of Boccaccio. These texts do, after all, issue from a group of merchant capitalists that compares with the *Decameron*'s first audience and matches Boccaccio's mercantile origins. And they reflect a comparably detailed understanding of the urban milieu that they seek to control and regulate. In unraveling a fraud case in 1391, for example, *Letter-Book H* takes us on a journey through the streets and suburbs of London almost as complicated as that of Andreuccio of Perugia through Naples (*Decameron*, 2.5). We follow a cloth merchant's servant through various wards, parishes and hostelries inside and outside the city walls until he is finally locked into a room at "'Le Walssheman sur le Hoope,' in Fletestret, in the Parish of St. Martin without Ludgate, in the suburb of London"; here he is finally parted from his master's merchandise by a con artist posing as a nobleman's servant.[27]

Such a detailed concern with the regulation and division of time and space in the city is a constant feature of the letter-books. When we read their narratives in sequence we begin to see how the lines of power in the city run. On folio cxiii of *Letter-Book H*, for example, we find the names of eleven women who have paid the sum of 13s 4d each for the privilege of maintaining market stalls at specific points around the High Cross of Cheapside for one year.[28] On the reverse side of the same folio (two pages later in Riley's *Memorials of London*, which breaks up the sequence of the manuscript) we find that these fees are to be diverted to one John Charney by virtue of his office as *venator communitatis London'*, "Common Hunt for the Commonalty of London." Common Hunt was responsible for overseeing the stables and kennels maintained for the use of the citizens of London. The art of city government here, then, consists in a masculine oligarchy selling city space to women traders so that London citizens can pursue their aristocratic pretensions outside the city walls through the art of hunting. Such models of expropriation were not, of course, made visible to the general public. The *Letter-Book* keeps to Latin here and only turns to the vernacular when it wishes the citizens, "foreigns," and aliens of London to take notice of its ordinances and proclamations.

I am not suggesting that Chaucer spent his evenings leafing through record books at the Guildhall. It is worth noting, however, that a good number of letter-book cases record the participation, as prosecutor or spokesman, of Ralph Strode, common serjeant of the city of London from 1373–85. Strode, who died in 1387, is very probably the "philosophical Strode" who is briefed to "correcte" the finished *Troilus and Criseyde*, "there nede is" (5.1857–58).[29] Chaucer himself appears in *Letter-Book G* in 1374 on the occasion of his leasing the city-owned house above Aldgate.[30] All in all, then, he had ample opportunity to experience and meditate upon the functioning and governance of urban space long before he left England for Florence and Milan.

Urban Narrative: Italian Precedents for Chaucer

Why, then, does Chaucer miss or pass up the possibility of developing the kind of urban narrative we associate with the Italian Trecento? It is worth noting, in pursuit of this question, that the local urban scenes of Dante and Boccaccio are set securely within great and long-pedigreed systems of ideological framing. Dante deploys the greatest framework imaginable: his sunken city is reached only by the path that leads us beneath the Trinitarian inscription of *Inferno* 3, which begins: "PER ME SI VA NE LA CITTÀ DOLENTE" ("Through me you enter the woeful city"). Here, beyond this inscription, the familiar mechanisms of urban justice are regulated with superhuman impartiality. Boccaccio, however, operates above ground within an ideological space that may be read in conjunction with a Florentine tradition of mercantile historiography.[31] This begins with Giovanni Villani, who assigns the moment of inspiration for his *Chronicle* to 1300, the year of Dante's imaginary journey through the afterlife, and makes a Dante-like attempt to square events in Florence with an all-encompassing, God-guided scheme of historical explanation. Matteo, who took up the *Chronicle* on Giovanni's death, is interested more in the city-state of Florence and less in any putative universal history of which it might form part. By the time we get to Goro Dati at the turn of the next century the Florentine state has become the transcendent subject of history: "The commune," says Dati, "cannot die."[32] The *Decameron* situates itself, in time of composition, revision, and ideological positioning, somewhere near the midpoint of this Trecento tradition of merchant-class chroniclers. The imaginative power of the afterlife makes itself felt, but the compelling confidence of Boccaccio's text is invested not in the interpretive power of religion but in the city-state's ability to regulate itself through its own urban mechanisms and to identify and expel those who threaten its internal equilibrium.[33]

Chaucer, like Boccaccio, explicitly rejects the Dantean option of writing a text with pretensions to universal knowledge.[34] Yet he is also denied the Boccaccian option of tapping a vernacular tradition that is gradually adapting the religious universalism of monastic chronicling to the market-driven exigencies of urban society. London was close to the center of chronicle writing in Chaucer's time, but was not the subject of it; there was no tradition of merchant-class chronicling in fourteenth-century England.[35] We might make an exception here for *Letter-Book H*, which suddenly turns into a chronicle of sorts in June 1381. On the same folio that records Ralph Strode's prosecution of a poulterer who had attempted to sell eighteen pigeons, "putrid and stinking, and an abomination to mankind," we hear of "the most wondrous and hitherto unheard-of prodigies that have ever happened in the City of London."[36] The hero of this narrative is "Sir William Walworth, the then Mayor"; the climactic scene is played out at Smithfield, where Mayor Walworth rides at Watt Tyler with peasants to one side of him and king, lords, knights, esquires, and citizens on the other. The narrative concludes, after the jousting mayor has unseated and slain the rebel captain, with the mayor and his accomplices being knighted in the field beneath the royal banner. When the letter-book scribe turns historian, then, he sounds more like a chivalric chronicler than a mercantile one. Such uncertainty of style is not at all typical of the Florentine tradition of merchant-class chronicling that precedes and follows the *Decameron*. There is, we have noted, continuous adaptation within this tradition to new political needs. Once Giovanni Villani's *Chronicle* has been silenced by the plague of 1348, the pressure to interpret every flood, fire, and falling chimney pot as a message from the Almighty eases considerably. But although later chroniclers are apt to identify the workings of Providence more closely with the exigencies of Florentine polity, they do not cut the cord that attaches them to the religious universalism of earlier generations. Boccaccio's representation of Florence in the *Decameron*, then, continues and extends a long-lived tradition of imagining and chronicling the city. Chaucer, in London, would find no equivalent resources.

Boccaccio was able to respond to the complex demands of postplague Florence with a brilliance and imaginative flexibility unknown to merchant-class chronicling. The Florentine republican regime of 1343–78 started out, we have noted, as one of the broadest-based regimes in the history of early modern Europe: shopkeepers, artisans, and tradesmen shared in the business of government with patrician merchants, bankers, and rentiers. But powerful class antagonisms remained. The greater guilds controling the major industries did not think that the principle of *libertas* should extend to include lower guildsmen; the shopkeepers and craftsmen of the lower guilds were keen to accentuate their own privileged status by keeping the lower classes out of office and preventing them from forming guilds of their own. No single group was trusted to hold office for very long and no citizens were trusted with the administration of justice; outsiders were hired on short, fixed-termed contracts. The republican regime, then, found itself subject to some basic and disabling ideological contradictions. It was keen to foster an ideal of *libertas* that put all members of a specific social group on level terms with one another. But although this might be achieved within the lowest and highest political forms of the commune, from the parish guild to the Signoria, the spaces between such constituent forms were strictly hierarchized. Some form of cultural production was required to challenge ideologies hostile to associative polity while concealing the internal divisions of such polity; hierarchized relations within the city should somehow be reconciled along a single plane of *aequitas*, of *unitas civium*. Boccaccio proved brilliantly adept at working such magic. His technique may be observed to particularly fine effect in the second *novella* of the *Decameron*'s Sixth Day.

Cisti the Baker and the Ideology of Associational Form

The *novella* begins with the narrator, Pampinea, questioning the logic of Fortune and Nature (and hence of class-structured society): Why do they sometimes assign a noble spirit to an inferior body or social calling? Pampinea insists that these powers show great wisdom in "burying their most precious possessions in the least imposing (and therefore least suspect) part of their houses, whence they bring them forth in the hour of greatest need" (6.2.5.; p. 485). Here, then, is an attempt to develop the notion of an intelligence buried deep within the lower reaches of Florentine society that will make itself heard at times of danger. In Pampinea's *novella* this intelligence is embodied by the unlikely figure of "Cisti fornaio," Cisti the baker.

The *novella* is set in 1300, the year in which a papal delegation visited Florence to make peace between two feuding factions, the Black and White Guelfs. Pope Boniface's representatives, who assumed the role of peacemakers, were in fact working to bring the propapal Blacks to power by exterminating the Whites. This is precisely what was to happen in November 1301, when Boniface turned to Charles de Valois and his army: the Whites were massacred or (like Dante) exiled, and the Blacks came to power. By beginning her *novella* with this papal delegation of 1300, then, Pampinea is indeed setting it at an "hour . . . of greatest need" for the citizenry of Florence.

According to Pampinea, the papal delegation was lodged during its visit to Florence under the roof of Messer Geri Spina, a prominent Florentine merchant and friend of the pope. Most mornings they would walk with their host past the Church of Santa Maria Ughi, beside which Cisti had his bakery. Cisti realizes that it would show "gran cortesia" (6.2.10) to offer Messer Geri and the papal envoys some of his delicious wine; "but, being conscious of the difference in rank between himself and Messer Geri, he considered it would be presumptuous of him to issue an invitation" (p. 486). And so he resorts to the stratagem of sitting outside his door each day, dressed in a freshly laundered apron, with white wine cooled in a bucket and spotless wineglasses. He drinks his wine just as Messer Geri is passing with the ambassadors: "He then seated himself in the doorway, and just as they were passing, he cleared his throat a couple of times and began to drink this wine of his with so much relish that he would have brought a thirst to the lips of a corpse [venir voglia a' morti]" (6.2.12; p. 486).

Cisti dares not speak across the difference in social rank that divides him from Messer Geri and the papal envoys, but in clearing his throat to drink he both draws attention to his lowly status (plebeians customarily spat and freed their throats from catarrh before drinking) and inscribes his social superiors within this common human desire to drink cool wine in hot weather. By the second day, Messer Geri has been seduced. Cisti fetches a bench from his bakery, and serves his guests from a small flagon of his best wine. This becomes a regular occurrence. When the diplomatic mission is concluded, Messer Geri holds a magnificent banquet, to which he invites some of the most distinguished citizens of Florence; he also invites Cisti, who cannot be persuaded to attend the "magnifico convito." [37] Messer Geri then orders one of his servants to take a flask to Cisti, so that each of his guests may be served with half a glass of the exquisite wine during the first course. The servant replaces the small flask with a huge one and presents it to Cisti. When Cisti sees this, he says, "My son, Messer Geri has not sent you to me" (6.2.20). Cisti, a man of noble qualities, can read this huge flask as a counterfeit sign; Messer Geri could not have sent it to him. The servant returns to Messer Geri, and reports Cisti's words. Messer Geri sends the servant back, briefed to repeat that he is sending the servant to *him*, Cisti; and if Cisti should give the same answer, he is to ask "to whom I am sending you" (p. 487). The servant, returning with the huge flask, does as he is told and so comes to ask the question:

"Adunque," disse il famigliare "a cui mi manda?"
Rispuose Cisti: "A Arno." (6.2.23–24)

"So then," said the servant, "to whom is he sending me?"
Cisti replied: "To the Arno."

When these words are reported back to him, Messer Geri demands to see the flask that his servant had presented to Cisti. On seeing the gigantic glassware, he immediately understands the force of Cisti's comment. Having scolded the servant, he sends him back to Cisti with the small flask. Cisti now acknowledges that the flask has been sent to him; he fills it up and sends it back. A few days later, he fills a small cask with wine of the same vintage and sends that along too. He then, finally, visits Messer Geri and explains the rationale for his actions. His visit is not, strictly speaking, necessary: the only thing he now needs to explain is the significance of sending Messer Geri his wine. In an extraordinary closing sentence, Cisti takes the opportunity to inscribe himself in what can only be described as a relationship of feudal vassalage:

"Ora, per ciò che io non intendo d'esservene più guardiano, tutto ve l'ho fatto venire: fatene per innanzi come vi piace." (6.2.29)

"Now, since I do not intend to be the guardian of the wine any longer, I have let it all be sent to you: do with it henceforth as you please."

Cisti suggests that as *guardiano* of the wine he has enjoyed *possessio* of it, and *usus fructi*, but now he returns it to the *dominium* of Messer Geri. Messer Geri, for his part, prizes Cisti's gift and thanks him "as profusely as the occasion seemed to warrant" (p. 488): he cannot appear to be in Cisti's debt, since this would disturb the dialectical mutuality of the feudal bond. But the bond can be acknowledged as a permanent one: "E sempre poi per da molto l'ebbe e per amico" ("And from then on he held him as a man of worth and as a friend for life," 6.2.30).

Boccaccio is not suggesting that Florence should resolve its political difficulties through a revival of the vassalic bond. There is, however, a kind of *eros* that grows between the two men as they come to recognize one another, one that is best expressed through the suggestive power of feudal relations. The language and structure of courtly love is, after all, deeply indebted to the founding metaphors of feudalism. The metaphors of postfeudal society in which we speak not of bonds but of contracts do not have the ideological force of feudal mutualities. But although he defers to the vertical plane of feudal hierarchizing, Boccaccio also insists upon the lateral, associative aspects of social relations: his *novella* sees a ceaseless movement back and forth across city space. It falls to Cisti, the Florentine baker, to alert Messer Geri to the importance of this lateral dimension. He initiates this process while Messer Geri is moving across Florence, in the company of papal envoys, between the headquarters of the White and Black Guelfs, the factions that have torn Florence apart for generations. Once these envoys have left the city, a new diplomatic mission is conducted across the face of Florentine society as the *famigliare* moves back and forth between the baker and the Black Guelf. Through this transfer of tokens and messages, which owes as much to the devices of courtly love as to the protocols of Florentine politics, Boccaccio suggests an ideal unity of the Florentine body politic in the face of external treachery.

Chaucer's Cook and the Limits of Associational Ideology

In moving from Florence to London, from Cisti the baker to Perkyn the apprentice, we should note that the teller of each tale is representative of the city about which they speak. Pampinea, the oldest of Boccaccio's women, is the guiding intelligence of Boccaccio's *brigata*. She conceives of the plan for an organized flight from Florence, works out the ground rules for the *brigata's* governance, and rules as queen for the First Day. Chaucer's Cook, who speaks twice of "oure citee" (1.4343, 4365), is the only pilgrim to associate the pilgrimage collectively with London. He is also the only pilgrim to be explicitly identified as a Londoner: the five guildsmen he serves as cook are assumed to be from London only on the basis of their association with him. But although he is twice identified as a "Cook of London" and is said to be a connoisseur of "Londoun ale" (1.382), the Cook identifies himself as originating not from London but from Ware, a town in Hertfordshire thirty miles due north of the city. Ware had been a notorious trouble spot since the 1350s, when attempts to enforce the Statute of Laborers had led to rioting; the vicar of Ware and a local hermit were indicted for preaching that the Statute was wicked. In 1381 a subsequent vicar of Ware led a good cross-section of his townsmen on an attack against John of Gaunt's castle in Hertford; they then marched on to London and took a prominent part in sacking Gaunt's palace at the Savoy.[38]

The name of Ware, then, comes freighted with suggestions of unruliness or violence imported to the city from the provinces. And some of the details with which Chaucer's Cook is credentialed as a Londoner have disquieting or unsavory connotations. The Host's suggestion that many of the Cook's pasties have been doctored recalls an ordinance of 1379: no pasty maker in the City of London shall bake in pasties "rabbits, geese, and garbage, not befitting, and sometimes stinking, in deceit of the people"; no one shall purchase such "garbage" from the cooks of Bread Street or from the cooks of great lords.[39] And the Cook's familiarity with the language of Flemings (" 'sooth pley, quaad pley,' as the Flemyng seith," 1.4357) reminds us of the large-scale slaughter of Flemings that went on in London in 1381. The Cook's incorporation of a Flemish proverb into his own discourse seems on the face of it benign, if not impressively cosmopolitan. But in 1381, according to one chronicle, such an awareness of linguistic difference became the mechanism that led to murder: on being asked to say "Breede and Chese" by the London mob, the Flemings would say "Case and Brode" (*kaas en brood*) and so seal their fate.[40] The fact that the Cook knows some Flemish, then, does not mean that he is a friend of Flemings. He might have learned the language in a brothel, since many London prostitutes were of Flemish origin.[41]

The opening couplet of the *Cook's Tale* brings us directly to an intricate structure of social and political relationships set within "oure citee," the unifying term:

> A prentys whilom dwelled in oure citee,
> And of a craft of vitailliers was hee.   (1.4365–66)

Two sets of political relationship are suggested here, one defined internally and the other externally. The first, that of the apprentice to his master (there can be no apprentices without masters), is one of strict subordination with some overtones of feudal mutuality. An apprentice was enjoined to respect his master as his lord, his "seigneur"; one young man, apprenticed to his uncle, is directed to hold the stirrup while his master mounts his horse as a mark of respect and obedience.[42] The apprentice, who is by definition a "foreign," or noncitizen, elects to work for his master for a specified number of years in the hope of learning his master's craft and of eventually being sponsored for citizenship by his master's guild. But this ideal of an orderly hierarchy within the guild structure is immediately brought up against the political hostility that sets one guild against the next: "And of a craft *of vitaillers* was he." It would hardly be possible, for a contemporary audience, to think of the London victuallers without thinking of their binary pairing the nonvictuallers, and of the affrays, riots, and disputes between these rival parties that fill the London letter-books in the 1380s.[43] But our attention is soon distracted from such matters by some vigorous lines of physical description:

> Gaillard he was as goldfynch in the shawe,
> Broun as a berye, a propre shorte felawe,
> With lokkes blake, ykembd ful fetisly.   (1.4367–69)

Such fruit, animal, and grooming imagery puts the *Riverside* annotator in mind of both Alisoun and Absolon from the *Miller's Tale*.[44] Interestingly, though, we are not invited to make comparisons between the apprentice and the *General Prologue*'s Squire, although certain points of description clearly overlap:

> So hoote he lovede that by nyghtertale
> He sleep namoore than dooth a nyghtyngale.   (1.98–99)

> He was as ful of love and paramour
> As is the hyve ful of hony sweete.   (1.4372–73)

The squire and the apprentice are young men of comparable age and of comparable sexual energy living in the shadow of powerful masters. But whereas the squire's sexuality is seen as charming and innocuous (and is not associated with the energy of a professional killer),[45] that of the apprentice is at once ridiculous and dangerous. It is ridiculous in that any attempts to regulate it through the elegant, *fetys* decorums of courtly behavior only serve to remind us that the apprentice is a churl: he is dark in complexion, short in stature. Yet if this energy is left unregulated it poses an immediate threat to civil society or, more specifically, to "the shoppe":

> At every bridale wolde he synge and hoppe;
> He loved bet the taverne than the shoppe.
> For whan ther any ridyng was in Chepe,
> Out of the shoppe thider wolde he lepe—
> Til that he hadde al the sighte yseyn,
> And daunced wel, he wolde nat come ayeyn.   (1.4375–80)

The chief threat to the sober world of commerce here would seem to be a restless personal energy that cuts across the threshold of "the shoppe." But as the passage continues, this reckless individualism suddenly shows associative tendencies and a capacity for planning and organization:

> And gadered hym a meynee of his sort
> To hoppe and synge and maken swich disport;
> And ther they setten stevene for to meete,
> To pleyen at the dys in swich a streete.   (1.4381–84)

The term *meynee*, used over thirty times by Chaucer, is a slippery but indispensable term occupying that liminal space between the shop and the street: its primary meaning is "family, household"; its second "a body of retainers, attendants, dependents, or followers; a retinue, suite, train"; its third "a company of persons employed together or having a common object of association; an army, ship's crew, congregation, assembly, or the like."[46] *Meynee* is itself a neutral term (deriving from the Latin *mansionem*) that is rarely employed in neutral contexts: specific *meynees* are generally figured as a force for good or evil, as constructive or destructive of social and moral order. Chaucer speaks in one place of "the ryght ordene hous of so mochel a fadir and an ordeynour of meyne," at another of "he Jakke Strawe and his meynee": the same term covers both God Almighty and the leader of the Peasants' Revolt.[47] The occasion of its deployment in the *Cook's Tale* is particularly complex: it is applied to a group of young men who come together to agree on a time and place in the city so that they can reconstitute themselves as an organized body; they will then engage in the random business of dice-playing. This, according to the Cook, poses a direct and immediate threat to the master's business, his "chaffare" (1.4389): the rolling dice soon lead to the "box ful bare" (1.4390), a diminution of the master's capital. But we should note that it is not so much the vice of gaming that the *Tale* insists upon as the root of social evil, but rather the act of association that makes such evil possible. This emphasis dominates again once the master has given the apprentice his walking papers:

> And for ther is no theef withoute a lowke,
> That helpeth hym to wasten and to sowke
> Of that he brybe kan or borwe may,
> Anon he sente his bed and his array
> Unto a compeer of his owene sort.   (1.4415–19)

This new association of wasters makes capital from its own excesses: as the *Tale* breaks off a new shop arises to challenge that of the master; the dangerous sexuality of Perkyn returns as the energy that spins the wheels of commerce:

> of his owene sort,
> That lovede dys, and revel, and disport,
> And hadde a wyf that heeld for contenance
> A shoppe, and swyved for hir sustenance.   (1.4420–22)

This late invocation of heterosexual prostitution by way of delegitimizing relations between lower-class men is a strategy familiar from the London letter-books. Many motifs from Chaucer's *Tale* are developed in a case heard before Mayor Brembre in 1385. This concerns a woman called Elizabeth, wife of Henry Moring, who, "sub colore" of the art of embroidery, retained various female apprentices and ran a prostitution ring. Things went well until one of the apprentices, under pressure from her mistress, stole a breviary from a chaplain she was sleeping with.[48] Any comic potential this story might have had was entirely lost on the mayoral court: Elizabeth is to be put upon the "thewe," the pillory for women, and then taken to "some Gate of the City, and there be made to forswear the City, and the liberty thereof, to the effect that she would never again enter the same." Through such dramas of punishment and expulsion the city authorities were able to suggest that their political interventions were motivated by a concern for the city's moral welfare. And by associating prostitution with unruly gatherings they are able both to discredit such gatherings and to find a pretext for breaking them up:

Also (Item)—whereas many and divers affrays, broils, and dissensions, have arisen in times past, and many men have been slain and murdered, by reason of the frequent resort of [compaignie], and consorting with, common harlots, at taverns, brewhouses of *huckesteres*, and other places of ill-fame [autres lieus deshonestes], within the said city, and the suburbs thereof; and more especially through Flemish women, who profess and follow such shameful and dolorous life [tiel orde et dolerouse vie].[49]

This proclamation of 1393 goes on to restrict prostitutes to two sites outside the city walls: Cock Lane in Smithfield and the Stews in Southwark. It specifically empowers city officers to remove the upper garment and hood of any prostitute they see outside these areas. If they bring these items of clothing to the Guildhall they "shall have the half thereof for their trouble." This drama of unveiling is consistent with what goes on at the end of the *Cook's Tale*. The wife of the compeer of Perkyn, the riotous apprentice, pretends ("for contenance") to be a respectable businesswoman, but as the couplet completes itself she is revealed to be a whore. Her discovered whoredom further discredits the association of apprentice Perkyn with "his owene sort" while justifying the suspicious, scrutinizing gaze of masterly and mayoral authority.

It seems that the more we attempt to contextualize Chaucer's *Cook's Tale*, the more strikingly it differentiates itself from the Boccaccian tale of Cisti the baker. In the Italian *novella* two men of differing class and culture meet, albeit fleetingly, at a common level of understanding. In the English *Tale*, the differences between master and apprentice prove so intractable that the master cuts the cord that binds them together. Whereas Boccaccio's narrative generates an associational ideology that will unite the city against external dangers, the social divisions within Chaucer's city widen dramatically as the *Tale* runs on. And two of the proverbs that frame and inform the Cook's narrative reflect an ideology not of association but of its opposite. The first, spoken by the Cook himself, borrows the wisdom of Solomon:

> "Ne bryng nat every man into thyn hous,"
> For herberwynge by nyghte is perilous.   (1.4331–32)

The text from Ecclesiasticus with which the Cook glosses the *Reeve's Tale* itself forms an excellent introduction to the fragmented and mistrustful London milieu he is about to evoke: "Bring not every man into thine house; for many are the plots of the deceitful man" (11.29). And the nugget of popular wisdom[50] that comes (mysteriously) to the master as he contemplates his wayward apprentice also counsels the wisdom of putting limits on forms of association:

> "Wel bet is roten appul out of hoord
> Than that it rotie al the remenaunt."   (1.4406–7)

This antiassociational rhetoric is remarkably consonant with that informing a mayoral proclamation of 1383. This proclamation, the earliest Middle English entry in the London letter-books, begins by situating king, mayor, sheriffs, and aldermen on a single vertical axis of power. It then goes to extraordinary lengths to find names for the kind of political association that threatens this hierarchy:

The mair, shirreues, and aldermen, and alle othere wyse wyth hem, that habbeth the gouernaille of the citee, under oure lige lord the kyng, by vertue of the chartre of oure franchise, comaundeth on the kynges bihalf, and on hire owene also, that noman make none congregaciouns, conuenticules, ne assembles of poeple, in priue nen apert, ne no more *craftes* than other men, with oute leue of the mair; ne ouer more in none manere ne make alliances, confederacies, conspiracies, ne obligaciouns, forto bynde men to gidre, forto susteyne eny quereles in lyuingge and deyengge to gidre; upon peyne of enpresonement.[51]

The proclamation goes on to give "euery fre man of the Citee" powers to arrest any such gathering "he may aspie": everything, in theory at least, from a parish guild meeting to the dice game in the *Cook's Tale*. London and Crown authorities had good reason to be nervous of "swich congregaciouns or covynes" in this period, of course.[52] The proclamation above dates from the turbulent period of Northampton's mayoralty.[53] The experience of 1381, when laborers had employed the associational mechanism of the "commissions of array" to organize themselves for their march on London,[54] was still a recent memory. And in 1388 Richard II was to issue writs at the Cambridge parliament requiring all guilds, fraternities, mysteries, and crafts to give an account of themselves.[55] Some London guilds, it seems, avoided making any kind of return; some London craft fraternities apparently tried to pass themselves off as parish guilds.[56] The parish guild of St. Bridget, Fleet Street, was anxious to point out that although it was called a fraternity, it was really not a fraternity, and that "theirs is no malicious gathering" even though they wear hoods on the Feast of St. Bridget's Translation. Besides, they have no money and no rents; some of the members named in the return are dead, others have moved away, and the rest, "since they heard the decision of the last parliament, have refused to pay anything towards keeping the premises made."[57] As the return runs on, this fraternity or guild of St. Bridget seems to evaporate before our eyes.

The mayors and aldermen of London, we have noted, were quick to claim that their authority descended directly from the king, especially when that authority was challenged or their dignity offended. A man who tells an alderman to kiss his *culum* (arse) is said to extend the same act of rebellion ("rebellionem") to his mayor and his monarch.[58] A butcher who objects to aldermen who ride on the pavement is speaking "in disparagement of our Lord the King" and is hence obliged to walk barefoot with a candle from Newgate through the Shambles (where his fellows ply their bloody trade) to the Guildhall Chapel.[59] But in borrowing authority from the king, the city oligarchy was, of course, making itself vulnerable to that very authority. In 1377 rumors spread that the city was about to be taken into the king's hands and the mayor replaced with a royally appointed captain. In 1392 Richard committed the mayor and sheriffs to prison and appointed his own warden. On February 20, 1388, Nicholas Brembre, mayor of London from 1383–86, was hanged by the Lords Appellant.[60] Such episodes remind us that although the London letter-books evoke an orderly, hierarchical vision of society, the class of merchant capitalists they (usually) represent was continuously engaged in political struggles with Crown, magnates, small masters, foreigns, aliens, and peasants. The signs of such struggles are visible not only in major political events of the kind noted above, but in the business of everyday life:

Whereas the foreign drapers [les drapers foreins] bringing woollen cloths to the City of London for sale, do sell the same in divers hostelries in secret, where they make many disorderly and deceitful bargains, as well between foreigner and foreigner [forein et forein], as between foreigner and freeman, to the great scandal and damage of all the City.[61]

The city is figured in this ordinance as an all-encompassing entity ("all the City") that is sensitive to acts of moral outrage; and yet this notion of a city is clearly predicated on acts of exclusion and disenfranchisement. Noncitizens were habitually referred to as "foreigns"; although a foreign might live in London he was not, in any meaningful political sense, a Londoner. So when foreigns got together within the walls of London this could only be interpreted by the city authorities as a threat to the city. In 1387, for example, an attempt by journeymen cordwainers to form a fraternity was taken as "a deed which notoriously redounds to the weakening of the liberties of the . . . city."[62] At such moments the mayoral oligarchy reveals itself as just one more associational form that is anxious to discourage attempts at association lower down the political scale. At other moments it acts to preserve one form of association by banning another. In 1396, for example, the mayoral court heard that "there had arisen no small dissension and strife between the masters of the trade of Saddlers, of London, and the serving men, called *yomen*, of that trade." This dispute centered on the right of the *yomen* to dress themselves in livery and meet as a fraternity. The *yomen* insist that they have been meeting like this since "time out of mind," and that their objects are religious. Their masters argue that this tradition is no more than thirteen years old,

and that under a certain feigned colour [colore] of sanctity, many of the serving-men [servientes] in the trade had influenced the journeymen among them [stipendiaros inter se excitabunt], and had formed covins thereon, with the object of raising their wages greatly in excess; to such an extent, namely, that whereas a master in the said trade could before have had a serving man or journey-man for 40 shillings or 5 marks yearly, and his board, now such a man would not agree with his master for less than 10 or 12 marks, or even 10 pounds, yearly; to the great deterioration of the trade.[63]

Here again, the decisive rhetorical gesture consists of ripping away a veil of apparent respectability or piety to reveal corruption and rascality beneath. This time, however, the unveiling process is credentialized not by a moral vocabulary or by the language of the church but by the language of the shop, an unadorned economic language that, in the mayoral court, carries the force of moral argument. This whole dispute, of course, is pitched very close to the ideological terrain of the *Cook's Tale*; further correspondences suggest themselves as the case progresses. Whereas apprentice Perkyn would leave the shop for street processions and weddings, these journeymen leave for funerals (a commonplace obligation for fraternity members):[64]

And further . . . the serving-men aforesaid, according to an ordinance made among themselves [inter eos factam], would oftentimes cause the journeymen of the said masters to be summoned by a bedel [bedellum], thereunto appointed, to attend at Vigils of the dead, who were members of the said fraternity . . . whereby the said masters were very greatly aggrieved, and were injured through such absenting of themselves by the journeymen, so leaving their labours and duties, against their wish.[65]

It is no great surprise to learn that the mayor and aldermen side with the masters in this dispute, determining that in future the *yomen* "should have no fraternity, meetings, or covins." It is evident that the masters would wish their *yomen* and workers to have no social life at all beyond the confines of the shop. Every conversation could spell trouble for business. And yet the pleasures and privileges of political association and of fraternity life are what every alderman, master, and master's wife lives for:

> It is ful fair to been ycleped "madame,"
> And goon to vigilies al bifore,
> And have a mantel roialliche ybore.   (1.376–78)

Chaucer here momentarily adopts the viewpoint of the women who are married to the five guildsmen in the *General Prologue*. Moments before he had set out the ambitions of the guildsmen themselves. Their qualifications for civic office are chiefly a matter of capital, property, and image (primarily self-image: note the atomizing "ech" and "everich," working satirically against the corporate pretensions of their being clothed "alle in o lyveree," 1.363):

> Wel semed ech of hem a fair burgeys
> To sitten in a yeldehalle on a deys.
> Everich, for the wisdom that he kan,
> Was shaply for to been an alderman.
> For catel hadde they ynogh and rente.   (1.369–73)

We have here two associational forms: the "solempne and . . . greet fraternitee" that employs the Cook, and the corporation of mayor and aldermen that this group dreams of becoming.[66] What, then, is the relationship of the Cook to these associational forms, real and imaginary? The Cook as described in the *General Prologue* is absorbed by his office: all lines but two are given over to boiling, tasting, roasting, simmering, baking and blancmange-making—except, of course, for that couplet devoted to the "mormal" (1.386, "a species of dry scabbed ulcer, gangrenous rather than cancerous") that he bears on his shin.[67] This sign of danger compounds with the unsettling suggestions concerning provenance and personal habits raised in the Cook's own *Prologue*.[68] And yet, once he has launched into his tale, we find him speaking lines worthy of a knight, alderman, or mayor:[69]

> Revel and trouthe, as in a lowe degree,
> They been ful wrothe al day, as men may see.   (1.4397–98)

The lower classes are viewed here from the elevated perspective of the *General Prologue*'s Guildhall dais (1.370). The argument is that the privileges and pleasures of association ("revel") can only be entrusted to those of proven virtue (dedicatees of "trouthe," such as masters, aldermen, and their wives). There is a catch-22 in this argument, since if "trouthe" is to have any social meaning it must be exercised as a public virtue; those forbidden any form of public association cannot, therefore, practice or embody "trouthe." Since the lower classes cannot aspire to "trouthe," what need do they have of "revel," or of any other form of association? Such logic (like "trouthe" itself) pretends to impartiality, universality, and verifiability ("as men may see"), but the state of angry enmity ("they ben ful wrothe") between the lower orders and social order is there only because the city authorities say it is so. Hostility to public virtue is legislated into the lower orders so that those of "lowe degree" can be legislated out of political existence.

Many critics have noted that the high-principled Cook of Fragment 1 sorts ill with the Cook who, at the beginning of Fragment 9, has reached the far side of revel and (the Host notes) is about to tumble:

> "Is ther no man, for preyere ne for hyre,
> That wole awake oure felawe al bihynde?
> A theef myghte hym ful lightly robbe and bynde.
> See how he nappeth! See how, for cokkes bones,
> That he wol falle fro his hors atones!
> Is that a cook of Londoun, with meschaunce?"   (9.6–11)

The fall of the Cook, when it finally comes, is strongly identified with the end of language. This end is presaged by the Cook's huge yawn that runs for six lines as the Manciple heaps abuse on him: the mouth is open, but emits no sound (35–40). The act of falling occupies the same narrative moment as the act of falling silent:

> And with this speche the Cook wax wrooth and wraw,
> And on the Manciple he gan nodde faste
> For lakke of speche, and doun the hors hym caste,
> Where as he lay, til that men hym up took.   (9.46–48)

The notion of being *wrothe* reappears here at the very moment of the Cook's falling. He too, it would seem, reveals himself to be a figure of "lowe degree" who, having reveled to excess, finds himself "ful wrothe" with *trouthe* and incapable of language, the ground of *trouthe* as a social virtue. The image of the drunken, voiceless Cook lying inert on the ground, thereby bringing the entire pilgrimage to a halt, does seem to validate all the letter-book arguments about the inability of the lower orders to function within an associative framework.

How, then, are we to reconcile this Cook of Fragment 9 with the Cook of Fragment 1? The first-Fragment Cook seems, in retrospect, a dummy of a character through which his masters ventriloquize the mores of craft masters and would-be aldermen. This makes him little better than the Summoner, who parrots terms learned from his masters in the law courts ("*Questio quid iuris*") without understanding them (1.637–46). But it is important to note that the Cook of Fragment 9 does not remain on the ground; his fellow pilgrims pick him up and set him back on his horse. Nor does he remain in enmity with the Manciple. He falls through drink, but through drink he rises or rides again: in taking the gourd from the Manciple and returning it to him, and in thanking him "in swich wise as he koude" (90–93), the Cook returns to some form of social consciousness. And the Manciple's gesture of reconciliation is figured as an explicit rejection of *wrothe*: "I wol nat wratthen hym, also moot I thryve!" (9.80). The Host, having laughed "wonder loud" at this rapprochement, observes:

> "I se wel it is necessarie,
> Where that we goon, good drynke with us carie;
> For that wol turne rancour and disese
> T'acord and love, and many a wrong apese."   (9.95–98)

This reference to "good drynke" might appear to suggest some reference to sacramental wine. But "good drynke" was also, we have noted, commonly associated with, employed as a facilitator of, "acord and love" in the meetings of craft and parish guilds and in sealing arbitration between aggrieved parties.[70] Since guild ordinances devote considerable space to the management of the *riotour* and *contekour*, the *rebelle* and *unbuxom*, it was evidently accepted that *drynkyng* might prove the instrument of both social integration and of individual rebellion. Chaucer, through his Cook, keeps both possibilities active. It is worth noting, however, that this reconciliation scene between Cook and Manciple immediately precedes the nonaccord between Apollo and his wife. The conciliatory mechanisms of guild-based behaviors seem preferable, in this final poetic fragment, to those that supposedly govern the noble household. Whereas the Cook is shoved back into the saddle, Apollo's nameless wife will remain dead on the floor, slain by her own lord and master.

Cooks and Canons: Chaucer's Londons

It is particularly interesting that Chaucer should choose the Cook and the Manciple to play out a reconciliation scene reminiscent of a guild-sponsored reconciliation or *drynkyng*: for both are men of "lowe degree," and both are Londoners (or "of Londoun"). Both men serve corporate organizations above their own station: Roger cooks for "a solempne and a greet fraternitee" and the Manciple purchases provisions for one of the London Inns of Court (1.567–86).[71] The *Cook's Tale* and the mayoral letter-books, we have noted, operate on the assumption that lower-class Londoners are incapable of peaceable association. The "acord and love" that breaks out between the Cook and Manciple (the last such reconciliation in the *Canterbury Tales*) would seem to discredit this assumption. Are we to conclude, then, that Chaucer begins his opus by endorsing the political outlook of London merchant capitalists and ends by celebrating the political capacities of the common man?

If Chaucer's opus were an organic and completed whole like the *Commedia* or the *Decameron*, we might be tempted to look for an orderly progression in its politics. But the *Canterbury Tales* is an uncertain sequence of fragments, and the fragments featuring the Cook are plainly at odds with one another. The *Tale* of Fragment 1 develops a strain of London discourse that we can associate with that of the Guildhall, but it comes to no conclusion; it breaks off incomplete. Fragment 9 starts up as if the Cook had never spoken, or told a tale: perhaps, as Larry Benson suggests, this indicates that Chaucer intended to cancel the Cook's appearance in Fragment 1.[72] Fragment 1 is itself ambivalent about the Cook: at one moment he suggests an ulcerated, low-life image and the next a figure who should sit at the Guildhall dais rather than wait on it. Each image found its illustrator: the Ellesmere Cook, with "his fleshhook, soiled apron, torn slippers, and bandaged shin" suggests—in Kolve's arresting phrase—"the livery . . . of labor and poverty and disease."[73] The Cambridge Cook (University Library MS Gg. iv. 27, fol. 193v.) is a prosperous, fur-trimmed citizen holding a large, elaborate whip; his legs are discreetly covered.

These images might be reconciled by arguing that whereas the Ellesmere artist is guided by the *General Prologue* portrait of the Cook, the Cambridge illustrator is responding to the discursive level of the *Cook's Tale*. But the tenuousness of such an argument might also suggest that London's diverse aspects and embodiments cannot be reconciled on a single imaginative plane. Perhaps the city can only be imagined as a discourse of fragments, discontinuities, and contradictions. But one last London narrative, foisted dramatically and mysteriously upon the pilgrimage in Fragment 8, remains to be considered: the *Canon's Yeoman's Tale*, which sees a canon-alchemist swindle a London chantry priest to the tune of £40.

The key motif of this *Tale* is betrayal. The canon in the *Tale* is obviously intent on betraying the trust the London chantry priest puts in him as an alchemist. But the would-be pilgrim canon, the Yeoman argues, is also betraying his own kind, that is, canons: such a man is a Judas to his community (8.1007–9). The narrator is himself engaged in a narrative of bad faith: he is betraying the professional secrets of the canon he has served for seven years, the man he acknowledged at the outset as "my lord and my soverayn" (590). He may also be betraying the pilgrimage and the readership. The suspicion that the canon of the first half of his *Tale* is the canon of the second is so strong that the Yeoman plucks it from the air—to deny it:

> This chanon was my lord, ye wolden weene?
> Sire hoost, in feith, and by the hevenes queene,
> It was another chanoun, and nat hee.   (8.1088–90)

Earlier, as the duplicity of the first canon had begun to emerge, the Host was moved to ask a key question:

> "Where dwelle ye, if it to telle be?"
> "In the suburbes of a toun," quod he,
> "Lurkynge in hernes and in lanes blynde,

Whereas thise robbours and thise theves by kynde
Holden hir pryvee fereful residence,
As they that dar nat shewen hir presence;
So faren we, if I shal seye the sothe."   (8.656–62)

By the beginning of the *Tale*'s *pars secunda*, the disease that infects the canon-alchemist has been carried from the blind alleys of the suburbs, the criminalized margins of civic life, to the city itself:

Ther is a chanoun of religioun
Amonges us, wolde infecte al a toun,
Thogh it as greet were as was Nynyvee,
Rome, Alisaundre, Troye, and othere three.   (8.972–75)

Nineveh was threatened with destruction; Troy was betrayed from within. What hope does London—New Troy—have of surviving this threat in its midst?[74] The argument is made that the city may escape betrayal through language by more language: the Yeoman alerts "us" (his word) to the second canon's duplicity so that "men may be war therby."[75] The discourse that saves us is the discourse of a *yoman* betraying his master. The form of the discourse adheres remarkably closely to depositions heard in the London Guildhall, and its tale of deception through magic or false science is no more fantastic than that of many letter-book narratives. But the notion of a *yoman* proposing to save a city, or a pilgrim body, by betraying his master's secrets ("Thou . . . discoverest that thou sholdest hide," his master warns him, 695–96) turns the operative assumptions of the Guildhall upside down. It also raises the possibility that Chaucer's Yeoman may be a Sinon, a foreigner who betrays a community by joining it belatedly and pretending to save it from ruin. It is worth recalling that in the last *bolgia* of Dante's Hell we first encounter two Tuscan alchemists and then (after a passage lamenting the ruin of Thebes and Troy) two arch-deceivers: "false Sinon, the Greek of Troy" and Master Adam, falsifier of the gold florin.[76] London, as New Troy, knew that the threat of economic disaster posed by alchemy and false coinage was every bit as serious as the threat of political betrayal.

The discourses of London in the *Canterbury Tales*, then, are freighted with suggestions of duplicity and bad faith. We have a Cook who sounds like two Cooks, one Yeoman, and two (perhaps one) canon-alchemists. It is a fitting irony of literary history that the two most authoritative texts in the *Canterbury Tales*' manuscript tradition perpetuate such ambiguities: Ellesmere contains the *Canon's Yeoman's Tale*, and Hengwrt does not.[77]

The conclusion this chapter seems bound for differs markedly from that offered by D. W. Robertson's celebrated *Preface to Chaucer*: "To conclude, the medieval world was innocent of our profound concern for tension. . . . We project dynamic polarities on history as class struggles, balances of power, or as conflicts between economic realities and traditional ideals. . . . But the medieval world with its quiet hierarchies knew nothing of these things."[78] The most cursory reading of London history or of London legal documents renders such statements unintelligible. There is no idea of a city for all the inhabitants of a space called London to pay allegiance to; there are only conflicts of associational, hierarchical, and antiassociational discourses acted out within and across the boundaries of a city wall or the fragments of a text called the *Canterbury Tales*. Florentine historiography, by contrast, experiences little difficulty in appealing to or assuming a notion of *unitas civium*; and Boccaccio's *Decameron* is able to imagine a momentary but decisive meeting, on level terms, of a powerful merchant-politician and a lowly baker.

The phrase that jumps the gap in Boccaccio's *novella*, bringing Cisti and Messer Geri Spina to full mutual recognition, is simply "A Arno" (to the Arno). Benvenuto da Imola, as early as 1379–80, points out that the Arno is only "un fiumicel" (as Dante describes it in *Purgatorio* 14). The fame of the river, which is not broad, nor easy to navigate, nor even full of fish, nonetheless runs throughout the world, thanks to the efforts of Dante, Petrarch, Boccaccio, and other Florentines.[79] In Spenser, the Thames is named some 28 times: in the *Faerie Queen*, it is both "wealthy" and "noble"; in the *Prothalamion* it occurs as the famous final line of every stanza, including the eighth, in which Spenser claims "mery London" as "my most kyndly Nurse" and as "native sourse" of his own life.[80] Nothing of this kind happens in the works of the London-born Chaucer; the Thames is never mentioned by name. In his *envoy* to Scogan, Chaucer does mention the English river (an altogether more imposing stretch of water than the Arno) but only as the unnamed facilitator of a court-centered political and geographic conceit:

> Scogan, that knelest at the stremes hed
> Of grace, of alle honour and worthynesse,
> In th'ende of which strem I am as dul as ded,
> Forgete in solytarie wildernesse.   (43–46)

Chaucer's addressee here is most likely Henry Scogan (c. 1361–1407), a squire in the king's household. All three of this poem's extant manuscripts feature the marginal gloss "a Wyndesor" at line 43 ("at the stremes hed"), and all three have "a Grenewiche" by line 45 or 46 ("th' ende of which streme . . .").[81] Scogan, then, is with the monarch at Windsor Castle some 35 miles upstream from London; Chaucer languishes in Greenwich, 6 miles downstream from London, "in solytarie wildernesse." The unnamed Thames is adduced here not as a phenomenon of nature but as a convenient metaphorical conduit for the flow of royal favors. In the limited geography of this *envoy*, the only distances that matter are those measured between "the stremes hed" of the royal court, and the "solytarie wildernesse" of Greenwich, where the sometime courtier feels himself "as dul as ded." London offers no reference point at all; the city here is unnamed, absent, and irrelevant.

Given Chaucer's delicately calibrated, long-term status as a royal servant (of London mercantile stock) working among merchant-capitalists at the London customhouse, it is perhaps unreasonable to expect his poetry to include a full-blooded endorsement or exemplification of urban ideology. But this is a dubious argument, since the *Canterbury Tales* contains many particular discourses that Chaucer would not wish to claim as his own. The Franklin, for example, is able to demonstrate the most convincing mastery of astrological terms while disowning such "supersticious cursednesse" (5.1272). The absence in Chaucer of the kind of urban ideology so brilliantly exemplified by Boccaccio is more convincingly explained, I would argue, by its absence on English territory and in English texts. In Chaucer's London (as in Chaucer's *Cook's Tale*), any discourse beginning with aspirations to inclusiveness soon comes to discover special allegiances and unbridgeable hostilities. One last trip to the Guildhall archive, specifically to an Anglo-Norman proclamation of 1391, makes this abundantly and painfully clear. Ex-mayor Brembre, hanged for treason by the Lords Appellant, has been dead for three years; ex-mayor Northampton has not held political office since 1383. The chief threat to city independence in the 1390s cannot be spoken, since it is the king himself. Mayor Adam Bamme must oblige this master, therefore, by locating threats elsewhere:

Whereas many dissensions, quarrels, and false reports [rumours] have prevailed in the City of London, as between trade and trade, person and person, because of diverse controversies lately moved between Nicholas Brembre, Knight [Nichol Brembre chivaler], and John Norhamptone, of late Mayors of the said city, who were men of great power and estate [de grant puissance et estat], and had many friendships and friends within the same; to the great peril of the same city, and, maybe, of all the realm.[82]

Here again, as in the *Cook's Tale*, we see that personal association of any kind, "as between trade and trade, person and person," and even including "friendship and friends," falls under suspicion: evils may be nurtured; "destruction and annihilation to the said city may readily ensue."[83] In addressing the inhabitants of London the proclamation must find some associative terms suggestive of a common interest. But even as it deploys such unifying terms ("common profit"; "of one accord in good love") the Guildhall text once again uncovers divisions in the working world and so divides itself from the body politic it presumes to serve and govern:

Desiring to maintain the peace of our Lord the King . . . for the common profit, they [the mayor and the aldermen] have ordained and established, that no man, great or small, of whatsoever estate or condition he be, shall speak from henceforth, or agitate upon any of the opinions, as to either of them, the said Nicholas and John, or shall by sign [ne pur signe], or in any other manner, shew that such person is of the one opinion or the other. But let the folks of the same city be of one accord in good love [en bon amour], without speaking, any person to another, on the said matter, in manner of reproof or of hatred; on pain, if any one shall speak or do against any of the points aforesaid, of imprisonment in Neugate for a year and a day, without redemption [pur un an et un jour sans redemption].

Unable to maintain a stable discursive level that can offer the sense or illusion of shared urban identity, the voice of the Guildhall falters here between vacuous promise and precipitous threat. Language itself is seen not as the chief guarantor of civic liberty (as it is in Florence) but as a revel that leads to Newgate. And the recent history of the city is defined chiefly as something not to be spoken. It is fitting, then, that the *Cook's Tale* of Fragment 1, like its London narrator in Fragment 9, should end by falling into silence. The absence or absenting of the city in Chaucer is not so much evasive as it is mimetic.

Chapter 7

"Deyntee to Chaffare": Men of Law, Merchants, and the Constance Story

Chaucer's Man of Law, another London-dweller, employs a stanzaic form favored by professional religious to affirm the Rome-centered authority of emperors and popes. Most critics have read his *Tale* as a religious narrative, although they have commonly been troubled by its indefinite genre[1] and by the resolutely secular opening both of its *prologe* (a full-blooded paean to wealth, particularly merchant wealth) and of the *Tale* proper (an eight-stanza business trip by Syrian spicers and drapers). This chapter intends to affirm the religious credentials of this *Tale*. My argument is that its particular expression of religious values is peculiarly that of a traditional religion seeking forms of compromise and accommodation with a vigorously emergent mercantile ethos. Words such as *creaunce* and *rekenynge* come to straddle secular and spiritual terms of reference; *tidynges* and *novelle*, the lifeblood of secular and religious courts, of mercantile trade, and of vernacular storytelling, draw their authors and bearers into the risky business of commodity production. In nosing into these waters, the *Man of Law's Tale* joins other contemporary texts, both English and Italian, that are attempting to find their way between theological systematizing and mercantile wealth: texts ostensibly as far apart as *Piers Plowman* and the magnificent chapter-house frescoes of Santa Maria Novella. Boccaccio's retelling of the European Costanza legend, *Decameron* 5.2, envisions a commerce-oriented society that sharpens, rather than relaxes, the gendered division of labor. Rather than representing a radical break with the English tale-world, however, Boccaccio's *novella* envisions a future latent, as English critics have uneasily anticipated, in those strange and unassimilable aspects of Chaucer's Custance story.

Chaucer's Man of Law, despite his use of rhyme royal, is not a cleric; his authority as *narrator* (such was his professional designation) derives from his membership of a secular association, the Order of the Coif. This Order models its ceremonial procedures on those of knighthood, but he is no knight; he looks for work in St. Paul's cathedral, but he is neither chaplain nor priest. Members of his Order are both revered and reviled, capable of inspiring awed admiration and murderous resentment in magnate and peasant alike. The Man of Law's power derives, in essence, from his monopolizing of a certain form of discourse, one found or asserted to be indispensable in both judicial and commercial contexts. It is to him that Chaucer entrusts the second and most extensive authorial signature of his *Canterbury Tales*.

Merchants in the *Man of Law's Tale*

Unlikely as it seems, Chaucer's Man of Law has something in common, if only in name, with the protagonist of the *Cook's Tale*: he, too, was once an apprentice.[2] He may even have been a reveler on the same London streets: his revels culminated in a procession so magnificent that it was sure to bring Perkyn and his compeers leaping from their shops.[3] On being called to be sergeant-at-law, after some twelve years as an "apprentice at the Bar," he had taken a formal and solemn farewell of his Inn of Court before being rung out of the society by the chapel bell.[4] He now passed into a more prestigious society, the Order of the Coif. This Order admitted, on average, one new member per year and included about a dozen practicing sergeants at any one time.[5] The Order's origins may be traced back to the time of Henry II (1154–89); by the end of the fourteenth century it formed "a close guild in complete control of the legal profession."[6] Sergeants made most of their money in the Court of Common Pleas (where they had exclusive rights of audience); much of their business here was concerned with the recovery of debts.[7] They were the recognized authorities on parliamentary law and were sometimes summoned to aid Parliament on difficult legal questions. They were counsel to the sovereign, acted as public prosecutors, and formed the pool of talent from which the justices of the highest courts were drawn. In turning from the Cook to the Man of Law, then, we rise precipitously up the social scale. This ascent between fragments[8] is not as memorable or dramatic as the move from Knight to Miller, but it measures no lesser social distance; the distance between Cook and Man of Law is, if anything, greater.[9]

The Host seems inclined to accept that the sergeants who "fed the Bench . . . led the Bar . . . were in the inner circle of the Great Men of the Realm" are "awe-inspiring personages,"[10] although his awe comes tinged with a self-assertiveness bordering on aggression. He cannot address the Man of Law without immediately becoming self-conscious about his own provisional status as "governour" of the pilgrim body; he puts the Sergeant in the dock, borrows his legal language, and holds him to the contract or "forward" (34, 40) of storytelling:

> "Ye been submytted, thurgh youre free assent,
> To stonden in this cas at my juggement,
> Acquiteth yow now of youre biheeste;
> Thanne have ye do youre devoir atte leeste."   (2.35–38)

The Man of Law responds by declaring his intention to tell a tale and so honor the principle of common accountability to law that he upholds from the bench.[11] The tale he tells, according to V. A. Kolve, meets a lack realized with increasing urgency during the four tales of Fragment 1, namely, "the possibility of an uncompromised Christian life and true Christian society, in which the absolute power of God and his love for those who serve him would stand revealed."[12] Chaucer's Sergeant-at-Law is billed in the *General Prologue* as a master of impeccable discourse, one who "koude endite and make a thyng, / Ther koude no wight pynche at his writyng" (1.325–26). Such seamless writing, which would prove resistant to nit-picking analysis or "pynching," was an essential professional asset for a Man of Law: the smallest flaw could render his legal documents invalid in the courts.[13] There seems little danger that his language, like that of the Cook or Yeoman, will distract us with ambiguities or lapse into silence. Predictably enough, then, the model of authority he employs seems straightforwardly hierocratic and downward-descending: God rules above and humankind, represented by Custance in her rudderless boat, wanders below. Custance does cover a huge amount of territory on the lateral plane—she travels for thousands of miles—but the vertical dimension is constantly drawn to our attention through pedagogical interrogations ("Who kepte hire fro the drenchyng in the see?" 2.485) and by references to planetary motion. Even water, the medium Custance moves in, is first encountered "descendynge" in this Fragment (2.23–24).

Kolve is surely right to propose that "a woman in a rudderless boat, afloat on the sea" is the image that first comes to mind when we think of this *Tale*. By focusing on this dominant image and its precious cargo of allegorical meaning (Custance's boat as the Ship of the Church), critics have come to celebrate the *Man of Law's Tale* as "a poem as emotional and solemn as it is dignified and exalted"; as "poetry . . . at its fullest dignity."[14] But this dominant image is not an uncontested one; there are other ships in the sea. The first vessels seen to cross the world in this *Tale* are not Christian at all, but are owned or commissioned by a guild or "compaignye" of Muslim drapers and spicers:

> In Surrye whilom dwelte a compaignye
> Of chapmen riche, and therto sadde and trewe,
> That wyde-where senten hir spicerye,
> Clothes of gold, and satyns riche of hewe.
> Hir chaffare was so thrifty and so newe
> That every wight hath deyntee to chaffare
> With hem, and eek to sellen hem hire ware.   (2.134–40)

In this first stanza the Syrian merchants are content to employ shipmen to transport their goods; the quality of their merchandise is guaranteed by the quality of previous shipments and by their past reputation for being trustworthy and honest, "sadde and trewe." But in the second stanza, reputation is not enough: the "maistres" of the company (2.141) are required to assemble and travel to Rome as a body on undisclosed business. All this is foreign or eccentric to Chaucer's sources, Trivet and Gower: both Trivet's Anglo-Norman *Chronique* and Gower's Middle English *Confessio amantis* begin the Constance story with the Emperor Constantine in Rome.[15] And when the Muslim merchants arrive in Rome in these two versions they are soon absorbed into Christendom by the power of Constance's preaching. According to Gower, God so favors Constance

> That al the wide worldes fame
> Spak worschipe of hire goode name.   (2.595–96)

Chaucer's merchants, by contrast, know nothing of Custance until they arrive at Rome. They do come to hear of her "excellent renoun" once they have been in Rome for "a certein tyme" (2.149–50), but there is no suggestion of their being converted. And although "the commune voys of every man" has much to say about her virtues, there is no mention of Custance preaching ("[ele] . . . lour prescha") or of her speaking "wordes wise."[16] The only account that the merchants hear of Custance is the *rekenynge* that the "commune voys" gives of her ("To rekene as wel hir goodnesse as beautee," 2.158). This term *rekenynge* is a curious one: in the *Canterbury Tales* it denotes the kind of detailed calculations associated (most commonly) with mercantile trade, astrology, or the state of the soul. It appears three times in the *General Prologue*: the Shipman is said to "rekene wel his tydes" (1.401); the Reeve makes his own "rekenynge" of his young master's stock value (1.600); and the pilgrims pay their "rekenynges" before leaving the Tabard (1.760). On the only other occasion that the Man of Law uses the term, he imagines a damned sinner who will wait too long to "rekene" his life (2.110). The most memorable fusion or confusion of commercial and religious *rekenynge* comes, of course, in the *Shipman's Tale*, where the merchant shuts himself off "to rekene with hymself" in his counting-house while his wife entertains a monk in the garden (7.1268).

The *rekenynge* that the "commune voys" makes of Custance is, we are bluntly informed, true. It is evidently important, however, that the merchants should see Custance for themselves. But this does not happen until they have finished loading their vessels; the sighting of Custance is then shipped aboard in a subordinate clause:

> And al this voys was sooth, as God is trewe.
> But now to purpos lat us turne agayn.
> Thise marchantz han doon fraught hir shippes newe,
> And whan they han this blisful mayden sayn,
> Hoom to Surrye been they went ful fayn,
> And doon hir nedes as they han doon yoore,
> And lyven in wele; I kan sey yow namoore.   (2.169–75)

The firm bid for closure made at the end of this stanza strengthens our sense that the narrative subject or "purpose" of this opening section centers not on the imperial court at Rome but on the merchant *compagnye* in Syria. After six stanzas we have returned to our eccentric point of origin; nothing has changed, except for the fact that the Muslim "maistres" have added the image of Custance to their inventory of cloths and spices. The commodity value of this image is soon realized when the sultan, in the very next stanza, summons the merchants to "espye" or elicit

> Tidynges of sondry regnes, for to leere
> The wondres that they myghte seen or heere.   (2.181–82)

This perennial desire for truthful *tidynges* is most fully acknowledged in the *House of Fame*, where the Chaucer *persona* names *tidynges* as the chief motive of his fantastic voyaging. At the end of this incomplete poem, in the House of Rumor, Chaucer presses forward, anxious to hear more of one particular *tidynge* he has heard from overseas (2131–36). This House is full

> of shipmen and pilgrimes,
> With scrippes bret-ful of lesinges,
> Entremedled with tydynges,
> And eek allone be hemselve.   (2122–25)

Pilgrims and shipmen are an excellent source of *tidynges*; but the credibility of the tales they unpack from their bags is always suspect. No sultan could have complete faith in a pilgrim from Rome, nor could he trust a mere shipman. But he could, it seems, believe a merchant, because a merchant's entire business depends on *creauncing*, the ability to attract capital by being creditworthy. The principle is succintly put by the merchant in the *Shipman's Tale*:

> "We may creaunce whil we have a name,
> But goldlees for to be, it is no game."   (7.1479–80)

The term *creaunce*, which appears five times as noun or verb in the *Canterbury Tales*, is used three times by the Shipman and twice by the Man of Law. The Shipman's *creauncing* is confined to commercial contexts (although the gloss on *creauncing* in the couplet above is addressed to a Christian monk). The Man of Law restricts the term *creaunce* to religious contexts—one Muslim, one Christian—although (as we have noted) he devotes much of his opening stanza to emphasizing the good name, the creditworthiness, of the merchants. This emphasis on the trust and capital invested in the Muslim merchants, which is unique to Chaucer, becomes more remarkable when it compounds with another departure from the sources. In Trivet and Gower, the merchants are summoned by the sultan to explain their change of faith. Why have they exchanged "creaunce" for "mescreaunce"?[17] In Chaucer, by contrast, the unconverted merchants are summoned only as a source of *tidynges*; their narrative is authorized by commercial and not religious *creaunce*. They lay out their story "ceriously," in great detail. The sultan is soon "caught" by their narrative; the "figure" of Custance is transferred to the sultan's "remembrance" (2.183–89).

The *tidynge* of Custance is shipped to Syria, then, within a purely commercial frame of reference which is indifferent to questions of religion. As soon as it lodges in the sultan's mind, however, it provokes a change of religious *creaunce*. This in turn signals a change of narrative personnel. After two stanzas on reading the stars (or on failing to read them), we see the sultan assembling his "privee conseil" to discuss the marital impediments of *disparitas cultus* with his canon lawyers.[18] The merchants, who dominated the Man of Law's first eight stanzas, have now disappeared; they are not heard from again.

The Man of Law's merchants are the agents of *amor de lonh*; their merchant ship is a strange variant of Cupid's arrow, the wooden vessel that carries the image of a woman to the mind of an unsuspecting male. Their action sets off a train of events that lasts many years, covers thousands of miles, and costs the lives of hundreds of people. Its most poignant summation comes, perhaps, in the third and final part of the narrative, as Custance's boat meets up with the Roman fleet. Custance is accompanied by her son, born of a marriage to a Saxon king; the Roman fleet is returning from Syria, where it has spent "ful many a day" burning, killing, and otherwise inflicting "meschance" on Syrians. All this originates from the transmission of a single *tidynge*. Why does Chaucer choose to make such a momentous narrative spring from a business meeting convened by a guild of Syrian spicers and drapers? This decision to add a new episode that accentuates the role of chance in human affairs is not uncommon in Chaucerian narrative.[19] When merchants are chosen as the subject of the new episode, however, the choice seems overdetermined: chance, or the control of chance, is the founding condition of mercantile business; the "bagges" of merchants, the Man of Law tells us, are filled with rolling dice (2.124–25).

Merchants in Fourteenth-Century England

Does this motif of gratuitously appearing and suddenly disappearing merchants in the *Man of Law's Tale* find any correlative in the politics of fourteenth-century England? Merchants come remarkably close to the center of political power in the last years of Edward III and the first years of Richard II. London merchants such as John Pecche, fishmonger, Adam de Bury, skinner, and Richard Lyons were frequently to be seen in and around the court circle of the elderly Edward III. Lyons, an illegitimate Fleming who had settled in London, is described as a vintner, although he traded in a wide range of commodities. He began lending money to the Crown in 1373, held high office in the city, and became warden of the London mint. With

William Latimer, Richard Sturry, John Nevill, and Alice Perrers, he formed the leading group of the King's *privata familia*.[20] Other London merchants played a prominent part in the emergency council of 1377, called after the French had captured the Isle of Wight and burned coastal towns in Sussex. The four London members of this council soon raised £10,000 for the war effort, backed by "autres certeins merchantz"; the city soon added £5,000. On December 14, 1377, the London merchants John Philpot and William Walworth were appointed joint war treasurers to ensure that the money raised was spent on fighting the French, rather than on financing the royal household. Philpot soon became impatient at the ineffectiveness of the royal fleet, fitted out a fleet of his own, and scored a major triumph by capturing John Mercer, a Scottish pirate in league with the French. This lent substance to Peter de la Mare's proud boast to the 1377 parliament at Westminster: "When the merchants of the realm were lords and masters [seigneurs et maistres] and had control and regulation of their own ships, the navy of the realm [la navye de roialme] was great and strong."[21]

But the merchants could not think of themselves as lords for long without being challenged by the established "seigneurs," the magnates who saw the military and political guidance of the realm as their own rightful business. John of Gaunt was evidently not thrilled to learn that Philpot's fleet was covering itself with glory while his own military expedition to Brittany was making little headway. As *gubernator* of the realm, Gaunt was handily placed to cut back the powers of the London merchants. In October 1378 Parliament met at Gloucester (any move out of London hurt the Londoners), removed Walworth and Philpot as war treasurers and abolished many of the monopolies enjoyed by the victualing trades. Lyons, Pecche, and Bury had already been impeached by the "Good Parliament" and ousted from their offices as aldermen; none of them ever held civic office again. Lyons died in the Rising of 1381; one chronicler remembers his foreign origins in noting that "Richard Lyons and many more of the Flemings were beheaded in diverse places of London."[22] Gaunt's opinion of the London merchant capitalists is eloquently summarized by the clerk who kept his register: Brembre and Philpot are referred to by nickname in a record of currency exchanges as "Nichol" Brembre and "Jankyn" Philpot.[23]

The structural problems symptomatized by these rapid changes of political fortune were not resolved in the later years of Richard II. Merchant capital, quick money, became ever more attractive to the royal household as traditional sources of Crown revenues dried up or took longer to appropriate.[24] The king recognized "the kyndenes & subsidie" of the city by allowing the mayor to butler his wine, "trustyng time commyng to have like kyndenes & subsidie":[25] but the presence or influence of merchants at court remained perennially irksome to the magnates. The merchants, for their part, were not inclined to view centralized government as something worth fighting for and paying for. When the French were cruising the Channel or threatening to sail up the Thames, merchants, like Chaucer's Merchant, recognized national defense as a top priority: "He wolde the see were kept for any thyng" (1.276). At other times they were less willing to finance the war effort or to subsidize a peaceful foreign policy.[26] They were not keen to get too close to military action themselves. In 1387, when the king summoned the city authorities to Windsor in order to seek help against the Appellants, the mayor and aldermen rehearsed a familiar plea to cover their inactivity: that craftsmen and merchants are unskilled in matters of war.[27]

English polity possessed no stable or established structures that could accommodate the fiscal and economic powers of the merchant class; it had not yet evolved the kind of compromise seen in the sixteenth century, whereby mercantile interests accepted limitations on their political powers in exchange for greater autonomy in the economic sphere. London returned four guildsmen to each parliament, but merchants were not (like sergeants-at-law) summoned to give specialized professional advice. Nor were they recognized as a separate *estate* by fourteenth-century parliaments; the first formal parliamentary reference to merchants as a separate order does not appear until 1442.[28] Without a secure and generally recognized political identity in national affairs, then, high visibility (political or economic) was ill-advised.

After 1388 corporate and individual loans from the mayor and commonalty of London to the Crown all but dried up. The execution of ex-mayor Brembre and the cessation of fighting in the Channel made London merchants even less inclined to advance money. In 1392 Richard sent a writ to his sheriffs instructing them to make a list of all persons qualified to take up knighthood. This was both a political and an economic initiative: knights were taxed at a higher rate. The reply that came back from London in 1392 echoed that returned in 1344, 1356, and 1366: nobody was so qualified. The qualification was £40 a year in rents; the city, which could raise thousands of pounds at short notice when its own immediate interests were threatened, was telling the Crown that it knew of nobody who enjoyed such an income. This response drove Richard to more drastic, and ultimately tyrannical, measures in his attempt to extract capital from London; any chance of a stabilized working relationship between Crown and city was lost.[29]

It is worth noting that although the merchant class was a permanent feature of medieval London, merchant family dynasties were not: capital was more easily dissipated than accumulated, and families rarely spent more than two generations in active trading.[30] The claim that no London merchant is guaranteed an annual income of £40 from rents may, then, be worth pondering. It was made as follows: that since tenements were often empty, and could hence be destroyed by fire or wind at any moment, citizens never knew the value of their property.[31] This argument taps stereotypical commonplaces about the inherent instability and perilousness of merchant activity that had been in circulation since classical and Patristic times, and had allowed the narratives of knightly and mercantile *aventure* to run together. Merchants could no doubt exploit their reputation for restlessness when it suited them; and they could always vanish on business. Their god is Mercury: Fulgentius interprets his name as *mercium curum*, "concern with wares." Mercury is also the god of eloquence, the god of theft, and the god who traverses huge geographical distances.[32] Merchants possess a gift to speak and a gift not to be found. The most mercurial narrative of the *Canterbury Tales*, which conveys a deep-seated restlessness in both stylistic and moral terms, is told by the Merchant. The last thing we learn about him in the *General Prologue* is that his name is not known:

> "For sothe he was a worthy man with alle;
> But, sooth to seyn, I noot how men hym calle."   (1.283–84)

Merchant Wealth, the Triumph of Aquinas, and the Building of the Chapter House

The need to recognize the impact of merchant capital on the political order of fourteenth-century England is registered by other Middle English texts, most memorably by *Piers Plowman*. In Passus 7 of B-text, as the Pardon from Truth is promulgated, the outlook for merchants seems bleak: the pope objects both to their use of time ("thei holde noght hir halidayes") and to the oaths that support their *creauncing* ("thei swere 'by hir soule' . . . / hir catel to selle").[33] But suddenly another document appears:

> Marchaunts in the margyne hadde manye yeres,
> Ac noon *A pena et a culpa* the Pope nolde hem graunte,
> For thei holde noght hir halidayes as Holy Chirche techeth,
> And for thei swere "by hire soule" and so "God moste hem helpe"
> Ayein clene Conscience, hir catel to selle.
> Ac under his secret seel Truthe sente hem a lettre,
> [And bad hem] buggen boldely what hem best liked
> And sithenes selle it ayein and save the wynnyng,
> And amende mesondieux thermyd and myseise folk helpe;
> And wikkede weyes wightly amende,
> And do boote to brugges that tobroke were;
> Marien maydenes or maken hem nonnes;
> Povere peple and prisons fynden hem hir foode,[34]
> And sette scolers to scole or to some othere craftes;
> Releve Religion and renten hem bettre.   (B.7.18–32)

Merchants, once nervous in the face of religious authority, are now urged to fully exercise themselves *as* merchants ("buggen boldely") and thereafter ("sithenes") to improve hospitals, assist the sick, repair roads and bridges, furnish dowries for young women as wives or nuns, provide food for poor people and prisoners, finance young scholars and apprentices and support and endow religious orders. Now, it seems, merchant enterprise and the work of the Church can be contemplated, albeit under a "secret seel," in the same narrative frame. This unforeseen, half-acknowledged, yet materially concrete compromise between religious authority and merchant capital bears direct comparison with another secret text from this period: the frescoes that adorn the Dominican chapter house of Santa Maria Novella (the Florentine church in which Boccaccio's *brigata* first gathers). This chapter house, built between circa 1350 and 1355, was financed by Buonamico di Lapo dei Guidalotti, a rich merchant wishing to commemorate the wife he lost in the plague of 1348. When Mico himself died in 1355 he elected to further "releve religion" by leaving over four hundred gold florins to finance frescoes; these were executed by Andrea Bonaiuti and his assistants between 1365 and 1367.

The immense scale of the chapter house and the ambitious art of *Programmbild* that adorns it add up to a magnificent experience of artistic space; Ruskin was led "to wonder that human daring ever achieved anything so magnificent." [35] But this space also tells of a slow and deliberate migration of merchant wealth into artistic and spiritual capital. Mico images this nicely as he lies by his own altar. He is now dressed in a Dominican habit, but (his tombstone tells us) it was his activity as a merchant that got this building built and painted: "Hic jacet Michus, filius olim Lapii de Guidalottiis, Mercator, qui fecit fieri et dipingi istud Capitulum cum Cappella, in habitu ordinis, anno Dni 1355, die 4 sbris. Requiescat in Pace." [36]

This tension between mercantile and religious *rekenynge* may be read not only in the history of the chapter house but also in the two frescoes that face each other across its great open space (plates 4a and 4b). [37] To the left of the main doorway (the west wall) we find the *Triumph of St. Thomas Aquinas*. The central and dominant figure here is St. Thomas, who is seated in his cathedra beneath a female personification of wisdom in a roundel, with an open book affirming the divine inspiration of the doctrine he purveys: "Therefore I prayed and prudence was given to me; I called for help, and there came to me a spirit of wisdom [spiritus sapientiae]." Aquinas sits as the middle figure in a line of patriarchs, prophets, evangelists, and apostles: the authors of Scripture. The Holy Spirit descends to him from the western quadrant of the ceiling; beneath his feet lie three vanquished heretics. Lower still, seated in a tier of Gothic stalls, are female figures representing the seven sacred and seven secular sciences from which his doctrine is built: we begin with grammar in the bottom right corner (left from where Aquinas sits) and work our way to the center through the rest of the trivium and quadrivium. We then move out to the far left corner (civil law) and work toward the center again through canon law and five species of theology. Each science has its exemplary figure: the

Plate 4. Andrea Bonaiuti and assistants. Frescoes, Dominican chapter house (Cappellone degli Spagnoli), Santa Maria Novella, Florence.

(a) *Triumph of St. Thomas Aquinas and Allegory of the Sciences* (west wall)

(b) Allegory of the Church and of the Dominican Order (east wall)

trivium is represented by Priscian, Cicero, and Aristotle; Justinian and Clement V represent, respectively, civic and canon law; Augustine represents the wisdom and strength required for the final mode of theology, apologetics.[38]

The west wall presents the elements of a completed system of thought, set beyond time, centered on the single figure of Aquinas. The opposite wall depicts this body of thought being carried to and through the world by Dominican friars. Space here, in the *Road to Salvation*,[39] is not organized by symmetrical planes; upward movement is achieved along uneven diagonals, and the only centered figure is the severe Christ Pantocrator at the apex. We move from time (at the bottom) through an earthly paradise (in the middle) to eternity (at the top), although our movement through time runs backwards as well as forwards: the figures crowned at heaven's gate have become "as little children" (Matthew 18.3). The bottom left quarter of the fresco is dominated by a futuristic representation of the new Florentine cathedral of Santa Maria del Fiore.[40] In front of the cathedral, to our left, we find every degree of professional religious from nun to pope; to the right every kind of layman, from beggar to emperor. Extraordinary care is taken in observing the details of costume and bearing that denote the precise social standing of each individual; the range of trades, occupations, and callings shown is remarkably diverse. A pilgrim with three signs sewn to his hat kneels next to a gartered knight, who thrusts his gartered leg forward in an assertive manner.[41] A nobleman feeds his falcon, a lady feeds her lapdog, and a magistrate strokes his chin, lost in contemplation. Beneath him three girls dance to a tambourine; four more dance to a bagpipe.

The attempt to represent the social experience of postplague Florence absorbs as much energy in this fresco as the effort to trace an allegorical journey. It has long been a popular pastime to assign the names of famous Florentines to the figures who stand before Santa Maria del Fiore.[42] Some figures, such as those plucking fruit from the trees or hiding behind hedges, seem to lie outside any allegorical schema. The many determined attempts to match motifs in the fresco with those in its supposed literary source, Friar Jacopo Avanti's *Mirror of True Penitence*, have not proved very convincing.[43] Literal and allegorical representations seem content to double up in the same visual space; the Dominican friars are represented both by realistic figures of friars and by the black and white dogs (*domini canes*) that run at their feet, guard the pope's sheep, or assault heretical wolves. And the style of these representations mixes touches of post-Giottesque naturalism with Gothic renditions of scholastic allegory. Such inconsistencies and stylistic promiscuities have been seen as expressive of a transitional period that has no name, that is no longer medieval but not yet Renaissance. New forms of representation betray the traditional content of scholastic allegory; old visual stereotypes are employed to express new aspects of social experience.[44]

The space between west and east walls, between the *Triumph of St. Thomas*

Aquinas and the *Road to Salvation*, was the ground upon which the friars of Santa Maria Novella met to regulate their internal affairs or to interrogate outsiders. The chapter house was often used as an inquisitorial court; Catherine of Siena was called upon to plead for herself there not long after the murals were completed.[45] Situated between the orderly, hierarchical vision of Aquinas and the broken planes and representational inconsistencies of the west wall, the friars act out their mission of bringing a timeless vision to a postlapsarian world.

But can there be such a clean break between the unchanging truth of doctrine and the vicissitudes of worldly experience as this schema suggests? Aquinas had been canonized at Avignon in 1323; in 1346 Pope Clement VI had proclaimed to a Dominican general chapter at Brives that no friar was to dare to depart from the common doctrine of Aquinas.[46] Bonaiuti's fresco suggests that the system of thought that finds its summation in St. Thomas is perfectly coincident with the inspiration of the Holy Spirit and the text of Scripture. But it is worth returning to and continuing with the verse of Scripture that Aquinas holds open for our inspection, Wisdom 7.7ff. This passage was appointed to be read on his feast day:[47]

> And so I prayed, and understanding was given me;
> I entreated, and the spirit of Wisdom came to me.
> I esteemed her more than sceptres and thrones;
> compared with her, I held riches as nothing.[48]
> I reckoned no precious stone to be her equal,
> for compared with her, all gold is a pinch of sand,
> and beside her silver ranks as mud . . .
> In her company all good things came to me,
> and at her hands incalculable wealth.
> All these delighted me, since Wisdom brings them,
> though I did not then realize that she was their mother.[49]
> What I learned diligently, I shall pass on liberally,[50]
> I shall not conceal how rich she is.
> For she is to human beings an inexhaustible treasure . . .   (7.7–9, 11–14)

Solomon, the supposed author and speaker of these verses, decides that wisdom is to be valued above wealth or secular power; the wisdom of this decision is attested to by the wealth and power that follow from it. The wisdom of Aquinas in making this same choice is confirmed by the same mechanism, the "good things" that it draws to itself. Merchant capital thus performs both a hermeneutic and a material function in the process of bringing Aquinas to the world. It confirms that his teaching is coincident with the wisdom of Scripture; and it memorializes this affirmation through the brick, paint, and plaster of the chapter house. But in doing this, it shoots the gap between east and west walls and, it would seem, contaminates the vision of St. Thomas in glory. For, as Thomas had once asked himself, "What else is commerce . . .

than securing something cheaply and wanting to sell it at a profit? . . . it was just such traders that our Lord drove out of the temple."[51] By this logic, it would seem, the friars would need to drive the merchants out of the chapter house. But then, of course, the vision of Thomas would disappear; the building would vanish.

But Thomas had more to say[52] on the subject of profit-making in the mercantile economy. Profit, "lucrum," which is recognized as the desired end of commerce ("negotiationis finis"), is not intrinsically honest or necessary, vicious or unvirtuous:

There is, therefore, nothing to stop profit being subordinated to an activity that is necessary, or even right. And this is the way in which commerce can become justifiable. This is exemplified by the man who uses moderate business profits [lucrum moderatum] to provide for his household, or to help the poor; or even for the man who conducts his business for the public good [propter publicam utilitatem]. (2a2ae.77, 4; p. 229)

By this reasoning, which ends with the kind of spending program envisioned in *Piers Plowman* B.7, the merchant renders himself legitimate as he transfers his accumulated "lucrum" to the poor, the public good, or the chapter house. But this emphasis upon the ways in which commerce can be rendered justifiable ("licita reddetur") diverts attention from the troubling interval preceding this moment of transfer (that is, from the accumulation and conservation of wealth). Aquinas shows no inclination to be trapped, finally, in this difficult theoretical no-man's-land. And so he concludes this *quaestio* by reestablishing the space that divides *spiritus sapientiae* from the ways of the world; reaffirming his clerical identity, he retreats (so to speak) to his centered and elevated vantage point on the east wall:

Clerics are bound to abstain not merely from things that are bad but from things that look bad. And engaging in commerce falls into this category, both because its aim is the making of earthly gains, which clerics should despise, and because of the likelihood of their falling victim to the vices of business men [negotiatorum vitia]. For as Ecclesiasticus says, *A merchant can hardly keep from wrongdoing.*[53]

Merchants, Men of Law, and the Ship of the Church

Merchant wealth, it seems, cannot be discretely represented in the religious art or literature of the late Trecento; it is made apparent only as it disappears into[54] an economy of Church-sanctioned images. Nor can its place in the totality of social, political, and spiritual life be adequately theorized. Aquinas cannot allow it to detain him for too long, since, he tells us, it would compromise his mental freedom: "Commercial activity engrosses a person too much in secular cares and thereby withdraws him from spiritual concerns."[55] And yet Aquinas does go on to consider the details of commercial exchanges, and the borrowing and lending of money. The merchants in *Piers Plowman* cannot find much cause for hope in the public document that Truth puts into Piers's hands. And yet the letter sent privately, under Truth's "secret seel," causes merchants to rejoice while men of law are left to despair:

> "And I shal sende yow myselve Seynt Michel myn angel,
> That no devel shal yow dere ne [in youre deying fere yow],
> And witen yow fro wanhope, if ye wol thus werche,
> And sende youre soules in saufte to my Seintes in joye."
>   Thanne were marchaunts murie—manye wepten for joye
> And preiseden Piers the Plowman, that purchased this bulle.
>   Men of lawe leest pardon hadde that pleteden for mede,[56]
> For the Sauter saveth hem noght . . .   (B.7.33-40)

This sudden juxtaposition of merchants and men of law may take us by surprise: we are not predisposed to associate men of law, who are royal appointees, with the trickeries and vagaries of *negotium*. The *Man of Law's Tale* invites us to identify such men with the hierarchic and hierocratic values of the Constance story, a narrative unified by the dominant allegorical referent of the Ship of the Church. But perhaps it is time to historicize this term: to consider what "Church" might have meant to a fourteenth-century audience.

When first we think of "Church," we tend to think of the sanctified space evoked by Kolve's exegesis of Custance's boat: a little spot of heaven on earth (or at sea). But no church on earth looks like this; churches can only be built and decorated through the kinds of historical compromise that can still be read in the chapter house of Santa Maria Novella. St. Paul's, the cathedral church of London, was never an empty space. Today it looks, from the inside, like a gift shop annexed to an imperial war museum.[57] The Middle Ages saw a similarly complex conjunction of religious, political, and commercial functions, although the commercial aspects were *more*, not less, visible; they extended into the body of the church itself. Unemployed clerics, Chaucer tells us, would hang around St. Paul's in the hope of being hired as fraternity or chantry chaplains.[58] Sermons preached outside the cathedral, at Paul's Cross, proved so popular that they became a means of making announcements about business matters, such as the repayment of debt.[59] Just north of the Cross, along Paternoster Row, worked the scribes, limners, bookbinders, parchmeners, stationers, and scriveners (plus apprentices and servants) of the London book trade.[60] And inside the cathedral London merchants could hire one of the dozen scribes who sat in the nave, ready to copy their documents, or hire a lawyer who specialized in debt cases, a man of law.

Chaucer notes in the *General Prologue* that his Man of Law "often hadde been at the Parvys" (1.310). Chaucerians persist in assuming that "the Parvys" should be glossed as "the porch of St. Paul's cathedral,"[61] but commentators with a background in legal history have long thought it much more likely that "the Parvys" refers to the pillars inside the cathedral (along the colonnaded north aisle).[62] On the grand day of their feast, newly created sergeants moved in procession to St. Paul's and made offerings at the rood of the north door and at the shrine of St. Erkenwald. Each new sergeant was then taken to the north aisle and assigned a specific pillar; this would become identified as the site of his business dealings with clients in the afternoons.[63] When Chaucer's Man of Law evokes the *navis ecclesiae*, then, he is describing his own place of work. For him the Ship of the Church doubles as a merchant ship, the place where he exchanges his professional expertise for money. Such an assessment is shared by Gower's *Mirour de l'Omme*, which views the custom of newly advanced sergeants giving gifts of gold rings with a jaundiced eye.[64] These lawyers give out a little gold, Gower observes, in the hope of making a lifelong return on their investment:

> Mais ils ont une acoustummance,
> Qant l'aprentis ensi s'avance
> A cell estat du sergantie,
> Luy falt donner une pitance
> Del orr, q'ad grant signefiance:
> Car l'orr qu'il donne signefie
> Q'il doit apres toute sa vie
> Reprendre l'orr a sa partie.   (24385–92)

> But they have a custom
> When an apprentice thus advances
> To the degree of sergeant:
> They make him give a little bit
> Of gold, which has great significance:
> For the gold that he gives signifies
> That he must afterwards, throughout his life,
> Take back gold for his own benefit.

The tension between the commercial and religious obligations intrinsic to a sergeant-at-law's professional identity is neatly exemplified by the oath he swore on entering office. Commercial concerns predominate here; the public must be protected:

Ye shall swear that well and truly ye shall serve the king's people as one of the serjeants at the law. And ye shall truly counsel them that ye shall be retained with, after your cunning. And ye shall not defer, tract, or delay their causes willingly for covetise of money or other thing that may turn you to profit. And ye shall give attendance accordingly. As God you help, and his saints.[65]

A sergeant-at-law was obliged to give counsel to anyone who sought him out for legal advice, regardless of that person's ability to pay for such counsel. Perhaps this is one reason why Chaucer's Man of Law found it convenient to appear "busier than he was": there was much more money to be made in the Court of Common Pleas.[66] The chief business of this court (to which Chaucer was frequently summoned in his later years) was debt collection.[67] The sergeants-at-law, who enjoyed a monopoly of Common Pleas business, were well aware that they were living especially dangerously in the late fourteenth century. One of their number, John Cavendish, was murdered during the Rising of 1381; seven more were sentenced to death for treason by the Merciless Parliament. Six of those accused in 1388 were pardoned and exiled to Ireland; the seventh was hanged in front of his wife and children, along with his apprentice.[68] Gower opens his *Vox clamantis*, Book 6, by promising to cry out against men of law "what the voice of the people cries out" ("quod plebis vox clamat clamo," 15). He then promptly subjects them to better than four hundred lines of virulent abuse: the lawyer or *causidicus*, he insists, "chooses to behave like a whore, who cannot love a man without looking for a present . . . give him gold, and you can have his body."[69] Like merchants, then, men of law may often have found it prudent, in the England of Chaucer and Gower, not to be easily found.[70]

The *Introduction to the Man of Law's Tale*

Fragment 2 opens with the Host performing the difficult mental arithmetic of an astrologer and then moralizing, quite seriously it would seem, on the irrecoverability of wasted time and the folly of idleness; it ends with the Man of Law misconstruing a religious text, written by a pope, to endorse the wisdom of rich merchants being rich. We begin with couplets, end with the rhyme royal stanzas favored by professional religious,[71] and traverse a remarkable range of commercial and religious referents. The centerpiece of this section, edited as the *Introduction to the Man of Law's Tale*, is the Man of Law's assessment of Chaucer as author. Critics committed to viewing or classifying the *Man of Law's Tale* as a decorous and single-minded statement of religious faith have found this heady cocktail somewhat difficult to swallow. But the *Tale* proper, I have argued, is itself mapped within a complex network of commercial and religious, laterally extending and downward-descending vectors. The *Introduction* gives us stylistic and thematic forewarning of ideological conflicts developed more subtly by the *Tale* to come.

The fragment opens at 10 A.M. on April 18, a moment at which meteorological time and mechanical time, Church time and merchant time, are in perfect alignment.[72] At this moment a six-foot man is as long as his shadow.[73] This also means, of course, that as time runs forward such perfect correspondence between body, body image, and the hands of the clock will be lost; shadows shorten and lengthen as (to medieval thinking) the sun moves on. So even as the Host speaks of philosophers who "Bewaillen tyme moore than gold in cofre" (2.26), natural and mechanical time are already telling different stories, situating us at different points in the cosmos. The attempt to measure time by gold was at the heart of medieval thinking on usury. By charging interest on a loan we are, in effect, selling time; and time belongs to God alone.[74] The merchant knows that "los of tyme shendeth us"; but he also knows that the usurer may help him to keep time at bay. Wealth and time are not, in the late medieval market economy, so absolutely incommensurate as the Host suggests.

The impeccable religious orthodoxy of the Host's musings is taken up by the Man of Law as he switches into rhyme royal. He begins by translating Pope Innocent III's meditations on the miseries of the poor with reasonable fidelity: "O miserabilis condicio mendicantis!"; "O hateful harm, condicioun of poverte!"[75] The figure of need (2.102–3), a personification embellished by the rhyming of "wounded" with "wounde hid," adds a hint of rhetorical preciosity not found in the source text's Latin prose; further embellishment is supplied in the next stanza by the half-line "needfulle in hir neede" (2.112). The Man of Law's poor man, who is granted direct speech, is more specific about the cause of his miseries than his counterpart in the Latin text: "Crist . . . / . . . mysdeparteth richesse temporal," he says (2.106–7), where the *De Miseria* has "Deum . . . non recte dividat" (1.14, 6–7). Where Innocent goes on to denounce the idea of valuing a person according to his material possessions, the Man of Law implicitly endorses this idea in a sudden, full-blooded celebration of mercantile wealth. Christmas, in this account, seems like a pagan festival designed to celebrate winnings in a dice game:

> O riche marchauntz, ful of wele been yee,
> O noble, o prudent folk, as in this cas!
> Youre bagges been nat fild with ambes as,
> But with sys cynk, that renneth for youre chaunce;
> At Cristemasse myrie may ye daunce!   (2.122–26)

We will have to wait for the next speaker in the Ellesmere order to give us a palliative for poverty that Innocent III would have endorsed.[76] Right-thinking Christians should endure poverty in patience: they should not deduce that since poverty is miserable, wealth is the source of happiness. The next Ellesmere speaker is, of course, the Wife of Bath. It certainly seems odd that the Wife, a figure firmly identified with the world of commerce and guildhall, should appear more orthodox in this matter than the great legal expert who precedes her. Such a crossover suggests, once again, that even the most authoritative of secular and religious figures cannot help but be complicit with the values and mechanisms of the mercantile world. The Man of Law, apostrophizing merchants in the last stanza of his *Introduction*, concedes the point explicitly:

> Ye seken lond and see for yowre wynnynges;
> As wise folk ye knowen al th'estaat
> Of regnes; ye been fadres of tidynges
> And tales, bothe of pees and of debaat.

I were right now of tales desolaat,
Nere that a marchant, goon is many a yeere,
Me taughte a tale, which that ye shal heere.   (2.127–33)

Merchants prove indispensable to the Man of Law both inside and outside
his *Tale*. Without fictional merchants, Custance would not have left Rome;
without a real one, the Man of Law would have no tale to tell.

The Man of Law on Chaucer as Author

In the middle section of his *Introduction*, the Man of Law identifies Chaucer
as an eager and long-practiced monopolist of English storytelling:

I kan right now no thrifty tale seyn
That Chaucer, thogh he kan but lewedly
On metres and on rymyng craftily,
Hath seyd hem in swich Englissh as he kan
Of olde tyme, as knoweth many a man;
And if he have noght seyd hem, leve brother,
In o book, he hath seyd hem in another.   (2.46–52)

This second authorial signature of the *Canterbury Tales* registers more serious claims than the first, while remaining, like the first, at once confident and
uneasy: confident in claiming an identity as a vernacular author, and uneasy
as to what kind of social and professional profile this might portend. In the
General Prologue, I have argued, Chaucer situates himself as one who aspires
to Dantean grandeur as a European *auctor* while keeping company with social
predators.[77] Here, in opening Fragment 2, Chaucer chooses to associate his
own activity as a vernacular author with the professional assessments, texts,
and procedures of men of law.[78] This associative process will be carried further by the *Tale of Melibee*, a narrative derived from an Italian *causidicus* and
probably first assigned to Chaucer's Sergeant, but then transferred to the pilgrim Chaucer himself. Why, then, does Chaucer choose to have the most
extended characterization of himself as purveyor of literary texts, as crafty
rhymer, proceed from the mouth of a man of law?

It is important to remember that although this portrait is jocular in tone,
it is spoken by a man said to be (by the pilgrim Chaucer) "war and wys," "of
greet reverence" (1.309, 312): not a reeve or a miller, but a *serviens ad legem*,
a sergeant-at-law. A man of law, we have noted, is a figure of considerable
cultural status; through his control of the written and spoken word he makes
and breaks fortunes and decides on matters of life and death. He was trained
through the study of *casus*: stories illustrating situations where the use of specific writs is appropriate, and reports of cases (real or imaginary) in which
litigants resort to particular types of action.[79] He is an assiduous student of
auctoritee; he knows every case and judicial decision that has been heard in
England since the time of William the Conqueror (1.323–24). He is also a

narrator: such is the name applied to him by the plea rolls when he argues a case as an advocate.[80] In traveling the assizes circuit, he supplied a vital linkage (one of major importance in the development of the modern state) between localized and centralized authority: a circuit judge dealt with cases that were deemed too difficult for the justices of the peace.[81] His civic importance is emphasized by suggested equivalence in rank to a knight;[82] contemporary orders of knighthood were eager to stress that the term *militare* meant not only "to fight" but also "to serve." [83]

Chaucer's most important and conspicuous acts of political service were performed in Kent (the area of jurisdiction traversed by the Canterbury pilgrimage) between 1385 and 1389: in 1386 he was elected Member of Parliament for Kent, and from 1385 to 1389 he served in the county as a justice of the peace. Such justices were empowered "to inquire by sworn inquest concerning all kinds of felonies, trespasses, forestalling, regrating, extortion, walking or riding armed in conventicles, lying in ambush to maim or kill, illegal use of liveries for maintenance, offences of hostelers . . . and offences of laborers against the labor laws." [84] His eighteen fellow justices were (as laid down by a statute of 1360–61) a distinguished tripartite group of magnates, gentry, and lawyers. The head or *seigneur* of the Kentish peace commissions was Sir Simon Burley, sometime teacher of Richard II, friend of Anne of Bohemia, and a powerful presence at court.[85] Other prominent magnates who served as justices of the peace for Kent with Chaucer include Lord Cobham, Lord Devereux, and Lord Clinton. It is not certain whether Chaucer was selected to represent the gentry ("des meultz vauez du countee") or the law ("ascunes sages de la ley"); gentry seems the most likely bet, although Chaucer's experience might have qualified him for both groups.[86] The seven members of the gentry group (excluding Chaucer) were typically wealthy landowners, knights who served as M.P.s or sometimes as sheriffs. All six of the lawyers who served with Chaucer were knights; five of them were already sergeants-at-law by 1385.[87] The *Man of Law's Tale* cannot be dated earlier than 1386.[88] The self-naming of Fragment 2, then, might be read as a bid to associate, perhaps equate, the vocation of an English author with the power and authority of a man of law.[89]

This suggestion might seem less fanciful if we recall how Chaucer weighs the worth of Petrarch as a poet at the opening of Fragment 4. Petrarch's "rhetorike sweete," the Oxford clerk says,

> Enlumyned al Ytaille of poetrie,
> As Lynyan dide of philosophie,
> Or lawe, or oother art particuler.   (4.33–35)

Poetry; philosophy; law; other specialized "art": there is a clear sense here that literary disciplines are commensurate, that excellence in one "art particuler" might be compared with excellence in another. The power of Petrarch's poetry, which is seen to illuminate and define an entire territory ("al Ytaille"), is here compared to the power of law, specifically to the writings of Giovanni da Lignano, a professor of canon law at Padua. Chaucer's Man of Law is not a canonist, but as an author, interpreter, and practitioner of common law he works at London and Westminster as a layman, rather than at Oxford or Cambridge as a clerk; this brings him much closer to Chaucer. Like Chaucer, he occupies a difficult but crucial place between royal power (he was appointed by royal writ) and the commercial world. He draws his expertise from the study of old texts, and like a poet he lives and perishes through his control of the written and spoken word. The man of law hanged for treason in 1388 was Robert Tresilian, one of the five sergeants Chaucer had served with as a justice of the peace for Kent; Thomas Usk (who refers to Chaucer's *Troilus* in his *Testament of Love*) was put to death in the same year.[90]

A sergeant-at-law, then, needed to convince his public and his sovereign that his writing and speaking is exercised for the public good. This puts him in company with the poet; so, too, does his use of fictions. When a *narrator* spoke for a defendant in court in the later fourteenth century, he was routinely expected to employ fictions: "Fictions can as well be used," we learn from a reporter of 1330, "and in some cases had better be used, to fill in between what has to be specified to round out a statement and what can be denied to rebut it."[91] In the practice called "giving color," the color given to a plaintiff (the claim attributed to him by a defending counsel) is often quite fictitious; actions and motivations are ascribed to the plaintiff that are utterly fanciful. Modern commentators admit that "it is incongruous that statements that were wholly false and known to be so should operate to turn the course of proceedings whose intent was to find facts and do justice." But "the men of law of that age who invented these things, and . . . who first adopted them . . . considered them good."[92]

Legal scholars have recently admitted that "the intellectual structure of pleading" (of the kind practiced by men of law in Chaucer's time) has been largely ignored by social, intellectual, and legal historians. We obviously have much to learn from the study of "this peculiar, artificial form of argumentation," a form of discourse that even the experts find difficult to follow.[93] For now we can at least notice that Chaucer's Man of Law, in his interchange with the Host, is first addressed as a defendant accused of debt (33–38). Debt collection, we have noted, was the chief business of the Court of Common Pleas, monopolized by the sergeants. The plaintiff is the pilgrimage, which requires him to deliver the tale he holds in his personal possession, which is rightfully common property. The Man of Law admits the principle of accountability to law in such cases ("Biheste is dette," 41) but denies the specific allegation: he cannot possess a tale because Chaucer has already made all English tales his own. Hence it is that a monopolist of one kind of discourse, the Sergeant-at-Law, comes to recognize the achievement of another.

In enumerating the tales Chaucer is supposed to have told, the Man of Law makes mistakes: he attributes some tales to Chaucer that Chaucer never told, and he leaves out others that Chaucer certainly did write. The inaccuracies of this passage (53–89) have long troubled critics who read it as an authorial inventory. But if we read it as a specific phase of legal pleading, the inaccuracies of its details need not surprise us. Medieval courts were keen for charges and claims to be set out concretely, but they also assumed that such charges could not be rebutted just by picking at details. Barristers were mindful, therefore, "that under these circumstances the details that were alleged need not all be accurate, need not all be true."[94]

It is important to recognize, then, that the catechistic simplicities of the *Man of Law's Tale*, a narrative that judges truth-telling by the most inflexible, eye-popping standards (2.671–72), have little to do with the courtroom practices of a man of law. And it seems reasonable to assume that a sergeant, as professional *narrator*, might acknowledge some kinship with Chaucer as a maker of fictions. Indeed, in Fragment 2, the Man of Law impresses us more as a hard-boiled literary professional than the pilgrim Chaucer ever does. His understanding of the value of literary creativity is evidently determined by the kind of texts ("caas and doomes," 1.323) he is accustomed to working with: once a tale is set down in ink and put into circulation it becomes (he suggests) the property of the teller and cannot be retold (2.45–52). Such an attitude is perhaps designed to represent the mentality of a small, elite associational group, the Order of the Coif, that had in the course of the fourteenth century come to professionalize itself by monopolizing its own discourse.[95] This process is paralleled in Italy during the Trecento by the formation of elite cadres of *litterati* dedicated to the recovery and study of ancient texts. Such groups, or *cenacoli*, represent the first modern attempts to professionalize the study of literature and to make this study a vital part of civic life. Many of these proto-humanists were, of course, lawyers. When the Man of Law names Chaucer as "Chaucer" (not as "Geoffrey"), he is affirming a civil rather than a spiritual identity.[96] When he observes that Chaucer's prolific making of English poetry has created scarcity in the market he is, by the standards of his own associational grouping, paying him a professional compliment.

The Man of Law's involvement with the commercial world, especially as it pertains to the circulation of fictional narratives, is not without its ironies. Although he might monopolize his own particular market—the right to speak as *narrator* in the Court of Common Pleas—his efforts to procure a tale fit for a pilgrim *compagnye* have drawn him to a commercial sector that he cannot control and knows nothing about. His celebration of wealthy merchants might be less enthusiastic if he knew that the story he learned from a merchant (1.131–33) is a real Jack of Dover (1.4347): twice written and twice told, once by a Dominican for an English princess, and once by Gower for the kind of English public the Man of Law is currently addressing.[97] The irony is further refined by the fact that the merchant gives him a tale set in the sixth century: this predates 1066, the year that marks the maximum historical depth of the Man of Law's professional competence (1.323–24), by half a millenium.

Chaucer, of course, knows more about merchants than the Man of Law does. He grew up among them in the Vintry, was appointed customs controller for the port of London in 1374 and continued to work with them after becoming justice of the peace for Kent. We have noted that Chaucer acknowledges merchants in the *House of Fame* as "fadres of tidynges" (129); and *tidynges* represent the essential raw material for a certain kind of poetry. But Chaucer also knows (and here he knows more than the Man of Law) that *tidynges* have two aspects. If a *tidynge* has a father it must also have a mother. She is found not in the House of Fame, but in the whirling twig-cage of Rumor. Her name is Aventure; her motherhood is likened to the sea:

> And loo, thys hous, of which I write,
> Syker be ye, hit nas not lyte,
> For hyt was sixty myle of lengthe.
> Al was the tymber of no strengthe,
> Yet hit is founded to endure
> While that it lyst to Aventure,
> That is the moder of tydynges,
> As the see of welles and of sprynges.   (1977–84)

"Aventure" is the term that merchants came to appropriate by way of suggesting the resemblance between their particular form of professional activity and the time-honored values of the knightly class.[98] Their good name, their capacity for *creauncing*, is founded upon their ability to distinguish good merchandise from bad, true *tidynges* from false ones. Chaucer shares something of their expertise. The Man of Law may persuade us that an English poet has something in common with an English man of law, but Chaucer convinces us that he never loses contact with the values of the mercantile world. Chaucer clearly *does* wish to be recognized as author, like Petrarch, whose singular excellence will be commemorated by a textual afterlife that will save his *entente* from the vagaries of time.[99] And yet, as he lives and writes in an unfolding historical present, Chaucer knows himself to be just one more writer in the market for *tidynges, novelle*, the raw material of storytelling (and the enabling precondition of mercantile trade).[100] This sense of the commercial aspects of fiction writing—storytelling as commodity production—places him much closer to Boccaccio than to Petrarch.

Constance Rerouted: *Decameron* 5.2

In the *Canterbury Tales*, I have argued, Chaucer draws the Constance story into closer contact with the commercial world by accentuating the instrumental importance of merchants as purveyors of narrative *matière*. This in turn invites us to consider the Man of Law in his professional aspect as *narrator*: not as the disinterested purveyor of a hierocratic, God-given vision of society, but as one performer among many in a mixed economy of religious, secular, ancient, and contemporary narratives. The motif of disappearing merchants finds its correlative in the national politics of fourteenth-century England: the merchant class cannot be made continuously visible as a significant political class because of the hostility of the magnates. In Boccaccio's Florence, however, this particular political configuration is inverted: it is the Florentine merchant-capitalists who frame the laws, guide the government (and finance the chapter house); the magnates are excluded from political life. How, then, will the Constance story come to be written within these new cultural and political parameters?

Decameron 5.2, narrated by Emilia, describes how Gostanza, a young woman of noble birth, falls in love with a craftsman called Martuccio. Gostanza's father rejects Martuccio's request for his daughter's hand on the grounds that he is "poor" (5.5; p. 418). Martuccio, indignant at this rebuff, sets sail for the Barbary (North African) coast and becomes a privateer. After some initial success he is captured by Saracens and imprisoned at Tunis. Gostanza, believing her lover to be dead, steals from her father's house at night, puts to sea in a tiny fishing boat, throws the oars and rudder overboard, and lies down to die. But her boat beaches on the Barbary coast at Susa; she is found by an Italian woman called Carapresa and taken in by a community of Saracen women craftworkers. Martuccio, meanwhile, is freed from prison for offering the king of Tunis a winning strategy in his war against a grandee from Granada. Martuccio rises to high estate at Tunis, Gostanza hears of his fame, and the lovers are reunited. They sail back to their homeland together and pass the rest of their lives "in the tranquil and restful enjoyment of the love they bore one another" (5.48; p. 423).

Boccaccio's Italian *novella* of Gostanza brings about a drastic *aggiornamento* of the European legend of Costanza. We move from the ancient world to the recent past (the story takes place "not so very long ago") and although the story still crosses the boundaries between Christian and Arab worlds its geographic range has shrunk dramatically. Chaucer's heroine travels thousands of miles over many years, from Rome to Syria via the eastern Mediterranean, then west and north to Northumberland, then back to Rome, back to Northumberland, back to Rome again. Boccaccio's lovers live in Lipari, an island on the Italian mainland side of Sicily. Tunis is only two hundred miles away; the trip from Lipari to Susa (modern Sousse, some seventy miles south of Tunis) takes Gostanza less than 24 hours (5.13; p. 419). The hundred-mile Mediterranean bottleneck separating Trapani (Carapresa's home town in western Sicily) from Tunis was much traveled in Boccaccio's time. Coral divers from Trapani worked in Tunisia and (one hardly need add) the Bardi, the merchant banking company that Boccaccio served as an apprentice in Naples, had offices and warehouses in Tunis.[101] We can believe Martuccio, then, when he claims to have spent time in Tunisia at an earlier stage in his life (5.30; p. 421); it is quite plausible that such a poor Italian craftsman should speak Arabic. And the fact that Gostanza, on being washed up on the Tunisian shore, is discovered by Carapresa, an Italian woman working for Saracen fishermen, is fortunate but not too fantastic.

In the *Man of Law's Tale*, we have noted, political and religious authority is still centered on Rome, although the eccentric opening in Syria poses something of a challenge to ancient Roman authority. At the beginning of *Decameron* 5.3, the *novella* immediately following the Gostanza story, it is clear that this authority has slipped and eroded over the centuries: "Rome," Elissa tells us, "was once the head and is now the rump of the civilized world" (4; p. 424). Boccaccio's displacing of Costanza's homeland from Rome to Lipari symptomizes this slippage of authority; and the clear line of separation between Christian and Arab cultures proposed by Chaucer's Custance narrative is less distinct in *Decameron* 5.2.[102] Boccaccio's Barbary is still figured as an alien realm, but it has become indispensable as a space in which Christian society might work out social and political conflicts that it cannot resolve through its own internal mechanisms. The most serious conflicts of this kind, here and throughout the *Decameron*'s Fifth Day, are grounded in class difference: protagonists (usually men) who have fallen in love above their station struggle to achieve their desires by overcoming the conservative constraints of hierarchical societies.[103] The masculine protagonist of *Decameron* 5.2 is driven out of his native society by the *non du père*, the word of denial with which a father blocks the way to alliance with his daughter, a woman of higher degree. Barbary then comes into play as the realm of tumbling dice, the place where he may dramatically improve his fortunes and so return to his *patria* at a higher social level. Moral considerations in Barbary are held in suspension, since every rapacious act may be seen as a blow struck for Christendom against the infidel. Martuccio may be some sort of merchant venturer, but he is no knight errant: he seeks out and plunders "every vessel that was weaker than his own" (5.2.6; p. 418).

What we have here might be read as the time-honored crusading spirit (Tunisia was repeatedly attacked by bands of Christian knights and was the object of a "Barbary Crusade" as late as 1390) calked onto, or evolving into, a brave new world of commercial opportunism.[104] Such a narrative takes us several steps down the road toward the European capitalist expansionism of later centuries, but it does not take us out of sight of the *Man of Law's Tale*. The point of departure for both narratives is a rejection of traditional Christian teaching on attitudes to poverty. Rather than counseling the patient acceptance of poverty, and of the humble but respectable place in society assigned to the poor, both narratives interpret poverty only as an absence: an absence of riches. Poverty is not to be praised or accepted, but cured. Folk apostrophised as "riche" and "ful of wele" are, according to the Man of Law, to be identified as "noble" and "prudent folk" (122–23). This suggestion that wealth might purchase social standing and moral reputation, which many Chaucer critics have stepped over in embarrassed silence,[105] is the dominant assumption driving the action of *Decameron* 5.2. Martuccio, adjudged "povero" (5) by the father of Gostanza, resolves never to return to his homeland, "se non ricco" (6). Through privateering, he and his companions become "ricchissimi" (7); the pursuit of riches supplants all other desires, and they resolve to become extraordinarily wealthy ("trasricchire," 7). When, finally, he has achieved fame and fortune in Barbary, Martuccio returns to Lipari on his own terms. No scene of reconciliation with the forbidding father takes place (he disappears after the opening paragraph) because none is needed: Martuccio has become so wealthy that he can now ignore the father and the conventional authority that he embodies.

The most precious mercantile commodity purveyed in Chaucer's Constance narrative, we have noted, is the *tidynge* that brings the image of Custance to the Syrian sultan. The transmission of *tidynges* also plays a vital role in Boccaccio's Gostanza story. The false *tidynge* that will set Gostanza on the high seas is so important that Boccaccio makes it both an allegorical personification (a tactic employed by Chaucer in the *House of Fame*) and a grammatical subject lying in wait behind a long subordinate clause:

In Lipari tornò, non per uno o per due ma per molte e diverse persone, *la novella* che tutti quegli che con Martuccio erano sopra il legnetto erano stati annegati. (5.2.8; emphasis mine)

To Lipari was brought, not by one or by two but by many and diverse people, the news that all those who were with Martuccio aboard the ship had been drowned.[106]

Novelle, the precise equivalent of the Middle English *tidynges*, were essential for the functioning of the Florentine merchant economy. News of distant markets, and of the political events that affected them, were eagerly sought out; this appetite for *novelle* may still be read in the many Trecento chronicles written by Florentine merchants. Boccaccio, of course, is as hungry for *novelle* as Chaucer is for *tidynges*: they represent the raw material of his art while lending their name to its chief narrative component. It is not surprising to learn, then, that in seeking out a narrative motif that will distinguish his Gostanza story from its European analogues, Boccaccio (like the Man of Law) turns to a merchant. The winning military strategy that Boccaccio has Martuccio offer the king of Tunis is borrowed from Giovanni Villani's *Cronica* (where it is attributed to Cassano, king of the Tartars).[107] Martuccio knows that a good *consiglio* (like a good *novella*) is a precious commodity that must be marketed very carefully if it is to realize its optimum value. It is not to be given away for nothing: Martuccio does not tell his gaoler what his *consiglio* is, only that he has one to offer; like the squire in the *Summoner's Tale* (3.2243–52), he will not speak until he can be sure of exchanging his opinion for personal profit. Even when he stands before the king, Martuccio takes pains to accentuate his own ingenuity and local knowledge before delivering the goods:

"My lord . . . years ago I spent some time in this country of yours, and if I rightly observed the tactics you employ in battle, it seems that you leave the brunt of your fighting to your archers. If, therefore, one could devise a way of cutting off the enemy's supply of arrows whilst leaving your own men with arrows to spare, I reckon that your battle would be won." (5.2.30; p. 421)

What Martuccio is doing here, of course, is carrying mercantile ethics to the battlefield: the day will be won by the side that best understands the law of supply and demand. His *consiglio* allows the Tunisians to win the war; his marketing of it ensures that the king will raise him to rich and powerful estate ("grande e ricco stato," 35; p. 422). In rising from craftworker to magnate, Martuccio changes places with the woman he loves: for Gostanza, born into the nobility of Lipari, is now a craftworker in Tunisia.

Female Friendship and Women's Work

Gostanza's change in social fortunes is perhaps the most remarkable aspect of Boccaccio's rewriting of the legend: for the heroine's loss of nobility in Christian society leads directly to her enfranchisement in Barbary. Her new freedom is experienced as friendship with women and is developed through the sharing of meaningful work. The first suggestion that Gostanza is capable of working comes as she is rowing herself *away from* her native island: "like most women on the island," we are told, "she had learnt the rudiments of seamanship" (5.2.11; p. 418). But the patriarchal structure of Lipari forbids her, as the daughter of a noble father, the productive use of this "arte marineresca," or of any other "arte" in which she is "ammaestrata" (11); she is also forbidden any personal involvement with men or women from the world of craft or mercantile labor. In Barbary, however, she is first discovered by an Italian woman at work: Carapresa sees her tiny fishing boat as she is "taking in nets that had been left in the sun by the fishermen for whom she worked" (5.2.15; p. 419). On first learning that she has landed in Barbary, Gostanza wishes herself dead: but on hearing Carapresa's name (*cara preda*, "precious gain") Gostanza takes it "as a good omen." Carapresa then takes Gostanza to the house of a "very kind Saracen woman" who takes her in and makes her part of a community of women craftworkers. This "bonissima donna saracina" (5.2.24; p. 420) greets her like a long-lost daughter; such a welcome forms a pointed contrast to the rejection Gostanza has just experienced from her father and the inflexible class structure of Lipari:

When the lady, who was getting on in years, had heard her story, she looked into Gostanza's eyes, burst into tears, gathered her in her arms and kissed her on the forehead. Then she led her by the hand into the house, where she lived with certain other women, isolated from all male company. The women worked with their hands in various ways, producing a number of different objects made of silk, palm, and leather, and within a few days, the girl, having learned to make some of these objects, was sharing the work with the others. Her benefactress and the other ladies were remarkably kind and affectionate towards her, and before very long they had taught her how to speak their language. (5.2.25–26; p. 420)

Emilia insists on the fact that these women live together without a single man, "senza alcuno uomo." Through working with the Saracen women Gostanza comes to learn their language and, at the same time, to forget Martuccio: by the time Martuccio's fame has spread from Tunis, "her love for him . . . was beginning to fade from her heart" (5.2.36; p. 422). Her lukewarm ("intiepidito") feelings for her former lover do heat up again, however, and the good Saracen woman, "treating her like a daughter," arranges a reunion. Gostanza and Martuccio present themselves to the king of Tunis, tell him their story, and ask permission to marry according to "la nostra legge," "our law," the Christian rite (44; p. 423). The king, who cares nothing for noble birth in Christian society, decrees that Gostanza has earned ("guadagnato," 45) the right to marry Martuccio, his distinguished counsellor. This exchange of social degree, in which the noble woman trades places with the craftworking man, will be held in place by "our law" once Martuccio and Gostanza return home as a married couple.

In Barbary, we have noted, Martuccio finds opportunities for social advancement denied to him by the inflexible, class-conscious limits of his native island. Does this suggest that Gostanza's Barbary, particularly her experience of female friendship and meaningful work, might be read as a critique of normative social relations in Christian culture? A wider reading of the *Decameron* will fully endorse such a reading. Friendship between women is almost unheard-of elsewhere in the *Decameron*; the great narratives of friendship, which rival the most celebrated heterosexual romances in their steady eroticism, are all fashioned after a Ciceronian male-male ideal.[108] As for work: no women of noble birth are allowed to work in Boccaccio's text. Indeed, the very writing of the *Decameron* is predicated upon the forced idleness of women, who "are forced to follow the whims, fancies and dictates of their fathers, mothers, brothers and husbands, so that they spend most of their time cooped up within the narrow confines of their rooms" (*Proemio*, 10; p. 46). When men fall in love, Boccaccio continues, "they can always walk abroad, see and hear many things, go fowling, hunting, fishing, riding and gambling, or attend to their business affairs [mercatare]," but women have no such resources for venting or putting aside their feelings. Boccaccio responds to his own compassionate analysis by offering women "succour and diversion" in the form of a text, but the writing of his *Decameron* serves as a way of keeping *him* busily employed as he affirms the housebound vocation of his female readership.

Gostanza's rowing away from her father, and her forgetting of her lover through the "grazia e buono amore" she experiences among women in Barbary, might be taken as the political unconscious of a long historical trajectory of which the *Decameron* forms part. As commercial production shifted from household to workshop and factory, and political power was increasingly associated with the public sphere, women gradually lost the high labor status[109] they had enjoyed in the traditional household and were penned back into the home (the household stripped of the economic and political power of the *oikos*). Denied meaningful work, women became habituated to a purely symbolic role: they were to symbolize the social and political importance of their fathers and husbands. When a woman in late medieval Florence entered the house of a new husband, the laws of dowry made her, symbolically speaking, as naked as Boccaccio's Griselde: all rights of property passed to her husband or remained with the family she was born into.[110] At the moment of union with a masculine beloved, women, politically speaking, experienced something akin to voicelessness and death. This, too, is eerily prefigured in Boccaccio's rewriting of the Costanza legend:

The girl was so delighted to see him [Martuccio] that she nearly died [morì]. Carried away by her feelings, she ran up to him and flung her arms round his neck; then she burst into tears, unable to speak [senza potere alcuna cosa dire] because of her joy and the bitter memory of her misfortunes. (5.2.41; p. 422)

In Chaucer, I have argued, the expanded and then abruptly curtailed role accorded to the guild of Syrian merchants registers a challenge to the stable, hierocratic values of the Constance legend: a legend, as Chaucer found it, written by a Dominican friar for the daughter of a king to celebrate her taking the veil (becoming a nun). In accentuating the instrumental importance of the mercantile economy, Chaucer reminds us that even his awe-inspiring Man of Law is touched by the commercial forces that structure his professional life. In Boccaccio's Constance *novella*, which issues from a society governed by craftworkers and merchant capitalists, the traditional script is entirely rewritten by the dynamism and opportunism of this new commercial economy. In this new text, the future is scripted differently according to gender. Martuccio's Lipari adumbrates the colonizing adventurism of later centuries by allowing a young man to leave as a poor craftworker and to return home rich and on his own terms. As men move outward from household production to the international market economy, women are driven indoors: Gostanza's Barbary represents the displacement of female aspirations to an exotic dreamland, the territory of romance. Denied meaningful crosstown friendships and direct participation in the productive process, women, penned indoors under the political command of husbands and fathers, form a new mass market, an ideal readership for masculine authors.

Chapter 8

Household Rhetoric: Violence and Eloquence in the *Tale of Melibee*

In the *Man of Law's Tale*, vertical vectors of religious and political power are crossed by lateral motion associated with mercantile trade and imperial politics. Named locations—Syria, Rome, Northumberland, Scotland, Wales, "the See of Grece" (2.464), "the Strayte of Marrok" (2.464–65)—quickly come and go. The next two chapters discuss two unlocated narratives that lead us, physically speaking, nowhere: the *Tale of Melibee* and the *Manciple's Tale*. These tales have no specific geographical location, only a *kind* of location: a household dominated by a powerful, irascible, and violent male. Since everything that happens in such a space addresses itself to him, his physical presence is (we are encouraged to believe) the narrative's location.[1] The most urgent priority for those located or trapped in such discursive space is to find a language that will hold off, divert, or dissipate the immediate threat of masculine violence. Such a language begins with the body, appeals to the body, and measures its success in the fate of bodies (dead or alive; beaten or sound). The victims of violence in these tales are women and, in the *Manciple's Tale*, a court-trained bird who sounds a lot like Chaucer. Violence and the language through which violence is deferred or brought on is the chief concern of both of these tales and of the *auctor* who stands behind them: Albertano of Brescia.

In the *Man of Law's Tale*, a woman traverses the world; in the *Melibee* and the *Manciple's Tale*, women never leave the house. Despite these very different itineraries, however, all of these women seem to move within similar discursive limits, suggestive of a world mapped uncertainly between religious, secular, and mercantile terms of reference. And Chaucer, in pursuit of his own social, professional (and emotional) identity, moves with them. For just as he identifies himself as an interested party within the international nexus of *tidynges* created by the *Man of Law's Tale*, so he repeatedly chooses to script and describe strategies for solitary women facing masculine anger within the closed limits of a *familia* or household: women such as Prudence, Virginia, Griselde, Alceste, and Apollo's nameless wife. Such imaginative identification seems especially acute in the middle of Fragment 7, where, immediately before he is called upon to speak *in propria persona*, he has himself seen as a social outsider (isolated, vulnerable, and subjected to masculine scrutiny). This is a different Chaucer from the figure who, in the *General Prologue*, boldly talked himself into the pilgrim *felaweshipe* through the art of conversation.[2] He stares at the ground; he is viewed as one who has drifted out of the social circle ("lat this man have place!" 7.699). And even as the Host attempts to reintegrate him into the *compagnye*, the Host cannot help but single out Chaucer's physical and emotional strangeness:

> "Approche neer, and looke up murily.
>   Now war yow, sires, and lat this man have place!
>   He in the waast is shape as wel as I;
>   This were a popet in an arm t'enbrace
>   For any womman, smal and fair of face.
>   He semeth elvyssh by his contenaunce,
>   For unto no wight dooth he daliaunce."   (7.698–704)

   This Chaucer is a person who cannot hold a level gaze ("looke up"), whose passivity is said to invite physical handling, whose body is read as his social being. And this, too, is an author portrait: a portrait, specifically, of an author about to speak for himself. Such emphases upon physical vulnerability and social isolation suggest the impress of political pressures requiring a new explanatory framework. The latter part of this book will draw us away from associational poetics, a form brilliantly exemplified by Boccaccio's Florence. The figure we are heading for now, as we move into territory traditionally regarded as the preserve of "Renaissance" self-representation, is Petrarch, darling of Lombard despots, poet laureate of European absolutism, and the hapless antihero of his own household politics.

Chaucer in Lombardy; Albertano in England

When Queen Alceste, in the *Legend of Good Women*, counsels the God of Love to forgive Chaucer for his egregious shortcomings as courtier and poet, she confronts her irascible spouse with a negative exemplum: he should strive *not* to imitate

> "tyraunts of Lumbardye,
> That usen wilfulhed and tyrannye."   (G 354–55)

Lombardy, as exemplified by the *Clerk's Tale*, the *Merchant's Tale*, the *Legend of Good Women* (and by a single stanza of the *Monk's Tale*) comes to represent for Chaucer a spatial metaphor for the tyrannical cast of mind: a place where the unbridled desires of masculine authority, "wilfulhede," become the chief instrument of state. Lombardy for Chaucer is both a real foreign territory, a place to which he had traveled on the king's business, and an imaginary place close to home. The *Legend* suggests that Chaucer was haunted by thoughts of becoming a victim of tyrannical violence. His best hope of survival is represented by the rhetorical powers of a skilled female advocate: were it not for Alceste, he argues, "I hadde be ded, withouten any defence" (G 182). Similar anxieties, and similar hopes of salvation through the powers of womanly rhetoric, may be read in the most extensive authorial signature of the *Canterbury Tales*: the *Tale of Melibee* (or, as Thynne has it, sharpening the autobiographical identification, the *Tale of Chaucer*).[3] Albertano, the original *auctor* of this text, was in fact a Lombard, bent on addressing the immediate problems of his native, precariously emergent, urban culture. The fate of his text, as we shall see shortly, exemplifies the grandest historiographical paradigm of this book with unnerving clarity. Designed to facilitate communal resistance to magnate violence, Albertano's Melibee story comes to find different meanings in a culture that sees magnate violence elevated to a form of state (hence making "Lombardy" synonymous with "tyranny").

Albertano (professionally active 1226–51) was one of the most popular and widely disseminated of all medieval authors. Sharon Hiltz lists more than three hundred Albertano manuscripts;[4] James M. Powell adds to Hiltz's list and speculates that the final count may well exceed five hundred.[5] The range of Albertano's influence extends from marginal and interlinear annotations lifted from his works to complete manuscripts dedicated to him alone. By the fourteenth century, however, an order of transmission for Albertano's works (as a complete manuscript, or as part of a manuscript) has established itself with remarkable consistency: first the *De doctrina dicendi et tacendi*, a short rhetorical treatise;[6] then the *Liber consolationis et consilii* (the tale of Melibee and Prudence); then the *De amore et dilectione Dei et proximi et aliarum rerum et de forma vitae* (a longer treatise on the pursuit of civic and religious virtue); then five sermons; then (quite often) some verses of Peter Damian, beginning "Episcopi, attendite, / Dei verba discernite" and addressed (when rubricated) "to all orders of men living in this world."[7] It was possible to learn a good deal about Albertano from the rubrics, incipits, and explicits accompanying his works. One fourteenth-century manuscript of English provenance tells us that Albertano, *causidicus* of Brescia (from the St. Agatha district), devised and delivered one of his sermons for "causidicos" and "notarios" by way of reforming their lives;[8] another, in its table of contents,[9] borrows from Albertano's own explicit to tell us that the *De amore*

was written and compiled by Albertano while held prisoner by the lord Emperor Frederick in the city of Cremona. He was put there for having been captain of Gavardo, defending this place for the good of the community of Brescia in August 1238, on St. Alexander's Day, when the citizenry of Brescia was being besieged by the aforementioned Emperor.

Emperor Frederick II, according to Dante, punished his political enemies by dressing them in capes of lead and then tossing them into boiling cauldrons.[10] For Burckhardt, Frederick was chief practitioner of a new form of statecraft: a despotism dedicated to "the transformation of the people into a multitude destitute of will and of the means of resistance"; an "absolute monarchy," organized "with the sole object of securing a concentrated power for the death-struggle in which he was engaged."[11] In this context, Albertano's defiance of Frederick on behalf of his native *communitas* of Brescia represents a twofold heroism, beginning with the sword and ending with the pen. Such heroism is made the more poignant by the shift in transmission order effected by fourteenth-century Albertano manuscripts. The text Albertano composed first (1238), the *De amore et dilectione Dei*, is placed last; the *De doctrina dicendi et tacendi*, composed second (1245), is placed first; the *Liber consolationis*, composed last (1246), is placed in the middle. The effect of this is double. First, we are alerted to the rhetorical aspects of Albertano's work. Since we begin with a short treatise on the art of speaking and of keeping silent, we are predisposed to read the *Liber consolationis*, the Melibee story, as a sustained exemplification of that art.[12] Second, following a hint offered by the title of the Melibee-Prudence dialogue, the *Liber consolationis*, we are encouraged to read the three works as a Boethian sequence: beginning with the art of speaking in public service, we end in prison with Albertano, contemplating "the love and pleasing of God (and of our neighbors)." Such a reordering gained added power from historical hindsight. The civic virtues that Albertano labored to exemplify and defend at Brescia had been wiped out by the Visconti, heirs to the despotic statecraft pioneered by Frederick II. Brescia, following its military defeat in 1337, was absorbed into the Lombard territory of the Visconti. The city statutes were rewritten in 1355 to ensure that all civic powers and jurisdictions should be translated to Bernabò Visconti, "magnificus dominus," and his heirs.[13] In 1363, having violently repressed an uprising, Bernabò built a fortress in the middle of the city and surrounded it with walls and ditches.[14] On the first folio of an Italian Albertano manuscript, earlier matter is scraped and wiped away to make room for the Visconti blazon: eloquent testimony to the fate of the civic culture that Albertano strove to nurture.[15]

There is no doubt that in writing the *Melibee*, Chaucer worked closely from the French translation by the Dominican Renaud de Louens.[16] It is also clear that he was familiar with Latin manuscripts of Albertano. The opening discussion of marriage in the *Merchant's Tale* borrows from the "De uxore diligenda" section of *De amore*, the same section from which both Ellesmere and Hengwrt scribes draw their glosses. William Askins has argued that the *Manciple's Tale*, like the *Merchant's Tale*, is "laced with references to Albertano's work from beginning to end"; his argument for the influence of the *De doctrina dicendi et tacendi* on the ending of the *Manciple's Tale* is particularly persuasive (13 parallel passages in the last 42 lines).[17] If Chaucer knew Latin manuscripts of Albertano (and he had dozens of opportunities to make their acquaintance, since they were scattered all over Europe), he would have known something about Albertano: the Brescian author was un-usually forthcoming about himself in his incipits and explicits. This was no accident: Albertano was keen to promote himself as a man of law and urban professional, dedicated to guild structures, to the life of his *commune*, and to employing private and public rhetoric as a palliative, even an alternative, to magnate violence.

Chaucer, we have noted, is willing to identify himself as an author with European pretensions (the sixth of six) in the communal setting of a pilgrim *compagnye*.[18] When he wishes to have himself *named* as an author, however, he turns to a Man of Law (who catalogues his works). When he wishes to speak *in propria persona* he turns to a tale translated from a man of law, a tale once intended (most critics agree) for his own Sergeant.[19] Chaucer and Albertano are in many respects kindred spirits: figures balancing allegiances to associational and hierarchical structures in the attempt to establish a new form of authorial identity. Each must have recognized the possibility, one accentuated by the transmission of Albertano in the fourteenth century, that this brave enterprise might meet with a Boethian ending. Skillful regulation of language and silence may bring violence to an end: such is the hope of the *Melibee*. But mismanaged speaking and silence may also bring violence to a peaceful household: such is the nightmare of Chaucer's last poetic fiction, the *Manciple's Tale*.

This chapter begins by resisting the traditional impulse to fit Albertano quickly into long-lived religious or *Fürstenspiegel* traditions. It is important to grasp the particular political conditions that shaped his writing; it is also vital to appreciate (as his fourteenth-century readers and copyists evidently did) his abiding concern with rhetorical performance. We also need to understand the relationship of rhetoric to the female body, or to ask: Why do Prudence and the Wife of Bath have so much in common? Finally, after much elaborate preparation, we need actually to read the *Tale of Melibee*. The unwillingness of our subjection to the text of *Melibee* teaches us something about the unpleas-antness of absolutist chamber politics, which typically demand subjection to the will and pleasure of a dominant godlike male. Perhaps this is why women, especially wives, were granted such generous roles as practitioners of house-hold rhetoric. But if the prospect of reading *Melibee* seems unpleasant, the practice of living it may prove worse: deadly for the wife housed with an angry, vengeful man, and catastrophic for the household she holds together. Such is the dark underside of the *Melibee* offered by the Manciple as the final poetic fiction of the *Canterbury Tales*.

Guilds, Magnates, and Go-Between Authors

Chaucer critics have traditionally spoken of the *Melibee* as a text securely rooted in the "mirror for princes" tradition.[20] Albertano's text was deliberately assimilated into this tradition: Reynaud de Louens, Chaucer's immediate source for the *Melibee*, prefaces his translation from the Latin by marking this moment of assimilation. He tells his noble female dedicatee ("ma treschere dame") that he has made a short treatise for the teaching of princes: "Je ay fait un traicté petit a l'enseignement [et au proufit] de mon [trescher] seigneur vostre filz et de touz autres princez et barons qui le vouldront entendre et garder."[21] This treatise, he tells her, was "fondé et extrait d'une ficcion ancienne que j'ay trouvee en escript." It is important to observe that Reynaud claims credit here not for translating a mirror for princes, a *Fürstenspiegel*, but for fashioning one from a "ficcion ancienne." Reynaud cuts his Latin source by about one-third, omits the names of *auctores*, adds citations from the Gospels and saints' lives, and makes other changes pertinent, in the view of this particular friar, to the particular circumstances of war-torn Burgundy in the 1330s. Such changes cannot obscure the residual otherness of Albertano's invention. Reynaud's *Livre de Melibee et de Prudence* reads like a palimpsest; Albertano's text and Albertano's Brescia continue to peer through, imperfectly assimilated to the northern European *Fürstenspiegel* tradition.

Albertano of Brescia's *Liber consolationis et consilii* was written not to instruct or win the favor of a prince, but rather to aid the survival of a struggling, emergent city-state culture. Albertano showed a lifelong dedication to the sworn association, or commune, of Brescia. The economic and political confidence characteristic of his native city in this period is attested to by a document of 1237 that lays out plans for urban expansion with remarkable detail, coherence, and far-sightedness.[22] The chief threat to such peaceable civic association came from *milites*, knights, who insisted on bringing seigneurial habits—especially the habit of dispensing summary justice—from their country domains to the city.[23] Albertano's *Liber consolationis* takes issue, above all, with the increasingly desperate problem of the urban vendetta,[24] and is peculiarly urban in character. The high towers that dominate his Italian skyline may disappear in translation, but the sense of insistent personal pressure generated by living in confined urban spaces remains. His hero, Melibeus, seems peculiarly a product of urban culture. He endures the social isolation of the *nouveau riche*: when he calls an assembly, he (unlike scions of established, aristocratic families) has no relatives to call upon.[25] Melibeus is a man who stands in need of counsel: he was defined as such by the *De amore*, Albertano's first prose treatise, in two epigrams borrowed from Godfrey of Winchester ("Melibee, you are to expect / Headlong ruin, while you are without counsel").[26] Melibeus and his kind need, in short, Albertano, "a sociologist of the medieval urban experience,"[27] a "new man" of the early Duecento.

Albertano of Brescia is usually referred to as a judge, or a man of law; his particular title (faithfully reproduced by manuscript rubrics) was *causidicus*. Although Gower uses this term with monotonous regularity as a synonym for "man of law" in his attack on the legal profession in *Vox Clamantis*, Book 6, *causidicus* was earlier applied to "the professional pleaders at Rome, who were not scholarly lawyers and indeed rather despised legal learning but orators, knowing only enough law to understand the advice they got from the juriconsults."[28] Albertano's function evidently extended to that of legal assessor and counselor, but his work remains primarily *rhetorical* in character: he never gets bogged down in the minutiae of legal learning, nor does he attempt to construct a legal basis for his arguments.[29] His concern with rhetorical practice is most obviously advertised and exemplified by the *De doctrina dicendi et tacendi*. This short work borrows from Alcuin's *Dialogus de arte rhetorica*, makes extensive use of Cicero, and structures itself by considering terms from the rhetorical *circumstantiae*: "who (speaks), what, to whom, why, in what way, when."[30] As his title implies, Albertano devotes as much space to the art of keeping silent as he does to the art of speaking. He advises his son Stephen, the addressee of this work, to imitate the cock who beats himself three times before he will crow about himself.[31] The wise man, he argues under "quando" ("when," the final section), will keep quiet until he sees his time; the wanton and imprudent man will pay no attention to the time of his speaking.[32] It is not surprising to discover Brunetto Latini borrowing from Albertano's discussion of *dicendi* and *tacendi* to augment his own discussion of the virtue of prudence.[33]

Albertano, like the Trecento Florentines we have discussed earlier, shows himself exceptionally conscious of language as the determining force of civic life. In reading a manuscript of Seneca's moral epistles, Albertano was moved to mark passages ripe for recycling into his own treatises with a striking series of mnemonic devices: knots, fabulous buildings, beasts, grotesques, a cock, a cowled and tonsured religious, and a two-faced bishop; he also made the following marginal annotation: "Nota sermo cum vita concordet" ("Note that speech should harmonize with life").[34] Attention to *ethos* was particularly appropriate for a legal advisor such as Albertano, who would travel in the service of a *podestà* to rule neighboring cities.[35] Such concern is carried forward in the first section of the *De doctrina*, where in exploring the subject of "Quis es qui loqueris" ("Who are you that would speak"), he offers an imaginative revision of a much-traveled Roman law maxim: "Quod omnes tangit ab omnibus approbetur" ("That which concerns everyone must be approved of by everyone") is wittily reworked as "Quod te non tangit, hoc te nullatenus angit" ("Do not lose sleep over things that are none of your business").[36] Albertano shows a particularly keen and historically precocious sense of himself as an urban professional. This implies establishing a particular place for oneself within the general division of labor: his three sons, each a dedicatee of one of his three treatises, are addressed as young professionals in the making.[37] Albertano himself, as a *causidicus*, was particularly devoted to his own professional body, the guild or confraternity of the Brescian *causidici*.

Albertano's concern with the professional conduct of his fellow guild members is inevitably self-interested: greater emphasis upon the difficulty of public speaking must accentuate the particular skills of the *causidici*; professional standards help secure professional monopoly. But the sermons preached by Albertano to his fellow guildsmen are, on the face of it, remarkable for their outward-focused altruism.[38] The *causidici* should be friends, even political allies, of the poor: "Almsgiving is the highest good [summum bonum] in man"; "We ought to liberate the poor, if possible, from the powerful"; "We ought to rise up to their help because of their misery."[39] Not everyone should be invited to the *convivium* or banquet that the confraternity is about to enjoy: just the good and the poor.[40] This does indeed seem revolutionary (as if Chaucer's Man of Law were to ride with the Plowman instead of the Franklin) until one grasps that the *pauperes* Albertano is speaking of here are, in fact, Franciscan friars. The Brescian *causidici* held their meetings in the Franciscan church of St. George the Martyr; Albertano's words at the *convivium* were followed by those of a friar, intent on feeding them "with spiritual food."[41]

We should not, on hearing that the *causidici* feasted with friars, immediately yield to the kind of cynicism cultivated by our reading of Chaucer, Langland, and Penn Szittya.[42] The fraternal orders were, in these early decades, still touched by the dynamism and idealism of their founders; the development of the kind of urban culture envisioned by Albertano required both the formation of professional elites and the development of a city-centered, rather than rural-monastic, spirituality. Albertano's preaching among friars during the boom period of the medieval economy might even be viewed as an Edenic moment in the history of medieval associational forms. For Chaucer such a moment was long past. Chaucer shows no inclination to recognize the virtues of friars in either rural or urban settings: Thomas Speght's story of Chaucer beating up "a Franciscane fryer in Fleetstreete" may be apocryphal, but it is not out of keeping with the spirit of his writings.[43] It is worth noting, however, that the association between Albertano and friars was preserved both by the French intermediary text Chaucer worked from and by Latin manuscripts in fourteenth-century England. Readers of these manuscripts are routinely informed that Albertano's sermons were delivered either to an audience of legal professionals or to a mixed and mutually acquainted company of lawyers and friars.[44] Albertano manuscripts in England were copied, housed, and circulated by friars. The Austin friars of York, for example, bound his three treatises and his sermons together with a life of St. Thomas Becket and classified it under pressmark K: canon law.[45] The Albertano manuscript Corpus Christi College, Cambridge 306 was owned by the Dominicans of London; Sidney Sussex 48 belonged to the Dominicans of Lancaster.

Albertano did not write with the intention of being absorbed into mendicant culture. He advertised links with the Franciscans by way of authorizing, or theologizing, his own profession. The Brescian *causidici*, like many other specialized groups in emergent urban cultures, were concerned, Jacques Le

Goff argues, "with finding religious justification for their activity and vocation, anxious to assert their dignity and obtain assurance of their salvation,
not in spite of, but rather because of, their profession."[46] Chaucer is similarly concerned, in the *Canterbury Tales*, with defining and justifying his own
profession of authorship even as he writes the text. He will not, like Albertano, advertise links with the friars. But he trusts that the *Melibee* in prose,
especially when complemented by the prose of the *Parson's Tale*, will win him
an authority that is both urbane and religious in its appeal; that will both
anchor and license his poetic fictions. It is worth noting that one fourteenth-
century Albertano manuscript of English provenance repeats this matched
pair of Melibeus and the Seven Deadly Sins. British Library Add. MS 6158
features Albertano's works in the usual (fourteenth-century) order[47] and ends
with a very short treatise "de septem peccatis capitalibus" (92v.). This fills up
just one and two-thirds columns of the double-columned page; the remaining space is given over to some Anglo-Norman verses, lecturing "You who
uphold the justice of law" on the importance of exercising power humanely.
The intent here is to flush Albertano out of the religious setting he had grown
accustomed to in English manuscripts and identify him, once more, as a man
of law.

Albertano adopts a variety of disguises and keeps some strange company
over the decades. In one late thirteenth-century manuscript his works appear
immediately after (and in the same bold, black hand as) documents pertaining
to the discovery of the relic of the Holy Blood at Fécamp.[48] A century later,
his Melibeus story is keeping company with rat poison recipes and strategies
for ridding hawks of lice (as offered to a teen bride by her aging Parisian
groom).[49] Such versatility may be attributed chiefly to the rhetorical character
of Albertano's writing, which shows a boundless ability to adapt itself to new
and different discursive contexts (hence generating new and different uses and
meanings). It also derives from Albertano's attempt to root himself in both
religious and secular aspects of urban culture while recognizing the claims and
powers of a dominant magnate class.

Chaucer, I believe, would have recognized Albertano's *Liber consolationis
et consilii* (even through vernacular intermediaries) as a work of counsel au-
thored not by a magnate but by someone (much like himself) confecting a
social and authorial identity from divergent bases of authority: a "new man."
It is worth dwelling on this term, one developed by Anne Middleton[50] and
deployed by Antony Black in the following review of arguments for counsel
in medieval political thought:

The argument for counsel or wisdom in government could be employed on behalf of
several practical programs. It could be employed on behalf of the supposedly traditional role of the baronage, or certain select barons, as the "natural counsellors" of the
king, a hereditary aristocracy; or, alternatively, on behalf of experts, men trained in
law, theology, or the liberal arts, a meritocracy (*sapientes, savi, prud'hommes*). These

two were liable to conflict: barons frequently objected to royal use of "new men," who in turn proclaimed the rights of merit against the accidents of birth.[51]

The monarchical setting evoked here, with its attendant magnate jealousies, would seem to fit Chaucer's situation as a member of the king's affinity.[52] And yet it does not seem plausible to suggest that Chaucer slotted the *Melibee* into the *Canterbury Tales* by way of advertising himself as a potential adviser to princes. The setting of the *Melibee* in the *Tales*, with its heterogeneity of social voices, suggests something different: that Chaucer effects a conjunction of court, religious, urban, and commercial worlds; that, from this peculiar vantage point, he is able to offer not counsel for princes but strategies for he or she who must speak with powerful men. His *Melibee* is not a *Fürstenspiegel*, but a handbook for go-betweens.

Friars and Wives; Persuasion and Confession

The most celebrated go-betweens in fourteenth-century court society were friars and wives.[53] Friars were royal confessors; wives enjoyed privileged access to the royal ear. Such intimate contact with the great and powerful made them doubly vulnerable, both to the displeasure of the great and to the jealousies of rivals. The Carmelite John Latimer, having celebrated mass before Richard II "in camera," denounced John of Gaunt as a traitor; he was subsequently murdered by a group of knights who, according to the *Westminster Chronicle*, subjected him to genital torture.[54] The early years of Henry IV were to see a number of Franciscans caught in complex networks of plotting, approving, and betrayal.[55] Women, of course, were subjected to forms of violence, particularly domestic violence, that were never recorded in courts of law. Traces of all this are to be found throughout Chaucer: in the Wife of Bath's deafness, in a long succession of assaults on women, in the extreme physical and scatological abuse wished on friars in Fragment 3. And, of course, in a classic divide-and-rule tactic, friars and wives are represented as professional rivals: the Friar mildly rebukes the Wife for preaching, or preambling; the Wife characterizes friars as rapists-in-waiting; Wife and Friar tell tales back to back.[56] The ground of their rivalry is, of course, rhetoric, *groping* and *glosing*, an art both of words and the body. This emphasis upon the embodied character of language, and the importance of real (rather than allegorical) bodies, is one of the most striking aspects of Albertano's *Liber consolationis*.

When he speaks of the poor, Albertano emphasizes the importance not just of almsgiving, but also of making actual, physical contact with the bodies of poor people.[57] Similarly, when he speaks of the body of Prudence, and that of her daughter, Albertano evokes a real, beaten body that provokes genuine rage in the husband: the kind of passion that represented the greatest historical danger to the vendetta-ridden fabric of Brescian society. Albertano seems to have had an exceptional capacity for envisioning women (political *pauperes* throughout the Middle Ages) as historical subjects. His *De amore* rejects the sumptuary legislation habitually found in guild rules and Orders of Penance; it offers a rule of moderation in both food and dress that makes no reference to gender.[58] His *Liber consolationis*, James Powell argues, attaches unusual importance to female advice:

It is not merely that Albertano placed a positive value on women, but he reversed the traditional role of relationships between men and women and did so consciously in order to emphasize certain "female" characteristics in the social order. This does not mean that he was uncritical of women. Indeed, he also noted the customary female vices and warns against them in the *De amore*. But the *Liber consolationis* passes over such criticisms, indeed refutes them.[59]

Most manuscripts of Reynaud de Louen's translation of the *Liber consolationis* entitle the work the *Livre de Melibee et de Prudence*. Some manuscripts have "*et de Prudence* sa femme" (my emphasis): which, as Mario Roques argues, "shows no hesitation to consider the real [réel], and not simply allegorical, character of the personage."[60] Such cognizance of the powers of wifely eloquence was shared by certain contemporary clerical writers. Monastic authors tended to associate women with spoken language and distrusted both. Silence should ideally reign in monasteries: "Like women and the devil," Sharon Farmer observes, "spoken language had the power to entice the monks away from their silent conversation with God."[61] But if women are born talkers (the monks reasoned), let them talk to the good: let them employ the arts of feminine persuasion, in which they naturally excel, to soften men's hearts. The Cistercian Conrad of Eberbach tells of a rich young noble knight who is led to follow the impulses of the flesh and so despise all laws, both human and divine; his wife, through tears, physical affection, and eloquence, finally persuades him to desist from his extraordinary acts of violence (arson, rape, treason, and homicide) and to confess his sins to a priest.[62] Friars and urban scholastics, unlike monks, were not unnerved by spoken language: they lived by it. Men such as Thomas of Chobham, who was associated with the Parisian circle of Peter the Chanter in the early thirteenth century, set out to devise a form of practical ethics that reflected the realities of a new urban and commercial environment.[63] The phenomenon of wifely eloquence, according to Thomas, should be put to good practical use. Wives should be preachers to their husbands, "because no priest is able to soften the heart of a man the way his wife can."[64]

Writers such as Thomas of Chobham, according to Sharon Farmer, closed the divide "between the material attractions of speech and its spiritual benefits." Thomas's positive treatment of the alluring qualities of wifely eloquence, Farmer continues, "is suggestive of an intellectual development that reached its greatest peak in the urban culture of the thirteenth century. Increasingly, scholastic inquiry and the urban environment created an interest in and affirmation of the realm of the empirical."[65]

Albertano of Brescia, writing in the same period, shows a similar determination to fuse material and spiritual aspects of language by exploring the empirical powers of wifely eloquence. He has a good deal in common with his Parisian counterparts. He is responding to the particular pressures of an urban milieu and a money economy;[66] he is influenced by the example of secular literature; he benefits from the fresh grasp of the powers of female eloquence that came in 1215, when lay confession was declared normative. Thomas of Chobham's *Summa confessorum*, a manual prepared to facilitate the newly regularized dialogue of confession, argues that wives "should employ persuasion, feminine enticements, and even deceit." Albertano's *Liber consolationis* adopts the dialogue form and redeploys it within a neighboring "realm of the empirical," matrimony. Prudentia takes on the role of confessor and leads her husband to true penitence, a renunciation of the passion that drives him to destructive acts. Exemplifying a wife who is not herself in the grip of strong passion, Albertano's wife steadily visualizes a goal to be achieved through rational argument. Such a wife is inclined to argue for the kinds of purposes of which confessors—friars, monks, or secular clergy—would approve. But such an exemplification inevitably suggests the possibilities of its opposite: a wife who uses "feminine enticements, even deceit" not for the purposes of the clergy but for her own designs; or a wife who, as a preacher to her husband, berates him for sins he never committed and drives him to an early grave. A wife could even, rather than lead her husband away from physical violence, drive him to it:

> "Slee the dogges everichoon,
> And brek hem, bothe bak and every boon!"   (7.1899–1900)

For Chaucer's Host the example of Prudence points, by way of contrast, to the violence and unruliness of his own wife (or, better, the violence and unruliness *in him* that she has the power to unlock). Many male Chaucer critics have been similarly unnerved by Prudence because (consciously or not) she reminds them of her negative antitype—the Wife of Bath—and because she threatens to uncover disequilibrium, if not violence and unruliness, within their own critical discourse.

Begetting and Beating: Prudence, Rhetoric, and the Wife of Bath

Chaucer's *Melibee* sees a mother and daughter, alone at home, attacked by three men who climb in through the windows. The wife is beaten; the daughter is severely wounded and left for dead. On returning to the house, the husband, Melibee, weeps, cries, tears his clothes and plots his revenge. The mother, Prudence, turns all her attention to Melibee. Her aim henceforth will be to dissuade her husband from perpetuating the cycle of violence with which the *Tale* has opened. Her means are rhetorical: she will say just what is necessary, from one moment to the next, to move Melibee's mind away from thoughts of vengeance and recrimination. The *Tale* will last just as long as (is synonymous with) the wife's rhetorical performance.

I begin with this simple, literal synopsis of the *Melibee* because the literal sense (what happens) is so quickly discarded by most critical accounts of the *Tale*. Chaucer, the masculine author, may be writing in hope of impressing a masculine patron (although a feminine patron is just as likely),[67] but what the *Tale* speaks of is a wife counseling her husband. Her dissuasion of Melibee from revenge brings a sequence of texts exploring the interactions of female eloquence with magnate violence to a triumphant high point. In the *Knight's Tale*, men fought over, or at the instigation of, women; in the *Wife of Bath's Tale*, women postpone and then dispense with male-on-male violence (a beheading). Now, finally, the urge to masculine violence is simply talked out of existence by the power of female (specifically wifely) eloquence.

Chaucer criticism has long been unsettled by the gender politics of the *Melibee*. Critics have sometimes attempted to deny the relevance of gender *tout court* by treating Prudence, Sophie, and Melibee as aspects of universal—masculine—mind, or by pointing to the precedent of Boethius's *Consolation of Philosophy*. But Prudence is different in kind from Philosophy; *prudentia* is a practical art, not an allegorical abstraction. And Chaucer's Prudence is no lady from the heavens, but a stay-at-home wife. The Danish scholar Thor Sundby, who edited Albertano of Brescia's *Liber consolationis et consilii* for the Chaucer Society in 1873, struggles to relate Prudence to his own particular understanding of what a woman and a wife should be. Melibeus, he argues, is readily recognizable as "an honest but rash and hotbrained young man of high rank."[68] "His wife, Prudentia, on the other hand," Sundby continues,

is painted as a strong and noble-minded but kindhearted and religious woman, far superior to her husband in knowledge and intelligence, though not unacquainted with those small and harmless, or at least well-meant, artifices and stratagems that are so characteristic of her sex. Unhappily, Albertano has identified her with himself to such a degree, that she not only quotes all sorts of authors, even Albertano himself, but reasons in judicial matters like an accomplished lawyer, equally versed in the Digest and the Decretals. Indeed if we did not remember her allegorical dignity, we might be tempted to use a modern term and call her a most terrible blue-stocking.[69]

Sundby begins here by approving of Prudence, but is unsettled by the antithetical relationship of "strong and noble-minded" to "kindhearted and religious" when it pertains to "woman." He then denigrates Prudence for her typically female "artifices and stratagems" while pretending to approve of them as womanly traits. He then becomes alarmed by the collapse of Albertano, the masculine author, into his female character. He ends by castigating Prudence for displaying what is found admirable in Albertano, namely, her learning: she is "a most terrible blue-stocking." Prudence evidently fills Sundby with turbulent and contradictory emotions: in short, she makes a

Melibee of him, much as Julian of Norwich unhinges Clifton Wolters.[70] This spectacle of self-possessed women throwing their masculine readers into confusion is quite familiar, of course: it simply rehearses the gender politics of the *Clerk's Tale.*

Sundby's allusion to "artifices and stratagems that are so characteristic of her sex" suggests the *modus operandi* of a specific part of the trivium: rhetoric, an art habitually associated with (even to the extent of being said to issue from) the female body.[71] The most famous exemplification of this in Chaucer comes, of course, in the discourse that flows unbidden at the beginning of Fragment 3 from the "joly body" of the Wife of Bath. The analogy between the Wife's "joly body" and the textual corpus she generates is sustained through rhetorical *dilatio* both in her confessional *Prologue* and in her *Tale* (a romance, a genre traditionally associated with *ars dilatandi*). The Wife's "copious discourse or dilated textual body" has been read as a direct challenge to the Parson and to the heavy curtain of his concluding text: "Alisoun of Bath," Patricia Parker argues, "ameliorates the harsh polarizations of apocalyptic judgment and eschatology and opens a space of dilation in which what we have come to call literature can have its place."[72] The art of dilation with which the Wife opens a space for textual and bodily pleasure also flushes out anxieties (in medieval clerics and modern male critics alike) concerning the all-enveloping, endless character of female discourse (and of the body that generates it). It is important to note (once again) that similar concerns have been voiced about Prudence: "What wife was ever so learned or so pedantic," Charles Muscatine asks, "as Prudence in Chaucer's *Melibee*?"[73] It is interesting that Muscatine, in posing this question, does not entertain the thought that Prudence might be considered a blood relative (even a distant one) of the learned, pedantic, wifely, and rhetorical Alisoun of Bath.[74] It is also worth noting that Muscatine's uneasiness with the narrative of the *Melibee* is expressed as a critique of Prudence. It is, of course, Melibee himself who determines the dilation of the text: once his passion has abated, Prudence is free not to speak.

The Wife of Bath and Prudence, I shall argue, have a great deal in common. If critics have failed to explore the import of such kinship, it is perhaps because they have brought to the text presuppositions about the kind of woman each of them is: Alisoun is the bourgeois, man-hunting wife; Prudence is the noble, continent spouse. Comparisons might begin with their common employment of rhetorical dilation as a means of creating a specifically feminine discursive space that *holds off* violent, even apocalyptic, masculine speaking. The Wife, we have noted, holds off the Parson and everything he stands for. Prudence holds off Melibee; she prevents his turbulent emotions from finding expression as political violence in the public realm. The Wife maps out a space for poetic pleasure under clerisy; Prudence creates a space for political life under the shadow of tyranny.

Prudence, like Alisoun of Bath, embodies her own discourse: she *is* prudence, the matter of which she speaks. Her bodiliness is established before her speaking. Prudence is represented first as a sexual creature (Melibeus "bigat upon" her) and next as the object of masculine violence (men "betten" her).[75] The Wife of Bath, of course, is both a sexual body from the beginning of her *Prologue* and a beaten body by the end of it.[76] Alisoun and Prudence have much in common as historical bodies in the world and of the world: their likeness compares with that of rhetoric and prudence, "for rhetoric and prudence alike are concerned with the contingent realm of human affairs."[77] This likeness, Victoria Kahn argues, was recognized by Aristotle (in both the *Rhetoric* and the *Nicomachean Ethics*) as "a faculty of judgment that is not logical or theoretical, but practical; that does not subordinate an object to a general rule or concept, but responds to the particular per se."[78] Prudence, Thomas Gilby argues, is to Aristotle "like a bridge flung out from necessary principles to contingent occasions in human living."[79] The decisive knowledge held in Prudence is experimental, elicited from the opinative or calculative part of the soul, not from the scientific. Such knowledge turns to the experience of individual things, and implies an appetite for things as they are in themselves, not as they might be in the mind. "Prudence itself," Gilby argues, "is an act of reason reaching past the general meaning to the reality beyond, past *quidditas carnis* to *ipsa caro*."[80] Not fleshliness in general but a particular, fleshly body: such is the emphasis established from the first by the narratives of Prudence and the Wife of Bath.[81]

The prudent person, seeking to effect change in the public world, must of necessity be a rhetor; ideally, rhetoricians should always be prudent in selecting the tropes and topics of their public discourse. Here Prudence and the Wife part company, for while it is easy to see how the rhetorical skills of Prudence are prudently employed, it is not self-evident how the Wife serves the public good, unless, of course, the pleasurable space of narrative that she opens up be acknowledged, following Glending Olson, as a public good.[82] Such a possibility cannot be argued for logically or overtly declared, but it is hinted at. Chaucer, after all, identifies with the voice of *Sir Thopas* before claiming authorship of the *Melibee*. Thynne's Chaucer may attempt to discriminate between "Chaucer's Tale of Melibee" and "the rym of Sir Thopas" (as if the latter were generated by its eponymous hero), but they are both, of course, tales of Chaucer, the poet of Prudence and Alisoun.[83]

A Preface to *Melibee*: Saving the Literal Sense

Melibee has often been paired with the *Parson's Tale* as a religious tale in prose and, as such, considered not fit to read: that is, deemed undeserving of the kind of sustained critical attention bestowed on a work of *literature*.[84] But *Melibee* is different in kind, literary kind, from the *Parson's Tale*.[85] It does not begin as a religious narrative. It makes a very late turn to orthodox Christianity (7.1868) and prefers the counsel of surgeons and lawyers to that of priests or bishops; its first *sententia* (7.977) is drawn not from the Bible but from Ovid, *Remedia amoris*. And it is first introduced to the pilgrimage in the wake of a casual but full-blooded religious oath whose effect is not at all pious:

> "Gladly," quod I, "by Goddes sweete pyne!
> I wol yow telle a litel thyng in prose
> That oghte liken yow, as I suppose,
> Or elles, certes, ye been to daungerous."   (7.936–39)

This oath is the first thing heard from Chaucer in response to the Host's pungent critique of his turdlike rhyming; it is doubtful whether this rush of impure affect should be authorized by reference to the sufferings of Christ on the cross.[86] And yet, remarkably, this same motif of "Goddes peyne" is deployed again just eight lines later by way of introducing a short excursus on literary theory:

> "As thus: ye woot that every Evaungelist
> That telleth us the peyne of Jhesu Crist
> Ne seith nat alle thyng as his felawe dooth;
> But nathelees hir sentence is al sooth,
> And alle acorden as in hire sentence,
> Al be ther in hir tellyng difference."   (7.943–48)

The example of "the peyne of Jhesu Crist," *the* subject of Christian religion, is clearly subordinated here to the main business of the sentence, the relationship of literal exposition to allegorical meaning, "tellyng" to "sentence."[87] This passage (7.943–66) has assumed portentous significance since D. W. Robertson attempted to draw the whole of the *Canterbury Tales* under its interpretive framework, one he assimilates to Augustinian metaphysics.[88] Most critics today are skeptical of Robertson's claim that the phrase "this litel tretys heere" (7.957) refers not just to the *Melibee* but to the whole of the *Canterbury Tales*. And yet Robertson has been successful in encouraging us to continue classifying, or preclassifying, *Melibee* as a religious tale. Rather than acknowledging that the subject of Chaucer's discussion is literary theory (the relationship of literal to allegorical senses), Robertson insists that the message is and is only *sentence*: "pay attention to the *sentence* of the Melibee because it affords a clue to the *sentence* of all the other tales which come before it." Such one-track insistence on *sentence* entails the erasure, or the rapid forgetting, of the literal sense. We do not concern ourselves with what happens in *Melibee*; we read past *Melibee* to a system of belief that lies somewhere outside and beyond it.

In attempting to establish the meaning of the term *tretys*, as in "this litel tretys heere" (7.957; see also 963), Robertson appeals to Dante's *Epistle to Can Grande*.[89] It is certainly worth turning to the *Epistle*, for a moment, to consider its deployment of the techniques of Scriptural exegesis. It is quite clear that the *Epistle* author is *not* interested in passing quickly from the *Commedia*'s literal sense to its allegorical meanings: indeed, it is worth noting that the third and final part of the *Epistle*, which exemplifies the art of exposition by analyzing the first 38 lines of the *Paradiso*, concerns itself exclusively with the literal sense.[90] Textual fabric (it is suggested) is worthy of long and studied attention; it is not to be regarded as a nut-shell, to be cracked and tossed away once the *sentence* within has been extracted.[91]

The *Epistle*'s boldest suggestion is that the work of a vernacular author might merit the kind and quality of attention, the range of exegetical techniques, hitherto devoted to the analysis of Scripture. This claim represents a significant landmark in the history of literary criticism and in the apologetics of vernacular authorship.[92] In the *House of Fame*, Chaucer registers the extraordinary claims of Dantean poetics even as, by way of recognizing the limitations of his own vernacular tradition, he retreats into extremes of self-parody.[93] Something similar appears to be going on as Chaucer prepares to deliver his *Melibee*. His meditation on the relationship of literal sense to allegorical *sentence* is pedantic and long-winded, full of awkward qualifications and prosaic formulas ("As thus," 7.955; "After the which," 7.964). And yet (as in the *House of Fame*) something serious is being said. Chaucer's argument is not that we should read through the *Melibee* to its allegorical meanings, but rather that his text forms a bridge between vernacular fiction and social, historical (and ultimately religious) truths. Fiction, even a fiction deficient in "imaginatively self-aware and generative use of language," deserves a hearing (must be respected at its literal level) before it is referred to or assimilated into discursive systems outside itself.[94] Chaucer's last line is of particular importance here: "And lat me tellen *al* my tale, I preye" (7.966; emphasis mine). That is: let me tell this tale *without interruption*. The interruption of a tale is always experienced as a form of violence, the premeditated cutting off of a speaking voice.[95] Women, of course, are not accorded powers of interruption in the *Canterbury Tales*. In *Decameron* 6.1 Madonna Oretta is made to feel physically ill by listening to a long-winded and incompetent masculine narrator, but she recognizes that cutting off his discourse would be experienced as a cut at his manhood.[96] The cutting off of *Melibee* would be an embarrassment and a disaster: a simulated embarrassment for the pilgrim Chaucer (one he has suffered already), but a real disaster for the social nexus that Prudence represents. If Prudence were interrupted in her work of managing and dissipating Melibee's rage, the threat of violence would continue to hang over us. Chaucer succeeds with *Melibee*, then, in identifying himself with a text of assured literal integrity, one that saves him from the violence of interruption.

If it seems fanciful to parallel so exalted a pair as the *Epistle to Can Grande* and the *Commedia* with the rear end of *Thopas* and the *Melibee*, it might prove instructive to consider another pairing: the *Vita nuova* and the *Convivio*.[97] The *Convivio* sees Dante deploying techniques learned and borrowed from Scriptural exegesis to analyze vernacular love poetry, his own prior texts. Dante does not cut straight to the chase of allegorical meanings; he lavishes a lot of time and attention on the literal sense of the *canzoni*, for (as he himself remarks) nothing can happen without or before the literal sense.[98] And when he does arrive at the discussion of allegorical meanings (revealing his secret love to be the Lady Philosophy), he does not encourage us to forget our experience of the literal sense of the *Vita nuova*. Above all, we do not forget the wasted body of the masculine lover, Dante, lamenting the absence of Beatrice.[99] It is remarkable, by contrast, how soon we (both author and audience) forget the wounded body of Prudence. We are predisposed to forget the wounded female bodies of *Melibee*, I would suggest, by the traditional understanding that the female body is and is only the literal sense: women, female figures, stand always in need of an interpreter, an exegete, an allegorist, to speak their meaning.[100] Two women are stabbed by three men in their house: What can this *really* mean?

In what follows, I would like to attempt a reading of *Melibee* that pays due attention to the literal sense. This does not mean that I read it only at the literal level as the touching domestic drama of Mr. and Mrs. Melibee. I just want to give the literal sense its due, to treat *Melibee* as if it were worthy of a literary-critical reading. To that end, I block out reference to particular historical events of the last two decades of the fourteenth century; I also stick largely to the English letter (rather than referring to prior texts in Latin and French). There have been many attempts to tether *Melibee* to contemporary events, ranging from John of Gaunt's Spanish campaign to the Merciless Parliament of 1387.[101] It is not part of my purpose to dispute such readings. Indeed, I would argue that the best of them usefully suggest how the immediate pressures of particular historical circumstances imbue *Melibee* with fresh commentative power. And this suggests, once again, that *Melibee* is primarily rhetorical in character. The text realizes its social power (and outlives the moment of its composition) as it is surrounded by fresh historical contingencies: new threats of war, new failed parliaments, new candidates to play the roles of irascible householder and prudent adviser.

Reading *Melibee*: Pain and Suffering; Female Bodies and Masculine Performance

I would like to begin my reading of the Melibee-Prudence story by briefly considering how its Latin avatar was read (and prepared for future readers) by one fourteenth-century Englishman. On f. 6r of British Library Add. MS 6158, a manuscript containing Albertano's three treatises in their usual fourteenth-century order, we find the "G" of the phrase "Garrulitas mu-

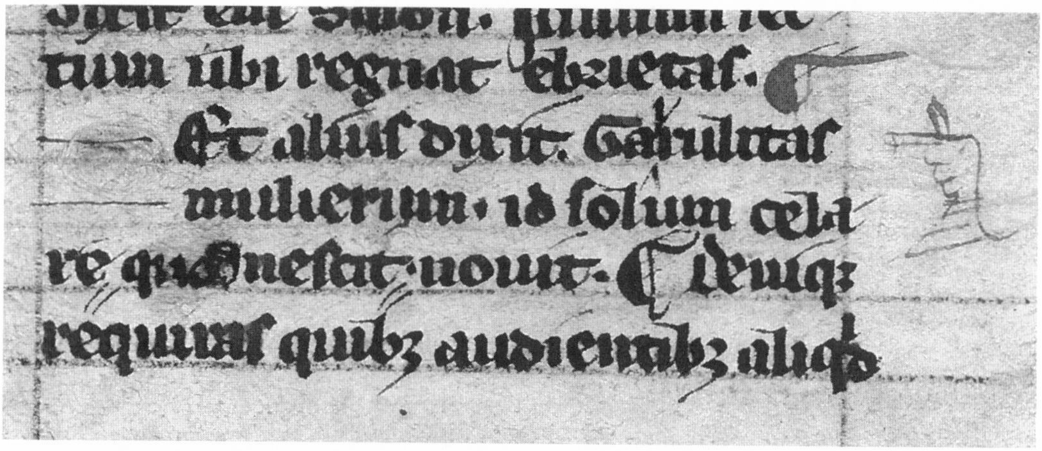

Plate 5. *Manicula* pointing to "Garrulitas mulierum." British Library Add. MS 6158, f. 6r. (detail).

lierum" accentuated in blue ink; a long pointing finger, in the same blue ink, points to the same phrase from the right hand margin (see plate 5).[102] The Latin text of the *De doctrina dicendi et tacendi* here reads: "Garrulitas mulierum id solum celare quod nescit novit" ("the janglerie of wommen kan nat hyden thynges save that they witen nought," 7.1062).[103] The very same one-liner is recycled a few folios later as part of the *Liber consolationis et consilii*;[104] when it shows up for a third time (on f. 12v.), it again attracts the interest of Add. 6158's finger-pointing reader. This second citation in the *Liber consolationis* is actually occasioned by Prudence's *refutation* of the charge that women cannot keep secrets (neatly translated by Chaucer).[105] Our menacing *manicula*, however, points specifically to the words "de pessimis mulieribus garrulis et loquacibus," those exceptional, beyond-the-pale women "that been jangleresses and wikkid" (7.1085). It is apparent, then, that at least one male reader/transmitter of the Melibee story in fourteenth-century England thought (and encouraged his readers to think) that it was at least in part a text about women.[106]

The physical violence at the opening of *Melibee*, like that at the opening of the *Wife of Bath's Tale*, has typically been read as a narrative premise: that which must be said to occur before the story proper can get under way. The rape in the *Wife of Bath's Tale* has, of course, drawn more critical attention of late. Readers have refused to let such an extreme act of physical violence fly past in the space of a couplet (and an awkward subordinate clause).[107] Rape becomes the subject: so too, I would argue, we should recognize that in *Melibee* the subject (for Albertano, for Chaucer, for ourselves) is physical violence. The physical violence with which the narrative opens is important both as a specific act inflicted by men upon female bodies and as a paradigm of the violence that might, at any point of the narrative, break out again.

To begin, then, at the beginning:

> A yong man called Melibeus, myghty and riche, bigat upon his wyf, that called was Prudence, a doghter that called was Sophie. /
> Upon a day bifel that he for his desport is went into the feeldes hym to pleye. / His wyf and eek his doghter hath he left inwith his hous, of which the dores weren faste yshette. / Thre of his olde foes han it espyed, and setten laddres to the walles of his hous, and by wyndowes been entred, / and betten his wyf, and wounded his doghter with fyve mortal woundes in fyve sondry places — / this is to seyn, in hir feet, in hire handes, in hir erys, in hir nose, and in hir mouth — and leften hire for deed, and wenten awey. (7.967–72)

The whole of this opening is developed *litteraliter*. The glossator's formula employed in line 972, "this is to seyn," *id est*, sometimes signals a switch to allegorical exposition, but here it introduces a more particular account of the literal sense. The literal sense of the opening sentence offers an image that is not to be imagined, begetting, in a stark representation of masculine-feminine (subject-object) relations that is disturbingly congruent with the account of violence that follows. Melibee next exercises his right to walk at large in the public domain, "the feeldes," and also the right to lock up his wife and daughter "inwith his hous."[108] But his very insistence on these divided domains renders him vulnerable to "his olde foes," who invade his house and wound his wife and daughter by way of wounding him.

Up to this point, and after this point, nothing is said of any pain that mother and daughter might feel. From the moment that Melibee returns to his house, sees the "meschief," and begins "to weep and crie," the attention of the narrative becomes absorbed by the sufferings of the masculine protagonist. Prudence, who has so far occupied the position of a grammatical object (things are done *to* her) becomes a grammatical subject only through the business of consoling him. Prudence's pain remains unspoken, hence unknown: Melibee's pain becomes the subject of the text. Or, to adapt terms from Elaine Scarry, Prudence can be assumed to experience pain; Melibee is seen to dramatize his suffering. Physical pain, Scarry argues, cannot be known outside itself, since, unlike any other state of consciousness, it "has no referential content. It is not *of* or *for* anything. It is precisely because it takes no object that it, more than any other phenomenon, resists objectification in language." When pain is forced down "avenues of objectification," pain is transformed into forms of consciousness other than itself, such as suffering, that are amenable to linguistic expression.[109] The pain of the female in Chaucer's *Melibee*, then, never speaks itself; the pain of the male (which is, in a fundamental and obvious sense, borrowed from the female) is linguistically objectified as suffering and hence found amenable to the language of consolation. Such a distinction obviously forms part of the greater division of labor: for as pain is unknowable and stays at home and is thus appropriately female, suffering is public and performative, and therefore masculine. The most terrible exemplification of this is the *Physician's Tale*. Virginia's pain can never be anything other than itself because it is denied any hope of objectification through social expression. Virginius converts Virginia's pain into a dramatic rendition of his own suffering, a public performance brought to a triumphant and theatrical conclusion in a Roman court of law. Virginia's pain remains unknown; her fragmented body is seen, finally, only as a prop supporting the public art of masculine suffering.

Melibee begins his particular performance by crying, weeping, and "rentynge his clothes," gestures of biblical extravagance that prepare for his identifying himself, twelve lines later, with Jesus Christ (weeping for Lazarus, 987). Prudence immediately accepts her role as counselor; Melibee's emotions now become the single object of attention. Recognizing that Melibee has feminized himself through weeping, Prudence turns her memory to Ovid,

where as he seith, / "He is a fool that destourbeth the mooder to wepen in the deeth of hire child til she have wept hir fille as for a certein tyme, / and thanne shal man doon his diligence with amyable wordes hire to reconforte." (7.976–77)

Seeing Melibee wholly absorbed in dramatizing his grief, Prudence initiates her own performance: the performance of rhetoric. She begins by recognizing the vital interplay of speaking and silence (the art of *dicendi et tacendi*, as taught by the treatise prefacing the Melibee story in fourteenth-century Albertano manuscripts). She begins with *tacendi*, recognizing that Melibee must be allowed to weep "for a certein tyme" before he can be considered amenable to arguments. The importance of maintaining silence is then underlined before the crucial moment of *dicendi*, linguistic intervention, is signaled:

For which resoun this noble wyf Prudence suffred hir housbonde for to wepe and crie as for a certein space, / and whan she saugh hir tyme, she seyde hym in this wise: "Allas, my lord," quod she. (7.979–80)

The crucial and characteristic phrase here, "whan she saw hir tyme," recurs at two further critical junctures in the narrative.[110] The first comes just after the moment when Melibee declares himself persuaded by those of his advisers who argue "that he sholde maken werre" (1050). The urgency of the situation here is conveyed through double emphasis on Prudence's powers of perception; she sees the situation, and she sees when to speak:

Thanne dame Prudence, whan that she saugh how that hir housbonde shoop hym for to wreken hym on his foes and to bigynne werre, she in ful humble wise, whan she saugh hir tyme, seide to hym thise wordes: / "My lord," quod she, "I yow biseche..." (7.1051–52)

The third and final appearance of the phrase comes at another crucial juncture: immediately following the moment at which Melibee surrenders the *maistrie* to his wife and Prudence foresees the possibility of achieving "a good conclusioun":

> "Dame," quod Melibee, "dooth youre wil and youre likynge; / for I putte me hoolly in youre disposicioun and ordinaunce."
>
> Thanne dame Prudence, whan she saugh the goode wyl of hir housbonde, delibered and took avys in hirself, / thinkinge how she myghte bringe this nede unto a good conclusioun and to a good ende. / And whan she saugh hire tyme, she sente for thise adversaries to come unto hire into a pryvee place. (7.1724–29)

The repetition of this phrase at crucial moments of Prudence's performance points to the preeminent importance of all that Sophistic rhetoric understands by the concept of *kairos*: the timeliness of an utterance and its appropriateness to the particular circumstances obtaining at the moment of speaking.[111] Recognition of *kairos* (or *quando*) as a guiding principle of the *Melibee* will surely clear up a great deal of critical confusion.[112] Daniel Kempton, for example, wonders why Prudence "contradicts herself" by citing advice from one *auctor* at one moment that is plainly at odds with a *sentence* cited earlier in her discourse.[113] The short answer is that circumstances have changed (the most pressing circumstances of the text being, of course, the emotions that run and collide within the body of Melibee). The citation of an *auctor* aims not to open the window onto universal truth, but rather to address the state of Melibee's emotions and to nudge them down the path toward "a good conclusioun." Even Melibee can recognize that the best *sentence* in the world can have no effect if it fails to address his current state of feeling:

> To thise forseide thynges answerde Melibeus unto his wyf Prudence: "Alle thy wordes," quod he, "been sothe and therto profitable, but trewely myn herte is troubled with this sorwe so grevously that I noot what to doone." (7.1001)

It is worth returning to Kempton's critique of the *Melibee* for a moment because it echoes both the dissatisfactions of other scholars and the critique delivered by Plato and Aristotle upon its *modus vivendi*, rhetorical performance:

> The operation of the discourse, then, makes the mediation of "auctour" perceptible as problematic. Contrary to our expectations, the diverse voices of "auctors" are not brought into accord among themselves, or into harmony with the single voice of "auctoritee," through exegesis on the part of Prudence, for example, or through her protracted disputation with Melibee; there is no synthesis of doctrine through the operations of dialectic, as there would be in a scholastic Book of Sentences. Most instances of contradiction are simply left uninterpreted.[114]

Kempton's critique here, like so many other negative reviews of *Melibee*, introduces epistemological standards that are quite alien to the text and to the work it proposes for itself: how to address the imminent threat of masculine anger; how to prevent it from spilling into the public domain through acts of violence. In adopting dialectic as his privileged term, Kempton follows the precedent of Plato and Aristotle, who express dialectic's privilege by emphasizing its subordination of rhetoric.[115] Rhetoric for Plato entailed the enunciation of truths already discovered through dialectic; for Aristotle, it was an imperfect system of reasoning, kept subordinate to science and dialectic. For both Plato and Aristotle (and evidently for Kempton, since he never names the term), rhetoric figures as the excluded term by which philosophy defines itself. Rhetoric is associated with ephemeral opinion, with the timing of opportunities, with bodiliness, with gesture, costume, and color—in short, with woman. Thus it is that Dame Prudence, even as she engages the emotions of her feminized spouse, continues to practice an art that remains essentially (so to speak) feminine. The only other instance of the "whan she saugh hir tyme" *topos* in the *Tales* suggests a calculation of public circumstances that has bodily satisfaction as its only *telos* (as May times her approach to Damyan).[116] Duke Theseus, by contrast, never needs to time his utterance since time, in the public domain he rules over, is supposedly his own.[117]

The last of the three passages quoted above by way of exemplifying the "whan she saw hir tyme" *topos* inevitably suggests further parallels between Prudence and the Wife of Bath: both are engaged in struggles for *maistrie* that demand a moment of masculine surrender. Melibee, recognizing that he is engaged in such a struggle, worries about the consequences of subjecting himself (and of being seen to subject himself) to a feminine art issuing from a feminine body:

"And also, certes, if I governed me by thy conseil, it sholde seme that I had yeve to thee over me the maistrie, and God forbede that it so weere!/For Jhesus Syrak seith that 'if the wyf have maistrie, she is contrarious to hir housbonde.'" (7.1058–59)

Inasmuch as rhetoric is associated with the body of woman, then, the negative and positive critique of woman in *Melibee* (7.1055–114) doubles as a critique of rhetoric itself and hence of the *Tale*'s most basic *modus operandi*. When Melibee finally submits himself to the curative power of his wife's verbal craft, he recognizes rhetorical enunciation ("wordes that been spoken discreetly by ordinance") as a power of mind *and* body: for, he notes, as Solomon says,

"'Wordes that been spoken discreetly by ordinaunce been honycombes, for they yeven swetnesse to the soule and holsomnesse to the body.'" (7.1113)

Reading *Melibee*: Household Rhetoric

It is clear, then, that Melibee's best hope of spiritual and bodily recovery lies in submitting to the powers of his wife. Such an arrangement would not (as Melibee argues at some length) be tolerated in the public realm, but this is a private arrangement, contracted between husband and wife within the household.[118] The healing powers that Prudence proposes to employ are those of a private rhetoric. The body she seeks to move bears a special relation to her own: she is married to it, is of "one flesh" with it. She is uniquely capable of turning Melibee's mood and, *per consequens*, his mind. It follows, then, that the public realm forms something of an obstacle to her designs. She feels compelled to invoke it and urges Melibee to recognize its claims, but what transpires among "the greet congregacion of folk" (7.1004) serves only to accentuate the need for household rather than neighborhood rhetoric. It is significant that the notion of "commune profit," the touchstone of political values in the *Parliament of Fowls*, is never introduced into the *Melibee*.[119] In the *Parliament*, the dilemma of the aristocratic birds (three suitors, one lady) can be debated in public (among commoners) because it does not pose a threat to public order; an immediate resolution is not strictly necessary. In *Melibee*, the need to find a cure for the distressed husband is of pressing urgency, since the malaise of one so "myghty and riche" threatens the whole body politic with the prospect of "werre." Such discussion cannot be entrusted to "a greet congregacioun" but must be conducted as chamber politics, a private dialogue between suffering husband and "noble wyf."

The *parlement* called in the *Melibee* proves counterproductive from Prudence's viewpoint because it is too broadly inclusive and because such a great audience frees up Melibee's emotions in sudden and surprising ways:

And by the manere of his [Melibee's] spech it semed that in herte he baar a crueel ire, redy to doon vengeaunce upon his foes, and sodeynly desired that the werre sholde bigynne. (7.1009)

Prudence argues explicitly against the wisdom of following majority opinion: Melibee should not incline his heart "to the moore part and to the gretter nombre" (7.1257), since

at congregaciouns and multitudes of folk, there as men take moore reward to the nombre than to the sapience of persones, / ye se wel that in swiche conseillynges fooles han the maistrie. (7.1259–60)[120]

The hallmark of folly, for Prudence, is that it operates on emotion, desire, *likynge*. At large public gatherings, Prudence argues, "every man crieth and clatereth what that hym liketh" (7.1069). A fool counsels "after his owene lust and his affeccioun" (7.1173); flatterers, Prudence tells Melibee, spy out "by youre wordes to what thyng ye been enclyned" and then proceed to direct their advice "to youre talent [rather] than to youre profit" (7.1250–51). Any counsel that is predicated on emotion "ne sholde nat, as to speke properly, be called a conseillyng, but a mocioun or a moevyng of folye" (7.1239). When Prudence finally tests Melibee on his powers of textual interpretation at the end of the *parlement* sequence, she finds that he flunks the test in spectacular fashion; he is still running high on emotion: "Lo, lo," she exclaims (making Melibee a text to be pointed at, a negative exemplum ripe for generalization), "how lightly is every man enclined to his owene desir and to his owene pleasaunce" (7.1283). It is imperative, then, that such a man be withdrawn from the public sphere and worked on in private by herself and a few choice advisers. Such a select grouping should be so jealous of its integrity that it will tell lies to strangers on the open road:

"For Piers Alfonce seith, 'Ne taak no compaignye by the weye of a straunge man, but if so be that thou have knowe hym of a lenger tyme. / And if so be that he falle into thy compaignye paraventure, withouten thyn assent, enquere thanne as subtilly as thou mayst of his conversacion, and of his lyf bifore, and feyne thy wey; seye that thou [wolt] thider as thou wolt nat go.'" (7.1309–11)

Such counsel is obviously antithetical to the generous and inclusive ethos that prevailed among the pilgrims at the Tabard. But it is remarkably prescient of what is to transpire in the next fragment when the same itinerant *compagnye* meets up with the mysterious Canon. As we have observed in earlier chapters, associational forms may define themselves through both internal solidarity and external hostility. The household regime that Prudence proposes to rule over is obviously prepared to define itself primarily through acts of exclusion. Some members of the "greet congregacion" are deemed worthy of a hearing, however, since they provide Prudence with a supply of arguments to work with. They also exemplify, through their struggles in the greater public world, the limitations of that world. The professional groups represented here are surgeons, physicians, advocates, and "olde wise." The surgeons argue that it is not in their professional interest "to norice werre" (7.1014; a somewhat specious argument, of course, since they depend on "werre" as a lawyer depends on crime). The advocate makes an eloquent plea for delay and restraint, finding an "ensample" of eloquent *ars tacendi* in Christ, who draws on the ground in silence before those wishing to condemn the woman taken in adultery (7.1021–34). The "olde wise" who attempts to counter the arguments of the war party finds himself interrupted, the victim of speech-breaking:

And whan this olde man wende to enforcen his tale by resons, wel ny alle atones bigonne they to rise for to breken his tale, and beden hym ful ofte his wordes for to abregge. (7.1043)

Albertano was himself, of course, an advocate (and, as time rolled on, an "olde wise"); his son John, dedicatee of the Melibee story, was a surgeon. The suggestion, once again, is that Albertano and the urban professionals he represents form a vital bridge between the public world and the tighter, more exclusive circles of the great. A similar suggestion, a similar social identity, may be inferred for Chaucer as author of the English *Melibee*. He does not propose to counsel the great and mighty face to face: he simply supplies arguments that may be deployed within the closed circle of the household, the *privata familia*. What he aspires *not* to encounter, that is, is the wrath of an intractable and irascible masculine ruler. When it comes to counseling powerful and angry men in Chaucer, men are nowhere to be found. This is a job best left to wives, such as Prudence, Griselde, and Alceste. The *Summoner's Tale* is littered with the bodies of men who either tried to counsel an "irous potestate" (3.2017) or who found no female advocate to save them from the depravities of an "irous, cursed wrecche" (3.2063). The only hope of averting the disasters that follow from the rigid anger of an absolute ruler lies, as Prudence argues, in "chaunge."[121] Since the idea of a man working "chaunge" in the breast of a more powerful male upsets all norms of heterosexual propriety, it follows that a woman, and a woman's body, must be placed in the line of fire.

When Melibee makes his first submission to Prudence, promising to "governe me by thy conseil in alle thyng," Prudence begins her lengthy anatomization of Melibee's spiritual state not with *superbia* (the usual order of penance, as exemplified by the *Parson's Tale*) but with *ira*, anger, the emotion that poses the most immediate threat in these particular circumstances. Anger, as expounded by Prudence, feeds forms of alienation and self-delusion that have severe social consequences:

"First, he that axeth conseil of hymself, certes he moste been withouten ire, for manye causes. / The firste is this: he that hath greet ire and wratthe in hymself, he weneth alwey that he may do thyng that he may nat do. / And secoundely, he that is irous and wrooth, he ne may nat wel deme; / and he that may nat wel deme, may nat wel conseille. / The thridde is this, that he that is irous and wrooth, as seith Senec, ne may nat speke but blameful thynges, / and with his viciouse wordes he stireth oother folk to angre and to ire." (7.1123–28)

Clearly, a powerful individual such as Melibee, when running on *ire*, is not fit to operate in the public realm. He needs to be closeted away and softened by the feminine arts associated with rhetoric and the female body. This does not mean he should be flattered. Flattery is seen by both the *Melibee* and the *Parson's Tale* as particularly dangerous and potentially destructive when applied to angry men.[122] He needs, rather, to be faced with the virtues that prove (according to the *Parson's Tale*) particularly efficacious in remedying *ire*: *mansuetude* or *debonairetee*, *pacience* or *suffrance*. Part of the technique of dealing with an angry man lies in charming violence out of him; part of it demands (ultimately) a willingness to absorb his violent impulses.[123] The woman who must stand in for absent virtue is thus accorded a very dangerous role. In Bosch's famous table-top representation of *ire* (which takes place beneath a scroll noting that "a nation lacking counsel is without prudence") the woman who restrains a man from attacking a male rival finds her dress trampled underfoot and her body uncomfortably close to the knife (see plate 6).[124] Her only weapons, according to the *ire* excursus of Chaucer's Parson, are *debonairetee* and *suffrance*:

Plate 6. Hieronymus Bosch, *Anger* (detail). From painted tabletop of the Seven Deadly Sins and the Four Last Things, Prado, Madrid.

Debonairetee withdraweth and refreyneth the stirynges and the moevynges of mannes corage in his herte, in swich manere that they ne skippe nat out by angre ne by ire. / Suffrance suffreth swetely alle the anoyaunces and the wronges that men doon to man outward. (10.655–56)

Ire suggests an excess of turbulent emotion that threatens to "skip out" of the bounds of personhood and leave a violent mark on the public realm. *Mansuetude* and *debonairetee*, by contrast, suggest inner stillness; *pacience* and *suffrance* suggest a willingness to maintain such stillness even when provoked by external insults and injuries. "Stillness" is a better term than "passivity" here, since it represents a state that the individual must consciously struggle to achieve. It denotes, nonetheless, what might be termed a feminine or feminized social positioning. When Criseyde is handed over to her father Calkas at the Greek camp, she is said to be "muwet, milde, and mansuete" (5.194): nonspeaking, unassertive, acted upon. When Emelye washes herself in Diana's temple, she does so "with herte debonaire" (1.2282): her attitude is not cheerful (as modern *debonaire* might encourage us to misread), but rather (as Patricia Ingham has it) "submissive." [125] For men, such a state of being is prescribed as a remedy for, or counterpoise to, *ire*; for women, as Felicity Riddy has shown, "peaceableness" is a feminine attribute inculcated through systematic training. [126] When a man needs to cultivate *mansuetude* and its associated virtues, then, he is best advised to mirror himself in a woman (an ideal woman). So it is that Prudence and Melibee remain closeted in dialogue, face to face, for almost seven hundred lines. It is only when Melibee has in-corporated Prudence, has seen her image in himself, that he can return to the public world. The allegorical drama fits neatly into that of the ideal house-hold: the faithful wife remains at home, *mansuete* as ever, until her spouse next brings home the *ire* he has accumulated from the *polis* and looks, once more, for a domestic cure.

Prudence deploys her household rhetoric with immense skill in seek-ing to discipline Melibee's "mannes corage." But what principle is to guide Melibee in the public world once he is no longer driven by anger? The answer (predictable enough, given Albertano's authorship) is the rule of law:

"For, as by right and resoun, ther may no man taken vengeaunce on no wight but the juge that hath the jurisdiccioun of it, / whan it is graunted hym to take thilke vengeance hastily or attemprely, as the lawe requireth." (7.1379–80)

This advertence to law is soon followed by an analysis of what happened to Melibee (or, better, an interpretation of what the event at the beginning of the text—the assault on his household—can mean to him now). That initiating event is treated as if it were a double-authored text: the three ene-mies were the immediate or "neer cause" of the assault, but the "fer cause" or ultimate *auctor* is God.[127] As discussion of causes passes to speculation over meanings, Prudence weighs in with a massive qualification concerning the interpretive powers she is about to exercise. Such a qualification, with its frank acknowledgment of "presumpciouns and conjectynges" to follow, is worth dwelling on:

"Now, sire, if men wolde axe me why that God suffred men to do yow this vileynye, certes, I kan nat wel answere, as for no soothfastnesse. / For th'apostle seith that 'the sciences and the juggementz of oure Lord God almyghty been ful depe; / ther may no man comprehende ne serchen hem suffisantly.' / Nathelees, by certeyne presump-ciouns and conjectynges, I holde and bileeve / that God, which that is ful of justice and of rightwisnesse, hath suffred this bityde by juste cause resonable." (7.1405–9)

The foundational assumption here is shared by monastic chronicling but (after Giovanni Villani) doubted by mercantile historiography: that contin-gent events may be rendered meaningful when reconciled with, hence read within, the all-encompassing framework of divine providence.[128] Prudence does not attempt or presume to spell out the terms of any such reconciliation. She simply shows Melibee how the text of his own past can be interpreted in such a way that it might become meaningful for him *now*. Her task remains, as ever, a rhetorical one. At *this* moment (she suggests) Melibee should ety-mologize his own name: he is a honeydrinker, one who has gorged himself on the "hony of sweete temporeel richesses." And so, "peraventure" (another qualification), Christ has decided to punish him: "the flessh, the feend, and the world" (which might be read as a synonym for that which he gorges upon, his own excess) has broken into his body and wounded his soul. This is who

Melibee is now, and it is clear what he needs to do next. He must understand that he cannot revenge himself on forces that he is himself complicit with (flesh, fiend, and world); and he needs to learn the correct attitude toward "temporel richesses." And so Prudence moves the dialogue forward into its next phase.

Many critics have been troubled by the argument that Prudence's allegorization of Melibee's enemies here makes nonsense of his ultimate reconciliation with this same trio: How can Melibee reconcile himself with the world, the flesh, and the devil? The simple answer is that Prudence's allegorization is only of local and limited effect: it serves to help Melibee see who he is and where he is at this stage of the dialogue. Melibee's identity, who he is at a particular moment, will continue to change until the work of the text (the task of working "chaunge" in Melibee) is completed. Dante, after all, *never* responds to the many requests for identification he meets with in traveling through the afterlife by speaking his own name: he defines himself always in terms of his self-understanding (where he is, what he has just come to recognize) at that particular moment of his unfinished journey.[129] Dante's self-understanding, of course, is never achieved alone. It is achieved through dialogue, beginning with one famed for his "parola ornata"—which is to say, rhetoric.[130]

The self-understandings of Melibee and of Dante-*personaggio* differ greatly in quality and kind; so too do the rhetorical strategies of their mentors. Dante's intellectual growth is gradual and incremental; he is always, or almost always, moving forward. Melibee makes some gains (expressed chiefly through his compliance with Prudence's counseling) but then regresses into the primitive emotionalism he set out from. It follows that Dante's text offers the kinds of readerly satisfactions associated with linear narrative. The *Melibee*, by contrast, can only derive its itinerary from the unstable *corage* of its eponymous hero. In this sense, the experience of reading *Melibee* is more lifelike, less securely sequenced and structured, than that of reading the *Commedia*. There is no guarantee that the rhetorical strategy of one sentence will ensure progress in the next. Whether we like it or not, we are tethered as readers to the subjective emotional responses of a powerful and angry male. If we are to persist with the text, we will need to practice the virtues of *mansuetude* and *debonairetee* exemplified by Prudence. By line 1521, we are well into the second half of the text. But we have also, in a fundamental sense, moved nowhere, as Melibee declares: "myn herte may nevere been in pees unto the tyme it be venged." This draws an exclamation from Prudence (a modest one) and a restatement of the most basic choice that faces Melibee in all his public actions:

"A," quod dame Prudence, "ye seyn youre wyl and as yow liketh, / but in no caas of the world a man sholde nat doon outrage ne excesse for to vengen hym. / For Cassidore seith that 'as yvele dooth he that vengeth hym by outrage as he that dooth the outrage.' / And therfore ye shul venge yow after the ordre of right; that is to seyn, by the lawe and noght by excesse ne by outrage." (7.1526–29)

Melibee may act on his emotions, according to his will and liking, and hence act tyrannically; or he may act "by the lawe." The whole of the *Melibee* is suspended at this moment of Melibee's choosing how to act; this is what the text is about. The struggle to ensure that Melibee makes the right choice, long and exhausting as it is, is one that Prudence (and her historical surrogates) cannot give up, for if the counseling process should stop, Melibee's emotions will be loosed onto the public world with disastrous consequences. Prudence, in this sense, has no power in choosing her role; and neither (for as long as we remain readers of the *Melibee*) do we. Most critical readings of the *Melibee* amount to strategies for nonreading: ways of imposing our own critical schemata and so exercising our own critical powers; ways of "skipping out" of the oppressive sensation of being held subject to the awful, monotonous logic of the text. And the logic of the text, we have noted, is wholly subjugated to the turbulent nonlogic of Melibee's emotions, his *wyl* and *lykynge*. To persist as a reader of *Melibee*, then, is to experience what subjection to Melibee-like rule means and feels like. Reading *Melibee* may seem like women's work, but female experience within such a masculine-headed household stands in for that of every political subject under absolutism.

The later phases of Prudence's counseling, in addressing Melibee's continued desire for revenge and his faith in riches, take us back to the very beginning of the text (its first subordinate clause) and the first definition of who or what Melibee is: he is "myghty and riche" (7.967). Melibee recalls this initial juxtaposition in boasting that "I am richer and moore myghty than myne enemys been" (7.1548). Prudence consequently challenges the assumption that riches can translate themselves into might: "I se wel," she says,

"that for the trust that ye han in youre richesses ye wole moeve werre and bataille. / I conseille yow that ye bigynne no werre in trust of your richesses, for they ne suffisen noght werres to mayntene." (7.1649–50)

Here, as elsewhere, Prudence's counsel is notably pragmatic—which is to say, again, that it is tailored to the dimensions of Melibee's intelligence and to his immediate need. Prudence does not critique the notion of *myght*, nor does she question the propriety of being rich and of growing richer. Her discussion of *richesses* actually allows a rationale for the vigorous pursuit of wealth and profit that seems to have stepped straight from the pages of Weber's *Protestant Ethic*. Prudence quotes from Cicero:

" 'And though the grete men and the myghty men geten richesses moore lightly than thou, / yet shaltou nat been ydel ne slow to do thy profit, for thou shalt in alle wise flee ydelnesse.' " (7.1587–88)

The more vigorously one flees idleness, then, the better one is doing. Such a rationale for the accumulation of wealth makes Thomas Aquinas (in the Spanish Chapel frescoes) look sluggish.[131] Aquinas, the purveyor of Wisdom, is content to sit and wait for riches to seek him out: Prudence, figured as the mother of Sophie, *id est* Wisdom, advises her husband, "myghty and riche," to get mightier and richer by fleeing from idleness just as fast as he can. Such counsel apparently would marry the manic energy of the Merchant (or of the *Shipman's Tale*'s merchant) to the "feithful bisynesse" of the Second Nun (8.24). But it is important to grasp that Prudence's excursus on "richesses" is not to be read as *doctryne*, but as one element of a rhetorical strategy whose aim is the prevention of war. If Melibee is content to define himself as "myghty and riche," he is likely to be swayed by the policy that will leave him mightier and richer. The peace policy, Prudence argues, is his best bet:

> "For Seint Jame seith in his Epistles that 'by concord and pees the smale richesses wexen grete,/and by debaat and discord the grete richesses fallen doun.'/And ye knowen wel that oon of the gretteste and moost sovereyn thyng that is in this world is unytee and pees./And therfore seyde oure Lord Jhesu Crist to his apostles in this wise:/'Wel happy and blessed been they that loven and purchacen pees, for they been called children of God.'"
>
> "A," quod Melibee, "now se I wel that ye loven nat myn honour ne my worshipe." (7.1676–81)

The success of the rhetorical strategy here is attested to by the exclamation, "A," that escapes from the mouth of Melibee as its arguments hit home. The first argument, attributed to St. James but actually from Seneca,[132] assures Melibee that the peace option will serve his desire to stay rich or grow richer. The second speaks to his desire to be "myghty," since he who supports "the gretteste and moost sovereyn thyng" will surely be regarded as *grete* and *sovereyn*. And in doing this, the third sentence suggests, he may count himself "happy and blessed." This last proposition is perhaps the most audacious example of Prudence's willingness to use any material that lies to hand (including the seventh Beatitude) to further the immediate needs of her argument.[133] The Vulgate says nothing about *purchasing* peace.[134] Prudence's usage of the verb neatly complements her earlier suggestion that riches cannot purchase, or maintain, war (7.1650). Prudence knows that Melibee will more easily be swayed by biblical arguments suggestive of sound and profitable commercial investment.

Melibee's exclamation (and it *is* an exclamation, although it goes unpunctuated as such by the *Riverside Chaucer*)[135] suggests that our hero is experiencing an emotional crisis. This is also a moment of crisis for the *Melibee*, the text that tracks his emotions. As Prudence's arguments hit home, Melibee sees that his long-nursed hopes for *vengeaunce* are receding rapidly. He therefore seeks to arrest this movement by forcing a rupture in his relations with Prudence: he accuses her of not caring for (literally, not loving) his public reputation, his "honour" and "worshipe." Such an accusation borrows the emotional force (in the household realm, the arena of marital interplay) of a charge of marital infidelity. It therefore threatens Prudence's right of continued existence in the household; the thought of dispensing with her and the virtues she mirrors back to him is evidently crossing Melibee's mind: "For right as men seyn that 'over-greet hoomlynesse engendreth dispreisynge,' so fareth it by to greet humylitee or mekenesse" (7.1686).

It is at this crucial moment that Prudence chooses to change her image: if Melibee thinks he can do without "humylitee or mekenesse," then he should see what the absence of these virtues might look like:

Thanne bigan dame Prudence to maken semblant of wratthe and seyde: / "Certes, sire, sauf your grace, I love youre honour and youre profit as I do myn owene, and evere have doon." (7.1687–88)

Prudence employs her rhetorical skill here, those powers of persuasion and seduction associated with the female body, to present Melibee with a "semblant," an image of something she herself is not, namely, wrathful. She now offers Melibee not a remedy to his anger but a mirror image of it. And she goes on to mirror, or speak back, the accusation of emotional betrayal that Melibee has just made to her: "For I knowe wel that ye been so hard-herted that ye wol do no thyng for me" (7.1695). In doing all this, Prudence vacates the strong, controlling position she has occupied since the dialogue began: in short, she affects to feminize herself and thereby to occupy the same subject positioning as Melibee. This presents her spouse with the opportunity of claiming the place she has just vacated. Melibee, sure enough, soon makes his first conciliatory speech (and shows the first signs of self-knowledge as one who is "angry and wrooth"):

Whanne Melibee hadde herd dame Prudence maken semblant of wratthe, he seyde in this wise: / "Dame, I prey yow that ye be nat displesed of thynges that I seye, / for ye knowe wel that I am angry and wrooth, and that is no wonder; / and they that been wrothe witen nat wel what they don ne what they seyn." (7.1697–1700)

In reconciling himself with Prudence, then, Melibee initiates the process that will lead to reconciliation with his enemies at the end of the text. To do this he needs to put himself under the tutelage of Prudence, but the moment of submission to his wife (what we might term the Wife of Bath *maistrie* moment) can now be seen not as capitulation from a weak position, but as an act of manly choice:

"Dame," quod Melibee, "dooth youre wil and youre likynge; / for I putte me hoolly in youre disposicioun and ordinaunce." (7.1724–25)

Prudence now turns her attention to the public world and, "whan she saugh hir tyme," arranges for Melibee's enemies to meet with her "in a pryvee place" (7.1728). Prudence never enters the public world herself, nor does she represent herself as anything other than the representative of Melibee. Even the "goodliche wordes" that so delight Melibee's adversaries are commended in terms designed to remind us of the recently etymologized name of her master: they show "the blessynge of swetnesse"; they are "sweete wordes" (7.1735,

1740). Melibee, sitting in his "court" (7.1806) with his enemies kneeling on the ground (7.1827) before him, has finally reattained the strong, masculinized position that, Elaine Tuttle Hansen has argued, makes an end to every tale in Chaucer.[136] Yet the text has one surprise left. Once Melibee's adversaries have left, promising to return and receive "sentence and juggement" (7.1830), Prudence "sees her time" one last time. Prudence is too prudent to assume that a drama is over just because the conventional signs of closure are being wheeled into place:

And whan that dame Prudence saugh hire tyme, she freyned and axed hir lord Melibee / what vengeance he thoughte to taken of his adversaries. /
To which Melibee answerde and seyde, "Certes," quod he, "I thynke and purpose me fully / to desherite hem of al that evere they han and for to putte hem in exil for evere." (7.1832–35)

This is, as Lee Patterson has observed, "a devastating moment."[137] The vehemence of Melibee's response (just a few lines after he has raised his enemies from the ground "ful benignely," 7.1827) represents a major regression: have we read so many pages, heard so many arguments, only to end up where we began? This possibility, the text suggests, remains forever active when we are caught in the chamber politics of a powerful and emotional male; *voluntas arbitrium* can exercise its arbitrary powers at any moment.[138] Prudence now has little time to work with, since "a certeyn day" (7.1829) has been appointed for judgment in court. She therefore modifies her tactics of persuasion by picking up the biggest club she can find, a threat of judgment greater than any threat that Melibee can wield:

Wherefore I pray yow, lat mercy been in youre herte, / to th'effect and entente that God Almighty have mercy on yow in his laste juggement. / For Seint Jame seith in his Epistle: "Juggement withouten mercy shal be doon to hym that hath no mercy of another wight." (7.1867–69)

This is clearly another "semblant" tactic: Melibee is encouraged to look at "God Almighty" in his most terrible aspect and see an image of himself as a merciless judge. It is this masculine image of the deity, rather than the feminizing *remedium* of *mansuetude* and *debonairetee, pacience* and *suffrance,* that finally moves Melibee and dissuades him from revenging himself on his enemies. This is not the only form of religious closure open to a literary opus: the *Troilus,* for example, moves past the judgmental aspects of the deity and ends by appealing, in its final line, to "love of mayde and moder thyn benigne" (5.1869). But the form of closure chosen for the *Melibee* does broadly predict that of the *Tales* itself, as Chaucer, *"the makere of this book,"* petitions to be "oon of hem at the day of doom that shulle be saved" (10.1092). Yet it would be wrong to infer, from these convergent moments of closure, that the *Melibee* and the *Parson's Tale* exhibit systematic similarities of form and function. The *Parson's Tale,* from the first, walks us along "the righte wey of

Jerusalem celestial" (10.80); its journey along "olde pathes" (10.77) leads from discussion of Penitence through a systematic account of seven sins and their remedies to a certain end. The *Melibee*, like the *Parson's Tale*, knows where it must get to, but it has no idea, at the outset, of the particular "olde pathes" (at what time, in what order, in what circumstances) down which it must travel. Its subject, and that to which it is subjected, is not the deity, or religious schemata, but the unstable emotions of an angry man who is and remains "myghty and riche."

From beginning to end, the *Melibee* is caught up in the secular realm (which is always subjected, in the Middle Ages, to the pervasive and definitional influence of religious discourses): the political and gendered spaces of household, court, and greater public world.[139] The last of its many rhetorical strategies happily succeeds in aligning the text at its moment of closure with religious orthodoxy. But the strategy of employing the argument of "juggement withouten mercy" is, like that of employing the seventh Beatitude, primarily *rhetorical*. What is important in *Melibee* is not that the male protagonist should grasp the essential or transcendent truth of the *sententiae* that are addressed to him, but that the arguments in which they are embedded should dissuade him from violent acts. Only the wife of such a man, the text suggests, can do the necessary emotional and intellectual work, face-to-face, that is needed to control his emotions; to ensure that anger does not translate into violence. Her ultimate concern is not with Melibee's welfare but with the *bonum commune*, the greater political society of which she and her spouse form part. But to achieve this end, she must operate within domestic space in much the same way as Alisoun of Bath (or Alice of Windsor)[140] work in the bedroom, retaining close contact between her body and that of her spouse. Such crucial combining of bodily proximity with linguistic skill is acknowledged by the Latin tomb inscription accorded to Richard II's queen, Anne of Bohemia:

> Jurgia sedavit—et pregnantes relevavit
> Corpore formosa—vultu mitis speciosa.

> She calmed quarrels and relieved pregnant [quarrels/women]
> Beautiful in body, kind and fair in face.[141]

The rapid movement here from acknowledgment of Anne's skills as a mediator in disputes to awareness of the female body to description of her physical person, and specifically of her face, is not gratuitous: it captures *in nuce* the specifically wifely powers exemplified by the protracted, face-to-face drama of the *Melibee*. (And the moment of Anne's death, marked by these verses, sees *Melibee's* grip on political *actualité*, as lived at out court, slacken; the text recedes deeper into written culture.)[142] Women, when alive and well in the *Canterbury Tales*, prove uniquely capable of preventing masculine anger from rigidifying into masculine violence. Ypolita, Emeleye, and "wommen alle" (1.1757) dissuade Theseus from the summary execution of the young Theban knights. Guenevere "and other ladyes mo" (1.894) dissuade Arthur from *quiting* the violence of rape with the violence of beheading. And Prudence crowns this development by easing the urge for magnate vendetta and achieving a peaceful end. The price of such success for women is that their complex and dangerous work of household rhetoric, vital to the health of the body politic, will not be acknowledged *as* political work; assumed to occur in private, it can expect no public acknowledgment. Prudence, after all, is an allegorical abstraction and not a real woman.

Chapter 9

After Eloquence:
Chaucer in the House of Apollo

Richard II's life after Anne of Bohemia began inauspiciously when, in a fit of rage, he shed magnate blood at her funeral.[1] Without the restraining effects of the wifely powers inscribed on Anne's tomb, without her human companionship, Richard II was likely to be a Melibee without Prudence. The unhappy possibilities of such a domestic scenario are first anticipated, and after 1394 exemplified, by the short poetic fiction that undoes all the good work of the *Melibee*: the *Manciple's Tale*. The need to read Chaucer's last poetic fiction within the hermeneutic frame of the *Melibee* is, I hope, obvious enough to warrant a short chapter rather than another long one.

The *Melibee* and the *Manciple's Tale*, we have noted, are the only fictions in the *Tales* to unfold without grounding themselves in a specific geographic locale. Their location is a person, an *irous* and powerful male whose passions dictate the narrative's course and duration. His setting is his household, in which he dramatizes his feelings, stages his suffering, at seeing his wife subjected to violence. The form of discourse that attempts to govern such domestic space is rhetoric, specifically those arts of *dicendi* and *tacendi* taught by *rhetores* such as Albertano of Brescia. Each tale is overshadowed by its relationship to law: the *Melibee* is derived from an Italian *causidicus* (and was originally intended for Chaucer's Man of Law); the Manciple is a minor official who works at the fringes of a London Inn of Court. And each tale is ultimately a "Tale of Chaucer": the *Melibee* is narrated by Chaucer the pilgrim; the *Manciple's Tale* features a loquacious, court-trained, avian Chaucer surrogate in the familiar triangulated relationship of lord and master, wife, and poet.[2]

"A Maunciple, and Myself"; Marsyas/Marcia

When read in conjunction with the *Melibee*, the *Manciple's Tale* is plainly a catastrophe. Everything learned in the treatise is forgotten in the fable: masculine anger turns to masculine violence; the wounded but eloquent Prudence yields to a wife who is nameless, silent, and (finally) dead; the household breaks up; the songster loses his voice and livery and is slung out of doors. This last experience of disgrace, ruin, and rustication leads us back in a full, Langlandian circle to the noncourtly opening of Fragment 1: to the Tabard and the open road, and to the poem's first authorial signature. Chaucer, in that first fragment, both authorizes and discredits himself by appearing at the back of the pilgrimage as "the sixth of six": he recognizes the highest poetic pretensions of Dante, Boccaccio, and Jean de Meun even as he rides in the company of five "miscellaneous predators."[3] He actually shares a line (and a weak alliterative bond) with the Manciple; beyond himself and the Manciple, the speaker of his last poetic fiction, there is nobody: "A MAUNCIPLE, and myself—ther were namo" (1.544).

A manciple was a minor official of the Inner or Middle Temple; his chief business was the buying of provisions for his Inn of Court.[4] Chaucer cele-brates the Manciple for his commercial variation of rhetorical *quando*, his ability to buy the right thing at the right time:

> For wheither that he payde or took by taille,
> Algate he wayted so in his achaat
> That he was ay biforn and in good staat.   (1.570–72)

Such powers of calculation, characterized by William Wordsworth as "shrewdness and clever worldly Prudence,"[5] extend to dealings with his "maistres" (1.576), the men of law who frequent his inn; this Manciple, Chaucer tells us, deceived them all ("sette hir aller cappe," 1.586). A kindred calculating spirit guides the Manciple in his shaming and displacement of, and final reconciliation with, the Cook in Fragment 9. He shames and silences the Cook through a display of "gentil" speech that, Louise Fradenburg argues, "removes us from the festival of pilgrimage and gives us the entrée to court—or to a travesty of the court"; the entry into court space is signified through the process of displacing the Cook "as the alienated body."[6] And yet, as the Host observes, it would be "to nyce" of the Manciple to think that he could permanently sever himself (as a professional provisioner) from relations with a London cook:

> "Another day he wole, peraventure,
> Reclayme thee and brynge thee to lure;
> I meene, he speke wole of smale thynges,
> As for to pynchen at thy rekenynges,
> That were nat honest, if it cam to preef."   (9.71–75)

Although the Host's metaphor here nods at courtly rhetoric—the Man-ciple as hawk; the Cook as the hand that the Manciple must fly back to—his gloss ("I meene") soon draws us back to commercial and legal consider-ations: *pynching* at *rekenynges*; "honest" as a synonym for "good business."[7]

The Manciple cannot carry the professional liability of being at odds with a London cook (or with a Southwark taverner, for that matter), and so he offers to share "a draghte of wyn" (9.83). This conciliatory initiative, which causes the Host to laugh "wonder loude" as "acorde and love" supplant "rancour and disese" (9.94–98), seems finally to end the cycle of pilgrim *quiting* that has run through nine fragments. This hardly represents a crowning moment for the ideological purity of associational form, however. The winning argument for reconciliation, as offered by the Host, speaks chiefly to professional self-interest. But so too do the winning argumentative strategies advanced by Prudence in the *Tale of Melibee*. And if a spirit of commercial calculation moves the Manciple, so too does it color the spiritual vision of his master, the Man of Law.

The return of the Manciple to speak Chaucer's last poetic fiction suggests that Chaucer, again Langland-like, never quite shakes off anxieties regarding the legitimacy or usefulness of his own social role. Chaucer and the Manciple share a line and have a lot in common; the Manciple mirrors both Chaucer's aspirations to social status and his dread of being deemed parasitical. Each tries to authenticate himself and his profession (household servant; vernacular poet) by hanging around men of law. Each attempts to imagine himself into court space, but each is known to be fundamentally rooted and invested in a non-noble world of commercial exchange. In the *Manciple's Tale* Chaucer has himself imagined, as poetic songster at the court of Apollo, as a bird in a cage. He speaks the words that his master teaches him (9.132), but there remains the terrible possibility that a different voice will escape from him, a native register ("Cokkow!") that marks him as a parasitic outsider even as, so to speak, he brings the house down.[8] He will thus be uncovered, unfeathered, unskinned, as one who professes wisdom while speaking "lewedly"; as someone betrayed, in short, by his own class origins.

Chaucer's choice of Apollo's court and household as the site of his *Tales'* last fiction heralds the return of anxieties first voiced in his most anxious of poems, that nervous breakdown in short couplets, the *House of Fame*.[9] In opening Book 3 of his dream poem, Chaucer had both appealed to and shied away from Apollo as the God-like patron of his poetic craft:

> O God of science and of lyght,
> Appollo, thurgh thy grete myght,
> This lytel laste bok thou gye!
> Nat that I wilne, for maistrye,
> Here art poetical be shewed.   (1091–95)

This appeal is, of course, based on the opening of Dante's third *cantica*:[10]

> O buono Appollo, a l'ultimo lavoro
> fammi del tuo valor sì fatto vaso,
> come dimandi a dar l'amato alloro.   (1.13–15)

> O good Apollo, for this last labor
> make me such a vessel of your might
> as you require for granting your beloved laurel.

Dante's anxiety, even as he makes such an appeal, is that he will end up as a "vagina" rather than as a "vaso," an upstart skinned for presumption rather than a vessel of divine power:

> Entra nel petto mio, e spira tue
> sì come quando Marsïa traesti
> de la vagina de le membra sue.   (1.19–21)

> Enter my breast, and breathe there
> as when you drew Marsyas
> from the sheath of his own limbs.

Chaucer's eyes must have passed over this passage because we find him imitating the very next tercet, Dante's appeal to "divina virtù" (1.22; "devyne vertu," 1101) and his promise to crown himself with laurel (1.22–27; 1101–9). Chaucer did not excise Marsyas or forget how he lost his skin; he simply transferred him away from a self-referential context to a safer place, the House of Fame. Or rather, her:

> And Marcia that loste her skyn,
> Bothe in face, body, and chyn,
> For that she wolde envien, loo,
> To pipen bet than Appolloo.   (1229–32)

This change of gender is very strange. As Alfred David observes, it is quite plausible to deduce from the *Commedia* (or from the *Teseida*) that "Marsïa" is a feminine noun: but as David further observes, Chaucer's "oune bok," the Ovidian *Metamorphoses*, would clearly have informed him that "Marcia" was masculine: so too, *inter alia*, the *Ovide moralisé*, Giovanni del Virgilio, and the third Vatican mythographer.[11] Chaucer, through ignorance or volition, chose to imagine Marsyas, *the* classic exemplum of the artist whose artistic presumption enrages a social superior, as feminine. How, then, might such a slippage of gender be glossed? When Chaucer is caught in the presence of a mighty or godlike lord, we might argue, he is feminized both by the pressures of hierarchical subordination and by his own performative anxieties.[12] But here again, as in the *Melibee* chapter, this impulse to instant allegorization (especially one that would fit a literal or historical man within an allegorical woman) might be resisted. If female Marcia dies as a presumptuous artist at the hands of a wrathful Apollo, masculine Marsyas might live.[13] Given that there are so many female victims of masculine violence in Chaucer, this seems a worryingly cogent proposition.[14] The poet and the wife, within the household, would appear to be natural allies: each practices a rhetorical art to please, and not enrage, a lord and master. In the *Melibee*, wifely eloquence saves private and public society; in the *Prologue* to the *Legend of Good Women*, it saves the poet Chaucer. How, then, might the masculine poet reciprocate by helping the wife? The *Manciple's Tale* provides a short and chilling answer.

Although Marsyas/Marcia makes no appearance in the *Manciple's Tale*, his/her spirit hovers over us early on in the form of citation chosen to commend the singing of Phoebus Apollo:

> Certes the kyng of Thebes, Amphioun,
> That with his syngyng walled that citee,
> Koude nevere syngen half so wel as hee.   (9.116–18)

Book 6 of Ovid's *Metamorphoses* tells how the seven sons of Amphioun are slaughtered by a hail of arrows fired by Phoebus Apollo as "archer-god" (the guise in which he first appears in the *Manciple's Tale*, 108–12); the grief-stricken Amphioun subsequently kills himself. Apollo takes up his bow at the urging of Latona, his mother; Latona is enraged by the boasting not of Amphioun, but of Niobe, Amphioun's wife.[15] Niobe does boast, in passing, of "the magic of my husband's lyre" (6.178–79), but there is no suggestion in Ovid of Amphioun seeking to compete with Apollo through his "syngyng." In Chaucer, it seems, Amphioun's fate at the hands of Apollo the archer-god assimilates him to the broader outline of the Marsyas/Marcia legend: one who tries to compete with a lord or a god at his own particular art. And here, once again, the anxieties surrounding the Marsyas role for a court poet such as Chaucer may be acknowledged without being explicitly recognized: identification *as* a potential Marsyas figure, for Chaucer, would not be prudent.

The complex resonances of the Amphioun citation, and the slipperiness of the movement from Marsyas to Marcia, suggest that the poet in the house of Apollo knows himself to be in a potentially treacherous game of survival. We seem here to anticipate the complex survival strategies of poets writing at the court of that sixteenth-century David, King Henry VIII.[16] And yet the duplicity and bad faith we find in this last poetic fiction were anticipated by the *Tale* which, in Ellesmere, immediately precedes it: the narrative of craft betrayal conducted between the Canon and his Yeoman. The protagonist of the *Canon's Yeoman's Tale* is said to stand, in his "infinite falsnesse," with the worst betrayers of the ancient world (Nineveh, Rome, Alexandria, Troy, 8.973–75). More unsettling for the reader, however, is the suspicion of betrayal by the Yeoman himself, who tells of a canon and swears ("in feith, and by the hevenes queene") that he is not speaking of *his* Canon: "It was another chanoun, and nat hee" (8.1089–90). In Fragment 8, the *compagnye* (and the reader) doubts whether it can trust the newcomer in its midst; in Fragment 9, a wife is betrayed within her own household by one she might have looked to as an ally.

Ars Tacendi, Ars Dicendi, and the Failure of Household Rhetoric

Chaucer takes considerable pains to invest his source tale of Apollo and the too-talkative bird with the claustrophobic intensity of domestic drama. In Ovid and the *Ovide moralisé*, the bird (a raven) flies from the house to tell Phoebus of his lover's infidelity. In Gower the raven is "kept in chamber" through the youthful whimsy of Cornide, Apollo's lady-love.[17] In Chaucer the raven becomes a caged crow under Apollo's tutelage; the lady Cornide or Coronis becomes a nameless "wyf." The phonic proximity of *cornix* to Cornide suggests an affinity of crow to wife that is both concealed (the wife is never named) and underscored through a curious paralleling of clauses:

> Now hadde this Phebus in his hous a crowe . . .   (9.130)

> Now hadde this Phebus in his hous a wyf . . .   (9.139)

This repetition serves to emphasize that crow and wife occupy equivalent political positions. Each is situated in Phoebus's house, under Phoebus's immediate political authority; each is itemized as property (Phoebus "hadde" them). It seems, then, that they might function as natural political allies. It is, in fact, imperative that they do so, since the *Tale* has introduced a crucial splitting of household functions—the division of eloquence from affect. In the *Melibee* affect and eloquence are united in the person of Prudence. In the *Manciple's Tale* the wife is granted the power to move, the ability to stir Phoebus's emotions, but not the power of speech. The crow is trained and entitled to speak, but his speaking is divorced from any understanding of its own affective power. The outcome of these domestic arrangements, of this new division of labor within the household, is (as the most rudimentary knowledge of Ciceronian rhetoric would lead us to expect) catastrophic.[18] Things look unpromising from the very beginning, since Phoebus trains his caged bird to mirror, imitate, and "countrefete" speech (9.134) but not to understand its emotional effects: a crucial defect, according to Albertano, since one should speak "only if you know not only your reason for speaking but also the impact your speech will have"; the effect ("effectum") of ill-considered speech "may prove horrible."[19] Albertano also insists (a little earlier in his *De doctrina dicendi et tacendi*) that "you who would speak must know in your soul who you are."[20] Such self-recognition would seem to be difficult for Phoebus's pet bird, which is consistently imagined as something other than itself: as a jay (9.132), like a swan (9.133), like and unlike a nightingale (9.136), as a scorpion's tongue (9.271); as, in short, an aggregation of rhetorical tropes. This strange bird knows the mechanics of speaking, but not the art of speech: "quis, quando, cui dicas; cur, quomodo, quando requiras."[21] The crow's deficiency in *ars dicendi et tacendi* reflects the limits of his master's knowledge. Phoebus Apollo, a god on earth, need not know how to *persuade* people to act in his own household: he needs only to command. It follows that in training his court bird he imparts no understanding of the calculative skills we have seen summarized as *kairos* and exemplified in the person of Prudence.

Prudence, we have noted, excels in seeing "hire tyme" for both speaking and silence; her first tactical decision is for silence, not speaking (as Melibee weeps like a bereaved mother, 7.977). In the *Manciple's Tale*, too, the first crucial decision is for silence, an option that Chaucer takes some trouble to accentuate:

> The white crowe, that heeng ay in the cage,
> Biheeld hire werk, and seyde never a word.   (9.240–41)

The crow's first betrayal of wife and master is made through silence, his second through speaking. More specifically, it comes in the form of a gloss on his own utterance ("Cokkow! Cokkow! Cokkow!"), an outburst that Phoebus defines as alien to his own courtly register ("what song is this?" 9.247). This glossing takes the form of a long, controlled descent down the hypotactic structures of courtly discourse that finally hits a brutal, monosyllabic bottom:

> "By God," quod he, "I synge nat amys.
> Phebus," quod he, "for al thy worthynesse,
> For al thy beautee and thy gentilesse,
> For al thy song and al thy mynstralcye,
> For al thy waityng, blered is thyn ye
> With oon of litel reputacioun,
> Noght worth to thee, as in comparisoun,
> The montance of a gnat, so moote I thryve!
> For on thy bed thy wyf I saugh hym swyve."   (9.248–56)

The immediate effect of this speech is to arouse violent emotion and to break the crucial, face-to-face relationship between lord and adviser, as Phoebus twists himself away; it also succeeds in ending the relationship between husband and wife:

> This Phebus gan aweyward for to wryen,
> And thoughte his sorweful herte brast atwo.
> His bowe he bent, and sette therinne a flo,
> And in his ire his wyf thanne hath he slayn.   (9.262–65)

The last line here recalls the infamous line 248 through both its monosyllables and its parallel alternation of substantives and possessive adjectives: "thy bed thy wyf"; "his ire his wyf." Words feed emotions that translate into deeds: a heart "brast atwo" can pick up "a flo" and kill with it. The term "flo," which draws attention to itself through its archaism and rarity, reminds us that arrows need feathers to fly straight.[22] Phoebus would shoot no arrows were it not for his feathered friend, the crow. And Phoebus himself has been struck by arrows, fired by the crow: "for words are like arrows," Albertano says, in his *De doctrina dicendi et tacendi*, "easy to shoot off, hard to retrieve."[23] It is fitting, then, that Phoebus should deprive the crow not only of his whiteness, his song, and his speaking, but also of his feathers (symbolic, perhaps, of his power to make words fly to their target, to turn words into deeds): "And pulled his white fetheres everychon" (9.304).

The line that follows the slaying of Phoebus's wife summarizes everything that happens next: "This is th'effect; there is namoore to seyn" (9.266). The "effect" or *effectus* of the tale, its "outcome, end,"[24] is already known. The time for efficacious speech is over. The rest of the narrative can only be a lot of "namoore to seyn." Phoebus accuses the crow of treachery ("Traitour," 271) and tells us what we have already learned from the *Melibee*, that an angry man without an eloquent adviser may commit violent acts:

> "O trouble wit, O ire recchelees,
> That unavysed smyteth gilteles!"   (9.279–80)

Phoebus again:

> "Smyt nat to soone, er that ye witen why,
> And beeth avysed wel and sobrely
> Er ye doon any execucion
> Upon youre ire for suspecion."   (9.285–88)

Phoebus regrets his ire, but he cannot cure himself of it. The person who was best able to model the feminine virtues instrumental to any *remedium contra peccatum Ire* ("mansuetude, that is debonairetee"; "pacience or suffrance") lies dead at his feet.[25] No adviser can step forward to challenge his warped recollection of his dead wife as one "to me so sad and eek so trewe" (9.275); nobody can prevent him from making the tale-telling crow the next and last victim of masculine *quiting*: "I wol thee quite anon thy false tale" (9.293).

The fate of the crow inspires the long *moralitas* that drags down the curtain on this short but violent household drama. These 45 lines evoke a different household setting (the Manciple at his mother's knee) through a strange impersonation that plays (to borrow a favorite trope from Albertano) like "musica in luctu" ("musik in wepynge").[26] Albertano's arresting phrase, which succinctly captures the folly of Chaucer's crow by pairing cheerful song with unhappy circumstances, comes near the end of his *De doctrina dicendi et tacendi* (and reappears near the beginning of his Melibee story). The Manciple's mother owes nothing to the late part of the *De doctrina* dedicated to *quando*, when to speak; the dense network of echoes and correspondences between her speech and the Latin text suggest she has not progressed beyond the first chapter (with its heavy and recurrent emphasis on *ars tacendi*). Albertano's later *De doctrina* chapters emphasize the importance of speaking: speaking the truth, speaking with style, speaking at the right moment. The final (*quando*) section is the most important, since it concerns the crucial moment of entering or not entering into discourse. This is the moment at which an inert aggregation of *dicta* may take on political life; the moment at which we graduate from the schoolroom of *ars dicendi et tacendi* to the historical world of Prudence and Melibee. Anyone who enters such a world with just one idea, one strategy to follow without reference to changing circumstances, will not survive. By concluding his *Tale* with rigid repetitions, then, the Manciple confirms that he too is an outsider to court discourse; he understands nothing of the crucial art of *kairos* or *quando*.

The particular dictum that the Manciple chooses to repeat ("hold your tongue") serves to accentuate his blindness to his own narration: for it was through holding his tongue, rather than through speaking, that the crow made his first and most crucial error. It also allows Chaucer to end by airing anxieties that speak to the perils of writing, as well as speaking, within the context of court and household:

> But he that hath *mysseyd*, I dar wel sayn,
> He may no wey clepe his word agayn.
> Thyng that is seyd is seyd, and forth it gooth,
> Though hym repente, or be hym nevere so looth.
> He is his thral to whom that he hath sayd
> A tale of which he is now yvele apayd.   (9.353–58; emphasis mine)

These lines (juxtaposing two *De doctrina dicendi et tacendi* dicta)[27] suggest that all the anxieties associated with speaking in the presence of the great are magnified for he (or she) who writes.[28] Although ill-timed words launched into the air have their consequences, they do (so the *House of Fame* assures us) fade away; words written down, however, endure, and leave a paper trail back to the author. Once the *makere* has loosed his text onto the world he cannot "clepe his word agayn," nor can he control the conditions of its transmission and reproduction. All this, Chapter 12 will argue, bodes ill for Chaucer in the *Prologue* to the *Legend of Good Women* as he falls under the shadow of another amorous, uxorious, *irous*, bow-wielding, godlike male, the God of Love. Once again, female eloquence will busy itself to save men from violence, but the song of the poet, as crystallized by the unhappy rhyming of "Creseyde" with (again) "mysseyde" (F 440–41), will once more suggest a failure of reciprocity. The eloquent wife must pursue her work as a protectress unprotected; her perennial vulnerability to physical violence is essential to the tortured erotics of absolutist chamber politics.

The *Manciple's Tale* concludes with the mother urging her son to give up his attachment to "tidynges." The *House of Fame* suggests, and the Man of Law confirms, that the quest for *tidynges* is an aspiring *auctor's* chief business; this therefore represents a demand for the end of poetry itself:

> "My sone, be war, and be noon auctour newe
> Of tidynges, wheither they been false or trewe.

> Whereso thou come, amonges hye or lowe,
> Kepe wel thy tonge and thenk upon the crowe." (9.359–62)

Even as these lines give out the last gasp of Canterbury fabling, they also hint, as does so much in this *Tale*, at a cyclical recursion to origins, one that moves here with the great regenerative cycle of the poem's opening *quando*: "Whan that Aprill" (1.1). In beginning this last fiction, Chaucer, I have argued, was haunted by the figure he found at the opening of Dante's last *cantica*: Marsyas/Marcia, the artist flayed by an angry masculine God. The ending of the *Tale*, through its unusual and insistent affirmation of the mother-son bond (and, specifically, of the mother's attempt to regulate the filial tongue), is remarkably congruent with the ending of the *Paradiso*. As he approaches the end of *his* poetic journey, preparing to move from speech to silence, Dante likens his *lingua* (tongue, language) to that of a breast-fed baby:

> Omai sarà più corta mia favella,
> pur a quel ch'io ricordo, che d'un fante
> che bagni ancor la lingua a la mammella.   (33.106–8)

> Now will my speech fall more short,
> in respect to that which I remember, than that of a baby
> who still bathes his tongue at the breast.

Through this extraordinary return to dependent babyhood, Dante recognizes the collocation of mother and child, infant tongue and female body, as the alpha and omega of vernacular poetics. Their shared language falls far short of the rhetoric that governs the world beyond the household, but without the mother tongue, the *lingua materna*, there would be no speech, and hence no poetic journey, at all.[29] Since mother and child form the primary linguistic community, the division of mother from child must be read as an act of personal cruelty with far-reaching social consequences. So whereas a dead wife brings household rhetoric to an end, a tortured wife facilitates symbolic expression of a new kind of political rhetoric: that of tyranny, the subject of our next chapter.

"Signes," "Tokenynge," and Tyranny

Locationless and semitransparent compositions such as *Melibee* and the *Manciple's Tale* take on much of their color and power from their particular textual and historical circumstances.[30] The circumstance that this chapter has considered most intensively for the *Manciple's Tale* is a formal one—namely, its placement as the final fiction of Chaucer's *Tales*. As such, it exploits its kinship with the *Melibee* to demonstrate, calamitously, the limitations of secular rhetoric. It thereby discovers the need for and the path to another long prose tract of quite different import: the *Parson's Tale*. However, the social and linguistic breakdown that makes an end of this fable, while providing a powerful rationale for the step to systematic religion, may speak to and gain urgency from life beyond the text. Formal analysis (while itself constitutive of historical meaning) seeks its complement in political narrative. Where, then, to look for a tale of wayward *tokenynge*, household rhetoric turned bad, in the 1390s?

It is difficult to imagine the youthful, godlike, *irous*, amorous and uxorious protagonist of the *Manciple's Tale* without thinking of that "flour of bachilrie" (9.125), Richard II. Memories of the youthful Richard as Phoebus personified (jousting in armor embellished with his grandfather's celebrated sun badge) seem almost *too* apposite, too dazzling to dwell upon.[31] But if we were to conduct a Kolvian experiment to assess the most striking visual icon of this tale,[32] we might settle on a more particular and less overwhelming image: the bow. Whereas Gower's version of the fable sees Phoebus dispatch his wife with a sword, a noble weapon, Chaucer sticks with the traditional bow and arrow.[33] By making Phoebus Apollo an archer-god, Chaucer invests him with some of the iconographic power of Cupid: there is, in fact, little to distinguish this figure from the *Legend's* God of Love. Crucially, however, the bow first appears not as an offensive weapon but as a "signe" (9.127), performing a semiotic function equivalent to that of a livery badge or a pilgrim "signe."[34] Phoebus bears a bow; all bows may thus come to summon mental images of Phoebus.

Such interplay between chivalric signs and natural phenomena was, as Lee Patterson has memorably demonstrated, a dangerous and closely regulated game in Ricardian England.[35] Disputes over signs as markers of chivalric pedigree and honor (on the field of battle, or in the Court of Chivalry) could and did prove ruinous or fatal. Defeat and disgrace could empty a particular "signe" of its meaning, or drain it of all positive valences. The bow of Phoebus, which from the beginning of the *Manciple's Tale* seems an alarming choice of "signe," comes to mean something quite different as the physical instrument of uxoricide. When this "signe" is repudiated and destroyed (9.269), a new one is created from the body of the hapless crow: his loss of song, white feathers, and absence from court will henceforth be read as "tokenynge" (9.302) of his guilt as an accessory to wife-slaying. Such is the fate, the *Tale* prompts us to moralize, of the courtier-songster who would "countrefete the speche of every man" (9.134).

Richard II's propensity for handing out signs and tokens is well-known: even the court of heaven, in the Wilton diptych, wears the "signe" of the White Hart. In 1387, while on a ten-month "gyration" through the north and midlands of England, Richard handed Cheshire archers badges of golden crowns by way of recruiting them into his retinue.[36] As the reign wore on, however, it was the bow itself that proved to be the most potent and terrifying symbol of Richard's personal authority. When Arundel was led to the block in 1397 he was escorted by the Cheshire archers.[37] Earlier in the same year, according to Adam of Usk, the same archers had terrified an open-air parliament with the prospect of imminent death. The prelates withdrew, says Usk, and then

the king's archers, who, to the number of four thousand, surrounded the parliament house, which was set up to this end in the middle of the palace-yard, thought that some quarrel or strife had arisen in the house; and, bending their bows, they drew their arrows to the ear, to the great terror of all who were there; but the king quieted them.[38]

Those who find themselves targeted by archers at such a moment must look to the king as the absolute arbiter of life and death. And at such a moment, the king's emotional disposition, his ability to master "ire," is of paramount importance; the wrong word or sign may prove fatal. The bow, then, comes to be recognized as a dangerously unstable "signe" in the later years of Richard II. When deployed as a "signe" of youthful prowess in hunting, or as homage to Cupid, it constitutes court space as *Hof*, a nexus of social relationships organized around a princely presence. When wielded as a weapon, it turns *Hof* into *Gericht*, a space for judicial judgment or even, in the hands of a tyrant, gratuitous death.[39] The same physical space generates differing and shifting rules; for those who cannot read the "signes" or govern their tongues, court life may prove a very short tale indeed.

While offering itself primarily as an exemplum of how not to survive at court, the *Manciple's Tale* does cleverly succeed in critiquing Phoebus as tyrant. A tyrant, according to medieval political theory, is a ruler who acts to satisfy his own immediate desires rather than to address the needs of the *bonum commune*.[40] When Phoebus kills his wife, he acts out of emotion; he behaves tyrannically. Nobody will accuse him of being a tyrant to his face: indeed, there is no point in doing so, since this may only inflame him to greater acts of tyranny. Nevertheless, the Manciple gives his readers all the material they will need to identify the archer-god as a tyrant. His twelve-line excursus on the semantics of tyranny is slipped in very cleverly as an analogy, ancillary to the main business of defining Phoebus's wife: is she to be called a "lemman" or a "lady"? While ostensibly subordinate to this trifling question, the Manciple's tyranny excursus actually functions as a powerful gloss to the violence that is about to happen:

> Right so bitwixe a titlelees tiraunt
> And an outlawe or a theef erraunt,
> The same I seye: ther is no difference.
> To Alisaundre was toold this sentence,
> That, for the tirant is of gretter myght
> By force of meynee for to sleen dounright,
> And brennen hous and hoom, and make al playn,
> Lo, therfore is he cleped a capitayn;
> And for the outlawe hath but smal meynee,
> And may nat doon so greet an harm as he,

> Ne brynge a contree to so greet mescheef,
> Men clepen hym an outlawe or a theef.   (9.223–34)

This miniature *Fürstenspiegel* is something of a *tour de force*: it is possible to work as an adviser to volatile princes, the text tells us, if you are clever enough. The adviser who holds up the mirror to Alexander here remains safely unnamed (it is, of course, Aristotle), and the whole performance is neatly bracketed away within the limits of *comparatio* (as if hoping for a subliminal and not confrontational encounter with the seigneurial mind). Set within such a subtly qualified discursive frame (affording, as we might say, a high level of deniability), the actual arguments advanced may be exceptionally blunt and direct: the only difference between the "titlees tiraunt" and the outlaw, as destroyers of "hous and hoom," is size of "meynee." The householder of greatest "myght" cannot be termed an "outlawe" because he makes law synonymous with his own personal power; law lives in his body and realizes itself through his actions. All this resonates with *fin de siècle* critiques of Richard II as egregious household builder and as self-appointed, self-embodied *lex*. In pairing the tyrant "capitayn" and the outlaw, men who "sleen dounright," burn down houses, and bring whole areas "to so greet mescheef," Chaucer may have been thinking primarily of Lombard despots and their *condottieri*. But such foreign tyranny, so powerfully imagined in Fragment 4, is held up chiefly as a mirror in which English polity will not wish to recognize itself.

Adultery, Political Crime, and the Poet's Survival

When Apollo calls the crow a "traitour," he is accusing him of political crime. This crime, as Apollo sees it, is perpetrated by the weapon of the tongue:

> "Traitour," quod he, "with tonge of scorpioun,
> Thou hast me broght to my confusioun."   (9.271–72)

The crow's untimely speaking is represented by his master as an act of disloyalty to his physical person. But the crow's first error, we have noted, was one of *tacendi*, not *dicendi*: he watches, rather than interrupts, the illicit liaison of "Phebus wyf" and "hir lemman" (9.238). What the crow is witnessing is in fact a political crime. According to a celebrated statute of 1352 — one recently invoked by newspaper editors in pursuit of Princess Diana stories — it was an act of treason "if a man should violate the companion of the king" ("Si home violast la compaigne le Roi").[41] The hapless crow, then, makes himself an accessory to treason both through silence and through speaking. His real crime, the source of all his troubles, is lack of timing. As for court birds, so for courtly authors: timing is all. The tragedy of Thomas Usk, as Paul Strohm so movingly tells it, is one of bad timing: Chaucer's instincts, it seems, were better than those of his fellow author or of his fictional crow.[42] Chaucer was plainly an adept in household rhetoric: as such, he could fully appreciate the precariousness of *ars dicendi et tacendi*. Through good timing, the art of *quando*, the wife of his *Melibee* prevents anger and violence from spilling out into the greater public world. Through bad timing, the Manciple's crow manages to kill the wife (the natural protector of poets in Chaucerian fiction), destroy the household, and lose his livery, his voice, and his place. Such final confusion, such catastrophic failures of self-recognition, anticipate the imaginings of Wyatt at the court of a later, more fully developed absolutism:

> For him death gripeth right hard by the crop
> That is much known of other, and of himself alas
> Doth die unknown, dazed with dreadful face.[43]

In Chaucerian fiction, however, one senses that the masculine poet and his surrogates are unlikely to die if there is a woman in the house.[44] And as a final fiction that hints at both terminal disaster and cyclical recurrence, that witnesses the collapse of familiar social structure, that returns us to an author among pilgrims who seems both sublimely energized and wracked by self-doubt (poet or predator?), the *Manciple's Tale* encourages us to look not forwards but sideways, even slightly backwards, to the texts of Chaucer's greatest contemporary.

Chapter 10

"Whan She Translated Was": Humanism, Tyranny, and the Petrarchan Academy

Truth is violent, it controls minds.
— Petrarch, *Familiares*, 17.10.18

The *Manciple's Tale* explores the causes and consequences of a momentary step into masculine tyranny: ill-timed words bring on ill-considered behavior that ends in physical violence, death, and social disintegration. Fragment 4 of the *Canterbury Tales*, which is situated entirely in "Lumbardye," imagines such momentary masculine excess as a form of state. Chaucer had heard talk of and then negotiated with such statecraft during his visits to Italy in the 1370s, experiences that enabled him to evaluate Petrarchan poetics within and as part of Lombard polity. Fragment 4's exploration of Lombardy, the terrain ruled by a regime that might be viewed as at once viciously tyrannical and proto-absolutist, begins with meditation on the figure and legend of "Fraunceys Petrak the lauriat poete" (4.31). It ends in Pavia, the Lombard city in which Boethius—Chaucer's preeminent master of dialogue, song, and reasoned persuasion—fell victim to tyranny and died under torture.

Chaucerian "Lumbardye" sees political dynamics once again articulated through gendered voices and bodies, close encounters that pit a masculine will to act against a vulnerable female eloquence. In the *Melibee*, an eloquent wife succeeds, through timely language and physical closeness, in outlasting a mighty man's desire for violent retribution. In the *Clerk's Tale*, the mighty man actually succumbs to his cruel desires. Wifely eloquence, and the wifely and motherly body that speaks it, now become the object of tyrannical, Nero-like investigation. But the work of female eloquence is not done: Griselde must labor to ensure that the effects of such tyranny are directed at and restricted to her own body, so sparing the greater body politic. Griselde's willingness to absorb Walter's violence realizes what remains, in the story of Melibee and Prudence, from moment to moment an unacknowledged political requirement.

Petrarch has something in common with Albertano of Brescia, a Lombard of an earlier political generation, in that he is celebrated and imitated for his "rethorike" (pronounced "sweete" by Chaucer's Clerk, 4.32). But those rhetorics are very different in scope. In Albertano's *Liber consolationis et consilii*, powers of rhetoric are deployed to save communal structures from violent destruction. In Petrarch's Lombardy, those structures have long since been destroyed by the willful violence of Petrarch's political patrons. The *fyn*, or final effect, of Petrarchan humanism and of Petrarchan poetics, I shall argue, is to announce and embellish the will of the state as embodied in the person of a single masculine ruler. Petrarch's fame is of paramount importance here: the Visconti may have gobbled up much of northern Italy, Brescia included, but Petrarch's power extends to "al Ytaile" (4.33). Poet and despot have much in common, much to offer one another. The trope that expresses their commonality of interests and strategies in most compelling fashion is that of their invention, translation, and violent subjugation of woman: woman as text; woman as political subject (or nonsubject, an entity little better than a slave). Such collusion of humanist poetics and absolutist power has a very long history, one that leads us to the first encounters between "America," figured as a naked native woman, and the European colonialists who invent, discover, and describe her.[1] The Griselde legend is a story that runs and runs.[2]

Time, Fame, and the Petrarchan Academy

The name of Petrarch has come to mean much more than the sum of texts that Petrarch wrote: it suggests a cultural movement called humanism. But the minute we admit the term "humanism" into any question the entire discussion threatens to escape all historical limits. Nobody knows where humanism begins or ends, although it seems to include writers as far apart as Mussato, Petrarch, Salutati, Bruni, and Valla. The proclivity of Petrarchan texts to detach themselves from the time, place, and circumstances of their composition is extraordinary: Petrarch was a generation older than Chaucer, but he is often still spoken of in "Renaissance" scholarly circles as if he were of the same historical generation as Wyatt and Surrey. It is vital to rehistoricize Petrarch if we are to understand the political and cultural work performed by his texts; in leaving him dehistoricized we only acquiesce to Petrarch's own rhetorical strategies. Any such attempt must begin by acknowledging the extraordinary power and complexity of Petrarch's textual afterlife; the Petrarch legend is itself a historical force to be reckoned with. Nicholas Mann, for example, has shown that fifteenth-century north Europeans knew and revered a "medievalized" Petrarch.[3] Petrarchan texts were shorn of their Stoicism and their more exotic classical instances were replaced by commonplace medieval dicta. The urge to read Petrarch as a Church Father accounts for his appearance in some manuscripts as "Franciscus Patriarca." This was the Petrarch that Lydgate revered: the orthodox medieval moralist. This Petrarch was always a Latin author. The only evidence of Petrarch's vernacular works circulating outside Italy before 1500 is Chaucer's translation of "S'amor non è" which forms part of *Troilus and Criseyde*.[4] And even this stray sonnet was later translated into Latin by Coluccio Salutati as "Si fors non sit amor."[5]

While north Europeans were striving to make Petrarch more "medieval," Italian humanists such as Salutati were working in the opposite direction. The early history of humanism, itself precarious and (excepting Salutati) devoid of forceful leadership,[6] struggled with Petrarchan texts that were delicately poised between opposite tendencies—between, for example, a yearning for monkish seclusion and a determination to intervene in public affairs. Florentine humanists under Salutati's leadership often found it disconcertingly difficult to reconcile Petrarch's political and cultural ideals with the values of Florentine republicanism. Petrarch had censured Cicero for his excessive fondness for public controversy, for valuing *negotium* above *otium*; in 1394 the humanist educator Pier Paolo Vergerio was moved to reply in Cicero's name.[7] Petrarch's own pronouncements on public affairs, while concerning themselves with historical particulars, were always liable to balloon away into Augustinian metaphysics. His traditionalist distrust of and contempt for worldly wealth required vigorous modification by later humanist figures, and his distaste for marriage, coupled with a notion of woman as "l'aura," the airy object and cipher of romantic quest, proved equally baffling. When speaking of women Petrarch was always liable to take a sharp turn into medieval misogyny, a tradition that differed markedly from the misogyny of later writers.

For Petrarch life was (to draw from the brilliant sequence of almost two hundred epithets he compiled on November 29, 1370) "imbecille potentia, pulchra deformitas, nuge serie" (feeble strength, beautiful deformity, serious foolishness).[8] But what are the historical and political implications of this tendency to evaporate, to escape from the pressures of a concrete historical moment? Such a paradoxical habit of mind, where one half of the mind hides from the other, is generously invoked by critics wishing to explain Petrarch's political thinking. Margaret Schlauch, for example, in considering why Petrarch "labored and wrote for a *renovatio imperii*," argues that he did this "for reasons probably unclear to himself."[9] Nobody would say this of Dante on empire. Perhaps this is because Dante's thought is taken as a historical terminus, whereas Petrarch's forms an origin, a point of departure. The true destination of Petrarchan thought, unclear to Petrarch himself, is made clear by the subsequent history of the movement he is bringing to light. This tendency to interpret the origins of humanism by reference to its ends has proven virtually irresistible. Perry Anderson, even as he attempts to trace "the lineages of the absolute state," seems unwilling to connect a vatic, time-transcending Petrarch with the absolutist regimes he actually worked for.[10]

Some effort must be made, then, to recover the historical moment of each Petrarchan utterance.

But if we could locate such moments, how close would this bring us to Chaucer? Chaucer's engagement with Petrarch precedes those Italian and north European traditions of reception that we have just adumbrated. Culturally and geographically, however, medieval England seemed like a strange and distant planet to Italian contemporaries. Leonardo Bruni could marvel at the enterprise of Florentine merchants, whose profession could lead them as far away as Britain, "which is an island in the ocean almost on the edge of the world."[11] Petrarch marveled at English successes in war against the French, but only as examples of how Fortune could allow a lesser kingdom to humiliate a greater one.[12] He was depressed to note, in the course of a diplomatic mission for the Visconti in 1360, how war with England had ruined the French countryside and brought the intellectual life of Paris to a standstill.[13] Petrarch later expressed his vigorous contempt for French intellectual traditions. The English had no traditions that could claim his attention, although he did acknowledge acquaintance with the *Architrenius* of the Englishman Jean de Hanville. This Petrarch described as the most tiresome thing he had ever read.[14]

On the other hand, the English, despite being perched at the edge of the world, had ample opportunity to learn about Petrarch. Avignon provided one source of information; the imperial court at Prague (with which Petrarch maintained strong ties) provided another.[15] Contacts between London and Prague were strengthened in 1382 when Richard married Anne of Bohemia. Anne had special reason to remember Petrarch since she was named after Anne, third wife of Charles IV, the only woman known to have received a letter from Petrarch. This letter, *Familiares* 21.8, took the form of a short treatise *de laudibus feminarum*, a legend of good women.[16]

Chaucer stood little chance of coming across Petrarch manuscripts in London since Petrarch exerted extremely tight control over the production and diffusion of his works. At the same time, he did nothing to discourage the spread of his own fame. Fame had been the theme of the oration he had delivered on being crowned poet laureate at Rome in 1341. In 1373 he received a letter from Boccaccio urging him to give up writing since he had written quite enough already; his younger admirers could take over. Petrarch found such a suggestion abhorrent: if (as Boccaccio maintained) he had now become world-famous this could only serve to spur him on to greater things.[17] The cult of Petrarch's fame was nurtured and spread by the curious institution alluded to by this chapter's title, the "Petrarchan Academy." By this I mean a small, consciously exclusive, masculine group of initiates dedicated to the pursuit of Latin culture: just such a group, in fact, as Petrarch describes in framing his Griselde story.[18] The two differing receptions of this story recorded by *Seniles* 18.3 both took place in Petrarch's presence. Most such gatherings around Petrarchan texts, however, took place in his absence, although Petrarch liked to think of himself as metaphysically present through the body of his text.[19]

I employ the term "Petrarchan Academy," then, to denote a complex cultural phenomenon[20] that was in part historical (Petrarch's admirers held meetings) and in part imaginary, expressive of a desire to escape history entirely: Petrarch dreamed of producing finalized texts of permanent value. Petrarch formed the center of this cultural entity and his followers formed its periphery. The most important of these peripheral Petrarchan groups were located at Florence and Naples. Although not formally constituted, these groups exhibited many institutional features. Membership was difficult to come by. Petrarch warned his followers against being imposed upon by men who claimed to be his friends.[21] When Francesco Bruni sought admittance to the Florentine circle it took some vigorous petitioning from Pandolfo Malatesta and then Francesco da Carrara before Petrarch would write Bruni a letter.[22] Petrarch maintained a policy of not writing to anybody who did not first write to him, but he answered every letter.[23] Writing to Petrarch subjected any command of Latinity to the severest scrutiny: correspondents such as Francesco Nelli suffered acute embarrassment on realizing their mistakes.[24] The best way of improving your *Latinitas* was, of course, to get hold of a collection of Petrarchan epistles; Petrarch's letters were eagerly copied and hoarded away, and many were stolen en route to their addressee. The dearest ambition of any Petrarchan circle was, paradoxically, to defeat the Petrarchan policy of *tarditas*, the postponed circulation of texts.[25] In 1361 four admirers at Sulmona decided to appeal to Petrarch for the preposthumous release of his Latin epic *Africa*. This appeal, penned by Barbato da Sulmona and transmitted via Boccaccio (who added a covering letter) was turned down flat. Petrarch had already entrusted Barbato with one passage of *Africa*, in 1343, on condition that he would not release copies. Barbato had broken his promise, and Petrarch, some eighteen years later, was still not ready to forgive him.[26]

Petrarch was further troubled by what we might call a number of anti-Academies: the French cardinals who reacted against Petrarch's belittling of France, for example, or the Aristotelians at Venice who decided that Petrarch was "illiterate" ("sine litteris").[27] It was the task of Petrarch's followers to keep him posted of all such murmurings.[28] What profit did such followers derive from their devotion? A number of them obtained important offices in Church or secular administrations (Petrarch complained in 1371 of having written endless letters of recommendation).[29] But many seemed content, like many adherents of more recent critical movements, to bask in the reflected glory of their distant master. And what benefit did Petrarch obtain from the demanding task of keeping these groups together through the nexus of his correspondence? The Academy provided a framework within which Petrarch could perpetuate the new philological standards he had established and (following the Dantean precedent of the *Epistle to Can Grande*) secure the terms of his own transmission to posterity. We see Petrarch committing himself to this process through his diligent editing, arranging, and rewriting (missive and final forms often differ) of his own letter collections. The *Familiares* opens with an address to posterity and closes with a letter to a friend of Petrarch's known as Socrates. This final letter opens up, toward the end, into a plural form of address and comes to rest with the individual reader: "te in finem, lector . . ." As individual readers we recognize that we are interchangeable with any other member of the posterity that Petrarch is addressing. As he composed the final letter Petrarch knew its first addressee to be recently dead. But many Petrarchan letters are addressed to men who had been dead for a millennium; and all Petrarchan letters, in their final form, were designed to outlive their addressees. Petrarch typically wrote not to solicit opinions or initiate debate but to publish finalized ideas.

Petrarch's epistles, though full of historical detail, tend to escape or erase the specific moment of their historical origin. The same may be said of Petrarch's other works, which, through a series of minute revisions extending over decades, conceal the chronology of their making. Petrarch's practice here forms an instructive contrast with that of Salutati (chancellor of the Florentine Republic from 1375–1406) who elected to let his works stand once written, thus revealing the lineaments of a personal history. Salutati also preferred to develop his ideas dialectically, through conversation, rather than announcing them in writing.[30]

The formation of the Petrarchan Academy, then, represents an attempt at self-classicizing, of exempting texts from the erosions of time. Time had been an urgent preoccupation for Petrarch since his youth, when he habitually marked passages relating to the flight of time.[31] Throughout his life Petrarch was constantly striving to stretch time out, to profit from every minute. Like the Emperor Augustus he read while being shaved or having his hair cut; he slept with pen and paper by the bed and sometimes wrote on horseback.[32] He felt compelled to calculate and account for how his time was controlled and spent, and he even struggled to erase the natural demarcations of daylight and darkness by working right through them: the "solitary man," Petrarch said, "knows how to join on night to day and day to night, and when the occasion demands it to combine the two, and in other ways to interchange the duties incident to each division."[33] This passage of *De vita solitaria* goes on to contrast the life of such a man, "whose whole year passes happily and peacefully as though it were a single day," with that of "voluptuous men of the city," who "in the midst of their wines and feasts, their roses and ointments, their songs and their plays . . . think a single day longer than a year and can scarcely pass a few hours without grumbling and annoyance." Petrarch himself was a professed lover of solitude who was forced to live in cities for most of his life. His attitude to time strangely couples an Augustinian yearning for transcendence (we should seek to escape time by sending our souls ahead of us to heaven)[34] with an outright commodification of time that allies him with those Florentine merchants whom he so fiercely condemned.[35] His final work, appropriately enough, was the *Triumphus eternitatis*, which was to succeed the Triumph of Time and rediscover Laura in heaven. This last poetic sequence, which Petrarch worked on for some thirty years up to his death at Arquà on July 18, 1374, systematically opposes the triad of forces that threaten the Academy from those that ensure its continuance: Physical Love, Death, and Time versus Chastity, Fame, and Eternity.[36]

This struggle in the life and writings of Petrarch between the limits and frustrations of earth-bound time and the airy expanses of fame and eternity is formulated with extraordinary precision by Chaucer's Clerk of Oxenford:

> "I wol yow telle a tale which that I
> Lerned at Padowe of a worthy clerk,
> As preved by his wordes and his werk.
> He is now deed and nayled in his cheste;
> I preye to God so yeve his soule reste!
>   Fraunceys Petrak, the lauriat poete,
> Highte this clerke, whos rethorike sweete
> Enlumyned al Ytaille of poetrie,
> As Lynyan dide of philosophie,
> Or lawe, or oother art particuler;
> But Deeth, that wol nat suffre us dwellen heer,
> But as it were a twynklyng of an ye,
> Hem bothe hath slayn, and alle shul we dye."   (4.26–38)

Here we have Petrarch discovered as a living source of poetic inspiration; Petrarch as a corpse; Petrarch as a poet laureate whose rhetoric illuminates a nation; and Petrarch laid low by death, a fate that unites him with us all. The cultural achievement of Petrarch is here accorded great respect, but is insistently brought up hard against the brute facts of mortality. The tone and logic of this passage are uneasy, unstable, almost tortuous: qualities that are typical of Petrarch's own musings on life, on death, and on textual afterlife.

Place and Time: Petrarch in Lombardy

Critiques of Paul de Man's "fatalism and avoidance of history," vigorously resisted by apologists such as Jonathan Culler, have necessarily been subjected to reassessment since details of de Man's own personal and textual history in German-occupied Belgium, 1940–44, have come to light.[37] Crass attempts have been made to explain, dismiss, or discredit everything that de Man subsequently wrote (and everything that can opportunistically be associated with it, including all forms of feminist and materialist theory) by referring it back to a corrupt point of origin.[38] Other critiques, equally irresponsible, have tended to relieve the wartime documents of their historical force by drawing them into a pantextual universe. Others have argued, in very different ways, that knowledge of de Man's wartime history changes everything and nothing.[39] Whatever conclusions are drawn, there is at least the recognition that the texts and the history need to be put into some relation, stand in some relation, to the life and work. Similar recognition, I am arguing, needs to be made for Petrarch. The cultivated uneasiness of his relation to fame, time, and history should be reassessed in relation to his historical presence at Milan as servant and ornament of the Visconti state.

Petrarch took pains to represent his entry into Visconti service, and hence into the ideological framework of the Florentine-Milanese conflict, as a complex tale of meditated triumph and casual seduction. His departure from Provence in 1353 and his crossing of the Alps into Italy seemed, in his own mind, hardly less momentous than the imperial descent into Italy envisaged by Dante. Petrarch figures himself as an Aeneas, carrying a precious burden on his back; this patrimony is his library, which includes some of his own compositions (*Fam* 15.3). Petrarch had no definite idea of his final destination in Italy; Mantua and Padua seemed promising. But he got as far as Milan and found himself suddenly and utterly seduced. Like his own Griselde, Petrarch is reduced to shyness and silence on being courted by a despot: "I blushed and remained silent; and by doing so I consented or seemed to have consented. There was nothing, or at least I could find nothing, to say against it" (*Fam* 16.12). The previous year Petrarch had spoken of Lombardy as being "oppressed by an undying tyranny," a place where "you will not find one place where a lover of virtue and tranquility may seek repose" (*Fam* 15.7). But it was the promise of repose that convinced Petrarch to remain at Milan: the Visconti could guarantee him time and security for his writing (*Fam* 16.11).

Petrarch offers the most detailed defense of (or confession to) accepting Visconti patronage in *Familiares* 17.10, written to Giovanni Aretino, chancellor of Mantua, on January 1, 1354. The letter is highly digressive (Petrarch admits to "evading and rambling"), but this digressive and evasive quality may be read (as de Man has been read) as part of its political statement.[40] Its chief theme addresses a central mystery of human behavior (and a familiar Petrarchan paradox): why do we desire and intend to do one thing and then do another? Paul and Augustine are Petrarch's chief authorities in this exploration of the divided self.[41] The outcome of the "internal warfare" suffered by Augustine was his decision to be baptized by Ambrose at Milan. This allows Petrarch to mythologize the scandal of his own presence at Milan as a temporary liminal paralysis; the suggestion is that he will soon cross the threshold and be free to move elsewhere. Petrarch further explains his paralysis by quoting from Paul, "the greatest of men in every respect": " 'I do not do the good that I wish to do, but rather the evil that I do not wish to do.' " He suggests that the cause of this tragic divorce between action and volition "lies in the mysterious punishment that has come upon men and some deeply hidden flaw in the sons of Adam." The "root" of this monstrousness lies in the fact that although the mind can command the body it cannot command itself: "The mind commands the mind to will, the mind is itself, but it does not do it." We can but hate ourselves: "Nothing is more vile to man than himself, nothing more venal than liberty."

The extreme political pessimism of this letter makes any form of social action seem pointless and self-defeating. We hardly need defend liberty from external threats since it is bound to be undermined and defeated from within:

We are not struck down from the outside, nor is it even necessary; for believe me, there is no need for well-trained troops or machines to attack the walls or secretly dig tunnels. Each man possesses within himself a destructive enemy, his companion amidst his pleasures, whom he surprisingly obeys and obstinately supports against himself. (*Fam* 17.10)

Petrarch cannot obey his better self, but he can obey a better man, one who exerts "the power over me of an absolute command and the force of imperial majesty." This man is Archbishop Giovanni Visconti, the absolute ruler who can defend the physical walls of Milan and hence protect the meta-phorical walls of Petrarch's selfhood. In this letter, then, Petrarch discovers himself to be a natural subject for despotic rule.

Petrarch joined the Visconti in 1353 just a matter of months after they had concluded a war with Florence. His Florentine friends were quick to voice their sense of outrage and betrayal. Most such protests came in the early months of Petrarch's residence at Milan, but they never stopped coming: Salutati wrote from Rome in 1369 attempting to prise Petrarch away from his despotic patrons, and Boccaccio wrote along similar lines in 1360 and again as late as 1373.[42] Some of Petrarch's Florentine critics were bluntly or ingeniously insulting. One Gano del Colle sent Petrarch a sonnet in which, according to a manuscript note, he exhorts Petrarch "to discharge himself from the tyranny of the lords of Milan and come to a place of liberty." Gano added insult to injury by sending a minstrel to sing the sonnet to Petrarch.[43] Petrarch hated minstrels and anything that smacked of minstrelsy and lower-class art: he changed the wording of one of his own *ballate* on realizing that it echoed a "plebeian song," and he censured Dante for writing verse that could be taken up by "ignorant oafs in taverns and market places."[44]

Petrarch claimed that the Visconti had offered him patronage and protec-tion without formal responsibilities. In fact he was about to enter the most intensive and time-consuming period of his political life. When he wrote to Giovanni Aretino he was already contemplating a winter crossing of the Alps on Visconti business. Petrarch found himself composing numerous letters for the Visconti, representing them on long and exhausting diplomatic missions, negotiating with the emperor (on many occasions), the French, the English, the Venetians and other minor powers. When Giovanni Visconti died on October 5, 1354, Petrarch was called upon to deliver an oration commemorating the passage of power to the three new lords of Lombardy: Matteo, Bernabò, and Galeazzo. On June 18, 1358, Petrarch rode with Galeazzo into Novara, recently recaptured from the Marquis of Monferrato, and proceeded to deliver an oration to the nervous populace. His text was "Convertetur populus meus hic" (Psalms 72.10). "Convertetur" (*convertere* meaning to convert, to exchange and, in Ciceronian usage, to translate) indicates the importance of repentance. "Populus" is a designation that not every group of men deserves; the Novarese are found deserving. "Meus" represents the status of Novara in relation to the Visconti. "Hic" is an emphatic adverbial form denoting special affection; Galeazzo has forgiven the city its faults and will henceforth take a close interest in its affairs.[45]

In the following year, 1359, the Augustinian friar Iacopo Bussolari took over the city government of Pavia and ousted the Visconti. He particularly outraged Bernabò by ordering the slaughter of all dogs: such creatures (wrote Petrarch at Bernabò's behest) deserved to meet a nobler death through hunting.[46] On being commanded to negotiate with Bussolari (by exchanging letters) Petrarch predictably exploits his familiarity with Augustine, particularly his doctrine of the two cities, earthly and heavenly (*Fam* 19.18). He also makes careful distinctions between the literal and allegorical senses of certain biblical verses (such as "I have not come to bring you peace but the sword") and offers a detailed profile of the true orator (who must unite rhetorical skill with concern for the public good). In deriding Bussolari's "ridiculous appetite for tyranny" Petrarch follows the example of other Viscontian propagandists who deflected a political lexicon habitually employed against the Visconti onto their enemies.[47] He had done this before, some six years earlier, in speaking of the "oppressed masses" of Genoa who turned to Giovanni Visconti, "this truly righteous prince," for assistance in resisting the establishment of a tyranny (*Fam* 17.4).

Humanist Landscapes; Rhetoric, Slavery, and the Female Body

The sharpest and most consistent criticisms of Petrarch's associations with despots came from Boccaccio, Dante's most dedicated admirer. Boccaccio first met Petrarch in 1350 when Petrarch stayed with him en route to and from Rome. In March 1351 Boccaccio traveled to Padua with official letters that revoked the notice of exile served on Petrarch's father in 1302, promised the restoration of confiscated patrimony, and offered Petrarch a university chair.[48] Petrarch declined this opportunity to return to Florence. Boccaccio's *Ut huic epistole*, dated August 15, 1353, is bitterly reproachful of Petrarch's move to Milan; it reminds Petrarch of the damning things he had said of Giovanni Visconti in Boccaccio's presence at Padua just two

years before.[49] Petrarch never answered this letter. Boccaccio's meetings with
Petrarch certainly exerted a powerful influence on Boccaccio's artistic development: he gave up composing vernacular verse and dedicated most of his
mature energies to Petrarchan-inspired Latin encyclopaedism. And yet Boccaccio always retained an impressive independence of political judgment. He
turned down Petrarch's offers of patronage (even though he was often indi-
gent) and maintained a long and active interest in the civic and diplomatic
affairs of Florence. Whereas Petrarch maintained an uneasy, ambiguous attitude towards Dante,[50] Boccaccio envisioned his Dantean discipleship as an
integral part of his civic politics. In 1350 (immediately before his first meeting
with Petrarch) he traveled to a convent at Ravenna to present Sister Beatrice,
Dante's daughter, with ten gold florins on behalf of the Florentine Compagnia di Or San Michele. In the summer of 1373, following a public petition, he
was called upon by the Florentine civic authorities to deliver the world's first
lecturae Dantis. And between these dates he composed three versions of his
short treatise in praise of Dante, the *Trattatello in laude di Dante*.

Boccaccio's *Trattatello* makes a noteworthy contribution to Florentine
political thought by tracing the originary interdependence of priesthood,
poetry, and political dictatorship.[51] The earliest poets, like their political
masters, dazzled the populace by embellishing the plain truth with "ornamenti"—in their case ornaments drawn from that style of writing previously
reserved to the praise of God. Through such rhetorical means poets managed to surround their masters with a mystifying religious aura and (says
Boccaccio) to "cause to be believed that which the princes wished to be believed" (1.136). The poet cannot legitimate the rule of a despot, then, but
he can gild it with the semblance of legitimacy by exploiting his rhetorical
skill to tap veins of religious feeling. Boccaccio's thesis, first devised c. 1351–
55, functions as a brilliant, Florentine critique—delivered in the course of
celebrating Florence's greatest poet—of any poet who would work hand-in-
glove with despots; it certainly casts Petrarch's alliance with the Visconti in a
harsh, clear light.

As the *Trattatello* sees it, then, it is above all the use of ornament that
unites the poet and the prince in their bedazzling of an impressionable public.
The prince recognizes in the poet the same skill that he employed in establishing his own power; it is quite natural that he should attempt to appropriate
such power to further his own purposes. This sense of mutual recognition
forms an interesting subtext to the famous story about Giangaleazzo Visconti,
who, when present as a boy at one of his father's banquets, was asked to
name the wisest man present. He singled out Petrarch without hesitation.[52]
And Petrarch himself also created a highly successful myth of his relations to
power. On the one hand, he claimed total independence. "What am I then?"
he asks himself in the course of *Seniles* 1.6, "a learner, but hardly even that; a
lover of the woods, wont to utter insipid words amid tall birches, or ply a frail

pen."[53] This accords with the famous poetic image of a Petrarch wandering "solo e pensoso" through "i più deserti campi" before expiring through the force of internal paradox.[54] But other letters suggest a different relationship to landscape, a landscape of power. Here, late in 1367, Petrarch recalls his youthful habit of wandering through Vaucluse at night:

You wonder at my confidence? I have never feared ghosts and shadows; I never saw a wolf in my valley; I had no apprehension of man. Plowmen sang in the fields, fishermen watched silently by the stream; they greeted me at whatever hour, knowing well that their lord was more than a friend to me, he was a dear brother, a father. Thus they were always my well-wishers, never hostile.[55]

The "lord" that Petrarch allies himself with in this early case is Philippe de Cabassoles, a powerful French landowner who later became a cardinal at Avignon. Petrarch's insistence on this alliance ensures that his encounter with the rural laborers is not companionable but hierarchical. Indeed, the notion of companionable encounters in a natural landscape seems foreign to Petrarch. Nature serves not to erase social distinctions but to help play them out. In 1372 he reminds Cabassoles of how, many years before, they would wander in the woods, far beyond the reach of the servants who came hunting for them at dinner time.[56] And in *Familiares* 19.16 he speaks of the "freedom" he is enjoying during a short spell of country life; of how "my humble neighbours eagerly bring me fruits from their trees, flowers from the meadows, fish from the streams, ducklings from the brooks, birds from their nests, hedgehogs from the fields, as well as hares and goats and wild pigs." Such energetic activity, here admired by the eye of a consumer, becomes elsewhere a cause for complaint, "for often celebrated lakes are disturbed by fishermen's nets, often famous forests are invaded by barking dogs" (*Fam* 17.10). Such contradictions (Petrarch is happy to consume the fruits of the landscape but is distracted by the business of harvesting them) suggest that the ideal landscape Petrarch sought throughout his life as the locus for his contemplation existed only in his verse or in his memory of Vaucluse.[57]

The country landscape of Petrarch's day was actually, historically, a dangerous place to inhabit. It was frequently traversed by armies and mercenary bands. Petrarch was therefore forced to spend most of his time among the restless and agitated city-dwellers he so despised. The city, for Petrarch, was (in a tortured imagistic inversion) a tempest, a sea of miseries; the countryside is our true harbor. Petrarch frequently yearns to set sail for this harbor, especially when buffeted by the rude shocks incident upon the urban division of labor:

Arise, come, hasten, let us abandon the city to merchants, attorneys, brokers, usurers, tax-gatherers, scriveners, doctors, perfumers, butchers, cooks, bakers and tailors, alchemists, fullers, artisans, weavers, architects, statuaries, painters, mimes, dancers, lute-players, quacks, panderers, thieves, criminals, adulterers, parasites, foreigners, swindlers and jesters, gluttons who with scent alert catch the odor of the market-place, for whom that is the only bliss, where mouths are agape for that alone. For on the mountains there is no smell of cookery.[58]

Petrarch here recoils from a whole Canterbury pilgrimage (or Langlandian tavern) of urban professions; but there can be no permanent escape to the countryside. This sad fact induced Petrarch to attempt one of his most audacious maneuvers: to turn the country and the city inside out. At Milan he took up gardening (with little success) and attempted to live as if he were, indeed, in the country. At Padua in 1373, having completed the Griselde story, he composed his own treatise on city and princely government. This treatise, which contains a good deal of diffuse complaining, objects to roving pigs, women who wail too loudly at funerals, and wheeled carts (that is, the vehicles that facilitate urban trade).[59] In the letter to Bruni examined above (*Seniles* 10.2), Petrarch objects to one further source of urban blight—slaves:

The disasters of Greece are long past, but those of the Scythians recent. From them we used to receive the annually great cargo of grain; but now the ships come loaded with slaves, whom their wretched parents sell under the pressure of hunger. Now an unwonted multitude of slaves of both sexes, offscourings of their race with horrid Scythian faces, invade this lovely city, as a turbid torrent flows into a sparkling river. If their purchasers were not more indulgent than I, with eyes less offended by ugliness than are mine, these repulsive youths would not crowd our streets, nor would they revolt visiting foreigners, accustomed to better sights, by their hideous aspect. They would still be plucking with their nails and gnawing, pale with hunger, the scanty produce of their stony fields, which Ovid once described. But enough of this.[60]

This chilling passage deserves some scrutiny as an authentic testimony to Petrarch's hard-core humanism, or neoclassicism, for as Perry Anderson has observed, "it was precisely the formation of a limpidly demarcated slave sub-population that . . . lifted the citizenry of the Greek cities to hitherto unknown heights of conscious juridical freedom. Hellenic liberty and slavery were indivisible: each was the structural condition of the other."[61] Such a dyadic system seems to structure Petrarch's sensibilities here: for it is his acute perception of the ugliness of the slaves that confirms his sense of his own exceptional vision. Ordinary eyes are not so sensitive to ugliness. It is entirely appropriate that Petrarch should end here with a footnote from Ovid: he is turning his eyes from ugliness toward the Academy, the institution where men of exceptional vision meet. Such men, it would seem, are drawn together across the centuries by uncommon powers of perception. But for Petrarch, as later for Matthew Arnold and F. R. Leavis, this acute sense of separateness is founded upon a radical unwillingness to countenance the harsher aspects of the urban commerce that sustains him.

Perhaps the most troubling aspect of this passage is Petrarch's willingness to view certain human beings as nonsubjects, as mere objects for unbridled hatred and disgust. This attitude toward slaves, the purest expression of political nonentity, has much in common with his attitude toward women. The only letter that Petrarch wrote to a woman congratulates the Empress Anne (mother of Anne of Bohemia, Queen of England) on the birth of a daughter; "better fortune often follows," Petrarch assures her, "upon a weak beginning."[62] Women are figured in Petrarch not as participants in a social discourse but as scattered fragments,[63] as an idea, disembodied, posthumous or metaphorical. And yet when women are present only by way of analogy or incidental metaphor, the female body is often figured as the object of social or commercial exchange or, more commonly, violence:

"Remove the frontlet from horses that are for sale," is an old caution. No sane man wants to marry a misfeatured girl because she is well dressed. If we tear off the front-let, or the mask rather, from those who are so gay in their purple, we shall clearly see their wretchedness.[64]

Such imagery of dressing and undressing, masking and cosmetic face-painting, a familiar feature of classical demonstrations or critiques of the func-tion of rhetoric, is a recurrent feature of Petrarch's polemical prose. Petrarch himself recognizes that the pursuit of rhetoric will inevitably color social prac-tice: "What is advantageously taught in the art of oratory, the art, that is, of speaking with propriety and elegance, has in our time been mischievously applied to the art of wicked and disgraceful living."[65] When imitation shifts from the literary to the social sphere the self becomes hopelessly dislocated: "No one is of a clear mind as to his costume, his speech, his thought—in short, as to what sort of man he would like to be, and therefore every man is unlike himself." This is an argument for the policing, the social control, of oratory and not a denial of its social character. In the right hands, the hands of the Prince or Academician, oratory may be practiced to advantage. In *Fami-liares* 22.1, dated September 11, 1362, Petrarch turns his attention to marriage (a subject of which, he freely admits, he has no experience). In evaluating a prospective wife one should consider "not so much her dowry and wealth as her family line and upbringing, not so much her elegant attire as her devotion [non tam ornatus elegantiam quam pietatem], and above all, not so much her bodily beauty as her mind." Petrarch is here advocating a kind of masculine *inventio* which, in gazing at or through the female body, may lay bare the essential qualities beneath. The female mind is valued, but only for its will-ingness to cast off any "ornatus elegantiam" it brings with it, laying bare the essential "pietatem" that may be subjected to masculine molding.[66] It is best to select a young virgin from a distant community:

For a noble maiden, devoted to you from an early age and distanced from her people's flatteries and old women's gossipings, will be more chaste and humble, more obedi-ent and holy; quickly casting off her girlish frivolity, she will don the seriousness of a married woman. In short, whether a virgin or a widow, once she joins you in the nuptial bed, hearing, seeing and thinking of you alone, she will be transformed into your image alone and will adopt your ways. (*Fam* 22.1)

As a woman assumes the lineaments of her master—making him, in effect, both husband and father—she attests ever more impressively to the excellence of his original choice, his judicious reading of her inner qualities. She functions as a semiotic object that points to a higher union, the marriage between the humanist and the landscape he inhabits. This is the mysterious alliance that is celebrated at the very end of *De vita solitaria*. Nature voices its approbation of everything that Petrarch has said:

These things I have addressed to you with such affection of mind that every rustle of the branches breathed upon by the wind and every ripple of the waters gushing from the ground about me seems to say a single thing: "You argue well, you counsel uprightly, you speak the truth." [67]

The Florentine humanists who were quick to praise Petrarch's championing of rhetoric were puzzled and disturbed by the antisocial character of his writings on women.[68] But the most sophisticated and extensive critique of this cultural complex—the relationship of the humanist enterprise to civil society, natural landscape, and the female body—is supplied by a Boccaccian text, *Decameron* 5.8. Nastagio degli Onesti, a noble, loves a woman of superior social rank. She despises him. At the urging of his friends, Nastagio leaves the city (Ravenna), but instead of seeking out a new city he camps in the countryside. One morning toward the beginning of May, Nastagio, like a good Petrarchan, dismisses his servants and wanders off into the landscape, lost in thought:

The fifth hour of the day was already spent, and he had advanced at least half a mile into the woods, oblivious of food and everything else, when suddenly he seemed to hear [gli parve udire] a woman giving vent to dreadful wailing and earsplitting screams. His pleasant reverie [dolce pensiero] being thus interrupted, he raised his head to investigate the cause, and discovered to his surprise that he was in the pinewoods. Furthermore, on looking straight ahead he caught sight of a naked woman, young and very beautiful, who was running through a dense thicket of shrubs and briars towards the very spot where he was standing. The woman's hair was dishevelled, her flesh was all torn by the briars and brambles, and she was sobbing and screaming for mercy. (5.8.14–15; p. 458)

The woman is pursued and then overtaken by a mounted knight and two huge dogs. Nastagio steps forward to defend her, but the knight (who identifies himself as a fellow citizen) explains that Nastagio is witnessing a God-given torment: the woman is being punished for scorning his love and rejoicing at his death. Nastagio steps back and the woman, kneeling and sobbing, is duly torn to pieces; the knight slashes open her back with a dagger, digs out her innards and throws them to the dogs. Soon, however, the girl

Plate 7. Alessandro Botticelli, *Nastagio degli Onesti* (third episode). Prado, Madrid.

rises to her feet as if nothing has happened and the hunt begins again. This happens every Friday. Nastagio realizes that this "ought to prove very useful to him" and arranges an outdoor banquet for the following Friday. The whole sequence is acted out again in front of Nastagio's lady and her family. The lady is so terrified that she manages (Boccaccio tells us) to turn her hatred for Nastagio into love; they marry without delay and settle down "to a long and happy life together" (5.8.44; p. 462).[69]

The potency of this myth for its masculine Renaissance readers is perhaps best attested by the four paintings Botticelli and his workshop made of this narrative, a sequence that spawned countless imitations.[70] (See plate 7, which depicts the third of Botticelli's sequence; the paintings were probably commissioned in 1483 by Lorenzo the Magnificent, the Medici despot who ruled Florence, as a wedding gift.)[71] The myth's predatory, unbridled energy seems expressive of a period when the rapid conquest of new texts (through a new humanist discipline) promised to liberate a power that could reshape the social world.[72] Mindful, as in our reading of *Melibee*, that a text representing violence to women is always *about* violence to women (whatever other levels of interpretation it might point to) we may pause for allegoresis. Masculine desire, of a specific social and educated level, finds itself locked out of social and erotic fulfillment and exiles itself from the city. Lost in thought (within a humanist landscape) a text comes to mind: one that sees the female body pursued by masculine desire.[73] This text is captured, laid open or transcribed (with a dagger), and consumed. The knowledge of this text, gained in private, may then be exploited to influence behavior within the public domain. Control of the text, figured as a woman, facilitates control of woman in society; allegorical reading thus neatly returns us to matters literal and historical.

Magnificence and Tyranny; Boccaccian Griselde

Boccaccio's most extreme example of such masculine control of a female body is provided by his *Decameron*'s very last tale. This sees a female villager subjected to extreme mental and emotional torments by her political overlord, a Lombard dictator. Petrarch, finding himself "delighted and fascinated"[74] by "so charming a story" ("tam dulcis ystoria") suddenly snatched up his pen one day in 1373 and (he tells Boccaccio) "attacked this story of yours" ("ystoriam ipsam tuam scribere sum aggressus"). By this time Petrarch had moved from Lombardy (although he remained on good terms with the Visconti) to Padua, the city that is justly celebrated as the cradle of humanism. The early Paduan humanists, or pre-humanists, such as Lovato Lovati (1241–1309) and his disciple Alberto Mussato (1261–1329) had seen their dedication to the revival of literary culture as part of their service to city republicanism. Mussato's Latin *Ecerinis*, hailed as the first secular drama to be written since antiquity, deliberately set out to celebrate the fight for liberty and self-government against the forces of tyranny.[75] Mussato was crowned with laurel by the commune of Padua in 1315 (an event that set the precedent for Petrarch's coronation at Rome in 1341) and a civic decree was passed requiring an annual reading of *Ecerinis* before the assembled populace. In 1328, however, the republic fell to the da Carrara, a dynastic dictatorship that remained in control of Padua until 1425.[76] Petrarch moved to Padua in 1368, serving Francesco da Carrara in many capacities. Petrarch's treatise on city government (or on princely government, since the prince now ruled the city) was written for Francesco da Carrara in November 1373, just months after the completion of the Petrarchan Griselde story. Francesco had been urging Petrarch to write something for him for some time. He was no doubt delighted to receive such a prestigious legitimation of his rule from Italy's new poet laureate. Padua could now forget Mussato and the ideal of civic self-government he stood for.[77]

For Petrarch and the various audiences described in *Seniles* 17.3, the meaning of the Griselde story is not, apparently, problematic. Petrarch acknowledges that the story "differs entirely from most that precede it" in the

Decameron, but he also notes that the rules of rhetoric dictate that the most important parts of a work come first and last. The first part of the *Decameron* describes (Petrarch notes) "that siege of pestilence which forms so dark and melancholy a period in our century." On turning to Boccaccio's account we discover that the Black Death has precipitated the complete breakdown of city law and familial obligations. Boccaccio's first story continues this theme of civic, judicial, and religious collapse as a city rejoices in the canonization of Ser Cepperello of Prato, "perhaps the worst man ever born" (1.1.15; p. 71). The second story sees a Parisian Jew riding to Rome to discover the pope and his clergy "doing their level best to reduce the Christian religion to nought and drive it from the face of the earth" (1.2.25; p. 85). The hero of these first two stories, in which the authority of all civic and religious institutions is severely problematized,[78] is God, whose truth stands above all this as "something immutable" and (since the human eye is "quite unable to penetrate the secrets of divine intelligence," 1.1.5; p. 69) utterly mysterious. Filomena, in opening the third story, proposes that since "we have heard such fine things concerning God and the truth of our religion, it will not seem inappropriate to descend at this juncture to the level of men" (1.3.3; p. 86). Storytelling remains at this more modest, human level for the duration—for as long, that is, as the *brigata* continues to occupy the temporary, provisional, marginal space it has mapped out for itself.[79] Many critics, however, have read *Decameron* 10.10 as a return to a more exalted sphere, a world in which God works his purposes through patient Griselde and the godlike Walter.[80]

Such a reading of *Decameron* 10.10 is Petrarchan. It is very difficult for readers (especially readers of Chaucer) to approach Boccaccio's *novella* without crossing the lines of Petrarch's interpretation. We should recall, however, that Boccaccio's narrator here is Dioneo, "a youth of matchless charm and readiness of wit" (Intr. 92; p. 64) who has invited the ladies to join him in "laughter, song and merriment" and to forget their troubles: "My own I left inside the city gates when I departed thence a short while ago in your company" (Intr. 93; p. 64). All tales told by Dioneo are, accordingly, comically critical of any authority that takes itself too seriously. Dioneo exploits his privilege of speaking last to ironize, subvert, or disperse the theme that has supposedly unified the day's storytelling. The theme proposed for the tenth and final day is liberality and magnificence.[81] The term *magnificenza* (as *Decameron* 10 defines it) denotes a form of liberality or giving that serves to enhance, rather than deplete, the power and resources of a great lord. In combining the mystifying suggestiveness of religious transcendence with the stark realities of social and economic power, magnificence is innately theatrical, a virtue realized through public spectacle.[82] Chaucer's Walter, it has been noted, is much more theatrical (even melodramatic) than the Petrarchan Valterius in staging the exercise of his own power.[83] The term "magnificence" occurs just five times in Chaucer.[84] As glossed by Chaucer's Parson, it is said to occur "whan a man dooth and parfourneth grete werkes of goodnesse." Magnificence is ascribed twice to the Virgin Mary, once to a Roman senator who is anxious to display his own power and importance, and once to Walter:[85]

> "My lord," quod she, "I woot, and wiste alway,
>   How that bitwixen youre magnificence
>   And my poverte no wight kan ne may
>   Maken comparison . . ."   (4.814–17)

Griselde here acknowledges the gulf of degree that divides the common subject from her magnificent lord. But the attribution to Walter here of "magnificence" is ironic, if not outright subversive. The drama of magnificence represents a liminal moment in which a lord offers some revelation, gift, or transfer that delights his subject and binds her closer to him. Here, however, the lord is about to strip Griselde of her court clothes and banish her from his presence. Where, then, does Walter prove himself magnificent in Boccaccio's tale? The crucial, climactic scene comes later, as Walter presents Griselde with her own children. The closest equivalent scene in *Decameron* 10 comes in the fourth *novella*, where a lover restores a lady (buried while pregnant and presumed dead) and her child to her husband. But Walter is only restoring what he himself has taken away. Only a Dioneo narrative could exemplify a lord said to act "liberalmente o vero magnificamente" in such perverse fashion.

An ancillary virtue exemplified in *Decameron* 10 is the restraint of desire by lords of high degree when the pursuit of such desire would threaten the *bonum commune*. The moral world of *Decameron* 10.5 (the *Franklin's Tale* analogue) is held together by this virtue. In the next story an elderly king gazes upon a near-naked girl, falls in love with her, arranges for her *raptus*, but then (after heeding the advice of a noble follower and at great personal cost) restrains his desire. The following story sees an "exquisitely beautiful" girl (10.7.4; p. 768) of low degree fall in love with King Peter of Aragon. Far from exploiting her vulnerability, Peter collaborates with his queen to cure the girl of lovesickness[86] and then sees her married "in truly magnificent style" (10.7.48; p. 775). He then jousts in the lists "as her loyal knight for as long as he lived." Such virtuous restraint, we are told at the very end of the *novella*, is rarely exemplified by modern *signori*:

"By deeds such as these, then, does a sovereign conquer the hearts of his subjects, furnish occasions to others for similar deeds, and acquire eternal renown. But among the rulers of today there are few if any who can train the bowstrings of their minds [l'arco teso dello 'ntelletto] upon any such objective, most of them having been changed into pitiless tyrants." (10.7.49; p. 775)

Such talk of "signori . . . crudeli e tiranni" (who, as in the *Manciple's Tale*, make the bow of the mind a killing instrument) could only prompt Florentines to think of those "tirauntz of Lombardye" threatening their borders.

(Italian republics were exceptionally sensitive to the problematics of tyranny and *utilitas publica*; the influence of their political theorizing was felt as far afield as Oxford, the Clerk's *alma mater*.)[87] After two more tales Boccaccio actually shifts the scene to Lombardy as Dioneo proposes not one more example of magnificence, but a counterexemplum:

"I want to tell you of a marquis, whose actions, even though things turned out well for him in the end, were remarkable not so much for their munificence as for their senseless brutality [non cosa magnifica ma una matta bestialità]. Nor do I advise anyone to follow his example, for it was a great pity that the fellow should have drawn any profit from his conduct." (10.10.3; p. 813)

Dioneo has no sympathy for Walter, who is described by his own subjects as a "cruel tyrant" and as "a cruel and bestial tyrant."[88] Walter's tyrannical tendencies are actually signaled by the first sentence of the storytelling proper, which states that he "spent the whole of his time hunting and hawking, and never even thought about raising a family, which says a great deal for his intelligence" (10.10.4; p. 813). Walter, in short, strives "moore for delit than world to multiplye" (7.3345). The comparison with Chauntecleer is appropriate since, in Dioneo's view, Walter's behavior amounts to "matta bestialità," a thorough confusion of the rational with the animal. This pursuit of personal pleasure at the expense of "comune profyt" identifies Walter quite clearly, for a late medieval audience, as a tyrant: for whereas a true king "strives for the *bonum commune*, the tyrant strives for his own good." Again, "the tyrant strives for a pleasurable [delectabile] good, whereas a true king strives for an honorable one." Tyrannical polity is truly perverse ("vero est dominium perversum").[89] These precepts are taken from Egidio Colonna, *De regimine principum*, a text that circulated widely in both Latin and French. Their sentiments are echoed in Nicholas of Oresme's *Livre de Politiques*, written for King Charles V of France in the 1370s. Oresme argues that "anyone who governs for his own benefit and against the common good, whether alone or in a group, can be called a tyrant."[90] For Egidio and Oresme, as for Aquinas and Brunetto Latini, the fate of the *bonum commune* remains the key issue.[91] Aquinas notes that a king becomes tyrannical in governing "for his own good, and not for the good of his subjects." And Henry Bracton, the thirteenth-century legal commentator, maintains that a ruler so guided by arbitrary will is no longer a king, "for there is no king where will [voluntas], not law, holds sway."[92] Such a conflict between the law of the land and kingly will and pleasure, subjected to detailed analysis in late medieval writings on tyranny,[93] was to be played out most dramatically in the final years of Richard II (and in his textual afterlife). It also figures prominently in Chaucer's representation of "the false tiraunt" Nero, who "brende Rome for his delicasie," who "gan delite" in his gem-covered clothes, and who ensured (following Dante's Semiramis to the letter) that "his lustes were al lawe in his decree."[94]

Once Dioneo's story has run its course, Panfilo, Boccaccio's tenth and final monarch, feels obliged to renounce his own power and to propose the dissolution of the *brigata*. In doing this, however, he is moved to commend the company for their disciplined maintenance of social order:

"From what I have seen and heard, it seems to me that our proceedings have been marked by a constant sense of propriety [onestà], an unfailing spirit of harmony [concordia], and a continual feeling of brotherly and sisterly amity [fraternal dimestichezza]. All of which pleases me greatly, as it surely redounds to our communal honor and credit." (10, Concl. 4–5; p. 825)

Such concern for the common good requires a sacrifice of selfish interests. The depressing circumstances of the plague license an exceptional indulgence in singing, dancing, feasting, and storytelling—anything within reason that will nurture cheerfulness and keep terror at bay.[95] Such strong medicine may "encourage unseemly behavior among those who are feeble of mind" (10. Concl. 4; p.825) but, as the king has observed, nobody has betrayed the *brigata* by following selfish impulses. Such vigilant concern for the integrity of the *brigata* suggests that this temporary institution represents more than a convenient framework within which to wait out the plague. It represents, rather, an active response to the moral, social, and political collapse of Florence: the communal spirit must be kept alive outside the city walls until the city is once more healthy enough to support its growth.[96]

The effect of the Black Death on Florence is rather like the effect of tyranny on any city: it is a disease that runs out of control, feverishly devouring the body politic. Such an association between plague and tyranny is at least as old as the *Oedipus Rex* of Sophocles. In *Paradiso* 19.115–32 Dante denounces European princes, whose selfishness, violence, and tyranny spell out (in acrostic form) "LUE": pestilence. Similar associations are relied upon in the prescription Aquinas writes for the Christian subject afflicted by tyranny: "Sin must therefore be done away with so that the plague of tyrants may cease."[97] This course of treatment is followed most faithfully by Griselde, who cultivates an inner purity that finally outlasts the torments that Walter plagues her with. Boccaccio's Griselde, then, is the faithful and enduring Christian subject. Walter is not to be compared to God, but he might be seen as an agent of God; he might, as a tyrant, be compared to the Black Death.

The 1348 pandemic was imaginatively linked for Boccaccio to an earlier phase of that "decade of disaster,"[98] the tyrannical regime of the Duke of Athens: Boccaccio's *De casibus virorum illustrium* sees a fictional Dante refer to this historical duke as "domesticam pestem," "a home-bred plague."[99] This duke, proclaimed *signore* of Florence for life in September 1342, was driven out of Florence by a united effort of all social classes in July 1343. It is particularly fitting that the *Decameron* should close with the defeat of Walter's tyranny since, as Boccaccio's fellow Florentines would recall, the Duke of

Athens was also a Walter (or Gualtieri)—Walter of Brienne. The final defeat of tyranny, like the longed-for abatement of plague, signals a return to Florence—a return to those liberties that Griselde and the Boccaccian *brigata* have endeavored to keep alive.

Humanist Insight; Petrarchan Griselde and Chaucerian Critique

My argument does not assume that Chaucer knew the Boccaccian Griselde story, although it is quite possible that he did. I am suggesting, however, that the political dimensions of Boccaccio's *novella*, its embeddedness in contemporary ideological debate, do have an important bearing on our reading of the *Clerk's Tale*. Petrarch's translation relieves Boccaccio's story of its specific historical urgency. Petrarchan Griselde is classicized, mythologized, and moralized as a timeless exemplum of obedience to God; Petrarchan readers are advised to "submit themselves to God with the same courage as did this woman to her husband" (p. 138). This implied analogy between Walter and God can be taken seriously in Petrarch's text because Walter's tyrannical proclivities are played down or passed over without comment. But Petrarch's Latin cannot entirely erase the historicity of Boccaccio's Italian text: signs of contradiction bubble to the surface when Petrarch's story is subjected to a historical reading. Chaucer, I am suggesting, was excellently qualified as a historical reader of Petrarch through his experience of Florence and Milan, his participation in political events in England, and his evident familiarity with the metaphors, tropes, and general rhetoric of ideological debate. Contradictions detected in the Petrarchan story are not just smoothed away but are critiqued or carried over into English and made part of the meaning of the Chaucerian *Tale*.

Part of Chaucer's meaning in translating Petrarch is that there can be no final translation. Despite the studied casualness with which he announces his own translating, Petrarch evidently sees his own work as a literary and historical terminus: future translation is obviated by a text that is good for all times and all places. Chaucer, I am arguing, sees the Petrarchan text as a response to a particular historical and political moment. As that moment recedes Chaucer needs to translate Petrarch into his own cultural present. Chaucer, unlike Petrarch, does not see his own narration as a unitary moment that can save itself from past and future translations. Once the Clerk's voice falls silent it will be supplanted by other voices that contest his individual pronouncements on politics, religion, and marriage and hence place them within the larger interpretive framework of the Canterbury pilgrimage. But even as the Clerk speaks we hear ghostly voices from earlier versions of the story: Boccaccio's politics reverberate within Petrarch's dehistoricized spirituality; Petrarch's unworldly allegorization struggles with the domestic exemplarism of the French tradition. The *Clerk's Tale*, like the *Melibee*, is a palimpsest.

The Petrarchan Griselde occupies a classicized, perpetual present that would displace past and future and so exempt itself from historical contingency; Chaucer's text questions the very possibility of occupying a "present" moment in its own narrating. Chaucer's translation restores Griselde to the movement of history.

Petrarch begins *Seniles* 17.3 with *inventio*, a detailed account of how he came across the Griselde story. The effect here is extremely odd, since Petrarch evidently wishes to distance himself from Boccaccio's *novella* even as he appropriates it. Petrarch recoils from the circumambient pressure of historical events, yet he cannot allow Boccaccio's Italian to make any serious claim on his attention:

Your book, written in our mother tongue [nostro materno eloquio] and published I presume, during your early years, has fallen into my hands, I know not whence or how. If I told you that I had read it, I should deceive you. It is a very big volume, written in prose and for the multitude [ad vulgus et soluta scriptus oratione]. I have been, moreover, occupied with serious business, and much pressed for time. You can easily imagine the unrest caused by the warlike stir about me, for, far as I have been from actual participation in the disturbances, I could not but be affected by the critical condition of the state. What I did was to run through your book, like a traveller who, while hastening forward, looks about him here and there, without pausing. (p. 137)

Boccaccio's book merges here with the busy, vulgar world that Petrarch can attend to only intermittently and distractedly. Petrarch's expert eye rests long enough on Boccaccio's text, however, to identify the one portion that merits isolation, translation, and the promise of a greater, less localized audience. Petrarch draws attention here to his exceptional insight, his ability to see through the plain clothes of Boccaccio's text to the naked beauty beneath. This beauty will be made visible to others by the rhetorical garments in which Petrarch will dress it. Such characterization of humanist vision, which sees the naked beauty of a woman beneath whatever rudiments of style an author has laid upon her, had been developed in detail many years before in a letter Petrarch wrote at Milan to a friend at Florence:[100]

Your letter, written in haste and on the spur of the moment, was nevertheless pleasing to my eyes and mind, indeed even more so; its appearance was that of a rather disheveled woman to her eager lover. I sighed, saying, "What would this have been had it seen itself in the mirror!" It bore witness to its hasty stuffing into an everyday dress and to its command to come to me in that fashion, as you were rising from dinner with Ceres and Bacchus struggling within you, to use your joking phrase. Yet its style revealed a sober and fasting author: nothing could be more modest or abrupt; the seriousness of the ideas was suitable for the occasion, the tone of the words sweet and tender. It behooved many women caught unawares to make use of shame, a trembling voice, uncombed hair, ungirt breasts, bare feet, and casual dress; often a casual simplicity has been preferred to fancy dress. Thus did the disheveled Cleopatra sway the imperial firmness of Caesar's spirit.

Here, once again, a Petrarchan discussion of reading and textuality sees the strangest confusion of the erotic, the rhetorical, the authoritarian, and the violent. The Petrarchan eye sees into everything: a male author rises drunkenly from the table, brings a disheveled woman into existence, and is pronounced "sober"; a female body is stuffed into a dress, commanded, dispatched, and then scrutinized by a man who gazes like "her eager lover"; and the persuasive power exerted by such surprised, half-naked women over masculine rulers is duly noted. Such Petrarchan passages are especially unsettling because they slip or drift between the metaphorical and the historical, between figures of speech and the experience of actual women. The final part of this passage does, apparently, move more decisively into history: the example of Cleopatra and Caesar is followed by those of Phaedra and Hippolytus, Sophonisba and Masinissa, Lucretia and Sextus Tarquinius. Griselde and Walter may obviously be added to this list. And yet the historical couples of *Familiares* 18.7 are bracketed within the limits of *comparatio*, existing only as parts of an extended rhetorical figure: what Petrarch is "really" talking about is his reading of the letter he is currently writing a reply to. Similar uncertainties have unsettled most readers of *Seniles* 17.3 and the tale Chaucer made from this "rhetorike sweete." Is Griselde (to repeat a question asked earlier about Prudence) rhetorical or real? Does her suffering have any historical basis or is it just pointing at something else?[101]

Petrarch's emphatic representation of the powers of his own eye finds an obvious equivalent within the *Seniles* story as Walter gazes upon Griselde. This scene, developed from a casual phrase in Boccaccio, is faithfully preserved in Chaucer's account:

> Upon Grisilde, this povre creature,
> Ful ofte sithe this markys sette his ye
> As he on huntyng rood paraventure;
> And whan it fil that he myghte hire espye,
> He noght with wantown lookyng of folye
> His eyen caste on hire, but in sad wyse
> Upon hir chiere he wolde hym ofte avyse,
>
> Commendynge in his herte hir wommanhede,
> And eek hir vertu, passynge any wight
> Of so yong age, as wel in chiere as dede.
> For thogh the peple have no greet insight
> In vertu, he considered ful right
> Hir bountee, and disposed that he wolde
> Wedde hire oonly, if evere he wedde sholde.   (4.232–45)

Walter's steady and deliberate gaze ("sette his ye") aligns and crosses between two carefully articulated social spaces: court space (extended through hunting—Walter gazes down from the saddle)[102] and village space. Walter's superior "insight" detects in Griselde a "vertu" which remains hidden to "the peple." Walter decides to appropriate such "vertu" by drawing it into his own immediate sphere. He has a dress and "other aornementes" made, estimating Griselde's physical dimensions from a girl of similar "stature" (4.253–59). He then rides to the village, secures Griselde's total obedience in thought, word, and deed, and then has her stripped of her old clothes. The effect of Griselde's new, court-manufactured clothes causes a public sensation:

> Unnethe the peple hir knew for hire fairnesse
> Whan she translated was in swich richesse.   (4.384–85)

Chaucer's use of the verb *translaten* here emphasizes Walter's power as both ruler and rhetor. As a ruler he is empowered to move Griselde across territorial boundaries. The means by which he demonstrates the exercise of this power are rhetorical: he first invents, comes across, Griselde, then reads her, and finally lays upon her the ornate clothes that make the excellence of his reading visible. This procedure is analogous to Petrarch's translation of Boccaccio's vernacular text into the *ornatus difficilis* of humanist Latin. Both Walter and Petrarch, who gaze with court-trained eyes, know that village or vernacular virtue is blind to itself. Such virtue can only be made visible if it is translated to court space in court language. Village or vernacular virtue only achieves meaningful social existence when gilded by the transforming power of the poet-potentate.

Such affinities of *modus operandi* perhaps help explain why Petrarch was so assiduously and successfully courted by Italian despots. They certainly return us to Boccaccio's theorizing, in his *Trattatello in laude di Dante*, of the function of poets within the first despotic regimes: both poets and princes hold the populace spellbound through their use of ornament. The source of such spellbinding, as Boccaccio explains, lies in religion, specifically in the symbols and sentiments of religion that poets and princes have annexed to their own spheres of influence. Religion, we have noted, plays no significant part in Boccaccio's Griselde story. But in Petrarch's translation it becomes (as it became in the political speeches Petrarch wrote for the Visconti) both powerfully intimidating and nebulously vague: a tool for tyranny. Walter is not God, but as Griseldes, his political subjects, we would be well advised to treat him as if he were.[103] We should all, says Petrarch (p. 138), strive to be Griseldes—an injunction that usefully distracts us from considering Petrarch as a Walter.

The cultural strategies of the Petrarchan Griselde story show signs of inconsistency that form their own internal and unconscious critique. Let us, for a moment, take Petrarch at his word. What would happen if we did strive to become Griseldes, and some of us succeeded? In Italian political debate of the late fourteenth century the *signoria* justifies its own historical inevitability by pointing to the factious, unruly, and disobedient character of the body politic. Citizens cannot rule themselves and so the despot steps in to rule them. Despotism exists to enforce obedience. But what happens when a despot confronts a subject who is utterly obedient? Such a subject undermines despotic self-justification; this is why Griselde unhinges Walter. Fortunately for Walter, however, nobody can see Griselde's singular qualities (except Petrarch, who describes them before Walter gets to the village) without his mediation, dressing, and translating. Once Griselde is relocated within Walter's court structure Walter can explore the limits of her obedience at his leisure, as his *delectabilia* dictates. If Griselde breaks Walter can relax and be generous: no subject is perfect; despotism recovers its ideological self-justification. But Griselde does not break, and this, for despotism, is scandalous. Fortunately, however, Walter is able to reincorporate Griselde into his political structure by taking her back into marriage. And this is, indeed, a formidable alliance: despotic power is wedded to natural virtue through the force of its own exceptional vision.

The *Clerk's Tale*: Five Critiques of Petrarch

Just how sensitive is Chaucer to this complex of humanistic vision, religious mystification, and tyrannous power? Let us consider five ways in which the *Clerk's Tale* might be read as an explicit critique of its Petrarchan source.[104] First, and fundamentally, Chaucer reverses the direction of Petrarch's literary translating. Although he locates the discovery of his source text at the very center of the Petrarchan Academy—the Clerk learned it from Petrarch at Padua—Chaucer chooses to restore this text to the vernacular. All the mysteries that Petrarch's Latinity conceals are laid open for general inspection.[105] Specific attention is drawn to this policy of removing obstacles that stand between the story and the common reader. The Host requests the Clerk to save his *ornatus difficilis* until he needs to impress the king at court:

> "Youre termes, youre colours, and youre figures,
> Keepe hem in stoor til so be ye endite
> Heigh style, as whan that men to kynges write.
> Speketh so pleyn at this tyme, we yow preye,
> That we may understonde what ye seye."   (4.16–20)

The Clerk immediately declares himself obedient to the Host's temporary authority ("Ye han of us as now the governance") and applies himself to his chosen "tale." Before he can get to Petrarch's "tale," however, he must cut a path through Petrarch's "heigh style" preface. Those high hills and mountains, which form "the boundes of West Lumbardye," are a cultural frontier that none but the gifted Latinist may cross. Chaucer's Clerk has no use for them:

> "And trewely, as to my juggement,
> Me thynketh it a thyng impertinent,
> Save that he wole conveyen his mateere;
> But this his tale, which that ye may heere."   (4.53–56)

The fact that the Clerk actually translates much of Petrarch's geography (4.44–51) before questioning its relevance (4.52–55) focuses attention upon the business of critiquing Petrarch: we see what deserves cutting before the cut is signaled. This suggests, as we approach Petrarch's tale (4.56), that the translation to come will be actively critical rather than passively faithful.

Chaucer's Clerk is translating a tale whose most dramatic events are enacted across a threshold of translation.[106] Chaucer's use of the verb *translaten* to describe Griselde's movement from village to court attire deserves some pondering. Chaucerian *translaten* and *translation* generally refer to movement between languages. The one exception, besides that of the *Clerk's Tale*, comes in the *Boece*, where it refers to the movement of money.[107] *Translation* in Chaucer is a term that is customarily hedged with nervous qualifications: it is an activity that calls for some sort of apology or explanation.[108] Most complete manuscripts of the *Canterbury Tales* end with a retraction, in which Chaucer abjures "my translaciouns and enditynges of worldly vanitees." Subsequently, however, "the translacioun of Boece de Consolacione, and othere bookes of legendes of seintes, and omelies, and moralitee, and devocioun" (10.1088) are pulled from the fire. It is not clear whether the *Clerk's Tale* is to be numbered with these works or with "the tales of Caunterbury, thilke that sownen into synne" (10.1086). Every translation contains a trace of impurity because no translator can guarantee a perfect transfer between languages—nobody, that is, except Christ, the "perfect translator of God's will to man."[109] Perhaps this is why Griselde puts down a signifier that points us to Christ[110] at the very threshold (Chaucer insists on the term by repeating it) that divides her from Walter:

> And as she wolde over hir thresshfold gon,
> The markys cam and gan hire for to calle;
> And she set doun hir water pot anon,
> Biside the thresshfold, in an oxes stalle.   (4.288–91)

The Incarnation sees the translation to the world of Christ, the unique and perfect sign whose signified is the Father. No gap divides the Father from the Son: they are consubstantial and without difference.[111] Chaucer's allusion to the Incarnation here (an addition to Petrarch's text) emphasizes the imperfection of the translation that Walter is about to make across the threshold that divides him from Griselde. We recall that the dress and ornaments that represent this translation cannot fit Griselde exactly or perfectly. They are transferred from the lineaments of another woman (4.256–57). All "heigh style" language has this property of transferability; the tropes and figures employed to praise one king can easily be turned to the praise of another.

Griselde fascinates Walter because no gap shows between her public face and her private feelings: she is "ay oon in herte and in visage" (4.711). This gap between face and feelings, which is observed in Walter throughout his testing of Griselde,[112] is a defining feature of life at court. The innocent who fails to perceive the rhetoricity of court behavior lays herself open to deception and betrayal. We may recall here, by way of example, the young falcon in the *Squire's Tale* who is betrayed by a tercelet who "dyed his colors" (5.511) so skillfully that she mistook them for nature.[113] Griselde suffers a similar ordeal of rhetorical betrayal, an ordeal she survives without once indicating that she is speaking or behaving rhetorically herself. Her face agrees with her thoughts and feelings; she is as "constant as a wal" (4.1047). Is Griselde un-rhetorical? Is she made of stone? Once her ordeal is terminated Griselde drops to the ground. Her public face falls with her and some time elapses before she "caught agayn hire contenaunce" (4.1110). It seems, after all, that Griselde contains a world of private feeling, an individuality that Walter, operating through the methods and assumptions of a passion-driven courtly rhetor, cannot comprehend or take possession of. Walter's experience here of his own imprisonment within the confines of artificial language parallels that of the early part of the *Vita nuova* as Dante struggles to realize his love for Beatrice through the tired tropes and mechanical formulae of conventional love poetry (7–16).[114] Eventually, from within a circle of women, Dante learns how to praise (rather than invent) Beatrice. A marvelous period of poetic creativity follows, in which Dante sees that Beatrice is possessed of an individuality too brilliant to be looked on (20–27). Beatrice then surprises Dante once again (she dies) and everything again changes (27–42). Dante knows that he cannot "have" Beatrice in any language; and Walter can never "have" Griselde.

For Petrarch, we have noted, the fact that Boccaccio's text is written "in our mother tongue" ("nostro materno eloquio") can only diminish its power. Chaucer reverses the direction of Petrarch's translating because he shares Dante's hope, if not his profound conviction, that the vernacular may prove uniquely adequate to human experience.[115] True enough, Dante feels compelled in the pit of hell to reach for a language more difficult than that learned at the breast:

> for it is not a task to take in jest
> to show the base of all the universe —
> nor for a tongue that cries out, "mama," "papa." [116]

As soon as he returns to the light, however, Dante resolves to put such "dead poetry" ("morta poesia") behind him.[117] The last two *cantiche* see a re-turn to the "lingua materna," the mother tongue that must somehow serve as the alpha and omega of Dante's ultimate vision.[118] Such an infantile tongue, still bathing at the breast (*Paradiso* 33.108), must prove weak in the face of eternity, although (Dante notes in his *Convivio*) it was the exercise of such a *lingua materna* that brought his mother and father together and hence brought Dante into being.[119] Dante opens *De vulgari eloquentia*, his treatise on the vernacular, by defining the vernacular as "that language which infants learn from those around them, when they first begin to articulate sounds;

or, more briefly, that which we acquire by imitating our nurses without needing any rule." [120] We later learn a secondary, artificial language "which the Romans called *grammatica*." Of these two the vernacular is the nobler language: "nobilior est vulgaris." This nobler language, the mother tongue, structures the primary linguistic community that Griselde governs. Griselde is "fair of eloquence": the people who "hire loved that looked on hire face" are happy to accept this as something "hevene sente" (4.410–13, 440). But Walter, unable to accept what is "hevene sent," estranges Griselde from her own children and thus violates that primary linguistic community. His illicit desire to crack Griselde's "eloquence" and discover the "Griselde" within leads him, in effect, to violate the womb—which makes him not a figure of an incarnating deity but a Nero, the worst of tyrants:

> His mooder made he in pitous array,
> For he hire wombe slitte to biholde
> Where he conceyved was . . .   (7.2483–85) [121]

The utter failure of Walter's perverse enterprise is followed by the re-union of mother, children, and father. This new linguistic community, which marries the natural virtues of the mother tongue to the artificial skills of the courtly rhetor, promises to generate an ideal language, an illustrious vernacular that will prove uniquely capable of serving the common good. [122]

Chaucer's second critique of Petrarch is coupled with the first. As he restores the narrative to the vernacular, the language of the commons, he also restores the commons to the narrative. The English poet shows an interest in the details and mechanisms of politics and government that goes far beyond his sources. This is evident from the first as the people try to divert Walter from "his lust present" to his responsibilities in securing the future. Without this intervention there would be no Griselde story, just pages of hawking and hunting. The commons, who seem every bit as nervous as the mice in Langland's Westminster, work through a representative Speaker, who begins by appealing to Walter's "humanitee" (4.92). This term, a unique Chaucerian usage, translates Petrarch's *humanitas* and brings with it some of the doubleness of the Petrarchan usage: the ruler is linked to his subjects by a common humanity, but is also divided from them by a more authentic understanding of what humanity is. This tension of affinity and difference is felt throughout this first political exchange between Walter and his subjects, particularly in their conflicting presuppositions about the origins of power. The people presume upon their right to initiate an affair of state (Walter must marry) but they presume too far in offering to choose a bride. Walter rebukes them for this second presumption, claiming that the right to make his own choice (in this as in all else) descends upon him from God:

> "I truste in Goddes bountee, and therfore
> My mariage and myn estaat and reste
> I hym bitake; he may doon as hym leste."   (4.159–61)

Does Chaucer's text mount any challenge to this descending model of authority? Walter, we have noted, lives "in delit" (4.68). But so does Griselde:

> Noght fer fro thilke paleys honurable,
> Wher as this markys shoop his mariage,
> There stood a throop, of site delitable.   (4.197–99)

The "delit" that Griselde lives in is that of an austere and time-honored simplicity. This is the "blisful lyf, a paisible and a swete" of Chaucer's *Former Age*, a simple life that preceded the rapacity of "tyraunts" and the building of "paleis-chambres."[123] The tranquillity of this "Etas Prima" was ruined by ambitious tyrants such as Nimrod who, being "desirous / to regne" (58–59), precipitated the fall of Babel and the confusion of tongues:[124]

> Allas, allas, now may men wepe and crye!
> For in oure dayes nis but covetyse,
> Doublenesse, and tresoun, and envye,
> Poyson, manslawhtre, and mordre in sondry wyse.   (60–63)

Griselde's life of moral, economic, and dietary simplicity evidently has a longer pedigree than Walter's life at the palace, with its "houses of office stuffed with plentee" (4.264). Walter's invasion of village space recalls the original, ruinous disruption to the life of "the peples in the former age" (4.2); his courtly rhetoric, structured on "doubleness," is an instrument of torture for Griselde as it is for many "men . . . in oure dayes" (60–61). Walter employs such rhetorical doubleness most skillfully in dividing Griselde from his (her) subjects. The commons recognizes that Griselde is concerned with its collective interests, "the commune profit" (4.431). But Walter informs Griselde that the commons have turned against her. They complain, says Walter, that "the blood of Janicle" will succeed to power (634); they constrain him to take another wife (800). Walter must take such words seriously; he is not free to behave like a commoner:

> "Swich wordes seith my peple, out of drede.
> Wel oughte I of swich murmur taken heede,
> For certeinly I drede swich sentence,
> Though they nat pleyn speke in myn audience."   (4.634–37)

> "I may nat doon as every plowman may."   (4.799)

Walter pretends to respect and be constrained by an ascending model of power, but this is a fiction, an invention to legitimize his own perverse designs. Not only, then, does Walter invent and appropriate Griselde; he also invents the people by speaking for them a fiction of his own devising. The commons are roundly condemned for their fickleness within Chaucer's text, but this critique is voiced by another part of the same social body across a line of rupture drawn by the tyrannical Walter himself. The people criticize the people since Walter stands beyond open criticism:

> "O stormy peple! unsad and evere untrewe!
> Ay indiscreet and chaungynge as a fane!
> Delitynge evere in rumbul that is newe."   (4.995–97)

Such lines suggest unease at the voice of the commons without quite disowning it as a political force. The court-centered partiality of this narration
hardly troubles to hide itself: whereas courtiers (and the poets who write for
them) hunger for *tidynges*, the "peple" are said to delight in "rumbul" (recalling the infamous peasant *rumore* of 1381).[125] The difference between a *rumbul*
and a *tidynge* is only one of number, distance, and degree: many voices far
away, as opposed to a few voices here at court. The commons, always vulnerable to misrepresentation in courtly discourse, is in Walter's case subjected to
impersonation as part of despotic statecraft. Elsewhere in Chaucer, however,
the commons is granted a useful commentative function that ultimately becomes active. The common birds in the *Parliament of Fowls* justly question
the naturalness of aristocratic sexual practice (or nonpractice); and the *Physician's Tale* suggests that "the peple" will indeed rise to depose tyranny, albeit
only after the killing of a suitably symbolic female innocent. The commons is
not celebrated as a political force in Chaucer (Prudence clearly has no time
for it),[126] but it is recognized as part of a complex political equation. No
equivalent recognition is to be found in Petrarch. For "the lauriat poete," the
commons or *vulgo* remains absolutely antithetical to the cultural values of
humanism.[127]

   Third, having restored the commons to the body politic, Chaucer restores
the female body to itself. Griselde's suffering begins when she becomes the
object of the tyrannical gaze, but self-realization begins here too, since, as
Sartre observes, to realize that you are being looked at is (at least) to realize
yourself.[128] It follows that Walter's perceptions, Walter's gazing out into the
world, must remain scattered throughout the world: there is nobody who can
look out at him and tell him who he is or even that he is.[129] This, then, is
the tragedy of the tyrannic gaze: that it cannot be met. Through his perpetual
gaze at the Other-as-object the tyrant (and the tyrannic humanist) excludes
himself from the possibility of human community.

   Griselde contains the effects of Walter's gaze, and later of his acts, within
herself; she never gratifies tyranny by becoming a spectacle of its own effects.
Petrarch's Valterius gazes wonderingly ("admirans") at Griselde's constancy
as he robs her of her second child. In Chaucer, however, the gaze drops as
Griselde finishes speaking:

> "Deth may noght make no comparisoun
> Unto youre love." And whan this markys say
> The constance of his wyf, he caste adoun
> His eyen two . . .   (4.666–69)

"Constance" means more of the same, the same as before. Walter sees this
when he gazes at Griselde, yet this sight, something he has seen all along, sud-

denly becomes unbearable. Perhaps he has seen, in Griselde's "constance," a mystery that he cannot fathom or possess; or perhaps he cannot countenance any visual sign of his own "mad bestiality." Walter, as he casts down his eyes, does not know what he has seen.[130]

Valterius adheres quite closely to Petrarch's own prescription for a happy marriage: find a devoted, good-hearted girl from far away who will wish to see, hear, and think of you alone and so be transformed into your image.[131] *Familiares* 22.1, addressed to a single man, recognizes no autonomous significance in female thought and feeling, and neither does Petrarch's *Seniles* story. The mental and bodily hurts of the Petrarchan Griselde apparently vanish into thin air, but in Chaucer they achieve powerful physical recognition just as soon as tyranny admits to final defeat. Griselde locks her own children back into herself in a fierce and passionate moment of physical reintegration (4.1079–1101). Although enacted publicly, at court, this is a wholly private moment from which (as Griselde swoons) Walter is hopelessly excluded. The next narrative moment, in which Griselde's children are drawn from her body with great care and difficulty (4.1102–3), has all the physical intensity of childbirth. The release or rebirth of these children signals the defeat of Walter's aspiration (a masculine fantasy old as Genesis) to mother or "bring forth" his own children without female participation.

Chaucer's fourth critique of Petrarch is formed by putting this Petrarchan narrative into the mouth of a logician. The essential opposition between the Oxford logician and Petrarch, the rhetor, is initially obscured by the fact of kinship beneath a religious dress: each is described as a "worthy clerk" (4.21, 27). But no logician, especially one bred on "Aristotle and his philosophie" (1.295), could happily tolerate the slippages of meaning that characterize Petrarchan rhetoric. In the winter of 1365–66 Petrarch learned that a group of Aristotelians at Venice had concluded that he was a good man, but an illiterate ignoramus.[132] Petrarch responded in 1367 with *De sui ipsius et multorum ignorantia*, a treatise characterizing current speculative philosophy as "petty, arid, pedantic, an endless exercise in dialectic punctuated by absurd and boring genuflections to a quasi-divinized Aristotle."[133] It seems, then, that in giving the Griselde story to an emaciated Aristotelian, Chaucer is enjoying an academic joke at Petrarch's expense. There is one member of the Canterbury pilgrimage who, we have noted, embodies all the signs of a rhetor: the Wife of Bath.[134] The Wife might be seen as the only motherly begetter of the *Clerk's Tale*. She spurs the Clerk into narrating and (as if to claim maternity) dramatically appears in the final stanza of the story proper (4.1170–76). The Wife is not only the most rhetorical of pilgrims but also, in her headlong pursuit of *delectabilia* and in her slavelike subjection (and Valterian testing) of husbands, the most (from a male perspective) tyrannical.[135]

The fifth and final aspect of this Chaucerian critique concerns questions of framing and closure. The manifold ways in which the *Clerk's Tale* fails to enforce its own closure have been widely recognized. The final events reported by the narrative—the death of the peasant Janicula in court space and the ascension to power of his grandson—are fraught with political and ideological difficulties; these are simply not discussed. We then have successive attempts at equating the readership to the figures in the text. The narrator first takes his cue from "Petrak" and his "heigh stile" story (4.1147–48) in proposing that we are all (or should be) Griseldes. We should steel ourselves "ful ofte to be bete" by the "sharp scourges of adversitee" that God sends us "for oure exercise" (4.1142–62). But then it appears that Griseldes are women, although only two or three are to be found in each town (4.1163–69). Finally, in a song sung "for the Wyves love of Bathe" (4.1170), we surprisingly rediscover the original Petrarchan formula: we are all Griseldes (4.1177–1212). But this time the "we" is exclusively masculine, as in the Petrarchan Academy all wives are Walters, tyrants who torture our Griselde-like bodies. By now it is not clear whether this is Chaucer speaking or Chaucer's Clerk, but by now it has ceased to matter. What does matter is that these terminating contradictions and incoherencies are seen to issue from similar qualities within the tale itself and, by extension, from within its acknowledged Petrarchan source.

Although the letter of Chaucer's closing stanzas restates an allegiance to Petrarch, the tone and spirit of this closure is Boccaccian. Whereas Petrarch's Walter ends "happy in his wife and his offspring" (p. 151), Boccaccio's Dioneo ends by wishing that Griselde "had found some other man to shake her skin-coat [il pilliccione] for her, earning herself a fine new dress in the process" (10.10.69; p. 824).[136] This conjunction of sex and commerce is most powerfully embodied by the last person named in Chaucer's story, the Wife of Bath. In pointing us back to the Wife, the Clerk, we have noted, is recognizing the true source of his impulse to narrate. He is also directing us to an ironic gloss on his own narration, particularly to that tyrannico-humanist act of vision. The *Wife of Bath's Tale* opens with a comparable act of seeing and translating: a mounted knight sees a woman and rapes her. The remainder of the Wife's *Tale* traces the lengthy and difficult process, under female judicial governance, of undoing or unwilling this tyrannical masculine act. The masculine weeping and wailing with which the *Clerk's Tale* closes is, for the Wife, the beginning of masculine wisdom.

Still in Lombardy: The *Merchant's Tale*

Such "wepyng and waylyng" forms an immediate point of departure for the Merchant (4.1213), another masculine Griselde who suffers the "passyng cruel-tee" of a wife. It is the *Merchant's Tale* that performs the most comprehensive critique of the *Clerk's Tale* and hence of its Petrarchan origins. The Merchant's opening line makes it clear that we have not yet left Lombardy. We have, to be precise, moved just ninety miles east-north-east, from Saluzzo to Pavia.

His *Tale*'s opening sentence also informs us that we are to consider (once again) a man who "folwed ay his bodily delyt / On wommen." The narrative then plays out the familiar pattern: a tyrannical male sees a female body, commands it, takes possession of it. But here the determining act of vision, likened to a sighting in a mirror in a marketplace, is seen as one of blindness and not of insight: "For love is blynd alday, and may nat see" (4.1598). Here, as in the *Clerk's Tale*, such deliberate gazing at a female object is presented as the legitimate outcome of a consultative political process. But here that process, the consulting of Placebo and Justinus, is evidently a crude facade that covers a naked act of will.

John of Salisbury initiates his discussion of tyranny in his *Policraticus* by emphasizing the great dangers of flattery at court. The victory of Placebo over Justinus signals a failure of vision and an unwillingness to hear the truth:

The flatterer is the enemy of all virtue and forms as it were a cataract over the eye of him whom he engages in conversation. He is the more to be avoided, as he never ceases harming under guise of friendship, until he has blinded keen vision and put out the modicum of light that seemed present. Added to this he stops up the ears of his listeners that they may not hear the truth. I hardly know of anything more disastrous than this.[137]

May is first seen in the *Merchant's Tale* as the familiar voiceless and apparently volitionless female object of masculine vision. But as the narrative progresses our viewing perspective changes. We are invited to lie down on our backs with May in her marriage bed, gazing up at her tyrannizing spouse (4.1849–54). Later May discovers her voice and January loses his vision. And when January recovers his eyesight (just as May is recovering her sexuality up a pear tree) a new interpretive order is established: men will see, but women will explain what men see.

What I am proposing, then, is that Chaucer's two tales of Lombard tyranny be considered as the kind of narrative sequence formed by the *Knight's Tale* and the *Miller's Tale*: the second tale, through judicious use of structural parallelism and grotesque realism, performs a humorous critique of the first. The somber, claustrophobic, courtly societies of Theseus and Walter yield to the cheerful, mobile market economies of Alisoun and May.[138] It was a stroke of genius to locate two Lombard tyrannies within such a unified narrative sequence: tyranny cannot tolerate two tyrants any more than it can tolerate two Griseldes. But when Chaucer traveled to Lombardy in 1378 he *had* discovered two tyrants: there was Bernabò Visconti (Petrarch's former patron) with whom Chaucer did business at Milan; and there was Bernabò's nephew and son-in-law Gian Galeazzo Visconti twenty miles south at Pavia.[139] This state of affairs could not last for long. Eventually it was January's townsman, the tyrant of Pavia, who won out against his "double allye" (7.2403). Bernabò, once the "scourge of Lombardy," *flagellum Dei*, dies an obscure death that merits just one stanza from Chaucer's Monk. Fragment 7 of the *Canterbury*

Tales repeats as history what was offered in Fragment 4 as poetic fiction: one foolish Lombard tyrant succeeds another.

Politics, Marriage, and Marriage "Agein"

There is much in Chaucer to exemplify the bad end that awaits overweening and tyrannical males. But there is also much encouragement for monarchs (magnates, or householders) in their perennial struggle to address the needs of the *bonum commune* rather than to follow the logic of their own *delit*. Theseus, we have noted, is offered several opportunities to step into tyranny when his personal desires conflict with the immediate needs of Athenian (or Theban) subjects. Melibee finally renounces the desire to revenge himself on his enemies; Walter finally overthrows his own tyrannizing of Griselde. Tyranny, for Chaucer as for medieval political theorists, is not a terminal disease, an irreversible state of mind. It is an aberrant mode of behavior that may be renounced as quickly as it is assumed. Tyranny is also, particularly for Chaucer, intimately connected with metaphors and flesh-and-blood practices of marriage. For Walter and Melibee, in very different ways, marriage provides both an entry into tyranny and a way out of it. For Theseus marriage to a former enemy of the state deprives him of the advisory function of an intelligent spouse, who (as exemplified by both Griselde and Prudence) is the best safeguard against tyrannical masculine tendencies. A monarch without an adequate wife is liable, like Theseus, to operate from an elevated position of sublime isolation: at the ill-fated tournament Theseus sits "as he were a god in trone" (1.2529). Richard II, late in his reign, sat on a specially elevated throne from dinnertime to vespers on feast days, speaking to nobody but observing all. Anyone chancing to meet his gaze was required to bow the knee.[140] Something of the terrible, isolated, and isolating quality of such a monarchical gaze may be gauged from the panel portrait now hanging in the south side of the nave in Westminster Abbey (plate 8). This image, seven feet high, suggests both blankness and acuity in its gaze, a look that both scrutinizes viewers and passes clean through them, a gaze that does not expect to be met or returned. It is possible that this panel was once paired with a portrait of Queen Anne, but this companion painting has not survived.[141] The absence of a counterbalancing spousal image must have been felt with increasing desperation as the reign wore on; Queen Isabella, still only eleven years old in 1400, could never have played Griselde or Prudence to Richard's Walter or Melibee.

The articles of Richard's deposition in 1399 play out dramatically the conflict between the laws of the land and the arbitrary will and pleasure of the king. They express an unwillingness to countenance the notion that the state could be embodied by a single individual; in Fortescue's terms, they reject the notion of *dominium regale* in favor of *dominium politicum et regale*.[142] Richard, it is claimed, ignored the laws and customs of the realm (which he swore to

Plate 8. *Richard II Enthroned* (c. 1395). Panel, Westminster Abbey, London.

uphold in his coronation oath), since "according to the whim of his desire he wanted to do whatever appealed to his wishes."[143] Sometimes, speaking with "harsh and determined looks," he claimed "that the laws were in his own mouth, sometimes he said that they were in his breast, and that he alone could change or establish the laws of his realm."[144] This crude formulation, in which Richard arbitrarily claims that his own body and the body politic are one and the same, implicitly rejects the metaphor by which Chaucer had urged him, in the "Balade Royal" known as *Lak of Stedfastnesse*, to imagine his relationship to his subjects:

> Dred God, do law, love trouthe and worthinesse,
> And wed thy folk agein to stedfastnesse.   (27–28)

In urging Richard to recognize the bonds of matrimony that tie him to his subjects, Chaucer imagines the "folk" as collective bride to Richard's "stedfastnesse," the virtue that holds *voluntatis arbitrium* in check. The adverb "agein" is significant here since it suggests that the sacramental bond uniting this ruler to his subjects as *sponsus regni* has come unraveled.[145] Walter welcomes Griselde as his wife "agein" once he has renounced his "merveillous desir his wyf t'assaye" (4.454). This second union surpasses the first in ceremonial splendour and symbolic importance; the tyranny of one-man rule yields, once again, to a marriage of hearts, minds, and political will:

> For moore solempne in every mannes syght
> This feste was, and gretter of costage,
> Than was the revel of hire mariage.   (4.1125–27)

This notion of a second marriage (or marriage "agein") suggests a certain congruence between the *Clerk's Tale* and *Lak of Stedfastnesse*, a ballade that was "made by our laureal poete" (according to John Shirley) "then in his last yeeres."[146] Chaucer's celebrated interest in the dynamics of unadulterous marriage—a subject supposedly foreign to the conventional concerns of romance and courtly *makynge*—is continuous with a political intelligence that carries to the greater historical world. As both metaphor and weathervane for the relations of monarch to populace, marriage is of compelling concern for a courtier-poet who—for reasons more complex than discussions of "patronage" can hope to comprehend—invests so much time, hope, and imaginative energy in the provision of wifely counsel. A mature and intelligent queen, such as Anne of Bohemia, represents a comforting historical correlative to figures such as Griselde, Prudence, and Alceste. A twelve-year-old bride brought from afar to succeed a wife of Griselde's stature, "so discreet and fair of eloquence" (4.410), would suggest a more troubled future. And an infant queen, or no queen at all, would loosen much of the purchase of Chaucerian fiction upon contemporary contingencies; the Griselde story, suddenly, would read like an outdated fable or extravagant romance in need of a new translation.

Petrarch's attitude to marriage, as we have seen, differs markedly from that of the English "laureal poete." Where Chaucer envisages dialogue between spouses, Petrarch imagines the domination of male over female, subjugation rather than conjugality. In addressing his political master on the importance of "law" (bracketed between fear of God and love of "trouthe and worthinesse"), Chaucer envisages a form of *dominium* that is both *politicum et regale*. Characteristic Petrarchan images of female subordination and dismemberment, by contrast, serve the needs of an emergent absolutist culture that, as we shall see in the next chapter, represented its power through images and practices of masculine sexuality run rampant. Such prodigal sexual display pays scant attention to the metaphorical and historical bonds of marriage.

Chapter **II**

All That Fall: Chaucer's Monk
and "Every Myghty Man"

~~~~~

De casibus tragedy, which concerns the fall of great men, is a genre that few men wish to read, least of all a reigning monarch or other "myghty man" at the peak of his powers. Typically, by the time he feels drawn to such reading, the time is too late; the genre is already reading or narrating him as just one more exemplum among many. For Shakespeare's Richard II, the desire to rehearse the genre comes at the midpoint of personal tragedy, not at its beginning:

> For God's sake, let us sit upon the ground
> And tell sad stories of the death of kings:
> How some have been deposed; some slain in war;
> Some haunted by the ghosts they have deposed;
> Some poisoned by their wives; some sleeping kill'd;
> All murder'd ...   (III.ii.155–60)

Such taxonomizing of great falls, as the fivefold "some" suggests, is reductive, repetitive, and dull—except, that is, at the single and crucial moment of the genre's extension. Shakespeare revitalizes the genre by having Richard II speak just as he is about to disappear inside it; just before, to risk a transiently modern analogy for the blood-hungry genre of *de casibus*, his personal interview with the vampire.[1] The genre may also work effects in the wider political world by suggesting, as the Earl of Essex was keen to suggest by sponsoring timely productions of *Richard II* just before the 1601 rising, that the logic of *de casibus* is about to home in on the royal jugular.[2] Similarly, I shall argue, the *Monk's Tale* brought imaginative power and frisson to Ricardian subjects simply by being read *as* a contemporary text. Great men have fallen; *great men are falling*—here the genre features as a modality not for the recording of history but for the experiencing of it; great men will fall. The *Tale* is thus energized chiefly by pressures external to its own formal constitution (thereby justifying another long chapter of historicist recuperation); except that the form of the *Tale* brilliantly exemplifies the crucial moment at which contemporary history (through the "modern instances") itself breaks into and breaks up the stabilized repetitions of oft-told tales. Chaucer shares with his Italian contemporaries a vivid sense that the whole meaning of a man's life is rewritten as he falls. And he shares with some of them a willingness to suggest that such renarration is always imminent; that it may be already in progress. It is not sufficient, then, to see the *Monk's Tale* as a repudiated experiment in Italian neohumanism. Discriminating between diverse Italian humanisms and their differing political agendas, the *Monk's Tale* forges a pressured and unfinishable narrative for English people living under, or in sight of, Richard II or any "myghty man."

This chapter begins by situating Chaucer's *Monk's Tale* in relation to its immediate Italian humanist antecedents: Petrarch's *De viris illustribus* and Boccaccio's *De casibus virorum illustrium*. Such a lineage reprises the political frameworks deployed in the *Clerk's Tale* chapter (Florentine republicanism; northern Italian despotism), but reverses their order. In this instance, Petrarch writes first and Boccaccio follows and critiques his example. My argument will be, again, that Chaucer aligns himself with Boccaccian revisionism and against a Petrarchan cultural project that proves congenial to despotic ideology. This alignment is explicit: although Chaucer does not mention Boccaccio (his main source) by name, his *pattern* of naming Petrarch and Dante (among ancients and moderns, respectively) conforms exactly to the precedent of Boccaccio's *De casibus*. Such allegiance is not, however, immediately apparent: for the Host, the self-nominated guardian of Chaucer's associational polity, is initially seduced by his own fantasy of "a myghty man," the Monk, who (so the fantasy runs) will ease the painful memory of past failures, public and domestic. Associational groupings, racked by internal stresses and divisions, are perennially vulnerable to the fantasy of surrendering to a "myghty man" who will put everything right.

Petrarch, Boccaccio, and the Lives of Great Men

Chaucer's Clerk, we have noted, prefaces his *Tale* by observing that Petrarch "is now deed and nayled in his cheste" (4.29). Twentieth-century Chaucer editors have been unwilling to let this comment pass uncontested: Petrarch "was never literally *nayled in his cheste*," asserts F. N. Robinson: "his body was laid uncoffined in a sarcophagus." The *Riverside Chaucer* maintains and elaborates this assertion by noting that Petrarch in fact was "placed in a sarcophagus of red stone, after the ancient manner."[3] Both editions then acknowledge the folly of their annotating by explaining what we already know: that the phrase *nayled in his cheste* "here means nothing more than dead and buried."[4] What compels these editors to make such awkward and unnecessary interventions; to stumble at Petrarch's grave? Their difficulty lies in accepting that Petrarch, the founding father of humanism, is (as Chaucer has it) simply dead and buried. Their impulse to exempt him from death and decay forms part of a very long tradition. Within years of Petrarch's death, admirers and dependents at Arqua had constructed an ornate funeral monument.[5] This impulse to monumentalize Petrarch, to detach him from his own place and time and imagine him speaking from somewhere outside history, has continued ever since. Morris Bishop, for example, concludes his lengthy study of Petrarch's life and times with the following assertion: "Petrarch has frequently been called the First Modern Man. I would go farther. I would call him one of the Eternal Men."[6]

Bishop here offers not a critique of the Petrarchan ideology of Great Men, *viri illustres*, but a wholesale consumption of it. It was the promise of being associated with "Eternal Men" that made north Italian despots so very keen to patronize Petrarch: for Petrarchan scholarship could distract attention from the immediate, often squalid and illegitimate, sources of their own personal power by associating them with a grand historical tradition of great men. The practice of writing of great men was for Petrarch a lifelong habit. Having begun his *De viris illustribus* in the late 1330s (at roughly the same time as the *Africa*), Petrarch continued writing, revising, and expanding it to the very end of his life. The particular narrowness of Petrarch's definition of the genre helps explain its popularity among Italian despots: Petrarch's *viri illustres* are essentially men of action, statesmen and military commanders; physicians, poets, and philosophers are not included.[7] Neither are women: the tradition is not to be confused with that of Fame, as exemplified by Boccaccio's *Amorosa visione*, the Petrarchan *Trionfi* (and by Chaucer's *House of Fame*).[8] Such a definition evidently proved congenial to the Visconti, Petrarch's longterm hosts. Around 1340, Azzo Visconti decorated a large hall of his newly built palace at Milan with portraits of "illustrious pagan princes of the world." The sequence included Aeneas, Hector, Hercules, and Attila the Hun; the only Christian represented, according to the chronicler Galvano Fiamma, was Charlemagne (plus, of course, Azzo Visconti himself).[9] Francesco da Carrara, Petrarch's last despotic patron, urged Petrarch in his final years to complete his *De viris* and to offer him advice on executing his own *Sala virorum illustrium* at Padua. He also requested Petrarch to produce a shortened version of the *De viris*, a *compendium*; this was probably used as a guidebook in showing guests around the great hall.[10] The only Trecento portrait to survive in this hall, now known as the Sala dei Giganti, is a portrait of Petrarch at work at his desk.[11]

Although he had received the laurels at Rome in 1341 for his poem *Africa*, it is the Latin prose of the *De viris* that came to epitomize Petrarch's more important cultural legacy (and his hopes for lasting fame).[12] Petrarch grew disenchanted with Scipio Africanus in later years; he invested more and more of his energy in narrating great Roman lives and developed a book-length passion for Julius Caesar. Such devotion to the warriors and statesmen of pagan Rome did not go unchallenged: in his *Secretum*, Petrarch has "Augustinus" challenge "Franciscus" on his obsession with finishing the *Africa* and *De viris*.

Franciscus acknowledges that his preoccupation with secular history may be delaying his journey to the *patria* of heaven. But, he argues, his desire to study cannot be bridled; the quicker he finishes his scholarly work, the sooner he can turn his attention to higher matters.[13] Further moral dilemmas arise when we consider Petrarch's declared intentions in conducting such scholarship and the uses to which it was put. Here is part of the preface for the *De viris* written at Valchiusa around 1351–53:

Illustrious men (who, according to what the most learned minds have passed down to us, flourished with a certain glory) and the praise of such men (which I have found scattered and dispersed through many different books): these things I have decided to collect together in a single place, forming, so to speak, an illustrious gathering. I would write more willingly, I must confess, of things *seen* rather than of things *read about*, things recent rather than ancient, so that distant posterity might receive from me news of this epoch as I have gathered information about ancient times from ancient authors. But I am grateful to our princes for relieving me of this labor (being one who is tired, avid for peace and quiet): for their doings provide my pen with material fit for satire rather than history. For even if I might honor certain of them distinguished enough by victories of late, these things are nonetheless to be credited to fortune and to the slothfulness of the enemy (and so are not to be seen as occasions of virtue or true fame).[14]

The princes that Petrarch makes fun of here are the Visconti: Luchino and Galeazzo had recently enjoyed some measure of military success.[15] Shortly after writing this, of course, Petrarch crossed the Alps and settled at Milan, accepting the patronage and protection of the *signori* he had so recently mocked. Following his move to Padua in 1368, Petrarch rewrote his *De viris* preface in order to recognize the virtues of his new patron, Francesco da Carrara.[16] His policy of *not* including soldiers and statesmen from modern times obviously suited Petrarch well. His text could travel with him from one despotic patron to the next without substantial revision. Petrarch did come under some pressure to include contemporaries: Francesco was keen to honor Manno Donati, a Florentine mercenary captain who died in the service of Padua, by having him inserted into the *De viris*. Petrarch managed to keep him out (probably by composing an inscription for his tomb); Francesco had Manno portrayed in his much-decorated palace.[17] Petrarch obviously found the cultural limitations of his military masters extremely irksome at times: his *De viris* preface complains of "militares viri" who, having restricted their leisure reading to one well-thumbed book, resent all departures from this single familiar account.[18] Such an attitude offered little encouragement for the comparative philological and codicological methods that Petrarch was attempting to develop.

Methodological discussion in the *De viris* preface proceeds by the familiar Petrarchan tactic of exclusion. We need not detain ourselves with kings of the Goths, Huns, and Vandals;[19] we do not need to know every detail of the domestic life of those *viri illustres* who merit our attention. Here as elsewhere, Petrarch classes women (as wives) at the same level as servants or slaves (and, in this instance, as dogs and vegetables):[20]

What does it concern us to know (for example) how many slaves [servos] or dogs an illustrious man might have had, how many packhorses, how many cloaks, what names his slaves might have had, what conjugal relations, skills, or savings; what foods he liked best, what means of transport, what ornamental trappings, what fashions, what sauces and (finally) what his favorite vegetables might have been?[21]

Petrarch does go on, however, to admit his own weakness for chronicling the habits and home life of great men; he is fond of recording their conversations and their pithy, elegant, or timely utterances. In what follows he will also give us, where possible, details of their physical stature, of their birth, and of their manner of death.[22] Such things, he argues, are pleasing to know, a source of sweetness in themselves.[23] This affable approach to the lives of great men forms a pointed contrast to the way Boccaccio opens his contribution to the genre in Book 1 of his *De casibus virorum illustrium*:

As I sought out what, from my scholarly work, I might be able to contribute to the public good [rei publice], an unbelievable amount of material suggested itself. However, my mind was particularly struck by the obscene longings of princes and of those who hold command in some way: their violent tricks, time-wasting leisure, insatiable avarice, bloody rivalries, precipitate and fierce vendettas, their endless, abominable crimes. And seeing that such crimes, following the command of the wicked, were spreading (unbridled) everywhere, corrupting all standards of public honesty, loosening the most sacred bonds of justice, overthrowing all virtues, and (what is unspeakable) seeing the character of the masses lured ignorantly into impious manners through execrable example; seeing all this, and perceiving that chance had brought me to just the place I desired to be, I immediately snatched up my pen to write against such men.[24]

Boccaccio represents the writing of the *De casibus* as a deliberate attempt to make his scholarly skills serve the public good, or the state (*res publica*). The state he served when writing the first version of his text (1356–60) was the Florentine republic; the greatest threat to its integrity was posed, as we have noted, by the *principes* or despots of northern Italy. Boccaccio certainly shows a strong prorepublican, antityrannical bias in narrating histories of ancient Rome: his version of the Virginia story (Chaucer's *Physician's Tale*) sacrifices all interest in family pathos (father stabs daughter with a butcher's knife) in order to concentrate on the political struggle of the plebeians against Claudius, an overweening *decemvir*.[25] But he does not adopt the harsh, polemical stance that is typical of Florentine antidespotic polemic. Rather than denouncing contemporary Italian despots, he seeks to engage their interest and persuade them to change by encouragement, exhortation, and negative example. This explains the exceptional importance of rhetoric for such an undertaking: Boccaccio mounts a vigorous defence of rhetoric in Book 6, immediately following his life of Cicero. It also accounts for the extraordinary and long-lived success of the *De casibus*, a text that survives in some 83 manuscripts, 3 printed Latin editions, and in no fewer than 28 translations in 5 different languages.[26] Boccaccio's text was prized by different, often antithetical, publics. One of the two most authoritative early manuscripts was owned by a Dominican friar of Santa Maria Novella in Florence; the other was written for Queen Giovanna of Naples.[27]

De casibus virorum illustrium was obviously inspired by the precedent of the Petrarchan *De viris*. Petrarch actually shows up at the beginning of Boccaccio's eighth book, just as Boccaccio has retreated to his sofa in a fit of boredom, self-doubt, and exhaustion. Petrarch, or this Boccaccian vision of Petrarch, upbraids Boccaccio as an "egregious Professor of Idleness" ("ociorum professor egregie," 8.1.7) and urges him to fix his attention on the prospect of future fame. By so doing, Boccaccio "will be separated from the common herd, and just as those who came before us helped us with their labours, so will we help those who come after" (8.1.26). Boccaccio shows an informed understanding here of Petrarchan *gloria*, a concept that proposes to create a society of gifted initiates across the centuries (while leaving the individual scholar alone in his study, supposedly innocent of any immediate historical context).[28] Petrarch's ghostly visit serves the purpose of getting Boccaccio back to his desk, but it does not succeed in breaking Boccaccio's relationship to the social and political world he inhabits. When Boccaccio thinks of the countryside, he (unlike Petrarch) manages to think of the people who actually live and work there: of how their weathered skin shows the effects of sun and rain; of how their sinewy bodies shake down acorns from oaks; of how they till the earth and "sweat with never-ending labor" ("laboribus assiduis insudare," 3.17.16). When he thinks of the power of kings he thinks of "the sweat of the people that makes royal honor shine" (2.5.2–3); rulers "should consider the people not as slaves, but as collaborators" — "non esse populos servos, sed conservos." And when he thinks of the immediate historical circumstances of his own political world—that of Florence—he thinks not of Petrarch but of Dante.

When Dante appears in the ninth and final book of the *De casibus* he comes accompanied by a great crowd of notable contemporary figures, headed by Philip the Fair, King of France from 1285 to 1314. Having identified Dante as a great poet, Boccaccio first addresses him as a great citizen of Florence (9.23.6–7). Brushing aside Boccaccio's praises, Dante urges him to address himself to the political task at hand: to speak of those who brought everlasting shame to Florence. The chief of these, following immediately behind him, Dante describes as "a home-bred plague [domesticam pestem], an everlasting blot on the name of Florence" (9.23.9).[29] Boccaccio looks at this newcomer "and recognizes him to be Walter, Duke of Athens and sometime pernicious tyrant of Florence" (9.23.11). He goes on to give a lengthy account of how the Florentines, weakened through a costly war with Pisa, contrived to put power into Walter's hands; of how the "magnates" encouraged him to seize personal power; of how Walter terrified the citizenry and took his tyrannical pleasure with adolescent boys, daughters, sisters, and wives; of how the tyrant was overthrown (and was finally murdered by a Florentine mercenary fighting for King Edward III at the Battle of Poitiers, 9.24.1–42).

The ninth and final book of Boccaccio's *De casibus* makes a significant departure from Petrarchan precedent by considering modern instances, rulers whose lives helped shape the present historical moment. The tyrannical Walter, for Boccaccio, is the most significant such figure, since his decline and fall ushered in the republic of 1343–78, the regime that Boccaccio served for most of his mature life. Dante is obviously Boccaccio's most important model here. The *Commedia* is peopled with the recent dead as well as with those from recent centuries and from the ancient world. And yet Boccaccio is keen to emphasize, in a dialogue with Fortune, that his mission differs markedly from that of Dante:

I now realize that I do not have the feathers of a bird with which I might penetrate the heavens and examine the secrets of God; and then, having seen them, reveal them to mortals. (6.1.9)[30]

Acknowledging that he lacks the God-given talent to reconnoitre the heavens, Boccaccio insists that his concern is with this world: with the distant and recent past and with possible, imminent futures. His last example, from 1356, nudges right up into the historical present. It tells of the capture of the French King John at Poitiers and his subsequent imprisonment in England. This is followed by a most eloquent and extensive appeal to contemporary rulers; they, surely, would not wish to join this miserable catalogue of death and disaster:

But you who hold sway over mighty empires, open your eyes and unplug your ears. And to ensure that a deadly sleep does not carry you off, stay wide awake, ignoring minor figures to consider kings: their tears, depositions, exiles, chains, imprisonments, tortures, execrations, deaths; and the shedding of blood, the broken bodies, scattered ashes; heirs driven across the world, royal plunderings, and kingdoms destroyed. (9.27.8)

Perhaps only the citizen of a republic could offer such an unblinking vision of the end of tyrannical kingship. Boccaccio's critique of tyranny was clearly prized for its boldness. In 1407, for example, it was put to good use by Jean Petit in his attempt to represent the assassination of Duke Louis d'Orléans, brother of Charles V, as tyrannicide.[31] Whereas Petrarch's *De viris* encourages the individual reader to look to the distant past for inspiration for personal virtue, and to hunger for future fame,[32] Boccaccio's text shapes the art of scholarly exemplification as a form of resistance to contemporary tyrannical rule.

Before moving on to Chaucer we must acknowledge one strain of writing in the *De casibus* that owes nothing to Dante or Petrarch but is resolutely Boccaccian. Pointedly situated at the beginning of Book 9, in the narrow space between the departure of Petrarch and the arrival of Dante, it has the force of what, with reference to Chaucer, we have termed authorial signature. It concerns the extraordinary dialogue between Boccaccio and Brunhilde, Queen of the Franks (534–613). Brunhilde experiences great difficulty in persuading Boccaccio to pick up his pen and take down her story: "Since my earliest youth," Boccaccio exclaims, "I have known women to be double-tongued" ("mulieres esse bilingues," 9.1.8). When Brunhilde finally begins telling her life story she finds that she is continuously interrupted by a stream of nit-picking objections from her masculine amanuensis:

". . . as a young girl I was given in marriage to King Sigibertus." I then said: "Be careful what you say! The name I've heard is Chilpericus or Childepertus."

She replied: "I know that some people share your opinion. But nonetheless I, as the end of the story showed . . ." (9.1.13–14)

Boccaccio continues to interrupt and interrogate Brunhilde ("Siste, queso"; "I beg you, stop!") until she loses all patience with him:

She, somewhat irritated, exclaimed: "God almighty! Who is this man, so swiftly transformed from ignoramus to fierce and all-knowing disputant? I'm sure he believes what he's saying, as if he could better tell what went on, after so many centuries, than can I, who was actually *there*." (9.1.17)

Brunhilde, speaking from the far end of history, articulates the crucial interrogative principle given contemporary expression by Chaucer's Wife of Bath ("Who peyntede the leon, tel me who?" 3.692). Her physical presence speaks to Boccaccio's struggles with textuality *as* a female body, a struggle fought out in the famous *novella* of "the scholar and the widow" (the *Decameron*'s longest story) and carried forward to the virulent misogyny of the *Corbaccio*.[33] Boccaccio's chief source for the Brunhilde story was, in his own estimation, unreliable. Rather than discussing the defects of this particular source (Paolino da Venezia), Boccaccio simply assimilates them to the unreliability of all feminine discourse and argues with Brunhilde. The Frankish queen has the last word in their dialogue, but it is said to owe more to the persuasive powers of female rhetoric than to historical fact:

Thus she spoke (and I became better disposed to please her). I write, I must confess, employing a source [testimonio] of dubious authenticity. And if it happens that something less than truthful be found, let it be attributed to she who so urgently begged me to write. (9.1.30)

Boccaccio's Brunhilde episode points up, with memorable and comical clarity, some of the difficulties facing the incipient humanist movement. Petrarch's insistence on confining his *De viris* to great figures of Roman an-

tiquity commits him to a mighty, masculine labor of reading and collation in
search of the best and most authoritative texts.[34] But all texts are female: texts
are born out of earlier texts and their defects multiply from one generation to
the next. The only narratives that can hope for independent, extratextual veri-
fication—that can escape the argument between Boccaccio and Brunhilde—
are those that deal with modern instances. But this raises a whole new set of
problems.

"Myn Owene Lord": Admiring and Rejecting Mighty Men

Chaucer's *Monk's Tale* raises textual problems more complex than those of any
other tale—a phenomenon that is in part expressive of unparalleled political
and historical complexities. Similarly complicated are its relations, acknowledged or occulted, to its own oral and literary sources: influences range from
Ovid and the Bible through Boethius and Vincent of Beauvais to Jean de
Meun's *Rose* and contemporary word of mouth.[35] Its most fundamental debt,
however, is explicitly recognized by the fifteen manuscripts employing the
Boccaccian title as epigraph or explicit: "De casibus virorum illustrium." But
although Boccaccio's title is appropriated by this textual tradition, it is the
name of Petrarch that actually appears within the body of the *Tale*, or tale
collection, itself. Those wishing to learn more about Cenobia, warrior-queen
of Palmyra, are directed to seek out Petrarch. Here, as in Boccaccio's dialogue
with Brunhilde, the encounter with a female historical figure prompts the
need for a display of stabilizing textual *maistrie*:

> Hir batailles, whoso list hem for to rede,
> Agayn Sapor the kyng and othere mo,
> And how that al this proces fil in dede,
> Why she conquered and what title had therto,
> And after, of hir meschief and hire wo,
> How that she was biseged and ytake—
> Lat hym unto my maister Petrak go,
> That writ ynough of this, I undertake.   (7.2319–26)

Anyone who searches for equivalent Petrarchan passages on this Syrian
queen will be disappointed; Chaucer is borrowing intensively from Boccaccio
at this point, not Petrarch. To make matters more complicated, Chaucer is
actually borrowing from Boccaccio's *De claris mulieribus*, although he does
rejoin the *De casibus* for the episode's final stanza.[36] Chaucer's substitution of
Petrarch for Boccaccio in this stanza forms part of the greater enigma of his
systematic suppression of the name of Boccaccio. Here, however, it is enough
to note that Petrarch is more than a literary source for Chaucer's Monk. He is
his "maister" (proudly unveiled at the end of a long and complex period). The
name of Petrarch is chosen to authorize, and characterize, the cultural undertaking of the *Monk's Tale*: for "discourse that possesses an author's name,"

Foucault argues, "is not to be immediately consumed and forgotten; neither is it accorded the momentary attention given to ordinary, fleeting words."[37] Petrarch is evidently more than a source to Chaucer's Monk; his name (to persist with Foucault) performs the office of the "author-function." Such a name, Foucault argues, in a discussion that dwells upon a *De viris illustribus*— that of Jerome—longer than upon any other text, "is more than a gesture, a finger pointed at someone; it is, to a certain extent, the equivalent of a description."[38] Petrarch's name, in the context of the *Monk's Tale*, may be read as describing Italian humanism as an emergent cultural tradition. Boccaccio is denied explicit recognition, perhaps through an economy of thrift, a calculation that his name lacks the suggestive, descriptive power of "my maister Petrak." And yet the *Tale* does recognize Boccaccio through its *incipit*, through its politics, and (I shall argue) through ingenious authorial signature.

Critical studies of the *Monk's Tale*'s affiliations with Italian humanism have tended to concentrate on literary sources in general and on tragedy in particular. This has tended to draw attention away from political contexts: the foundational character of the Petrarchan *De viris* has not been sufficiently recognized, whereas the Petrarchan *De remediis utriusque fortune* has been much discussed for its Senecan understanding of tragedy.[39] The *De remediis* is certainly an important and much-traveled text, but it has little to do with the genre of *vires illustres* that leads to the *Monk's Tale* (a narrative performance rejected by the Host precisely because it offers "no remedie," 7.2784).[40] The *De remediis* has been succinctly characterized as "a guide to conduct by a critical examination of the four major 'passions,' joy and hope, sorrow and fear";[41] the sentiments expressed by its dialogue between Dolor and Ratio were thought orthodox enough (in their first extant Middle English translation) to keep company with religious works such as *A Tretis of Mayndenhod* and *The Clowde of Unknowyng*.[42] The political contexts within which the quiescent sentiments of the *De remediis* were conceived would repay attention, of course: written under Visconti patronage at Milan, the text was ultimately dedicated to Azzo di Correggio, "tyrant of Parma, a figure with an abominable historical record."[43] But as a corrective to previous neglect, it seems more germane to situate the *Monk's Tale* in the political and historiographical lineage that runs from the *De viris* through the *De casibus* to the *Canterbury Tales*. Such a lineage repeats the elements of the Griselde story but revises their sequence (as Boccaccio and Petrarch swap places). Petrarch writes in praise of great men and is rewarded by the great despots of northern Italy; Boccaccio writes of the fall of great men, hence furthering republican critiques of despotic polity; Chaucer writes the *Monk's Tale*.

Chaucer's *Monk's Tale* follows the *Tale of Melibee* in Fragment 7; like the *Melibee*, it has often fallen foul of attempts to divide secular politics (on the one hand) from religious discourse (on the other).[44] Its *Prologue* opens by sustaining the gender politics of the *Melibee* through the Host's characterization

of his wife as an antitype of Prudence. "Goodelief, my wyf," according to
Herry Bailey, is a vigorous advocate of domestic violence:

> "By Goddes bones, whan I bete my knaves,
> She bryngeth me forth the grete clobbed staves,
> And crieth, 'Slee the dogges everichoon,
> And brek hem, bothe bak and every boon!'" (7.1897–90)

Goodelief's wrath pursues Herry into the public sphere: he must "out at
dore" to avenge his wife for putative insults in church; he is fearful of slaying
"som neighbor." He is "perilous with knyf in honde": yet he fears his wife,
who is "byg in armes." Compared to her, he is (in her words) a "false coward,"
"a milksop," "a coward ape"; Goodelief should take his knife, and he should
take her distaf "and go spynne!" (7.1901–21). And having told us all this, the
Host summarily dismisses it and turns to the Monk:

> "But lat us passe awey fro this mateere.
>   "My lord, the Monk," quod he, "be myrie of cheere,
> For ye shul telle a tale . . ." (7.1923–25)

The Host continues to address the Monk, then gaze upon him, for some
41 lines. First he concentrates upon the Monk's putative name and title:
"my lord," "myn owene lord," "my lord daun John," "daun Thomas," "daun
Albon" (7.1924–30). Next he wonders about his rank and function at the
monastery before deciding that he must be "a maister" and "a governour"
(7.1938–40). All this remains speculative: the Host is not so much interested
in establishing the Monk's actual name, rank, and title as he is in exploring
his own fantasies. Such fantasies soon turn physical as the Host notices the
Monk's "ful fair skyn," his "brawnes and bones," his "wel farynge" personhood. Physical observation leads to sexual speculation: this Monk would have
made "a tredefowel aright" (an "excellent copulator of fowls") [45] since he is
evidently possessed of exceptional sexual powers:

> "Haddestow as greet a leeve as thou has myght
> To parfourne al thy lust in engendrure,
> Thou haddest bigeten ful many a creature." (7.1946–48)

Herry Bailey imagines the Monk to be a strong man and a virile man:
a man, in short, who might command the physical and sexual potency to
stand up to, stay indoors with, Goodelief, his wife. [46] The "tredynge" of ordinary husbands like himself, to Herry's mind, is "fieble"; compared to the
Monk, laymen are "shrympes." Such fantasies are of particular significance for
the associational polity of the pilgrimage because the Host is its designated
"governour" (1.813). As we observed in Chapter 2, the Host was prone to take
an overly masterful view of his own importance in the process of incorporating the pilgrim body: described as one who "of manhod . . . lakkede right
naught" (1.756), Herry initially conceived his task as enforcing "assent" to

"my juggement" (1.777–78). His tendency to confuse the visceral reactions of his own body with the interests of the corporate body he supposedly governs poses dangers for the *compagnye* throughout the *Tales*. In Fragment 6, for example, when the *Physician's Tale* brings him to the brink of cardiac arrest ("cardynacle," 6.313), he turns in desperation to "thou beel amy," the Pardoner, desperate for some "myrthe or japes" to restore him (his body) to health. Similarly, in Fragment 7, the narrative leaves him in a state that calls for immediate treatment. Forced to contemplate his own life ("This is my life," 7.1913), Herry is overcome by a sense of sexual and marital, hence social, failure. And so he delivers himself into the hands of a strong man, a "maister" or "governour"—or rather, to his own fantasy of a virile man, since the Monk has yet to speak.

When the Monk does speak, of course, he disappoints. The Host feels bound to depose him (in some manuscripts), or to help with the deposition (in others).[47] Neither the Monk (whom the Host considers more than a man) nor the Pardoner (less than a man) can sustain the saving fantasies conceived by the Host at moments of personal crisis. Their repudiation, which itself repudiates a momentary blurring of homosocial/homosexual boundaries, promises a return to stable social/sexual order.[48] But the man making these judgments—Herry Bailey—can himself hardly be considered the model of an efficacious masculine heterosexuality. Unable to establish peaceable relations within his own domestic sphere, he rushes into the public domain, "perilous"—like the enraged male householder on Bosch's table-top—"with knyf in honde" (7.1919; see plate 6). And yet this is the self-nominated *governour* of Chaucer's corporate, associational body of storytellers. It is not surprising that the society evoked by such storytelling seems often so violent and confused. The men and metaphors selected to describe and regulate it are driven by a masculine heterosexuality that projects violence and confusion wherever it looks.

Male-dominated associational polity is notoriously vulnerable to fantasies about strong and masterful men. The stresses, strains, and conflicts of communal life may prove so intolerable that the promise of turning all responsibility over to a single *governour* becomes impossible to resist. Such was the experience of Florence in 1343 (as narrated by Book 9 of Boccaccio's *De casibus* and by numerous variant accounts in Florentine historiography). The surrender of a body politic to a single masculine *maister* is inevitably experienced, at least in part, sexually. It follows, then, that the failure of such a ruler is typically expressed in sexual terms: sexual fantasy is followed by sexual disappointment. In Boccaccio's account, the Duke of Athens rapes, pillages, seduces. All this depends not on historical evidence but on the playing out of a metaphor of sexual seduction that caused Florence to yield herself in the first place.

The failure of Chaucer's Monk is not one of virility. His seed, his supply of new *vires*, seems inexhaustible. One wonders, with Helen Cooper, "if the Monk need stop when his hundred is up."[49] And yet his narrating proves barren: its "substance" cannot take root because, as the Host observes, it affords no pleasure, "no desport ne game." The excess of masculinity ascribed to the Monk is seen, finally, to issue in a solitary and repetitive narration that makes no concessions to group pleasure and heterogeneity and hence, according to the Host, "anoyeth al this compaignie" (7.2789). Critics have noted that the Monk (unlike Chaucer the pilgrim) refuses the offer of a second chance at narrating when his first proves unsatisfactory.[50] Several have argued that the Monk has narrated himself into a state of terminal *acedia*,[51] what we might term depression or boredom: the state Boccaccio has reduced himself to by Book 8 of his massive *De casibus*. Boccaccio, we have noted, is driven back to work only by the appearance of Petrarch, his contemporary *maestro* or *maister*. Petrarch spurs his pupil to strive for future fame by writing of the ancients. But he fails to imbue Boccaccio with much sense of the present utility of his work, its relevance within his immediate political circumstances. Boccaccio, like Chaucer's Monk, remains a solitary figure as he returns to his desk. He has a host of people to write about, but no one to talk to. His work will not discover an immediate political purpose and context until the arrival of Dante, his fellow Florentine, in the final book.

Boccaccio's *De casibus* offers both imitation and critique of its Petrarchan model, the *De viris illustribus*. Chaucer follows Boccaccio in concentrating on the fall, rather than on the lives, of great men; and he seems similarly concerned to interrogate the vertical space that sets *vires illustres* apart from, or over, the rest of humanity. Adam, his first human exemplum, falls

> out of hys hye prosperitee
> To labour, and to helle, and to meschaunce.   (7.2013–14)

The fall of Adam, the necessary or foundational moment of human history, entails the beginning of "labour": that is, what most of the pilgrims do and how they are defined. Since the fall of Adam cannot be reversed without denying the necessity of the Incarnation, it seems difficult to deny labor as a necessary aspect of the human condition. Those who forget the necessity of labor seem fated to return to it: in the very next narrative, Sampson falls from the estate of "almyghty champioun" (7.2023) to that of miller: "they made hym at the queerne grynde" (7.2074). Those who presume to raise themselves too high find that vertical separation from human society soon turns to horizontal distance. Balthasar

> was out cast of mannes compaignye;
> With asses was his habitacioun.   (7.2215–16)

The values of "compaignye" remain normative throughout this *Tale*; the most vividly imagined falls in estate are played out on a horizontal plane.

Nero, for example, runs out of doors on hearing the noise of popular rebellion to find himself

> Allone, and ther he wende han been allied
> He knokked faste, and ay the moore he cried
> The fastere shette they the dores alle.   (7.2530–32)

Nero finally seeks the company of "chirles two," sitting by a fire in a garden, and begs them to kill and decapitate him. But even this last-ditch attempt at human association, it seems, is too much to ask; Nero is forced to kill himself ("Hymself he slow," 7.2549). Similarly, the concluding moralization of "Balthasar" insists that loss of "lordshipe" is most keenly felt through the losing of "freendes, bothe moore and lesse" (7.2243). Chaucer's Monk, who remains strangely detached from the "compaignye" he rides with, makes no "freendes" through his storytelling. His failure enacts something of a mimetic fallacy: in telling of the fall of *viri illustres*, this physically "myghty" and putatively virile Monk reenacts their isolation from human "compaignye" through the monotony of his narrating, and so becomes doomed to repeat their fate. He is finally brought down by an alliance of burgess and knight (a classic revolutionary combination). He will not speak again.

The grounds for repudiation of the Monk are evidently both political and stylistic, but to what extent does this represent a rejection of Italian-inspired humanism *tout court*? In struggling with this question, Renate Haas wishes to suggest that Chaucer is offering "ingenious criticism" of certain aspects of Italian humanism. But her Monk never quite becomes a fully-fledged humanist. He is, successively, a "small-scale humanist"; a "would-be humanist"; a "sham humanist"; a "mini-humanist." [52] The narratives he tells, I have argued, point to the logic of his own fall as a narrator. But any possibility of his coming to resemble, even for an instant, a humanist without adjectival qualification is always already defeated by the most basic condition of his tale-telling: speaking in the vernacular to the kind of mixed and socially heterogeneous group that "my maister Petrak" would avoid at all costs.

As in the *Clerk's Tale*, Chaucer takes pains to represent the *Monk's Tale* as a text caught moving from Latin into the vernacular. The Latin title, the unusual *ababbcbc* verse form, the talk of feet and *exametron*, the lengthy periods that often run on for half a stanza or more, the references to putative sources such as Lucan and Suetonius—all these suggest that something complex and learned is being attempted. And yet the poem's diction often seems at odds with its cultural pretensions, or with the lofty register of humanist Latin. The account of Hercules, for example, begins convincingly enough in classicizing, fame-hungry style:

> Of Hercules, the sovereyn conquerour,
> Syngen his werkes laude and heigh renoun.   (7.2095–96)

But just three stanzas later, Latinate register dips unmistakably into romance formula:

> A lemman hadde this noble champioun,
> That highte Dianira, fressh as May.   (7.2119–20)

The life of Julius Caesar, which Petrarch developed as the book-length jewel of his *De viris* project, is disposed of by Chaucer in just six stanzas. Following an abbreviated account of Caesar's "chivalrie" and "knyghthod," Chaucer has him end his life thoughtfully by covering up his private parts as he lies dying on the Capitol floor (7.2671–726).[53] Such treatment has more in common with the narrative technique of Chaucer's pilgrim nuns, or with the cultural level of the average parish guild, than with any humanist *cenacolo*. And yet even such attempts to approximate the diction and exemplary concerns of popular vernacular narrative cannot ingratiate this *de casibus* sequence with the pilgrim *compagnye*. The *Monk's Tale* falls, or moves uncertainly, between its attempt to develop and sustain an elevated "heigh style" that approximates humanist Latin and the pull of a native vernacular.

Pressuring the Present: Chaucer's "Modern Instances"

In attempting to translate humanist Latin to the understanding of an English-speaking pilgrim *compagnye*, the *Monk's Tale* runs counter to the cultural project of the Petrarchan *De viris*. Rather than constructing narratives of antiquity that stabilize the past as a secure point of reference for a troubled present, Chaucer translates the past into the vernacular, the fluid and unstable idiom of the here and now. This tendency to dwell upon the making and undoing of history in the present moment is exemplified by Chaucer's most significant departure from the Petrarchan model: his decision, following Boccaccio, to add "modern instances" to his ancient, biblical, and classical *exempla*. There are four of these. The longest of them, "De Hugelino Comite de Pize," is imitated from the *Commedia* (with a few hints from Boccaccio)[54] and ends by pointing to Dante:

> Whoso wol here it in a lenger wise,
> Redeth the grete poete of Ytaille,
> That highte Dant, for he kan al devyse
> Fro poynt to point; nat o word wol he faille.   (7.2458–61)

With this citation, the *Monk's Tale* offers a precise mirroring of Boccaccio's *De casibus*: first we have the appearance of Petrarch, associated with figures from antiquity; then Dante appears, associated with figures from more recent times (who continue to exert immediate influence on the present). Boccaccio's "modern instances," we have noted, appear midway through the final book of the *De casibus* and are sustained to the end. Most Chaucer editors

since Tyrwhitt have placed Chaucer's "modern instances" after "Cenobia" and
before "Nero": but the most authoritative Chaucer manuscripts, including
Ellesmere and Hengwrt, have them at the end.[55] Editors and commentators
generally appeal to aesthetic criteria when defending this shift. The talk of
"tragediës" at the end of the "Croesus" is said to bring us full circle, to the
Monk's opening remarks on this topic. This is a somewhat problematic argument, of course, since the *Tale* is about to be interrupted ("Hoo! . . . namoore
of this!"). It is difficult to interrupt a completed tale.

Rather than rehearsing arguments for and against the medial or final
position of the *Monk's Tale*'s "modern instances," arguments that tend to pit
manuscript authority against appeals to aesthetics, we might consider what is
at stake in such debates.[56] My argument will be that the decision to include
"modern instances," to write an open-ended *de casibus* history, entails endless
textual destabilization. "Ugolino" is something of an exception: this "Comite
de Pize," dead for a century, never exerted much influence in England. But
the inclusion of "Ugolino," always *the* Dantean signature piece for English
poets,[57] allows Chaucer to align himself both with Dante and with Boccaccio's turn to the modern, for Dante is the great *maestro* in exploring the effects
of recently completed lives on contemporary history. Chaucer's "Ugolino"
is quite long (seven stanzas): his audience requires considerable background
knowledge, since this "Roger" was not a household name. His other "modern instances"—Peter of Spain, Peter of Cyprus, and Bernabò Visconti—are
short. But so are "Lucifer" and "Adam": some characters need little introduction; some names are more suggestive than others. Bernabò and the two Peters
were remembered as colorful and evocative figures in royal, Bohemian, and
Lancastrian circles. Their political ambitions frequently crossed and intersected English aspirations; their sudden and violent demise, rendered with
such brevity by Chaucer's Monk, was bound to prove more difficult to assimilate than the oft-chronicled deaths of Sampson and Hercules.

The story of King Pedro of Castile and Leon, "worthy Petro, glorie of
Spayne" (7.2375), has all the makings of a great *de casibus* narrative: a famous
victory in alliance with the Black Prince at Nàjera in 1367, acclaimed as a triumph greater than that of Crécy or Poitiers;[58] a squalid death two years later
at the hands of a bastard half-brother, Enrique da Trastamare. But Chaucer
confines "Petro" to just two stanzas, one essaying the kind of wordplay on
names and chivalric symbols ("Mauny" becomes "mau ni," or "wicked nest,"
7.2386) perfected by Dante and the other rehearsing brotherly betrayal, a
perennial Chaucerian theme:

> O noble, O worthy Petro, glorie of Spayne,
> Whom Fortune heeld so hye in magestee,
> Wel oghten men thy pitous deeth complayne!
> Thy bastard brother made the to flee.   (7.2375–78) [59]

Chaucer may have opted for brief treatment of his "modern instances" on the assumption that his courtly audience could fill in the details. But brevity was also sound policy where contemporary politics were concerned; last year's enemy may become next year's ally. It suited Chaucer, when he first wrote these stanzas, to speak of "worthy Petro" and hence ignore his more familiar epithet, "the Cruel," an appellation earned for reputedly poisoning both his wife and his father's mistress.[60] "Petro" was still to be counted "worthy" in 1371, two years after his death, when John of Gaunt married his daughter Constance; Gaunt henceforth styled himself "Roy de Castille et de Leon Duc de Lancastre" in all documents until 1388.[61] On July 9, 1386, Gaunt set sail for Castille with his wife, daughters, and 7,000 men. On September 17 his daughter by Constance, Catherine or Catalina, reconciled hostile factions by marrying the grandson of Enrique of Trastamare, the "bastard brother" who had murdered Pedro.[62] Since Gaunt based claims to Castilian territories on this union, it must have seemed unwise to a poet like Chaucer, who valued his Lancastrian connections, to proclaim the illegitimacy of Don Enrique's lineage.[63] And so, in an important group of manuscripts (that includes Hengwrt and Ellesmere) we find the Monk's original line "Thy bastard brother made the to flee" rewritten as: "Out of thy land thy brother made thee flee" (7.2378).[64]

Chaucer's interest in the historical events associated with the "Peter of Spain" stanzas is strikingly personal. He had been dispatched to Spain in 1366 on a diplomatic mission that may have included direct dealings with Pedro; his wife, Philippa, certainly spent time in the household of the Duchess Constance in the early 1380s; and his son Thomas most probably sailed from Plymouth with Gaunt and entourage in 1386.[65] Chaucer was well placed, then, to see the fall of Pedro as part of greater and longer-lasting cycles of historical tragedy: the premature death of the Black Prince;[66] the destructive potential (for Spain, as later for Italy) of free-floating mercenary troops left hungry for work during lulls in the Hundred Years' War; the disastrous consequences, for the Iberian peninsula, of being dragged into the Anglo-French conflict.[67] The meaning and consequences of Pedro's assassination in 1369 soon became a hot issue for Spanish historiographers; his fortunes were to rise and fall until his final rehabilitation by Queen Isabella I (1451–1504) and King Philip II (1527–98).[68]

The fall of Chaucer's second "worthy Petro," Peter of Cyprus, was even more poignant to the English court in that it evoked the memory of a single brilliant decade, the 1360s. Pierre de Lusignan, scion of the family dynasty from Poitou in western France that had colonized and controlled the indigenous Greek population of Cyprus since the 1190s, made a stirring impression on his visit to England in 1363.[69] Pierre was embarked on an extensive tour of central and western Europe in that year, seeking financial aid and military assistance for a new Crusade; numerous English knights and men-at-arms joined his cause. In 1365 Pierre captured Alexandria, an event hailed by Petrarch as "magnum opus et memorabile" (and by Terry Jones as "a pointless piece of vandalism").[70] In 1369, just four years after this world-renowned conquest, Pierre was murdered, as Chaucer's Monk tells us, by "his owene liges" (7.2394). Pierre's vassals were evidently exasperated by crippling war taxes, by having foreign troops and nobles on Cypriot soil, and by the adverse effect that the sack of Alexandria had on trade.[71] Chaucer, supposing that the murderers were motivated by "envie" of "chivalrie," condemns the murderers and hence aligns himself with Machaut, Froissart, Christine de Pisan, and Philippe de Mézières.[72] Philippe, who served as chancellor of Cyprus from 1360 until 1369, kept Pierre's memory bright by holding him up as the model Christian campaigner for his new crusading society, the Order of the Passion of Jesus Christ. This Order attracted many English adherents, including (by 1396) the Despenser brothers, the earls of Huntingdon and Rutland, the dukes of York and Gloucester, John of Gaunt, and Sir Lewis Clifford (one of Chaucer's closest friends).[73] The exemplary and monitory poignancy of Pierre's fall, *de casibus* style, is preserved by the 1384 *Ordo*, now Bodleian Library, Oxford MS Ashmole 813: "Les trés vaillant et en puissance de subiiees petit Roy de cypre et de Jherusalem . . ." ("The very valiant although weak in the power of his subjects king of Cyprus and Jerusalem . . .").[74]

The impression that Peter of Cyprus was a posthumous name to conjure with is reinforced by Chaucer's *General Prologue*, where the Knight is said to have fought "at Lyeys" and "Satalye" (1.58) and to have been "At Alisaundre . . . whan it was wonne" (1.51). The fact that the Knight was present at three of Pierre's campaigns leads Muriel Bowden to the very brink of suggesting that he (somehow) *is* Peter of Cyprus.[75] Donald Fry conjectures that the Knight was so upset by hearing "the tragedy of Pedro of Cyprus, his old commander" that he felt compelled to interrupt the Monk.[76] This seems somewhat fanciful, although it is worth noting that Chaucer does suggest some degree of social kinship between the Knight and the two "worthy" Peters by insisting on that same adjective: the *General Prologue* Knight is "a worthy man"; "worthy . . . in his lordes werre"; "honoured for his worthynesse"; "ilke worthy knyght"; "worthy" (1.43, 47, 50, 64, 68). The possibility that the fall of "worthy" Peters might somehow, for whatever reason, precipitate the Knight's interruption (and so end the *Tale*) again suggests the destabilizing effect of intercalating "modern instances" with ancient tragedies.

Besides a reputation for "chivalrie," there is another aspect of Peter of Cyprus that might have commended him to Chaucer, namely, his reputation as an artistic patron. The Lusignan dynasty had a long tradition of artistic patronage. Aquinas composed a *De regimine principum* (c. 1255) in honor of Hugh III (ruled 1267–84); Hugh IV (1324–59), Pierre's father, was the dedicatee both of a treatise on kingship by the Byzantine scholar Theodou-

los Magistros and of Boccaccio's celebrated *Genealogia deorum gentilium*.[77]
Froissart, in *Le joli Buisson de Jonece*, acknowledges "bienfés" received from
Pierre, "De Cyppre le noble roi."[78] But the most extensive and heartfelt compliments to Pierre were paid by Chaucer's first poetic mentor, Guillaume de
Machaut. James I. Wimsatt has convincingly demonstrated how the tradition
of *marguerite* poems (that leads directly to Chaucer's worship of the "dayesye"
in the *Prologue* to the *Legend of Good Women*) originates in Machaut's warm
regard for Peter of Cyprus.[79] Pierre's devotion to the *marguerite* represented
both good policy (Cyprus was particularly rich in pearls) and near-comical
obsession: the king dressed in pearls, wore a pearly crown, built a pleasure-
house called "Marguerite," and had both a daughter and a "wonderful mule"
named Marguerita.[80] In his sixth complaint, Machaut made the association
of patron and symbol part of his poetic fabric: the initial letters of the first
stanza spell out "MARGUERITE/PIERRE."[81]

Machaut's most extraordinary act of literary homage to Pierre was not
begun until after the king's sudden fall in 1369. News of Pierre's death moved
Machaut to write his *Prise d'Alixandre*, an account of Pierre's life in some
8,977 lines of verse.[82] The French poet elected, once again, to acknowledge
his devotion to Pierre by building his name into the fabric of the poem. This
time, however, he took things further by merging or marrying Pierre's name
with his own in an anagram:

> ADIEU MA VRAIE DAME CHIERE;
> POUR LE MILLEUR TEMPS GARDE CHIER.

Unscrambled, the anagram simply puts the two men side by side without further comment: "Guillaume de Machaut; Pierre roi de Chipre et de
Jherusalem."[83]

Winthrop Wetherbee has noticed that the *Monk's Tale* takes a particular
interest in the difficult predicament of *litterati* who are forced to serve self-
willed, irascible, or pathological masters.[84] Men and women of letters may be
destroyed by their patrons (as Nero slew Seneca); they may be dragged down
when their patrons take a *de casibus*–style fall. Machaut, however, offers something rather different by willingly identifying himself with a man who has
already fallen. This is a moving gesture. Clearly aware of Pierre's defects (he
critiques his tyrannical tendencies),[85] Machaut devotes several years of his life
and almost nine thousand lines to creating a "life," and hence an afterlife, for
his friend and patron. The remarkable precedent of the *Prise*, a work Chaucer
must have known,[86] makes the skeletal brevity of the *Monk's Tale* all the more
poignant:

> *De Petro Rege de Cipro*
> O worthy Petro, kyng of Cipre, also,
> That Alisandre wan by heigh maistrie,

Ful many an hethen wroghtestow ful wo,
Of which thyne owene liges hadde envie,
And for no thyng but for thy chivalrie
They in thy bed han slayn thee by the morwe.
Thus kan Fortune hir wheel governe and gye,
And out of joye brynge men to sorwe.   (7.2391–98)

Chaucer may have admired Machaut's *Prise*, but he here turns his back on it in decisive fashion: for, as Angela Dzelzainis has argued, "there is no suggestion in the *Prise* of a mechanistic principle at work which governs the rise and fall of princes."[87] It has been suggested that Chaucer may have drawn his account of Pierre de Lusignan from the "modern instances" in Christine de Pisan's *Livre de la Mutacion de Fortune*, a suggestion made the more intriguing by the fact that she, like Chaucer's Monk, juxtaposes accounts of the two Peters, he of Cyprus (23,301–42) and he of Spain (23,343–52).[88] This theory falls with the unfortunate consideration that Christine did not get to work on her *Livre* until late in 1400 (when Chaucer was dead and buried).[89] Nonetheless, the rapidity with which Christine turns from triumphs over the pagan to domestic "envie" and betrayal to the fatal movement of Fortune is remarkably congruent with Chaucer:

Les Sarrazins, que trop heoit,
Moult dommaga, tant qu'il vesqui;
Mais la tres faulse Envie, qui
Ot surpris mesmes son lignage,
Le fit mourir (Ce fu dommage!)
Car, de sa main, son propre frere
L'occist. Ainssy, fortune amere
Luy nuissi, quant bien hault l'ot mis;
Ainssi le fait a ses amis!   (23,334–42)

The Saracens, whom he greatly hated,
he greatly injured and so conquered;
but the very false Envy, who
had overwhelmed even his own lineage,
made him die (that was a pity!)
for, by his own hand, his own brother
killed him. Thus bitter Fortune
brought him down, having set him high;
Thus does she treat her friends!

Christine de Pisan, like Chaucer's Monk, feeds Peter of Cyprus into the meatgrinder of *de casibus*-style history.[90] Christine was extraordinarily well connected across Europe: she would have known as much as Chaucer did about the brilliant rise and sudden fall of Pierre de Lusignan. *De casibus* history, particularly when applied seriatim to "modern instances," is not designed to give a life its full measure of recognition. It is intent, rather, on reiterating the fatal gesture that brought that life suddenly to an end. Its affective power is achieved, through what it assumes in but conceals from its audience: familiarity, extending to intimate acquaintance, with the "myghty man" who is wheeled in only to be brought down. The Knight's cry of "Hoo!" and his plea for "namoore of this" testifies to the potential of the genre's affective power as well as to its remorseless monotony.

News Just In: The Fall of Bernabò

Chaucer's single stanza on Bernabò Visconti, the most notorious tyrant of his time, pushes the *Monk's Tale* closer to the present and, in so doing, further destabilizes the text while suggesting its open-endedness. Bernabò Visconti died late in 1385, more than sixteen years after the two Peters. The death of Bernabò evidently spurred Chaucer to supplement and revise (or perhaps even to initiate) his "modern instances." Some manuscripts, we have noted, have them at the end; some locate them in the middle, between "Cenobia" and "Nero." To complicate matters further, one manuscript has all four "modern instances" in both final and medial positions; another features all four in medial position and repeats the really modern "modern instances" (the two Peters and Bernabò) at the end (after line 3956).[91] Chaucer's decision to have the Knight (rather than the Host) interrupt the Monk may have come at the same revisionary moment. But we cannot really know: despite the ingenious schemata devised by Manly, Rickert, and Fry, we must recognize (with Ralph Hanna III) that the placement of the "modern instances" may owe more to a plurality of scribes than it does to a single authorial intent.[92]

The very complexity of the schemes adduced to explain Chaucer's composing and revising of the *Monk's Tale*[93] would seem to attest to the destabilizing influence of the "modern instances." The Bernabò stanza, as the most modern of the modern, takes this principle further: it *seems* imperfectly digested into the *de casibus* format. Haldeen Braddy noted that this stanza, unlike the others, "lacks formal reference to the moral concerning Fortune." To Kittredge the question "Why sholde I nat thyn infortune *account*?" (7.2401; italics mine) seemed "eminently suggestive of an addition."[94] The stanza seems caught between the first flush of *tidynges* and the fully digested accounting of formal narrative. Kittredge suggests that Chaucer was moved to "dash off his vigorous stanza in the margin of his own copy of the *Tragedies*" just as soon as he heard of Bernabò's demise.[95] This is plausible, if not provable, but the mimetic *effect* of belated composition is certainly a distinctive feature of the stanza; like the alchemical Canon and his Yeoman, it appears to scrape into the frame of the narrative at the very last minute. Bernabò, the greatest tyrant of the age, has recently died (we know not "why ne how," 7.2406). What are we (the court, the king) to make of this? Kittredge proposes that news of Bernabò's fall was brought to Westminster in January 1386 by an unnamed "armiger," a member of Sir John Hawkwood's company.[96] Hawkwood was one of Bernabò's numerous sons-in-law; he and his followers would certainly have taken a close interest in his fortunes. But the connections between the Visconti and the English court (especially Henry of Derby)[97] were so numerous that it is not necessary to try to pin down a single source of *tidynges*. Bernabò's daughter Caterina had been offered in marriage to Richard II; his niece Violanta had actually married (and soon after buried) Chaucer's first patron, Lionel, duke of Clarence. And Chaucer himself, of course, had direct personal experience of Lombardy and the tyrants who ruled there. His earliest images of Lombardy were mediated by geographic distance and by various forms of political, literary, and cultural mythmaking. In 1378, however, Chaucer had been able to judge Lombard polity for himself when sent "ad partes . . . Lumbardie versus Barnabo dominum de Mellan,"[98] briefed to seek the assistance of Bernabò and Hawkwood in England's war with France.[99] But this opportunity did not mean that Chaucer was finally able to separate the Bernabò of fiction and legend from the "truth" of a historical personage. What he experienced in Lombardy was the cultivation of fiction and legend as an instrument of state.

Before the Fall: Tyrannical Legend as an Instrument of State

Bernabò's political position was exceptionally strong at the time of Chaucer's visit to Milan. His brother Galeazzo died at Pavia on August 4; Galeazzo's successor, Gian Galeazzo, was only 27 years old and had an undistinguished track record as politician and soldier.[100] Bernabò, it seemed, was set fair to unify the Visconti state under his personal authority. This process of making himself the sole and absolute embodiment of power within his own expanding territories had been underway for many years. So too had been the process of finding dramatic forms of representation for this incipient absolutism. In 1360, for example, Bernabò required all the citizens of Parma, from all social classes, to kneel in the street and render homage to him as he rode through the city; failure to comply brought capital punishment.[101] In 1369, an archbishop who refused to follow Bernabò's orders to ordain a certain monk was forced to kneel at Bernabò's feet and endure a pointed lecture, or interrogation:

Don't you know, moron, that I am Pope and Emperor and Lord in all my territories? And that not even God can do what he likes in my territories—nor do I intend him to be doing anything.[102]

This anecdote, which is preserved as part of an attack on Bernabò by Pope Urban V, recalls a *novella* by the Florentine Franco Sacchetti that confirms Bernabò's determination to command both sacred and secular authorities. In this *novella*, the first of six in the *Trecentonovelle* featuring Bernabò as protagonist, Bernabò finds a miller whom he considers more learned than an abbot he is interrogating. He promptly decrees that they should exchange jobs: the miller becomes an abbot, and the abbot a miller. This fictional abbot had first attracted Bernabò's attention, and aroused his displeasure, by neglecting to feed two of his hunting dogs adequately.[103] The passion of the historical Bernabò for hunting was legendary. In 1372, having conquered Reggio, Bernabò declared that every city official should send him a certain number of well-bred dogs every year. Anyone caught hunting at Reggio in the area Bernabò had reserved to himself would have their eyes put out. Anyone who informed on illegal hunters would be awarded 50 gold florins.[104]

It is, we have noted, impossible to make clear distinctions between the legendary Bernabò of *novella*, poem, and anecdote and the historical figure. Some of the best anecdotes are supplied by official annals, records, and decrees. This blurring of the historical and the imaginary to create a figure of terrifying and enigmatic potency was an essential element of Bernabò's statecraft. If all authority were to reside in one person, that person would need to be larger than life and omnipresent: present through decrees, *novelle*, and images, if absent in person. The most famous such image of Bernabò is the equestrian statue by Bonino da Campione, now in the Castello Sforzesco at Milan, that once stood in the Milanese church of San Giovanni in Conca (plate 9).[105] This is generally described as a funeral monument, but the statue was in place long before Bernabò's death in 1385. The chronicler Pietro Azario, who had completed his *Liber gestorum in Lombardia* by 1364, was unnerved to discover that Bernabò had had this image of himself—armed, helmeted, and mounted on a warhorse—placed on the church's main altar.[106] A contemporary Frenchman, visiting Milan, recoiled with shock on seeing this same "abominable idol" surmounting the altar of a church.[107] His reaction can be fully understood not by viewing photographs of the statue but by standing beneath it. Looking up from the ground, little can be seen of the barbaric figure of Bernabò, standing stiffly in his stirrups as he gazes to the far horizon. The viewer sees more of the virginal female figures of Justice and Fortitude, fashioned on a smaller scale on either side of the horse, and the gigantic equine penis that hangs between them.

This image of a despot and a giant marble penis bestriding a church altar looks forward not only to absolutist polity but to spectacular displays of virility under fascism.[108] Bernabò, however, was interested not just in display, but in progeny as building blocks of statecraft: at one count, he was credited with 36 living children and with 18 women in various stages of pregnancy. His official consort, Regina della Scala, bore him 5 sons and 10 daughters. Legitimate offspring were employed to further the extensive networking of the Visconti through Europe, especially northern Europe: Bernabò's legitimate daughters were married to a duke of Austria, two dukes of Bavaria, a count of Württemberg, a king of Cyprus (son of the *Monk's Tale*'s "worthy Petro"), and to Lionel, duke of Clarence, Chaucer's first master.[109] His daughter Caterina

Plate 9. Bonino da Campione, *Tomb and Equestrian Statue of Bernabò Visconti.*
Castello Sforzesco, Milan.

married his nephew (her cousin) Gian Galeazzo Visconti. Legitimate sons and daughters sometimes shared a complicated wedding day, as on August 12, 1367, when his daughter Taddea married Stephen, son of Duke Stephen of Bavaria, and his son Marco married Isabella, sister of Duke Stephen and daughter of Duke Frederick of Bavaria.[110] Illegitimate daughters married *condottieri* from outside the state, such as Hawkwood, and illegitimate sons became *condottieri* in the service of the state.

For Bernabò, the development of absolutist polity entailed not the denial of the worst excesses traditionally attributed to despots—unbridled sexual appetite, extreme and violent anger, cruelty, willfulness, sudden and arbitrary changes of mind—but the cultivation of them.[111] If all authority was to be derived from the mind and person of the prince, all attention must habitually turn to the prince and away from law, custom, and conventional expectations. This lesson is understood by the first *novella* in a manuscript section entirely devoted to Bernabò stories.[112] In riding between Pavia and Milan, Bernabò comes to a wooden bridge over a river. The bridge is blocked by a peasant and his heavily laden ass. Bernabò's sergeants shout at him: "Turn back, for the Lord is here." The peasant immediately heaves his ass into the river to clear the way and do honor to his lord. Bernabò summons the peasant and asks him to account for his actions. The peasant complies, and Bernabò orders *him* to be thrown into the river. Bernabò explains: it would not have bothered him, he says, if the peasant had behaved like a peasant, but he could not be allowed to boast (*vantare*) of having thrown his ass into the river to honor the lord. "And," the *novella* concludes, "the peasant struggled to drag himself away, half-dead and totally broken in body; his ass he lost."

The performance and report of such violent and arbitrary acts formed part of the long and painful educative process through which *cives* were transformed into *subditi Domini*.[113] Subjects were forbidden to speak of a Guelf or Ghibelline lord, but should speak only of one lord: "ipse dominus vivat."[114] Such relentless insistence upon the term *dominus* did not pass without notice: the humanist Gabrio de' Zamorei observed that "these tyrants no longer wish to be called 'Lord Peter,' 'Lord Martin,' but simply 'the Lord': 'the Lord wishes' and 'the Lord ordains.'"[115] The aim, of course, was to suggest the godlike qualities of the ruler by merging fear of the Lord with fear of the despot. The Visconti were frequently accused of heresy and blasphemy by the pope. In 1371, for example, Bernabò was declared a heretic and made the target of a papal crusade; the whole of Europe was canvassed for money.[116] But the Visconti were anxious to dramatize their own zeal for piety: on June 10, 1378, Gian Galeazzo decreed that blasphemers against the saints should stand naked in a public place and be doused with three buckets of water; those who blasphemed God and the Virgin would lose their tongues.[117] The suggestion, again, is that an act of impiety directed at the godhead will be punished as if it were an insult to the prince.

Insults, threats, and conspiracies against the laws that emanated from the Visconti prince were similarly punished as if they represented a physical assault on the prince's person. The rationale for this has been neatly summarized by Foucault in his survey of the spectacle of torture and public execution staged by the absolutist regimes of Renaissance Europe: "Besides its immediate victim, the crime attacks the sovereign: it attacks him personally, since the law represents the will of the sovereign; it attacks him physically, since the force of the law is the force of the prince."[118] The ensuing "liturgy of punishment" must be seen as "a spectacle not of measure, but of imbalance and excess . . . an emphatic affirmation of power and of its intrinsic superiority" (p. 49). The longest such spectacle of atrocious and terminal torture to be found in *Discipline and Punish* is 18 days (p. 54). Foucault terms this "an infinity of vengeance," but it lasted less than half as long as the infamous "Lenten observance of Galeazzo." (Galeazzo Visconti, we should recall, was Petrarch's principal patron during his years in Visconti service.) The "liturgy of punishment" envisaged by this savage *quaresima* was to last 40 days and 40 nights. This might seem more than any human body could withstand, but the survival of the condemned was ensured by alternating each day of torment with a "day of repose."

According to the chronicler Azario, Galeazzo devised and published his "Lenten observance" by way of terrifying (*perterrere*) prospective traitors.[119] Detailed, day-by-day instructions are laid out in the document Galeazzo sent to his rectors in cities that might anticipate acts of rebellion. Tortures are to be administered little by little ("paulatim"): floggings and repose for the first week, then the drinking of water, vinegar, and slaked lime, then the loosening of limbs on various machines of torture. Dismemberment begins on the twenty-third day with the removal of one eye from the head ("unus oculus de capite"). The second eye is not to be removed: it is important in such spectacles that the victim be able to observe his own physical disintegration.[120] On day 25 the nose is cut off; hands, feet, and testicles are then removed, one at a time; and on day 39 the sexual organ ("membrum") is cut off. Day 40 is a day of repose; the next day the victim is hanged from a cart and then put on a wheel. Azarius follows his long quotation from the document by observing that many people were subjected to this treatment in 1362 and 1363.[121] In a document dated February 1, 1364, Bernabò prescribes a similar but extended course of treatment, with two-day intervals between amputations.[122]

The prison in the castle at Pavia was known as La Lunga Dimora, "the long stay"; Bernabò's infamous Milanese prison was called the Malastalla. Bernabò freed prisoners whenever his wife gave birth. On learning that some prisoners were being released before the appointed time, Bernabò wrote to the *podestà* of Milan instructing him that the prison's custodians were to incur the same penalties as those they had released.[123] The citizens of the conquered commune of Como were informed by a decree inserted into their statutes by

Galeazzo on October 9, 1370, that those who plotted against the state would be suspended by one leg until they were dead, "so that others may be terrified by this example."[124] One political rationale for such a culture of terror was that it promoted social cohesion and equality: all subjects are united in their fear of the lord and by their subjugation to the princely *arbitrium*. This principle is neatly exemplified in a Bernabò story that Pietro Azario folds into his *Liber gestorum* (pp. 143–45).

Bernabò is out hunting one day, and in his furious and headlong pursuit of his quarry he becomes detached from all his noble followers. He wanders through a dark and marshy wood of dead trees until he comes upon a poor, ill-dressed rustic whom he greets with the words "Ave frater." The laborer says he is in dire need of God's aid, because he has been ruined. Bernabò gets down from his horse and asks his *amicus* to explain. The rustic complains of having a devil for a lord ("diabolum pro Domino") who has driven him to ruin through the ruthless expropriation of his wealth. To this "dominus Bernabos" replies: "Certainly such a lord did wrong."

Bernabò and the rustic then negotiate the price to be paid for leading Bernabò out of the wood. The rustic asks for one Milanese groat to recompense his loss of labor; he demands payment in advance, since the officials of the aforesaid devil, his master, are wont to cheat him. Bernabò cuts off one of his silver trappings and hands it to him. He persuades him to climb up onto the horse, arguing that the rustic has eaten so little that his weight is negligible. As they ride along, Bernabò engages him in conversation:

"Brother, you have told me bad things about your Lord. What then is said in your brotherhood of your Lord who is at Milan?"

The rustic replied: "He is spoken of better, since although he may be savage [ferus] he keeps the peace, and if he did not I and other poor men would not dare to enter the remote parts of the dead wood in order to work. And he preserves good justice and that which he promises he holds himself to; this other Lord does just the opposite."

Bernabò continues interrogating the rustic until they emerge from the wood and approach a fortress, where they encounter a huge search party. On discovering the identity of his interlocutor, the rustic is frightened to death ("ad mortem timuit"); he wishes himself dead, and as they enter the fortress he expects to be put to death ("poni in exterminio"). Bernabò laughingly tells his knights and rectors of his adventures with the rustic ("gesta cum rustico"); the terrified rustic is accorded royal treatment. The next day Bernabò commands that he be presented with a groat and promises to fulfill any petition he may care to put. The rustic asks for his life and, on further prompting, for the restoration of his plots of land. Letters are sent to the offending *castellanus*, the rustic regains all his property and lives in peace.

This narrative of a self-revealing dialogue with a mysterious stranger encountered in a deserted place draws from folkloric origins that are also tapped by Chaucer's *Friar's Tale*. Bernabò, like Chaucer's yeoman, is dressed for hunting. Bernabò wears black, and the rustic at first fears that he may be an impure spirit ("spiritus immundus.") This image of Bernabò as a devil, who may be encountered by any of his subjects in any part of his *dominio*, however obscure, is as useful to the purposes of Visconti propaganda as the association between the Visconti lord and the Lord of the Christian religion. Other motifs of Visconti propaganda are active in the tale. Bernabò's cruelty is justified as a necessary instrument of distributive and retributive justice. The lord of Milan is shown to be a powerful ally of the simple laboring man in his struggles with the iniquities of local feudal arrangements. But the most convincing feature of the tale is the abject terror of the *rusticus* before Bernabò: he is evidently more terrified when Bernabò is fêting him in his fortress than he is when speaking to a mysterious, devillike knight in a dark wood.

In the *Liber gestorum in Lombardia* the legend of Bernabò is already well-developed, and Bernabò was to live for more than twenty years after this date. It is not known how much personal contact Chaucer had with Bernabò in 1378. It seems fanciful to imagine, with Donald Howard, the English poet and the Lombard despot achieving some degree of intimacy through shared bookish interests.[125] Chaucer may have dealt exclusively with ministers and notaries and have had no direct contact with Bernabò at all. But Chaucer experienced the legend and power of Bernabò on every street corner, as manifested through anecdotes, statutes, statuary, sites of punishment, ceremony, and display, and above all by the specific configurations assumed by courtiers, administrators, and subjects around the center, visible or invisible, of the princely *arbitrium*.[126] During his visit to Lombardy, in short, Chaucer lived within the ambit of a power more absolute than anything hitherto experienced in England.

After the Fall: Death Rewrites the Legend

On May 6, 1385, Gian Galeazzo Visconti rode into Milan with Iacopo dal Verme and some of his German mercenaries, having apparently persuaded his uncle and father-in-law Bernabò that he wished to pay him a courtesy call en route to a pilgrimage site at Varese. Bernabò was surrounded and imprisoned and was dead and buried by the end of December.[127] His imprisonment and death is recorded by almost every chronicler in Italy, by chroniclers in England and France, by *canterini*, sonneteers, *novellatori*, by Visconti and Florentine propagandists, by religious moralists, and by Chaucer's Monk. The fall of Bernabò was an event so momentous and exemplary for medieval Europe that the "event" itself disperses into heavy-layered determinations of political rationalization, religious moralization, and genre.

The three *cantari* of Milanese (or north Italian) provenance that narrate Bernabò's end (presumably to a large popular audience soon after the event) sacrifice all sense of historical detail or plausibility to the expectations of their genres. Matteo da Milano's 62 *ottave*, preserved within a holograph manuscript of Giovanni Sercambi's *Cronica*, have Bernabò mugging a pious friar who has come to visit him and stealing from the prison in disguise; he is recognized by a small boy and reincarcerated. Matteo does, however, have Bernabò address himself in an *ubi sunt* lament. The other two *cantari* are written almost exclusively within this neo-Boethian theme *de diversitate Fortunae*: each begins with a *vanto*, which exalts the virtues and magnificence of Bernabò; each ends with a *lamento* of his fall, his lost riches and lost honors, and with a confession of his guilt.[128]

An anonymous Florentine chronicler writing at the time of Bernabò's death is quick to assert that Bernabò was punished for his manifold sins by "God, the just avenger." Coluccio Salutati, chancellor of Florence, soon after argued that Gian Galeazzo had acted rightly in deposing a confirmed tyrant like Bernabò.[129] But Goro Dati, who began his account of the years 1380–1405 around 1409, represents Bernabò as a victim of treachery and murder who was nonetheless allowed a decent interval by the will of God to free himself from material possessions and repent and atone for his sins.[130] This shift in emphasis is already evident in the curious sentence with which Sacchetti prefaces the first of his Bernabò *novelle*: "This lord was, in his time, more feared than any other lord; and although he may have been cruel, there was nonetheless in his cruelty a great deal of justice" (4.3). This justification of Bernabò's cruelty as an instrument of justice recalls the words of the rustic in Azario's *Liber gestorum*. But Sacchetti and Dati are interested in commemorating the justice and piety of Bernabò only by way of discrediting the man who displaced him. Once Bernabò is dead, the Visconti threat to Florence is embodied by Gian Galeazzo. According to Dati, Bernabò died in prison not as a fallen tyrant but as a repentant sinner. By murdering his own kin in his lust for earthly power, Gian Galeazzo, in contrast, pledged himself to the devil.[131]

News of Bernabò's death came to Chaucer from out of this complex network of shifting political imperatives. How does Chaucer construct the meaning of this event?

De Barnabo de Lumbardia

> Off Melan grete Barnabo Viscounte,
> God of delit and scourge of Lumbardye,
> Why sholde I nat thyn infortune acounte,
> Sith in estaat thow cloumbe were so hye?
> Thy brother sone, that was thy double allye,
> For he thy nevew was and sone-in-lawe,
> Withinne his prisoun made thee to dye—
> But why ne how noot I that thou were slawe.   (7.2399–406)

Donald Howard argues that "when Chaucer called Bernabò Visconti 'god of delit and scourge of Lombardie' he was not necessarily calling him a tyrant."[132] But that is exactly what he was doing. One of the defining characteristics of tyranny for medieval political thought, we have noted, is the pursuit of pleasurable (*delectabile*) good rather than the cultivation of *bonum commune*.[133] "Scourge" suggests not so much "chastisement or reform"[134] as it does wholesale destruction of the kind practiced by Attila the Hun, *flagellum dei*. And the name of "Lumbardye" is so strongly associated with "tyrannye" elsewhere in Chaucer that throughout the stanza we half-expect it to show up in a rhyming position. There is little in this stanza, then, to further the search for signs of personal regret at the demise of a former acquaintance. Howard's biographism continually prompts him to make neat distinctions between a subjective emotional experience and its public representation (as, in this instance, a *de casibus* stanza). But *de casibus*, like any other ideological construct, is a form through which the world is hermeneutically and emotionally engaged, not a passive receptacle for predigested experience. This point is beautifully exemplified by a letter written by Franco Sacchetti, dated February 10, 1386, which struggles to recapture the experience of a last, face-to-face encounter with a now-fallen Bernabò:

Tanto signore e sí altero tiranno, con tanti geniti, e con tanta potenza e con tante parentele di príncipi e di regi, quanto era il Signore Melanese, in questo anno in un pícciolo punto, come ha perduto lui e tutta sua famiglia, e le famose città che tenea! Certo quand'io mi ricordo come io il vidi poco piú che 'l terzo anno passato, e quanto era nel supremo de la rota, e come è caduto, quasi fuori di me stesso mi trovo.[135]

Such a lord and such a lofty tyrant (with so many offspring, and with such power and with so many princes and kings among his relatives) as was the Lord of Milan has this year, and at one small point in time, lost both his entire family and the famous cities that he held in his grasp! Really, when I recall how I saw him little more than three years ago, and how he was on the very top of the wheel, and how he has fallen, I find myself almost beside myself.

There is a strength of feeling here, typified by the Hoccleve-like phrase "I find myself almost beside myself," that drives Sacchetti to the very limits of expressive possibility. The arresting juxtaposition of "anno" and "piccìolo punto," extensive and fleeting time, see him struggling to articulate the aporetic mystery of *de casibus*. Soon, however, this moment itself passes, swept away by the genre's controlling metaphor. The same figure wheels its way through the Monk's entire *Tale*, and although no formal or apostrophic reference is made to Fortune (as Braddy observes),[136] the third and fourth lines of the Bernabò stanza certainly bend to her metaphoric force field. This stanza, I have argued, conveys the *effect* of being a late arrival, imperfectly digested into the *de casibus* framework. But such is the power of the genre that there is hardly a moment before news of a fall becomes encoded in, experienced through, the genre's terms and metaphoric machinery. It changes the meaning of a life at the very moment of its fall or demise; it lies in wait like a political *memento mori*.

Chaucer, like Sercambi, notes that Bernabò perished through the offices of a "double allye," one who was close to him in blood and marriage. But whereas Sercambi goes on to denounce this murder ("the act was cruel"),[137] Chaucer makes little of it. The theme of domestic and family betrayal among the great has become so commonplace in Chaucer's *de casibus* narratives that denunciation or lament might seem otiose. There is little here, then, to suggest any private or subjective reaction on Chaucer's part to the most spectacular and (excepting the capture of King John by the English) widely remarked fall in postpandemic Europe. His "accounte" of Bernabò ends on a note of indeterminacy that foregrounds personal ignorance of the historical record ("noot I"). But this may itself represent an eloquent commentary on tyranny. In his remorseless effort to magnify and multiply his own bodily image through statute, statuary, and sexual intercourse, Bernabò's great enemy is death. Beyond death, his great equestrian statue becomes a funeral monument (a sarcophagus was soon added) and his name becomes synonymous not with power, but with the fall from power. Chaucer's text denies the uniqueness of Bernabò's physical presence by allocating him just one stanza and then serializing this as just one *de casibus* exemplum among many. His "Bernabò" offers nothing of the Petrarchan promise, so attractive to contemporary despots, to recover and perpetuate the life of great men. His last word to the Lombard tyrant accentuates only his incapacity to prevent the memory of Bernabò from draining away through the cracks of history at the moment of his death: "But why ne how noot I that thou were slawe."

The Fall of Richard II: Before and After

Chaucer's last words on the most famous tyrant of the age are eerily prescient of the thousands of lines waiting to be written on the death of Richard II in 1399. Richard too was to die obscurely. According to one account, he died of grief and starvation on St. Valentine's day; according to another he was clubbed with an ax at mealtime, having, in a fit of rage, stabbed the squire who carved his meat with a table knife. The first account is of Lancastrian provenance and the second is French.[138] Neither of them can be assumed to be accurate, since their interest lies not in recording the facts of history but rather in manufacturing competing narratives of history for their own political ends. The French, like the Florentines in 1385, suddenly change their minds about their worst enemy: the more kingly and peace-loving Richard is made to appear, the more illegitimate and damnable is the pretender who usurps his place. English rescripting of Richard's death is spectacularly intensive in the months and years following Henry's accession, but the process is still playing itself out on the London stage some two centuries later.

The imaginative confusions attendant upon the crucial *de casibus* moment—the "pìcciolo punto" dividing before from after—were to haunt Lancastrian attempts at controling and surviving the fall of Richard II. The Deposition Articles, we have noted, accentuate the scandal of Richard's claim to embody the laws (and by extension the state) in his own physical person.[139] To signal the collapse of such pretensions, the Lancastrians needed to produce and exhibit a dead kingly body (while, through their own governmental regime, demonstrating that the state was alive and well). King Henry IV, while willing to demonstrate the vitality of his state apparatus by persecuting and burning Lollards, was unwilling to countenance the spectacle of a dead king. In 1402 Henry issued a set of special commissions to local gentry, urging them to stop loose talk in taverns and other "congregations" against the new dynasty.[140] Sightings of Richard were nonetheless reported from all over: the rebellious Percys argued for his existence in Cheshire in 1403; the Earl of Northumberland affected to think of him as alive in 1406 (although he had accused Henry of his murder); and as late as 1418, Sir John Oldcastle was to claim that King Richard was alive and well and living in Scotland.[141] The Lancastrians, in short, were unable or unwilling to narrate Richard as a *de casibus*–style fallen prince after 1400. In opening their first parliament of 1399, the new regime was not prepared to countenance Richard as a "myghty man": his rule was actually likened to government by infants and widows.[142] The wheel of Fortune, so to speak, was jammed *at* the "picciolo punto," the mysterious point between before and after. The motion of *de casibus* was held in arrest, and all kinds of strange specters flew from the machinery. Not until Henry V disinterred Richard's body from Langley Abbey and transferred it to Westminster could his ghost be laid and the legend of his life be kept under control.[143]

The *de casibus* history of the *Monk's Tale* foretells something both of the mechanics and the problematics of Richard's fall in 1399. The moment of the fall will become the narrative *telos* of the life, prompting a rewriting of every earlier "accounte." And the need to fix and control the precise circumstances of death, the "why" and the "how" (7.2406), will continue to press upon the Lancastrians until, finally, they produce the body and unite it with its vacant monument; *de casibus* cannot do its work until its princely subject is known and shown to be dead. As it nudges ever closer toward the present, then, *de casibus* narration maintains an increasingly complex, dialectical relation with historical events. It determines to a considerable extent just how the fall of a "myghty man" will be experienced, but it requires other forms of discursive practice in the public realm (public execution, funeral, *tidynges*) to activate the simple and brutal mechanics of its genre.

In reading the *Monk's Tale*, particularly its "modern instances," we seem to experience only the shadow or skeleton of a text. Only through a process of historical recuperation can we recover some sense of its contemporary power to move, persuade, and instruct. And even in striving to achieve this, we grasp that the *Monk's Tale*, like the *Melibee*, changes its meaning with each newly situated reading. How, then, might the *Monk's Tale* have been read, have functioned, in that narrow chronological space between the addition of the last "modern instance" (the fall of Bernabò) and the fall of Richard? The limits of this period (1386–99) exactly coincide with what one historian has designated the "first tyranny" (1386–87) and "second tyranny" (1397–99) of Richard's reign.[144] In this period the Monk's recurrent image of the despot toppled from his lofty and "myghty trone" (2143), desperately seeking the most basic associative kinship (like Nero with the "cherles" in the garden), might well have caused court and country to wonder about Richard II. Richard himself was much preoccupied in this period with the cult and literary record of his great-grandfather, Edward II, who had been deposed, imprisoned, and murdered in 1327.[145] Richard wanted Edward to be recognized as a saint: in 1395 he sent Pope Boniface IX a book of Edward's "miracles" supporting his case for canonization. Richard's championing of Edward suggests an attempt to find religious sanction for behavior that has, in medieval and in modern times,[146] been deemed tyrannical. His alliances and his later rivalries with the Visconti might also suggest a desire to emulate the style and ambitions of the most notorious despots of the age. The *Monk's Tale*'s "modern instances," particularly the fall of Bernabò, might have been deployed as curb or bridle to such overweening ambitions—a book of grim *Realpolitik* to put beside the book of "miracles" ascribed to a deposed king of England.

Viewed from a long historiographical perspective, the *Monk's Tale*, like Boccaccio's *De casibus*, seems skeptical of the notion that any "myghty man" can flourish in "hye estaat" while rejecting "mannes compaignye" (7.2188, 2215), or that he may incorporate the full measure of state power in his own person: if Bernabò Visconti could not survive (the text seems to argue), the chances for an English monarch with tyrannical or absolutist aspirations seem slim indeed. As we have noted, the cruelty and ruthlessness that, for Burckhardt, were the enabling preconditions of the new Renaissance individualism were first exemplified by "tirauntz of Lumbardye."[147] Bernabò Visconti behaved cruelly, ruthlessly, tyrannically; his methods of propagating and dramatizing his own power were often crudely physical. His personal excesses, however, were acted out within and as part of a political framework that showed something of the infrastructural strength of later absolutist regimes.[148] The tyranny of Richard II, on the other hand, unfolded without the supporting context of such an infrastructure. Richard could not stabilize his relations with either the merchant capitalists of London, whose financial support was crucial, or with the magnates who finally deposed him. The tyrannical style he affected in later years was both behind its time and ahead of it, a doubly tragic anachronism.

Lydgate's *Fall of Princes*

Some fifty years after Chaucer's experiment with Boccaccian *de casibus* history, a second attempt was made to introduce the Italian humanist genre into English by Lydgate's *Fall of Princes*. Many of the difficulties and contradictions of Lydgate's massive essay in this genre—36,365 lines, a length that "appals criticism"[149]—are anticipated by the *incipit* from the first leaf of one of its earliest manuscripts:

Here begynneth the book callyd I. Bochas descriuyng the falle of Pryncys pryncessys and othir nobles translatid in to Inglissh bi Iohn Ludgate Monke of the Monastery of seynt Edmundes Bury atte commaundement of the worthi prynce Humfrey duk of Gloucestre begynnyng at Adam & endyng with kyng Iohne take prisonere in Fraunce bi Prynce Edward.[150]

As a monk of Bury St. Edmund's—one of the most powerful Benedictine foundations in Britain—Lydgate may have supposed himself a natural continuator of Chaucer's "myghty man," the Monk (whose "fall of pryncis," 1.249, he evidently took as offering native inspiration). Lydgate acclaims Chaucer as Chaucer's Monk had acclaimed Petrarch: as "my maistir" (1.246, 275, 328, 351). Lydgate's first imaging of his own authorial activity is modestly artisanal: he aligns himself, in his own writerly struggles, with "men off crafft," specifically "potteres" who are forced to break and discard many defective "vesselis" before making a good one (1.8–18). Only when he makes contact with Chaucer, "cheeff poete off Breteyne" (247), does he dare to imagine that poetic "makyng" might be judged "sovereyne," something to command the attention of "al this land" (1.250–51); much as Petrarch, in the estimation of Chaucer's Clerk, had "enlumyned al Ytaille" (4.33). The power of authorly fame to serve and illumine national interest is propounded further as Lydgate goes on to speak, with rare neohumanist enthusiasm,[151] of Seneca, Cicero, Petrarch, and Boccaccio:

> And all these writers, thoruh ther famous renoun,
> Gret worshipe dede vnto ther nacioun.   (2.272–73)

This crucial linkage between the "renoun" of writers and the status or "worshipe" of a nation was one that the Lancastrians had long been willing to exploit (and Lydgate and Hoccleve to exemplify).[152] In Humphrey, duke of Gloucester, Lydgate must have thought that he had found the ideal patron, a great man who would recognize his efforts to maintain contact with continental humanism while writing English in the national interest. Duke Humphrey (who actually wrote in French)[153] has been much celebrated as the first patron of Italian humanist letters in England and as the effective founder, through his gift of books, of the Oxford library that still bears his name.[154] But he was no otherworldly booklover. As the younger brother of Henry V—

and hence Protector of England during the minority of Henry VI—Duke Humphrey, like the Visconti before him and Wolsey after, viewed the discourse of humanism as an instrument of state. Humphrey was never prepared to be the passive recipient of Lydgate's industry. He evidently took an active role in the compositional process by lending books and making suggestions for additions, amendments, and excisions. He also managed to keep Lydgate in a subservient role by being stingy with his *largesse*. In pursuing his patron through the whole length of the *Fall of Princes*, Lydgate becomes ever more exhausted and alienated from his own intellectual labor.[155]

Lydgate plainly falls victim to the contradiction at the heart of his enterprise: that of trying to write of past *viri illustres* while a contemporary "myghty man" wields a pen and scraper at his side. Petrarch writes in a way that contemporary princes find congenial while managing to keep them out of the compositional process; Boccaccio engages the same *signori* in open ideological warfare. Lydgate, however, lets the lunatic-in-chief run his asylum. Rather than functioning as an instrument to curb and dissuade the excesses of the great, Lydgate's *Fall* becomes a kind of general handbook or encyclopaedic advice manual for rulers and governors. Boccaccio's powerful critique of tyranny and apologia for tyrannicide—preserved by Laurent de Premierfait's French prose translation, Lydgate's immediate source—is excised and replaced by a general account of the body politic from John of Salisbury's *Policraticus* (kindly provided by Duke Humphrey's library).[156] Premierfait's condemnation of the mistreatment of agricultural laborers (directed to a patron, the duke of Berry, who had suppressed a peasants' revolt "with barbaric severity")[157] is passed over by Lydgate, who prefers to invent a whole new category of *de casibus* fall: churls, or those "cherlissh of nature" (4.2659), who rise to power but are then thrown down.[158] Lydgate, we should remember, was a "Monk of the Monastery of seynt Edmundes Bury": the institution that, in 1381, had its prior decapitated by a rebel force of, according to the *Anonimalle Chronicle*, "more than ten thousand men."[159]

Lydgate is keen to discourage the notion that the misfortunes of the great might prove gratifying to "lowere peeple." Such falls, he insists, should stand as a warning not just to princes, but to "vicious folk off euery comounte" (1.206–10). And even when the mighty fall, it seems, there is a mightier man in charge: God, who "as a meek father" wields his "yerde of castigacioun" and "can ful faderli chastise" (1.194–97). The impulse to feminize God the Father here (by describing him as "meek" even as he wields his big "yerde") might be taken as half-recognition that He is usurping a woman's place: namely, that of Fortune, the traditional agent of rise and fall in the *de casibus* tradition. Lydgate, who finds ample space for misogynistic digression in the course of his 36,365 lines, comforts princes with the thought that their fall, should it come, will be skillfully managed by someone in their own kingly and masculine image.

Perhaps the most telling indication that Lydgate's *Fall* is dead on arrival as a critique of princely excesses is provided by its "begynnyng at Adam & endyng with kyng Iohne take prisonere in Fraunce bi Prynce Edward." Lydgate begins at the beginning of history but ends in 1356, some eighty years in the past. Unlike Boccaccio (and certain English continuators of the *Fall*), Lydgate (or his patron) decides against putting pressure upon princes and despots by including "modern instances," reminders of great men, like themselves and known to themselves, who have fallen to their ruin. Lydgate makes no advance on Boccaccio's chronology (and by stopping at the capture of King John by the Black Prince manages to end by reminding the British Crown of past triumphs rather than of present shortcomings). It is hardly surprising, then, that Lydgate's *Fall of Princes* should survive complete chiefly in upmarket manuscripts, prestige productions "of the kind that would have been admired rather than read."[160]

Comparison with Lydgate makes it clear that Chaucer's essay in the *de casibus* genre does not offer itself for cooptation by princes or state powers. It belongs where it begins and ends, outside the court and within the mixed *compagnye* of Canterbury pilgrims. (The text may well be read by or to the court, but it comes to them, so to speak, from a distance.) The hierocratic vision that the Monk attempts to impose upon his historical material (and upon the pilgrimage) is decisively rejected, but the disturbing and destabilizing impact of "modern instances" upon the text is fully registered before narration is called to an end. And while that narration was in progress, nudging ever closer to the contemporary interests of the English court, the *Monk's Tale* remained both the dullest and most dynamic of Chaucer's works. Such a master narrative (king, magnates, and householders might have thought) could suddenly extend itself at any moment; could feed itself by writing, and hence taking, their lives.

Fallen Princes and Ruined Texts

Comparison with Lydgate further emphasizes the singularity of Chaucer's decision *not* to press claims for the "renoun" of poets, and the "worshipe" they might bring a "nacioun," even as he engaged with the texts and authorial legends of Italian humanism. The *Monk's Tale* makes no claims for poetry or authorship as an instrument of state. Through his historical experience of Italy (and the consequent experience of writing the *Knight's Tale*) Chaucer grasped the logic of state-sponsored patronage: that the poet taken up by the state would find his *makynge* shaped and constrained by the state's changing needs.[161] Further: the fortunes of state-sponsored poetry follow the fortunes of the state. This last proposition, as we have seen, certainly formed part of Petrarch's calculations. In having himself seduced into the patronage of a "myghty man" at Milan, Petrarch hoped that his work could be conducted in security, free from the political vagaries that beset republics. Later in life Petrarch was keen to establish a library at Venice so that his life's work could be concentrated at one site and preserved by the Venetian republic for scholarly posterity. Shortly after June 1370, however, he had all his books transported to Padua so that he could pursue his scholarly work into old age under the protection of Francesco da Carrara. When he died four years later, Petrarch had effectively invested his hopes for a secure textual afterlife in a despotic rather than a republican polity.

Shortly after Petrarch's death on July 18, 1374, most of his books were seized by agents of the Carrara and removed to the seigneurial palace. Lombardo della Seta, a favored but mediocre pupil of Petrarch's, assumed the role of literary executor; custody of Petrarch's manuscripts (then accounted less valuable than his books) passed to Francescuolo da Brossano, spouse of Petrarch's illegitimate and never-named daughter Francesca. Francescuolo was a man of middling talents who had procured various administrative positions with Petrarch's various despotic patrons. When Petrarch died, the management of his writings became the chief source of cultural and political capital for Lombardo and Francescuolo. While requests for Petrarchan texts rained in from all over Europe—everyone knew, as Chaucer's Oxford Clerk knew, that Petrarch had died "at Padowe" (4.27)—Lombardo wasted valuable time better spent on editorial work on completing the *De viris* (and its abridgment, the *Compendium*) as a gift for his political master. Vital work of transcription was entrusted to copyists judged by Giuseppe Billanovich to be "mediocri e mercenari." [162] Things were muddled still further in 1384 when Francescuolo removed himself and many Petrarchan texts to the freshly conquered city of Treviso; here he took up a bureaucratic post similar to the one he had held under the Visconti at Pavia. Four years later, Padua fell to troops led by the *condottiere* Giacomo dal Verme and Francesco da Carrara was captured at Treviso; Paduan territories were carved up between Venice and the Visconti. Gian Galeazzo, who had recently disposed of Bernabò, looted the library at Padua and dragged Petrarch's books off to Milan. Petrarch's dream of a secure textual afterlife was thus destroyed by the very form of polity he had entrusted it to: a disastrous fulfillment of the kind of *de casibus* fall envisaged by Boccaccio's *De casibus* and (even as it was actually happening) by the *Monk's Tale*.

"Ad Hoc Specialiter Inductus": Witnessing the Fall of Richard II

Shakespeare's account of the fall of Richard II, which sees him rehearsing the literary genre that is about to claim him, finds a striking medieval counterpart in the Lancastrian *Chronicon Adæ de Usk*.[163] Adam, like so many of the writers encountered in this chapter, attempts to see into the dark heart of *de casibus* at the very moment of its activation. But from the first, when he places Richard's fall in relation to that of Arundel in 1397, he is seeing, thinking, and writing *through*, rather than before or outside, the terms of *de casibus*:

On Saint Matthew's Day (September 21), just two years after the beheading of the earl of Arundel, I, the writer of this history, was in the Tower, wherein King Richard was a prisoner, and I was present while he dined, and I marked his mood and bearing, having been taken thither for that very purpose [ad hoc specialiter inductus] by Sir William Beauchamp. And there and then the king discoursed sorrowfully in these words: "My God! a wonderful land is this, and a fickle [mirabilis terra et inconstans]; which hath exiled, slain, destroyed, or ruined so many kings, rulers, and great men, and is ever tainted and toileth with strife and variance and envy"; and then he recounted the histories and names of sufferers from the earliest habitation of the kingdom. Perceiving then the trouble of his mind, and how that none of his own men, nor such as were wont to serve him, but strangers who were but spies upon him, were appointed to his service, and musing on his ancient and wonted glory and on the fickle fortune of the world [de mundi fallaci fortuna], I departed thence much moved at heart. (p. 30; p. 182)

By the very act of narrating *de casibus*, Adam's Richard II convinces readers and onlookers that he is a fallen prince. As such, he feels his native earth move beneath his feet as a "terra . . . inconstans"; he senses himself surrounded not by "familiars" but by spying strangers. Adam himself, of course, is one of these outsiders. He has been brought to the Tower expressly for the purpose ("ad hoc specialiter inductus") of watching, reading, and recording— "explorando"—the manners and gestures of the fallen king. Adam can in no way *meet with* the king, who is already envisioned as a textual entity: the logic of *de casibus*, as exemplified by the flight of friendless Nero in the *Monk's Tale*, requires each "myghty man" to fall alone, without benefit of human *compagnye*. And although Adam can watch and narrate, he cannot interpret, except within the terms already provided by *de casibus* itself: "de mundi fallaci fortuna." The fall of Richard II, then, is written before it happens.[164] The *Monk's Tale*, lying in wait like a funeral monument, furnishes script and stage directions; all Adam of Usk need do is fill in the *ubi* and *quando*, the where and when, before departing thence, "much moved at heart."

Chapter 12

"If That Thou Live":
Legends and Lives of Good Women

Chaucer's *Legend of Good Women*, particularly its *Prologue*, shares the *Monk's Tale*'s interest in the dynamics of kingship and despotism but locates itself, in *de casibus* terms, before the fall. And, like the *Monk's Tale*, the *Legend* (while grounded in the poetic traditions of Machaut, Froissart, and Deschamps) follows Italian humanist precedents in collecting and framing ancient and classical lives. Boccaccio's *De mulieribus claris* is Chaucer's most obvious inspiration here, although he may also have heard of Petrarch's short treatise *de laudibus feminarum*, dedicated to an empress, Anne of Bohemia (the woman after whom the English queen, wife of Richard II, was named). In a landscape suggestive of Edenic (if not prelapsarian) natural beauty, the *Prologue* to the *Legend* conducts an extended exploration of absolutist poetics. By this I mean both the cultural forms deployed by an all-powerful figure to dramatize his own authority and the strategies developed by a poet to survive (as a poet, or at all) in such circumstances.

These two aspects of "absolutist poetics" come together some three hundred lines into the *Prologue*, when Chaucer, seemingly unaware that a court structure has suddenly configured itself in his presence, is called to account by a figure more "myghty" than any in his *Monk's Tale*. This "myghty god of Love" (F 226; G 158) is reminiscent of the jealous and irascible sun-god who dominates the *Manciple's Tale*: "corowned with a sonne," his face shines so brightly that it can hardly ("unnethes") be looked upon (F 230–33). And yet Chaucer knows that he is being looked at "ful sternely": "his loking," he tells us, "dooth myn herte colde" (F 239–40). Chaucer is out of place. He has adopted a position too close to this god's beloved ("myn oune floure," F 316); he has written slanderously of this god's servants (F 323); he is a heretic and worse than a worm (F 318, 330). And, since he is seemingly unlettered in such circumstances (he cannot read the social signs; he cannot grasp that this daisy-dotted ground is shifting from court of love to court of law, from *Hof* to *Gericht*), he seems likely to destroy himself the moment he opens his mouth.

Left to his own devices, he will surely perish at the hands of a wrathful, god-like ruler likened to "tirauntz of Lumbardye" (F 374). Condemned both as poet and as political subject, he stands in desperate need of the right social and rhetorical strategies.

Boccaccio's *De mulieribus*, I shall argue, provides no path out of such a predicament. Boccaccio did not interest himself in absolutist poetics. His advice to a poet living under the shadow of despotic authority was that he should change the polity he lived under.[1] But Petrarch, as we shall see, promises to be more helpful on this subject. Valued by Lombard tyrants as an illustrious cultural figure, Petrarch was careful not to let such greatness challenge that of his political masters. While willing to be crowned and fêted as emperor of poets, Petrarch simultaneously cultivated a quite different persona through his letter collections, particularly his *Familiares*. Such self-representation was developed in part through the struggle to define humanist culture (an enterprise that forced Petrarch, paradoxically and often comically, into intimate relations with the *vulgus* he affected to despise). The humorous, domestic, and otherworldly aspects of such self-representation proved to be of great utility in Petrarch's development of a *modus vivendi* under despotic authority. Criticism, dazzled by the Petrarch legend, has failed to notice that Chaucerian and Petrarchan court and domestic personae have much in common. Indeed, there are moments when the two poets seem to exchange the roles that literary history has assigned them. Petrarch, conventionally portrayed as the lofty and singular "laureate poete," seems married to the masses, a Canterbury *compagnye* of vernacular voices that counterdefine humanism while providing its material infrastructure. And it is Chaucer rather than Petrarch who offers strategies from the most desperate predicament of absolutist poetics, namely, the dream of a solitary poet trapped in the immediate presence of a godlike, masculine monarch who misinterprets his *makynge* and finds it personally and sexually insulting.

In representing his personal dealings with despots and "myghty men," Petrarch typically decides both to be his own advocate and to speak from a variety of "feminized" subject positions. Chaucer, by contrast, typically seeks to position an eloquent wife between himself and the sovereign or god-like masculine figure who dominates his social world. Alceste, the eloquent wife of the F *Prologue*, has a historical surrogate beyond the text in Anne of Bohemia; and Bohemia, I shall argue, represents a congenial cultural and political ground for Chaucer that saves us from the terrifying alternative of an Anglicized "Lumbardye." With the death of Queen Anne in 1394, however, Chaucer's delicate strategies for wifely eloquence lose something of their purchase on historical reality. In attempting to save the literary text from the movement of history, the revisionary gestures of the G *Prologue* turn from a Dantean acceptance of temporality to a Petrarchan longing for transcendence. Chaucerian polity, in G, contemplates its own redundancy even as it reinvests its hopes in a post-historical literary afterlife.

Boccaccio, Petrarch, and Legends of Good Women

Boccaccio's *De mulieribus claris* survives, in whole or in part, in more than ninety manuscripts (including a holograph manuscript in the Biblioteca Laurenziana, Florence).[2] Boccaccio wrote his first draft in the summer of 1361, added a dedication to Andreola Acciaiuoli in June 1362, and continued modifying the work, with slight expansions, until his death in 1375.[3] The 106 lives of the *De mulieribus* run in more or less chronological order, beginning with Eve, "citizen of Paradise" (1.5), and ending with Queen Giovanna I of Naples (ruled 1343–82). The second chapter is on Semiramis, Queen of Assyria (celebrated, as in Chaucer's *Legend*, for her defensive fortification of Babylon);[4] chapters 3–40 are dedicated to figures from mythology and ancient poetry. Chapters 41–100 feature (with just three exceptions) women from the ancient and secular world, from Lavinia to Zenobia; this last legend was translated from the *De mulieribus* by Chaucer and transferred to his *Monk's Tale*.[5] Boccaccio's last six lives feature women from the Middle Ages, beginning and ending with women (Pope Giovanna; Queen Giovanna) who share his first name (Giovanni, Iohannes).[6]

Boccaccio's late turn to "modern instances" clearly reproduces the movement of his own *De casibus virorum illustrium*. He begins his *Proemio* by acknowledging both the ancient tradition of writing compendia "de viris illustribus" and the text in this genre on which Petrarch, "preceptor noster," is currently at work (1). Soon, however, Boccaccio announces his intention to turn from praise of men to praise of women:

If men are to be praised when, with the strength allotted to them, they have achieved great things, how much more deserving of praise are women (considering how, by nature, they are endowed with softness and physical weakness and sluggish intelligence) if they have shown manly spirit, daring to take on and accomplish outstanding feats through ingenuity and virtue, things that would be most difficult even for men? (*Proemio* 4)

This pattern of putting women in their political place while affecting to praise them is repeated throughout the *De mulieribus*. A little later in his *Proemio*, Boccaccio argues that his expansion and elaboration of female lives will prove useful and pleasurable to men and women alike, especially to women, who are largely ignorant of historical matters (8). And at the end of his *Conclusio*, Boccaccio admits that he may at times have been drawn along by excessive pleasure ("affectio," 5) in narrating. Boccaccio certainly takes interest and pleasure in the minutae of female lives in ways that recall Petrarch's evocation of great men in his *De viris*. The sense of political urgency that we noted at the very beginning of his *De casibus*, however, stands in marked contrast to the leisurely tone set by the *De mulieribus* in its opening period (addressed to Queen Giovanna):

Not long ago, outstanding woman [mulierum egregia], while a little removed from the uncultivated multitude and almost freed from other concerns, I wrote a little book in singular praise of the female sex (more for the pleasure of my friends than as a great service to the state). (*Dedica* 1)

Whereas the masculine lives of the *De casibus* were written to help secure the state, *res publica*, against the threat of tyranny, the female lives of the *De mulieribus* are offered as a pastime to be enjoyed once the security of the state has been assured. The *De mulieribus* does show signs of Boccaccio's characteristic intelligence and skepticism in political matters: the Flora story, for example, sees a Roman prostitute proclaimed a goddess (much as Ciappelletto, in the *Decameron*'s first *novella*, is proclaimed a saint).[7] But the explicit exclusion of postclassical women who have resisted "the tortures of tyrants" (*Proemio*, 11; one thinks of Griselde) helps ensure that this version of history will narrate women's experience *within* preordained political categories, rather than telling of their role in challenging and changing them. The real political work of the *De mulieribus*, then, is achieved through its paradigms of gender. Women's history, it argues, is to be written and read in a leisured manner at one remove from the public realm where the fate of communities and nations is actually decided.

Petrarch, in all the hundreds of letters through which he structured, sustained, and instructed members and political patrons of the incipient humanist movement, wrote to a woman just once (on May 23, 1358). The recipient of this letter was Anne of Bohemia, empress and third wife of Emperor Charles IV. Petrarch had visited Prague and spent time with Anne in 1356. Two years later, Anne wrote to him in person announcing the birth of her first child, a daughter (Elizabeth). Petrarch wrote back a long letter of congratulation, *Familiares* 21.8, which is, in effect (as his own rubric suggests) a short treatise *de laudibus feminarum*. The Petrarchan "I" that addresses the Empress Anne (or "Augusta," as he calls her) is learned, lofty, almost imperious: this is the Petrarchan voice that posterity best remembers. Petrarch begins by congratulating Anne on "the great wisdom" she displays in her letter "for such a young person." He acclaims her childbirth as an event of universal import: Christ, he says, "has cheered your youth with solemn fertility not only for yourself but for the entire empire." Anne need not be disappointed that her first child is a girl since "better fortune often follows upon a weak beginning" (3). Petrarch then sets out to demonstrate that "the female sex is noble not only for child-bearing, but for its intellect, its manifold virtues, and for the glory and accomplishments of the empire." Having named women who were of importance in founding learned traditions, verse forms, and alphabets (Minerva, Isis, Carmenta, Sappho, Proba), Petrarch proceeds to discuss a long sequence of ancient and illustrious women. Then, seemingly anxious "lest antiquity claim all the credit," Petrarch turns his attention to "our own time" ("apud nos," 15). The only woman he actually names in this short modern excursus, however, is the Countess Matilde di Canossa; all other women remain as generic wives or daughters or have their names concealed under *le nom de père*. Soon returning to his favorite topic of ancient Roman women, Petrarch ends with Livia: she proved to be the ideal consort for Caesar Augustus, "sharing not only his bed but his deliberations and his entire life"; Anne may prove to be her equal. Petrarch concludes with a final note of congratulation, hoping that this daughter may have been sent by heaven "as a token [literally, 'earnest-money'] of a more noble birth and a more complete joy" ("arram nobilioris partus et gaudii plenioris," 30): meaning again, of course, a masculine child.

Petrarch and Boccaccio are keen to ensure that their uncovering of ancient female lives need not be taken to challenge current social (patriarchal) arrangements. Both tend to emphasize the pastness of female power: contemporary women are simply not as illustrious as their ancient counterparts. Such an emphasis pushes both of them toward a gender essentialism that each finds difficult to sustain through his own self-representation. Boccaccio's authorial "I" shows a perennial drift toward fictional cross-dressing. For whatever reason (his own well-documented fleshliness; his sense of legal and artistic illegitimacy), Boccaccio feels compelled to imagine himself in a woman's place or (more simply) as a woman.[8] Petrarch, in one voice, adopts a militantly masculine tone in speaking across Europe to address the imperial household as an equal: he, too, has been crowned at Rome. But in other parts of the *Familiares* (letters intended only for cultivated men, hidden behind a high wall of complex Latinity), Petrarch confesses to lapses in personal authority that grow more egregious (and more comical) the deeper he wades into scholarship. It is abundantly evident, for example, that Petrarch rarely felt himself to be the master of his own household. In dramatizing this sense of displacement from his own domestic sphere, Petrarch may easily have availed himself of the misogynistic tropes recycled by Chaucer's Wife of Bath and Boccaccio's *Corbaccio*. But for Petrarch there was a voice that articulated cultural (political, personal) otherness more compellingly and completely than that of woman: that of the *vulgus*, particularly the urban proletariat.

Domestic Petrarch: Married to the Mob

Petrarch professed to prefer living in rural solitude, but the demands of his political patrons, his ambitions for the humanist movement, and the war-ravaged state of the Italian countryside forced him to be a city-dweller for most of his life.[9] This drew him, inevitably, into intimate, long-term relations with the urban proletariat, a class for which he affected disgust. His household could offer no retreat from the *vulgus* since it needed to be staffed. While the great man was rapt in study, his domestic servants would (so he tells us) rob him shamelessly. Petrarch tried to keep his mind above such distractions. One day, however, his domestic servants quarreled in his presence, brandishing knives, over the sharing out of Petrarch's own property. Sacking these servants on the spot, Petrarch was clearly outraged: "I had truly been a father to them, whereas they were not sons to me but rather plotters, assassins, and domestic thieves."[10] Subsequently, however, Petrarch felt lonely and unsafe in a large, unprotected house and was forced to move.[11] The Petrarchan household simply could not function efficiently without domestic servants to attend to the numerous visitors, relatives, and copyists who lived with him; and he needed them to form a protective curtain between his study and the outside world. They protected him from unwelcome and untimely visitors when he was active and from doctors when he was ill. *Seniles* 3.8 tells of how he was trapped in bed by a physician afflicted with excessive "verbositas": he was only able to get rid of him by feigning a relapse.[12] On May 7, 1371, Petrarch was laid low by fever. Doctors gathered at his bedside, decided that death was imminent and that his only hope lay in being bound with cords so that he could not sleep. Petrarch's household, however, had standing orders either to ignore what doctors recommended or to do the precise opposite. When these doctors returned on the following morning expecting to find Petrarch dead they found him busy writing.[13]

The poet's behavior must have seemed eccentric, sometimes comical, to those who shared his household. He slept only six hours a night and habitually rose before dawn; but he was afraid of sleeping alone and a servant was obliged to sleep with him and (with much grumbling) to get up at an unearthly hour. Bookishness, for Petrarch as for Chaucer, is a defining trait, a quality that wins them a place in the world and yet excludes them from it. Relationships with books characterize the peculiar source of both their strength and their weakness, a complex liaison neatly mythologized by *Familiares* 21.10. One day Petrarch walked absentmindedly into his study and caught a volume of Cicero with the edge of his gown.[14] This Cicero (kept on the floor by the door for ready reference) fell over and bruised his left leg. Petrarch upbraided the book ("Quid rei est, mi Cicero, cur me feris?") but the same thing happened to his "unlucky left leg" (as one of his servants called it) on the following day and at least twice thereafter. The leg swelled and a poisonous tumor developed. Laid up for weeks, Petrarch was forced to depend on his household servants and to subject himself to doctors. These doctors put him through a particularly painful course of treatment. Petrarch complained that his beloved Cicero "has now wounded my leg as he once did my heart."[15] This confession of personal inadequacy contains hints of two-way sexual betrayal: Petrarch ignores the world for books, and the world—through the physical agency of a book—bites back at him. If we do detect sexual overtones here (as Petrarch lies in bed like some wounded lover) they serve chiefly to remind us how thoroughly Petrarch's letters exclude the erotic. This Petrarch is seemingly an outsider to love; rather than the erotic torments of the *Canzoniere*, we find sufferings that are chiefly social, cultural, and political. The chief source of such suffering, it seems, is Petrarch's relationship to the *vulgus*.

Petrarch's exposure and subjection to the workaday world was an inevitable, albeit much lamented, consequence of his ambitions for humanist culture. He relied upon merchants to carry books in their bales, messengers to deliver his correspondence, and a variety of contacts living in various parts of Italy, France, Germany, Spain, Greece, and Britain to further the search for Cicero manuscripts.[16] Petrarch bargained with peasants at Rome who dug up Roman coins and with the Calabrian Leontius Pilatus (described as beastly, slovenly, greedy, insolent, and unreliable) for Latin translations of Homer's Greek epics;[17] he also made desperate efforts to track down a pawned copy of Cicero's *De gloria*.[18] And in a remarkable passage, directed to his brother Gherardo, Petrarch is forced to acknowledge his dependence on artisanal labor in textual production even as he attempts to distance himself from it:

An architect does not mix the mortar but orders it to be mixed; a military commander does not sharpen swords, a ship's captain does not plane a mast or the oars, nor did Apelles saw boards or Polyclites ivory or Phidias marble. The proper work [suum opus] of the plebeian intelligence is preparing that which the noble intelligence will consume. Thus in our time, some scrape parchment, others write books, others correct them, others, if I might use a common word, illuminate them, others bind them, others adorn the covers; the noble intellect aspires to higher things, flying beyond the humbler ones.[19]

Petrarch, then, knew himself to be married to the *vulgus* as surely as Walter is married to Griselde. He needed them (it?) to provide the material infrastructure requisite for transcendent flights of humanism; he needed his *idea* of them in order to articulate, by counterdistinction, the idea of his own elite program. The last sentence of what may be regarded as Petrarch's very last text—his will—can only end by both invoking and repudiating the *vulgus*:

Ego Franciscus Petrarca scripsi, qui testamentum aliud fecissem, si essem dives, ut vulgus insanum putat.[20]

I, Francesco Petrarca, have written this, and would have drawn up a different testament if I were rich, as the mad rabble believes me to be.

The marriage metaphor seems apt in describing Petrarch's relation to the *vulgus* because Petrarch was evidently fascinated even as he was alarmed by a succession of colorful and eccentric characters. In *Familiares* 18.6, for example, Petrarch speaks of a "seniculus" who shares his household and "speaks stones." This old man could be a Scotsman or a slave from north and east of the Black Sea slaving port of Caffa; for Petrarch he is simply a nameless object of wonder:

In my own house lives an old fellow who, though born at the fringe of the inhabited world beyond which there are no men, is still a man, possessing a man's soul and appearance; but he behaves so inhumanly that he either growls like a bear or snarls like a wild boar when he wants to show affection. In short, his behavior is so rough, so thoroughly barbaric, that he seems to bite when he licks; you would consider most appropriate for him not the great prophet's words to the effect that his eloquence flows like dew, but rather those of the comic poet that he speaks with words of stone. Stone, I say, which is bare and hard, with which he strikes the mind in an incredible fashion, wearying and saddening the heavens with his awful thunder.[21]

In *Familiares* 20.12 Petrarch tells of the comforting presence [22] of another extraordinary character, a man of 85 who "had almost returned to childhood"; his speech "would evoke laughter even among mourners." Fond of engaging in religious and philosophical disputes and of employing outrageous linguistic barbarisms and solecisms, the old man would tap his forehead and declare: "It is here, here, that I have my books and my knowledge." [23] Petrarch was similarly captivated by Enrico Capra, a goldsmith from Bergamo who became a fanatical admirer of Petrarch, filled his house with Petrarchan busts and portraits, and finally gave up his craft in favor of studying at the local *gimnasium*.[24] During his first summer at Milan, Petrarch was accosted in the street, trapped under a blazing sun, by an interminably talkative old soldier who would not let him pass until he gave him a message (any message) to take to Florence. A month or so later Petrarch was visited at home by an interminably talkative old monk who spoke without pause until the city clock (a recent innovation) struck a late hour. Realizing that the monk and the soldier were one and the same person, Petrarch named him Bolanus (after a character in Horace, *Satires* 1.9).[25] Bolanus continued to perform valuable services for Petrarch as a messenger although he continued to cause him some awkward moments. One day in January 1360, for example, he turned up at Petrarch's door at a late hour with a crowd (*turba*) of companions in a rainstorm: "at his noisy arrival," Petrarch remarked to Socrates, "this solitude became a veritable public square." [26]

There are many saving moments in the *Familiares* when Petrarch seems to view himself, so to speak, from the cultural far side. His gardening habit, for example, makes for an extended narrative of bookish incompetence: the humanist struggling to imitate the natural man. Shortly after arriving at Milan in 1353, Petrarch spent several days planting spinach, beetroot, fennel, and parsley. He then added details of this to his gardening notes in a manuscript containing the *De agricultura* of Palladius. Several weeks later, on reviewing his handiwork, he sadly noted that not a single seed had sprouted. On April 4, 1357, Petrarch planted six laurel trees and an olive brought from Bergamo, making careful notes about climatic conditions and the state of the moon. And once again, a brief note follows: all dead. Petrarch later made efforts to acquire Varro's *Res rusticae*. Perhaps he thought it would bring him better luck. He must have seemed an odd figure, standing in the garden of Sant'Ambrogio surveying shriveled trees and seeds that will not sprout. He was obviously led to such an unlikely situation by a purely literary ideal that, he hoped, would bear fruit in the tradition of Vergil's *Georgics*.[27]

Petrarch's ineptitude in the domestic (and gardening) realm, then, is self-cultivated and deliberately documented. This invites his correspondents to read his neglect of personal affairs both as indifference to political intrigue and as a sign of his singleminded devotion to the transcendent pursuit of scholarship:

As I see it, I am no better a householder than a politician [yconomicus quam politicus]; the love of solitude and literature has completely deprived me of all that, nor do I entertain any hope of changing my ways in the future. Despite my daily attempt to learn something, it is too late to develop a skill utterly unknown to me; and so, let my private affairs go as they will or as they can, provided that I escape safely even though stripped naked [licet nudus].[28]

Competence and Ineptitude; Petrarch, Chaucer, and Life at Court

The forms of self-disclosure essayed in Petrarch's letters are not to be confused with the intimacies of a modern diary, a quite different mode of rhetorical self-fabrication. Some letters are addressed to fictional or classical personages; some were never dispatched; and some (as comparison of final and missive form reveals) were extensively revised for inclusion in the *Familiares* and *Seniles*. The oscillation between competence and ineptitude, practical ability and bookish otherworldliness, that is so characteristic of these texts does not seem to herald the invention of a newly interiorized, newly self-doubting, Renaissance "self." It seems, rather, to parallel forms of self-construction that are actively pursued by Petrarch's fourteenth-century contemporaries, Machaut and Chaucer.[29] In the *House of Fame*, the poem that plays out the immediate shock of his exposure to Italian culture, Chaucer's mind turns to the familiarity of domestic space even as it is called heavenward ("in mannes vois," 556) by the Dantean eagle:

> And called me tho by my name,
> And for I shulde the bet abreyde,
> Me mette "Awak," to me he seyde
> Ryght in the same vois and stevene
> That useth oon that I koude nevene.   (558–62)

The voice and sound of the "oon" that Chaucer could name, we are led to assume, belong to his strong-lunged wife: a figure both intimidating yet (given the soaring ambitions of the imperial and pedagogical eagle), comfortingly domestic. Eighty lines later, as Chaucer is dragged heavenward, this distinction between greater public and lesser domestic realms is revived again, this time by the imperial bird:

> "Wherfore, as I seyde, ywys,
> Jupiter considereth this,
> And also, beau sir, other thynges:
> That is, that thou hast no tydynges
> Of Loves folk yf they be glade,
> Ne of noght elles that God made;
> And noght oonly fro fer contree
> That ther no tydynge cometh to thee,
> But of thy verray neyghebores,
> That duellen almost at thy dores,
> Thou herist neyther that ne this;
> For when thy labour doon al ys,
> And hast mad alle thy rekenynges,
> In stede of reste and newe thynges
> Thou goost hom to thy hous anoon,
> And, also domb as any stoon,
> Thou sittest at another book
> Tyl fully daswed is thy look."   (641–58)

The eyes of Jupiter—the deity associated with Theseus in the *Knight's Tale*—penetrate the heavens and enter Chaucer's "dores." Chaucer is evidently a dullard: having spent all day doing the books at the customhouse, he spends all evening going through more books at home. Jupiter pities Chaucer (and has him whisked heavenward) because he can discover no "tydynges."[30] The discovery of "tydynges," for Jupiter, would seem to be the preeminent aim for a creature such as Chaucer, a *makere* of "bookys, songes, dytees" (622). The chief recipient of such compositions would naturally be "Cupido," or the God of Love, Jupiter's "blynde nevew" (617). "Tydynges," the exact English equivalent of the Italian term *novelle*, suggests stories of immediate, contemporary import; "tydynges" are the lifeblood of both love life and court life (and hence of political life). "Newe thynges" (654) are what lovers and political rulers—such as the sultan in the *Man of Law's Tale*—are forever desperate to discover. It is the insatiable appetite for *tidynges* and *novelle* that sends Chaucer across the heavens (a journey he evidently takes no interest in) and Petrarch across the Alps and down the canals of war-torn Italy. The unspoken secret of Petrarch's household is that it is not the *vulgus* but his political masters who break up the happy home; they have little genuine interest in humanist scholarship, or "olde bokes," except as a repository of tropes that they, or Petrarch, can take on the road to do political business with.

The private household, for Chaucer and Petrarch, cannot be imagined as a refuge from the gaze of their political masters. It is a place where large cultural pretensions are seen to collapse and personal foibles stand revealed. It does offer a measure of protection, but it is no hiding place from the perils of the greater household that that lies beyond its threshold: the seigneurial court.

Court life, especially when constellated around a figure with absolutist proclivities, is densely and precariously rhetorical. August ceremony may totter into outrageous farce. Petrarch evidently lived through many such moments. On October 5, 1354, his patron and political master, Giovanni Visconti, died, leaving Lombardy to be governed by his three nephews, Matteo, Bernabò, and Galeazzo. Petrarch was requested to deliver a commemorative oration which would precede the investiture of the three brothers as co-rulers of Lombardy. This was a tense and awkward moment in Visconti history: no despotic regime could survive long if divided three ways. Petrarch duly embarked on his oration, only to be interrupted by the court astrologer who insisted that the time had come to hand the brothers their symbols of office; delay would be dangerous. Petrarch stopped speaking at once, thereby unnerving the astrologer completely. He asked Petrarch to go on for a while, but he insisted that he had finished. As the audience grew restless (some snickering, some indignant), the astrologer grew agitated. Suddenly, he exclaimed "hora est," "the time has come."[31]

Chaucer must have lived through or heard tell of many such moments of impending breakdown in the presence of the famously foul-tempered Richard II. In 1385, to cite just one early example, Richard became so incensed with the archbishop of Canterbury that he drew his sword; the men who restrained him from killing the archbishop were so terrified by the "rex iratus" that they leapt from the royal barge into the archbishop's boat. And since no monarch can afford to be seen as the centerpiece of a farce, the archbishop was subsequently obliged to kneel before the king and sue for his pardon.[32] Courtiers, at such moments, must exercise great ingenuity in saving their monarch from suggestions of ineptitude or illegitimate action. Petrarch was obviously adept at this, as when he likens Galeazzo's gout to the pains of stigmata suffered by St. Francis of Assisi.[33] Gout pains drove Galeazzo to desperate straits. One evening in the autumn of 1365, while Petrarch was dining with Galeazzo at Milan, news arrived of a healer approaching from the Canton Valais. Galeazzo sent a white horse with an armed escort to hasten his arrival and obediently swallowed his egg-based concoction. But Galeazzo's gout only worsened under this treatment; the healer now maintained that the only hope of cure lay in certain books of magic that he intended to go off and search for.[34] A gout-ridden Visconti tyrant could not have been much easier to deal with than a gouty Henry VIII. Petrarch did what he could in 1365 by writing a lengthy diatribe against physicians (*Seniles* 5.3); this was added as a supplement to his *Invective contra medicum*. Such writing served a vital function in exposing the ineptitude of doctors; the heat of the invective draws

attention away from a prince pursuing any quack in his desperate search for a
remedy.

Petrarch was of immense value to the Visconti because he brought suggestions of legitimacy both through his competence (as the crowned heir to
Roman cultural tradition) and his ineptitude. When he first moved to Milan
in 1353, Petrarch wore the fashion-conscious clothes of a courtier. Later on,
however, he began persuading himself to adopt "a common and modest,
even 'philosophical' dress," [35] steeling his mind against "the shame of wearing
worn-out clothes." By dressing as a threadbare philosopher, Petrarch obviously offered little social competition for the mighty princes he served. And
in one extraordinary text, *Variae* 56, Petrarch grasps how his own social ineptitude, his need of a "myghty man," can allow a young prince to dramatize
his saving power and hence be legitimized as an instrument of God.[36] The
letter opens by tracing a grand and sustained historical vision: the succession
of illustrious legates who served ancient Rome. The scene then shifts to the
coming of a modern Roman legate: Cardinal Albornoz, representing Innocent VI and the papal curia. When the papal legate approaches Milan on
September 14, 1353, Petrarch is chosen to join the ceremonial greeting party.
But as the Milanese contingent moves out of the city, Petrarch is rendered
deaf, blind, and voiceless by the incredible clouds of dust thrown up by car-
riage wheels and horses' hooves. Confused by this tumult, Petrarch's horse
lets its hind legs slip over the edge of a precipice. Petrarch, however, remains
oblivious of the fact that he is in mortal danger:

But that great-hearted young man, to whom (unless the fates cut off the beginning
web of succession) the rich inheritance of Milan and Liguria is promised, and than
whom (unless love defeats my judgment) among favored youths none is better, none
more refined, before all others was warning me, calling me by name, that I should
watch out.

At this delicate narrative juncture, Petrarch holds his story in suspension
with a long meditation on whether it is better, or not, for an individual to
know of the peril he is in. Returning to the precipice, he tells us that he
was then saved from destruction more by an invisible force than by his own
efforts. This saving power soon takes the physical form of the young *signore*,[37]
who commands his servants to unhorse while himself coming to the rescue
not just with words (Petrarch emphasizes) but with his own hands.[38] Yet
again, Petrarch suspends his narrative at the brink: if he were to have fallen
then, he would now be dead; he was rescued only by virtue of Christ stretch-
ing out his hand ("manum," vol. 3, p. 462). All this goes to show, he tells Nelli,
that humans are blind, subjected utterly to the force of fate. He then goes on
to tell of his meeting with the papal legate.

This narrative, written just a few months after Petrarch's controversial
move to Milan, has the force of an apologia for living under despotism. Deaf,

blind, and voiceless, Petrarch situates himself in a liminal drama in which he is powerless to act or even to grasp his own predicament. He is saved only by the dramatic intervention of a seigneurial hand (subsequently likened to the hand of God) that sets him on firm ground. Without such a hand, Petrarch would no longer be with us; everything that follows is owed to this fateful intervention. All this is strongly reminiscent of the liminal drama played out in *Familiares* 16.12, written just three weeks earlier, which sees a Griselde-like Petrarch, blushing and voiceless, seduced by the Visconti lord who first offered him a home.[39] In *Variae* 56, Petrarch again discovers and reveals himself as the natural subject of absolutist rule.

"And as for Me . . . and Nothing I"

The precarious and sustained predicament of *Variae* 56—the poet, in the midst of a courtly ceremony, hangs over a cliff, oblivious to his own danger— forms an obvious and compelling analogue to the self-representation essayed by Chaucer's *Prologue* to the *Legend of Good Women*. The *Legend* was perhaps first written between 1386 and 1388, a period that has been taken to represent the apogee both of Chaucer's involvement in public affairs and his career as "a poet of the court." [40] It certainly postdates, following the honeymoon period of the early 1380s, the first attribution of autocratic tendencies to Richard.[41] It is at a period of rapid change and exceptional political instability, then, that Chaucer is moved to represent himself as a courtly *makere* at the edge of the abyss. Unlike Petrarch, however, he identifies the abyss with the very center of the social structure in which he struggles to function: the ruler of the court, the youthful, irascible, and "myghty god of Love" (F 226).

The first two hundred lines of the *Prologue* to the *Legend of Good Women* are remarkably uneventful. Chaucer declares his devotion to old books, abandons books to worship a daisy, admires a landscape, listens to birds, and then returns to his bed and falls asleep. Such procedures are familiar from Chaucer's earlier dream poems and their French antecedents, although the lack of dramatic interaction here is quite exceptional. The opening phases of Chaucerian dream poems typically function as overtures to the work; here the groundwork for the later association of Alceste with the daisy is laid out in detail. But if the thematics of this opening are to prove significant, so too is its *modus agendi*. The relative absence of dramatic content tends to draw attention to the functioning of language itself and to the struggles of the poet to shape diction, control referentiality, and generate intelligible meanings. If control of language is to prove crucial in negotiating with the "myghty god of Love," we realize that Chaucer, or the Chaucer persona, walks on dangerous ground from the very start. His opening couplet, prefacing discussion of the limits of personal experience and the utility of books (F 1–28), establishes

the certainty of the joys of heaven and pains of hell, and (as their necessary
precondition) the inevitability of final judgment.

Chaucer first turns attention to himself in an elliptical and apologetic
manner ("And as for me . . ." F 29), defining himself not as a maker of books
but as a reader or devotee of them (he holds them "in reverence," F 32). But
when May comes he soon turns apostate ("Farewel my bok and my devocioun!"), drawn by "gret affeccioun" to "reverence" a new object of desire:
the daisy, "of alle floures flour" (F 39–53). In seeking to praise this bloom,
however, he immediately runs up against the limits of language—or at least
of the language available to him:

> Allas, that I ne had Englyssh, ryme or prose,
> Suffisant this flour to preyse aryght!   (F 66–67)

Faced with this impasse, Chaucer calls upon members of two courtly
factions for assistance: lovers who "ben with the leef or with the flour" (F
72).[42] But he then immediately helps himself out by turning to a text that
few, if any, English devotees of the flower or the leaf would be familiar with:
Boccaccio's *Filostrato*. This citation is both unambiguous (Chaucer closely
imitates the opening of the second stanza of Boccaccio's opening book)[43] and
treacherous, a secret betrayal of his imagined audience: for it was his imitating of the *Filostrato* in the *Troilus* that supposedly provided the occasion for
the present corrective exercise, the *Legend of Good Women*. It is from this duplicitous position that Chaucer moves directly from imitation of the *Troilus*'s
source text (F 84–85) to heartfelt protestations of loyalty to the lady; she is (he
tells her) "The maistresse of my wit, and nothyng I" (F 88). Chaucer claims
to be "nothyng" (even as he drifts back to imitating the *Filostrato*)[44] because
his voice, his every word, responds to her direction; she plays him like an
instrument:

> My word, my werk ys knyt so in youre bond
> That, as an harpe obeieth to the hond
> And maketh it soune after his fyngerynge,
> Ryght so mowe ye oute of myn herte bringe
> Swich vois, ryght as yow lyst, to laughe or pleyne.
> Be ye my gide and lady sovereyne!   (F 89–94)

If Chaucer is to be reckoned a poet, then, his current status (in the symbolic
presence but physical absence of the lady who gives him voice) is nothing
at all: "nothing I." Rather than lapsing into silence or nothingness, however,
the narrator forces a fresh start: "But wherefore that I spak . . ." (F 97). Why
did he just spend a hundred lines speaking of the importance of old books (F
98–100)?

> That shal I seyn, whanne that I see my tyme;
> I may nat al at-ones speke in ryme.   (F 101–2)

This strange deferral at least serves to recognize the art of "whanne" or *quando*, saying the right thing at the right time, as the most crucial principle of household or courtly rhetoric. As the *Prologue* progresses, however, we continue to doubt whether this Chaucer figure possesses the mastery of language requisite for its successful deployment. Kneeling before the daisy before dawn, Chaucer waits for it to unclose before the sun, "that roos as red as rose" (F 112): suddenly he has two flowers to contend with, one bracketed within the figure of *comparatio* and one presumably real, but in need of an allegorical referent. We also have two "roses," one verbal, one substantive, a doubling (underscored by alliteration) that both compares a greater thing to a lesser, dependent one (a sun to a rose) and distracts attention from daisies, "of alle floures flour." Such infelicitous doubling reminds us of the struggles of another would-be courtly rhetor: the Squire, who recognizes principles of *ars dicendi* even as he proceeds to fall short of them:

> Accordaunt to his wordes was his cheere,
> As techeth art of speche hem that it leere.
> Al be that I kan nat sowne his stile,
> Ne kan nat clymben over so heigh a style,
> Yet seye I this . . .   (5.103–7)

Chaucer in the *Legend* obviously has much in common (besides equivalent rank: both are squires) with the youngest storyteller of the *Tales*. Each finds courtly language drawing attention to itself as it trips over the artificialities of its own deployment; each has terrible trouble in applying the tropes and figures of rhetorical craft to the description of the natural world. "Comparisoun may noon ymaked be," cries Chaucer, struggling to put the smell of a daisy into words (F 115–24). Immediately afterwards, however, he deploys *comparatio* and every other trope that lies to hand in attempting to evoke the coming of summer. This passage continues to play as an overture to the poem to come, although its themes are realized more as accidents of style than as the substance of narrative argument:

> Forgeten hadde the erthe his pore estat
> Of wynter, that hym naked made and mat,
> And with his swerd of cold so sore greved;
> Now hath th'atempre sonne all that releved,
> That naked was, and clad him new agayn.
> The smale foules, of the sesoun fayn,
> That from the panter and the net ben scaped,
> Upon the foweler, that hem made awhaped
> In wynter, and distroyed hadde hir brood,
> In his dispit hem thoghte yt did hem good
> To synge of hym, and in hir song despise
> The foule cherl that, for his coveytise,

> Had hem betrayed with his sophistrye.
> This was hire song: "The foweler we deffye,
> And al his craft."   (F 125-39)

The seasonal cycle is here figured in social terms as a change of "estat," effected through the agency of lordship: tyrannical winter wreaks havoc with his sword and reduces all to nakedness, while benign summer (personified as the sun) relieves and re-leaves his subjects by offering new clothes (a traditional obligation of good lordship). Such natural artifice encourages the birds to mate, and to sing a song of political liberty against the "coveytise" and "sophistrye" of another artificer, the "foule cherl" fowler. All this is penned by a poet-artificer, a craftsman deploying rhetorical figures while pretending to aspire to the ideal of fashioning a "naked text in English" (G 86). Chaucer is at once bird and birdcatcher: as what might be termed *auctor*, he lays out his duplicitous poetic tropes; as what might be termed Chaucer-protagonist or persona, he walks through the landscape of his own poem in apparent ignorance of the traps laid in the text he speaks.[45] For example, not all birds within the collectivity of birds are trustworthy: the "tydif" is said to pursue "newefanglnesse" (F 154, one of the key terms in Wyatt's lexicon of courtly betrayal).[46] Such unfaithful birds finally win an "accord" with their mates, swearing "on the blosmes to be trewe" (F 157-59). The blossoms of May, of course, will not last until September, a consideration buried beneath a rapid recapitulative gloss on the bird's love affair. This begins with an extraordinary concentration of courtly artificialities; the whole history of courtship is dispatched in just four lines, featuring five allegorical personifications (seven if we promote "innocence" and "myght," which seem just as deserving as "Mercy" and "Ryght"):

> Al founde they Daunger for a tyme a lord,
> Yet Pitee, thurgh his stronge gentil myght,
> Forgaf, and made Mercy passen Ryght,
> Thurgh innocence and ruled Curtesye.   (F 160-63)

The poet steps back from this compacted history as soon as he speaks it, invoking the name of an *auctor* to gloss what he means, which differs, apparently, from what he says. This is followed by a firm bid for narrative closure, beginning with a familiar summarizing formula ("And thus") and ending with a chorus of universal "acord":

> But I ne clepe nat innocence folye,
> Ne fals pitee, for vertu is the mene,
> As Etik seith; in swich maner I mene.
> And thus thise foweles, voide of al malice,
> Acordeden to love, and laften vice
> Of hate, and songen alle of oon acord,
> "Welcome, somer, oure governour and lord!"   (F 164-70)

The narrator is clearly moved here by a desire to proclaim all elements of social discord resolved by the univocal acclamation of a single authoritative figure. This is, of course, familiar as the strategy that brings earlier dream poems (the *Parliament of Fowls*; the *House of Fame*) to an end. In the *Legend*, however, the same device is employed just as the dream is about to begin. Such premature placement of narrative resolution invites us to examine this "accord" more closely. Summer is "governour and lord" for the moment; when the season changes the "tydif" will return to his "malice," the fowler to his traps, and the earth to the "pore estat" evoked just forty lines before. The desire to live in May "alwey" is tempered by the realization that such a landscape will, "day by day," disappear (F 175–77). The fantasy of living in perennial May might be read here as a response to the daily pressures of life at court, a structure constituted in Chaucer's England not by any one physical locality but by a nexus of relationships centered on a single authoritative figure. Such a complex cannot be fixed or stabilized because it is organic, actualized by a medium that is (in Dante's famous formulation) forever moving toward flowering or decay: human language.[47] It is unrealistic to seek a position of neutrality within such a structure, since this would amount to a position outside language. This, however, is just what Chaucer's narrator tries to map out for himself shortly before entering the dream. He chooses no side in the factional debates of the court; he will praise the merits of the flower against the leaf

> No more than of the corn against the sheef;
> For, as to me, nys lever noon ne lother.
> I am withholden yit with never nother;
> Ne I not who serveth leef ne who the flour.   (F 190–93)

It might seem gratuitous to apply the term "faction" to defenders of the flower or the leaf in Maytide games, but it is surely naive to underestimate the ways in which such debates might have rehearsed or developed, albeit in humorous vein, political and sexual alliances at court. It is worth noticing that Chaucer actually strengthens the linkage with factional politics here by employing the term "withholden," which is, as Lee Patterson has demonstrated, a key term used in indentures of retaining in this period.[48] Chaucer's line F 192 might then be translated as follows: "I am as yet retained by neither one party nor the other." This can hardly be taken as a statement of studied political neutrality, since it both draws attention to the practice of retaining (an increasingly controversial subject in late Ricardian England) and suggests that Chaucer might "yit" be in the market.[49]

All hopes of social neutrality or invisibility are immediately dispersed once Chaucer enters the dream and falls beneath the gaze of the God of Love:

> For sternely on me he gan byholde,
> So that his loking dooth myn herte colde.   (F 239–40)

Within the compass of such "loking," the dreamer is already fixed within a court structure, although he persists in thinking of himself as a neutral observer until he is called to account some seventy lines later. Turning his attention to the god's "noble quene," he is moved to fulfill his recognized social function as poet by meditating a *balade* in her honor. It is clear to the poet that when he speaks of "my lady" in this *balade* he is referring to "this lady free" (F 248), queen to the God of Love. But he does not name her, since he is as yet ignorant of her identity. When detached from its immediate context here in this court space, then, the identity of this *balade*-lady who may "disdeyn" the most beautiful beings of antiquity (two men, positioned first and third, and eighteen women)[50] remains in doubt: a circumstance that will have painful repercussions for the poem's *makere* later on. It is worth emphasizing (since most critics seem to overlook the point) that in the F text the *balade* is not sung by the dreamer, nor by anyone else: it "may ful wel ysongen be" by the queen (F 270), but it is not. The only song performed here is that "songen in one vois" by the ladies who follow the queen (F 296–99).

These women singing in unison are said to be those women who, since God made Adam, were "trewe of love" (F 290). These ladies, whose number is said to be very great (F 285–89), deliberately form themselves into a court structure, arranging themselves "a-compas enviroun" around the royal couple "as they were of estaat, ful curteysly" (F 305). The court of Love is now formally constituted, a circumstance of which the dreamer seems sublimely ignorant. Still apparently thinking of himself as a neutral and invisible spectator, the dreamer fails to grasp that within such a courtly configuration, mapped by the strict observance of social degree, he is himself turned spectacle. Holding to his station by the God of Love's "oune floure," he becomes absurdly and presumptuously overvisible. Once the deity's gaze falls upon him, the dreamer is subjected to intensive interrogation as the court shifts from *Hof* to *Gericht*, from court of love to court of law. Charges are leveled: the dreamer profanes the God's "relyk" by his mere presence; he slanders his "olde servauntes"; he has disseminated "heresye" through his translating of the *Roman de la Rose*; his account of Criseyde erodes trust in women. And, suddenly, he is called to speak in his own defense:

> "Of thyn answere avise the ryght weel;
> For thogh thou reneyed hast my lay,
> As other wrecches han doon many a day,
> By Seynt Venus that my moder ys,
> If that thou live, thou shalt repenten this
> So cruelly that it shal wel be sene!"   (F 335–40)

The charge here is both apostasy and treason, since the God of Love clearly arrogates both religious and secular authority to his own person.[51] The outlook is bleak: the dreamer must speak to save himself, but words may inflame his accuser, a son of Venus, rather than mollify him. The god may then act cruelly, that is, tyrannically; the dreamer might not live long enough to hear his own penance.[52] The dreaming Chaucer, at this crucial point in the poem, hangs over the abyss. Rhetoric and political acumen are his only hope, but such skills, as we observed in painful detail before the dream began, are absent from his repertoire. Even as he occupies center stage at court, this dreamer thinks that he plays no part in court politics. And even as he prepares to speak in his own defense, he seems not to know, as we do, that the content and timing of his own tropes lie beyond his control. He is bound to destroy himself the minute he opens his mouth.

Petrarch, we have noted, chooses to represent himself being saved from mortal danger by the power of masculine lineage (as the son and heir of his *signore* takes hold of his bridle). Chaucer, by contrast, looks for salvation in a female speaker:

> Thoo spak this lady, clothed al in grene,
> And seyde, "God, ryght of youre curtesye,
> Ye moten herken yf he can replye
> Agayns al this that ye have to him meved."   (F 341–44)

In Chaucer's revision of the *Legend*, the G text, we were told early on (and then frequently reminded) that "this lady" is Alceste. The lines in G corresponding to F 341–44 continue this disambiguating trend:

> Thanne spak Alceste, the worthyeste queene,
> And seyde, "God, ryght of youre curteysye,
> Ye moten herkenen if he can replye
> Ageyns these poynts that ye han to hym meved."   (G 317–20)

In F, however, the lady's identity remains concealed until close to the end of the *Prologue* (508–19). This encourages the F audience to play the familiar *marguerite* game of guessing the lady's identity: just who might this "dayeseye" be? Speculation is held suspended between fictional and historical terms of reference. Representation of the God of Love, who is said to be "corowned with a sonne" and possessed of a face "so bryghte" that it cannot be looked upon (F 230–34) must, at some level of consciousness, have encouraged associations with Richard II.

The king, like the sun, is the vital presence of life at court; courtiers and subjects open and close like flowers in the light and darkness of his favor and absence. Richard II was evidently concerned to have himself portrayed as a dazzling, sunlike presence; the sunburst, which adorns his robes on his tomb effigy,[53] was a favorite personal symbol. If the sunlike and sun-crowned God of Love evokes associations with Richard, then, it follows that the "dayesye" might point to his queen, Anne of Bohemia. The seeds for such an association are planted early on in the F *Prologue* when the daisy is acclaimed as "of alle floures flour" (F 53). If the God of Love's queen is to be seen "ryght as a dayesye" (F 218), then she is associated not just with a flower but with the flower of flowers: in short, with the empress of flowers. This chain of association is made explicit shortly before the dream begins; the daisy is said to be "the emperice and flour of floures alle" (F 185).

Anne of Bohemia was the daughter of an emperor (Charles IV); her mother, Elizabeth of Pomerania, traveled to Rome to be crowned empress in 1363.[54] She was half-sister to the emperor's son, King Wenceslaus; and she was also the great-granddaughter of Emperor Henry VII, the most crucial political figure in Dante's *Commedia*. This last association may have inspired Chaucer's deft citation from *Inferno* 13.64–66, a tercet designed to remind us of Dante's perennial concern with the imperial household:

> Envie ys lavendere of the court alway,
> For she ne parteth, neither nyght ne day,
> Out of the hous of Cesar; thus seith Dante.   (F 358–60)

The Dantean speaker imitated by Chaucer here is Pier della Vigna (c. 1190–1249), a member of Frederick II's household who, among other things, negotiated the marriage of the emperor with Isabella, sister of Henry III of England, in 1234–35. Pier, also a poet, became the emperor's most intimate political advisor, but suddenly fell into disgrace and was arrested, imprisoned, and blinded, the victim (according to Dante) of calumny. In prison he committed suicide, supposedly by smashing his head against a wall.[55] Chaucer's citation of this tercet in the *Legend* (a poem that hinges on crucial misinterpretations of a poet's work by an irascible and godlike master) is tantalizing, but is not clear how much or how little Chaucer actually knew of *Inferno* 13.[56] It is certain, however, that Chaucer was learning a great deal about the art of calumny and betrayal at court in this desperate period. We have noted that his hopes for social and personal survival are elsewhere in his work heavily invested in the practice of wifely eloquence. In the *Legend*, such hopes are associated with a woman who comes "out of the hous of Cesar." The cultural and political significance of Anne of Bohemia has been grossly underestimated (or unestimated) by Chaucer's critics and biographers; she certainly brought more to England than sidesaddles, pins, and extravagant headgear.[57] Critical reactions to Anne are somewhat reminiscent of the attitude maintained by old-fashioned source study toward the *Filostrato*: foreign texts (and foreign persons) only come alive as they enter English territory. The problem is exacerbated in the case of Anne in that she was "only" a sixteen-year-old girl when she set foot in England. It seems worthwhile, then, to enquire who she was and what she might have brought with her.

"Out of the Hous of Cesar": Anne of Bohemia

The question of who Anne was before she was queen of England, posed to the historical sources currently available, returns a predictable answer: the daughter of the Emperor Charles IV. But this answer can be held at bay, for a moment, by considering two pictorial representations still visible at Prague. The first is the famous Zlatá Brana or Golden Portal on the south side of St. Vitus's cathedral, at the heart of the Hradčany or Prague Castle complex. The decorative front wall of this portal, built by Petr Parléř in 1367, features a mosaic in colored stone and gilded glass (now much faded): Charles IV and Elizabeth of Pomerania, Anne's parents, kneel to either side of a Last Judgment. Emperor and empress, in this representation, share the same horizontal plane, but just a few hundred yards to the northeast, within St. George's Basilica adjoining the former Benedictine convent,[58] we find a female figure dominating the vertical axis (see plate 10). On the tomb of Prince Vratislav I, the convent's founder, a mitred bishop is painted kneeling, less than willingly, before an abbess—an image recording the prerogative of the princess abbess (who was selected from the royal family or high aristocracy) to crown the Czech queen. English politics and pictorial representations would require Queen Anne to adopt kneeling and intercessionary postures before King Richard II, but we cannot assume that Anne came from Bohemia to England with no sense of the politics of such postures, or with no capacity for imagining alternatives.

Charles was in every sense a dominating personality: he ruled as emperor from 1346 to 1378, fathered 11 children with 4 wives over 42 years,[59] and presided over one of the most brilliant and well-connected courts and cities of postpandemic Europe.[60] The Black Death affected Bohemia and Moravia in 1348–50 less severely than most parts of western Europe. Prague actually experienced a significant growth spurt in the second half of the fourteenth century. Charles attempted to strengthen this dynamic urban culture by undermining the nobility's position as the traditional interpreters of law.[61] His attempt to introduce a written constitution would certainly have given rise to a new class of urban and legal professionals whose competence was defined by education rather than by birth—an initiative in keeping with the principles and practices disseminated through the writings of Albertano of Brescia. Prague, where Anne grew up, was a remarkably cosmopolitan city, the biggest of all European cities east of the Rhine. Nové Město (New Town) was founded in 1348 to provide for a rapidly expanding population made up predominantly of Czech speakers of rural provenance. Staré Město, north of Nové Město on the east bank of the Vltava, gained rights for a town hall in 1338 and a university ten years later. German was the most favored language here and at Malá Strana, the "Lesser Side," a town that had grown up across the river on the slopes beneath the Prague castle complex.[62] The Jewish com-

Plate 10. Tomb of Prince Vratislav I. Painted wood, St. George's Basilica, Prague.

munity of Prague, which proved exceptionally influential and resilient over the centuries, expanded into the area now known as Josefov (north of Stare Město) during the twelfth century; the extraordinary Staronova Synagogue was one of the first Gothic structures in Prague.[63] French culture continued to exercise an important influence. John of Luxemburg, Anne's grandfather, had been an infrequent visitor to Prague, preferring to divide his time between Luxemburg and the court of the French King Charles IV. He removed his eldest son, Wenceslaus, from Prague in 1323, when he was seven, to have him educated at the French court. At the time of his son's confirmation in France, John changed his name from Wenceslaus to Charles.[64]

Charles's new name spoke eloquently to his ambition of becoming a second Charlemagne, cynosure of a pan-European culture: this ambition is still legible in the disposition of architecture and civic space in Prague today. The multilingual Charles did not feel obliged to promote one vernacular culture at the expense of others. He was certainly a vigorous supporter of Czech and encouraged numerous translation projects, including a Czech Bible undertaken by monks of a Slavic-speaking cloister he himself had founded in 1348. But he did not seek to advance Czech by downplaying German; indeed, his court proved vital for the development of German in this period. His distinguished chancellor, Johann von Neumarkt (1310–80; also known as Jan ze Středy), translated numerous prayers, documents, and religious works into German and devoted his *Buch der Liebkosung* to the emperor.[65] Charles himself wrote (in Latin) both a life of his ancestor St. Wenceslaus (Václav), patron saint of Bohemia, and an autobiography that reads like a mirror for princes and has been described as "a literary effort unique among mediaeval rulers."[66] He gave an imperial and royal charter for a university at Prague in 1348, staffed his chancery with scholars, and offered particular encouragement to the writing of history, especially Bohemian history. He was fluent in Czech, German, French, Latin, and (according to Petrarch) Italian.[67]

Charles IV and Petrarch took a very particular interest in one another since their cultural and political roles were complementary: if Charles were heir to the Roman emperors, then Petrarch was his contemporary Vergil. Their twelve-year letter exchange plays out across Europe like an unrequited love affair, in which Petrarch assumes a passionate and impatient, one might say "feminized," role.[68] Petrarch is forever exhorting Charles to descend on Italy and take charge of affairs (backpedaling only when the local interests of his despotic patrons are threatened).[69] The poet moves between acclaiming his emperor and denouncing him with the passion and vehemence of a spurned lover. When things go well (as when Charles visited Italy in 1354), Petrarch acclaims him personally ("michi") as king not of Bohemia but of the world; as emperor of Rome; as Caesar himself: "Iam michi non Boemie sed mundi rex, iam romanus imperator, iam verus es Cesar." When things go badly (as Charles heads back to his "barbaric kingdoms" in 1355), Petrarch, feeling he has been cut with a sword, is full of reproaches: "Farewell, O Caesar, and consider what you are leaving behind and where you are headed."[70] Less than a year later, however, things are patched up, as the exigencies of Visconti foreign policy shift again: Petrarch sets off in pursuit of the emperor in Basel (where he fails to find him) and Prague (where he spends about a month in the company of the emperor, Empress Anne, and their court). Here he discovers "nothing more human than Caesar" and, in Caesar's entourage, "men of consummate kindness and courtesy, as though born in Attic Athens."[71] A later, petitionary letter, which reads like a love letter to "Caesar" but is actually a letter of reference for a friend, opens with the simple declaration: "Love makes even timid people daring."[72]

Petrarch and the emperor were evidently drawn together both by scholarly interests and by a shared fascination with (and investment in) the cult of great men. Petrarch was flattered to learn that his name was revered on the far side of the Alps and to discover that the emperor, in conversation, "wished to have a chronological account of my entire life from the day I was born to the present time."[73] The emperor, having already written his own *vita*, was particularly keen to get his hands on the Petrarchan *De viris illustribus*. Petrarch, like a romance heroine contemplating the yielding of her favor, promises it to him "provided your virtue persists and my life as well." Pressed to explain, Petrarch declares that Charles will have proved himself worthy both of the book and its dedication when, with deeds and a valorous spirit, he writes himself into the company of illustrious men ("rebus gestis et virtute animi illustribus te te viris ascripseris").[74] Charles's desire to possess and be part of the *De viris* was neither renounced nor satisfied; a later letter from Johann von Neumarkt indicates that the *De viris illustribus* continued to be discussed and longed for at the imperial court.[75]

Charles IV and his court occupy an important structuring role in Petrarch's *Familiares*: letters to Prague grow more frequent through the course of the work, and those addressed to Charles often occupy a prominent position (at the beginning or end of particular books).[76] The Bohemians, for their part, attached particular importance to Petrarch as a vital part of what Ferdinand Seibt has termed the "mythische Legitimation des Kaisertums."[77] Petrarch met with the emperor during both of his descents into Italy (1354, 1368); he marshaled his brilliant philological skills to disprove the authenticity of documents prejudicial to imperial interests; he could be called upon to exercise his powers as a Count Palatine, an honor accorded him during his visit to Prague.[78] Since Petrarch enjoyed close relations with the court as well as the emperor, reminiscences and textual traces of Petrarch were certain to outlast the death of Charles in 1378. For the young Anne of Bohemia, the poet's name would have been closely bound up with the memory and mystique of her father. In the realm of imperial culture, Petrarch was the one true counterpart to the Emperor Charles IV.

A recent bibliographical guide to medieval studies lists the term "Bohemia" under the organizational heading "Central Europe," thereby subordinating medieval culture and geography to categories from postwar or cold war Europe. Postpandemic and imperial Bohemia is central to Europe rather than Central European (a category that lumps it in with Bulgaria, Armenia, and the Balkans).[79] From such a viewpoint, then, England must have seemed to Anne and her followers (as it seemed to contemporary Italians) eccentric in its geography, politics, and culture.[80] Bohemians who had accompanied the emperor through Lombardy in 1368 and lodged with Bernabò might have recalled the massive English contingent that accompanied Lionel, duke of Clarence, to Milan for the famous wedding.[81] But the English would have been more immediately associated with the long and ruinous war with France: John of Luxemburg, Anne's grandfather, had been killed fighting (or bystanding: he was blind at the time) for the French at Crécy in 1346. Anne was to arrive in England with no dowry, and English commentators such as Walsingham were quick to complain about the expense of maintaining Anne "cum suis Boemiis," especially when they embarked on a tour of English monasteries "in excessivo numero."[82] Walsingham also complains about how the Bohemians, "patriotae Reginae," were quick to forget their native land once they had tasted the sweetness of English hospitality.[83] Given such xenophobic resentment, the Bohemians must surely have welcomed signs of cultural continuity that might have made Prague seem not so very far away. Chaucer's writing, I would suggest, provided one such hopeful sign. Anne and her retinue, who formed part of a sophisticated, multilingual culture that valued both Latin and vernacular composition, arrived in England speaking French.[84] (Anne's supposed dependence on vernacular texts and "glossed gospels" for her reading of the Bible was to be eagerly exploited by Lollard propagandists.)[85] Chaucer's writing, particularly his earlier, courtly poems, was strongly influenced by French models; his *Book of the Duchess* owed a particularly heavy debt to the most popular French *dit* of the fourteenth century, Machaut's *Le Jugement du roy de Behaigne*.[86] There is no doubt that Chaucer owned (or had ready access to) a manuscript of this poem, which tells how a historical monarch—Anne's grandfather, John of Luxemburg, King of Bohemia—comes to deliver a judgment at a specific site, the Castle of Durby. Machaut followed John all over Europe as his private secretary from c. 1323 until the late 1330s; his work continued to be influential at Prague throughout the fourteenth century (albeit the music rather than the poetry).[87] Machaut's second major patron, Peter of Cyprus, was well-known to the Bohemians and attended the wedding of Charles and Elizabeth of Pomerania, Anne's mother, at Krakov in 1363.[88] Froissart speaks of Peter (and he speaks of him at considerable length) being in Prague "et là environ" in 1363, shortly before his celebrated visit to England.[89]

The decline and fall of Peter of Cyprus was, as we have seen, one of the four "modern instances" included in the *Monk's Tale*. It is plausible that Chaucer was encouraged to write this essay in the Italian humanist genre, and to advertise it with the rubric "De Casibus Virorum Illustrium," by hearing talk of the Petrarchan *De viris illustribus*. Such talk was as likely to emanate from Bohemians in England as from Italians in Milan or Florence since, as we have noted, the Petrarchan *De viris* was the object of particular desire in Prague. No Bohemian, so far as we know, had ever seen the *De viris*, since it was bottlenecked in Padua by the jealous guardians of Petrarch's estate.[90] Chaucer was therefore at liberty to work from a Boccaccian model but to suggest the effect of a Petrachan text by having readers or auditors discover "my maister Petrak" (7.2325) in the middle of it. The inclusion of "modern instances" in the *Monk's Tale* would have been as topically poignant for the Bohemians as it was for the English. Anne's young half-brother Wenceslaus, like her husband Richard, was finding it very difficult to succeed as a young ruler following a long-lived monarch.[91]

Chaucer's decision to write the *Legend of Good Women* as a recompense for *Troilus and Criseyde* might similarly have been influenced by Bohemian connections. The opening book of the *Troilus* has generally been read as paying a compliment to the newly arrived Queen Anne. As Stephen A. Barney argues,[92] the case for deliberate allusion is considerably strengthened by use of the word "now":

> Right as oure firste lettre is now an A,
> In beaute first so stood she, makeles.   (1.171–72)

It is problematic to suggest too close an association between a contemporary queen and an ultimately unfaithful heroine, but consciousness of this fact may well have prompted the writing of the *Legend* as a palinode to the *Troilus* (a precedent clearly suggested by Machaut's two *Jugement* poems, where *Behaigne* is complemented, or reversed, by *Navarre*).[93] But inspiration for the *Legend* might again have derived from Bohemian recollections of Petrarchan texts, here specifically of the little treatise *de laudibus feminarum* addressed to Anne of Bohemia, third wife of the emperor. This unfortunate Anne died in childbirth (probably along with her third child) on July 11, 1362, at the age of 23; our Anne of Bohemia, born of the fourth empress three years later, was named in her memory.[94] Part of this memory must surely have been talk or material evidence of the letter that Petrarch had written to the young Empress Anne. Chaucer, once again, was stirred to compose the kind of neo-Italian humanist encyclopaedic text that might claim "Petrak" as its "maister." And once again he employs a Boccaccian model, the *De mulieribus claris*, since Petrarchan texts were very hard to come by. His choice of Alceste, the dead queen of the *Book of the Duchess*, might have been influenced by knowledge of how Anne came to be named. And, at the risk of gilding the daisy, it is perhaps worth noting that Anne's father devotes a whole chapter of his autobiography to the virtues of the *margarita* or pearl, the gem that, for all those soaked in French literary tradition, adds symbolic luster and pious suggestion to the English "dayesye."[95] The association between Alceste as "dayesye" and Alceste as pearl is made explicit by Chaucer in F 215–25, where she is said to wear a white crown "of perle fyn."

Such suggestions of the various ways in which Chaucer's court-based writing might have served, meshed, or intersected with Bohemian interests are designed not so much to encourage further study of sources and influences (although much is clearly needed) as to draw attention to a remarkable congruence of cultural fields. The congruence is not specifically between Bohemian and English culture, but rather between the Bohemians and Chaucer, for there was nobody in England more capable than Chaucer, through his particular political, diplomatic, and literary experiences in France, Italy, and elsewhere, of grasping the full internationalist dimensions of Bohemian style.[96] "Style" is a term that hangs ambiguously, often ephemerally, between literary and political terms of reference.[97] It is quite clear that the style of Richard's monarchy—in dress, culture, and political ambition—owed much to his marriage to the Bohemian daughter of an "emperice." It is also possible to show, by tracing lines of manuscript transmission, that certain productions of English culture (as diverse as Latin satire and Lollardy) were, sooner or later, carried back to Bohemia.[98] It seems legitimate, then, to see Chaucer's texts offering themselves, in both their literary and political styles, as an imaginative bridging of London and Prague.

Anne of Bohemia's education in English culture and politics was quite advanced before she reached London and Westminster in December 1381.[99] One of her chief instructors was Sir Simon Burley, a longterm associate of Chaucer's and a member of the so-called "Chaucer circle" in the 1380s.[100] Burley had taken a leading part in negotiating Anne's marriage with Richard and had accompanied her to England. Three days after landing in England, however, Anne passed (at Canterbury) from the care of Burley to the supervision of Thomas of Woodstock, Richard's uncle, later duke of Gloucester.[101] Burley, who had been entrusted with Richard's education by Edward III and was still described as "meastre del roy" in 1380,[102] was evidently popular with both Richard and Anne. But his access to the royal couple became more problematic when, at the insistence of the parliament of November 1381, two guardians (Sir Michael de la Pole and Richard, earl of Arundel) were appointed "to attend the king in his household and to counsel and govern his person."[103] Anne and Richard were married on January 14, 1382.

Very little time elapsed after her arrival in England before Anne, or the name of Anne, was pressed into service as a *mediatrix* seeking mercy or favor from the king on behalf of his wayward subjects. In 1382–83, many individual pardons to 1381 rebels were said to be granted at the queen's request; in 1382, Anne's nominal intervention supposedly saved Wyclif from the Council.[104] A charter of 1389 pictures Anne kneeling before Richard (within the R that begins his name) on behalf of the citizens of Shrewsbury (plate 11). Anne continued to play this role, one traditionally assigned to English queens,[105] for the rest of her life. In 1391, the Grand Master of the Teutonic Knights wrote to her (and separately to John of Gaunt) urging her to influence Richard in adhering to the terms of a treaty; in 1392, she knelt before Richard in Westminster Hall, making formal intercession on behalf of the citizens of London.[106] It is evident that at most such intercessory moments, Anne is simply acting out a scripted role in a public drama that is not of her making. But it is rash to suppose Anne incapable of assuming an active role, or to assume (as does one historian) that she was valued chiefly for her docility and charm.[107]

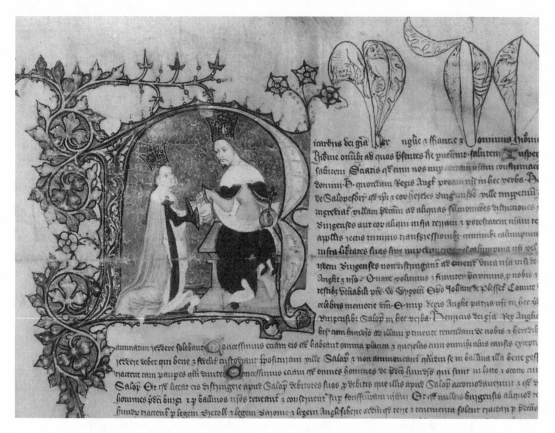

Plate 11. *Richard II and Anne of Bohemia*. Illuminated initial, Charter of Richard II to Shrewsbury (1389). Shrewsbury Museums, MS I.24.

Her reported commissioning of a book of heraldry, the *Tractatus de armis* of the mysterious Johannes de Bado Aureo, may indicate an ambition to read the signs in disputes such as the Scrope-Grosvenor controversy (the six-year Court of Chivalry epic that erupted in 1385).[108] And, like the rebels of 1381, or like the wife in the *Shipman's Tale*, she may have been perfectly capable of envisioning an active role within political structures that assumed only passive compliance.[109] If she could play Mary and Esther, merciful *mediatrix* and wise counselor,[110] in public, she was evidently capable of assuming such roles in private: in the household (a location at once public and private) and in the bedchamber (one of the most notable Chaucerian sites for female eloquence). Chaucer's evident conviction that wifely eloquence represents the chief hope of facing down a powerful, irascible spouse is clearly shared by the citizens of London, or at least by the poet who writes on their behalf: "Quod vir non audet, sola potest mulier" ("What a man does not dare, a wife alone can do").[111]

"Y Aske Yow this Man": Chaucer, Alceste, Queen Anne

F 342—Alceste's first intervention for Chaucer before her irate, godlike husband—is clearly a moment deserving of the thickest description. The first thing to notice (once again) is that the saving voice in Chaucer is female. Petrarch, in his relations with Anne's father, keeps women out of the picture, preferring (as in his dealings with other great men) to play the woman himself. Chaucer, in representing his relations with a figure of equivalent authority, chooses to position an eloquent wife between himself and his lord. He clearly felt licensed to do this both by immediate political contingencies and by political tradition: he too could imagine an English-speaking queen, a sage and merciful *mediatrix*, who would intervene on his behalf. But there is more to be said about Chaucer's personal devotion to a fictional figure, Alceste, who stands in some relation to a historical queen, Anne of Bohemia:[112] Chaucer might be considered as a suitor. The fact that nobody thinks to take Chaucer seriously as a suitor might well be read as testimony to the brilliance of his protective coloring. How can such a "worm" be taken seriously? But such a "worm," as the irascible god himself points out, is found very near the bud. What, then, does such a suitor have to offer? An appreciation, unmatched by any man in England, of the kind of cultural terrain a Bohemian abroad might recognize and feel welcomed by. What might his reward be? Perhaps the freedom to stand in the place he has already unwittingly occupied; and also the license, "whan this book ys maad," to "yive it the queene, / . . . at Eltham or at Sheene" (F 496–97).

There is no need to assume, with Lydgate, that Chaucer wrote this poem expressly "at request off the queen."[113] But even if the *Legend* never left his desk, it remains remarkable for its intimate *imagining* of relations between an eloquent queen and a productive poet. This intimacy between poet and queen is suggested by the possibility of secret communication between them (as Chaucer evokes a cultural terrain more familiar to the queen than to her husband) and by the perennial question of whose voice occupies whose body at any given moment. As devotee of the "dayesye" within the poem, we have noted, Chaucer claims that his voice is really hers: like fingers on a harp, she plays his heart and brings forth whatever "vois" she chooses (F 89–93). But it becomes clear as the poem progresses that language has complex and dangerous political connotations that escape Chaucer's control or comprehension. When the time comes for Chaucer to defend himself from the accusations of an outraged spouse who stands at the brink of tyranny, the conceit that his "vois" is directed by the lady will have to be abandoned: to save him, she must speak not through him but instead of him. Yet every word she speaks, of course, is scripted by the historical Chaucer, who stands in some relation (however distant) to the historical Anne of Bohemia. Given such complexities and dangers, where timely use of language seems the only guarantee of salvation or betrayal, and such subtle overlaps between poetic and historical worlds, it is not surprising if we occasionally call to mind relations between a later poet and a later Anne under the shadow of a later (and more terrible) absolutist monarch: Thomas Wyatt, Anne Boleyn, and Henry VIII.[114]

Alceste's defense of Chaucer before the God of Love must surely rank as one of the most brilliant set-pieces of political rhetoric ever written. Although it begins with a hundred-line monologue (F 342–441), it nevertheless suggests the dialogic qualities of the *Melibee* by seeming to respond to the shifting emotional state of its addressee. It would be otiose to trace every twist and turn of this rhetorical performance, since this would tend to repeat the thematic concerns of the *Melibee* chapter. But it is worth noting how Alceste fights to establish, or to redefine, the circumstances of her utterance and how she achieves the brilliant feat of practicing the arts of *dicendi* and *tacendi at the same time*. Her crucial intervention (to recap a little) comes as the God of Love considers turning Chaucer from a spectacle of foolishness to a spectacle ("wel be sene!") of cruelty:

> "By seynt Venus that my moder ys,
> If that thou lyve, thou shalt repenten this
> So cruelly that it shal wel be sene!"
> Thoo spak this lady, clothed al in grene,
> And seyde, "God, ryght of youre curtesye,
> Ye moten herken yf he can replye
> Agayns al this that ye have to him meved."   (F 338–44)

Chaucer must speak, says Alceste; he deserves the right of "replye." But, knowing that if Chaucer does "replye" he will certainly destroy himself, Alceste continues talking for a hundred lines, monopolizing the *dicendi* while imposing *tacendi* on Chaucer. The first problem she addresses is the confusion of *Hof* and *Gericht* (always a danger when the same authority rules over both). She begins by separating out these functions, appealing first to her spouse's "curtesye" (*Hof*) and then to his sense of judicial procedure ("that ye have to him meved," *Gericht*). It is difficult for a God of Love (and son of Venus) to be always mindful of his obligation to govern by due process of law, "by right" (351); but it is also difficult for anyone to remind him of this duty, since, being a god (and absolute ruler) he knows everything. Alceste solves this dilemma even as she expresses it through the indispensable courtly trope (much favored by the Knight, and botched by the Squire) of *occupatio*:

> "And yf ye nere a god, that knowen al,
> Thanne myght yt be as I yow tellen shal:"   (F 348–49)

Alceste next returns to the problematic *Hof-Gericht* divide by considering the topic of flattery, one of much concern to political theorists such as John of Salisbury and Albertano of Brescia. The "losengeour," or flatterer, systematically exploits the confusion of *Hof* and *Gericht* by attempting to turn the former into the latter: that is, he drums on the ears of his monarch at court in order to win his "daliaunce" and then to move him against those he envies (F 352–56). And so we come to Alceste's first major defense of Chaucer. Her general strategy is to separate the intentions, fruits, and uses of Chaucer's *makyng* from the historical individual who is supposedly responsible for them (F 362–72). In denying Chaucer any defining moment of authorial intent, Alceste encourages the God of Love to view "Chaucer" as what we might term an "author function": to let the axe fall on the neck of the historical Chaucer would be unduly essentializing, endowing the flesh-and-blood Chaucer with a historical grandeur that he could never actually command. If this formulation seems too indebted to modern literary theory, it might be rephrased in terms of medieval understanding of legal ownership (in which the notion of "absolute ownership" is very rare). Chaucer never "owned" the writings that bear his name: he might claim *usus fructi* of the tropes that cycle through his writing, but never *dominio*.[115]

Alceste now develops a remarkable parallel between the relations of kings to *makeres* and the relationship of monarchs to subjects, beginning with an infamous negative exemplum:

> "This shoolde a ryghtwis lord have in his thoght,
> And be nat lyk tirauntz of Lumbardye,
> That han no reward but at tyrannye.
> For he that kyng or lord is naturel,
> Hym oghte nat be tiraunt ne crewel
> As is a fermour, to doon the harm he kan.
> He moste thinke yt is his lige man,
> And is his tresour and his gold in cofre."   (F 373–80)

No king should diminish himself by behaving like a tyrannical tax-gatherer ("fermour"); he must think that *such a man as Chaucer* ("yt") is his liegeman, his treasure and his money in the bank. The text does not make such high claims for Chaucer quite so directly, of course (although he remains the most logical choice as referent of the pronoun "yt"). Alceste's discourse is evidently drifting from the immediate scene of intercession and judgment to more general but no less concrete political reflections in which "yt" stands in for political subjects in general. Such subjects are evidently those of Richard II's England rather than the God of Love's dreamland: the discussion of the need to honor and advance magnates (evocatively described as "half-goddes," F 387) while respecting the rights of lesser subjects (F 384–90) seems particularly apt for the 1380s. But most timely and eloquent of all is the naming and repudiation of "tirauntz of Lumbardye": Anne of Bohemia must surely have come to represent for Richard (as for Chaucer) the living antithesis of the Lombard option. Before his marriage to Anne was arranged,

Richard's diplomats were actively pursuing a union between the English monarch and Caterina Visconti.[116] Instead of having Emperor Charles IV as a father-in-law, illustrious and deceased, Richard might have ended up with Bernabò, infamous and alive. Having observed Bernabò and his polity at first hand, Chaucer was well equipped to imagine how a Lombard absolutist model might play on English soil; the nightmare of Fragment 4 would be much closer to home. Anne/Alceste, therefore, represents the historical alternative to such a fate; no wonder she sends Chaucer zipping into the fields.

Alceste's next move, effected so elegantly that it is possible to miss its extraordinary boldness, is to convince an absolute ruler, her spouse, of the virtue of silence and inaction:

> "In noble corage ought ben arest,
> And weyen every thing by equytee,
> And ever have reward to his owen degree."   (F 397–99)

The practice of "arest" is obviously vital to a king in his struggle to master his passions and remain "ryghtwis"; it is the quality—commended by Dante's Aquinas as part of his discourse on "regal prudenza," "kingly prudence"—that differentiates Theseus from Walter (and, one hopes, Richard II from "tirauntz of Lumbardye").[117] The whole of Alceste's speech is a form of "arest": it prevents Chaucer from speaking (while insisting on his right to speak) and allows the God of Love to recover himself—his kingly self. It also continues to offer both monarch and subject clues as to what their next speeches and actions should be. Chaucer's role is laid out first: he should simply beg for mercy "ryght in his bare sherte" (F 405). The God of Love, for his part, should be "sumwhat tretable," remembering (and here Alceste interpellates her spouse most cleverly) that no death sentence is involved in this case (F 409–11). Chaucer has attempted to be loyal to Love in his poetry, however ineptly, as the catalogue of his works suggests (F 417–30). Since he "mysseyde" in his *makynge*, he should now make amends in kind (and under a tighter rein): responsibility for *inventio* should be taken from him, and all phases of his literary production should be dictated by the God of Love ("as ye wol devyse," F 431–41). Having argued long and hard for Chaucer's right to reply, Alceste has now relieved him of the need to speak. The only speech she has envisaged for him is a suit for pardon (F 403–6). Sensing that even this may be too much to ask, however, she speaks it herself (taking the opportunity to remind her spouse that she, like Anne of Bohemia, had a life before she ever set foot in his kingdom):

> "I, youre Alceste, whilom quene of Trace,
> Y aske yow this man . . ."   (F 432–33)

Alceste's request is immediately granted by her spouse, who, judging from the judiciously qualified quality of his first sentence, has evidently regained

his composure (F 443–46). Although Alceste has alerted him to his responsibilities within the court as *Gericht*, the framing of her final appeal enables
him to speak *höflicherweise*: he grants the queen's request (like a good king
in a romance) purely out of devotion to her. No mention is now made of
Chaucer's rights under law. Chaucer is addressed in just one line, where he is
brusquely directed to thank the queen. Chaucer does so, but with appalling
lack of tact; he actually manages to subordinate the God of Love (to "God
above," and to his wife) twice in the space of three lines:

> "Madam, the God above
> Foryelde yow that ye the god of Love
> Han maked me his wrathe to foryive."   (F 456–58)

Chaucer immediately makes things worse by attempting to reopen a judicial procedure that has evidently come to an end, and by taking issue with
some of the lines of defense that Alceste employed to save him. Whatever his
sources might have meant, he claims, he always had a firm grip on his own
authorly intent, his "menynge" (F 470–74). Alceste soon calls a halt to such
"arguynge" (a term, like "counterpleted," drawn from the lexicon of legal
procedure):[118]

> "For Love ne wol nat countrepleted be
> In ryght ne wrong, and lerne that at me!
> Thow hast thy grace, and hold the ryght therto."   (F 476–78)

Since Love is the absolute arbiter on matters of love, there can be no questioning of his judgments: Chaucer must accept the social and judicial reality
of his "trespas" and serve the life sentence of supervised "makyng" that is
handed down to him (F 479–84). The suspicion that the God of Love's court
is governed by political rather than philosophical perceptions is confirmed
some fifty lines later when a new charge is leveled against Chaucer: that he neglected to include Alceste in his *balade* "Hyd Absolon" (F 537–43). It is quite
clear, from the context provided three hundred lines earlier, that this *balade* is
intended to praise "this lady fre," Alceste. But, as Chaucer the dreamer has recently learned, authorly "entente" and "menynge" are difficult to hang on to
once a text enters public circulation: when the God of Love heard the *balade*
it seems that nobody was on hand to gloss "my lady" as "Alceste." Chaucer
has also learned, however, that "Love ne wol nat countrepleted be" (F 476):
he holds his tongue, swallows some reasoned but unwarranted abuse, and gets
on with making his "Legende." The *Prologue* closes with the poet's despotic
master exercising extremely close control over his "makynge": he prescribes
content ("goode women"), sources ("thy bookes"), form (rhyming meters),
starting point (Cleopatra), and mode of treatment (exemplary; epitomiz-
ing—"the grete"—with a marked tendency toward *abbreviatio* rather than
amplificatio).

Such tight control suggests that *makyng* in such a context will prove just as claustrophobic and restrictive as it is at the court of Theseus: the temple walls writ (but only slightly) longer. And the dreamer Chaucer, one realizes, seems particularly ill-qualified to assess "the grete" of lives of ladies (inevitably) at court. His own readings of court space suggest that he belongs in the study or the marketplace rather than within the *familia regis*. His reaction to learning that Alceste is to be identified with his special flower seems particularly crass:

> "Wel hath she quyt me myn affeccioun
> That I have to hire flour, the dayesye."   (F 523–24)

Chaucer now understands why Alceste has stood up for him: she has repaid ("quyt") his devotion to her symbol, the daisy. Court life, in this view, is reduced to *commercium*, commercial exchange: the idea that Alceste's mediation, like that of the Virgin Mary, cannot be bought or deserved at any price remains a mystery beyond his grasp. His very ignorance of this point is designed to assure us, as cultured courtly readers, that his need for Alceste (and her surrogate beyond the text) remains as great as ever.

Past and Present: Chaucer as Petrarchan Humanist

The rewriting of the so-called F text of the *Legend of Good Women* as so-called G (uniquely preserved by Cambridge University MS Gg. 4.27) reiterates an issue of growing importance for this book: the ways in which a text, over time, comes to mean different things as circumstances change; the ways in which contemporary history may break into and embed itself in a literary construct or, as in the case of G, demand both expansion and excision. The ultimate effect of the G revision, I shall argue, is an attempt to save or withhold the text from history by denying it the force of occasion and by fixing it in a past that is sharply separated from the single viewpoint of an all-knowing present. As the agent of such a revision, the G-author (whom I take to be Chaucer) follows the precedent of Petrarchan humanism, turning his back on the vernacular poetics of Dante, Boccaccio, and the *Canterbury Tales*.

The delicate courtly scenario of the F-text *Prologue* could hardly survive if Alceste were to kneel to one of the "half-goddes" (F 387) who attend the God of Love while the god himself stands uselessly by. Something analogous to this, however, is said to have happened to Richard II and Anne of Bohemia in 1388 (that is, almost as soon as the F-text had been written). Sir Simon Burley, Richard's childhood tutor and his matchmaker with Anne, was impeached for treason by the Lords Appellant. The two junior appellants—Derby and Nottingham—interceded for Burley, but their senior partners—Gloucester, Arundel, and Warwick—proved obdurate.[119] Queen Anne went on her knees before the earls of Arundel and Gloucester begging for the life of Burley, who (in the laconic words of the *Traïson et Morte*) "nonetheless had his head chopped off."[120] Adding insult to injury, Arundel responded to the queen's entreaties by telling her that she would do better to pray for herself "et pour vostre mary." The all-powerful royal husband is not now one to be prayed to, but (at the direction of one of his own magnates) to be prayed for. The insult maintains contact with the courtly world of the *Legend* through the choice of epithet chosen by Arundel to address the queen: "Mamie," "my lady-friend."[121]

There is no doubt that Burley was resented for his links with the Bohemians: he was explicitly charged with showing them undue favor.[122] There can be little doubt, too, that Anne was personally attached to Burley, the courtier who had escorted her to England before transferring her to Gloucester's care in 1381. The helplessness of king and queen before the events of 1388 makes the delicate politics and rhetoric of the F *Prologue* seem anachronistic—properly the stuff of dream poetry—almost as soon as they were written. The deaths of Burley and his fellow chamber knights, commonly characterized as the first political executions in England for more than half a century,[123] made any kind of attachment to the royal household and its courtly politics seem highly dangerous. As signs of trouble grew more abundant during and after the parliament of October 1 to November 28, 1386, Chaucer systematically distanced himself from the royal circles. By 1388 he had resigned from his controllership of customs (a royal appointment), given up his exchequer annuities, and left his dwelling above Aldgate. Such astute reading of historical signs (a talent not to be guessed at from the self-representation of the F *Prologue*) enabled him to survive 1388 when lesser talents, such as Thomas Usk, did not.[124]

If the events of 1388 threatened the delicate mechanisms of the F *Prologue*, the death of Anne of Bohemia in 1394 made them worse than obsolete: a painful reminder of lost options. Anne, who represented the chief source of continuity in the much-damaged royal household, came to assume increasing importance for Richard after 1388.[125] Their marriage seems to have been, to borrow Caroline Barron's felicitous phrase, a "companionate" one.[126] The death at Sheene on June 7, 1394, of the "benignissima domina" (as Adam of Usk calls her) was experienced as a sudden and unforeseen disaster by Richard, who ordered that the entire manor be destroyed ("fecit extirpari"); there is no evidence that he ever visited the site again.[127] Anne's demise also marks, I would argue, a disastrous terminus for Chaucerian polity, the subject of this book. As we have seen, so many of the hopes for the stability of male-headed households hang upon the office and performance of eloquent wives. Anne of Bohemia, while she lived, represented an important historical correlative for the wives who fight out political battles in a whole host of Chaucerian texts. The absence of Anne makes the future look about as bright as it does for Apollo and his court-trained crow once Apollo has killed his wife. The likely consequences of Richard attempting to rule without his queen were soon glimpsed in an extraordinary scene that took place as Anne lay in her coffin at Westminster Abbey. Arundel, one of the Appellants who had pressed for the death of Burley, absented himself from the funeral procession from St. Paul's, arrived late at the Abbey, and then asked to leave early on urgent business. Richard, outraged, struck him violently on the head, causing his blood to flow freely and pollute the church.[128] Richard without Anne is a Melibee without Prudence: outrage at insult and injury to a much-loved wife, in that wife's absence, is doomed to lead to a renewal of violence. The particular cycle of intermagnate violence initiated in 1388 and rehearsed at Anne's death was not completed until 1397, when Richard had Arundel escorted through London by his Cheshire archers and beheaded on Tower Hill.[129] Gloucester, having been reminded of his failure to spare Burley when the queen kneeled before him, died at Calais soon after.[130]

The timing and circumstances of Anne's death were particularly unfortunate for Chaucer. Anne's death on June 7, 1394, the feast of Pentecost, must have made the pentecostal imagery of the *Summoner's Tale* seem wholly distasteful: the unholy wind that descends over the twelve spokes in the convent is a joke that, for the moment, does not bear repeating.[131] The bright idea of associating this tale with Holderness, held by Queen Anne "ad terminum vitae suae," must also suddenly have seemed a liability, especially when the Duke of Gloucester arrived in Holderness soon after the death of Anne, "circa festum Pentecostes," to claim the *dominium* as his own.[132] Even Chaucer's choice of name for his peasant protagonist was ill-fated. The new claimant to Holderness was, as the monastic chronicler tells us, "serenissimus princeps dominus *Thomas* Wodstok, dux Gloucestriae."[133] The *Summoner's Tale* could evidently survive such strokes of coincidence and dumb luck: but the F *Prologue* of the *Legend* was another matter. Chaucer had, after all, associated the very moment of his completing the text with the queen and the place she died, a bond made tighter through the effect of rhyme:

> "And whan this book ys maad, yive it the quene,
> On my byhalf, at Eltham or at Sheene."   (F 496–97)

Chaucer would also, I believe, have found the suggestive associations he had forged between Alceste as "perle" and "dayesye" and "the quene" very difficult to shake. In October 1396, when Richard traveled to Ardes to receive his new, infant queen from King Charles VI, he had his male attendants dress in the livery of his dead queen, Anne of Bohemia, while he himself wore a hat of hanging pearls.[134] It is clear that Richard explicitly associated the pearl with Anne because he gave the French king a collar of pearls from the livery of the dead queen, worth 5,000 marks.[135] It could be that Chaucer's suggestive association of Anne with his pearl-crowned queen, Alceste, had proved so successful that Richard was moved, at this crucial moment, to wear the *margarita* in her memory. It is more likely, of course, that Chaucer's *Legend* is simply refining and recycling motifs and associations originated from royal circles. Either way, allusion to "the quene" within a context soaked in *marguerite* tradition seems certain to have stirred memories of Anne of Bohemia years after her death.

In his *Book of the Duchess*, Chaucer actually introduces the image of a historical site that quite literally speaks the memory of a loving, courtly marriage destroyed by death. As the "hert-huntynge" in that poem ends, the king rides homeward to

> A long castel with walles white,
> Be Seynt Johan, on a ryche hil.   (1318–19)

"Johan" may be taken as representing John of Gaunt, "long castel" as Lancaster, "white" as Gaunt's deceased wife Blanche, and the "ryche hil" with Richmond, their castle in Yorkshire. But whereas in the *Duchess* Chaucer is moved to introduce a building that evokes memories of a deceased and much-loved wife, in the *Legend* (in a gesture analogous to Richard's repudiation of Sheene) he elects to tear one down, or out: the F 496–97 couplet that invokes Sheene is excised. So too is the characterization of the daisy as "of alle floures floure" (F 53) and as "emperice" (F 185); so too thoughts of "my lady sovereyne" (F 275). In fact, a whole succession of cuts are made that weaken both the mystery and political suggestiveness of Alceste; she is, from the start, both a known and a diminished quantity. The refrain of the *balade* critiqued for its nebulousness in F ("My lady cometh") is rewritten in G as "Alceste is here"; the risk that the God of Love will misjudge Chaucer's intentions is thereby neatly removed (G 525–28). The general effect of the G revision is to preserve both text and author from those linguistic traps that made F such dangerous and exhilarating territory: all those lines on the *tydif*'s "newefanglnesse," on the betrayals of bird courtship (and of personification allegory), and the final, dubious acclamation of Summer as "governour and lord" (F 154–70) are simply cut. Ambiguities that remain seem less topical and therefore less threatening: a considerable passage of time has evidently passed between F and G. In F, May has just begun (108), but in G it is almost over (89). Chaucer, in G, "begynnyst dote" (261); he belongs now among "olde foles" (G 262), busying himself with "olde bokes" that speak of "olde women" (301). Indeed, the *Legend* now seems to think of itself as an old book, a text that has become familiar and hence less remarkable. There is no talk now of the lady authoring the text through Chaucer since the excursus from the *Filostrato*, F 84–96, is cut entirely. There is, however, much more talk of *auctors* in general. Even the God of Love seems to have grown more bookish and orthodox in his thinking:

> "This knoweth God, and alle clerkes eke
> That usen swiche materes for to seke.

> What seith Valerye, Titus, or Claudyan?
> What seith Jerome . . . ?"   (G 278–81)

These lines form part of the greatest single addition to G (267–312), a passage that makes a concerted attempt at pushing experience back into "the world of autours" (308). All this distracts from the sense of *occasion* so vividly generated by F: if this text were tied to any specific historical moment, the sense now is, it lays—like some old romance—far back in the past.[136] The God of Love's lengthy speech about old books, delivered just before Chaucer is called upon to speak and defend himself, serves to diffuse the tension generated by F at this most crucial juncture. In F, we have noted, the deity stands on the very brink of losing self-control and threatens death and cruelty (F 339–40). Such extreme language is moderated in G: the God of Love calls for Chaucer's "answere" in G at line 267, but then goes on (in a forty-line excursus) to develop a reasoned critique of Chaucer's *makynge* suggestive of irritation rather than outrage. Alceste's intervention in G 317 is less dramatic because it seems less urgently required.

At this point, I would suggest, the G-text loses contact with (or washes its hands of) contemporary history. The hope that an irate son of Venus would moderate his anger on his own initiative (rather than relying on the rhetorical skill of his queenly spouse) seems a pious wish indeed after 1394. In his poem or dream world, Chaucer elects to erase lines that might point to an Alcestian surrogate beyond the text. In the historical world there was, indeed, nobody to point to but the monarch himself (plus, in 1396, a seven-year-old queen). While Anne was alive, Richard could feed and stage his own importance by having the daughter and sister of an emperor kneel before him; the lion rises above the eagle.[137] Once Anne was dead, however, Richard felt compelled to retain the prestige of her imperial pedigree by becoming Holy Roman Emperor himself. To do this he needed to depose Anne's brother, the Emperor Wenceslaus. As early as 1394, Richard was sending gifts to the imperial electors; by 1397 he had made four of them his pensioners (including the influential archbishop of Cologne, who became his vassal and liegeman).[138] His affectation of imperial style may be seen in the Wilton diptych, where eagles alternate with white harts on his robe; in the extraordinary carved head at York Minster, said to represent Richard II as emperor-designate;[139] and in his characterization in the roll of the Hilary Parliament in 1397 as "entier Emperour de son Roialme d'Engleterre."[140] To advance his ambitions, Richard was willing to support (but then to repudiate) the Franco-Florentine war against Gian Galeazzo Visconti, "tyrant of Lombardy"; to encourage yet another "Visconti marriage," this time between Henry of Derby and Lucia, another of Bernabò's daughters; and to become the author (rather than the attentive reader) of *de casibus* tragedy by deposing his own brother-in-law.[141] The self-deluding grandiosity of such schemes must have driven the author of the *Clerk's Tale*, the *Melibee*, the *Manciple's Tale*, the *Monk's Tale*, and the *Legend of Good Women* close to despair (or into retirement).

The G revision does make some effort to adjust to new political realities. One expansion (360–64) emphasizes the importance of listening to the "excusacyons" of subjects, and of respecting parliamentary procedures ("here compleyntes and petyciouns"). The very need to make such a plea suggests that tyrannical or absolutist tendencies are in the ascendant. The term "tyrannye," used to describe "tyraunts of Lumbardye" in F, is now coupled with "wilfulhede" (suggestive of the term *voluntas arbitrium*).[142] New emphasis is laid on kingly tradition in the evocation of oaths sworn by kings before their lieges "Ful many a hundred wynter herebeforn": the tendency of tyrannous polity, as we have seen, is to effect a violent rupture with the past. Such traces of resistance in G are heartening, but they cannot alter the dominant impression that the death of Anne and the diminution of Alceste have sapped the text of its political vitality and its occasional (that is, historical) force. Time has passed, and the poet "begynnyst dote" (261). Taking his place among "olde foles" whose "spiryt fayleth" (262), his chief concern becomes the saving of his text from temporal vicissitudes and its delivery to posterity as a finished book. This effort to save a text by a process of revision that stabilizes the present by confining historical indeterminacies to a carefully distanced past marks the closest Chaucer ever comes to adopting a Petrarchan or neohumanist poetic. Dante, in opening his *Convivio*, explicitly refuses either to repudiate or revise his youthful work, the *Vita nuova*, in the light of later experience: "Ché altro si conviene e dire e operare ad una etade che ad altra."[143] His *Commedia* also stands unrevised even after the death of the Emperor Henry VII has vitiated the political hopes with which it set out; the frustrations and disasters of unfolding history, perhaps most poignantly captured in *Paradiso* 30, 136–38, are integral to its power as a vernacular text. Petrarchan *tarditas*, by contrast, refuses to release texts to the movement of history until they promise to be, through a process of private revision, unassailably finished. Petrarch's technique, followed by Chaucer in G, is to make the present a secure point of reference against the newly essentialized otherness of a now distant past.[144] Such a technique serves regimes keen to assert the unquestionable givenness of present political arrangements better than it suits those that would trace continuities between past and present.

The Wilton diptych, that most enigmatic and beautiful of texts from the last years of Richard II, speaks both to the English monarch's immediate absolutist and imperial ambitions and to his sense of continuity with a political and religious tradition of English kingship. As one of three kings kneeling before the Virgin and child, he claims his figurative place both among the magi and in a line of succession leading from the English royal saints Edmund and Edward the Confessor to himself. The Lancastrian dynasty, given its violent usurpation of the throne, had little choice but to downplay the significance of historical continuity and to accentuate the overwhelming reality of new political (and religious) circumstances. The emphases of Petrarchan human-ism, elaborated within the contexts of northern Italian despotism, seem quite in keeping with the ideological needs of such an enterprise. Chaucer's G-text, in its repudiation of Dantean temporality, reads like a Lancastrian text *avant la lettre*.

After Wifely Eloquence: The Passing of Chaucerian Polity

The F-text of the *Prologue* to the *Legend of Good Women*, much like the Wilton diptych, gains much of its poignancy as an artefact through our knowledge that its delicate balancing of symbolic claims is, almost at the moment of its completion, about to be swept away. The Lancastrians will attempt to legitimate themselves in matters of religion not by celebrating the continuity of royal bloodlines but by turning the machinery of state to the persecution of religious dissent. Wifely rhetoric will contribute little to the testing and tempering of Lancastrian policy: Henry IV had little time or inclination to develop court life with his second wife, Joan of Brittany; Henry V (who spent much of his brief married life outside England) paid for his wife's dowry by seizing that of his stepmother (once his prospective mother-in-law) whom he charged with witchcraft.[145] Chaucer's dedication to exploring the domestic dynamics and political efficacy of female eloquence, then, seems peculiarly a phenomenon of the years of Richard's first marriage, 1381–94. Such dedication is not shared by his Italian contemporaries. Boccaccio, we have noted, sees the business of writing *de mulieribus claris* as a pastime to be enjoyed once the serious business of *res publica* has been taken care of. Petrarch, with the single exception of his short *de laudibus feminarum* treatise, excludes women from the international networks of correspondence represented by his letter collec-tions. When, in his personal dealings with "myghty men," Petrarch discovers a need for traditionally feminine roles (the powerless, Griselde-like subject; the hopeful or spurned lover; the romance heroine, offering and withholding her favors) he plays them himself. Only Chaucer, it seems, is moved to keep positioning an eloquent wife between an irate masculine master and himself and the public world. When he hangs over the abyss, as he does in the F *Pro-logue*, he is saved not by the strong hand of masculine bloodlines (as Petrarch is saved at Milan), but by the timely intervention of wifely eloquence.

Anne of Bohemia, I have suggested, is a historical surrogate of vital im-portance for Chaucer's elaboration of the role of Alceste. The arrival of Anne and her fellow Bohemians prompted Chaucer to explore a rich new cultural ground: a vital conjunction of his awakening interest in Italian neohumanism and his long-term dedication to the courtly poetics of Machaut. The abiding presence of Anne, the daughter and sister of an emperor, also symbolized a historical alternative to the polity pursued by "tyraunts of Lumbardye," a form of rule where masculine "wilfulhede" and self-aggrandizement turn a deaf ear to the moderating persuasions embodied in the person of an eloquent wife. The loss of such a wife, or the lost possibility of imagining one, is a disaster that Chaucerian polity cannot survive.

Chaucer's dedication to imagining wifely eloquence is, in the comparative and diachronic perspectives developed by this book, the most singular aspect of his oeuvre. This is not a phenomenon limited to his court-based writing. Eloquent wives who influence or determine the outcome of events are a perennial feature of all kinds of Chaucerian text. Differences between Chaucer's court and noncourt writing have, I think, been unnecessarily exaggerated. The Wife of Bath, for example, is a remarkable crossover phenomenon: she represents the mercantile and manufacturing world, but tells a tale that hinges (twice) on wifely eloquence at court and is cited in a courtly near-*balade* as a familiar authority on marriage.[146] The royal household itself, through its exemplary relation of king to queen, may be read as a model both of relations between monarch and subject and (in a structure reproduced throughout the kingdom) between masculine household head and feminine spouse. Attempts to identify the origins of literature with court structures seem to me to fall victim to the court's own ideology of self-sufficiency. The court, like the fragile project of Petrarchan humanism, knows itself to be dependent on sources of supply beyond itself both for purposes of ideological counter-definition and for its own material infrastructure (that is, food, drink, and clothing).[147] When the king is dwelling at London or Westminster, "at Eltham or at Sheene," the Tabard at Southwark (where the associational form of Chaucer's pilgrimage takes shape) falls within court space and so becomes subject to one-sided expropriation.[148]

Chaucer's dedication to particular eloquent wives—Alceste and Alisoun, Griselde and May—seems ultimately to express something larger than allegiance to a particular form of courtly or noncourtly polity. Their moments of utterance read like epiphenomena of a greater narrative that speaks, perhaps, to Chaucer's sense of writing a new *lingua materna*; or issue, perhaps, from psychological depths that other critics are better qualified to fathom.[149] This book can insist, however, that Chaucer's dedication to wifely eloquence is a singular historical phenomenon, one to which Chaucer himself draws attention. The "sixth of six" topos, we have noted, was adopted by Chaucer (following the precedent of Ovid, Jean de Meun, Boccaccio, and Dante) as a form of authorial signature. In the *Troilus*, Chaucer's self-definition as the sixth of six expresses his most exalted ambitions in a tradition of great *auctors*; in the *General Prologue*, it draws attention to the oddity of his social positioning among the most marginal and parasitical of pilgrims. But the last of his "sixth of six" signatures seems, all things considered, to make the most convincing claim on him: "Welcome the sixte, whan that evere he shal" (3.45). Given his lifelong devotion to wifely eloquence, Chaucer and his *Tales* are clearly the person and the moment, the man and "whan," that the Wife of Bath is riding forth to find.

Conclusion

Fundamental Chaucerian processes of *felaweshipe*-formation and despotic staging are rediscovered in Shakespeare; disruptions to and intensifications of such processes, however, remain memorably disorienting for a medievalist reading forward in time. Cultural differences between Shakespeare and Chaucer seem to emerge mysteriously, lacking immediate political correlatives; revolutions in poetic and dramatic form resist easy alignment with revolutions in forms of polity. Elizabethan England does not, in fact, represent a revolutionary period in the extended history of English state forms; it sees, rather, steady and unspectacular consolidation.[1] The cultural and psychological disjunctions of *Hamlet*—a play that strains at the structuring frameworks of an imagined medieval world—lag more than a half-century behind the revolution in state forms effected under Henry VIII. The Henrician revolution has been narrativized many times from many differing literary, political, historical, and (especially) religious viewpoints. Here I would like to identify just two political moments that effect radical disruption of the historiographical *longue durée* traced by this book and to adumbrate their playing out through Shakespeare. The first such moment, predictably enough, is the spoliation and abolition of guilds in the 1540s. The second is the execution of Anne Boleyn, queen of England, on May 19, 1536.

Reading forward into Shakespearean polity brings further and particular complications, for staged representations of even the most intensively despotic regimes—as in *The Tempest*, for example, or *Measure for Measure*—are achieved through the collaborative efforts of an associational grouping: a company of actors.[2] We must, as always, remember that such associational forms—taverns, companies of actors—are historically contingent. The tavern of 1601, for example, differs from that of 1381 (or from places in which audiences might gather today—after a play, before a soccer riot, or in dreaming of rebellion). But awareness of *aspects* of continuity in social structure over centuries might usefully counterbalance the tendency, current in much Shakespeare criticism, to evaluate social spaces (such as taverns) on the Shakespearean stage primarily as epiphenomenal mirrorings of the stage-world itself.[3]

───⌀

Two national surveys, the 1389 Chancery returns and the 1548 Certificate, summarize vast political differences while serving ostensibly similar purposes: the surveying of local associational cultures by centralized royal authority. In the 1389 returns, we have noted, the guilds describe themselves: their dedications to specific saints, their prayers, cultural customs, and *drynkyng* habits, their provision for the sick and needy, their methods of internal self-regulation, their strategies for the promotion and maintenance of *felaweshipe* and good *compagnye*.[4] In 1548, however, the guilds give no account of themselves but are described by officials of the Court of Augmentations. Moving systematically through the whole country, which is divided up into 24 circuits, the commissioners rarely pause to note even the names of saints that particular altars and chapels might be dedicated to. Guilds are commonly listed after their church, and their particular activities (the hiring of priests, donations to the poor and prisoners, the provision of lamps and lights) are tallied as items of expense. The 1548 Certificate, in short, is a basic reference work intended as a guide for the disposal of property.[5]

The most singularly impressive aspect of fourteenth-century guild culture is the confidence—a confidence shared by and exemplified through the formation of Chaucer's Tabard *compagnye*—that a group of men and women may come together and regulate themselves as a corporate body without reference to external authority. The forming of associational groupings is thereby nurtured as a political practice and experienced as a natural social habit.[6] The growth, flourishing, and demise of guilds in particular localities attests to the presence of cultural and economic energies not necessarily coincident with the strict delineations of parish boundaries. The wholesale destruction of guilds, colleges, and chantries in the 1540s—coupled with a strengthening of centralized religious authority, disseminated through the parish pulpit— forms part of a greater destruction of the associational habit of mind.[7] Such systematic alienation from local custom and familiar modes of social relationship—pioneered, as we have seen, by those despotic regimes of northern Italy that sponsored Petrarch's eloquent expressions of self-estrangement—is carried further by ambitious enclosers, who (in the words of Ralph Robynson, translating Thomas More) reduce whole towns to rubble "and leaue nothing stondynge but only the churche, to make of it a shepehowse."[8] An uprooted household takes to the road not as a *compagnye* with the specific *telos* of a pilgrimage (and, more significantly, with a specific point of return) but as vagrants heading into a destructured unknown: "Away they trudge," observes Robynson, "out of their knowen and accustomed houses, fyndyng no places to rest in."[9]

It is ironic that More, even in lamenting the destruction of long-established communal structures, himself envisages no place in his utopian society for traditional sites of *drynkyng* and voluntary association:

Ther be nether wyn tauernes, nor ale houses, nor stewes, nor any occasion of uice or wickednes, no lurking corners, no places of wicked councelles or vnlawfull assembles; but they be in the present sight, and vnder the iyes of euery man.[10]

More's tactic here of tainting all sites of popular association with suggestions of sexual impropriety is no different from what we have seen from the mayoral court of medieval London. What is different, however, is this suggestion that every nook, cranny, and corner of English society lies under "the present sight" of external authority. This persistent sense of a society under surveillance is the most memorably disconcerting aspect of Shakespeare's intensive imagining of a Chaucerian, or rather immediately post-Chaucerian, world: *Henry IV*, Parts I and II.

Part I opens with a twofold evocation of a Chaucerian *telos*. King Henry IV, in his opening speech, adumbrates a journey to Jerusalem, while Sir John Oldcastle/Falstaff,[11] in his opening scene, plots a robbery on the very road traveled by Chaucer's pilgrim *compagnye*:

there are pilgrims going to Canterbury with rich offerings, and traders riding to London with fat purses. (I.ii.125–27)

This initial citation of *the* Chaucerian itinerary develops, over the course of ten acts, into an exploration of genuine Chaucerian breadth: from brief imaginings of pilgrims and merchants (traveling in opposite directions) to detailed accounts of city, court, and countryside. Shakespeare's imagining of rural locations in these plays strips away all suggestion of the power and mystery with which Chaucer's countryside comes charged. Oldcastle, a fat man sending thin men to their deaths, rapes rural communities as equably as Father Gianni screws the peasant's wife in *Decameron* 9.10; Shallow and Silence, country justices, dream of bygone days in the city while Feeble, Wart, and Shadow are "pricked."[12] And even though Sir John and the justices are themselves representatives and appointees of court and city culture, their deficiencies are to be taken as an argument for investing the royal-headed center with even greater powers. So it is that at the end of Part II, Henry IV's projected journey to Jerusalem is actually completed without his leaving Westminster. Whereas Chaucer's *compagnye* must travel away from court and capital through the Kentish countryside to Canterbury, finally envisaged as a figure of "Jerusalem celestial" (10.51), Shakespeare's dying monarch need not venture through "the Wild of Kent" (*1 Henry IV*, II.i.55); he need only change rooms in his own palace. The authoritative religious *telos* of Jerusalem, once "vainly" supposed to lie down the road to Canterbury and beyond, is now discovered as part of the English monarch's own dwelling: "In that Jerusalem shall Harry die" (*2 Henry IV*, IV.v.238, 240).

Oldcastle's appearances in villages and on the fringes of battlefields serve
to define him as a displaced urbanite, native to a tavern culture continuous with that of Chaucer's Tabard. His fleshliness may issue from a strange
literalization of a long-established critique of Lollards: that they are literal,
hence fleshly, readers.[13] As a womanish fleshly body, as a fleshly reader, and as
the singer of pisspots and Arthurian song (" 'When Arthur first in court' —
/ Empty the jordan — ")[14] Sir John is a close relative of Chaucer's Dame Alice.[15]
He is further medievalized through associations with the carnivalesque and
with the Vice and Gula figures of an antecedent (barely expired) dramatic
tradition;[16] and he greets his senior paramour, Chaunticleer-like, as "Dame
Partlet the Hen."[17] Shakespeare's "Hostess," like Chaucer's "Host," governs
loosely over an associational space that generates unusual verbal energy. Here,
in confronting Sir John, Hostess Quickly captures a transient place, time, and
promise with extraordinary precision:

Thou didst swear to me upon a parcel-gilt goblet, sitting in my Dolphin chamber,
at the round table by a sea-coal fire, upon Wednesday in Wheeson week, when the
Prince broke thy head for liking his father to a singing man of Windsor, thou didst
swear to me then, as I was washing thy wound, to marry me, and make me my lady
thy wife. (2 Henry IV, II.i.86–92)

And yet it is the very precision of this vernacular that spells its demise
(as the head-punching Prince within the speech finds a surrogate without
in the Chief Justice): for in the presence of this Justice, humorless embodiment of impersonal *lex*, Hostess Quickly's speech assumes the character of a
legal deposition. By the end of Part II (just in time for the coronation) the
Eastcheap tavern company has been broken, with Doll Tearsheet dragged off
for "whipping cheer" (V.iv.5). But there is never a moment in the *Henriad*
when tavern space is not subjected to the surveillance envisioned by More: "I
know you all," the Prince declares to the tavern-dwellers (even before entering
their tavern, Part I, I.ii.195). And having crossed the Eastcheap threshold, the
Prince is more typically a spy than a companion, subjecting tavern space to
a series of interrogations regarding its precarious relation to external, royal-
headed authority. Nothing of this kind happens in Chaucer: royal justice,
in the person of the Man of Law, plays no part in the internal regulation of
the *felaweshipe*; the invasive outsider, personified by the alchemical Canon, is
himself interrogated and found unworthy to join the *compagnye*.

What Harry wants from Eastcheap is its simplest constitutive quality,
something not found in the aristocratic domain. "Company, villainous company," Sir John laments, "hath been the spoil of me" (Part I, III.iii.9–10): but
it is precisely the mysterious practice of *compagnye*, as maintained through
Chaucer's ten Fragments and discovered more locally in Shakespeare, that the
young king-to-be seeks and needs. For the Prince, companionship with the
likes of Poins — "such vile company as thou art," Part II, II.ii.49 — is disgrace-

ful. But to Sir John, companionship with the same man is a mystery and a source of wonder:

I have forsworn his company hourly any time this two and twenty years, and yet I am bewitch'd with the rogue's company. If the rascal have not given me medicines to make me love him, I'll be hang'd. (*1 Henry IV*, II.ii.15–18)

Hostess Quickly is similarly surprised by the power and longevity of a companionship of even greater (but still precisely recorded) longevity. "Well, fare thee well," she says to Sir John:

I have known thee these twenty-nine years, come peas-cod time, but an honester and truer-hearted man—well, fare thee well. (*2 Henry IV*, II.iv.382–84)

Viewed in the context of the endless internecine rivalries of Lancastrian magnate politics, 28 years is a very long time indeed: a time here measured not by the fall of kings, but (as in Chaucer's famous opening period) by the rhythm of the natural world. This, then, is what Harry wants. *Compagnye*, discovered as a long-lived nexus of local and personal relations, must be expropriated from its immediate context and imagined at the national level: "When I am King of England," the Prince declares, "I shall command all the good lads in Eastcheap" (Part I, II.iv.12–13). To this end, the associational forms of old Eastcheap must be hunted and dragged from the stage while the simulacrum of its *felaweshipe* is converted to royal service. This process attempts to force its triumphant and newly foundational moment at Agincourt as the English monarch moves among his "band of brothers":[18] the displaced remnant of Eastcheap, plus representative figures from Scotland, Ireland, and (especially) Wales.[19] Thus the nation as an imagined entity is formed through the destruction of local communities and the simultaneous engorging of their ideological gloss:[20] for, as Benedict Anderson notes, "the nation is always conceived as a deep, horizontal comradeship. Ultimately it is this fraternity that makes it possible . . . not so much to kill, as willingly to die for such limited imaginings."[21]

Shakespeare's evocation of the culture that dies with Sir John is so potent that we might want to connect it with memories of Catholic and guild-rooted Stratford and Coventry, worlds but recently vanished.[22] Such nostalgia may be genuine and personal; the tapping and organizing of nostalgias has proved essential to the process of state building, of imagining a nation—particularly an English one.[23]

⁓

The beheading of Anne Boleyn effects radical discontinuity with, rather than reconfiguration of, social strategies exemplified through Chaucer. Adam of Usk, thinking of an earlier Queen Anne, remembers her as "reginam benignissimam, licet sine prole defunctam."[24] Anne of Bohemia's childlessness is here recorded after estimation of her personal qualities, almost as a footnote to them. But the failure of the later Anne to provide a male heir is remembered as a tragic circumstance, contributing to her death. Anne Boleyn, second wife of Henry VIII, miscarried a son on January 29, 1536; on May 19 of the same year she was beheaded on Tower Green. Anne Boleyn was the first queen of England to be publicly executed.[25]

Once a king's killing of his queen is admitted as a political possibility, Chaucerian strategies for wifely eloquence lose all historical grounding. A wife does die, of course, at Chaucer's court of Apollo; but the Manciple's murdering god-on-earth is filled with remorse the moment his anger expires.[26] Henry VIII, by contrast, was keen to dramatize the steady deliberateness of the princely *arbitrium*. At the conclusion of Anne's trial, the mode of her death was left to "the king's pleasure": she would die either by burning or beheading. Having decided on the latter, Henry took a studied personal interest in the technology of Anne's death (shipping in a sword specialist from Calais). He was alive to the drama of the situation to the extent that, according to Chapuys, he composed a tragedy for the occasion that he would take from his pocket for people to read. And he was not unwilling to remind his next queen of his queen-killing pedigree: when Jane Seymour exercised her eloquence later in 1536 on behalf of the abolished abbeys, Henry warned her to keep out of politics and to remember Anne Boleyn.[27]

Chaucer's *Prologue* to the *Legend of Good Women* recognizes that a courtier may be destroyed by confusions of love court with law court, *Hof* with *Gericht*.[28] In Chaucerian fiction, the erring poet is rescued by an eloquent queen who proves to be an expert reader of courtly signs; but in the Henrician court, the queen is herself entrapped by the trivial processes of courtly interchange. The familiar gallant suggestion that a courtier might love his sovereign's wife is suddenly accorded treasonable intent; a kind look from a queen to a young musician or a dropped handkerchief suddenly betokens adultery. As an accused queen, Anne could find no mediator. The man described as "the closest friend King Henry had"—Henry Norris, groom of the stool and chief gentleman of the privy chamber—was himself to die at Tyburn as one of Anne's putative lovers.[29] And the girl that Anne attempted to employ as mediatrix between herself and her husband—her daughter, the Princess Elizabeth—was less than three years old.[30]

It is perhaps not surprising that Elizabethan gender politics seem so alien when approached from the reading of Chaucer. Texts set to circulate in the court of a queen whose mother, a queen, was killed by her kingly father speak perforce a strange new idiolect.[31] Rather than rehearsing such confusion further, I would like to make an end here by moving forward to one last revision of a Chaucerian text: *Two Noble Kinsmen*. Attributed to Fletcher and Shakespeare, this Jacobean reworking of the *Knight's Tale* was in repertory in 1619 while under active consideration for performance at court. The play stages pairings and crossings of sexual imagining that make *A Midsummer Night's Dream* look like a robust model of heterosexual normativity: "We are one another's wife, ever begetting," says Arcite to Palamon, "New births of love" (II.ii.80–81). Love between men is now the driving force of the drama; love between women—even Amazon women—is judged a thing of youth, pale in comparison to the force of feeling between Theseus and Pirithous.[32] Love of men for women follows chiefly from matters of property, deed, and title; womanly love for men has undergone massive dilution of its stirring affect and rhetorical power. It takes three kneeling Theban queens, plus Hippolyta and Emilia, more than two hundred lines of intensive petitioning to persuade Theseus to act against "cruel Creon" (I.i.40); and it takes more persuasion than Hippolyta and Emilia can muster to save Palamon and Arcite, discovered fighting in the forest, from the wrath of Theseus. This failure of wifely eloquence, signaled by the extraordinary intervention of a masculine petitioner, seals a massive shift away from the court and household politics of the Chaucerian world:

Emilia: By your own virtues infinite —
Hippolyta: By valor,
        By all the chaste nights I have ever pleas'd you —
Theseus: These are strange conjurings.
Pirithous: Nay, then I'll in too. [*Kneels*]
        By all our friendship, sir, by all our dangers,
        By all you love most — wars . . .
                                        (III.vi.199–203)

Such weakening of female eloquence forms part of a massive tightening of male-headed authority throughout the public sphere. The insistent penetration of associational groupings, observed through the *Henry IV* plays, is carried even into the forest. Whereas the artisans of *A Midsummer Night's Dream* could at least rehearse their performance unaided, the countrymen of *Two Noble Kinsmen* are pressured from without and within:[33] by Theseus, who discovers them in the forest, and by the Paedagogus, who (while speaking scraps of Latin that they cannot understand) oversees their every act:

        And I, that am the rectifier of all,
        By title paedagogus, that let fall
        The birch upon the breeches of the small ones,
        And humble with a ferula the tall ones,
        Do here present this machine . . .   (III.v.109–13)

The infantilization of the lower orders, glimpsed throughout *A Midsummer Night's Dream*, is here taken to its logical conclusion by this Schoolmaster's disciplining of his "good boys" (143). It is not surprising, then, that a

love-struck jailer's daughter—acclaimed as "a dainty mad woman," III.v.72—
may meet with the rustics and blend right into their dancing culture; become,
in effect, one of them.

The function of women in *Two Noble Kinsmen* is no longer to speak
and persuade, nor even to be fallen in love with, but rather to be seen. In a
play that begins with conquest, a rationale for further and greater conquest
is evolved through a simple but far-reaching amendment of the Chaucerian
text; specifically, through the promotion of what in Chaucer was simply a
throw-away line of love casuistry to the status of central argument. This line,
in the *Knight's Tale*, is actually just half a line, spoken by Palemon: "I loved
hire first" (1.1146). In *Two Noble Kinsmen*, this half-line is changed by just
one word: "I *saw* her first" (II.ii.160). This claim, initially scorned, is soon
elaborated to an argument for exclusive ownership:

> *Palamon:*   I saw her first.
> *Arcite:*   That's nothing.
> *Palamon:*   But it shall be.
> *Arcite:*   I saw her too.
> *Palamon:*   Yes, but you must not love her.
> (II.ii.160–61)

The energy with which Palamon goes on to elaborate his claim suggests
that there is more at stake here than seeing a girl in a garden. It is as if some
vast new continent has swung into view; he who sees first possesses all, as if by
divine right:

> *Arcite:*   Who shall deny me?
> *Palamon:*   I, that first saw her; I, that took possession
> First with mine eye of all those beauties in her
> Reveal'd to mankind.
> (II.ii.166–69)

Arguments concerning "the birthright of this beauty"—a woman considered born only at the moment of her being seen—are advanced throughout
the play and are finally summarized by Theseus: "The right o' th' lady," he tells
Palamon, is Palamon's, "for you first saw her" (V.iv.116–17). In a sense, then,
this is a play with but one moment of drama, recorded as the claim "I saw her
first." Speeches are extraordinarily long and full of extreme bodily affect because the underpinning assurances of an oath-based culture—as exemplified
by the *Knight's Tale*—are gone. Associational forms, rooted in a guild-based
culture, have also disappeared. The body of the masculine courtier now extends and contorts itself through new forms of rhetorical persuasion.[34] The
female body, divorced from time-honored recognition as rhetorical power
incarnate, is remarked chiefly as the object of masculine sight and discovery.

As such—a body assumed to have no significant history or language prior to the moment of its being sighted—it prepares the way for, becomes complicit with, the discovery of bodies further afield. Such bodies and such women will come to devise forms of resistance in new worlds quite different from, yet historically continuous with, that of Chaucer.

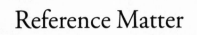
Reference Matter

Notes

Preface

1. A notable exception here is Walter Cohen, *Drama of a Nation: Public Theater in Renaissance England and Spain*. For a candid review of the expansionism, temporal and territorial, of Renaissance and early modern criticism, see Leah Marcus, "Renaissance/Early Modern Studies," esp. p. 42. See further Ella Shohat and Robert Stam, *Unthinking Eurocentrism: Multiculturalism and the Media*, a spirited (albeit conventionally medieval-hopping) critique of conventional historical teleologies.

2. One of the anxieties fueling the energetic efforts of the Chaucer Society, the Early English Text Society, and other bodies was the need for a secure, and securely English, point of origin for the great nation that grew to become Victorian England. Ruskin and Tennyson were among the first 75 subscribers to the Early English Text Society, which was founded in 1864; see *Frederick James Furnivall: A Volume of Personal Record*, p. xlvi. This urge to define and protect a specific cultural and racial legacy informs the vastly influential work of C. S. Lewis, who in a famous essay (1932) attempts to protect a native Anglo-Saxonism from the enervating effects of Italian literary invasion—obscurely associated with threats embodied by D. H. Lawrence, George Moore, and Marie Stopes, the pioneering founder of birth control clinics ("What Chaucer Really Did to *Il Filostrato*"). It was in the Oxford of C. S. Lewis in 1936 that Denys Hay, having expressed a desire to study the Italian Renaissance, was informed by his tutor "that only girls did that: I was to concentrate on the manly Middle Ages" (*Renaissance Essays*, p. 137; see also p. 398).

Victorian values continue to inform the choices made by Harold Bloom for his *Modern Critical Views* volume of essays on Chaucer (1985). Bloomian Chaucer is a site for the projection of an intense nostalgia; the medieval text promises to fill a present sense of loss with an originary fullness of the letter. This is, of course, familiar: the Victorian founding fathers of Chaucer Criticism, writing in the midst of their own incomprehensible social and political upheavals, assigned an Edenic purity and simplicity to Chaucer. It is quite appropriate that Bloom's *Modern Critical Views*, which returns us to Chaucer as the great Creator of Characters, should begin with G. K. Chesterton. (Bloom's *Modern Critical Views: Dante*, by contrast, recruits contemporary theory-literate Italianists like Barolini, Freccero, and Mazzotta to lead us through a postmodernist inferno.) John Burrow's *Ricardian Poetry* (1971; reissued in Penguin, 1992), a book of considerable importance in the development of English

Chaucer criticism, keeps the Victorian heritage alive by adopting something akin to the Tennysonian palace of art as its founding metaphor. Burrow contemplates the works of Chaucer, Gower, Langland, and the *Gawain*-poet "as if they were pictures hanging round the walls of a room devoted, in an imaginary museum, to the 'Ricardian School'" (p. 9). Burrow refers to Tennyson three times on the first page of his book and three times thereafter.

3. Most studies of Margery Kempe confine themselves to Part 1 and have little to say about the late travels of Part 2. But for Margery, domestic and foreign spheres form part of a continuous religious, cultural, and political experience. From a single point at Lynn, one can still observe key reference points of Margery's life: the Guildhall, the church of St. Margaret, and the lane leading down to a river that suggests—through the peculiar bowing of its horizon—the allure of the beyond.

4. This book, with its tautological appeal for a "diachronic history," does little to undo the forgetting of the Anglo-Saxon and post-Conquest period. On this phenomenon, see Allen J. Frantzen, *Desire for Origins: New Language, Old English, and Teaching the Tradition.*

5. Judith Butler, *Gender Trouble*: "Feminist critique ought to explore the totalizing claims of a masculinist signifying economy, but also remain self-critical with respect to the totalizing gestures of feminism. The effort to identify the enemy as singular in form is a reverse-discourse that uncritically mimics the strategy of the oppressor instead of offering a different set of terms" (p. 13). It is instructive to ponder the complex consequences of substituting the term "medievalist" for "feminist" and "Renaissance" for "masculinist" in Butler's first sentence. See further, Luce Irigaray, *Speculum of the Other Woman,* p. 141.

6. See now *GLQ: A Journal of Lesbian and Gay Studies,* ed. Carolyn Dinshaw and David M. Halperin.

7. See *The Civilization of the Renaissance in Italy,* trans. S. G. C. Middlemore, vol. 1, p. 143; the German of Burckhardt, *Die Kultur der Renaissance in Italien,* ed. Horst Günther, reads as follows: "Im Mittelalter . . . der Mensch aber erkannte sich nur als Race, Volk, Partei, Korporation, Familie oder sonst in irgend einer Form des Allgemeinen" (p. 137).

8. Lee Patterson's list of medieval "selves" is extraordinarily impressive, *inter alia,* for its sheer length: see "On the Margin: Postmodernism, Ironic History, and Medieval Studies," pp. 100–101. For a spirited critique of the repetition by early modernists of tired old commonplaces concerning the Middle Ages, see David Aers, "A Whisper in the Ear of Early Modernists; or, Reflections on Literary Critics Writing the 'History of the Subject.'"

9. In this account, the passage from feudal polity to absolute monarchy is one that repeats itself, with local variations, across the face of eastern and western Europe. It begins with a weakening of the reciprocal obligations binding peasant to lord, lord to seigneurial overlord. It sees a general movement from dispersed and parcelized sovereignties toward the formation of a single unified absolute state. It is achieved not through the abandonment of feudal forms of domination, but rather through a selective intensification of them. It ends with standing armies (which, augmented with foreign mercenaries, were more or less continuously employed in international warfare), a permanent bureaucracy, codified law (in which Roman absolutism seeks to displace the mutuality of feudal and Germanic custom), national taxation (from

which the seigneurial class effectively exempts itself), the enclosure of the country-side, the displacement of landholding peasantry, the absolute ownership and free transfer of private property, and the sacralization of the royal head of state. For a review and brief bibliography of writings on absolutism, see Perry Anderson, *In the Tracks of Historical Materialism*, pp. 24–27. See also the sequence of two works by Anderson himself: *Passages from Antiquity to Feudalism* and *Lineages of the Absolutist State*. For an important critique of the various and ill-defined ways in which the term "feudalism" is assumed or applied, see Susan Reynolds, *Fiefs and Vassals: The Medieval Evidence Reinterpreted*. For a recent critique of the concept of "absolutism," see Nicholas Henshall, *The Myth of Absolutism: Change and Continuity in Early Modern European Monarchy*.

10. Perry Anderson, in his *Lineages of the Absolutist State*, observes such differences in painstaking detail. Seven of his chapters are devoted to western Europe and seven to eastern Europe (including one on "The House of Islam"; he also has chapter-length notes on "Japanese Feudalism" and "The Asiatic Mode of Production"). Randall Collins, in his excellent *Weberian Sociological Theory*, balances accounts of western Europe against an account of developments in medieval China.

11. *The Governance of England: Otherwise called "The Difference Between an Absolute and a Limited Monarchy,"* ed. Charles Plummer, p. 112. For further discussion of *quod placuit principi* ("what is pleasing to the prince has the force of law"), see Fortescue, *De Laudibus Legum Anglie*, ed. S. B. Chrimes, pp. 24–26, 78–80 (where the prince is informed that "the laws of England do not sanction any such maxim"). Fortescue was chief justice of the King's Bench under Henry VI.

12. See Foxe, ed. Josiah Pratt, vol. 6, pp. 45–46. If there is any *grand récit* of English absolutism, this episode clearly runs contrary to it.

13. Stephen Greenblatt, for example, elects to structure his *Marvelous Possessions* "largely around anecdotes, what the French call 'petites histoires,' as distinct from the *grand récit* of totalizing, integrated, progressive history, a history that knows where it is going" (p. 2).

14. Jean Baechler, *The Origins of Capitalism*, p. 115. Baechler writes that "every philosophy of history that is based on the idea of a linear and necessary evolution seems to me uninteresting . . . because it rests upon a *petitio principii*, namely that the only possible history is the one that in fact resulted. To declare the necessity of one outcome is only to avow one's inability to explore other possibilities" (p. 115). See further Hendrik Spruyt, *The Sovereign State and Its Competitors*.

15. See Walter Benjamin, *Illuminations*, pp. 245–55.

16. See David Wallace, "Carving Up Time and the World: Medieval-Renaissance Turf Wars; Historiography and Personal History."

17. See Jameson, *The Political Unconscious*, p. 19; Bennington, "Demanding History," p. 23.

18. Jameson opens *The Political Unconscious* in characteristically forthright fashion by speaking of "the political perspective" as "the absolute horizon of all reading and all interpretation" (p. 17). Soon, however, in contemplating the recovery and narrative sequencing of such an all-inclusive perspective, he turns poetic, dramatic, and metaphorical: "Only Marxism can give us an adequate account of the essential *mystery* of the cultural past, which, like Tiresias drinking the blood, is momentarily returned to life and warmth and allowed once more to speak, and to deliver its long-

forgotten message in surroundings utterly alien to it. This mystery can be enacted only if the human adventure is one" (p. 19).

19. Marx, *Capital,* vol. 1, trans. Fowkes, pp. 873, 877, 892.

20. Ibid., p. 892. For a more extended analysis of Marx's dilemma here and his awareness of it, see Wallace, "Carving Up Time."

21. Engels cheerfully declares in his Preface that "the entire subject-matter on the peasant risings and on Thomas Münzer is taken from Zimmermann" (p. 7). In his second edition, written in 1870, Engels makes a spirited effort to credentialize Zimmermann: "The same revolutionary instinct, which prompted him to champion the oppressed classes, made him later one of the best of the extreme Left in Frankfurt." In 1875, the third edition, this effort is humorously qualified: "It is true that since then he is said to have aged somewhat" (p. 7).

22. In the recent *Cambridge History of Medieval Political Thought,* for example, the first reference to the political status of women (which pictures a husband chasing slave-girls) is also the last; the volume runs to more than eight hundred pages. See Henry Chadwick, "Christian Doctrine," p. 16.

23. The Florentine chronicler Goro Dati, for example, compares a despot's return to tyranny with the return of a woman (albeit terrified by memories of the pains of childbirth) to sexual excess. Such an appeal to the nature of women, while bracketed within the rhetorical limits of *comparatio,* is itself a political statement, one that borrows from and affirms traditions of medieval misogyny. See, for full citation of Dati's metaphor, Louis Green, *Chronicle into History: An Essay on the Interpretation of History in Florentine Fourteenth-Century Chronicles,* p. 120. The accentuation of masculine dominance over the female body in despotic polity refines a trope that may be considered foundational to all medieval textual practice: see Carolyn Dinshaw, *Chaucer's Sexual Poetics,* pp. 3–24.

24. On vanished space and lost time, see Julia Kristeva, *Strangers to Ourselves,* esp. pp. 4, 9; Louise Fradenburg, " 'Voice Memorial': Loss and Reparation in Chaucer's Poetry."

Introduction

1. See *Chaucer Life-Records,* ed. Martin M. Crow and Clair C. Olson, pp. 32–40, 53–61, 148–270; Wendy Childs, "Anglo-Italian Contacts in the Fourteenth Century."

2. Marx, *Capital,* vol. 1, trans. Fowkes, p. 876.

3. Anderson, *Lineages,* p. 10.

4. See *The Statutes of the Realm, 1235–1713,* ed. Luders et al., vol. 1, pp. 319–20. For discussion of this statute (and associated fourteenth-century developments posing "a new challenge to the household as a site for the production of gendered identities"), see Strohm, *Hochon's Arrow,* pp. 121–44 (p. 127); and for extensive discussion of the 1352 statute and its long-term effects, see J. G. Bellamy, *The Law of Treason in England in the Middle Ages;* E. Kay Harris, *Lancelot and Guenevere in Malory's Morte Darthur.*

5. The most recent work of this kind is Paul A. Olson, *The "Canterbury Tales" and the Good Society.*

6. For some intelligent reflections on such problems, see Jean Dunbabin, "Government," esp. pp. 477–79.

7. I was so struck in reviewing *The Cambridge History of Medieval Political Thought c. 350–c. 1450,* ed. J. H. Burns, for *Studies in the Age of Chaucer.*

8. See R. W. and A. J. Carlyle, *A History of Medieval Political Theory in the West*, vol. 5, pp. 417–19.

9. See, for example, Janet Nelson, "Kingship and Empire," an essay that discloses political thought through skillful analysis of Carolingian, Anglo-Saxon, and Anglo-Norman poems, prayers, and chronicles.

10. See, respectively, Baron, *The Crisis of the Early Italian Renaissance*; Burckhardt, *Die Kultur der Renaissance*.

11. Boethius died in Lombardy (imprisoned at Pavia).

12. Anderson, *Lineages*, pp. 148–49.

Chapter 1

1. *Chaucer*, p. 174.

2. Pearsall compares Chaucer's experiences in Italy with those of English academics in the United States in the 1950s or early 1960s, or with "the open-mouthed response of Eastern Europeans when confronted in the late 1980s with the wealth of the West" (*Life of Chaucer*, p. 103). Howard equates Chaucer's first experience of Italy following his winter crossing of the Alps with Gawain's accommodation at Bertilak's castle: an equation that once again defines Italy as a realm of magic and deceptive appearances (*Chaucer*, p. 175). For the argument that "a work of art has meaning and interest only for someone who possesses the cultural competence, that is, the code, into which it is encoded," see Pierre Bourdieu, *Distinction: A Social Critique of the Judgement of Taste*, p. 2; see also Bourdieu, *The Field of Cultural Production*, p. 7.

3. As will become evident later in this chapter, the notion that foreigners are invariably bedazzled by the splendors of Florence is itself a cultivated and long-lived product of Florentine city-state ideology.

4. See Glending Olson, "Geoffrey Chaucer"; Pearsall, *Life of Chaucer*, pp. 106–7.

5. See Strohm, *Social Chaucer*, esp. pp. 10–13.

6. See Ruth Bird, *The Turbulent London of Richard II*, pp. 43–50.

7. While John of Gaunt was leading his ill-starred expedition to Brittany, merchant capitalist John Philpot fitted out his own fleet and secured a major coup in capturing John Mercer, a Scottish pirate in league with the French who had inflicted great damage on English shipping. See Bird, *Turbulent London*, pp. 46–47; D. W. Robertson, *Chaucer's London*, pp. 90–91.

8. See Caroline M. Barron, "The Tyranny of Richard II," pp. 7–18. For differing views of how discourses of tyranny and incipient absolutism are mediated through *Piers Plowman*, see Anna P. Baldwin, *The Theme of Government in Piers Plowman*, esp. pp. 7–23; Helen Jewell, "*Piers Plowman*—A Poem of Crisis," pp. 75–78.

9. See Chris Given-Wilson, *The Royal Household and the King's Affinity*, p. 223. The Cheshire archers were joined by some 75 archers of the Crown.

10. The *locus classicus* of this reading of Chaucer, especially in relation to Italian culture, is C. S. Lewis, "What Chaucer Really Did to *Il Filostrato*."

11. Chaucer, as controller of customs, was obliged to monitor the activities of Nicholas Brembre, a customs collector for the port of London. Chaucer was appointed to a Kentish peace commission (guarding against the threat of French invasion) in 1385; Sir Simon Burley and Chief Justice Robert Tresilian also served on this commission. See *Riverside Chaucer*, pp. xx, xxii–iv.

12. See *Chaucer Life-Records*, ed. Martin M. Crow and Clair C. Olson, pp. 62–

63, 275; *Riverside Chaucer*, p. xxv. Anthony Goodman speaks of Chaucer as a retainer of Derby in 1395–96: see *The Loyal Conspiracy*, p. 156.

13. *Forms of Nationhood: The Elizabethan Writing of England*, p. 13. As we will see later in this chapter, such a redefinition of "freedom"—one requiring a sharp break with local and familiar structures—was transacted by the deracinated humanists who labored for the Visconti.

14. See Wendy Childs, "Anglo-Italian Contacts," pp. 67–68; *Riverside Chaucer*, p. xx; *Chaucer Life-Records*, pp. 148–270; Pearsall, *Life of Chaucer*, pp. 96–101, 210–14, 221–23.

15. See Mann, *Sources of Social Power*, vol. 1, pp. 424–25, especially table 13.2, "English state finances, 1155–1452: average annual revenue at current and constant (1451–75) prices."

16. See Mann, *Sources of Social Power*, vol. 1, pp. 427–28, 432, especially table 13.3, "Average annual sources of revenue in three reigns, 1272–1307 and 1327–99 (in percent)." For the reign of Richard II, percentages are as follows: customs, 38; hereditary crown revenues, 28; lay taxation and subsidies, 25; clerical taxation and subsidies, 9.

17. See Joan M. Ferrante, *The Political Vision of the Divine Comedy*, pp. 313–14; Armando Sapori, *The Italian Merchant in the Middle Ages*, p. 51.

18. See Childs, p. 68; *Chaucer Life-Records*, pp. 148–76.

19. See *Chaucer Life-Records*, pp. 32–40.

20. See *Chaucer Life-Records*, pp. 165, 55, 54.

21. *Chaucer Life-Records*, p. 54; the term "sibien" is interlineated.

22. See Christian Bec, "Il mito di Firenze da Dante al Ghiberti," p. 15.

23. See Gene A. Brucker, *Florentine Politics and Society 1343–1378*, pp. viii, 397–412; Brucker, *The Civic World of Early Renaissance Florence*, pp. 3–13.

24. This work has been edited as *Le bellezze di Firenze* and is published as an appendix to Giovanni Villani, *Cronica*, ed. F. G. Dragomanni, vol. 4, pp. 292–300.

25. See David Wallace, *Chaucer and the Early Writings of Boccaccio*, pp. 147–48; *Poeti minori del Trecento*, ed. Natalino Sapegno, pp. 349–456; *Cantari del Trecento*, ed. Armando Balduino, pp. 9–10.

26. Boccaccio served on the Ufficio della Condotta from May 1 to August 31, 1355. See Vittore Branca, *Boccaccio: The Man and His Works*, p. 102.

27. See Brucker, *Florentine Politics*, pp. 58–60.

28. These figures are for 1371: see Brucker, pp. 61–62. For a more detailed history of these offices, see Davidsohn, *Storia di Firenze*, vol. 5, pp. 134–60, 569–80.

29. See Brucker, *Florentine Politics*, pp. 28–29, 33; Davidsohn, *Storia di Firenze*, vol. 5, p. 402. On the survival of feudal mores within medieval Florence, see Marvin B. Becker, *Medieval Italy: Constraints and Creativity*, pp. 1–7.

30. For what follows on *ammonizione*, see Brucker, *Florentine Politics*, pp. 87–89, 99–103, 170–71, 370–73.

31. See Brucker, pp. 90–91, 98–99.

32. Ibid., p. 68.

33. See *Paradiso* 16.50, 55–56; Brucker, pp. 52, 124. For a detailed analysis of the "novi cives" and their impact on Florence in 1343, see Marvin B. Becker, *Florence in Transition*, vol. 2, pp. 93–149. Becker notes that the political crises of the 1350s and 1360s caused Matteo Villani and Boccaccio to revise their opinions: the nobility now posed the greatest danger to the *libertà* of the republic (pp. 111–12).

34. See Eleonora Carus-Wilson, "The Woollen Industry," vol. 2, pp. 651–52.

35. For a useful survey and discussion, see Samuel Cohn, "Florentine Insurrections," pp. 143–64.

36. Becker, *Florence in Transition*, vol. 2, p. 152.

37. See Becker, *Florence in Transition*, vol. 2, p. 152.

38. Boccaccio's most vehement antifeminist satire, the *Corbaccio* ("evil crow"), has been associated with Florentine sumptuary statutes of 1355 and 1356: see the translation of both text and statutes in Giovanni Boccaccio, *The Corbaccio*, ed. and trans. Anthony K. Cassell.

39. Lee Patterson describes the *Shipman's Tale* as "the most Boccaccian of the *Canterbury Tales*"; his reading of this tale—which traces the circulation of capital within a good faith/bad faith credit economy rather than chasing sources and analogues—sustains this claim admirably. See *Chaucer and the Subject of History*, pp. 349–66 (p. 361).

40. This paragraph owes much to John S. Henderson, *Piety and Charity in Late Medieval Florence*: see esp. pp. 196–237; for Sacchetti, see pp. 226–27.

41. "The Domestic Enemy: the Eastern Slaves in Tuscany in the Fourteenth and Fifteenth Centuries," p. 322. Origo's *Speculum* article of 1955 is both impressive in its erudition and alarming in many of its assumptions and narrative strategies. Her title translates Petrarch's phrase *domestici hostes*; for Petrarch's aesthetic and political responses to slavery, see Chap. 10 below. Medieval Ragusa (Dubrovnik), like Florence and ancient Athens, combined the institution of slavery with republican government: see Susan Mosher Stuard, "To Town to Serve: Urban Domestic Slavery in Medieval Dubrovnik," pp. 39–40. See also now John Bryan Williams, *From the Commercial Revolution to the Slave Revolution: The Development of Slavery in Medieval Genoa*.

42. See Origo, "Domestic Enemy," pp. 323–24, 336; William D. Phillips, Jr., *Slavery from Roman Times to the Early Transatlantic Trade*, pp. 88, 105–6; David Wallace, *Boccaccio: Decameron*, pp. 1–4, 17–22; Christiane Klapisch-Zuber, "Women Servants in Florence during the Fourteenth and Fifteenth Centuries," pp. 68–74. Klapisch-Zuber notes that about 98 percent of domestic slaves in Florence were women (p. 68).

43. A typical deed of sale described an *ischiavetta*'s origin, price, stature, skin color ("black, *ulivigna*, white, rosy, or even greenish"), shape of face, form of eyes, plus scars, tattoos, and physical defects: see Origo, pp. 333, 336. On Genoese taxonomies of skin color, see Phillips, *Slavery*, p. 106.

44. The text of this sonnet appears in Origo, pp. 363–64, n. 107.

45. The speaker here, Aglio degli Agli, reports this analogy in a letter; he first used it, he says, by way of attempting to placate his jealous wife. See Origo, p. 344.

46. See John Boswell, *The Kindness of Strangers: The Abandonment of Children in Western Europe from Late Antiquity to the Renaissance*, pp. 415–27; Klapisch-Zuber, "Women Servants," pp. 69–70. Boswell argues that the establishment of these hospitals may well have encouraged a higher level of abandonment (p. 418). The mortality rate was appallingly high: in the late fourteenth century, half the children abandoned at San Gallo, the oldest of the Florentine hospitals, died within the first year (p. 421).

47. On the dimensions of and limits to wifely rule in the Florentine household, see Klapisch-Zuber, "Women Servants," pp. 59–61.

48. Origo, "Domestic Enemy," pp. 329, 325; see also Phillips, *Slavery*, pp. 97–104.

49. See Williams, *Slavery in Medieval Genoa*, p. 211.

50. For reflection on ways in which Chaucer's traversing of a Kentish landscape with his pilgrim *compagnye* excludes and acknowledges memories of 1381, see Steven Justice, *Writing and Rebellion: England in 1381*, esp. pp. 230–31.

51. Easter fell on April 17 in 1373: see Howard, *Chaucer*, pp. 180, 196.

52. See Brucker, *Florentine Politics*, p. 100; Davidsohn, *Storia di Firenze*, vol. 4, pp. 196–97.

53. Although this conflict had originated as a battle for status between patrician neighbors, the Albizzi drew support from the Parte Guelfa and the most powerful houses of the ruling oligarchy, whereas the Ricci tended to ally themselves with lesser patrician houses and the mercantile and artisanal *gente nuova*. See Brucker, *Florentine Politics*, pp. 124–26, 202–4; Becker, *Florence in Transition*, vol. 2, p. 131.

54. See Brucker, *Florentine Politics*, pp. 248–61; Becker, *Florence in Transition*, vol. 2, pp. 130–37.

55. Quoted in Brucker, "The Medici in the Fourteenth Century," pp. 12–13.

56. Quoted in Brucker, *Florentine Politics*, p. 308.

57. See Richard C. Trexler, *The Spiritual Power: Republican Florence under Interdict*, p. 130; Trexler, *Public Life in Renaissance Florence*, p. 234.

58. See Brucker, *Florentine Politics*, p. 310; Trexler, *Spiritual Power*, pp. 36–43.

59. Brucker, *Florentine Politics*, p. 331.

60. See Brucker, pp. 331–32; Trexler, *Spiritual Power*, pp. 149–52.

61. See Brucker, *Florentine Politics*, pp. 340–86; Brucker, "The Florentine *popolo minuto* and its political role, 1340–1450," pp. 155–83; N. Rodolico, *I Ciompi: una pagina di storia del proletariato operaio*. For the political history of Florence during and after the Ciompi regime, see Brucker, *Civic World*.

62. Ferdinand Schevill, *History of Florence*, p. 261. Schevill attributes the fall of the 1343 regime in part "to the mistakes of the small people," but in greater part "to the operation of blind social forces beyond the control of feeble men" (p. 261).

63. Antony Black, "St. Thomas Aquinas: The state and morality," p. 66.

64. Quoted in Trexler, *Spiritual Power*, p. 159.

65. Gregorio Dati, *L'istoria di Firenze*, ed. Luigi Pratesi, 97, p. 74: "cioé che il Comune non può morire e il Duca era uno solo uomo mortale, chè finito lo stato suo."

66. Nicolai Rubenstein, "The Beginnings of Political Thought in Florence: A Study in Mediaeval Historiography," p. 198.

67. See Quentin Skinner, "Ambrogio Lorenzetti: The Artist as Political Philosopher," pp. 12–14, 34. Skinner emphasizes that the vision of self-governing republicanism was developed in Italy much earlier than has been hitherto recognized; it predates "by at least a generation the earliest availability of the Aristotelian texts" (i.e., the *Politics* and the *Ethics*). This emphasis upon Seneca, Cicero, and Macrobius (the kind of texts Chaucer was familiar with) closes the gap between Chaucer and the kind of political theory elaborated in the Italian republics; it also makes Chaucer's usage of Albertanus of Brescia seem less anachronistic: "The political theory of the Renaissance, at all phases of its history, owes a far deeper debt to Rome than to Greece" (p. 56).

68. See Brucker, *Florentine Politics*, p. 128. The phrase first appears in the *Consulte e Pratiche* records of July 1351. For a sustained effort to relate the *Decameron* to the

politics and ideology of postpandemic Florence, see David Wallace, *Giovanni Boccac-cio: Decameron*. References to the *Decameron* follow the edition of Vittore Branca, which forms vol. 4 of Boccaccio, *Tutte le opere*, ed. Branca; translations, unless other-wise indicated, follow the text of G. H. McWilliam (1972). In-text citations refer first to the Italian text by day, *novella*, and section, and then to the English translation by page number.

69. See Henderson, *Piety and Charity*, pp. 282–92. Henderson calculates that the company fed some 4,000 mouths in the first three weeks of June 1347.

70. This policy proved so popular that many householders followed the lead of the municipal authorities and bricked up members of their own families. It also proved successful: the mortality rate at Milan was less than 15 percent, probably the lowest in Italy. See Robert S. Gottfried, *The Black Death*, pp. 48–49, 122–24.

71. See Vittore Branca, *Giovanni Boccaccio: Profilo biografico*, in Boccaccio, *Tutte le opere*, ed. Branca, vol. 1, pp. 85–99; Aldo D. Scaglione, *Nature and Love in the Late Middle Ages*.

72. See Glending Olson, *Literature as Recreation in the Later Middle Ages*.

73. On the death of friars, see Brucker, *Florentine Politics*, p. 9. On the signifi-cance and limits of female initiative in organizing this group, see Wallace, *Decameron*, pp. 23–25. For intriguing short notes on the all-female Compagnia di Santa Caterina di Siena, which met at Santa Maria Novella in the sixteenth century, see Ludovica Sebregondi, "A Confraternity of Florentine Noble Women."

74. See Wallace, *Decameron*, pp. 25–31; Wallace, "Chaucer's Body Politic: Social and Narrative Self-Regulation," pp. 221–40 (pp. 226–28 and fig. 1).

75. In 2.4, for example, Landolfo is described as being "a very rich man indeed. But being dissatisfied with his fortune, he sought to double it" ("disiderando di raddopiarla," 2.4.5.; p. 136). This sudden desire (note the verb *disiderare*) appears all the more powerful, phenomenal, for not being glossed or explained.

76. See Wallace, *Decameron*, pp. 77–84; 106–7; *Decameron*, "Conclusione dell'autore."

77. See Chap. 6 below.

78. For a more detailed account of this *novella* as part of an extended discussion of the countryside in Boccaccio and Chaucer, see Chap. 5 below.

79. See Strohm, *Hochon's Arrow*, pp. 33–56; Justice, *Writing and Rebellion*, pp. 205–8.

80. See Patterson, *Subject of History*, pp. 244–46, 280–321.

81. See Raymond Cazelles, "The Jacquerie" (a French peasant revolt of 1358); Samuel Cohn, "Florentine Insurrections, 1342–1385, in Comparative Perspective"; Michel Mollat and Philippe Wolff, *The Popular Revolutions of the Middle Ages*.

82. In the 1370s, English peasants and artisans were organized into military units by government-sponsored "commissions of array" that sought to enforce the Statute of Laborers or to prepare against possible French invasion. Ironically, the frequency of such exercises was to help the 1381 rebels maintain discipline and cohesion as they marched on London. See A. F. Butcher, "English Urban Society and the Revolt of 1381," p. 101; Hilton, *Peasants' Revolt*, p. xxxvi.

83. See Trexler, *Spiritual Power*, pp. 64–65; George Holmes, *The Good Parlia-ment*, pp. 124–26, 179–80.

84. Chaucer left for Lombardy on May 28, 1378, and returned to London on September 19. See *Chaucer Life-Records*, pp. 58–59.

85. See Ettore Verga, *Storia della vita milanese*, p. 109.

86. See Schevill, *History of Florence*, pp. 259, 283; Brucker, *Civic World*, pp. 46–75.

87. See Lauro Martines, *The Social World of the Florentine Humanists*, pp. 272–73.

88. The seminal work here is Hans Baron, *The Crisis of the Early Italian Renaissance: Civic Humanism and Republican Liberty in an Age of Classicism and Tyranny*.

89. "Invectiva contra eum qui maledixit Italie," in Francesco Petrarca, *Prose*, ed. G. Martellotti et al., p. 790: "Quid est enim aliud omnis historia, quam romana laus?"

90. See Gigliola Soldi Rondinini, "Visconti e Sforza nelle terre padane: origine e sviluppo di uno stato regionale," pp. 7–11. The Visconti were not immediately able to establish dynastic rule and extirpate the della Torre. In 1302 they were temporarily forced to leave Milan.

91. See Gianluigi Barni, "La formazione interna dello Stato Visconteo," esp. pp. 17–40; Corrado Argegni, "Dal Verme, Jacopo," vol. I, pp. 222–23.

92. See Given-Wilson, *Royal Household*, pp. 213–21.

93. See *Chaucer Life-Records*, pp. 55–56.

94. See Jones, *Chaucer's Knight: The Portrait of a Medieval Mercenary*. For a sustained and splendid attempt to situate the *Knight's Tale* within and as part of the history of the English nobility, see Patterson, *Subject of History*.

95. Italians found the name "Hawkwood" difficult to pronounce and transcribe: variants include Hacoud, Haukovd, Aukud, Agudo, Aguto, and Acuto (hence the name "John the Sharp"). See Joseph Jay Deiss, *Captains of Fortune: Profiles of Six Italian Condottieri*, p. 117.

96. See May McKisack, *Fourteenth Century 1307–1399*, p. 346; Geoffrey Trease, *The Condottieri: Soldiers of Fortune*, pp. 41–43. Hawkwood's social origins were not as humble as one might assume from his father's profession: tanners often owned some land and enjoyed considerable local status. John Hawkwood was, however, a younger son.

97. Hawkwood achieved this by breaching embankments, flooding the imperial camp and washing away much of the emperor's equipment and supplies. See Trease, p. 78.

98. See Michael Mallett, *Mercenaries and Their Masters*, pp. 40–41; Trease, pp. 90–92.

99. "François Sforza: De condottiere a Duc de Milan," p. 7. For intelligent reflections on the term "bastard feudalism" and its application to English contexts, see Strohm, *Social Chaucer*, pp. 13–23.

100. See Trease, *Condottieri*, pp. 151–54.

101. See the edition by A. T. P. Byles, p. 123.

102. For an impassioned modern response to the phenomenon of medieval mercenaries, see Jones, *Chaucer's Knight*, pp. 13–30.

103. See Mallett, *Mercenaries*, pp. 21–23; *Purgatorio* 5.91–93.

104. See M. H. Keen, *The Laws of War in the Middle Ages*, pp. 156–85; McKisack, *Fourteenth Century*, pp. 140–41; *Chaucer Life-Records*, pp. 23–28.

105. See Mallett, *Mercenaries*, pp. 79–80.

106. *Il Trecentonovelle*, ed. Antonio Lanza, 181.2–4 (p. 406); my translations. Sac-

chetti was born sometime between 1332 and 1334 and died in August 1400, probably from the plague. Lanza suggests that the general design of the *Trecentonovelle* was conceived around 1384–85, and that it was written between 1392 and 1399 (p. xxix). The wars mentioned below that pitted Padua and Verona against Milan and Venice were fought in 1388–89.

107. Larner, *Italy 1216–1380*, p. 218.

108. See Mann, *Social Power*, vol. 1, p. 432. For a general analysis of the economic impact of the war, particularly of the "transfer of wealth" effected by taxes levied upon town and country, see Richard W. Kaeuper, *War, Justice, and Public Order*, p. 104.

109. Origo, *Merchant of Prato*, pp. 11–12. The merchant quoted is Datini.

110. See *Riverside Chaucer*, p. 829 (note to 1006–7). Chaucer's only other use of the term is *Parson's Tale*, 10.769, where he speaks of "pilours and destroyours of the godes of hooly chirche." The term *pilour* derives from OE *pilian*, to plunder, rob.

111. See Peyronnet, "François Sforza," p. 7; Branca, *Boccaccio medievale*, pp. 134–64.

112. See Patrizia Mainoni, "I mercanti milanesi in Europa," p. 78; Bruno Viviano, "Ospedali e organizzazione della beneficenza a Milano dal 1277 al 1535," pp. 56–57.

113. See Mainoni, "Mercanti milanesi," p. 82; Jones, *Chaucer's Knight*, pp. 28–30. Jones presses his case too far in suggesting that the reference to Milan might cause the reader to identify the Knight as a one-time member of the White Company (p. 30).

114. See "Le manifatture lombarde," unattributed in Villa, ed., *Lombardia delle signorie*, p. 97; Mainoni, "Mercanti milanesi," pp. 77–78.

115. Origo, *Merchant of Prato*, p. 12.

116. See Enrico Guidoni, "Appunti per una storia dell'urbanistica," vol. 1, p. 153. Guidoni speaks of Milan under the Visconti as "una specie di 'grande macchina' urbana."

117. See Viviano, "Ospedali," p. 72.

118. Peyronnet, "François Sforza," p. 9.

119. See Luisa Chiappa Mauri, "Aspetti del mondo rurale lombardo nel Trecento e nel Quattrocento," pp. 101–16.

120. See John E. Martin, *Feudalism to Capitalism*; Marx, *Capital*, vol. 1, pp. 875–83.

121. See Cohn, "Florentine Insurrections," p. 145; Trexler, *Public Life in Renaissance Florence*, p. 4.

122. The most painful, pitiful, and convincing example of this is *Decameron* 9.10. See further, Chap. 5 below.

123. See Mauri, "Mondo rurale," pp. 106, 112.

124. See *Storia di Milano*, dir. Giovanni Treccani degli Alfieri, vol. 6, pp. 451–52.

125. See Anna Antoniazzi Villa, "Dinamismo economico dello stato visconteo-sforzesco," pp. 31–38.

126. See *Storia di Milano*, vol. 6, pp. 478–79.

127. See G. S. Rondinini, "Visconti e Sforza," p. 13.

128. Ibid., p. 14.

129. See Patrizia Mainoni, "I mercanti milanesi in Europa," p. 78.

130. Bonvesin de la Riva, *Grandezze di Milano*, p. 80; Paredi's edition of Bonvesin's *De magnalibus Mediolani* is accompanied by an Italian translation.

131. See Mainoni, "Mercanti milanesi," p. 77.

132. Ibid., p. 78.

133. On the forms of agreement worked out between the Tudors and the urban oligarchies of sixteenth-century England, see Robert Tittler, "The Emergence of Urban Policy, 1536–58," pp. 74–93; W. G. Hoskins, *The Age of Plunder: King Henry's England 1500–1547*, p. 101.

134. *Humanist Scholarship and Public Order: Two Tracts Against the Pilgrimage of Grace by Sir Richard Morison*, ed. David Sandler Berkowitz, p. 30.

135. See G. S. Rondinini, "Visconti e Sforza," p. 16.

136. See G. Romano, "Regesto degli atti notarili di C. Cristiani dal 1391 al 1399," pp. 295–96.

137. See Ettore Verga, *Storia della vita milanese*, p. 102; *Storia di Milano*, vol. 4, pp. 372–75; vol. 6, p. 459.

138. For more on this infamous statue, see Chap. 11 below.

139. See Angelo Turchini, "La Lombardia centro artistico internazionale," pp. 116–17; Verga, *Vita milanese*, p. 103.

140. See Guidoni, "Appunti," vol. 1, p. 162; *Storia di Milano*, vol. 6, pp. 468–69.

141. Galvano Fiamma, *Opusculum de rebus gestis ab Azone, Luchino et Johanne Vicecomitibus*, ed. Carlo Castiglioni, pp. 15–16.

142. Ibid., pp. iv, v.

143. *De Genesi ad litteram* 9.9.14 as cited and translated in R. A. Markus, "The Latin Fathers," p. 110.

144. Janet Coleman, "St. Augustine: Christian Political Thought at the End of the Roman Empire," p. 52.

145. See the photographic illustration in Aldo Castellano, "Il postgotico lombardo e le origini del Duomo di Milano," p. 156.

146. See Castellano, pp. 167, 174; anon., "Due secoli di architettura lombarda," in Villa et al., ed., *Lombardia delle signorie*, p. 193.

147. Ibid., p. 191; Giuliana Ferrari, "Gli spettacoli all'epoca dei Visconti e degli Sforza: dalla festa cittadina alla festa celebrativa," p. 219.

148. Ferrari, "Spettacoli," p. 219.

149. See Fiamma, *Opusculum*, p. 22 (referring to Christmas 1336). Note also, from the preceding paragraph, that in September 1336 Azzone Visconti orders citizens from all his territories to bring lengths of silk cloth to the cathedral at Milan, "ad honorem Virginis" (the feast of the Nativity of Mary). On the *trionfi*, see Ferrari, "Spettacoli," p. 226.

150. See Ferrari, "Spettacoli," p. 219.

151. Matteo Villani, *Cronica*, ed. Dragomanni, 9.103. See also *Storia di Milano*, vol. 5, p. 410.

152. Matteo Villani ridicules the land and its title in fine fashion (*Cronica* 9.103).

153. This motto appears in frescoes at Milan and Pavia, and in manuscript illuminations by Anovelo da Imbonate, Giovannino dei Grassi, and Belbello da Pavia. See Chamberlin, *Count of Virtue*, p. 34; Turchini, "Centro artistico," pp. 129–32; *The Visconti Hours*, ed. Millard Meiss and Edith W. Kirsch, *passim*.

154. See Pietro Toesca, *La pittura e la miniatura nella Lombardia*, pp. 172–81; Mario Salmi, *La miniatura italiana*, p. 40.

155. The manuscript of the so-called *Visconti Hours* is in two volumes bearing the signatures Banco Rari (BR) 397 and Landau Finaly (LF) 22. Both volumes are now

in the Biblioteca Nazionale, Florence. LF was given to the Biblioteca in 1947, and BR was acquired from the Visconti family in 1969. Kirsch thinks it "probable" (p. 23) that the Book of Hours was begun to celebrate the birth of Gian Galeazzo's son and heir, Giovanni Maria, on September 7, 1388. All signs of the work of Giovannino and his workshop end on LF 54; Belbello's work was probably completed by the early 1430s: see *Visconti Hours*, ed. Meiss and Kirsch, pp. 24–28. For a more recent and detailed consideration of datings and attributions, see Antonio Cadei, *Studi di miniatura lombarda: Giovanni de' Grassi, Belbello da Pavia*, pp. 41–105, 130–32.

156. The folio originally opposite BR 150 and now missing contained a fourth portrait in its lower margin (Meiss and Kirsch, eds., commentary on BR 105).

157. *Visconti Hours*, BR 115.

158. See Dillian Gordon et al., *Making and Meaning: The Wilton Diptych*, pp. 27, 58. One of the Magi in Paris, Bibliothèque Nationale, MS lat. 757 (a Visconti manuscript) wears a personal badge of Gian Galeazzo in an *Adoration of the Kings* (f. 293v.): see *Five Illuminated Manuscripts of Giangaleazzo Visconti*, ed. Edith W. Kirsch, pp. 9, 36, and fig. 57.

159. In an illuminated book of hours, now British Library, King's MS 9, Henry scrawls a love note to Anne Boleyn beneath a miniature of a bloodstained Man of Sorrows. Anne responds by writing an encouraging reply, on a different folio, beneath the Annunciation (f. 66v., and f. 231). See Eric W. Ives, *Anne Boleyn*, pp. 7–8 and plate 27.

160. This inventory is preserved in the paper MS AD XV.18.4, Biblioteca Braidense, Milan, and has been published in G. D'Adda, *Indagini storiche sulla Libreria Visconteo-Sforzesco del Castello di Pavia*, pp. 3–91. The library was gradually dispersed in the course of the fifteenth century as many books were transferred to Milan; many volumes, especially those in French, were taken to Paris following the fall of the Sforza and the French occupation of the dukedom. Thanks to the cataloguing work of Paulin Paris, *Les Manuscripts François de la Bibliothèque du roi*, vol. 7, it is possible to verify the evidence offered by the 1426 inventory and "to achieve a precise account of the character of the fourteenth-century Viscontian library" (*Storia di Milano*, vol. 5, p. 572; my translation).

161. See *Storia di Milano*, vol. 5, pp. 581–82; for this process of assimilation, see Nicholas Mann, "Petrarch and Humanism: The Paradox of Posterity."

162. See Maria Pia Andreolli Panzarasa, "Il Petrarca e Pavia viscontea," p. 64.

163. See Howard, *Life of Chaucer*, p. 228; Rodney K. Delasanta, "Chaucer, Pavia, and the Ciel d'Oro," pp. 117–21; William E. Coleman, "Chaucer, the *Teseida*, and the Visconti Library at Pavia," pp. 92–101; Robert A. Pratt, "Chaucer and the Visconti Libraries," pp. 191–99. It seems fair to speculate that Chaucer spent some time at Pavia, which is twenty miles south of Milan, because Galeazzo died at Pavia on August 4, 1378, and was buried at Pavia soon after. All business would obviously have centered on Pavia during this period.

164. *Storia di Milano*, vol. 5, p. 574.

165. Ibid., vol. 5, p. 575.

166. Such as, for example, the vigorous monorhymed quatrains of Bonvesin de la Riva: see Bonvesin de la Riva, *Volgari Scelti*, ed. and trans. P. S. Diehl and S. Stefanini.

167. My translation from the Latin in Marco Vattasso, *Del Petrarca e alcuni suoi amici*, p. 43.

168. Zamorei, who was one of the first examiners at the university founded at Pavia in 1361, served Archbishop Giovanni as *vicario* and may have helped persuade Petrarch to take up residence at Milan in 1353. See Vattasso, *Del Petrarca*, pp. 57, 45.

169. Translated from the Italian translation of the Latin original in *Storia di Milano*, vol. 5, pp. 358–59. For the original, see Giulini, *Memorie spettanti alla storia . . . di Milano*, vol. 5, p. 387.

170. Zamorei also wrote a metrical inscription for the tomb of Isabelle of Valois, who died on September 3, 1373: see Vattasso, *Del Petrarca*, pp. 44–45.

171. The portrait is referred to at the end of the sixteenth century; the painting, which was apparently completed by 1367, was still to be seen in the seventeenth century. See Vattasso, *Del Petrarca*, pp. 60–61.

172. For example, Bracci comes up with the conceit that the wringing of hands and endless cries over Galeazzo's death are so loud that his poem may not be heard. See Antonio Medin, "I Visconti nella poesia contemporanea," p. 739.

173. Ibid., p. 761.

174. See *Familiares* 13.6 in Francesco Petrarca, *Rerum familiarum libri*, trans. Aldo S. Bernado, 3 vols. For the Latin text, see Francesco Petrarca, *Le Familiari*, ed. V. Rossi and U. Bosco.

175. For a detailed account of this process, see Chap. 12 below.

176. For consideration of links between Petrarch and the imperial court of Charles IV, Anne's father, see Chap. 12 below.

177. See *Troilus and Criseyde* 1.400–420. For excellent commentary on this "Canticus Troili," an adaptation to French-style *ballade* form of the Petrarchan sonnet (132) "S' amor non è," see James I. Wimsatt, *Chaucer and His French Contemporaries*, pp. xi–xii; Thomas C. Stillinger, *The Song of Troilus*, pp. 165–206. Stillinger explores the relationship of *Troilus* 5.638–44, rubricated as "Canticus Troili" in many manuscripts, to a second Petrarchan sonnet (189), "Passa la nave mia."

178. See Wallace, "Chaucer's Continental Inheritance," p. 21.

179. Jacob Burckhardt, *The Civilization of the Renaissance in Italy*, trans. S. G. C. Middlemore, vol. 1, p. 143.

180. Denys Hay observes that in Renaissance historiography between Burckhardt and Baron, "the Renaissance is neither explained nor interpreted. It is treated as a collection of self-evident phenomena, ultimately requiring no justification" (*Renaissance Essays*, p. 137; see also p. 398).

181. *Annales* 25, pp. 1394–99. Hans Baron, writing in 1960 to celebrate the centenary of Burckhardt's *Kultur*, states that over the last forty years the work has become "a classic read in all western countries." See "The Limits of the Notion of 'Renaissance Individualism': Burckhardt After a Century," now in Hans Baron, *In Search of Civic Humanism*, vol. 2, p. 155. On the triumph of Burckhardt over Ranke in Germany after World War II, as proclaimed by Friedrich Meinecke, see Hugh Trevor-Roper, "Burckhardt," pp. 377–78.

182. William Kerrigan and Gordon Braden, *The Idea of the Renaissance*, p. xi. This volume was awarded the Bainton Book Prize by the Sixteenth-Century Studies Conference.

183. The longevity and significance of this formulation has been recognized by Lee Patterson, "On the Margin: Postmodernism, Ironic History, and Medieval Studies," p. 95. Aers, "Whisper," pp. 195–96.

184. Braden, "It's Not the Years, It's the Mileage," p. 673.

185. Ibid., p. 673. Braden, who is responding to a collection of essays by Renaissance scholars, notes: "I actually see little in these essays that goes significantly outside the territory sketched 120 years ago by Jacob Burckhardt" (p. 672).

186. See Alison Brown, "Jacob Burckhardt's Renaissance," p. 26; Hay, "Place of Hans Baron," p. 141.

187. Burckhardt, *Die Kultur der Renaissance in Italien: Ein Versuch*, ed. Horst Günther, p. 11; this phrase is translated by Middlemore as "great intellectual process" (vol. 1, p. 21). In-text citations by page will refer first to the translation by volume and page, and then to the original German.

188. In discussing "Mohammedan usages" ("mohammedanischer Routine"), Burckhardt speaks of "those cruel and vexatious methods without which, it is true, it is impossible to obtain any money from Orientals" (vol. 1, p. 24; *Kultur*, p. 13).

189. Burckhardt, *Civilization of the Renaissance*, vol. 1, p. 144; *Kultur*, p. 139.

190. "No doubt it was often hard," Burckhardt concedes, "for the subjects of a Visconti to maintain the dignity of their persons and families, and multitudes must have lost in moral character through the servitude they lived under. But this was not the case with regard to individuality" (vol. 1, p. 144; p. 139). For an attempt to evaluate such passages in the context of nineteenth-century narratives of nationalism and imperialism, see Wallace, "Carving Up Time and the World," pp. 3–8.

191. "Political impotence," Burckhardt argues, "does not hinder the different tendencies and manifestations of private life from thriving in the fullest vigor and variety. . . . The private man, indifferent to politics [der politisch indifferente Privatmensch] and busied partly with serious pursuits, partly with the interests of a *dilettante*, seems to have been first fully formed in these despotisms of the fourteenth century" (vol. 1, p. 144; pp. 139–40).

192. Burckhardt, *Civilization*, vol. 1, p. 28, quoting from *Seniles* 14.1. This short political treatise written under despotic patronage later enjoyed independent circulation as (ironically enough) *De republica optime administranda*.

193. Hans Baron, "Moot Problems of Renaissance Interpretation: An Answer to Wallace K. Ferguson," p. 27.

194. Ibid., p. 28.

195. Perry Anderson, *Lineages of the Absolutist State*, pp. 148–49; see above, p. 7. See also August Buck, "Hans Baron's Contribution to the Literary History of the Renaissance," p. lvii.

196. See Susan Wittig, *Stylistic and Narrative Structures in the Middle English Romances*, esp. p. 179.

197. Burckhardt, *Civilization*, vol. 1, p. 144; *Kultur*, p. 139.

198. For detailed discussion of this phenomenon, see Chap. 11 below. Chaucer identifies Petrarch as "my maister" within the *de casibus* tragedies of the *Monk's Tale* (7.2325).

199. For a succinct overview of the friendship and two-way influence between Nietzsche and Burckhardt, which lasted from 1870 to 1889, see Trevor-Roper, "Jacob Burckhardt," pp. 373–76.

200. Burckhardt, *Civilization*, vol. 1, p. 146; *Kultur*, p. 143.

201. See Nicholas R. Havely, "The Self-Consuming City: Florence as Body Poli-

tic in Dante's *Commedia*"; Joan Ferrante, *The Political Vision of the Divine Comedy*, pp. 132–97.

202. Baron, "Moot Problems," p. 34; and *Crisis*, p. xxv.

203. For helpful synopses of Baron's arguments, see Hay, "Hans Baron in Renaissance Historiography," pp. 139–49; Buck, "Hans Baron and Renaissance Literature," pp. xl–xliv. For a succinct account of the evolution of Baron's thinking, see Ferguson, "Interpretation of Humanism," pp. 14–25. See also John A. Tedeschi and Andrew W. Lewis, "Bibliography of the Writings of Hans Baron 1924–1969," pp. lxxi–lxxxvii; Bernard Guenée, *States and Rulers in Later Medieval Europe*, pp. 230–33.

204. Baron, "Articulation and Unity in the Italian Renaissance and in the Modern West," p. 135.

205. Baron, "Cicero and the Roman Civic Spirit in the Middle Ages and Early Renaissance," p. 88.

206. Baron, "Moot Problems," p. 28. In his "Roman Civic Spirit" essay of 1938, Baron confects a *curriculum vitae* for Petrarch that entirely elides his long years of service, as a mature scholar of European stature, to northern Italian despotism: "Petrarch," Baron argues, "was the heir both to the culture of the Italian city-states and to medieval traditions. Although a Florentine citizen, he was born and bred in exile; he preferred, *during his decisive years* [emphasis mine], life in the isolated Alpine valley of Vaucluse in southern France to that of a Florentine citizen; he was in contact with the Franciscan movement and even more with the monastic literature of the twelfth century. So it fell to his lot to wage the historic conflict . . ." (p. 85). As he delivered these lines in Manchester, we should note, Baron was himself newly arrived in exile from Berlin.

207. Baron, "Moot Problems," p. 27. I refer to this article with some frequency because Baron is attempting to summarize his arguments and defend his methodological thinking in the face of a pointed critique by Wallace K. Ferguson ("Interpretation of Humanism").

208. Burckhardt, *Civilization*, vol. I, p. 143; *Kultur*, p. 137.

209. Changes to family structure in the early modern period, which see the replication of church and state authority through the notion of a masculine "household head," may be traced through the orchestrated rise of St. Joseph (from powerless *senex* to *sedulus administrator*): see David Herlihy, *Medieval Households*, pp. 127–30. See further Lawrence Stone, *The Family, Sex, and Marriage in England, 1500–1800* and the essay cluster "Recent Trends in Renaissance Studies: The Family, Marriage, and Sex," ed. Stanley Chojnacki.

210. Baron, *Crisis*, p. xxvi.

211. Lauro Martines, *Power and Imagination: City-States in Renaissance Italy*, pp. 262–300. For a critique of later humanist education plans, which set out to produce "a small, politically active minority who were heirs to a mature foreign culture," see Anthony Grafton and Lisa Jardine, *From Humanism to the Humanities* (p. 220).

212. See *La lirica toscana del Rinascimento anteriore ai tempi del Magnifico*, ed. F. Flamini, p. 60.

213. See *Storia di Milano*, vol. 5, p. 592; vol. 6, p. 539. Salutati must have found it embarrassing later in his career to recall having written that Bernabò's fall was moved by the finger of God and that Gian Galeazzo was a good and merciful prince, moved by the suffering of people under tyranny.

214. See Tenenti, "Etudes anglo-saxonnes," p. 1399; Gene Brucker, *Renaissance Florence*, pp. 169–70. Marvin R. Becker notes that as the Florentine territorial state grew and "the literature and the art of the period proclaim the glories of serving the state, the records of the Florentine treasury disclose that thousands of ordinary citizens preferred to pay the substantial fine of twenty-five lire rather than assume the responsibility of public office." See "The Florentine Territorial State and Civic Humanism in the Early Renaissance," p. 137.

215. Brucker, *Civic World*, p. 12.

216. For more on this, see Chap. 6 below.

217. Baron, "Moot Problems," p. 31.

218. See Ferguson, "Interpretation of Humanism," pp. 19–20. The excursus is made in Hans Baron, "A Sociological Interpretation of the Early Renaissance in Florence," pp. 427–48.

219. Baron, "Moot Problems," p. 33.

220. In 1396 Richard sealed a 28-year truce with France; in 1397 he promised to send an English force to support the Franco-Florentine war against Gian Galeazzo. The commons refused to offer any assistance in financing this venture. Richard was soon seduced into believing that the German electors, with papal support, were prepared to make him Holy Roman Emperor if he would give up his alliance with France. In 1398, Gian Galeazzo expected Henry of Lancaster to arrive in Lombady, marry Lucia Visconti (daughter of Bernabò) and lend him military assistance with 200 lancers, 5 knights, and 500 archers. Henry stayed in Paris, which pleased the French. He set sail for England from Boulogne towards the end of June 1399. Lucia Visconti was still entertaining hopes of marrying Henry as late as May 1399. See McKisack, *Fourteenth Century*, pp. 476–77, 492; Anthony Tuck, *Crown and Nobility 1272–1461*, p. 208; *Storia di Milano*, vol. 6, p. 40; G. Romano, "Un matrimonio alla corte de' Visconti," pp. 603–5.

221. See J. G. A. Pocock, *The Machiavellian Moment: Florentine Political Thought and the Atlantic Republican Tradition*, pp. 55–66 (with the references to Seigel, Garin, Struever, Martines, Becker, Molho); Quentin Skinner, *The Foundations of Modern Political Thought. Volume One: The Renaissance*, pp. 71–112; P. O. Kristeller, *Studies in Renaissance Thought and Letters*, pp. 38, 359; Charles Trinkhaus, *The Scope of Renaissance Humanism*, pp. 4–20.

222. *Florentine Politics and Society*, p. 3. Strictly speaking, Brucker is referring to the decade 1338–48. But things did not improve much in 1348. For a convenient summary of work by Becker, Herlihy, Waley, and De la Roncière which views the 1340s as a watershed period, see Randolph Starn, "Florentine Renaissance Studies," pp. 682–83.

223. Tenenti takes Baron to task for the "simplifications excessives" in his attempt to show how humanist culture bears the imprint of contemporary social and political events (and of little else): "Etudes anglo-saxonnes," p. 1397.

224. Becker, "Territorial State," p. 137.

225. A point often missed: there is nothing in Boccaccio's *Conclusione* to suggest that the completion of the storytelling schema signals or coincides with the end of the plague.

226. Quoted from a letter by Burckhardt in Baron, *In Search of Civic Humanism*,

vol. 2, p. 165. The opening paragraph of Burckhardt's *Kultur* speaks of "a civilization that is the mother [Mutter] of our own" (vol. 1, p. 21; p. 11).

227. Baron, *Search*, vol. 2, pp. 161–62. On the importance of Goethe to Burckhardt, see Trevor-Roper, "Burckhardt," pp. 363, 370.

228. These narratives—the *Canterbury Tales* of Clerk, Merchant, and Monk, plus the *Prologue* to the *Legend of Good Women*, are considered in my last three chapters.

229. Plummer's observations form part of the introduction to his edition of Sir John Fortescue's *The Governance of England*, pp. 15–16; they are quoted in K. B. McFarlane, "Bastard Feudalism," p. 161.

230. McFarlane, "Bastard Feudalism," pp. 161, 162. For an application of McFarlane's terms of analysis to legal history, see J. G. Bellamy, *Bastard Feudalism and the Law*. For a critical assessment of the usefulness and limitations of McFarlane's terminology, see Strohm, *Social Chaucer*, pp. 15–21.

231. McFarlane, "Bastard Feudalism," p. 169. This newfound "freedom of choice" did not, of course, extend down to the lowest ranks of society except as part of a new, proto-capitalist ideology of the freedom and mobility of labor.

232. Shortly before his famous evaluation of Chaucer's *Troilus and Criseyde*, Sidney observes: "Yet confesse I alwaies, that as the fertilest ground must be manured, so must the highest flying wit have a Dedalus to guide him" (*Defence of Poesie*, 1595 ed., not paginated; see also *Sir Philip Sidney*, ed. K. Duncan-Jones, p. 242, lines 1225–26, 1240–44).

233. *Arte of English Poesie*, ed. Willcock and Walker, p. 145.

234. "Our maker therfore at these dayes shall not follow *Piers Plowman* nor *Gower* nor *Lydgate* nor yet Chaucer, for their language is now out of use with us: neither shall he take the termes of Northmen . . . nor in effect any speach used beyond the river of Trent, though no man can deny but that theirs is the purer English Saxon at this day" (*Arte of English Poesie*, pp. 144–45).

235. *Arte of English Poesie*, p. 145.

Chapter 2

1. See *The Waste Land* 2.170–72, in *Collected Poems 1909–1962*, p. 69. Cross-reference with Chaucer's *General Prologue* is initiated by the very first line of Eliot's poem: "April is the cruellest month . . ."

2. The index to Caroline D. Eckhardt, *Chaucer's General Prologue to the "Canterbury Tales": An Annotated Bibliography 1900 to 1982*, contains no fewer than thirteen entries under "portrait gallery" (p. 459); no entries are recorded under *compagnye* or *felaweshipe*. In his influential *Ricardian Poetry*, John Burrow contemplates the works of Chaucer, Gower, Langland, and the *Gawain*-poet "as if they were pictures hanging round the walls of a room devoted, in an imaginary museum, to the 'Ricardian School'" (p. 9). For Tennyson's "Palace of Art," a poem obviously indebted to locales from the *House of Fame* and the *Knight's Tale*, see Hallam, Lord Tennyson, ed., *Works of Tennyson*, vol. 1, pp. 172–86.

3. There were many other sites for schooling in collective behavior in fourteenth-century England in various social, ecclesiastical, educational, judicial, and festival contexts: see Barbara A. Hanawalt, *Growing Up in Medieval London*; Hanawalt, *The Ties That Bound*, esp. pp. 257–67; Justice, *Writing and Rebellion*; Mary Flowers Braswell, "Chaucer's 'Court Baron': Law and the *Canterbury Tales*." Nonetheless, it

is the contention of this chapter and the next that the *mores* of guild behavior are particularly germane to the understanding of Chaucer's *General Prologue*.

4. For more on the pleasures, strategies, and gender politics of narrative dilation, see Chap. 8 below.

5. *Canterbury Tales*, p. 55.

6. Critics differ as to whether "nature" in line 11 should or should not be capitalized: see, for example, Eckhardt, *Prologue Bibliography*, entries 597, 631. *Riverside Chaucer* prints "nature" and glosses "the personified goddess Natura" (p. 799).

7. *Canterbury Tales*, p. 55.

8. "Magis igitur homo est communicativus alteri quam quodcumque aliud animal." St. Thomas Aquinas, *De regimine principum ad regem Cypri*, ed. R. M. Spiazzi, p. 258.

9. Dante, *Il Convivio*, ed. Maria Simonelli, 1.1.8.

10. "Thus we observe that it is by contrivance [per aliquam industriam] that [man] supplies his necessities, for instance food and clothing: nature starts him off with reason and hands, but not with the complete product, unlike other animals who are sufficiently provided with nourishment and covering" (St. Thomas Aquinas, *Summa Theologiae*, ed. T. Gilby et al., vol. 28, p. 10 [I a 2 ae. 95, 1]). Jill Mann observes that in medieval estates satire "there is nothing like Chaucer's continued insistence on the assembly of skills, duties and jargon that characterizes an estate" (*Estates Satire*, p. 15). "The *Prologue*," Mann concludes, "proves to be a poem about work" (p. 202).

11. Compare lines 30–41 with 715–24, 747–50.

12. John Russell, *The Boke of Nurture*, in *The Babees Book*, ed. Furnivall, lines 1025–28. This instructional text on household management, which survives whole or in part in five manuscripts, was written or copied by a "John Russelle," sometime servant of Humphrey, duke of Gloucester (died 1447). See *Boke of Nurture*, lines 1228–29; Jonathan Nicholls, *The Matter of Courtesy*, pp. 18, 159–60, 191.

13. See 1.837, 1.3118. Russell allows that a "knyght / digne and demure" may keep company with an unmitered "abbot & prioure" (1058–59). Chaucer's *General Prologue* describes the Monk as "A manly man, to been an abbot able" (1.167).

14. Bataille, "Sovereignty," vol. 3 of *The Accursed Share*, vol. 2, pp. 197, 198, 284.

15. For more on this, see Chap. 11 below. The Host's fantasies about "My lord, the Monk" (7.1924) show prescient understanding of Bataille's notion of the "sovereign" individual. As one absolved from the labor (including sexual labor, in marriage) of "borel men" (7.1955), the Monk achieves health, wealth, and a phenomenal sperm count; as a truly "sovereign" individual, the Monk should share, rather than hoard, such prosperity (7.1943–62).

16. Aquinas, *De regimine principum*, ed. Spiazzi, p. 258 (744); translation follows Aquinas, *Selected Political Writings*, ed. A. P. d'Entrèves, p. 3.

17. "All medieval authors," Jean Dunbabin argues, "took it for granted that legitimate authority was grounded in the people" ("Government," p. 515). It was the task of monarchical theorists to argue that such authority had, at a certain moment in the past, been transferred to a single ruler and could not now be recalled.

18. Jeannine Quillet, "Community, Counsel, and Representation," p. 522; C. Petit-Dutaillis, *Les communes françaises, caractère et évolution des origines au XVIIIe siècle*, p. 35.

19. See *Legend of Good Women*, F 170 ("Welcome, somer, oure governour and

lord!"), F 1060 ("That hadde founde here lord, here governour?"); *Franklin's Tale*, 5.1031 ("He seyde, 'Appollo, god and governour'").

20. As Walsingham noticed, Gaunt's influence over the government of England actually diminished after his father's death: see Anthony Goodman, *John of Gaunt*, p. 71.

21. See *Oxford Latin Dictionary*, *gubernator*. *OED* defines *governor* (1) as "a steersman, pilot, captain of a vessel"; see also *MED*, *governour* (5).

22. Chaucer's Shipman has also been commended for his knowledge of "her-berwe" (1.403). We should note, however, that the modern sense of *harbor* as a place of shelter for boats represents only one of the meanings of ME *herberwe* (*MED herberwe* 1 [c]), which is applied to many different places of shelter, lodging, or sojourn.

23. See *Le Songe du Vieil Pèlerin*, ed. G. W. Coopland. Coopland assigns the writing of this long text (over 340 folios) to the period 1386–89 (1.124).

24. *Songe* 2.116–25. For helpful commentary on this passage, see Dora M. Bell, *Etude sur Le Songe du Vieil Pèlerin*, pp. 101–12.

25. For more on this, see my Conclusion below.

26. The English ship of state actually shows up in *Le Songe du Vieil Pèlerin* as "la nef Malvoisine," the unneighborly vessel that threatens the French "Souveraine" (2.122). For a more detailed account of the "ship of state" metaphor in medieval English contexts, see Stillinger, *Song of Troilus*, pp. 195–206. Stillinger examines the possibilities of this metaphor in *Troilus and Criseyde*.

27. See *MED*, *reportour*.

28. *Hoccleve's Works*, ed. F. J. Furnivall, vol. 1, pp. 110–39. The lines immediately following those cited below are obviously indebted to Chaucer's *General Prologue* 1.731–36: "Who so þat shal reherce a mannes sawe, As þat he seith / moot he seyn & nat varie" (764–65). Hoccleve is here defending himself from the charge of antifemi-nist intent in writing his *Epistle of Cupid*.

29. For the hierarchy of author, commentator, compiler, scribe as discussed by St. Bonaventure, see A. J. Minnis, *Medieval Theory of Authorship*, pp. 94–95.

30. John A. Alford, *Piers Plowman: A Glossary of Legal Diction*, p. 127. Alford is quoting from H. C. Black, *Black's Law Dictionary*, 5th ed.

31. See Alford, *Glossary*, p. 151. For more on *narratio* (as applied to the Man of Law), see Chap. 7 below.

32. *Complete Works of Chaucer*, vol. 5, p. 817: "de alto in basso"; "de haut en bas."

33. These observations are commonplaces of the history of medieval political thought; Jean Dunbabin remarks, most eloquently, that such thinking "has the character of ordinary light—it is diffuse, spreads widely, is blocked by obstacles, casts shadows and merges into obscurity. As a consequence, it is hard to describe" ("Government," p. 498).

34. See *MED*, *felauship(e)*, which commands a remarkable range of definitions, including 2(c), sexual intercourse; 5(a), a band of associates or companions; a company of pilgrims; 6(b), a craft fraternity; a guild; 7(a), one of the heavenly companies of angels, saints, saved souls, etc; also, the whole heavenly community.

35. See Black, *Guilds and Civil Society*, p. 27.

36. Communion (*communio*) and community (*communitas*) both derive from the Latin term *communis*, common; *compagnye* is derived from the late Latin *compa-nio*, one who shares of the same bread.

37. See Henry Chadwick, "Christian Doctrine."

38. Augustinus argues, in his *Summa de potestate ecclesiastica*, that the power of the keys makes a pope superior to the angels; he could, if he so wished, simply float up to heaven and rule from above. See Michael Wilks, *The Problem of Sovereignty in the Later Middle Ages: The Papal Monarchy with Augustinus Triumphus and the Publicists*, pp. 358–59.

39. See Black, *Guilds and Civil Society* (which refers us to *Decretals* 47.22.1), p. 22.

40. Ibid., p. 63; see also J. Fleckenstein, ed., *Investiturstreit und Reichsverfassung*, pp. 321–62.

41. See D. E. Luscombe, "Introduction: The Formation of Political Thought in the West," p. 162; R. C. Van Caenegem, "Government, Law and Society," p. 210.

42. For the argument that the importance of Aristotle *can* be exaggerated, see Quentin Skinner, "Lorenzetti: The Artist as Political Philosopher," p. 56.

43. Quillet, "Community," p. 526. See also Ellen Meiksins Wood and Neal Wood, *Class Ideology and Ancient Political Theory: Socrates, Plato, and Aristotle in Social Context*: "*Koinonia*—variously translated as community, association, society, partnership, fraternity—is any group whose members have something in common, from mankind in general to a business arrangement. . . . Each form of *koinonia* is characterized by a particular kind of friendship or good will (*philia*), the bond that holds together its members. The *philia* binding the members of the household is a species of innate affection, while the friendship uniting the citizens of the *polis* is *homonoia*, or concord, more in the nature of agreement as to ends and values, a kind of contractual understanding" (p. 227).

44. Quillet, "Community," p. 528.

45. See D. E. Luscombe and G. R. Evans, "The Twelfth-Century Renaissance," pp. 312–13.

46. *De Genesi ad litteram* 9.9.14, as cited by R. A. Markus, "The Latin Fathers," p. 110.

47. Janet Coleman, "St. Augustine: Christian Political Thought at the End of the Roman Empire," p. 59.

48. See Chap. 10 below.

49. D. W. Robertson, *A Preface to Chaucer: Studies in Medieval Perspectives*, p. 243.

50. The first major section of *A Preface to Chaucer* (after the Introduction) is "Some Principles of Medieval Aesthetics" (pp. 52–137); the second is "Late Medieval Style" (pp. 138–285). It is worth remembering that D. W. Robertson's *Preface* (1962) was prefaced by his complete translation of Augustine, *On Christian Doctrine* (1958).

51. The most important theoretical treatment of guilds appears in Otto von Gierke, *Das deutsche Genossenschaftsrecht*, esp. vols. 1 and 2. Gierke himself notes that a theory of association in early Germanic law can only be abstracted from the study of concrete customs and usages (vol. 2, pp. 12–14). Much has been translated from Gierke, but little from these first two volumes until very recently: see now Otto von Gierke, *Community in Historical Perspective*, ed. Antony Black, trans. Mary Fischer.

52. See Black, *Guilds*, pp. 1, 14; see also *Convivio* 1.1.6–15, where Dante develops an extended gustatory metaphor in serving up the banquet of his text.

53. See Gierke, *Genossenschaftsrecht*, vol. 1, p. 221; Black, *Guilds*, pp. 13, 18, 55.

54. Black, *Guilds*, p. 11; Black's analogy here of the guild as a cell of the socioeconomic body is a helpful one.

55. See Gierke, *Genossenschaftsrecht*, vol. 1, pp. 359–80; Black, *Guilds*, p. 13; Pierre Michaud-Quantin, *Universitas: Expressions du mouvement communautaire dans le moyen âge latin*, pp. 149, 165–66.

56. See Gierke, *Genossenschaftsrecht*, vol. 1, p. 453.

57. I agree with Carl Lindahl's suggestion that "the most relevant real-life analogue [to Chaucer's *felaweshipe*] . . . is the parish guild": see *Earnest Games: Folkloric Patterns in the Canterbury Tales*, p. 25. In the Gild of Holy Trinity, St. Botolph's, Aldersgate, London, Lindahl finds "surrogates for the entire Canterbury cast—with the possible exception of the Shipman, Miller, and Reeve" and notes that "there are some temptingly close parallels" (between this parish guild and Chaucer's *felaweshipe*, p. 29). The real imperative here, however, is not to find a guild that is inclusive enough to stand comparison with Chaucer's *felaweshipe*, but to establish the common assumptions Chaucer's pilgrims bring to the *felaweshipe* from their experience of many different (rich or poor, craft or religious) guilds.

58. See Chap. 3 below.

59. Antony Black, prodded by the spirits of Quentin Skinner and Karl Popper, *inter alia*, offers a fine rolling critique of Gierke and Durkheim: see *Guilds*, pp. xi, 12–13, 26–29, 61–62, 223–36.

60. Black, *Guilds*, p. 28.

61. See J. L. Bolton, *The Medieval English Economy 1150–1500*: "Down to about 1300 the trend is clear, expansion in most sectors of the economy" (p. 180). See also Georges de Lagarde, *La naissance de l'esprit laïque*, vol. 1, pp. 174–83; Black, *Guilds*, pp. 7, 33, 58.

62. See Anthony Giddens, *Durkheim*, p. 62; Black, *Guilds*, pp. 229, 232.

63. Emile Durkheim, *The Division of Labor in Society*, trans. W. D. Halls, p. 331.

64. Durkheim offers a succinct account of these two forms of *solidarité* in the opening pages of his "Introduction à la sociologie de la famille" (1888), now in Emile Durkheim, *Textes*, ed. Victor Karady, vol. 3, pp. 9–34: "L'une [solidarité mecanique] . . . est due à la similarité des consciences, à la communauté des idées et des sentiments, l'autre . . . est au contraire un produit de la différenciation des fonctions et de la division du travail. Sous l'effet de la première, les esprits s'unissent en se confondant, en se perdant pour ainsi dire les uns dans les autres, de manière a former une masse compacte qui n'est guère capable que de mouvements d'ensemble. Sous l'influence de la seconde, par suite de la mutuelle dépendance où se trouvent les fonctions spécialisées, chacun a sa sphère d'action propre, tout en étant inséparable des autres" (p. 10). For a fuller account, see his *De la division du travail social*; for helpful synopses, see *Durkheim on Politics and the State*, ed. Anthony Giddens, pp. 2–3; Coser, Introduction, Durkheim, *Division of Labor*, pp. xiv–xvi.

65. Coser observes that Durkheim changed his mind on this point after writing the *Division du travail* (his doctoral dissertation): in modern societies, *conscience commune* "is still needed so as to assure overall coordination and integration of the society as a whole" (Introduction, *Division of Labor*, p. xix).

66. Coser, Introduction, *Division of Labor*, p. xxi.

67. Durkheim, *Division of Labor*, trans. Halls, "Preface to the Second Edition,"

p. xli; Durkheim is quoting from Lavasseur, *Les classes ouvrières en France jusqu'à la Revolution*.

68. This question is both engaged and resisted to the very end of Paul Strohm's *Social Chaucer*: see, for example, pp. 178–82.

69. Durkheim, *Division of Labor*, trans. Halls, p. 288, n. 16. These are the last words of Book 2. In Book 3, Durkheim turns from theoretical norms to historical pathology: from the way societies should be to the way things are.

70. Traugott Lawler (employing a different kind of critical language) might put himself in this category, since he sees "a movement in the direction of oneness" running through the poem (*The One and the Many in the Canterbury Tales*, p. 147).

71. Mann, *Estates Satire*, p. 200.

72. Schirk's film encourages us to admire the range of professional skills with which its handsome protagonist, the Chairman, negotiates his way past a factionalized and refractory committee. Through this focusing on professional technique, the cut and thrust of committee, Schirk tempts us to forget, momentarily, the final solution that these skills are deployed to secure: the mass exterminations of the final solution. See *The Wannsee Conference*, screenplay by Paul Mommertz, directed by Heinz Schirk (1987).

73. See Black, *Guilds*, p. 6–9, 18, 33.

74. See Durkheim, *Division of Labor*, pp. 200–225, esp. p. 201: "This art of drawing together morally can only bear fruit if the real distance between individuals has itself diminished, in whatever manner. Moral density cannot therefore increase without physical density increasing at the same time."

75. On the strange kinship conjoining the Wife and the Pardoner (who interrupts the Wife at 3.63), see Carolyn Dinshaw, *Chaucer's Sexual Poetics*, p. 156; H. Marshall Leicester, *The Disenchanted Self*, pp. 35–217, esp. pp. 161–77.

76. Brunetto, an Italian, was moved to write his *magnum opus*—the *Tresor* alluded to at *Inferno* 15.119—in a vernacular that was not his mother tongue.

77. See Nicole Oresme, *Le Livre de politiques d'Aristote*, ed. A. D. Menut. Oresme notes that in the days of Julius Caesar it was regarded as a great deprivation not to participate in the "divins sacrifices": "Et estoit ce que nous disons *excommunicacion*, qui signifie estre hors de communicacion. Et selon les droits canons, ce est tres grande paine. Et ce est signe que communicacion politique est tres naturele et tres convenable a humaine creature" (p. 49, f. 8a).

78. Quillet, "Community," p. 536, translating Scotus, *Opus oxoniense*, 2, d. 1, q. 1, n. 17. Georges de Lagarde characterizes the notion of *personalitas* developed in this passage of Scotus as "un isolement magnifique et un peu effrayant" (*La naissance de l'esprit laïque*, vol. 2, p. 237).

79. See Quillet, "Community," pp. 536–37.

80. Pearsall, *Canterbury Tales*, p. 58.

81. See David Wallace, *Chaucer and the Early Writings of Boccaccio*, pp. 50–53; Wallace, "Chaucer and Boccaccio's Early Writings," in *Chaucer and the Italian Trecento*, ed. Piero Boitani, pp. 150–51.

82. I borrow this term from Anne Middleton, "William Langland's 'Kynde Name': Authorial Signature and Social Identity in Late Fourteenth-Century England"; my understanding of "authorial signature" owes much to Middleton (in print, and in conversation) here and throughout this book.

83. Durkheim, *Division of Labor*, trans. Halls, p. 4. The quotation opens by citing Secrétant, *Le principe de la morale*.

84. Dinshaw, *Chaucer's Sexual Poetics*, p. 120.

85. For a fine account of this tradition, see Dinshaw, *Sexual Poetics*, pp. 3–27. "Chaucer," writes Dinshaw, "attempts to discern the consequences for literature and literary tradition, and the effects on lived lives, of understanding literary endeavor as masculine acts performed on feminine bodies" (p. 25).

86. On the importance of the Wife's vocation as "a clothier, dealer in *textus*" (Dinshaw, *Sexual Poetics*, p. 113), see Peggy Knapp, *Chaucer and the Social Contest*, pp. 114–28.

87. For more on this, see Chaps. 4 and 10 below.

88. The former strategy of presenting Margery as the illiterate and therefore hapless victim of clerical culture has yielded recently to more sophisticated accounts of a Margery who proves capable of understanding and hence redeploying the strategies of clerks and of authorizing her own voice. See Karma Lochrie, *Margery Kempe and Translations of the Flesh*, esp. pp. 97–134; Beckwith, *Christ's Body*, pp. 78–111.

89. "The Wife of Bath," Dinshaw notes, "would seem to be Chaucer's favorite character; she is to him "a source of delight" (*Sexual Poetics*, p. 116).

90. The bitter conflict between the scholar and the widow in *Decameron* 8.7 stages the conflict between the masculine "power of the pen" and the female body in extremely vicious terms (an instructive contrast to the Chaucer-Wife relationship); it ends with the widow's skin being "rent asunder like a piece of flaming parchment" (*Decameron*, ed. Branca, 8.7.114; discussed in Wallace, *Decameron*, pp. 87–91). Although this *novella* is the longest of the entire *Decameron*, it was not long enough for Boccaccio, who rewrote it several years later as his *Corbaccio*. This contains some of the most virulent antifeminist material ever penned; it represents Boccaccio's farewell to vernacular fiction. On the Petrarch-Laura relationship, see Nancy J. Vickers, "Scattered Woman and Scattered Rhyme," and Chap. 10 below.

Chapter 3

1. The great majority of surviving returns is now in the Public Record Office, London, C. 47, bundles 38–46. To the 471 documents listed by H. F. Westlake (*Parish Gilds*, pp. 137–238), two returns were added in 1972 and seven in 1975 (472–480). For a description of the physical condition of the three bundles (549 items) as Toulmin Smith and Lucy Toulmin Smith surveyed them in the late 1860s, see their edition of *English Gilds*, pp. xliii–xlvi. Four English returns from London guilds are to be found among the Rawlinson manuscripts in the Bodleian Library, Oxford; they have recently been edited and discussed by Laura Wright and Caroline R. Barron. See Barron, "The London Middle English Guild Certificates of 1388–9."

2. Gervase Rosser, "Communities of Parish and Guild in the Late Middle Ages," p. 32.

3. The appropriateness of guild behaviors to the formation of Chaucer's *compagnye* might be underlined by further reference to Rosser's excellent article: "Although infinitely various in detail, the guilds were essentially very simple organisms, easily formed and readily adaptable to changing needs" ("Communities," p. 32).

4. Rosser notes that "after c. 1300 the jealousy of established mother churches

and the constraints of ecclesiastical bureaucracy set limits on new parochial creations; the tally of approximately 9,000 English parishes formed by 1300 was not to be substantially altered before the nineteenth century" ("Communities," p. 31).

5. See *The Register of the Guild of the Holy Trinity, St. Mary, St. John the Baptist and St. Katherine of Coventry*, ed. Mary Dormer Harris, pp. ix–xxv. See further the companion volume to this study, *The Records of the Guild of the Holy Trinity . . .* , ed. Geoffrey Templeman.

6. See *Register*, ed. Harris, p. xxii. Russell is mentioned in three public documents, c. 1413. Harris remarks that "the number of women members of the [Trinity] Guild is extraordinary" (p. xxii).

7. Public Record Office, C. 47/40/120. The modesty of this guild is suggested by the size of its return (a single strip measuring 20 by 30 cm. inscribed with just eleven lines in Latin, plus a heading telling us that the certificate was written by the guild's chaplain). See further *Parish Gilds*, ed. Westlake, p. 120; Rosser, "Communities," p. 35.

8. See *Parish Gilds*, ed. Westlake, p. 120. The "hogglers" of rural Somerset, who organized themselves into guilds, were similarly concerned to maintain "hoggling lights" in their parish churches. Hogglers have been defined as "the lowest order of laborer with spade or pick, in tillage or in minerals": see *Church-Wardens Accounts of Croscombe, Pilton, Yatton, Tintinhull, Morebath, and St. Michael's, Bath*, ed. Bishop Hobhouse, p. 251.

9. See *English Gilds*, ed. Smith and Smith, pp. 22–24. I have regularized some of the more eccentric features of Toulmin Smith's transcriptions.

10. Jeannine Quillet, "Community, Counsel, and Representation," p. 538.

11. The Guild of the Assumption, Wiggenhall, Norfolk, for example, prays first for "holy chirche," then for "oure lord Kynge Richard of yngelond, and for alle þe baronyge," then remembers the pope and the patriarch of Jerusalem, the reconquest of the holy land and "þe frutte þat is on þe herthe, þat god sende it soche wedurynge þat may turne cristen men to profyt." See *English Gilds*, ed. Smith and Smith, pp. III–13.

12. For an account of the various ways in which guild officers responded to the demands of the royal Chancery in 1388–89, see Jan Gerchow, "Memoria als Norm: Aspekte englischer Gildestatuten des 14. Jahrhunderts." Gerchow argues that it was the more sophisticated, long-established guilds that furnished returns in English; poorer and smaller (often rural) guilds had to travel to London to have their returns drafted by chancery clerks (who wrote in Latin). See further Barron, "London Certificates," p. 4.

13. Some guilds were puzzled or alarmed by the inquiry; others from one neighborhood collaborated in framing individual or collective responses. For a succinct overview of the range of responses to the writ, see William R. Jones, "English Religious Brotherhoods and Medieval Lay Piety: The Inquiry of 1388–89," pp. 649–50.

14. Caroline Barron speaks of "the explosion of the guild movement" in fourteenth-century England ("Parish Fraternities," p. 14).

15. See Chap. 1 above.

16. I concentrate here on the returns of 1389. For broader discussion of the political and economic function of craft guilds in this period, see Heather Swanson,

"The Illusion of Economic Structure: Craft Guilds in Late Medieval English Towns."
For accounts of the 1389 returns that identify and begin to repair the many defects
and *lacunae* of the Toulmin Smith and Westlake volumes, see Barron, "Parish Fraternities"; Barbara Hanawalt, "Keepers of the Lights: Late Medieval English Parish
Guilds."

17. Joshua Toulmin Smith was born in Birmingham in 1816. His father was a
nonconformist educational and economic reformer; young Toulmin wrote an introductory Latin textbook for the Birmingham Mechanics Institute when he was just
seventeen. He journeyed to the United States in 1837, lived in Detroit, Utica, and
Boston, and in 1839 published *The Discovery of America by the Northmen in the Tenth
Century*. Returning to England in 1842, he was called to the bar in 1849 and developed an interest in fossils. Elected first president of the Geologists Association,
Toulmin Smith delivered an inaugural address on January 11, 1859, and promptly lost
all further interest in this subject. His interest in English local government, politics,
and history was galvanized by the threat of a cholera epidemic in Highgate in 1847.
He spent many years campaigning on the issue of local sanitation, wrote a book
on "the parish" and established the *Parliamentary Remembrancer* (1857–65), a weekly
record of actions in Parliament. He also wrote on or campaigned for "the reform
of the corporation of London, the sewerage and administration of the metropolis,
highway boards, the maintenance of public footpaths, the functions of the coroner's
court, the volunteer movement, parish rights and duties, and the church-rate." On
April 28, 1869, he drowned while bathing in the sea at Lancing, Sussex; his *English
Gilds* was completed and published after his death. (Biographical details here follow
The Dictionary of National Biography, ed. Leslie Stephen and Sidney Lee, vol. 53, pp.
94–95; this entry was written by Lucy Toulmin Smith.)

Every aspect of Toulmin Smith's academic work issued from, and flowed back
into, his interest and engagement in local and national politics. As he looked upon
the three bundles of the 1389 returns, written by diverse hands on parchment of
all shapes and sizes, he saw "the Englishman's independence, and the diversity of
character following thereupon . . . stamped upon them" (*English Gilds*, p. xxv). The
belief in national self-determination and self-governance that made him a passionate
supporter of the Hungarian Uprising of 1848–49 persuaded Toulmin Smith to revere
the 1389 returns as a new Magna Carta, an Ur-text for English liberty, self-help, and
collective responsibility. His hope in editing them (as Lucy Toulmin Smith explains
it) was that "the perplexing problems presented by modern Trades-unionism, and
the dangers to enterprise and manly liberty threatened by its restrictive rules," would
yield before this vision of "the ancient principle of association, more than a thousand
years old" (p. xiii).

18. H. F. Westlake opens his *Parish Gilds*, which contains an "analysis" or brief
synopsis of each of the 1389 returns, by claiming that Toulmin Smith "had little
sympathy with the mediaeval Church"; he therefore "mistook the true character of
the societies whose records he examined, and denied the existence of the religious
motives which, as I shall hope to show, played so large a part in their formation"
(p. v). Westlake proceeds to outline the history of "a gild system which, though not
religious in character, was yet destined in part to become so" (p. 21). During the
three centuries following the Norman Conquest, he argues, English guilds "gradually

became merged in the governing authority of the borough and lost their separate identity." Those not swallowed up by borough authorities survived as "a rather exclusive club for social or convivial purposes or for the furtherance of a particular trade monopoly, or else emphasized the devotional side of its former state and became a religious gild. The last-named development," Westlake continues, "is the only one that need be noticed" (p. 21). This attempt to characterize parish guilds as purely religious institutions (so separating them from craft guilds) is carried forward in later pages. Cardinal Gasquet's characterization of the guilds as "the benefit societies of the Middle Ages" (p. 39) is summarily dismissed; comparisons between certain guilds and " 'the Friendly or Benefit Societies of our working-classes' " (p. 39) are ruled irrelevant. The fact that only 154 of the 507 returns (quite a decent percentage) promise help in money or kind to those in need is cited by way of denying that "the term *Benefit Society* is in any way applicable" (p. 41).

Westlake is arguing a very delicate case. He wishes to foreclose any comparisons between medieval guilds and the associative and self-help structures of industrialized England. This leads him to argue that although parish guilds might have had secular origins they were, by 1389, being formed "for spiritual rather than material benefits" (p. 43). Westlake suggests his own spiritual credentials by locating himself, at the end of his Preface, at "The Cloisters, Westminster Abbey" (p. vi). But this, of course, presents him with a political problem: if the fourteenth-century guilds were entirely "spiritual" in their orientation, what justification could Henry VIII, the head of the Church that Westlake identifies himself with (locates himself in) have claimed in abolishing them? This dilemma leads Westlake into some ingenious revisionist history. In 1389, he tells us, the church of St. Botolph's, Aldersgate, contained two modest guilds dedicated to religious purposes. By 1450, these guilds had merged and "the brotherhood had developed into an organization never contemplated by its founders," since "the business aspect" is now "at least equal to the religious" (p. 72). Two pages later, he advances the general rule "that as a guild grew in numbers it lost in spirituality" (p. 74). This prepares us for the argument that "by the middle of the reign of Henry VIII the guilds, in the towns and larger villages at least, had lost their older democratic character" (p. 120). Westlake thus opens his final chapter, "The Passing of the Guilds," by readmitting talk of political causation; he closes it, however, by returning to a spiritual register: "The old simple spirit of devotion, which had led men and women to unite together to express that spirit in corporate fashion, had passed for ever" (p. 136).

19. For helpful discussion of distinctions between merchant, craft, and religious guilds, see Ben R. McRee, "Religious Gilds and Regulation of Behavior in Late Medieval Towns," pp. 109–10. McRee reviews taxonomical difficulties in a long footnote, asking: "How, for example, should a gild composed of tanners be classified if it had no craft statutes and limited itself to religious activities?" He notes, further, that "medieval record keepers . . . did not differentiate among the various types of gilds, referring to all types interchangeably as gilds, fraternities, or brotherhoods" (p. 119, n. 13).

20. In Westlake's account, the Act for Dissolution of Colleges (37 Henry VIII c. 4) seems almost an irrelevance: the guilds passed away peacefully (almost, one might say, in their sleep), their historical mission accomplished. For Toulmin Smith,

however, the same Act represents "a case of pure, wholesale robbery and plunder, done by an unscrupulous faction to satisfy their personal greed, under cover of law. No more gross case of wanton plunder to be found in History of all Europe. No page so black in English History" (*English Gilds*, p. xlii, n. 1). Such an account of the suppression of the guilds reminds us, of course, that Toulmin Smith was a Victorian liberal who was not a member of the Church of England; he was, in fact, a Unitarian.

21. J. J. Scarisbrick began his first Ford lecture at Oxford in 1982 by proposing that, "on the whole, English men and women did not want the Reformation and most of them were slow to accept it when it came. . . . To speak of a rising groundswell of lay discontent with the old order, of growing 'spiritual thirst' during the latter Middle Ages . . . is to employ metaphors for which there is not much evidence" (*The Reformation and the English People*, p. 1). In his second lecture, Scarisbrick explored the social and political consequences of the 1547 Act. The dissolution of the guilds, he argues, was a loss for women: "There was no other institution in late-medieval society in which lay women could stand on their own feet, be separately listed as autonomous human beings or (at least in theory) hold public office." The loss of guilds also entailed the loss of a traditional structure in which "rich and far-from-rich, male and female, laymen and cleric could meet and rub shoulders as nowhere else" (p. 25). This second lecture, entitled "The Importance of the Lay Fraternities," points us back to Westlake and Toulmin Smith with its very first footnote: it proves impossible, once again, to speak of 1547 without referring back to 1389.

A historiographical trajectory comparable to that of Scarisbrick, traced in a more incendiary style, is offered by W. G. Hoskins, *The Age of Plunder: King Henry's England 1500–1547*. Hoskin signals (and almost exhausts) his argument on the first page in asserting that when Henry VIII acceded to the throne in 1509, England "was still medieval in every important respect" (p. 1).

22. Eamon Duffy, *The Stripping of the Altars*, pp. 131–54, 454–56.

23. The historian Cornelius Walford, writing after the Smiths' edition and before Westlake's study, published a study of the guilds in 1879 as part of an encyclopaedia of life insurance. "Needless to say," observes Barbara Hanawalt, "he found them to be a precursor of the nineteenth-century insurance societies and mutual benefit funds" ("Keepers of the Lights," p. 23). Bishop Hobhouse, on the other hand, shared Westlake's inclination to dwell upon the guilds' religious aspects. For Hobhouse, Victorian editor of Somerset church records, all social groupings and class distinctions are swallowed up and forgotten within the parish church, a structure that is imagined as both local and universal (or at least national): "On all these days [holidays] the laborer, though born in serfdom, was free, bound only to the service of his Divine master. He donned his best clothes, he joined his fellow-guildsmen, he marched under banners to the church as the common home of the highest and lowest" (*Church-Wardens Accounts*, pp. xx–xxi).

24. Lucy Toulmin Smith, born in Boston, Massachusetts, in 1838, settled in Highgate with her parents in 1842 and lived there for more than fifty years. Following her work on *English Gilds*, she went on to edit a wide range of important medieval works for French, German, and English publications. In 1894 she was elected librarian of Manchester College, Oxford; she was (according to the *DNB*) "the first woman in England to be appointed head of a public library." Her house in Oxford became a meeting place for scholars from all over Europe. "At the same time," *DNB*

assures us, "she was an accomplished gardener and housewife" (*The Dictionary of National Biography Supplement, January 1901–December 1911*, vol. 3, pp. 341–42).

25. For Lucy Toulmin Smith, the phenomenon of female participation in the guilds was obviously bound up with the issue of her own occluded labor in bringing *English Gilds* into print. LTS, as she signed herself, felt bound to play the role of the dutiful Victorian daughter, "conscious of the imperfections and omissions that must necessarily occur in my part of the work," who could only end with a pathetic plea: " 'She hath done what she could' " (p. xlvii). At the same time, of course, she knows herself to be the greatest living expert on the English guilds (having worked with her father in the archives) and fiercely resents the fact that Furnivall, founder of the Early English Text Society, should have turned to a "gentleman" to write an introductory essay for the volume. This "gentleman," Dr. Lujo Brentano of Bavaria, cheerfully admits knowing next to nothing about English guilds (p. liii), an assertion borne out by his writing. The "General Introduction" that Furnivall asked him to write is downgraded in the volume to the status of a "preliminary essay"; the real Introduction is written, after all, by Lucy Toulmin Smith.

26. Lucy Toulmin Smith's Introduction contains many complex asides that attempt to balance responsibilities incumbent upon a Victorian daughter against the desire for a revisionary history. "It is worth noticing," she argues, "who were the persons who composed the Gilds. Scarcely five out of the five hundred were not formed equally of men and women, which, in these times of the discovery of the neglect of ages heaped upon woman, is a noteworthy fact. Even where the affairs were managed by a company of priests, women were admitted as lay members; and they had many of the same duties and claims upon the Gild as men" (p. xxx).

27. *Calendar of Close Rolls, 1385–1389*, p. 624. For writs seeking proclamations to be made in other parts of England, see PRO C.47/46/481 (Cambridgeshire, Huntingdonshire, Surrey, and Sussex); C.47/46/482 (Wiltshire, Yorkshire, and Northamptonshire). These two documents were found unnumbered in a check through C.47 bundles 38–46 in 1988.

28. See Chap. 1 above and Chap. 9 below.

29. See J. A. Tuck, "The Cambridge Parliament of 1388," pp. 227–30.

30. See Tuck, "Cambridge Parliament," pp. 236–38.

31. The 1388 petition (preserved in the *Chronicle* of the Monk of Westminster) seeks to ban laborers from carrying weapons and to expose beggars who pose as pilgrims (article v, items g and k, as tabulated in Tuck, "Cambridge Parliament," p. 228).

32. The royal servants who read the returns did draft new legislation leading to a statute of 1391 that brought land left to fraternities within the scope of mortmain legislation: see Barron, "Parish Fraternities," p. 21; Barron, "London Certificates," p. 12.

33. See Chap. 6 below.

34. This claim is based upon the following analysis of the founding dates of parish guilds, as recorded by the 1389 returns and reported by Westlake, *Parish Gilds*, pp. 138–229. The nine returns discovered since Westlake's book was published are not considered here; all nine, according to Ben R. McRee, are "in extremely poor condition" ("Religious Gilds," p. 119, n. 15).

TABLE I

Founding Dates of Guilds (All Returns)

Date	Number	Percentage
Before 1300	13	2.5
1300–1309	7	1.4
1310–1319	6	1.2
1320–1329	9	1.8
1330–1339	16	3.1
1340–1349	33	6.5
1350–1359	42	8.3
1360–1369	55	10.8
1370–1379	78	15.4
1380–1389	59	11.6
"Recently"	14	2.8
No Record	176	34.6
Total	508	100.0

TABLE 2

Founding Dates of Guilds (Returns with Recorded Date)

Date	Number	Percentage
Before 1300	13	3.9
1300–1309	7	2.1
1310–1319	6	1.8
1320–1329	9	2.7
1330–1339	16	4.8
1340–1349	33	9.9
1350–1359	42	12.7
1360–1369	55	16.6
1370–1379	78	23.5
1380–1389	59	17.8
"Recently"	14	4.2
Total	332	100.0

35. It is worth noting that women as well as men founded guilds: see Barron, "Parish Guilds," pp. 31–32.

36. *English Gilds*, ed. Smith and Smith, p. 54. It is interesting to note, in light of iconographic representations of the "Ship of the Church" (in which the crucifix forms the mainmast), that this "Shipmanesgilde" of Lynn is dedicated to the Exaltation of the Holy Cross. See *English Gilds*, p. 54 ("Statuta de Gilda Exaltacionis sancte Crucis, vocata Shipmanesgilde, de Lenn"); V. A. Kolve, *Chaucer and the Imagery of Narrative: The First Five Canterbury Tales*, pp. 308–25.

37. *English Gilds*, p. 6 (Guild of St. Katherine, Aldersgate, London).

38. *English Gilds*, p. 96; see also p. 21 (Guild of St. Katherine, Norwich).

39. Westlake, *Parish Gilds*, p. 171.

40. *English Gilds*, ed. Smith and Smith, p. 65.

41. PRO C. 47/46/465; *A Book of London English*, ed. R. W. Chambers and Marjorie Daunt, p. 42.

42. *English Gilds*, ed. Smith and Smith, p. 10. This practice of recovering bodies is quite common; the radius of acceptable mileage for recovery varies from guild to guild.

43. *English Gilds*, ed. Smith and Smith; p. 110.

44. *Parish Gilds*, ed. Westlake, p. 44.

45. Members of the Guild of the Assumption, Wiggenhall (Norfolk), pray "for oure fadere saules, and for oure modere saules, and for þe criste saules þat ben in þe bitter payne of purgatore, and for al þe brethire saules and sisturres þat to þis fraternitee longes." Christian names of members of this guild include Johannes (5); Robertus (2); Adam (1); Thomas (2); Galfridus (1); Ricardus (1); Laurence (1); Cicillia (2); Angneta (2); Asselyn (1); Beatrix (1); Isabella (1); Katerina (2); Margareta (1); Alicia (3); Elena (1); one unnamed female. See *English Gilds*, ed. Smith and Smith, pp. 112–13.

46. As late as 1535, the soul of Thomas, fool in the family of Lady Anne Graye, was admitted to the famous Guild of the Holy Cross, Stratford-on-Avon, at a cost of twenty pence: see *Parish Gilds*, ed. Westlake, p. 115.

47. See Barron, "Parish Fraternities," p. 31.

48. *Letter-Book H*, f. clxxii, in *Memorials of London*, ed. H. T. Riley, pp. 480–81 (and see Chap. 6 below).

49. *English Gilds*, ed. Smith and Smith, p. 5 (Guild at the Church of St. James, Garlikhithe, London). Newcomers to the Guild of St. Katherine, Aldersgate, London swear "vpon a book to þe brotherhede"; in joining the Tailors' Guild, Norwich, members swear "þat alle þese Comenaunts a-forsaid sshulle ben holden ferme and stable . . . and þer-to harn þei sworon on the halidom [relic]" (*English Gilds*, pp. 6, 36).

50. Ibid., p. 23 (Guild of St. Christopher, Norwich).

51. Ibid., p. 67 (Guild of St. Katherine, Lynn).

52. Ibid., p. 3. For a fine account of Langland's complex assessment of the social and spiritual possibilities of fraternities, "sektes of susterne and of brethurne" (*Piers Plowman*, C.XVI.293), see James Simpson, "'After Craftes Conseil clotheth yow and fede': Langland and London City Politics," esp. pp. 117–20, 127.

53. *Parish Gilds*, ed. Westlake, p. 146.

54. See ibid., p. 237; this return is reported to be in bad condition. Barbara Hanawalt notes that in poorer parishes, the church house, located next to the parish church, functioned as both tavern and community center: see "Keepers of the Lights," p. 31.

55. See, respectively, *Parish Gilds*, ed. Westlake, p. 168 (Guild of St. Anne, St. Peter's Parish in the Skin Market, Lincoln); *English Gilds*, ed. Smith and Smith, pp. 69 (Guild of St. James, Lynn), p. 79 (Guild of St. John the Baptist, Bishop's Lynn).

56. *Parish Gilds*, ed. Westlake, p. 166.

57. See *MED*, *potel* (a), (b), (d).

58. *English Gilds*, ed. Smith and Smith, p. 70.

59. Ibid., p. 84.

60. See ibid., p. 30 (Guild of the Pelterers, Norwich); and *Parish Gilds*, ed. Westlake, p. 166 (Corpus Christi, Hultoft).

61. See *Parish Gilds*, ed. Westlake, p. 220 (Holy Trinity and Holy Cross, Daventry), and *English Gilds*, ed. Smith and Smith, p. 84 (Guild of the Holy Cross, Bishop's Lynn).

62. *English Gilds*, ed. Smith and Smith, p. 84 (Guild of the Holy Cross, Bishop's Lynn).

63. Ibid., pp. 3–5 (Guild at the Church of St. James, Garlickhithe, London).

64. Ibid., pp. 78–79. Abusive epithets of choice among London merchants were "harlot," "carl," and "whoreson": see Thrupp, *Merchant Class*, p. 166.

65. The oldest extant English mystery cycle is N-town, a sequence of 41 plays compiled in a manuscript dating from no earlier than 1468: see David Staines, "The English Mystery Cycles," p. 80.

66. For a succinct account of this guild and of all guilds in medieval York, see Alexandra F. Johnston, "English Guilds and Municipal Authority," pp. 79–80. For a transcription and translation of the return of the Pater Noster Guild, see *Records of Early English Drama: York*, ed. Alexandra F. Johnston and Margaret Rogerson, vol. 2, pp. 645–48, 863–66; see also vol. 1, pp. 4–5, for further evidence of guild-related dramatic activity (in 1386–87). On York guilds, see further Eileen White, *The St. Christopher and St. George Guild of York*. The guilds of St. Christopher and St. George, neither of which appear in the 1389 returns, were both in existence by 1394; they had amalgamated by 1466. The St. Christopher Guild was incorporated on March 12, 1396, during Richard II's visit to York (White, pp. 2–5).

67. See *Parish Gilds*, ed. Westlake, p. 177 (Guild of St. Martin, Stamford), pp. 34, 122, 155 (Guild of St. John the Baptist, Baston, Lincolnshire). Female members of the Baston guild could be excused from dancing on St. John Baptist's Day on grounds of poor health, old age, or urgent business.

68. Jones, meditating on English guild dedications, argues that "early medieval cults were very particularistic, showing strong regional affections in their choice of patron, whereas fourteenth-century hagiology focused on the veneration of a relatively few, internationally renowned saints" ("Religious Brotherhoods," p. 657).

69. See Hanawalt, "Keepers of the Lights," p. 26. Holy Trinity was second in popularity (14 percent), followed by Corpus Christi (10 percent), St. John the Baptist (10 percent), Holy Cross (8 percent), and All Saints (5 percent): see Hanawalt, p. 27.

70. See *English Gilds*, ed. Smith and Smith, p. 117: "to go to þe kirke wit is brethere wit a garlond of hoke Lewes."

71. See *Parish Gilds*, ed. Westlake, p. 233.

72. Ibid., p. 144.

73. Ibid., pp. 175, 221–22. Both of these guilds were long-established: the Louth guild reports a foundation date of 1329; the Northampton guild reports "time without memory."

74. Ibid., pp. 204–5. The preamble of this 1389 return is in Latin, the rest in English.

75. Ibid., p. 205. Compare the language of the *Prioress's Tale*: "this innocent" (7.538, 566, 635); "this martir" (680); "O martir" (579); "this child" (621, 640, 650), etc.

76. See Donald Attwater, *A Dictionary of Saints*, p. 342. According to Attwater, this is the first recorded accusation of ritual child-killing by Jews in England; Hugh of Lincoln died in 1255.

77. In London, St. Katherine was outranked in popularity only by the Virgin; of the eight Cambridge guilds listed in the 1389 returns, two are dedicated to St. Katherine, two to the Trinity, and four to the Virgin. See Barron, "Parish Fraternities," p. 32; *Cambridge Gild Records*, ed. Mary Bateson. Some thirty guilds have been

identified for medieval Cambridge: see *Records of Early English Drama: Cambridge*, ed. Alan H. Nelson, vol. 2, pp. 798–801.

78. *Parish Gilds*, ed. Westlake, p. 203 (Guild of St. Katherine, Church of St. Simon and St. Jude, Norwich).

79. My translation from the Latin in *Cambridge Gild Records*, ed. Bateson, p. 78. For a detailed account of Cambridgeshire guilds (of which there were at least 350), see Virginia R. Bainbridge, *Guild and Parish in Late-Medieval Cambridgeshire, c. 1350–1558*.

80. See Attwater, *Dictionary of Saints*, pp. 209–10.

81. Ibid., p. 210.

82. *English Gilds*, ed. Smith and Smith, p. 47 (Guild of St. Thomas of Canterbury, Lynn; Church of St. Nicholas).

83. *Parish Gilds*, ed. Westlake, pp. 197–98.

84. See David Wallace, "Pilgrim Signs and the Ellesmere Chaucer," pp. 1–3; see further Duffy, *Stripping of the Altars*, pp. 410–12.

85. *Parish Gilds*, ed. Westlake, pp. 17, 168–69. See also p. 167 (Guild of Corpus Christi, St. Michael-on-the-Hill, Lincoln).

86. *English Gilds*, ed. Smith and Smith, p. 177 (Guild of the Resurrection of Our Lord).

87. *Parish Gilds*, ed. Westlake, p. 158.

88. *English Gilds*, ed. Smith and Smith, pp. 157, xxxvi.

89. The journal *Confraternitas*, published semiannually by the Society for Confraternity Studies since spring 1990, offers an excellent conspectus of European traditions and local variations.

90. Westlake speculates that this text, and its vernacular avatars, "must have suggested many a gild dedication" (*Parish Gilds*, p. 127). Its influence is evident in the *Interpretacio nominis Cecelie* and in the *Second Nun's Tale* (to about line 345): see *Riverside Chaucer*, p. 942.

91. *Tractatus adversus Iudaeorum inveteram duritiem*: see Jeremy Cohen, *The Friars and the Jews: The Evolution of Medieval Anti-Judaism*, pp. 28–30.

92. Ibid., p. 28.

93. The hospital of St. Mary of Rouncival was established c. 1231 as a cell or priory of the hospital of Our Lady, Roncesvalles, in Navarre. Henry III granted protection in 1229, and William Marshall, earl of Pembroke, endowed the foreign community with houses in Charing. The hospital evidently thrived until the mid-fourteenth century, when the Black Death and the war with France weakened the community and disrupted its communication with the continent. Finally the papal schism (1378) caused the administration to shift from foreign to English hands, for in 1379 the hospital was seized as a property of the schismatic alien. On May 8, 1382, Richard appointed a clerk, Nicholas Slake, warden of the hospital. On July 18, 1382, a yeoman of the Chamber was empowered by royal writ to arrest certain procurators of the hospital for diverting alms collections to their own use. An investigation followed, and in 1383 the hospital was restored to the mother-institution in Navarre. See James Galloway, *Historical Sketches of Old Charing*, pp. 1–27, 37–41; *Parish Gilds*, ed. Westlake, pp. 92–96; Alfred L. Kellogg and Louis A. Haselmayer, "Chaucer's Satire of the Pardoner," p. 271; Samuel Moore, "Chaucer's Pardoner of Rouncival," pp. 59,

65. The hospital fraternity, on whose behalf the Pardoner is supposedly working, was founded in 1385 "in no spirit of insolence . . . nor for any seditious purpose"; the members claim in the 1389 return to "have no assemblies or quarrels but exist solely for devotion . . . and for the safety of souls" (*Parish Gilds*, ed. Westlake, pp. 92, 187).

94. See the exchange between the friar and Thomas in the *Summoner's Tale*, 3.2126–28 (Thomas speaks first): "Ye sey me thus, how that I am youre brother?" / "Ye, certes," quod the frere, "trusteth weel. / I took oure dame oure lettre with oure seel." For discussion of the consequences of this exchange, see Chap. 5 below. Janette Richardson notes that "Thomas and his wife were members of a lay confraternity attached to Friar John's convent" (*Riverside Chaucer*, p. 878). Richardson is technically correct in using the term "confraternity" here, since in England the term "was used to mean 'association with,' an outside group joined in some way, but not completely, to a larger body" (Barron, "Parish Fraternities," p. 17). Usage of the term was rare in England: "Only one of the 150 or so London parish fraternities ever calls itself a confraternity" (Barron, p. 17). In Florence, however, the term was used much more loosely and frequently: see Henderson, *Piety and Charity*, pp. 1–9.

95. *English Gilds*, ed. Smith and Smith, p. 195 (Guild of the Palmers, Ludlow). Toulmin Smith appends an endearing footnote to his translation of this passage: "The beginning of this ordinance will hardly be thought true unless the original is given. This is as follows: — 'Si vero masculus quisquam voluerit, ut est moris, ejusdem defuncti vel defuncte nocturnis vigiliis interesse, hoc fieri permittatur, *dumtamen* nec monstra larvarum inducere, nec corporis vel fame sue ludibria, nec ludos alios inhonestos, presumat aliqualiter attemptare.' These remarkable words imply two things; *first*, that ghosts and other sprites can be called up after death; *second*, that this may be hindered by the strength of human law . . ." (and so on, with generous references to Old Icelandic sagas). Westlake throws a wet blanket over such speculation by pointing out that *monstra larvarum inducere* is better translated as "put on hideous masks" than as "call up the shape of demons" (*Parish Gilds*, p. 19). He generously concedes, however, that "the Rule hints at revelries of an improper character" (p. 19).

96. The women are said to be aged between 18 and 27 (*Intr.* 49; p. 58); each of the three "giovani" is at least 25 (*Intr.* 78; pp. 62–63).

97. Boccaccio devotes a good deal of space to these two topics: see *Intr.* 13, 28–42; pp. 51, 53–57.

98. 6. *Intr.* 4; p. 480.

99. See Chap. 1 above; and on the relationship of humanism to slavery (as articulated by Petrarch), see Chap. 10 below.

100. I give these alternatives (court and *cenacolo*) by way of suggesting that the *Decameron*'s *brigata* owes something to both. The kind of court circle Boccaccio experienced, or heard about, as part of the monarchical culture of Angevin Naples had already received idealized expression in a number of works, most notably his *Filocolo*. On returning to Florence, Boccaccio joined a succession of protohumanist *cenacoli*: see *Chaucer's Boccaccio*, ed. and trans. N. R. Havely, pp. 1–12; Wallace, *Early Writings*, pp. 23–36, 65–67; David Anderson, *Before the Knight's Tale*, pp. 4–8; *Medieval Literary Theory and Criticism, c. 1100–1375: The Commentary Tradition*, ed. A. J. Minnis and A. B. Scott, with the assistance of David Wallace, pp. 453–58.

101. On this delicate subject of "Germanic tradition," see Black, *Guilds*, esp. pp. 61–62. Black notes that "in Italy, Roman and Germanic influences would appear to

have been of about equal weight; in the rest of Europe, the Germanic far outweighed the Roman. It would seem that urban political sentiment and policy was inspired by a conviction that the town was a community in the Germanic genre, analogous to the guild: a group formed by the will of its members and thereby legally valid" (p. 61).

102. See Vittore Branca, *Giovanni Boccaccio: Profilo biografico*, vol. 1, pp. 186–87.

103. See Henderson, *Piety and Charity*, pp. 38–46. Henderson offers an excellent, detailed account of both the *disciplinati* and the *flagellanti*; he also examines (pp. 196–237) the *Compagnia della Madonna d'Or San Michele*, a *laudesi* company that enjoyed exceptionally wide support from men and women in Florence and the *contado*.

104. See Henderson, *Piety and Charity*, pp. 34–35, 113–54. For illuminating discussion (with musical texts) of these groups, see Blake Wilson, "Music and Merchants: The *Laudesi* Companies in Early Renaissance Florence."

105. He can only be *suspected* to be a flagellant ("degli scopatori," 3.4, 5) because the *disciplinati* were secretive about their membership. Boccaccio describes his flagellant, Puccio, as "uomo idiota e di grossa pasta."

106. 7.1, 5; p. 523. The "lauda di donna Matelda" is evidently a song in honor of Mechtilde of Magdeburg, a mystic whose cult and writings were diffused by the Dominicans in Italy. Santa Maria Novella (where Boccaccio's *brigata* first assembles) was a Dominican church.

107. Wilson notes that "Florentine *laudesi* were typically lower guildsmen, artisans involved in a local trade. They were bakers, carpenters, goldsmiths, barbers, lanternmakers, but most were involved in the great Florentine wool industry: washers, dyers, and independent master weavers, clothcutters, and burlers" ("Music and Merchants," p. 162).

108. See Henderson, *Piety and Charity*, pp. 87; Brian Pullan, *Rich and Poor in Renaissance Venice*, pp. 34, 51.

109. See John S. Henderson, "Confraternities and Politics in Fifteenth-Century Florence," pp. 53–72; Henderson, *Piety and Charity*, p. 442.

110. See Henderson, *Piety and Charity*, pp. 61, 280; N. Rodolico, *I Ciompi*, pp. 45–46.

111. Barron, "Parish Guilds," p. 30. It is worth noting, however, that many guilds were more broadly inclusive, at least in the fourteenth century. The Guild of St. George, Norwich, "comprised wealthy and eminent people in the city and county, both lay and ecclesiastical, and also craftsmen and laborers and even the poor brethren and officers in receipt of alms" (*Records of the Gild of St. George in Norwich, 1389–1547*, ed. Mary Grace, p. 23). In 1452, however, attempts were made to restrict the admission of county members to persons of noble blood or outstanding importance and to exclude craftsmen and people of low degree. Many members of the Paston family belonged to this guild.

112. Sidney, *The Defence of Poesie*, 1595 ed. (unpaginated); see also *Sidney*, ed. Duncan-Jones, p. 242, lines 1240–44.

113. Caroline F. E. Spurgeon, *Five Hundred Years of Chaucer Criticism and Allusion, 1357–1900*, vol. 1, p. 89. Becke's 1549 edition is a reprint of T. Matthew's Bible of 1537: see Derek Brewer, ed., *Chaucer: The Critical Heritage*, vol. 1, p. 102.

114. Spurgeon, *Five Hundred Years*, vol. 1, p. 89.

115. Ibid.

116. Becke's Bible edition is dated 1549; Latimer preached his sermon on March 15, 1549; Cranmer's sermon is tentatively assigned to 1549: see Spurgeon, *Five Hundred Years*, pp. 88–89.

117. See Scarisbrick, *Reformation*, pp. 85–88; Duffy, *Stripping of the Altars*, pp. 377–447; *English Gilds*, ed. Smith and Smith, p. 135.

118. John Leland, *Commentarie de scriptoribus Brittanicis* (c. 1540; first printed 1709) as excerpted and trans. in Brewer, *Critical Heritage*, vol. 1, pp. 91–96.

119. Brewer, *Critical Heritage*, vol. 1, pp. 91, 95.

120. This process may be observed with the assistance of Herbert G. Wright, *Boccaccio in England from Chaucer to Tennyson*.

Chapter 4

1. For the suggestion that the *Knight's Tale* might be read as a *summa* of Chaucer's earlier, court-centered career, see Patterson, *Subject of History*, p. 181.

2. The most extreme arguments for Theseus as "a typical Italian tyrant" have been made by Jones, *Chaucer's Knight* (pp. 192–216); for synopses of dissenting reviews by Jill Mann, V. J. Scattergood, David Aers, and John M. Fyler, see Monica McAlpine, ed., *Chaucer's "Knight's Tale": An Annotated Bibliography, 1900 to 1985*, p. 322. For helpful synopses of other critical arguments concerning Thesian politics, see Mark Allen and John H. Fisher, eds., *The Essential Chaucer*, pp. 106–11; John Leyerle and Anne Quick, eds., *Chaucer: A Bibliographical Introduction*, pp. 134–39; McAlpine, *Chaucer's "Knight's Tale."*

3. See Kenneth Muir, *The Sources of Shakespeare's Plays*, pp. 66–67; *Narrative and Dramatic Sources of Shakespeare*, ed. Geoffrey Bullough, vol. 1, pp. 368–70, 374, 377–84. References to Shakespeare in the text follow the *Riverside Shakespeare*, ed. G. Blakemore Evans.

4. References to the *Teseida* follow Boccaccio, *Tutte le opere*, ed. Branca, vol. 2. For a fine account of the consequences of Chaucer's cutting and suppression of Hippolita's "masculine" traits, see Susan Crane, *Gender and Romance in Chaucer's "Canterbury Tales,"* esp. pp. 18–23.

5. For a sustained comparison, see Wallace, *Early Writings*, pp. 78–94. For tags involving stars and roses, see specifically pp. 81–82; for evocations of *cortesia*, see pp. 87–89. My argument is that the *Teseida* and *Filostrato*, which are both written in the *ottava rima* stanza of the *cantare* tradition, "draw inspiration from the *cantare*" (p. 32); I do not claim that the *Teseida* is a *cantare* narrative. I would suggest, however, that disinclination to countenance the possibility of any *cantare* (or other popular narrative) influence lead David Anderson (*Before the Knight's Tale*) and Barbara Nolan (*Chaucer and the Tradition of the Roman Antique*) to present a *Teseida* that is too solemn, scholarly, and monogamously classical. Piero Boitani, in his "Style, Iconography, and Narrative: the Lesson of the *Teseida*," argues that the *cantari*, among other sources, "had shown the way" (Boitani, ed., *Chaucer and the Italian Trecento*, p. 186). The *Teseida* is peppered with tags and narrative gambits familiar from popular tradition; there can be no doubt that Chaucer, given his own familiarity with tail-rhyme, recognized them as such. The evocation of Emilia on her wedding day, for example, contains details that are more reminiscent of the Miller's description of Alisoun than of anything in the *Knight's Tale*: "Ella aveva la bocca piccioletta, tutta ridente e bella

da basciare" ("She had a cute little mouth, all smiling and nice to kiss"; compare *Miller's Tale*, 1.3261–62, 3268–69).

6. The longest reprise of this register comes in the description of Arcite's joyful "observaunce to May" in *pars secunda*; it is, however, overshadowed by the secret, listening presence of Palemon. "Sooth is seyd," observes the Knight, "That feeld hath eyen and the wode hath eres" (1.1521–22, a dictum not found in the *Teseida*); his evocation of an outdoor Maytime scene does not deliver us from the keyholes and corridors of court.

7. Theseus, it will be recalled, "rente adoun bothe wall and sparre and rafter"; he "dide with al the contree as hym leste" (1.990, 1004).

8. See "The *Knight's Tale* and the Crisis of Chivalric Identity," in Patterson, *Subject of History*, pp. 165–243.

9. See Chap. 1 above.

10. I part company here with Jill Mann's recent account of "the figure of Theseus in the *Knight's Tale*" as "the fullest development of an ideal of feminized masculinity" (*Geoffrey Chaucer*, Feminist Readings Series, p. 171). For an evaluation of "the risks and the benefits of gender instability" (of the kind symptomized by Mann's phrase "feminized masculinity") see Hansen, *Chaucer and the Fictions of Gender*, esp. p. 17.

11. See David Burnley, *Chaucer's Language and the Philosophers' Tradition*, pp. 25–28 and *passim*.

12. See Burnley's analyses of *crueltee* in *Philosopher's Tradition*, pp. 14, 30, 32, 43, 68, 157, 164, 184–85, 189. For an analysis of *Knight's Tale* 1.1303–8 (in the context of discussion of pagan fatalism), see A. J. Minnis, *Chaucer and Pagan Antiquity*, pp. 133–35.

13. Cambises insists on the importance of "myne eyen sight" by employing the phrase twice in quick succession: 3.2060, 2071.

14. See *De monarchia*, where Dante argues that "a universal ruler has nothing left to desire, since his jurisdiction is bounded only by the Ocean"; hence it follows that the "monarcha" is the only mortal immune to "cupiditas" (*Monarchia*, ed. Nardi, 1.11, 12).

15. See *House of Fame*, 405–26; see also Walter Scheps, "Chaucer's Theseus and the *Knight's Tale*," p. 24. The faithless men listed before Theseus are Demophon (another "duk of Athenys," 388–96), Achilles (398), Paris (399), Jason (400–401), and Hercules (402–4). Aeneas follows Theseus; his abandonment of Dido is excused by reference to the call of duty (427–32).

16. See Ovid, *Metamorphoses* 8.169–82; *Heroides* 10 ("Ariadne Theseo"). "When we turn to Statius's account of Theseus," Scheps observes, "it is as though Ovid had never lived" ("Chaucer's Theseus," p. 22).

17. See *Franklin's Tale*, esp. 5.1583–84 ("for elles moot I selle / Myn heritage").

18. See John Livingston Lowes, "The Prologue to the *Legend of Good Women* Considered in Its Chronological Relations," pp. 803–5; *Riverside Chaucer*, p. 1071. For an analysis of the *Legend of Ariadne* that makes detailed comparisons with the *Knight's Tale* (and so covers some of the same ground as my next few paragraphs), see Patterson, *Subject of History*, pp. 239–42. Patterson pays particular attention to the ideal of *gentillesse* and to the pattern of betrayal and revenge.

19. Ovid, *Heroides* 10.1.

20. On *Decameron* 10.10, see Chap. 10 below; on Gower's epithets for Richard II in his *Cronica Tripertita* (added as a sequel to the *Vox Clamantis*), see Burnley, *Philosophers' Tradition*, p. 12.

21. See *Heroides* 4.36. It is worth noting that Phaedra's passion for Hippolitus is represented as a political disaster for her whole court: "Serviat Hippolyto regia tota meo!" (4.164: "Let my whole court be slaves to my Hippolytus!" p. 57).

22. See, for example, *Scriptores rerum mythicarum latini tres Romae nuper reperti*, ed. G. H. Bode, Mythographer 1:204, 35–36: "Theseus de Hippolyta, regina Amazonum, genuit Hippolytum." In a gloss to *Teseida* 3.25, Boccaccio describes Hippolitus as "figliuolo di Teseo" (but does not name his mother). Boccaccio goes on to describe how the young man was killed in fleeing from his father's anger, but was then brought back to life by the physician Esculapius (p. 335).

Piero Boitani, in his study of Chaucer's possible acquaintance with Boccaccio's glosses, argues that "any student of probability would conclude that the chances are that Chaucer knew the commentary, or at least part of it" (*Chaucer and Boccaccio*, p. 114; see further pp. 113–16, 190–97). Six of the twelve extant fourteenth-century manuscripts of the *Teseida* contain Boccaccio's glosses, and six do not (see Boitani, p. 116).

23. On the limitations of Theseus's wisdom, see Minnis, *Chaucer and Pagan Antiquity*, pp. 128–35.

24. This subject is considered in detail in Chap. 8 below. For an excellent account of the mediatory roles played by queens in fourteenth-century politics, see Strohm, *Hochon's Arrow*, pp. 95–119.

25. For a detailed exploration of the *Hof-Gericht* distinction (as exemplified by the *Prologue* to the *Legend of Good Women*), see Chap. 12 below.

26. In his gloss to *Teseida* 1.5.7, Boccaccio writes: "Amazon: the Amazons are women who, all their men having been killed, gave themselves to arms, and made each one of themselves cut off her right breast since it impeded the drawing of a bow; and therefore are they called Amazons, which is as much to say 'without breast'" ("amazone, che vuole dire quanto senza poppa," p. 255). On the phenomenon of academic men defining native women by, even as, their breasts, see Trinh T. Minh-ha's account of the public interrogation of Sojourner Truth by "a threatened white doctor in the audience" (*Woman, Native, Other: Writing Postcoloniality and Feminism*, p. 100).

27. See lines 1801–3, discussed above ("Se how they blede! Be they noght wel arrayed? / Thus hath hir lord . . .").

28. The speech given to Egeus in the *Knight's Tale* is modeled on words spoken by Teseo himself in the *Teseida* (in opening the long political speech of the final book, 12.6). Chaucer goes to some trouble, then, in foregrounding the patrilinear linkage in statecraft between Egeus and Theseus, father and son; Boccaccio's "vecchio Egeo" (12.49.5; 12.82.2) does not speak at all in the *Teseida*'s last book.

29. My translation of *Trattatello in laude di Dante*, red. 1.134–36, in *Medieval Literary Theory and Criticism c. 1100–c.1375*, ed. A. J. Minnis and A. B. Scott, pp. 493–94. For further discussion of this passage see Chap. 10 below.

30. See *The Book of Memory*, esp. pp. 71–79. Carruthers describes the process whereby a speaker memorizes a speech by associating specific parts of a building or background with particular topics or words of the discourse to come.

31. This process is considered in detail in Chaps. 8 and 12 below.

32. See Chap. 12.

33. See Chap. 9.

34. Louis Adrian Montrose, "Shaping Fantasies: Figurations of Gender and Power in Elizabethan Culture," p. 45.

35. The political embarrassments in Chaucer are actually more acute than they are in Shakespeare: Hippolyta marries Theseus, and her sister and fellow Amazon-in-exile, Theseus's sister-in-law, marries a Theban, a sometime follower of the tyrant Creon.

36. See Montrose, "Shaping Fantasies," esp. pp. 35–45.

37. See E. Talbot Donaldson, *The Swan at the Well: Shakespeare Reading Chaucer*, pp. 7–18.

38. "An Haberdasshere and a Carpenter, / A Webbe, a Dyere, and a Tapycer"; I rely here on the glosses supplied by the *Riverside Chaucer*, p. 29.

39. I am indebted here to the glosses provided by Wolfgang Clemen in *Shakespeare*, ed. Sylvan Barnet, p. 533.

40. Donaldson has a field day in analyzing passages such as this one (thereby positioning himself with, often outperforming, the theater critics of the Thesian court). He characterizes, for example, the juxtaposition of lily white lips and a cherry nose as "an eye-catching anomaly, if a splotchy one" (p. 12).

41. Chaucer's long association with the wool business was recognized in 1387 when he was dispatched to Flanders on royal business, briefed "to negotiate a reopening of a free wool trade with the Flemish weaver cities of Bruges, Ghent, and Ypres" (Olson, *Good Society*, p. 52).

42. On Chaucer's strategy of self-infantilization in *Sir Thopas*, see Lee Patterson, " 'What Man Artow?': Authorial Self-Definition in *The Tale of Sir Thopas* and *The Tale of Melibee*," esp. pp. 129–35. Patterson's reading of Chaucer here is remarkably congruent with the one I am attributing to Shakespeare in *A Midsummer Night's Dream*: "He [Chaucer] is the originator of a national literature in a culture that lacks both the concept of literature and a social identity for those who produce it. . . . his solution to this dilemma is to adopt the identity of another socially marginalized and temporally anomalous figure: the child—but a child with a difference" (p. 135).

43. See *Merchant's Tale*, 7.2125–31. The pat rhyming of "woot" and "hoot" here, coupled with the maladroit repetition of "sleighte," seem prescient of Bottom's poetics.

44. See *Narrative and Dramatic Sources of Shakespeare*, ed. Bullough, vol. 1, pp. 373–76; Shakespeare, *A Midsummer Night's Dream*, ed. Harold F. Brooks, p. lix.

45. "I am not he," Wyatt tells his fellow-courtier John Poyntz, to "Praise Sir Thopas for a noble tale / And scorn the story that the knight told" (*Collected Poems*, ed. Daalder, p. 102, lines 43, 50–51).

46. See *Records of Early English Drama: Coventry* (henceforward cited *REED: Coventry*), ed. R. W. Ingram, p. 563. For a study of guilds in Coventry, c. 1518–25, see Charles Phythian-Adams, *Desolation of a City: Coventry and the Urban Crisis of the Late Middle Ages*, esp. pp. 99–117. On John Shakespeare as a whittawer, and on links between Coventry and Stratford established through common interests in cloth-making industries, see S. Schoenbaum, *William Shakespeare: A Compact Documentary Life*, pp. 5–6, 16–17.

47. Foxe, *Acts and Monuments of Martyrs*, as cited by *REED: Coventry*, ed. Ingram, pp. 207–8.

48. *City Annals*, as quoted by *REED: Coventry*, ed. Ingram, p. 294. This "suddaine Earthquake" reportedly caused "amazednes of the people & caused them to make there earnest prayers vnto Almighty god. And this yeare the padgins were layd down."

49. See *REED: Coventry*, ed. Ingram, p. 292–93. For the possibility that Shakespeare, then fifteen, might have witnessed the cycle of which this play formed part — "one of the last performances of the great cycle of Mystery plays acted by the craft guilds" — see Schoenbaum, *Documentary Life*, p. 111.

50. See *REED: Coventry*, ed. Ingram, pp. xxiii, xliii, 149. For the later history of English weavers, see E. P. Thompson, *The Making of the English Working Class*, pp. 297–346.

51. See PRO SP/1/142 as cited in *REED: Coventry*, ed. Ingram, pp. 148–49.

52. See Phythian-Adams, *Desolation of a City*, pp. 62–63, 253–54. On Coventry guilds, see *Records of the Guild of the Holy Trinity*, ed. Templeman, and *Register*, ed. Harris.

53. Phythian-Adams, *Desolation*, p. 19.

54. Ibid., pp. 27, 30, 50, 62.

55. Ibid., p. 33.

56. See *REED: Coventry*, ed. Ingram, pp. 564–65; Phythian-Adams, *Desolation*, pp. 102, 104, 212.

57. In the opinion of Brooks, the Arden editor, "it seems likely that Queen Elizabeth was present when the *Dream* was first acted" (p. lv; Brooks goes on to speculate, pp. lv–lvii, on the various weddings that may have furnished an occasion for the play's first performance).

58. See Schoenbaum, *Documentary Life*, pp. 16–54; "Shakespeare, William," in *DNB*, vol. 51, pp. 348–54; Stanley Wells, *Shakespeare: A Dramatic Life*, p. 5. John Shakespeare, father of the poet, enters the historical record "ingloriously" (as Schoenbaum puts it, p. 17) on April 29, 1552, in paying a shilling fine for amassing an unlawful midden heap in Henley Street, Stratford.

59. For the argument that "only the Mystery plays of the cathedral towns, which he had perhaps himself witnessed as a boy in Coventry, afforded a precedent for drama on the Shakespearian scale," see Schoenbaum, *Documentary Life*, p. 161.

60. Ibid., p. 37.

61. Montrose observes that the two wedding-night performances that Theseus chooses *not* to have performed propose to act out "the extremes of reciprocal violence between the sexes" in scenarios that would inevitably suggest parallel incidents in the life of Theseus: see "Shaping Fantasies," p. 45.

62. See *General Prologue*, 1.447–48: "Of clooth-makyng she hadde swich an haunt / She passed them of Ypres and of Gaunt."

63. Even in thinking of the "tricks" that "strong imagination might play," it seems, Shakespeare's mind turned to Chaucer and to his most famous masculine lover. Such imagination, Theseus argues, "if it would but apprehend some joy, / It comprehends some bringer of that joy" (V.i.19–20). Shakespeare is surely thinking here of *Troilus and Criseyde*, 5.1115–62, where Troilus stands on the walls of Troy, look-

ing for Criseyde, finally transforming a "fare-cart" to her image; see *A Midsummer Night's Dream*, ed. Brooks, p. 104.

64. Here again, however, some qualifications are in order. Puck, with the very first *abab*-rhymed lines following Theseus's parting words, stirs memories of Bottom's drama (why else a lion?) and evokes peasant labor: "Now the hungry [lion] roars, / And the wolf [behowls] the moon; / Whilst the heavy ploughman snores, / All with weary task foredone" (V.i.371–74).

65. In beginning her tale, the Wife recalls a place and time when "this land" was full of "fayerye" and of dances featuring "the elf-queene" with "hir joly compaignye" (3.859–61). For fuller consideration of this passage and of the importance of its rural setting, see Chap. 5 below.

Chapter 5

1. On the preeminent importance of craft and parish guilds for, respectively, economic policing and social cohesion in medieval towns, see Richard Holt and Gervase Rosser, eds., *The Medieval Town: A Reader in English Urban History 1200–1540*, pp. 9–18. The church, for Holt and Rosser, was "always an ambivalent force for social integration in the medieval town" (p. 13).

2. For some succinct demographic estimates, see Paul Strohm, "The social and literary scene in England," p. 1.

3. Randall Collins, *Weberian Sociological Theory*, p. 57.

4. Robert Brenner's seminal article first appeared as "The Agrarian Roots of European Capitalism," pp. 16–113; it reappears in revised form as part of *The Brenner Debate: Agrarian Class Structure and Economic Development in Pre-Industrial Europe*, ed. T. H. Aston and C. H. E. Philpin.

5. The term *lond* is also worth investigating; it is often used by Chaucer as if it were interchangeable with *contree*.

6. C. C. Dyer, "Power and Conflict in the Medieval English Village," p. 28.

7. It is worth remembering that many people in rural settlements engaged in nonagricultural activities. At the manor of Halesowen, west of Birmingham, villagers busied themselves with "manufacture of textiles, metalworking, leatherworking, woodworking, building, food production and ale-brewing" (Zvi Razi, *Life, Marriage, and Death in a Medieval Parish: Economy, Society, and Demography in Halesowen 1270–1400*, p. 7). Inhabitants of London and its suburbs, on the other hand, kept "horses, cattle, pigs, and all kinds of poultry" (Ernest L. Sabine, "City Cleaning in Mediaeval London," p. 20). For some general remarks on "the separation of town and country," see Susan Reynolds, *English Medieval Towns*, pp. 87–90. Reynolds notes that "a good many town-dwellers had spent their childhood or, if they were apprenticed young, at least their early childhood in the country" (p. 89).

8. Paul A. Olson, *Good Society*, pp. 39–40.

9. Olson concedes that the Franklin is a figure who operates "in both the city and the country"; he argues (somewhat desperately) that the London Manciple is included in the country group "because Temple lawyers often tended the estates of rural lords" (pp. 40, 41).

10. See *OED*, *country*; Raymond Williams, *Keywords: A Vocabulary of Culture and Society*, p. 81.

11. See "'No Man His Reson Herde': Peasant Consciousness, Chaucer's Miller, and the Structure of the *Canterbury Tales*," in Lee Patterson, ed., *Literary Practice and Social Change*, pp. 113–55. The article appears, in modified form, in *Chaucer and the Subject of History*, as "The *Miller's Tale* and the Politics of Laughter" (pp. 244–79).

12. See Geoffrey Chaucer, *The Canterbury Tales: Nine Tales and the General Prologue*, ed. V. A. Kolve and Glending Olson, p. 92.

13. PRO C.47/46/465. For a full edited version of this return, see *London English*, ed. Chambers and Daunt, p. 42. Chambers and Daunt print "hurtyng of an ax," rather than "hurtynge of an ey."

14. All members of the London goldsmith's fraternity contributed to a single alms fund to aid artisans suffering from blindness (an occupational hazard) and other disabilities: see Thrupp, *Merchant Class*, pp. 29–30. For a succinct survey of such practices, see Karl H. Van D'Elden, "The Development of the Insurance Concept and Insurance Law in the Middle Ages."

15. See PRO C.47/45/380; Westlake, *Parish Gilds*, p. 220.

16. PRO C.47/46/465; see also *London English*, ed. Chambers and Daunt, p. 43.

17. The term *fantasye* is applied both by Nicholas and Alisoun (1.3835) and by the neighbors (3840) to the old carpenter's account of his own misadventure. The London Carpenters insist, in their 1389 return, that any "brother or soster" who shall "be atteint of any falshede" will be expelled from the guild (PRO C.47/46/465; *London English*, ed. Chambers and Daunt, p. 43).

18. See R. H. C. Davies, "An Oxford Charter of 1191 and the Beginnings of Municipal Freedom."

19. See Bird, *Turbulent London*, p. 15.

20. This scenario is constructed from ordinances of hurers and fullers found in *Memorials*, ed. Riley, pp. 400–402, 549 (both *Letter-Book H*). The letter-books, as Sabine coyly remarks, reveal "not a few instances of vilely obnoxious filth" ("City Cleaning," p. 19). Wrangles between guild apprentices/journeymen and pages seeking to water horses in the Thames are said to be so intense that "they are then on the point of killing one another" (p. 549). Hurers and cappers show up again in *Letter-Book I* (1404), where they claim in a petition that "they have been at divers times slandered and reproved, as well in the said city as in divers country-places within England and without, for divers false works" (*Memorials*, ed. Riley, pp. 558–59).

21. See *London Assize of Nuisance 1301–1431. A Calendar*, ed. H. M. Chew and W. Kellaway, pp. 160–61. For more on the working environs of St. Paul's, see Chap. 7 below.

22. See *Memorials*, ed. Riley, p. 538 (Ordinances of the Blacksmiths, 1394). A lyric in British Library MS Arundel 292, dated to the mid-fifteenth century, employs alliterative technique to fine effect in evoking the noisy, dirty, and smelly environs of a smithy. The poem complains early on of night work: "Swarte smekyd smethes smateryd wyth smoke / Dryue me to deth wyth den of here dyntes. / Swech noys *on nyghtes* ne herd men neuer" (*Secular Lyrics of the XIVth and XVth Centuries*, ed. R. H. Robbins, 2d ed., p. 118; emphasis mine).

23. See J. A. W. Bennett, *Chaucer at Oxford and Cambridge*, p. 55.

24. For more on this, and on the problematic relations of "native" to "nonnative" in urban culture, see Chap. 6 below.

25. See Michael Gibson, *Peter Bruegel*, pp. 153–58; Margaret A. Sullivan, *Brue-*

gel's Peasants. This painting features some striking grotesque or world-upside-down images: plates of food are carried on a door, lifted from its hinges for the occasion; one of the food carriers sports a spoon in his hatband (signaling the dominance of the belly over the brain). The lord of the manor sits on an upturned tub, engrossed in conversation with a professional religious. Two bagpipers stand by the guests, one of them carrying a very long knife on a leather strap around his waist. Many motifs from this painting are shared by *The Peasant Dance*, a work from the same late period (see Gibson, *Bruegel*, pp. 153–54, 159–62). The bagpiper here dominates the left half of the painting. This camus-nosed piper remains wholly undistracted by the man who presses for attention on his left; his two piggy eyes refuse to shift their squinting gaze from the viewer. A huge knife hangs from his waist; its handle, outlined against the white of his smock, was clearly made to be gripped by a very large fist.

26. For a detailed survey of traditional associations between the horse and passion or the flesh, see Kolve, *Imagery of Narrative*, pp. 235–56.

27. See also 1.4129–30. Most medieval proverbs, and many modern ones, pass on the encapsulated, time-tested wisdom of village and barnyard. In 1559 Peter Bruegel chose to illustrate 92 Flemish proverbs in one extraordinary crowded scene (see Gibson, *Bruegel*, 44–46). One man fills in a well after the calf has drowned; a second casts roses before swine; a third keeps a nest egg, and so on. Bruegel's mode of representation here tends, of course, to deny peasant communities the possibility of deploying discourse at anything other than a literal and bodily level.

28. See Bartlett Jere Whiting, *Chaucer's Use of Proverbs*, pp. 7–9, 86–88; the peasant Reeve is famously sententious in his *Prologue*. The *Reeve's Tale* features 7 proverbs (5 of them spoken by John) plus 12 proverbial phrases in its 404 lines. The most prolific speaker of proverbs in the *Tales* is the Wife of Bath, with 14 in her *Prologue* but, interestingly, only 2 in her *Tale*).

29. *Esement* is a technical, legal term meaning compensation or redress; extended to the sexual sphere, its meaning would stretch to include comfort, refreshment, relief.

30. On the process through which the domesticated pig, "which almost never trespassed onto the pages of chivalric literature," was taken to represent the essence of peasant society, see Milo Kearney, *The Role of Swine Imagery in Medieval Culture*, pp. 215–22 (p. 221).

31. The phrase "a pig in a poke," defined by *Brewer's Dictionary* as "a blind bargain," refers to the practice of selling a cat in a bag under the pretence that it is actually a suckling-pig. If the poke is opened, the cat "is let out of the bag" and the trick disclosed. English proverbs warning against buying sacked pigs have been dated as early as 1325 ("Wan man yevit the a pig, opin the powch") and the Wycliffite *De blasphemia*, c. 1400, warns that "To bye a catte in tho sakke is bot littel charge": see *Brewer's Dictionary of Phrase and Fable*, ed. Ivor H. Evans, p. 852; Barlett Jere Whiting, *Proverbs, Sentences, and Proverbial Phrases*, P192 (p. 458), C102 (p. 74). As for *two* animals of the same species in one sack: Wycliffite writers were fond of speaking of "doggis in a poke," as in "Anticrist hath put diverse doggis in the poke of his obedience" (Whiting, D324, p. 139).

32. The phrase "of heigh parage" is employed twice by the Wife of Bath (and by nobody else): see 3.250, 1120.

33. "But certeynly, a yong thyng may men gye, / Right as men may warm wex

with handes plye" (*Merchant's Tale*, 4.1429–30; May gets "warm wex" into her own hands in 4.2117). See also *A Midsummer Night's Dream*, I.i.47–51 (and Chap. 4 above).

34. See *Sources and Analogues of Chaucer's Canterbury Tales*, ed. W. F. Bryan and Germaine Dempster, pp. 144–47.

35. The Mugnone Valley is the site where Calandrino's legendary simplemindedness is first exploited: see *Decameron* 8.3; Wallace, *Decameron*, pp. 91–98.

36. See 9.6.12; p. 711. The bed offered to the Florentines is actually described not as the best available, but as "il men cattivo," "the least awful"; Boccaccio's young noble masculine Florentine storyteller assumes the viewpoint of his young noble masculine Florentine counterparts in the *novella*.

37. See *Decameron*, ed. Branca, p. 1496.

38. See Chap. 1 above.

39. See Kolve, *Imagery of Narrative*, pp. 246–48. Kolve describes the image of Phyllis riding Aristotle as "one of the most popular secular images in all of medieval art" (p. 247); the so-called "Birth Tray: Triumph of Love" by the Master of Cassoni (Victoria and Albert Museum, London) featured on the cover of the Penguin *Decameron* includes a particularly attractive example of this motif.

40. For a fuller account of this *novella*, see Wallace, *Decameron*, pp. 62–63.

41. See Trexler, *Public Life*, pp. 3–5: "The conquering city replaced the old local ritual of community with its own, introducing the cult of its patron saint into the countryside, which in its worshipping this new saint effectively celebrated its own loss of sovereignty. . . . Thus the city-state was born from the city: a holy enclave surrounded by a desacralized country" (p. 5).

42. See John M. Manly, *Some New Light on Chaucer*, pp. 225–34; Muriel Bowden, *A Commentary on the General Prologue to the Canterbury Tales*, pp. 214–15; Francis F. Magoun, Jr., *A Chaucer Gazetteer*, pp. 29–30; D. W. Robertson, Jr., " 'And for my land thus hastow mordred me?': Land Tenure, the Cloth Industry, and the Wife of Bath."

43. See Mary Carruthers, "The Wife of Bath and the Painting of Lions"; Robertson, "And for my land . . . ?"; Patterson, *Subject of History*, p. 281.

44. *Western Society and the Church in the Middle Ages*, p. 286. See also Lester K. Little, *Religious Poverty and the Profit Economy in Medieval Europe*, pp. 197–217, esp. p. 203: "the sociological fact was that just by staying in cities the friars were fairly well assured of support." For a wide-ranging account of antifraternal exegesis, see Penn R. Szittya, *The Antifraternal Tradition in Medieval Literature*.

45. They are employed by T. S. Eliot as the epigraph to his *Love Song of J. Alfred Prufrock*.

46. For a remarkable account of Dante and Vergil, "simultaneously so close and so separated," see Kenelm Foster, *The Two Dantes*, pp. 156–253 (p. 156).

47. See also Langland, *Piers Plowman*, ed. Pearsall, C.XX, 295–311, where Lucifer reasons against the imminent coming of Christ: "For bi riht and by resoun þe renkes þat ben here / Body and soule beth myne" (300–301).

48. V. A. Kolve goes against critical tradition in considering the *Friar's Tale* as a religious narrative of serious import: see his " 'Man in the Middle': Art and Religion in Chaucer's *Friar's Tale*." His thorough survey of recent criticism leads him to remark that "it has somehow lost its identity as a religious tale" (p. 5).

49. Paul Strohm sees the following passage as "a kind of debased version of *im-*

mixio manum" (*Social Chaucer*, p. 99); he reads Chaucer's poetry generally (and the tales of Friar and Summoner in particular) as symptomatic of "a society in which vassalage has been replaced by an array of more casual relations epitomized by sworn brotherhood"; such a society "includes a critique of those relations" (p. 96).

50. For detailed accounts of these phenomena across many cultures and centuries, see *Männerbande—Männerbünde: Zur Rolle des Mannes im Kulturvergleich*, ed. Gisela Völger and Karin V. Welck.

51. *Women in the Medieval English Countryside: Gender and Household in Brigstock before the Plague*, p. 5. Judith Bennett enlarges the scope of her revisionary thesis in her "Medieval Women, Modern Women: Across the Great Divide": "The notion of a great and negative transition for women over these centuries [1300–1700] is now faced with too many anomalies to be sustained" (p. 150).

52. I consider this double movement of rejection/inscription as part of the dilemma of Margery Kempe, in "Mystics and Followers in Siena and East Anglia," pp. 169–91, esp. pp. 185–86.

53. Ernesto Laclau, "Metaphor and Social Antagonisms," p. 256.

54. See Rita Copeland, "Why Women Can't Read: Medieval Hermeneutics, Statute Law, and the Lollard Heresy Trials."

55. "Wepentake and an hondred is al oon" (John of Trevisa, trans., *Polychronicon Ranulphi Higden* [1387] as cited in *OED, wappentake*, 1a).

56. See *Yorkshire Sessions of the Peace, 1361–64*, ed. Bertha H. Putnam, p. 36. The term "libertas de Holdernesse" appears in the margin of an account of the session held at Hedon on July 26, 1361. The town of Hedon was created c. 1140 by excising some 300 acres from the Earl of Aumale's manor of Preston in Holderness (which covered over 5,000 acres): see K. J. Allison, *The East Riding of Yorkshire Landscape*, p. 237.

57. Allison, *East Riding*, p. 99.

58. This phenomenon (in the East Riding and elsewhere) is typical of the fifteenth and early sixteenth centuries: see ibid., p. 104.

59. See John V. Fleming, "The Antifraternalism of the *Summoner's Tale*," p. 689.

60. I employ the term "peasant house" (rather than "hovel" or similarly disparaging terms) because, as Barbara Hanawalt reminds us, "the word *house* means both a structure and the people living in it." In medieval England, Hanawalt continues, "the *husbond* was the bondsman who held the house, and the word *husbandry* also derived from this root"; the term *house* "had similar emotional ties as *haus* in Germany and *ostel* in France" (*Ties That Bound*, p. 31).

61. On wifely *chidyng*, see the *Wife of Bath's Prologue*, 3.278–81, 419–22. On the importance of wifely rhetoric in interrupting cycles of masculine violence, see Chap. 4 above and Chap. 8 below. On parallels between friars and wives as rhetors and confessors, see Chap. 8 below.

62. See Nicholas Havely, "Chaucer, Boccaccio, and the Friars," pp. 256–57; W. A. Hinnebusch, *The History of the Dominican Order*, pp. 257–60; David Knowles, *The Religious Orders in England*, vol. 2, pp. 71–72, 145–48. McKisack notes that Richard II wrote to the chancellor of Oxford on several occasions when it was thought that graces favoring the friars were being refused maliciously (*Fourteenth Century*, p. 504). In the late fourteenth century, Carmelites ousted the Dominicans from the positions that they had enjoyed as ambassadors and royal confessors for more than a century;

John of Gaunt, Henry IV, and Henry V all employed Carmelite confessors (Havely, p. 257; Knowles, vol. 2, p. 145).

63. For an exploration of *ire* as the protagonist of Fragment 3 (passing from one body to the next), see Wallace, "Chaucer's Body Politic," pp. 222–25. The *Codex regularum* of St. Francis notes that friars should welcome insults and injuries as opportunities to practice humility and forgiveness: see Fleming, "Antifraternalism," p. 699.

64. For discussion of these ties and of the iconographic traditions that were promulgated through such confraternities, see John V. Fleming, "The *Summoner's Prologue*: An Iconographic Adjustment."

65. See *Decameron* 6.10.10: "quegli che alla nostra compagnia scritti sono" ("those of you who are enrolled as members of our confraternity," p. 506).

66. A case for the value of deconstructive criticism as a postponement of violent acts is made (fleetingly, in conversation with Derrida) by Imre Salusinszky, *Criticism in Society*, p. 22.

67. See Walter Ullmann, *Law and Politics in the Middle Ages*, esp. p. 170. In reviewing the successive acts of legal interpretation that effect closure in the *Summoner's Tale*, it is useful to recall the ideals articulated by R. W. and A. J. Carlyle: "We may, indeed, say that it was the characteristic defect of mediaeval civilization that it was, if anything, too legal; but as the men of the time saw it . . . liberty, true liberty, was not something contrary to law, but rather was to be found in law itself" (*A History of Medieval Political Theory in the West*, vol. 5, p. 36). At the same time, it is worth recalling how far the administration of justice in fourteenth-century England had departed from such ideals: see Barbara Hanawalt, *Crime and Conflict in English Communities, 1300–1348*.

68. John Fleming notes that Jankyn's system for the twelve-part division of the fart "very carefully follows the principles for the division of communal property outlined in the fourth clause of the brief Carmelite Rule written by Albert of Vercelli" ("Antifraternalism," p. 699).

69. Assizes of Jerusalem, "Assises de la Cour des Bourgeois," xxvi, as cited in Carlyle, *Political Theory*, vol. 5, p. 37. Henry de Bracton, d. 1268, was a royal justice under Henry III and was long believed to be the author of *De legibus et consuetudinibus Angliae*.

70. It is important to note that such productive genius is found (and retained) within the feudal village. Linda Georgianna has argued that it is the friar who represents the "mode of free enterprise, with its strong emphasis on accounting procedures and competitive market forces" ("Lords, Churls, and Friars," p. 156). But within the economy of the *Tale*, the friar is parasitical upon (rather than the embodiment of) "competitive market forces."

71. For a fascinating account of the proceedings of a particular manorial court, see Razi, *Life, Marriage, and Death*, esp. pp. 12–16 (a reconstruction of the "personal file" of one villager, Richard le Bond, who appears in the court rolls 25 times between 1326 and his death in 1349); see further Braswell, "Chaucer's 'Court Baron.'"

72. I am indebted for what follows to the succinct overview of recent work provided by Dyer, "Power and Conflict," pp. 27–32.

73. See Thomas of Burton (and others), *Chronica monasterii de Melsa*, ed. E. A.

Bond, vol. 1, p. 92. Thomas of Woodstock, Duke of Gloucester, had a claim to Holderness that he pressed with eager haste on Anne's death in 1394: see Chap. 12 below.

74. "Pursuit by hue and cry," Kay Harris argues, "provided a way to equate capture in the mainour [in possession of physical evidence of the crime] with capture in the act" (*Proving Treason and Attainting Traitors*, pp. 82–83); see further A. Esmein, *A History of Continental Criminal Procedure with Special Reference to France*, p. 61.

75. "The rysyng of the comuynes in londe, / The pestilens, and the eorthe-qwake" (of 1382) are to be read, according to a lyric preserved in British Library Add. MS 22283, as "tokenes" of "grete vengaunce and wrake" to come "for synnes sake" (*Political Poems and Songs*, ed. Thomas Wright, p. 252); versions of this twelve-stanza lyric are also to be found in Bodleian Library, Oxford MS 3938 (Vernon) and in National Library of Wales, Aberystwyth, MS Peniarth 395.

76. See *Peasants' Revolt*, ed. Dobson, p. 173. I am indebted to Paul Strohm for generous assistance with this paragraph.

77. *Peasants' Revolt*, ed. Dobson, p. 274.

78. André Réville, *Le Soulèvement des travailleurs d'Angleterre en 1381*, p. 255.

79. See *Peasants' Revolt of 1381*, ed. Dobson, pp. 22–23, 123–31.

80. Paul Strohm observes that chroniclers of the 1381 Rising insist on imagining the rebels as rural even though the perpetrators of most of the events they describe are urban-identified: see *Hochon's Arrow*, pp. 36–39.

81. See Helen Cooper, *Pastoral: Mediaeval into Renaissance*, esp. p. 152. Cooper notes that Spenser's "frequent acknowledgment of Chaucer as his master in the *Calender* is backed by fewer echoes than even Barclay's work [eclogues] contains" (p. 153).

82. See *Riverside Chaucer*, pp. 650–51. The first half of this poem is heavily indebted to Boethius, *Consolation of Philosophy*, 2.m.5; in Cambridge University Library MS Ii.3.21, this poem is written in Chaucer's *Boece*, immediately following Bo. 2.m.5 (see *Riverside Chaucer*, p. 1083).

83. Raymond Williams, *The Country and the City*, p. 48.

84. Williams, *Country and City*, p. 33.

85. Quoted in Richard Halpern, *The Poetics of Primitive Accumulation: English Renaissance Culture and the Genealogy of Capital*, p. 72.

86. See Roger B. Manning, *Village Revolts: Social Protest and Popular Disturbances in England, 1509–1640*; Alan G. R. Smith, *The Emergence of a Nation State: The Commonwealth of England 1529–1660*, pp. 68–69.

87. Karl Marx, *Capital*, vol. 1, trans. Fowkes, p. 885. Various aspects of this proposition are upheld or qualified by Corrigan and Sayer, *Great Arch*, p. 97.

88. E. P. Thompson, *The Making of the English Working Class*, pp. 237–38.

89. "Introduction," *Medieval Town*, ed. Holt and Rosser, p. 12.

90. On the importance of liminal sites for rites of transition, see the pioneering work of Arnold van Gennep, *Les rites de passage* (1908), translated as *The Rites of Passage* by Monika B. Vizedom and Gabrielle L. Caffee. The liminal sites of both the *Friar's Tale* and *Pardoner's Tale* prove to be thresholds between life and death. That of the *Wife of Bath's Tale* turns out to be the familiar *limen* of marriage; so too that of *Clerk's Tale*, 4.288–89 ("And as she wolde over hir thresshfold gon, / The

markys cam . . ."; see also van Gennep, *Rites of Passage*, p. 20). For the argument that "pilgrimage itself has some of the attributes of liminality in passage rites," see Victor Turner and Edith Turner, *Image and Pilgrimage in Christian Culture*, pp. 1–38 (p. 34).

91. See *OED*, *mystery* (1: theology and religion) and *mystery* (2: service, trade, occupation); *MED*, *mister* and *misteri(e)*. Medieval Latin *misterium*, an altered form of *ministerium*, became confused with *mysterium*, "theological mystery" (derived from the Old French *mistere*, secret); the term *maistrie* offered further opportunities for confusion.

92. See, for example, Bowden, *Commentary*, pp. 84–88.

93. See D. W. Robertson, *A Preface to Chaucer: Studies in Medieval Perspectives*, pp. 242–43.

94. See Chap. 6 below. The term *covyne* occurs nowhere else in the *Canterbury Tales*; it occurs just once in *Boece*, in the highly charged political context of Book 1, prosa 4: "Certes me semyth that I se the felonous covynes of wykkid men habounden in joye and in gladnesse" (pp. 305–7).

Chapter 6

1. Donald Howard surmises that events in London in 1381 gave Chaucer "a sense of what it was like in a besieged city and how it would have felt to see Troy burning in its final hours" (*Chaucer*, p. 331).

2. In *Vox clamantis*, Book 1.

3. See Chap. 3 above.

4. On the phenomenon of the returned pilgrim (which merits more extensive consideration) see Turner and Turner, *Image and Pilgrimage*, p. 15.

5. See *Riverside Chaucer*, ed. Benson, note to line 4422, p. 853. I shall argue later in the chapter that the *Canon's Yeoman's Tale, pars secunda*, may be read as a London fiction.

6. See Chap. 1 above.

7. For this and other records of "Herry Bailey," see J. M. Manley, *Some New Light on Chaucer*, pp. 78–82. Manley lists seven other records featuring "Herry Bailey" (in diverse spellings); he appears twice as a Member of Parliament for Southwark (50 Edward III; 2 Richard II) and twice as a special coroner viewing dead bodies (1392, 1393).

8. See V. A. Kolve, *Chaucer and the Imagery of Narrative*, p. 259; Muriel A. Bowden, *A Commentary on the General Prologue to the Canterbury Tales*, pp. 187–88. The first plea of debt is entered in 1377.

9. See Laura Wright, "OED's Tabard, 4. (?)," a detailed study of the Accounts of London Bridge which ends by proposing that "the sign of *The Tabard* in the *Canterbury Tales* signifies 'The Ale-Tank'" (p. 157).

10. Martha Carlin, *The Urban Development of Southwark, c. 1200–1550*, p. 439.

11. Quoted in ibid., p. 467.

12. Ibid., p. 7.

13. See Chris Given-Wilson, *The Royal Household and the King's Affinity: Service, Politics, and Finance in England 1360–1413*, pp. 15, 22–23, 28–29, 34–35.

14. See Carlin, *Southwark*, 550–53; Sylvia L. Thrupp, *The Merchant Class of Medieval London (1300–1500)*, pp. 1–3; *Memorials of London*, ed. H. T. Riley, p. 492. Riley translates from the Latin of *Letter-Book H*, f. ccx, which records pleas held at the Lon-

don Guildhall before Mayor Nicholas Extone in January 1387. The need for "good governance" in London is of paramount importance since "there is a greater resort, as well of lords and nobles, as of common people, to that city, than to any other places in the realm, as well on account of the Courts there of our said Lord the King, as for transacting business there" (p. 492).

15. *Letter-Book H*, f. ccx (1387) in *Memorials*, ed. Riley, p. 492.

16. *Memorials*, ed. Riley, p. 536 (1394); *Letter-Book H*, f. ccxci.

17. *Memorials*, ed. Riley, p. 465 (1382); *Letter-Book H*, f. cxlv(a). I follow Riley's transcriptions and translations from *Letter-Book H*, add significant phrases (English, French, and Latin; abbreviations silently expanded) from examination of the manuscript, and note any errors or omissions detected in Riley. See further *Calendar of Letter-Books . . . Letter-Book H. Circa A.D. 1375–1399*, ed. Reginald R. Sharpe, p. 184.

18. *Letter-Book H*, now at the Corporation of London Records Office (London Guildhall), is in general carefully ruled and written; generous, 2.5″ margins are left for summarizing (sometimes moralizing) Latin titles for each entry.

19. F. cxxv(b); *Memorials*, ed. Riley, p. 444. Riley does not note that the text switches from Latin to Middle English for the phrase "this is the tonge of John Warde" (which he renders in modern English). Should this performance be counted as a dramatic record? On the problematics of such questions, see Teresa Coletti, "Reading REED: History and the Records of Early English Drama," esp. p. 268.

20. See David Aers, *Community, Gender, and Individual Identity: English Writing 1360–1430*, pp. 20–35; Miri Rubin, *Charity and Community in Medieval Cambridge*, pp. 291–93. Such discriminations were formulated and enforced as part of the reaction to the labor shortages occasioned by the Black Death. They mark the decline of a long-lived tradition of uncalculating alms-giving and the rise of a new work-oriented ethic.

21. During the Pardoner's modeling of false preaching, his tongue and hands become objectified as tools of a deceptive trade: "Myn handes and my tonge goon so yerne / That it is joye to se my bisynesse" (6.398–99).

22. *Letter-Book H*, f. ccx (Latin); *Memorials*, ed. Riley, pp. 490–94; *Calendar*, ed. Sharpe, pp. 295–96.

23. This delicate drama takes up an entire folio of *H*; ample space is left on the verso side (about one-third of the page), perhaps for later additions and amendments.

24. *Letter-Book F*, f. ccxxiv (Latin); *Memorials*, ed. Riley, p. 520.

25. See *Memorials*, ed. Riley, pp. 536, 466; *Letter-Book H*, ff. ccxci, cxlv.

26. See *Inferno* 17.52–78. On the representation of commutative justice in Dante, see Anthony K. Cassell, *Dante's Fearful Art of Justice*.

27. See *Decameron* 2.5; Wallace, *Decameron*, pp. 39–41; *Letter-Book H*, f. cclviii and *Memorials*, ed. Riley, pp. 523–25.

28. See *Memorials*, ed. Riley, p. 435, *Calendar*, ed. Sharpe, pp. 132–33; the year is 1379. The same entry records the names of seven women who paid either 10s or 6s 8d for the right to sell their wares near "Le Brokenecros" by the north door of St. Paul's. On the office of Common Hunt, see Thrupp, *Merchant Class*, pp. 241–42.

29. On the lawyer and logician Ralph Strode as "a very interesting addition to the Chaucer circle," see Pearsall, *Life of Chaucer*, pp. 133–34.

30. See Stephen A. Barney, note to *Troilus* 5.1856–59, in *Riverside Chaucer*, p. 1058; *Letter-Book G*, f. cccxxi as translated in *Memorials*, ed. Riley, pp. 377–78;

Chaucer Life-Records, pp. 144–47. Ralph Strode lived in the corresponding dwelling above Aldersgate between 1375 and 1382. Chaucer was probably granted the Aldgate dwelling rent-free "as a favor from the city to the king or other royal patron" (Pearsall, *Life of Chaucer*, p. 97).

31. See Green, *Chronicle into History*; Christian Bec, "Il mito di Firenze da Dante al Ghiberti," vol. 1, pp. 3–26; Donald Weinstein, "The Myth of Florence," pp. 15–44; Charles T. Davis, "Il Buon Tempo Antico," pp. 45–69. For an instance of Boccaccio's use of a *novella* almost certainly deriving from Villani, see Chap. 7 below.

32. *L'istoria di Firenze di Gregorio Dati dal 1380 al 1405*, ed. Luigi Pratesi, p. 74. Dati records that the citizens of Florence, in facing Gian Galeazzo Visconti in 1402, "sempre si confortavano con una speranza che pareva avere loro la cosa sicura in mano, cioé che il Comune non può morire e il Duca era uno solo uomo mortale, chè finito lui, finito lo stato suo" (cap. 97).

33. For detailed discussion of this process, see Chap. 5 above; David Wallace, "Chaucer's Body Politic: Social and Narrative Self-Regulation."

34. "Wot I wel," Chaucer writes in opening his *Legend of Good Women*, that "ther nis noon dwellynge in this contree / That eyther hath in hevene or helle ybe" (F 4–6); see further Piero Boitani, "What Dante Meant to Chaucer," esp. p. 125.

35. See Antonia Gransden, *Historical Writing in England, vol. 2, c. 1307 to the Early Sixteenth Century*, p. 61; John Taylor, *English Historical Literature in the Fourteenth Century*, pp. 14–16.

36. See *Letter-Book H*, f. cxxxiii, and *Memorials*, ed. Riley, pp. 448–51; *Calendar*, ed. Sharpe, pp. 165–66.

37. *Decameron* 6.2.18. Note the tension here between the substantive *convito* or *convivio*, a term emphasizing common participation in a shared meal, and the adjectival *magnifico*, suggestive of sharp inequalities of wealth and resources.

38. See Andrew Prescott, "London in the Peasants' Revolt: A Portrait Gallery," pp. 128–29. Trespass actions of John of Gaunt and John Butterwick list rebels from five counties. The group from Ware (Herts) is by far the largest (43 rebels); the next largest group is from Manningtree, Essex (17).

39. *Letter-Book H*, f. cxviii (Anglo-Norman); *Memorials*, ed. Riley, p. 438; *Calendar*, ed. Sharpe, p. 139.

40. See MS Cotton. Julius B II as edited by C. L. Kingsford in *Chronicles of London*: "And many fflemmynges loste hir heedes at that tyme, and namely they that koude nat say Breede and Chese, But Case and Brode" (p. 15). This chronicle covers the years 1189–1432 and concludes with Lydgate's verses on the reception of Henry VI in London in 1432. Kingsford dates the manuscript 1435 (pp. viii–ix).

41. See E. J. Burford, *Bawds and Lodgings*, p. 78.

42. See Thrupp, *Merchant Class*, p. 17.

43. See Ruth Bird, *The Turbulent London of Richard II*, esp. pp. 52–101.

44. See Douglas Gray's note to 1.4367 in *Riverside Chaucer*, p. 853.

45. The Knight, the Squire's father, is credited with having killed at least eighteen men (1.43–78). It is worth noting that Chaucer makes the relationship of Knight to Squire a natural one (father to son), whereas the master-apprentice relationship exists only on paper.

46. See *OED*, *meinie*. The other fourteenth-century meaning noted is "4. The

collection of pieces or 'men' used in a game of chess." *MED* records a comparable range of meanings under *meine*.

47. See *Boece* 4, *prosa* 1, 41–42; *Nun's Priest's Tale*, 7.3394. See further Paul Strohm, " 'Lad with revel to Newegate': Chaucerian Narrative and Historical Meta-Narrative," esp. pp. 166–67.

48. See *Letter-Book H*, f. cxciv(b); *Memorials*, ed. Riley, pp. 484–86; *Calendar*, ed. Sharpe, pp. 271–72. For a more legitimate example of female apprenticeship, see *Calendar*, ed. Sharpe, pp. 185–86, where the daughter of a deceased "wolmongere" is first made a ward of John Munstede, draper, and then apprenticed as a "thredwomman" to John Appleby and his wife Johanna.

49. *Letter-Book H*, f. cclxxxvii(a); *Memorials*, ed. Riley, p. 535. See also *Calendar*, ed. Sharpe, p. 402. This entry is in Anglo-Norman; the word "huckesteres" is Middle English.

50. We find the same proverb in the Kentish dialect of Dan Michel of Northgate's *Ayenbite of Inwyt* (completed 1340): "A roted eppel amang þe holen: makeþ rotie þe yzounde. yef he is longe þer amang" (ed. Richard Morris, vol. 1, p. 205).

51. *Letter-Book H*, f. clxxii(a); *Memorials*, ed. Riley, p. 480. Riley omits the crucial word "craftes" (italicized in my text). His transcription is otherwise accurate, although I have corrected his habit of heavy capitalization by following the manuscript.

52. *Letter-Book H*, f. clxxii(a); *Memorials*, ed. Riley, p. 481 (same document).

53. See *Calendar*, ed. Sharpe, p. 226; Bird, *Turbulent London*, pp. 63–85; Paul Strohm, "Politics and Poetics: Usk and Chaucer in the 1380s"; Simpson, "Langland and London City Politics," pp. 120–26.

54. See A. F. Butcher, "English Urban Society and the Revolt of 1381," p. 101.

55. See Chap. 3 above.

56. See Caroline M. Barron, "The Parish Fraternities of Medieval London," pp. 20–21.

57. *Parish Gilds*, ed. Westlake, p. 182.

58. See *Letter-Book H*, f. ccxiv(b). The short summary in the manuscript margin speaks of the malefactor's "rebellionem" against his alderman. See further *Memorials*, ed. Riley, pp. 500–502; Sharpe, *Calendar*, p. 323.

59. See *Letter-Book H*, f. ccxxvi; *Memorials*, ed. Riley, pp. 502–3.

60. For details of these episodes, see Given-Wilson, *King's Affinity*, p. 52; Bird, *Turbulent London*, pp. 24–25, 86–101; Caroline M. Barron, "The Quarrel of Richard II with London 1392–7," pp. 173–201.

61. *Letter-Book H*, f. cccxxvii(a); *Memorials*, ed. Riley, p. 551; *Calendar*, ed. Sharpe, p. 449–50. This Anglo-Norman document of 1399 apparently records an ordinance made during the mayoralty of Richard Whityngton (1398). This is the last numbered folio in *Letter-Book H*, with the exception of f. cccxxxi. Two of the three folios immediately preceding cccxxxi have been cut out; one half of the other, cut vertically, has been removed.

62. *Letter-Book H*, f. ccxix (Latin); and *Memorials*, ed. Riley, p. 496; *Calendar*, ed. Sharpe, pp. 311–12.

63. *Letter-Book H*, ff. ccix(b)–cccx(a); *Memorials*, ed. Riley, p. 542–44 (p. 543); *Calendar*, ed. Sharpe, p. 431.

64. See Chap. 3 above.

65. *Letter-Book H*, f. cccix(b); *Memorials*, ed. Riley, p. 543.

66. As Britton J. Harwood rightly observes, these 5 guildsmen stood little chance of becoming aldermen of London: of the 260 aldermen elected in fourteenth-century London, only 9 were from the lesser companies these guildsmen represent ("The 'Fraternitee' of Chaucer's Guildsmen," pp. 413–17).

67. Douglas Gray, note to 1.386, in *Riverside Chaucer*, p. 814.

68. Mormals were attributed, by some authorities, to generally intemperate or unclean habits. One critic argues that they were runny rather than dry; they were said to smell strongly (Gray in *Riverside Chaucer*, p. 814). On the notion of "danger" as employed here, see Mary Douglas, *Purity and Danger: An Analysis of Concepts of Pollution and Taboo*. The sign of danger confirms, of course, the need for social regulation and cleansing.

69. A good number of mayors and aldermen in Chaucer's London were knights; others refused to be knighted since they did not wish to be moved into a higher tax bracket.

70. For the use of drink to seal an arbitration or as a price for peace, see *Calendar of Early Mayor's Court Rolls of the City of London at the Guildhall, 1298–1307*, ed. A. H. Thomas, pp. 16, 34.

71. S. E. Thorne argues that when lawyers came to London in the fourteenth century they would band together to rent a house and "hire a cook and a manciple": see "The Early History of the Inns of Court with Special Reference to Gray's Inn."

72. See *Riverside Chaucer*, pp. 951–52.

73. Kolve, *Imagery of Narrative*, p. 264.

74. According to the Benedictine chronicler Walsingham, Nicholas Brembre, sometime mayor of London, had intended to massacre thousands of his fellow citizens, rename London "New Troy," and proclaim himself duke of the city. See Thomas Walsingham, *Historia Anglicana*, ed. Henry T. Riley, vol. 2, pp. 173–74.

75. "And" (he adds as a curious afterthought) "for noon oother cause, trewely" (8.1306–7).

76. See *Inferno* 29–30.

77. Norman Blake argues that the *Canon's Yeoman's Prologue* and *Tale* are spurious and does not include them in his Hengwrt-based edition: see *The Canterbury Tales by Geoffrey Chaucer: Edited from the Hengwrt Manuscript*, pp. 6, 9. Critics generally agree that they were written late in the Canterbury period: see John Reidy's note in *Riverside Chaucer*, p. 946. Their case is supported by Riley's observation that "this title, *yoman*, first appears in the City Books about this period": Riley is commenting on an entry for 1396 in *Letter-Book H* (ff. cccix(b)–cccx(a); *Memorials*, p. 542). Riley speculates that the term may be "an abbreviation of the words 'yong man'" (p. 542). But it seems clear that the term refers to rank rather than age: a *yoman* is a nonliveried member of a company or trade.

78. *A Preface to Chaucer: Studies in Medieval Perspectives*, p. 51. Robertson later wrote a whole book on London, prefaced by the strictures that preface *A Preface to Chaucer*: "We should expect, then, to find in medieval London an hierarchical classless society" (*Chaucer's London*, p. 5).

79. In his commentary on *Purgatorio* 14, which offers a sustained, dramatic account of the course of the Arno, Benvenuto meditates on the first hemistich of line 17

as follows: "*un fiumicel*, scilicet Arnus; et bene dicit, quia Arnus non est fluvius magnus, nec navigabilis, nec piscosus: est tamen famosus, quia labitur per famosas terras; et quia viri famosi dederunt sibi famam ipsum describentes, sicut Dantes, Petrarcha, Boccaccius, et alii florentini, qui discurrunt per mundum multum" (*Commentum super Dantis Aldigherii comoediam*, ed. J. P. Lacaita, vol. 3, p. 376).

80. *Faerie Queen*, ed. Thomas P. Roche, Jr., 3.9.45.2 ("wealthy *Thamis*"), 4.11.24.3 ("noble Thamis"); *Prothalamion*, in *Poetical Works*, ed. J. C. Smith and E. de Selincourt, lines 127–29 (p. 602).

81. The form of spelling for these glosses followed here is that of Bodleian Library, Oxford, Fairfax 16 (adopted by George B. Pace and Alfred David as base manuscript for their edition of the poem in Geoffrey Chaucer, *The Minor Poems*, Part 1, pp. 149–60).

82. *Letter-Book H*, f. cclix(a); *Memorials*, ed. Riley, pp. 526–27 (p. 526); *Calendar*, ed. Sharpe, p. 364.

83. F. cclix(a); *Memorials*, p. 526.

Chapter 7

1. A. S. G. Edwards, in his "Critical Approaches to the *Man of Law's Tale*," shows that critical confusion over the *Tale*'s genre began in medieval manuscripts before extending into contemporary criticism (p. 87).

2. All lawyers who were not sergeants-at-law were referred to as apprentices: see Edward H. Warren, "Serjeants-at-Law: The Order of the Coif," p. 915. The most important book-length study of sergeants-at-law was, until recently, Alexander Pulling, *The Order of the Coif*; but now see J. H. Baker, *The Order of Serjeants at Law*.

3. Baker describes this procession as, "from the public point of view, . . . the grandest spectacle ever provided by the legal profession" (pp. 89–90). After a lavish feast, which lasted seven days in Fortescue's time, the new sergeants processed through Cheapside, stopping at the church of St. Thomas of Acres en route to St. Paul's (Baker, pp. 101–2).

For the earliest description of the revels at the Inns of Chancery and Inns of Court, see Sir John Fortescue, *De laudibus legum Angliae*, ed. S. B. Chrimes, pp. 117–21. Fortescue was called to be sergeant-at-law in 1438; the *De laudibus* was written between 1468 and 1471. It has been argued that the provision of legal education at the Inns of Court was a fifteenth-century development: see S. E. Thorne, "The Early History of the Inns of Court with Special Reference to Gray's Inn," now in his *Essays in English Legal History*, pp. 137–54; and E. W. Ives, "The Common Lawyers." But see Paul Brand, "Courtroom and Schoolroom: The Education of Lawyers in England Prior to 1400." Brand marshals an impressive array of manuscript evidence to support his conclusion that "courtroom and classroom were already both playing a part in the education of common lawyers in 1300 just as they did in Fortescue's day" (p. 165). See also J. H. Baker, "Learning Exercises in the Medieval Inns of Court and Chancery," in his *The Legal Profession and Common Law*, pp. 7–23; Brand, *The Making of the Common Law*.

4. See Warren, "Serjeants-at-Law," pp. 933–34; Isobel McKenna, "The Making of a Fourteenth Century Sergeant of the Lawe," p. 248.

5. See Warren, "Serjeants-at-Law," pp. 914–16, and McKenna, pp. 253, 258—both now largely superseded by Baker, *Serjeants at Law*, pp. 140–250, which provides a

chronicle of "countors of the bench" and "serjeants at law" that runs from the reign of Edward I to that of Victoria (pp. 140–250). During the reign of Edward III (1326–77), 64 sergeants-at-law were created, compared with 22 under Richard II (1377–99) and 12 under Henry IV (1399–1413); the last sergeant was sworn in 1875. The Order of the Coif, which included sergeants-at-law, king's sergeants, and justices, took its name from the distinctive white coif that its members were required to wear (even in the presence of the sovereign); the Ellesmere manuscript depicts Chaucer's Sergeant in his coif and in a short robe (his traveling costume).

6. Theodore Plucknett, *A Concise History of the Common Law*, 5th ed., p. 223.

7. See McKenna, "Making," p. 255; Warren, "Serjeants-at-Law," p. 925.

8. Ellesmere's placing of the Man of Law's *Introduction* and *Tale* (Fragment 2) immediately after the *Cook's Tale* is followed by all the manuscripts in the *a* and *b* orders; *c* and *d*, plus Harley 7334, place *Gamelyn* between Ellesmere's 1 and 2. Hengwrt runs 1–3–2. The so-called "Epilogue of the Man of Law's Tale" appears in just three manuscripts. See Ralph Hanna III's textual notes in *Riverside Chaucer*, pp. 1120–22. *Gamelyn* may have been intended to provide a full tale for the Cook, although it is worth noting that "the poem mirrors accurately and in some detail the uncertain, though gradually developing, processes of justice in the fourteenth century" (Edgar F. Shannon, "Mediaeval Law in *The Tale of Gamelyn*," p. 463).

9. A sergeant-at-law ranked just below a knight bachelor; the resemblance between the coif and a knight's helmet (*coif de fer*) was emphasized in heraldic representations. The Order of the Coif was, it seems, the earliest Order created by an English sovereign; it predates the Order of the Garter by almost two centuries (see Warren, pp. 941, 919). The Miller is obviously more prosperous and politically powerful than the Cook.

10. Warren, "Serjeants-at-Law," pp. 911–12. See also Fortescue, *De laudibus legum Anglie*, ch. L, where sergeants-at-law are said to possess "not only a degree, but also a certain estate, not less eminent or solemn than the degree of doctor, which is called the degree of serjeant-at-law" ("datur tamen in illis nedum gradus sed et status quidam gradu doctoratus non minus celebris aut solempnis, qui gradus servientis ad legem appellatur," pp. 120–21).

11. Derek Pearsall notes that the second word spoken by the Man of Law, *depardieux* (2.39), is "appropriate to a man who would have spent much of his time pleading in the courts in Anglo-French" (*Canterbury Tales*, p. 257).

12. *Imagery of Narrative*, p. 297.

13. See McKenna, "Making," p. 261.

14. See, respectively, Edward A. Block, "Originality, Controlling Purpose, and Craftsmanship in Chaucer's *Man of Law's Tale*"; Kolve, *Imagery of Narrative*, p. 297. Not every critic has found such pleasure in this poem and its dominant image: according to Carolyn Dinshaw, "reading the *Man of Law's Tale* can be a trial much like Constance's, as she floats on the sea, rudderless, for 'yeres and dayes': the text is bewildering, disorienting, and seemingly endless" (*Sexual Poetics*, p. 88).

15. I follow the texts of Trivet and Gower as conveniently available in *Sources and Analogues of Chaucer's Canterbury Tales*, ed. W. F. Bryan and Germaine Dempster.

16. See, respectively, Trivet, *Chronique*, p. 165; Gower, *Confessio*, line 606.

17. See Trivet, *Chronique*, pp. 165–66; Gower, *Confessio*, lines 611–15.

18. See Paul Beichner, "Chaucer's Man of Law and *disparitas cultus*," pp. 70–75.

19. See Jill Mann, "Chance and Destiny in *Troilus and Criseyde* and the *Knight's Tale*," pp. 75–92.

20. See Bird, *Turbulent London*, pp. 1, 18–21; Given-Wilson, *Royal Household*, pp. 149–55.

21. *Rotuli Parliamentorum* 3, p. 7, quoted in Bird, p. 46 (my translation).

22. Bird, *Turbulent London*, pp. 28–29, quoting from *Gregory's Chronicle*.

23. Thrupp, *Merchant Class*, p. 259.

24. See Given-Wilson, *Royal Household*, p. 127.

25. Thrupp, *Merchant Class*, pp. 259–60, quoting from the coronation roll of Richard II.

26. See Barron, "Quarrel of Richard II with London," p. 179.

27. See *Calendar*, ed. Sharpe, p. 321; Bird, *Turbulent London*, p. 91.

28. See Thrupp, *Merchant Class*, pp. 292–93. Thrupp notes that merchants were summoned to Parliament for professional consultation in an earlier period. The 1442 reference to merchants comes in a sermon before Parliament given by the chancellor, Bishop Stafford, who splits the commons into three: merchants, cultivators, and artificers and common people ("ac communitate populosa").

29. See Barron, "Quarrel of Richard II with London," pp. 178–79; Thrupp, *Merchant Class*, pp. 275–77. Thrupp estimates that there were "not much above" 1,200 landed knights in 1324; a century later the number had fallen "to barely a quarter of this figure" (p. 276).

30. See Thrupp, pp. 311–13.

31. See T. F. Tout, *Chapters in the Administrative History of England*, vol. 3, pp. 479–81; Thrupp, *Merchant Class*, pp. 276–77.

32. See Ferrante, *Political Vision*, p. 328.

33. *Piers Plowman B-Text*, ed. Schmidt, 7.20, 21–22.

34. The Kane-Donaldson edition of B-Text includes the following line immediately following Schmidt's line 30: "Fynden [swiche] hir foode [for oure lordes loue of heuene]" (p. 371).

35. *Mornings in Florence: Being Simple Studies of Christian Art for English Travellers*, p. 101.

36. Quoted in James Wood Brown, *The Dominican Church of Santa Maria Novella at Florence*, p. 146.

37. See Roberto Salvini, "Il Cappellone degli Spagnoli," in *Santa Maria Novella*, ed. Umberto Baldini; this has some good color plates. See also Raimond van Marle, *The Development of the Italian Schools of Painting*, vol. 3, pp. 425–43; Eve Borsook, *The Mural Painters of Tuscany*, pp. 140–41 and plates 35–38; Miklòs Boskovits, *Pittura fiorentina alla vigilia del Rinascimento 1370–1400*, pp. 32–33; Alastair Smart, *The Dawn of Italian Painting 1250–1400*, pp. 124–25; Hans Belting, "Wandmalerei und Literatur im Zeitalter Dantes—Zwei öffentliche Medien an einer Epochenschwelle."

38. Salvini provides a detailed schematic chart ("Il Cappellone degli Spagnoli," pp. 102–3); see also Diana Norman, "The Art of Knowledge: Two Artistic Schemes in Florence," p. 226.

39. Such is the title given by Borsook, *Mural Painters*, p. 140. Different critics give different titles for the frescoes on the east and west walls; none is definitive.

40. Building began under Arnolfo di Cambio in 1296, although the vault of the nave was not completed until 1378; the aisle vaults were finished two years later. The

famous Brunelleschi dome was not completed until 1436, some seventy years after this fresco was painted. Andrea Bonaiuti had taken part in a competition to complete Arnolfo's work; the dome he gives us is his own vision of what the cathedral-in-the-making should look like. See Salvini, "Cappellone," p. 106; *Italy*, ed. Franz N. Mehling, p. 240.

41. See Harold Goad, "The Suggested Portrait of an Englishman in the Frescoes of the Spanish Chapel," pp. 10–14. Goad draws attention to the "red Lancastrian roses" that adorn the "hood and caperone" of this figure, and to his "shining golden garter" (p. 11). We should note that this fresco, painted *al secco*, has been much retouched over the centuries.

42. Vasari spots not just Petrarch, standing next to a knight of Rhodes, but also Petrarch's Laura, dressed in green, "con una piccola fiammetta di fuoco tra il petto e la gola." See Giorgio Vasari, *Le Vite de' più eccellenti architetti, pittori, et scultori italiani, da Cimabue insino a' tempi nostri*, ed. Luciano Bellosi and Aldo Rossi, p. 157.

43. See Salvini, "Cappellone," pp. 92–93.

44. See Belting, "Wandmalerei," pp. 53–54.

45. See Borsook, *Mural Painters*, p. 141.

46. See W. A. Wallace and J. A. Weisheipl, "Thomas Aquinas, St.," vol. 14, p. 109.

47. See Wood Brown, *Dominican Church*, p. 156. English text follows *The New Jerusalem Bible*; Latin follows *Biblia Sacra*, ed. B. Fischer et al.

48. "et divitias nihil esse duxi in comparatione illius."

49. "et ignorabam quoniam horum omnium mater est."

50. "quam sine fictione didici et sine invidia communico."

51. St. Thomas Aquinas, *Summa theologiae*, Blackfriars ed., vol. 38, 2a2ae.77, 4 (p. 227). Aquinas is quoting from Cassiodorus, *Expositio in Psalt.*, on *Psalm* 70, 15.

52. "Sed contra est . . ." ("On the other hand . . . ," p. 227).

53. Aquinas, 2a2ae.77, 4; translation lightly revised from that of Blackfriars ed., p. 231.

54. Aquinas argues that money is meant to be consumed in its use: "Quaedam res sunt quarum usus est ipsarum rerum consumptio" (2a2ae.78, 1; p. 234). Money that has been given in exchange for the creation of artefacts is entirely consumed at the moment of exchange; its prior existence can only be inferred back from the artefacts themselves.

55. *Summa*, 2a2ae.77, 4; p. 231. *Quaestio* 78, on the sin of usury, follows directly.

56. This line in the Kane-Donaldson edition of B-Text reads as follows: "Men of lawe leest pardon hadde, [leve þow noon ooþer]" (p. 371).

57. On the ideological importance of such supposed muddling, see Corrigan and Sayer, *Great Arch*: "In England, a (slowly and incompletely) rationalizing state continued (and continues) to be legitimated by primarily traditional forms of authority: the power of symbol, ritual, custom, routine, ways in which things have 'always' been done, in which the very bizarreness and anachronism of the forms is its own legitimation, protecting them from 'rational' scrutiny" (p. 193); "the supposed 'anachronisms' of English polity and culture lie at the heart of the security of the bourgeois state in England—to the present day" (p. 202).

58. See *General Prologue* 1.509–11: "And ran to Londoun unto Seinte Poules / To seken hym a chaunterie for soules, / Or with a bretherhed to been withholde"; McHardy, *Church in London*, pp. 14–15.

59. See Thrupp, *Merchant Class*, pp. 187–88.

60. See C. Paul Christianson, "Evidence for the Study of London's Late Medieval Manuscript-Book Trade," pp. 90–92 (and figure 10).

61. See Bowden, *Commentary*, pp. 166–67; *Riverside Chaucer*, pp. 29 and 811.

62. See Baker, *Serjeants at Law*, pp. 103–4; Warren, "Serjeants-at-Law," pp. 935–37; Pilling, *Order of the Coif*, pp. 2–3; McKenna, "Making," pp. 251–52.

63. See Baker, *Serjeants at Law*, pp. 101–4.

64. The practice of new sergeants giving out gold rings is first recorded in 1362: see Baker, *Serjeants at Law*, p. 95. References to Gower follow *The Complete Works of John Gower*, ed. G. C. Macaulay. Book 6 of Gower's *Vox clamantis* opens with a virulent and extensive (400 lines plus) attack on the legal profession.

65. Baker, *Serjeants at Law*, p. 88. Baker's modernized transcription is from the flyleaf of a fifteenth-century register of writs (BL MS Harley 1859, f. 1). See also Edward Foss, *The Judges of England*, vol. 1, p. 24.

66. See Warren, "Serjeants-at-Law," p. 925; *General Prologue* 1.322.

67. Thomas Pynchbek, a sergeant serving as chief baron of the Exchequer, signed a writ for Chaucer's arrest on charges of debt in 1388. Chaucer was summoned to appear at the Court of Common Pleas later in 1388 to answer a plea of debt by Henry Attwood, a London innkeeper; he was summoned again in 1389, 1390, 1393, 1394, 1395, 1398, and 1399: see Crow and Olson, *Chaucer Life-Records*, pp. 384–401. Such a track record led J. M. Manly to suggest that, with the line "Ther koude no wight pynche at his writyng" (1.326), Chaucer recalls Sergeant Pynchbek and his kind with no great affection (*Some New Light on Chaucer*, pp. 147–57). This thesis is rejected by William Askins, who points out, *inter alia*, that Pynchbek enjoyed strong Lancastrian connections ("The Anxiety of Affluence: Chaucer's Man of Law and His Colleagues in Late Fourteenth-Century England," pp. 9, 35). Askin's remarkable paper contains an appendix, described as "a work in progress," consisting of biographical profiles of persons nominated sergeant-at-law between 1362 and 1396.

68. See Alan Harding, "The Revolt Against the Justices," pp. 178–83; Robert Gottfried, *Bury St. Edmunds and the Urban Crisis: 1290–1539*, pp. 233–34; Goodman, *Loyal Conspiracy*, pp. 20–27, 44–45; J. R. Maddicott, *Law and Lordship: Royal Justices as Retainers in Thirteenth- and Fourteenth-Century England*, pp. 59–68; Askins, "Anxiety of Affluence," pp. 2, 8, 23, 39.

69. *Vox clamantis*, ed. Macaulay, 6.43–44, 46: "Vult sibi causidicus servare modum meretricis, / Qui nisi sit donum nescit amare virum, / . . . / Aurum si sibi des, corpus habere potes."

70. J. R. Maddicott, in his study of the king's justices, situates them in an "amorphous world, where bribery and corruption merged imperceptibly with back-stairs influence and the traditional exercise of patronage" (*Law and Lordship*, p. 2).

71. See Derek Pearsall, "Chaucer's Religious Tales: A Question of Genre," pp. 16–17; Barbara Nolan, "Chaucer's Tales of Transcendence: Rhyme Royal and Christian Prayer in the *Canterbury Tales*," pp. 21–38.

72. See Jacques Le Goff, "Merchant's Time and Church's Time in the Middle Ages," in his *Time, Work, and Culture in the Middle Ages*, pp. 29–42.

73. This according to the *Kalendarium* of Nicholas of Lynn, a text Chaucer also employed in writing the *Nun's Priest's Tale* and the *Parson's Prologue*. See Patricia J.

Eberle, note to *Riverside Chaucer*, p. 854 (lines 1–14) and Sigmund Eisner, ed., *The Kalendarium of Nicholas of Lynne*, pp. 29–34.

74. See Jacques Le Goff, *Your Money or Your Life: Economy and Religion in the Middle Ages*, esp. pp. 39–41; Le Goff, "Merchant's Time," p. 30.

75. Lotario dei Segni (Pope Innocent III), *De miseria condicionis humane*, ed. Robert E. Lewis, 1.14, 3–4; *Man of Law's Tale*, 2.99.

76. See *Wife of Bath's Tale*, 3.1177–1206, a passage that attracted a good number of Latin glosses; *De miseria*, 1.14, 16–26, especially lines 16–18: "O shame! A person is valued according to his wealth, when wealth should be valued according to the person."

77. See Chap. 2 above.

78. For an investigation of the possible sources of Chaucer's considerable legal knowledge, see Joseph Allen Hornsby, *Chaucer and the Law*, esp. pp. 7–30.

79. See Brand, "Courtroom and Schoolroom," p. 151.

80. See Baker, *Serjeants at Law*, p. 22. The formal complaint of a plaintiff was known as a *narratio* by the twelfth century; the French term was *count*, hence *countor*, the equivalent of *narrator*. Professional advocates began to speak the *narratio* or *count* on behalf of the plaintiff by 1200, if not before: see Baker, pp. 8–9.

81. See Corrigan and Sayer, *Great Arch*, pp. 33–39.

82. Bartolus (whose teachings gained a hearing at Oxford through Albericus Gentilis, an exiled Perugian) maintained that doctors of law were *milites* for legal purposes: see Baker, *Serjeants at Law*, p. 18; Skinner, *Foundations*, pp. 62–65. Baker points out, however, that although the Order of the Coif obviously drew inspiration from knighting ceremonies, sergeants were invariably placed after knights in public records (pp. 18, 52).

83. See Georges Duby, *The Chivalrous Society*, p. 175; Baker, *Serjeants at Law*, p. 26.

84. "Chaucer as Justice of the Peace for Kent 1385–1389," in *Chaucer Life-Records*, ed. Crow and Olson, p. 349.

85. For more on Burley, see Chap. 12 below.

86. For discussion of Chaucer's classification among the JPs and the reasons for his appointment, see *Chaucer Life-Records*, ed. Crow and Olson, p. 362, and the references therein. The Anglo-Norman phrases are from the statute 34–5 Edward III, c. 1 (1360–61).

87. The sixth, Sir William Brenchley, was made a sergeant before May 1389. In 1390, along with William Rickhill (another of the six) he served on the commission investigating the robbery of Chaucer by highwaymen at Hatcham. See *Chaucer Life-Records*, pp. 361, 477, 487.

88. The use of Nicholas of Lynne's *Kalendarium* makes 1386 the earliest possible date: see Eberle, note in *Riverside Chaucer*, p. 854.

89. On the phenomenon of authorial self-naming, see Middleton, "Kynde Name"; and Chap. 2 above. Middleton argues that "internal signature was . . . more pervasive, formally sophisticated, and diverse in vernacular writings of the thirteenth through the fifteenth centuries than at any other time in European literature before or since" (p. 24).

90. For a succinct and moving account of Usk, who "had a remarkable and

touching faith in the power of the written word to reorganize social reality," see Strohm, *Hochon's Arrow*, pp. 145–60 (p. 145).

91. Donald Sutherland, "Legal Reasoning in the Fourteenth Century: The Invention of 'Color' in Pleading," p. 190. On the relations of pleading procedures to Year Books and Plea Rolls, see W. F. Bolton, "Pinchbeck and the Chaucer Circle in the Law Reports of 11–13 Richard II," pp. 401–2.

92. Sutherland, "Color," pp. 184, 187.

93. Morris S. Arnold et al., Introduction to *Laws and Customs of England*, pp. xiv–xv. For a convenient selection of texts facilitating the study of such argumentation, see J. H. Baker and S. F. C. Milsom, *Sources of English Legal History: Private Law to 1750*.

94. Sutherland, "Color," p. 190.

95. For the progressive narrowing and exclusivity of the Order of the Coif in the course of the fourteenth century, see Baker, *Serjeants at Law*, pp. 14–15.

96. See Middleton, " 'Kynde Name,' " pp. 62–67, for an elaboration of the argument that "the two names, first and last, virtually divide between them one's spiritual and civil identity" (p. 62). Chaucer is addressed as "Geffrey" in *House of Fame*, 729.

97. On Chaucer's access to Trevet, see Robert M. Correale, "Chaucer's Manuscript of Nicholas Trevet's *Les Chronicles*"; on Chaucer's use of the Constance story in the *Confessio amantis*, see Peter Nicholson, "The *Man of Law's Tale*: What Chaucer Really Owed to Gower."

98. See Michael Nerlich, *Ideology of Adventure: Studies in Modern Consciousness, 1100–1750*, vol. 1, pp. 108–82.

99. For more on this, see Chap. 12 below.

100. The need for reliable information technology within highly complex and far-flung international markets may be deduced from Le Goff, *Time, Work, and Culture*, pp. 34–35.

101. See C. Trasselli, *Sicilia, Levante e Tunisia nei secoli XIV e XV*, cited by Branca, ed., *Decameron*, p. 1270.

102. The very clarity of this line of cultural difference creates the possibility for some sympathetic mirroring of Christian/Muslim dilemmas; Roger Ellis writes sympathetically and well of the "thraldom and penance" faced by both Custance and the Sultaness (*Patterns of Religious Narrative in the Canterbury Tales*, p. 146).

103. See Wallace, *Decameron*, pp. 61–67. It is worth noting that in the *Proemio* Boccaccio identifies himself as a man of low degree ("bassa condizione," 3) who has loved a woman above his station.

104. See J. R. S. Phillips, *The Medieval Expansion of Europe*, p. 146. Phillips notes that schemes for the destruction of Moslem commerce put forward by crusaders in the thirteenth and fourteenth centuries were fulfilled, albeit "unconsciously," by the firepower of sixteenth-century European fleets (p. 249).

105. See, for example, J. D. North, *Chaucer's Universe*. In hurrying past the poverty stanzas to concentrate on the *Tale*'s astrological superstructure, North pauses only to comment that their theme "has little obvious bearing on the tale" (p. 484). Their theme, as I see it, posits a direct challenge to the astrological *calkulynge* that fills North's pages; it suggests a different framework for interpreting the causality and meaning of historical events. Astrology plays no part in Boccaccio's *novella*; his Gostanza never appeals to God while afloat on the ocean.

106. My literal translation; for a more elegant rendering, see McWilliam: "Word was meanwhile brought to Lipari . . ." (p. 418).

107. See Giovanni Villani, *Cronica*, ed. Dragomanni, 8.35. The advice offered in Villani and Boccaccio runs as follows: let the archers' bows be fitted with exceptionally fine strings, and let special arrows be made with narrow notches. When each side has fired off their arrows they will gather up those fired by the enemy. But the narrow-notched arrows cannot be fired by the thicker strings, whereas the thin strings can accommodate any size of arrow. "Thus," Boccaccio's Martuccio concludes, "your own men will have an abundant supply of arrows, and the others will have none at all" (p. 421).

108. The most famous example of this is *Decameron* 10.8, in which Sophronia (who never speaks) is transferred from the Greek Gisippus to the Roman Titus. See also Joy Hambuechen Potter, "Woman in the *Decameron*."

109. I employ the term "labor status" here as defined by Martha C. Howell: "Labor status refers simply to the degree to which a person's role in economic production grants him or her access to economic resources—those of production, distribution, or consumption." See Howell, "Women, the Family Economy, and the Structures of Market Production in Cities of Northern Europe During the Late Middle Ages," p. 199.

For some case studies of this process of reducing women's economic powers in the *oikos* (household), see Martha Howell, *Women, Production, and Patriarchy in Late Medieval Cities*; Merry E. Wiesner, *Working Women in Renaissance Germany*; and see the essays in *Women and Work*, ed. Hanawalt. The classic account of women's experience of the transition from preindustrial to capitalist society is Alice Clark, *Working Life of Women in the Seventeenth Century*; for a succinct critique of this work, see Hanawalt, Introduction, *Women and Work*, pp. vii–xviii. Hanawalt observes that "while the authors [of *Women and Work*] have not found a golden age for women's work, those whose studies stretch up to the sixteenth century have found that medieval women had more access to high-status and independent employment than women did later" (pp. xiv–xv). For a critique of this position, see Bennett, "Medieval Women, Modern Women: Across the Great Divide." See also Joan Kelly-Gadol, "Did Women Have a Renaissance?" and (as a critique and elaboration of Kelly-Gadol's question), Merry E. Wiesner, "Women's Defence of Their Public Role."

110. See Christiane Klapisch-Zuber, "The Griselda Complex: Dowry and Marriage Gifts in the Quattrócento," in her *Women, Family, and Ritual in Renaissance Italy*. In late medieval Florence, Klapisch-Zuber argues, "a woman was virtually excluded from a share in the paternal estate. Her father or her brothers dowered her 'appropriately,' but they made every effort to keep her from removing any of the lands that constituted the nucleus of their patrimony" (p. 214). Her husband's family, for their part, "acquired rights over the bride, her labor, and her descendants" (p. 215).

Chapter 8

1. It is important to remember that the great households of medieval England were organized around a person, not a place. The royal household, which was frequently on the move, "was the sum of persons employed in it by the king, and its sole function was to serve the needs of the king" (Given-Wilson, *Royal Household*, p. 29).

The verge of this household was defined as extending out to a distance of twelve miles from the kingly person at its center (Given-Wilson, p. 37).

2. See 1.31–32, and Chap. 2 above.

3. See William Thynne's edition of 1532, conveniently available in *Chaucer*, ed. D. S. Brewer, *The Works, 1532, with Supplementary Material*.

4. See Albertano of Brescia, *De amore et dilectione Dei et proximi et aliarum rerum et de forma vitae*, ed. Hiltz, pp. 290–325. Hiltz's edition of the *De amore* is from a single manuscript, University of Pennsylvania MS Latin 107; her aim is to provide "a readable rather than a critical text of the treatise" (p. xix).

5. James M. Powell, *Albertanus of Brescia: The Pursuit of Happiness in the Early Thirteenth Century*, p. 14, n. 22.

6. An edition of this text, entitled *Ars loquendi et tacendi*, is provided as an appendix to Thor Sundby, *Brunetto Latinos levnet og skrifter*, pp. lxxxv–cxix. This edition is extremely unreliable, since it is "based on six of the thirty early prints of this work and without reference to any of the hundreds of manuscripts in which the work is found" (William Askins, "Chaucer and the Latin Works of Albertano of Brescia," appendix, p. 1). Askins provides a "trial translation" of the *De doctrina*, prefaced by an extremely valuable discussion of Albertano manuscripts in England and the influence of Albertano on Chaucer.

7. "De omnibus ordinibus omnium hominum in hoc saeculo viventium rubrica," in *L'opera poetica di S. Pier Damiani*, ed. Margareta Lokrantz, pp. 144–50.

8. Cambridge University Library, MS (1040) Ee.IV.23, f. 289v. The *ora*, district or quarter, of Santa Agata lay on the western edge of Brescia. Two fifteenth-century English Albertano manuscripts pick up on this mention of Saint Agatha and offer illustrations of the saint: Magdalen College, Oxford, Lat. 7; London, Lambeth Palace, Lambeth 384.

9. Corpus Christi College, Cambridge, 306; see M. R. James, *A Descriptive Catalogue of the Manuscripts in the Library of Corpus Christi College, Cambridge*, vol. 2, pp. 103–4. The table of contents is in the original hand; my translation. The *explicit* to the *De amore* in Cambridge University Library, MS (1040) Ee.IV.23, sharpens suggestively Boethian qualities through the effect of brevity: Albertano "compilavit ac scripsit" this text "cum esset in carcere domini imperatoris" (f. 289r.). In Gonville and Caius College, Cambridge, MS 61, a full-length *explicit*, accentuated by red underlining, takes up almost half a column (f. 481r.).

10. See *Inferno* 23.66; on the punishment of the "capa plumbea" as employed by Frederick and others, see *Inferno*, ed. Singleton, p. 397.

11. *Civilization of the Renaissance*, vol. 1, pp. 24, 92.

12. The Peter Damian verses that are often appended to the sequence of Albertano's works also serve, I would argue, to accentuate the rhetorical character of Albertano's writing. These verses, in 44 four-line stanzas, concern themselves with "all orders of all men living in this world" (*Opera poetica*, p. 144, rubric). Social groupings addressed (and offered nuggets of advice regarding proper conduct) include bishops, deacons, canons, plebeians, teachers (also beaters) of small children, scribes, notaries, lawyers, counselors, hypocrites, drunkards, lay people, wives, rich people, soldiers marching to war, married women, widows, young girls (and potential adulterers). The effect of this is to focus attention away from general rhetorical principles (as

exemplified by Albertano) and toward the needs of particular audiences, or subsets of an audience. The pattern for such a procedure is surely that of Pope Gregory's *Cura pastoralis*, an extraordinarily influential treatise on preaching (mostly) that concludes with a list of 36 pairs of social types that might be preached to: men and women; young and old; poor and rich; silent and talkative; married and single; those with (and those without) experience of the flesh, etc. On Gregory's *Pastoral Care* and its place in rhetorical tradition, see James J. Murphy, *Rhetoric in the Middle Ages*, pp. 292–97.

13. See Vasco Frati, ed., *Brescia nell' età delle signorie*: "Et quod in ipsum magnificum dominum eiusque heredes omne imperium et iurisdictio dicti communis et populi translatum esse intelligatur" (p. 72).

14. See Frati, ed., *Brescia*, p. 72.

15. See Bibliothèque Nationale, MS Lat. 3345. The manuscript was copied at the end of the thirteenth or beginning of the fourteenth century; the Visconti arms were added in the later Trecento. The manuscript contains the three treatises (in their usual fourteenth-century order), five sermons, and the Peter Damian verses.

16. See J. Burke Severs, "The Tale of Melibeus," in *Sources and Analogues*, ed. Bryan and Dempster, pp. 560–614. This includes discussion of Chaucer's translating from Renaud and an edition of *Le Livre de Mellibee et Prudence*. Chaucer made a lifelong habit of employing vernacular intermediaries or substitutes when faced with a Latin text: as Derek Pearsall notes, only two of the Canterbury pilgrims (Parson and Prioress) are given tales that are entirely from Latin sources (*Life of Chaucer*, pp. 241–42).

17. "Latin Works," p. 11.

18. See Ch. 2 above.

19. See *CT* 2.96 ("I speke in prose, and lat him rymes make") and discussion of this line in *Riverside Chaucer*, p. 854.

20. For detailed consideration of the relationship of *Melibee* to this tradition, see Burnley, *Philosophers' Tradition*, pp. 46–55; Patterson, " 'What Man Artow?' " pp. 139–50; Larry Scanlon, *Narrative, Authority, and Power: The Medieval Exemplum and the Chaucerian Tradition*, pp. 206–15.

21. I follow the text established by Mario Roques (based on Paris, Bibliothèque Nationale, Français 1555) in "Traductions françaises des traités moraux d'Albertano de Brescia," p. 496. Roques offers variant readings, which I do not reproduce.

22. For an account of this document, which was incorporated into the *Liber potheris*, see Enrico Guidoni, "Appunti per una storia dell' urbanistica nella Lombardia tardo-medievale," vol. 1, pp. 127–36. The best and most recent account of Italian magnates and their impact on Duecento urban culture is Carol Lansing, *The Florentine Magnates: Lineage and Faction in a Medieval Commune*.

23. See Daniel Waley, *The Italian City-Republics*, pp. 95–103; Larner, *Italy in the Age of Dante*, pp. 87–105.

24. This observation (and much of what follows in this paragraph) is indebted to Powell, *Albertanus*, esp. pp. 74–89.

25. Chaucer's Prudence suggests that Melibee call upon "thy trewe freendes and alle thyn lynage whiche that been wise" (7.1001): but no blood relatives are specified among the "greet congregacioun" that assembles (7.1004–7).

26. Cited by Powell, *Albertanus*, pp. 78–79; my translation.

27. Ibid., p. 80.

28. See Gower, *Vox clamantis*, ed. Macaulay, 6.21, 27, 37, 43, 51, 55, 58, etc. (and see Chap. 7 above); David M. Walker, *The Oxford Companion to Law, causidicus* (p. 193).

29. See Powell, *Albertanus*, pp. 11, 89. Powell notes that the *Liber consolationis* cites sources from Roman and canon law more extensively than any of his earlier works (p. 76).

30. "Quís, quid, cui dicas, cur, quomodo, quando." See Powell, *Albertanus*, pp. 61–62. On the classical rhetorical scheme of the *circumstantiae* and its medieval avatars, see Rita Copeland, *Rhetoric, Hermeneutics, and Translation in the Middle Ages*, pp. 66–76. For the influence of the circumstances on early medieval literary theory, see A. J. Minnis, *Medieval Theory of Authorship*, 2d ed., pp. 16–17, 19.

31. See Albertano, *De doctrina dicendi et tacendi*, ed. Sundby, Prologue: "Tu igitur, fili carissime, quum loqui desideras, a temet ipso incipere debes, ad exemplum galli, qui antequam cantet, ter se cum alis percutit in principio." Translations from this text will follow Askins, "Chaucer and Albertano," Appendix, p. 5. See also *Dei trattati morali di Albertano da Brescia*, ed. Francesco Selmi: "Tu addunque, figliuolo carissimo, quando tu ài volontà di parlare da te medesimo, dei incominciare a simiglianza del gallo, lo qual si percuote tre volte innanzi che canti" (p. 2).

32. "Homo sapiens tacebit usque ad tempus: lascivus autem et imprudens non observabit tempus" (*De doctrina dicendi et tacendi*, 6).

33. See Brunetto Latini, *Li livres dou Trésor*, ed. Francis J. Carmody, 2.62–67 (pp. 236–45).

34. See Claudia Villa, "La tradizione delle 'Ad Lucilium' e la cultura di Brescia dall' età carolingia ad Albertano," pp. 28–39 and plates I.2–IV.1 (showing annotations and drawings in Albertano's hand to Biblioteca Queriniana, Brescia, MS B.II.6); Carruthers, *Book of Memory*, esp. pp. 245–49; Powell, *Albertanus*, pp. 41–42.

35. Albertano served his fellow Brescian Emmanuele Maggi, *podestà* of Genoa, as legal counselor in 1343: see P. Guerrini, "Albertano da Brescia"; Powell, *Albertanus*, p. 3. Guerrini thinks it very likely that Albertano served other Brescian *podestà* in the same capacity, "ma non se ne hanno prove" (p. 669).

36. See Powell, *Albertanus*, p. 63 (where "Quod te non tangit . . ." is more soberly translated as "What doesn't concern you in no way should cause you concern"). The legal formula "quod omnes tangit" rose from obscure beginnings as an anthologized maxim in Justinian (where it applies only to guardian-ward relationships) to celebrity status in the Middle Ages as chief pillar of a theory of consent that was basic to corporate theory and the practice of representative government.

37. See Powell, *Albertanus*, pp. 1–4, 64, 74.

38. See Albertano of Brescia, *Sermones quattuor: edizione curate sui codici bresciani*, ed. Marta Ferrari.

39. As cited in Powell, *Albertanus*, pp. 97–98.

40. Ibid., p. 99.

41. Ibid.; *Sermones*, ed. Ferrari, p. 39.

42. See *The Antifraternal Tradition in Medieval Literature, passim.*

43. Quoted from Speght's 1598 life of Chaucer in *Chaucer Life-Records*, ed. Crowe and Olson, p. 12, n. 5.

44. See Cambridge University Library, MS (1040) Ee.IV.23, ff. 289v., 293v.

45. See *The Friars' Libraries*, ed. K. W. Humphreys, pp. xv, 11, 40. This information is gleaned from an inventory of books owned by the Austin Friars of York made in 1372; the inventory survives as a single folio (5) of Trinity College, Dublin, MS 359. Humphreys deduces that the fourth item listed under item 135 as "liber eiusdem" is a work by Martin of Braga; but the "formula vite honeste" almost certainly refers to one or more of Albertano's sermons.

46. *Time, Work, and Culture in the Middle Ages*, p. 115. Le Goff's discussion of emergent professions (as represented in confessors' manuals) remains useful despite his wholesale recycling of Burckhardtian dicta: "The time of the individual had not yet come, however. The individual was a creation of the modern world, of the Renaissance. . . . Each man's new consciousness of himself came to him only through the *estate* to which he belonged, the professional group of which he was a part, or the trade in which he was engaged" (p. 114).

47. The sermons are followed by the familiar Peter Damian verses, "Episcopi attendite"; there is also a schematic pairing of sins with the social groupings most likely to commit them (merchants and perfidy; rape and knights; pride and Templars / rich wives, etc.).

48. Gonville and Caius College Library, Cambridge, MS 61 (perhaps connected with Steyning in Sussex, a cell to Fécamp Abbey): see M. R. James, *A Descriptive Catalogue of the Manuscripts in the Library of Gonville and Caius College, Cambridge*, vol. 1, pp. 54–55. The tract on the Holy Blood is reportedly nearly identical to that contained in British Library, MS 1801 (librarian's note, Gonville and Caius College Library). The works of Albertano are accorded an extraordinary amount of vellum in Gonville and Caius 61: some 253 folios, in double columns of (mostly) 30 lines in a volume measuring 12.5 inches by 8.5 inches. In a section of Cambridge University Library, MS Ii.VI.39 dating from the early fifteenth century, Albertano's *De doctrina dicendi et tacendi* is again written at a rate of 30 (single-column) lines per page, but on pages measuring just 5 inches by 3.5 inches.

49. See *Le Menagier de Paris*, ed. Georgine E. Brereton and Janet M. Ferrier, pp. 131, 169. The bride is fifteen; the husband must be at least fifty (pp. xxi–xxii). The *Menagier* follows the French version of the *Liber consolationis* by Renaud de Louens. The husband/author, who speaks of the injury that Prudence "et sa fille avoient souf-ferte en leur propre corps," is plainly a literal, rather than an allegorical, reader. Earlier in the manuscript he recites the Petrarch-derived Griselde story by way of teaching his wife "a avoir pacience" (p. 72).

50. See Middleton, "Chaucer's 'New Men' and the Good of Literature."

51. Black, *Political Thought in Europe, 1250–1450*, p. 156.

52. For a detailed account of Chaucer's place in the Ricardian faction, see Strohm, *Social Chaucer*, pp. 24–46.

53. For a fine account of the petitionary and intercessory powers of fourteenth-century queens (Philippa, Anne, Alceste), see Strohm, *Hochon's Arrow*, pp. 95–119. Arguing that "the European zenith of queenly authority occurred in the twelfth century" (p. 95), Strohm goes on to examine the more attenuated public role played out by fourteenth-century queens.

54. *Westminster Chronicle*, ed. Hector and Harvey, pp. 68–80 (1384); Tuck, *Richard II and the English Nobility*, pp. 92–94.

55. See E. F. Jacob, *The Fifteenth Century*, pp. 27–29.

56. See 3.831, 880–81. It is the Pardoner who refers to the Wife as "a noble prechour" (3.165); the Friar acknowledges only that she has delivered "a long preamble of a tale" (3.831).

57. As Powell notes (*Albertanus*, p. 96), Albertano actually cites the example of Jesus cleansing the leper through touch; he may (in preaching among Franciscans) have been mindful of the attitude of St. Francis toward the leper.

58. Ibid., pp. 47–48.

59. Ibid., p. 77.

60. Mario Roques, "Traités móraux," p. 495; my translation.

61. "Persuasive Voices: Clerical Images of Medieval Wives," p. 539.

62. *Exordium magnum Ordinis Cisterciensis* 5.12, *PL* 185, pp. 1147–49; citation followed from Farmer, "Persuasive Voices," p. 536, n. 50.

63. The standard study of this milieu is John W. Baldwin, *Masters, Princes, and Merchants: The Social Views of Peter the Chanter and His Circle.*

64. "Nullus enim sacerdos ita potest cor viri emollire sicut potest uxor" (*Summa confessorum* 7.2.15, as cited by Farmer, "Persuasive Voices," p. 517).

65. Farmer, "Persuasive Voices," p. 542.

66. Baldwin notes that the Parisians took little notice of the peasantry: "The fields without the walls of Paris where the peasant toiled were beyond the ken of Peter the Chanter and his circle" (*Masters, Princes, and Merchants,* vol. 1, p. xii).

67. For careful assessment of the "considerable evidence" that Chaucer's *Melibee* "was made for Richard II," see Patterson, " 'What Man Artow?' " p. 139.

68. Albertano of Brescia, *Liber consolationis et consilii,* ed. Thor Sundby, p. xvi.

69. Albertano, *Liber consolationis,* ed. Sundby, p. xvii; I have amended Sundby's eccentric punctuation. Sundby is moved to add that Albertano "did not, of course, dream of such a thing as Woman's Emancipation" (p. xvii).

70. See Julian of Norwich, *Revelations of Divine Love,* trans. Clifton Wolters. Wolters, an Anglican cleric, is strangely compelled to adopt the posture of a Catholic inquisitor when discussing Julian's writings: "This is wishful thinking and not the teaching of the Church" (p. 37); "As she stands Julian is wrong" (p. 37). "Julian's heresy" is subsequently attributed to a happy home life and upbringing (p. 38).

71. See John A. Alford, "The Wife of Bath versus the Clerk of Oxford: What Their Rivalry Means"; Rita Copeland, "The Pardoner's Body and the Disciplining of Rhetoric"; Tzvetan Todorov, *Theories of the Symbol*; R. Howard Bloch, *Medieval Misogyny and the Invention of Western Romantic Love.*

72. Patricia Parker, *Literary Fat Ladies: Rhetoric, Gender, Property,* p. 16. Parker acknowledges her indebtedness here to Lee Patterson, " 'For the Wyves love of Bathe': Feminine Rhetoric and Poetic Resolution in the *Roman de la Rose* and the *Canterbury Tales,*" esp. pp. 676ff.; and see further Michel Foucault, *Language, Counter-Memory, Practice,* pp. 116–17. For an account of "the Wife of Bath's performance" as "at once enormously affirmative and adversative," see Dinshaw, *Sexual Poetics,* pp. 113–31 (p. 116).

73. Muscatine, *Chaucer and the French Tradition,* p. 207.

74. On the Wife as rhetor, see Alford, "The Wife of Bath versus the Clerk of Oxford"; see also Todorov, *Theories of the Symbol,* pp. 74–77.

75. On linkages "between sexuality, disciplining of the body, and the discipline of rhetoric," see Copeland, "Pardoner's Body," p. 138.

76. The Wife is described in the *General Prologue* as "somdel deef" (1.446), a trait that may be read as a sign of a beaten body in light of the ending of her own *Prologue* ("And with his fest he smoot me on the heed," 3.795).

77. Victoria Kahn, *Rhetoric, Prudence, and Skepticism in the Renaissance*, p. 9.

78. Ibid., p. 30. Kahn gives references to *Nicomachean Ethics* 6.1141b 14–22; 1142a 25.

79. Thomas Gilby, "Prudence," p. 925.

80. Ibid., p. 927. Gilby is here speaking of Aristotle as processed by Aquinas. In the course of a useful and wide-ranging survey of prudence, J. D. Burnley remarks that "to speak of prudence as a virtue in the modern sense of the word is misleading: it is rather to be conceived as a kind of knowledge upon which actions are based" (*Philosophers' Tradition*, p. 53).

81. Noting Aquinas's distinction between the virtue of prudence and *prudentia carnis* ("the prudence of the flesh," worldly wisdom), Burnley goes on to observe that "since the desirable and less-desirable kinds of prudence function in the same way, differing only in their ends and intentions, it is inevitable that when the lower kind of prudence is given praise due to the higher kind, connotations of that higher virtue may be ironically present in our minds" (*Philosophers' Tradition*, pp. 56–57). Once we begin to think of Prudence and Alisoun within the same conceptual frame it is difficult to think of one without recalling the other.

82. Glending Olson, *Literature as Recreation in the Later Middle Ages*.

83. V. J. Scattergood has suggested that the phrase "into the feeldes," added to the second sentence of *Melibee* ("Upon a day bifel that he for his desport is went unto the feeldes hym to pleye," 968), is designed to recall the outdoor location of *Thopas* 7.909–15 and hence establish continuity between the two works: see "Chaucer and the French War: *Sir Thopas* and *Melibee*," p. 288. I would add that the phrase "Upon a day bifel" suggests continuity with *Thopas* by solving (both echoing and completing) its unfinished last line ("Til on a day," 918). The completed form of *Thopas* 7.918 may be predicted from 7.748: "And so bifel upon a day"; see J. A. Burrow, *Essays on Medieval Literature*, pp. 60–65.

84. See, for example, Pearsall, *Canterbury Tales*: "Since they [*Melibee* and the *Parson's Tale*] are not cast as stories, and therefore do not draw upon the imaginative power that resides in stories, and since they are in prose, and demonstrate little interest in the imaginatively self-aware and generative use of language most commonly associated with poetry, they are not, according to certain quite useful distinctions, 'literature' at all" (p. 246). Pearsall later characterizes *Melibee* as "a fat dung-heap" (p. 288).

85. I employ the term "literary kind" as defined by Alastair Fowler, *Kinds of Literature: An Introduction to the Theory of Genres and Modes*. Fowler employs the term "kind" as a synonym for "historical genre" (p. 55).

86. The term *daungerous*, much favored by the Wife of Bath and the *Romaunt of the Rose*, also suggests an appeal to worldly rather than to religious sensibilities.

87. Chaucer's twofold reference to the physical pain suffered by Christ clearly offers a thematic parallel to the pain about to be suffered by two women. Although "the peyne of Jhesu Crist" is not the grammatical subject of its sentence, it can hardly be treated as a topic of secondary importance. So too (Chaucer seems to imply) the physical pain of Prudence and her daughter should not pass without notice.

88. See Robertson, *A Preface to Chaucer*, pp. 368–69; and *Riverside Chaucer*, p. 923.

89. See *A Preface to Chaucer*, p. 368.

90. See Dante Alighieri, *Epistolae*, ed. C. G. Hardie; *Medieval Literary Theory*, ed. Minnis and Scott with Wallace, pp. 441–42.

91. In a series of *lecturae Dantis* begun in October 1373 Boccaccio follows the *Epistle*'s example by paying detailed and particular attention to the literal sense of Dante's poem. He concludes his literal exposition of *Inferno* 10 by declaring that "this canto has no allegory whatsoever" (110); a similar claim is made for *Inferno* 11 (88). See *Esposizioni sopra la Comedìa di Dante*, ed. Giorgio Padoan, in Boccaccio, *Tutte le opere*, ed. Branca, vol. 6.

92. See *Medieval Literary Theory*, ed. Minnis and Scott with Wallace, pp. 444 and *passim*.

93. See Wallace, "Chaucer's Continental Inheritance," pp. 20–25.

94. Pearsall, *Canterbury Tales*, p. 246 (see note 84 above).

95. *Stans puer ad mensam* (Lambeth MS 853) advises: "Intrippe no man where so thou wende, / No man in his tale, til he haue maade an eende" (in *The Babee's Book*, ed. F. J. Furnivall, p. 31, lines 69–70).

96. For more on this *novella* (and on the difficult art of a woman interrupting a man), see Wallace, *Decameron*, pp. 69–70. For early and late medieval writings on the public ideal of masculine speaking and female silence, see Dinshaw, *Sexual Poetics*, pp. 18–19.

97. Much might be said, of course, about the *Convivio* and Albertano's *oeuvre* as parallel attempts, within an Italian city-state structure, to imagine and so create an intellectual elite that does not reproduce the cultural and social patterns of the magnate class.

98. See *Convivio*, ed. Simonelli, 2.1.9.

99. In thinking of Beatrice in glory, Dante weeps such copious tears "that my eyes were ringed with dark red, which happens as a result of some illnesses which people suffer" (Dante, *Vita nuova*, trans. Barbara Reynolds, 39.24–26, p. 95). Translator Reynolds informs us that "in cases of nephritis (kidney disease) red, puffy patches appear round the eyes, similar to the effect produced by excessive weeping" (p. 119). This eccentric endnote splendidly exemplifies a tendency among Dante critics to treat the body of the Dante-narrator of Dantean fiction with the seriousness befitting a historical personage; less attention (and little medical speculation) is devoted to the body of Beatrice.

100. See Rita Copeland, "Why Women Can't Read: Medieval Hermeneutics, Statutory Law, and the Lollard Heresy Trials"; Dinshaw, *Sexual Poetics*, pp. 3–27; Susan Gubar, "'The Blank Page' and the Issues of Female Creativity."

101. See, respectively, Leslie J. Hotson, "The *Tale of Melibeus* and John of Gaunt"; William Askins, "*The Tale of Melibee* and the Crisis at Westminster, November, 1387."

102. The indentation at this point of f. 6r. is caused by a flaw in the vellum.

103. BL Add. MS 6158, f. 6r. See (with a different word order) Albertano, *De doctrina dicendi et tacendi*, ed. Sundby, 3.6; the talk of drunken men is here equated with the *garrulitas* of women. My Middle English translation here follows that obligingly provided by John H. Fisher as part of his text of *Melibee* (7.1062); the line does not actually appear in any Middle English manuscript. See *The Complete Poetry and Prose*

of Geoffrey Chaucer, ed. John H. Fisher, p. 257 (7.1062, a modest emendation of *The Works of Chaucer*, ed. Skeat, vol. 4, p. 204, line 2252). Skeat argues for his translation on the basis that the missing clauses "are absolutely necessary to the sense" (vol. 5, p. 206); *Riverside Chaucer* elects to fill the gap with lines from Renaud de Louens (p. 220).

104. See Albertano, *Liber consolationis*, ed. Sundby, p. 13.

105. "And as to youre fourthe resoun, ther ye seyn that the janglerie of wommen kan hyde thynges that they wot noght, as who seith that a womman kan nat hyde that she woot; / sire, thise wordes been understonde of wommen that been jangleresses and wikked" (7.1084–85).

106. This reader does, of course, have other interests: on f. 12r., for example, he points to lines advising those in authority not to give sons, wives, brothers, or friends any power over them (see Albertano, *Liber consolationis*, ed. Sundby, p. 12; *Melibee* 7.1060).

107. Carolyn Dinshaw notes that "the rape is, in fact, Chaucer's own innovation to the traditional stories that inform his tale, a deliberate alteration that argues for its significance in the whole of the Wife's performance" (*Sexual Poetics*, p. 115).

108. The phrase "into the feeldes" (an addition in Chaucer) need not necessarily imply an excursion to the countryside (since the various "feeldes" in and around London were much frequented as sites of play and recreation).

109. Elaine Scarry, *The Body in Pain: The Making and Unmaking of the World*, pp. 5–6.

110. See 7.1051, 1728 (discussed in the next few paragraphs); the phrase "And whan that dame Prudence saugh hir tyme" (7.1832), which also occurs at a crucial juncture, is discussed below. The phrase "And whan *he* saugh *his* tyme" (emphasis mine) occurs just twice in the *Canterbury Tales*, both times in the avowedly un-rhetorical (but actually highly rhetorical) *Franklin's Tale*. Each instance of its deployment heralds a carefully premeditated speech at a crucial juncture in the narrative, namely Aurelius's first declaration of love for Dorigen (966, introducing 967–78) and his subsequent claim to her love once "the rokkes been aweye" (1308, introducing 1311–38).

111. My understanding of *kairos* is indebted to James L. Kinneavy, "*Kairos*: A Neglected Concept in Classical Rhetoric"; to Susan C. Jarratt, *Rereading the Sophists*; and, more generally, to Rita Copeland.

112. For discussion of principles and strategies pertaining to *quando*, the final section of Albertano's *De doctrina dicendi et tacendi*, see below, pp. 252–56.

113. Daniel Kempton, "Chaucer's Tale of Melibee: 'A Litel Thyng in Prose,'" p. 268.

114. Ibid., p. 268.

115. I am much indebted here and for what follows in this paragraph to Jarratt, *Rereading the Sophists*, esp. pp. 64–66.

116. See *Merchant's Tale*, 4.2001–2: "And whan she saugh hir tyme, upon a day / To visite this Damyan gooth May."

117. See Chap. 4 above.

118. For a comparable agreement of divided *maistrie* (the wife to rule in private, the husband to appear to rule in public, retaining "the name of soveraynetee"), see *Franklin's Tale*, 4.744–52.

119. For a discussion of Chaucer's returning "again and again to the idea of 'commune profit,'" see Pearsall, *Life of Chaucer*, p. 148.

120. Prudence is not arguing that fools are in the majority "at congregaciouns." She is suggesting, rather, that a few talented fools are able to sway the majority. She thus acknowledges that she and the fools work from the same tool chest of rhetorical techniques.

121. See especially 7.1223–31, where the verb *chaungen* is employed six times.

122. See *Parson's Tale*, 10.612–18. Flattery may be considered as misapplied rhetoric that perverts the vital process of self-recognition: "Flatereres been the develes enchauntours; for they make a man to wene of hymself be lyk that he nys nat lyk" (10.615). It is considered among "the vices of Ire," the Parson explains, "for ofte tyme if o man be wrooth with another, thanne wole he flatere som wight to sustene hym in his querele" (10.618).

123. Alisoun of Bath, once again, provides parallel commentary on the feminine and bodily strategies of rhetoric: she controls her first three husbands by mixing techniques of charming and bridling (3.219–21); to achieve *maistrie* over her *irous* fifth husband, however, she has to take a blow to the head.

124. For illustrations and discussion of Bosch's painted table-top, now at the Prado, Madrid, see Ludwig von Baldass, *Hieronymous Bosch*, pp. 15–27 and plates 1–9. Baldass assigns the table-top paintings to the 1470s; Tolnay suggests the influence of miniatures in Netherlandish manuscripts of Augustine's *City of God* (Baldass, *Bosch*, p. 22). The verses beginning "gens absque consilio e[st] sine prudentia" are from Deuteronomy 32.28–29.

125. *Chaucer Glossary, debonair(e)*.

126. See Felicity Riddy, "'Women Talking About the Things of God': A Late-Medieval Subculture," p. 116.

127. On the idea of the *duplex causa efficiens*, which sees God as the first mover of a text and the human *auctor* as its moved and moving agent, see Minnis, *Medieval Theory of Authorship*, pp. 75–84.

128. See Chap. 6 above.

129. To say "I am one who, when / Love inspires me [quando / Amor mi spira], takes note" is appropriate for the terraces of the *Purgatorio* (24.52–53), but would be untimely and out of place in *Paradiso*. Consider further the forms of response offered to the question "who are you?" (following, for example, *Inferno* 28.43, 32.88, or *Purgatorio* 1.40).

130. See *Inferno* 2.67 in conjunction with Brunetto Latini's *Rettorica* as discussed in Wallace, *Early Writings*, p. 59.

131. See Chap. 7 above.

132. Sharon Hiltz DeLong suggests that "Seint Jame" derives from "Seint Jaques" in Chaucer's French source, an error for "Seneques." She also points out that the term "unytee and pees" in 7.1678 expands the French, which speaks only of "paix"; the concern with "unytee" might be read as particularly urgent in fourteenth-century England (*Riverside Chaucer*, p. 928).

133. Prudence appeals here to what Takami Matsuda has termed "professional prudence," characterized as "a kind of professional worldly wisdom with no spiritual depth which the Manciple, the Reeve, the Miller, the Shipman, and perhaps the Mer-

chant in the *General Prologue* abundantly possess" ("Death, Prudence, and Chaucer's *Pardoner's Tale*," pp. 323, 324).

134. See Matthew 5.9: "Beati pacifici quoniam filii Dei vocabuntur."

135. Exclamation marks are, of course, a matter of editorial discretion. The celebrated "A" exclaimed by Palemon on seeing "Emelya" (1.1077–78) is awarded an ! by the *Riverside Chaucer*.

136. See Elaine Tuttle Hansen, *Chaucer and the Fictions of Gender*.

137. Lee Patterson, " 'What Man Artow?' " p. 157.

138. Such is the unhappy state of affairs explored by the *Clerk's Tale* (see Chap. 10 below).

139. The essayists in *Women and Literature*, ed. Carol Meale, are particularly skilled at breaking down supposed divisions between secular and religious institutions: see especially pp. 62, 65, 110.

140. Access to and influence over Edward III by Alice Perrers, "Aliciam quae fuit uxor Willelmi de Wyndesore," was widely condemned by monastic chroniclers, especially Walsingham (*Gesta abbatum monasterii Sancti Albani*, ed. H. T. Riley, vol. 3, p. 249). Alice attended Edward III on his deathbed at Sheen in June 1377; she died just a few months before Chaucer (her will being dated August 20, 1400). For a lurid, moralizing, and intermittently reliable account of Alice Perrers as mistress of Edward III, see F. George Kay, *Lady of the Sun*.

141. Royal Commission on Historical Monuments (England), *An Inventory of the Historical Monuments in London*, vol. 1, *Westminster Abbey*, p. 31. The inscription dedicated to Richard, which accompanies that of Anne, twice refers to him as "prudens" (p. 31).

142. On the relationships of the *Melibee* to written and manuscript culture, see Seth Lerer, " 'Now holde youre mouth': The Romance of Orality in the *Thopas-Melibee* Section of the *Canterbury Tales*"; A. J. Minnis, *Medieval Discussions of the Role of Author* (discussed by Lerer, pp. 194–95, n. 24). On the importance of Anne of Bohemia as a historical surrogate for Chaucer, and on the effects of her death, see Chap. 12 below.

Chapter 9

1. On Anne of Bohemia, see Chap. 12 below; for Richard's wounding of Arundel, see p. 372.

2. For detailed consideration of the crow as court poet, see Louise Fradenburg, "The Manciple's Servant Tongue: Politics and Poetry in *The Canterbury Tales*," pp. 86, 103–8. Fradenburg's fine article offers detailed reference to earlier studies of this *Tale*. On the white crow's voyeurism ("spying and reporting on a sexual love from which he is excluded") as an additional aspect of Chaucerian self-representation, see A. C. Spearing, *The Medieval Poet as Voyeur*, pp. 136–39 (p. 139).

3. See Chap. 2 above. The phrase "miscellaneous predators" is from Pearsall, *Canterbury Tales*, p. 58.

4. The Manciple's interest in timely purchasing is just one of the many things he has in common with his *maistre*, the Man of Law, a great "purchasour" (of land) whose "purchasyng" cannot be invalidated (1.318, 320).

5. William Wordsworth in a letter to Dora Wordsworth of 1840 as cited by *The Manciple's Tale*, ed. Donald C. Baker, Variorum Chaucer, vol. 2, part 10, pp. 19–20.

6. Fradenburg, "Manciple's Servant Tongue," p. 96.

7. The term *pynching* suggests one more link between servant and master, Manciple and Man of Law: see 1.326 ("Ther koud no wight pynche at his writyng") and discussion in Chap. 7 above.

8. Chaucer's poetic diction has often been discussed as a fusion of "vigorous wild stock" with "other more literary and sophisticated styles" (Burrow, *Ricardian Poetry*, pp. 12–21 [p. 21]; see further, Wallace, *Early Writings*, pp. 148–50).

9. See Wallace, "Chaucer's Continental Inheritance," pp. 20–25.

10. For more detailed discussion of Chaucer's imitation of Dante here, see A. C. Spearing, *Medieval to Renaissance in English Poetry*, pp. 27–29; Wallace, "Chaucer's Continental Inheritance," pp. 22–23; J. A. W. Bennett, "Chaucer, Dante, and Boccaccio," p. 107.

11. See Alfred David, "How Marcia Lost Her Skin: A Note on Chaucer's Mythology." Ovid's *Metamorphoses* are described as Chaucer's "oune bok" by the pedagogical eagle in *House of Fame*, 712.

12. For analysis and critique of such terms of reference, see Hansen, *Fictions of Gender*, pp. 15–25, 37–39. For a sophisticated account of "sovereign love," see Fradenburg, *City, Marriage, Tournament: Arts of Rule in Medieval Scotland*, pp. 67–83.

13. My understanding of the will to survive has been influenced by Fradenburg, "Chaucer and the Politics of Salvation."

14. On the tendency of Chaucerian fiction to bring "a woman to represented life so that she may be killed off, lost, silenced, and erased," see Hansen, *Fictions of Gender*, p. 56.

15. See Ovid, *Metamorphoses*, ed. Goold, 6.165–312.

16. On Henry VIII as the biblical David, see John N. King, "Henry VIII as David"; on Lombard despots as David, see above, pp. 46–47.

17. See *Sources and Analogues of Chaucer's Canterbury Tales*, ed. Bryan and Dempster, pp. 701–11.

18. The opening of Albertano's *De inventione* argues that "wisdom without eloquence does too little for the good of states, but . . . eloquence without wisdom is generally highly disadvantageous and is never helpful" ("eloquentiam vero sine sapientia nimium obesse plerumque, prodesse nunquam") (1.i, trans. H. M. Hubbell, p. 3).

19. A fuller citation proves helpful here: "Requiras, quis erit effectus tuae locutionis; nam quaedam ab initio videntur bona, quae malum effectum habent. Quaeritur non solum principium; sed etiam finem et effectum requirere debes" ("You should consider the impact of your speech. Your intentions may seem good when you begin to speak, but the effect of your speech may prove horrible. In all good, apparent evil can be discovered. So speak only if you know not only your reason for speaking but also the impact your speech will have," Albertano, *De doctrina dicendi et tacendi*, 1.5).

20. "Tu requires in animo tuo, quis es, qui loqui velis" (1.1).

21. This summary verse, from Trinity College, Cambridge, MS 1450 (a fifteenth-century manuscript from Glastonbury Abbey) opens an English verse redaction of Albertano's *De doctrina dicendi et tacendi*; Askins describes this redaction as "unrecognized" ("Chaucer and Albertano," p. 9).

22. Although *flo* (OE *flā*) offers many excellent rhyming opportunities, Chaucer uses it only once (here) in his writings, elsewhere preferring the term *arwe*. The term

survives in late medieval ballads and romances; it is very rare by the seventeenth century.

23. "Verba enim sagittis sunt quasi similia: facile dimittuntur, difficile retrahuntur" (1.5). This commonplace metaphor, painfully literalized by the Manciple, is again brought to mind by the moralization that closes his tale ("Thyng that is seyd is seyd, and forth it gooth," 9.355, discussed below).

24. Patricia Ingham's excellent gloss of this particular usage in *A Chaucer Glossary*, *effect* (p. 43).

25. *Parson's Tale*, 10.654 (and introductory rubric).

26. Albertano, *De doctrina dicendi et tacendi* 6, Intr.; *De consolatione et consilii* 2, p. 10; *Melibee*, 7.1045. Chaucer's rendition in the *Melibee* supplies an important forward gloss for the *Manciple's Tale*: "For soothly, he that precheth to hem that listen nat heeren his wordes, his sermon hem anoieth. / For Jhesus Syrak seith that 'musik in wepynge is a noyous thyng'; this is to seyn: as much availleth to speken bifore folk to which his speche anoyeth as it is to synge biforn hym that wepeth" (7.1044–45).

27. See *Riverside Chaucer*, p. 954. The phrasing of Albertano's *De doctrina dicendi et tacendi* 3.1, which may be paired with *Manciple's Tale*, 9.357–58, is particularly suggestive of the ways in which an author may be made a prisoner of his own circulated discourse: "[consilium] revelatum vero te in carcere suo tenet ligatum" (p. 493: "an act of counsel revealed keeps you in *its* prison").

28. Albertano concludes his *Ars dicendi et tacendi* by remarking (6.4) that his treatise will serve as a guide to written composition as well as to speech; just substitute *dicas* for *facias* in the summary verse ("Quis, quid, cur facias . . .").

29. For further discussion of the *lingua materna*, see the next chapter.

30. Lack of fixed location and paucity of formal content are both typical and controversial features of rhetorical, or rhetoric-intensive, texts: see Copeland, "Pardoner's Body," pp. 138–42.

31. See Patterson, *Chaucer and the Subject of History*, p. 187; Juliet R. V. Barker, *The Tournament in England*, pp. 69, 185. Richard had sunbursts pounced on the robes of his tomb effigy: see *Wilton Diptych*, ed. Gordon, p. 53. The same motif was also a favorite device of the Visconti.

32. See Kolve, *Chaucer and the Imagery of Narrative*.

33. See Gower, *Confessio Amantis*, ed. Macaulay, 3.800–801: "And he for wraththe his swerd outbreide, / With which Cornide anon he slowh." Ovid, the *Ovide moralisé*, and Machaut (in the *Voir Dit*) all supply Phoebus with a bow and arrow: see *Sources and Analogues*, ed. Bryan and Dempster, pp. 701–16.

34. On the terminology of "pilgrim signs," see David Wallace, "Pilgrim Signs and the Ellesmere Chaucer," pp. 1–3.

35. See Patterson, *Subject of History*, pp. 179–98.

36. See McKisack, *Fourteenth Century*, p. 447.

37. Ibid., p. 481. For further evidence of the prominent role taken by Cheshire archers in Richard's reign, see McKisack, pp. 449, 475, 484, 487.

38. Translation from *Chronicon Adæ de Usk* by Duls, *Richard II in the Early Chronicles*, p. 84. The Monk of Evesham says that the archers actually began to shoot, but the king stopped them: see Duls, p. 84, n. 53. Caroline Barron notes that all surviving chronicle accounts for the years 1395–99 were written *after* Richard's deposition

and are therefore colored by the needs of Lancastrian propaganda ("The Deposition of Richard II," pp. 132–49). Comparisons drawn between Chaucer's Phoebus and Richard II *after* 1399 would certainly have harmonized sweetly with Lancastrian representations of the deposed monarch.

39. See the exemplum of "irous Cambises," who asserts his arbitrary will and pleasure against "a lord of his meynee" by slaying his son with an arrow (*Summoner's Tale*, 3.2043–73). For further discussion of the *Hof/Gericht* distinction—a distinction elided by the English term "court"—see Chap. 12 below.

40. This subject is explored more extensively in the next chapter.

41. 25 Edward III Stat. 5.c.2, in *The Statutes of the Realm*. For detailed consideration of the short-term motives and long-term consequences of this statute, see Bellamy, *Law of Treason*, pp. 59–176; Strohm, *Hochon's Arrow*, pp. 121–28; Harris, *Proving Treason*.

42. See Strohm, *Hochon's Arrow*, pp. 145–60. On Usk's relationship to court culture and "the Chaucer circle," see Pearsall, *Old and Middle English Poetry*, pp. 194–97.

43. 163, "Stand whoso list upon the slipper top," in Wyatt, *Collected Poems*, ed. Daalder, lines 8–10.

44. We should note, however, that Wyatt does not actually die the violent, court-related death he is so apt to imagine. Anne Boleyn is executed (supposedly within sight of Wyatt's prison cell in the Tower) on May 19, 1536; released in June, Thomas joins his father Sir Henry in entertaining Henry VIII at Allington Castle on July 31.

Chapter 10

1. See Michel de Certeau, *The Writing of History*, frontispiece and pp. xxv–vi; Louis Montrose, "The Work of Gender in the Discourse of Discovery," figure 1 and pp. 3–7; Ella Shohat and Robert Stam, *Unthinking Eurocentrism*, pp. 9, 14, 142–43.

2. "If there is no more 'earth' to press down/repress, to work, to represent, but also and always to desire (for one's own) . . . then what pedestal remains for the existence of the [always and only masculine] 'subject'?" (Luce Irigaray, *Speculum of the Other Woman*, p. 133; see further, pp. 139–40).

3. See Nicholas Mann, "Petrarch and Humanism: the Paradox of Posterity."

4. Ibid., p. 295; Geoffrey Chaucer, *Troilus and Criseyde: A New Edition of "The Book of Troilus,"* ed. B. A. Windeatt, pp. 110–13; Piero Boitani, "Petrarch's *Dilectoso Male* and its European Context"; Robin Kirkpatrick, *English and Italian Literature from Dante to Shakespeare*, pp. 51–56.

5. See E. H. Wilkins, "Cantus Troili," p. 169.

6. See Ronald G. Witt, *Hercules at the Crossroads: The Life, Works, and Thought of Coluccio Salutati*, p. 416.

7. See Quentin Skinner, *Foundations of Modern Political Thought*, vol. 1, p. 108.

8. *Seniles* 11.11 as excerpted by E. H. Wilkins, *Petrarch's Later Years*, pp. 196–97.

9. Margaret Schlauch, "Chaucer's Doctrine of Kings and Tyrants," p. 148.

10. See Anderson, *Lineages of the Absolutist State*, p. 149. Later in this chapter Anderson describes the sovereignty of the *signoria* (the model of polity Petrarch dedicated himself to) as being "always in a deep sense illegitimate," resting "on recent force and personal fraud" (p. 162).

11. From Bruni's *Oration* of 1428, translated by Skinner, *Foundations*, p. 74. See also Wendy Childs, "Anglo-Italian Contacts in the Fourteenth Century," pp. 65–87.

12. See Petrarch, *Familiares* 15.7 (dating from 1352). References to the Latin text of the *Familiares* follow the editions of Vittorio Rossi and Umberto Bosco; English translations follow *Rerum familiarum libri*, tr. Aldo S. Bernardo. See also *Seniles* 10.2 (from 1367), translated and slightly abridged in *Letters from Petrarch*, tr. Morris Bishop, pp. 262–73 (p. 270).

13. See *Familiares* 22.14.

14. See Wilkins, *Later Years*, pp. 236, 239; *Invectiva contra eum qui maledixit Italie*, ed. P. G. Ricci; Winthrop Wetherbee, *Platonism and Poetry in the Twelfth Century*, pp. 242–58 (for the *Architrenius*).

15. In 1357 two of Petrarch's most trusted associates found themselves in London. Bernabò Visconti had convinced himself that Pandolfo Malatesta (to whom Petrarch sent a copy of the *Canzoniere* in 1373) was involved with one of his *amours*. Pandolfo managed to escape to Prague and Sagremor de Pommiers, one of Petrarch's most trusted messengers, was sent in pursuit to uphold the Visconti honor. Sagremor pursued Pandolfo from Prague to London and challenged him to single combat at court on seventeen successive days. Pandolfo failed to show up and Edward III signed a document recording these events. See Janet Coleman, "English Culture in the Fourteenth Century," p. 59; E. H. Wilkins, *Petrarch's Eight Years in Milan*, pp. 132–34, 148–49.

16. See Chap. 12 below.

17. See *Seniles* 17.2 (*Letters from Petrarch*, tr. Bishop, pp. 301–2, contains a short translated excerpt). This letter announces *Seniles* 17.3, containing the Griselde story, which proves (says Petrarch) "how far I am from accepting counsels of inactivity" (p. 302).

18. See Anne Middleton, "The Clerk and His Tale: Some Literary Contexts," pp. 130–35; Charlotte Morse, "The Exemplary Griselde," pp. 55–66.

19. See *Familiares* 18.10, a letter in which Petrarch lays down the conditions for an ideal social and literary gathering or *convivium*.

20. This phenomenon may be amusingly and instructively compared to the peculiar cultural entity that organized itself around Lacan: see Catherine Clément, *The Lives and Legends of Jacques Lacan*.

21. See Petrarch, *Familiares* 20.5 (August 27, 1358).

22. See Wilkins, *Later Years*, pp. 13–14.

23. See Petrarch, *Seniles* 16.3; Wilkins, *Later Years*, pp. 14, 221.

24. See *Lettres de Francesco Nelli a Pétrarque*, ed. Henry Cochin, pp. 24–26.

25. Petrarch explains this policy in *Seniles* 6.5.

26. See Wilkins, *Later Years*, pp. 33–34.

27. See Wilkins, *Later Years*, pp. 161, 92.

28. It was Salutati, then stationed at Avignon, who reported to Petrarch on the reception of his letter deriding the French and warned him that the French cardinals planned to commission a rejoinder: see Berthold L. Ullmann, *The Humanism of Coluccio Salutati*, pp. 80–81. A young Florentine monk informed Petrarch of criticisms leveled at the Mago passage of *Africa* by certain Florentines: this occasioned the lengthy and indignant *Seniles* 2.1, addressed to Boccaccio (who was not one of the critics).

29. See Wilkins, *Later Years*, p. 209.

30. See Witt, *Hercules*, pp. 417–18.

31. See *Familiares* 24.1 (in which Petrarch refers to his own youthful marginalia).

32. Ibid., 21.12.

33. Francis Petrarch, *The Life of Solitude*, trans. Jacob Zeitlin, p. 180.

34. See *De vita solitaria*, ed. G. Martelloti, in Petrarca, *Prose*, Liber II, p. 586: "Dum corpora nostra peregrinatur ab urbibus, peregrinentur a corporibus animi, premittamus illos ad celum."

35. For important discussions of changing conceptualizations of time in this period, see Jacques Le Goff, *Time, Work, and Culture in the Middle Ages*, esp. pp. 29–52; J. G. A. Pocock, *The Machiavellian Moment*, esp. pp. 53–55.

36. See Kenelm Foster, *Petrarch: Poet and Humanist*, p. 19.

37. See Jonathan Culler, "Criticism and Institutions: The American University." Culler argues that Frank Lentricchia, in *Criticism and Social Change*, "convicts Paul de Man and post-structuralism of fatalism and avoidance of history" in a critique "notable mainly for its shrillness" (p. 82). Culler's piece was published in 1987; the wartime journalism became known in October of that year. For facsimiles (not quite complete) of the journalism, see *Wartime Journalism, 1939–1943: Paul de Man*, ed. Werner Hamacher, Neil Hertz, and Thomas Keenan; see also the companion volume, ed. Hamacher, Hertz, and Keenan, *Responses: On Paul de Man's Wartime Journalism*. See also Lindsay Waters and Wlad Godzich, eds., *Reading de Man Reading*, a volume that straddles the moment of disclosure: one contributor "knows," the others do not.

38. Plentiful examples are to be found in Hamacher et al., *Responses*, a volume containing an extraordinary range of the good, the bad, and the awful. It is interesting to note how the de Man "crisis" forces a change in the conventional regulatory procedures of academic practice. The editors explain that their first act in November 1987 was to write to "fifty or so" people who seemed qualified "to produce particularly cogent and informed commentary" (p. vii). Many responded; others sent unsolicited essays. The decision was taken to publish everything submitted, without "monitoring," with no limits on length and with no editorial intervention. An extraordinary space opens up: the volume finally appears as a double-columned quarto of 477 pages; the contributors appear in alphabetical order.

39. Derrida writes: "In the several months to follow, the very young journalist that he will have been during less than two years will be read more intensely than the theoretician, the thinker, the writer, the professor, the author of great books that he was during forty years. Is this unfair? Yes, no" ("Like the Sound of the Sea Deep Within a Shell: Paul de Man's War," in *Responses*, p. 126). Catherine Gallagher, having asked "What has been learned from the revelations about de Man?", concludes: "Everyone learned everything he already knew" ("Blindness and Hindsight," in *Responses*, p. 207).

40. The problematics of defense and/or confession again find instructive parallels in the debate over de Man's wartime journalism. Frank Lentricchia proposes (at least according to an account in *The Nation*) that deconstruction functions as a lifelong defense or confession of a hidden personal and textual past (in that it makes *all* linguistic acts equally unreliable). Geoffrey Hartman suggests that de Man rejected the confessional mode because "confession is an alibi through which one constructs a narrative of self-overcoming, of progressive enlightenment, and hence of present

innocence" (Gallagher, "Blindness and Hindsight," p. 206; Gallagher offers a neat balancing of Hartman against Lentricchia). Petrarch, as a devotee of Augustine, was strongly attracted to the confessional mode that Hartman rejects, but he could hardly *confess* to accepting Visconti patronage in 1354, since he was not about to abjure it.

41. Petrarch's *Secretum* stages an energetic dialogue between Franciscus, a personification of Petrarch, and Augustinus. See the edition by Enrico Carrara in *Prose*, ed. Martellotti, pp. 22–215.

42. See Wilkins, *Petrarch's Later Years*, pp. 171, 173–74, 243; *Petrarch's Eight Years at Milan*, pp. 207–8.

43. See Wilkins, *Eight Years*, p. 9.

44. Ibid., pp. 116–17; *Familiares* 21.15 as translated by Foster, *Petrarch*, p. 29.

45. See Wilkins, *Eight Years*, pp. 167–69.

46. Ibid., pp. 197–98; W. F. Butler, *The Lombard Communes: A History of the Republics of North Italy*, pp. 462–64.

47. See Rubinstein, "Florence and the Despots," p. 35.

48. See Branca, "Giovanni Boccaccio: Profilo biografico," vol. 1, pp. 83–87.

49. See Giovanni Boccaccio, *Opere latine minori*, ed. A. F. Massèra, pp. 136–40.

50. See Foster, *Petrarch*, pp. 27–30.

51. This passage of the *Trattatello*, 1.134–36, is translated and discussed in Chap. 4 above.

52. See Bueno di Mesquita, *Giangaleazzo*, pp. 10–11.

53. Translated by Wilkins in *Petrarch's Later Years*, p. 18.

54. See Francesco Petrarca, *Rime sparse*, ed. Giovanni Ponte, 35 (p. 83).

55. *Seniles* 10.2, translated in *Letters from Petrarch*, trans. Bishop, p. 268.

56. See *Seniles* 16.4. Petrarch exhibits a strange compulsion to advertise his control of eating habits. Strange, but medieval: see H. L. Dreyfus and Paul Rabinow, eds., *Michel Foucault: Beyond Structuralism and Hermeneutics*, p. 229.

57. The real, historical Vaucluse offered Petrarch no hope of refuge in later years; his old home there was burned down. "Now venture to hope for safety in the dark recesses of the Closed Valley! Nothing is closed, nothing is too high or dark for thieves and bandits!" (*Seniles* 10.2 in *Letters from Petrarch*, trans. Bishop, p. 269.)

58. Petrarch, *De vita solitaria*, trans. Zeitlin, p. 312.

59. See *Seniles* 14.1; Wilkins, *Later Years*, pp. 252–56.

60. Probably written in Nov. or Dec. 1367; *Letters from Petrarch*, trans. Bishop, p. 273.

61. *Passages from Antiquity to Feudalism*, p. 23. On the relationship of Florentine *libertas* to the Levant slave trade, see Chap. 1 below.

62. For more on this letter, *Familiares* 21.8, see Chap. 12 below. The anxiety for a male heir was and is, of course, a harsh fact of life for any woman in monarchical or intensively patriarchal society. But a reading of *Familiares* 21.8 does suggest that women's power has diminished over the centuries. Women figure importantly at the beginnings of literacy, art, and history, but their power recedes in the Christian epoch; history becomes masculine, recovering from its own "weak beginning."

63. See Nancy J. Vickers, "Diana Described: Scattered Woman and Scattered Rhyme."

64. Petrarch, *De vita solitaria*, trans. Zeitlin, p. 312. See also the *Wife of Bath's Prologue*, 3.289–92. The "old caution" derives from Jerome: see *Chaucer: Sources*

and Backgrounds, ed. Robert P. Miller, p. 412. For more on violence to the female body as the precondition for Petrarchan poetic utterance (and political metaphor), see Margaret Brose, "Petrarch's Beloved Body: 'Italia mia,'" esp. pp. 9–10 and the bibliographical note at p. 17, n. 4.

65. Petrarch, *De vita solitaria*, trans. Zeitlin, pp. 172–73.

66. This fantasy of masculine molding was shared by men, such as Francesco Datini of Prato in 1393, searching for young and pliable female slaves: see Origo, "Domestic Enemy," pp. 329–30.

67. Petrarch, *De vita solitaria*, trans. Zeitlin, p. 312.

68. See Skinner, *Foundations*, pp. 88–89. Buonaccorso da Montemagna's Latin debate on nobility, translated by John Tiptoft as *The Declamacioun of Noblesse*, takes a more enlightened view of a woman's rights, particularly her right to study. See R. J. Mitchell, *John Tiptoft (1427–1470)*, which includes Tiptoft's translation (pp. 215–41).

69. Boccaccio's Italian maintains a logic of male/female, subject/object relations that is lost in translation: "Nastagio sposatala e fatte le sue nozze, con lei più tempo lietamente visse" (5.8.44).

70. Prof. Vittore Branca is coordinating an international scholarly project that will catalogue some 8,000 Renaissance illustrations of Boccaccio's works.

71. See Botticelli, *Complete Paintings*, ed. Michael Levey and Gabriele Mandel, p. 97. The first three paintings of the sequence are now in the Prado, Madrid; the fourth is the Watney Collection, Charlbury.

72. See Pocock, *Machiavellian Moment*, pp. 60–64. On the peculiar challenges faced by female humanists, see Margaret L. King, "Book-Lined Cells: Women and Humanism in the Early Italian Renaissance."

73. When Actaeon gazes upon the naked Diana bathing he is torn apart by his own desires (hounds): see Vickers, "Diana Described," pp. 97–99. The Nastagio story draws energy from this myth, which Trecento men found so compelling, both by mirroring it and by exacting revenge upon it: here men watch in safety and woman is torn to pieces.

74. Quotations from *Seniles* 17.3 follow the edition of J. Burke Severs, *The Literary Relationships of Chaucer's "Clerk's Tale,"* pp. 254–327. Translations from this text follow *Chaucer: Sources and Backgrounds*, ed. Miller, pp. 136–52.

75. See Roberto Weiss, *The Dawn of Humanism in Italy*, pp. 1–10; Skinner, *Foundations*, vol. 1, pp. 38–39.

76. See John Larner, *Italy in the Age of Dante and Petrarch*, pp. 137–38.

77. One last political irony: the Milanese humanist Giovanni Manzini probably employed Mussato's *Ecerinis* as the model for his neo-Senecan tragedy celebrating the defeat of Antonio della Scala by the Visconti in 1387. See Rabil, "Humanism in Milan," p. 237.

78. Proponents of the "descending" theme of government claimed that their temporal or spiritual authority devolved directly from God: see Ullmann, *Law and Politics*, p. 31. But in these narratives the downward chain of command would seem to be utterly broken: authority can only originate (in accordance with the "ascending theme of government") from below, in the human (civic) world.

79. See Wesley Trimpi, *Muses of One Mind*, pp. 328–29; Olson, *Literature as Recreation*, pp. 164–204.

80. For a succinct critique of past critical attitudes (and of Walter's claims to

divinity) see Giuseppe Mazzotta, *The World at Play in Boccaccio's Decameron*, pp. 122–30.

81. "Si ragiona di chi liberalmente o vero magnificamente alcuna cosa operasse intorno a' fatti d'amore o d'altra cosa" (10.1, rubric).

82. English readers will associate magnificence with the person, court, and theater of Elizabeth I, although Skelton's *Magnyfycence* forms an interesting evolutionary stage between medieval morality drama and the court politics of Henry VIII. See John Skelton, *The Complete English Poems*, ed. John Scattergood, pp. 140–214. For backgrounds to sixteenth-century Magnificence, see Rosamund Tuve, *Allegorical Imagery: Some Mediaeval Books and Their Posterity*, pp. 57–60, 79–82, 98–99. Hoccleve associates the virtue of magnificence with the person of Henry V in the *balade* appended to his *Regiment of Princes* in 1411: see *Selections from Hoccleve*, ed. M. C. Seymour, p. 52, line 15; see also the final stanza of his *Male Regle* (ed. Seymour, p. 23, line 441).

83. See Robin Kirkpatrick, "The Griselda Story in Boccaccio, Petrarch and Chaucer," p. 243.

84. See *Canterbury Tales* 2.1000; 4.815; 7.1664; 8.50; 10.736.

85. Chaucer's text is closer to the French translation at this point than it is to Petrarch. The French sees Petrarch's "magnitudinem" and "humilitatem" as social as well as moral categories: "entre ta grant magnificence et mon humilité et povreté." See Severs, pp. 278–79.

86. See Mary F. Wack, *Lovesickness in the Middle Ages*, p. 109.

87. The celebrated jurist Bartolus of Sassoferrato, whose teachings gained a hearing at Oxford through the exiled Perugian Albericus Gentilis, complemented his treatise on city government with a treatise on tyranny: see Skinner, *Foundations*, vol. 1, pp. 62–65; Ullmann, *Law and Politics*, pp. 108–10. Such analysis of tyranny in the postclassical world is as old as Isidore of Seville. But there is a fresh urgency behind Bartolus's account, reflected by his more complex taxonomy: tyrannies may be open (*manifesti*), disguised (*velati*), or concealed (*taciti*), categories that are further subdivided and subjected to detailed analysis. Such analyses, which served the Florentines well in their ideological battles with the Milanese, were finally subsumed into the most famous treatise of all, Coluccio Salutati's *De Tyranno* of 1400. See Ullmann, *Law and Politics*, pp. 110, 233; Schlauch, "Chaucer's Doctrine," p. 147; Skinner, *Foundations*, vol. 1, pp. 53–56. See also Ephraim Emerton, *Humanism and Tyranny: Studies in the Italian Trecento*, which contains translations of Salutati, *De Tyranno*, and Bartolus, *De Tyrannia*.

88. *Decameron*, trans. McWilliam, pp. 819, 823. McWilliam's translations of the phrases "crudele uomo" (10.10.39) and " 'crudele e iniquio e bestiale' " (10.10.61) are accurate because the epithet "cruel" was routinely applied to tyrants: see Burnley, *Philosophers' Tradition*, esp. pp. 29–43; Susan M. Babbitt, *Oresme's Livre de Politiques and the France of Charles V*, pp. 80–81.

89. Egidio Colonna (Aegidius Romanus), *De regimine principum*, ed. H. Samaritanius, 3.2.6. Egidio notes that the unbridled pursuit of *delectabilia* may induce a tyrant to violate a subject's rights by violating his wife or daughter; he also speaks of the perverse intent ("intentionem perversam") of the tyrant (3.2.7). For an account of "totalitarian Law" as "an obscene Law, penetrated by enjoyment, a Law which has lost its formal neutrality," see Žižek, *Sublime Object of Ideology*, p. 77.

90. Babbitt, *Oresme*, p. 81. Babbitt translates here from Oresme's gloss to Aristotle, *Politics*, 2.22.

91. See Schlauch, pp. 137–40; Skinner, pp. 44–48; Babbitt, pp. 69–97. For the importance of the *bonum commune* to fourteenth-century English writers, see Anne Middleton, "The Idea of Public Poetry in the Reign of Richard II," pp. 94–101; Carol Falvo Heffernan, "Tyranny and *Commune Profit* in the *Clerk's Tale*."

92. Translated from Schlauch, pp. 137, 136.

93. See Michael Wilks, "Chaucer and the Mystical Marriage in Medieval Political Thought," for references to John of Salisbury, Aquinas, Bracton, and Ockham (p. 517).

94. See *Monk's Tale*, 7.2537, 2479, 2470, 2477 (and *Inferno* 5.56: "che libito fé licito in sua legge").

95. See Olson, *Literature as Recreation*, pp. 165–83.

96. Brunetto Latini, in discussing Aristotle's views of city government, emphasizes at the outset that "if each man follows his own individual will, the government of men's lives is destroyed and totally dissolved" (*Trésor*, ed. Carmody, p. 223, trans. Skinner, *Foundations*, p. 44).

97. "Tollenda est igitur culpa, ut cesset a tyrannorum plaga"; cited by Schlauch, p. 138. For a more extensive extract from this passage of *De regimine principum*, Book I, see *The Political Ideas of Thomas Aquinas*, ed. Dino Bigongiari, p. 192.

98. Brucker, *Florentine Politics and Society 1343–1378*, p. 3. Brucker is referring to the period 1338–48.

99. See Chap. 11 below.

100. See *Familiares* 18.7, addressed to Francesco Nelli and dated Apr. 1, 1355.

101. It is interesting to note that the two readings Petrarch appends to his tale answer such questions in precisely opposite ways. The friend from Padua is so moved by tears of compassion that he cannot continue reading. The friend from Verona refuses to weep a single tear because he believes "that this is all an invention." Petrarch himself, not uncharacteristically, refuses to accept responsibility for the tale's fictional or historical status: readers wishing to know whether all this is "a history or a story [an historiam an fabulam]" will be referred to the author, Boccaccio.

102. John of Salisbury argues that in nurturing wild beasts for hunting the lordly hunter deprives "farmers of their fields of grain, tenants of their allotments, the herds and flocks of their pasturage." John notes that some hunters "inspired by this form of vanity have gone to such extremes of madness as to become enemies of nature [hostes naturae], forgetting their own condition and scorning divine judgment by subjecting God's image to exquisite torture" (John of Salisbury, *Policraticus*, trans. M. F. Markland, pp. 6–7; *Policraticus*, ed. C. C. I. Webb, 1.4, 396 a–b).

103. The Visconti were accustomed to seeing themselves represented in saintly or godlike postures in the art they commissioned: see Chap. 1 above.

104. For a detailed comparison of Chaucer's *Tale* and the Petrarchan source, see Severs, *Literary Relationships*, pp. 215–48 and the works cited in Leyerle and Quick, *Chaucer: A Bibliographical Introduction*, pp. 158–60. Derek Pearsall remarks on Chaucer's exceptional fidelity to Petrarch's Latin (*The Canterbury Tales*, pp. 265–66). This certainly makes Chaucer's infidelities easier to spot.

My proposal that the *Clerk's Tale* forms a critique of Petrarch and Italian humanism parallels Renate Haas's reading of the *Monk's Tale*. The Monk, who acknowledges

Petrarch as "my maister" (7.2325), takes great pride in introducing the humanist-revived genre of tragedy to England, a cultural innovation that enjoys little success among the Canterbury pilgrims. See Haas, "Chaucers Tragödienkonzept im Europäischen Rahmen," pp. 451–65.

105. On the importance of the Clerk's *sermo humilis*, see Kirkpatrick, "Griselde Story," pp. 246–48.

106. For a fine account of the costs and strategies of *translation* in this tale, see Carolyn Dinshaw, "Griselde Translated," in *Chaucer's Sexual Poetics*. "In the narrative representation of the *Clerk's Tale*," Dinshaw argues by way of concluding the penultimate section of her chapter, "*translation*—interpretation, all figuration itself—is a turning away from female experience" (p. 148).

107. See *Boece* 2.5, 21.

108. See *Prologue* to the *Legend of Good Women*, F 324, 329, 370, 425, and G 341; *Astrolabe*, Intr. 63. The Second Nun defines her "translacioun" as "feithful bisynesse" (8.24–25).

109. Eugene Vance, *Mervelous Signals: Poetics and Sign Theory in the Middle Ages*, p. 316.

110. See James I. Wimsatt, "The Blessed Virgin and the Two Coronations of Griselde," pp. 188–92.

111. See Vance, *Mervelous Signals*, p. x.

112. See 4.512–15, 671–72, 892–93, 1030–31.

113. See *Squire's Tale*, 5.558–61. This account of treachery through courtly rhetoric is offered by a young Squire who is himself betrayed by the complexities of rhetorical art.

114. See *Vita nuova* in *Opere minori di Dante Alighieri*, vol. 1, ed. G. B. Squarotti et al. For recent, detailed explorations of this topic, see Robert Pogue Harrison, *The Body of Beatrice*; David Wallace, ed., *Beatrice Dolce Memoria, 1290–1990: Essays on the "Vita Nuova" and the Beatrice-Dante Relationship*.

115. See Wallace, "Chaucer's Continental Inheritance," pp. 33–34; Wallace, *Chaucer and the Early Writings of Boccaccio*, pp. 15, 103–4, 137–40.

116. *Inferno* 32.7–9 in the translation of Allen Mandelbaum.

117. *Purgatorio* 1.7. On the subject of "morta poesia," see Robin Kirkpatrick, *Dante's "Inferno": Difficulty and Dead Poetry*.

118. See the discussion of *Paradiso* 33.106–8 in Chap. 9 above.

119. See *Convivio*, ed. Simonelli, I.xiii.4.

120. *De vulgari eloquentia*, ed. P. V. Mengaldo, I.i.2.

121. Juxtaposition of the *Monk's Tale*'s "vicious" Nero and the *Clerk's Tale*'s Walter should end all speculation that the latter can in any way be read as a figure of the Christian God.

122. The reunion of Griselde and Walter, in other words, forms the core of the linguistic community ideally envisaged by Dante's *De vulgari*.

123. See *The Former Age*, in *Riverside Chaucer*, ed. Benson, pp. 650–51, lines 1, 33, 41.

124. For Nimrod as tyrant, see Michael Wilks, *The Problem of Sovereignty in the Later Middle Ages*, p. 540. See also *Inferno* 31.34–81.

125. See Chap. 5 above. The revisionary thrust of this paragraph is indebted to a reading of Justice, *Writing and Rebellion*, esp. p. 227.

126. When Prudence advises Melibee to assemble "thy trewe freendes and thy lynage which that been wise," her spouse "leet callen a greet congregacioun of folk" (7.1002, 1004). Prudence later explicitly critiques such "congregaciouns and multitudes of folk, there as men take moore reward to the nombre than to the sapience of persones"; in such assemblies, "fooles han the maistrie" (7.1259–60).

127. Since *volgo* culture is strictly antithetical to humanist values, however, it proves indispensable to the structuration of humanism. The (often comical) consequences of this are explored in the next chapter.

128. See Jean-Paul Sartre, *Being and Nothingness*, trans. Hazel E. Barnes, pp. 340–400, esp. pp. 352, 384. But see also Jacques Lacan, "Of the Gaze as *Objet Petit a*," in *The Four Fundamental Concepts of Psycho-Analysis*, ed. J.-A. Miller, pp. 74–77.

129. "If there is an Other . . . then I have an outside, I have a *nature*" (Sartre, *Being and Nothingness*, p. 352).

130. For a powerful account of the effects of undropped female gazing on masculine would-be observers, see Sarah Stanbury, "Feminist Masterplots: The Gaze on the Body of *Pearl*'s Dead Girl." "The woman's directed gaze," Stanbury argues in her final paragraph, "recasts maternal power, both desired and disavowed" (p. 110).

131. See *Familiares* 22.1.

132. "Virum bonum, ydiotam ferunt"; "me sine litteris virum bonum." Quoted from the *De ignorantia* by Wilkins, *Later Years*, p. 92. For the Latin text, see *Opere latine di Francesco Petrarca*, ed. Antonietta Bufano, vol. 2, pp. 1025–1151. For a convenient translation, see *The Renaissance Philosophy of Man*, ed. Ernst Cassirer et al., pp. 47–133.

133. Foster, *Petrarch*, p. 151 (summarizing from passages of *De ignorantia*). I accept the central thesis of John Alford's "The Wife of Bath versus the Clerk of Oxford" (that this rivalry enacts a time-honored conflict between logic and rhetoric) but not the suggestion (p. 114) that Petrarch has a foot in both camps. Petrarch knows and shows himself to be a rhetor, a Wife rather than a Clerk.

134. See Chap. 8 above.

135. In his *envoy* to Bukton, Chaucer warns a male friend that, once married, he will be "thy wives thral," citing as his authority "the Wyf of Bath" (*Riverside Chaucer*, ed. Benson, pp. 655–66).

136. Joy Hambuechen Potter observes that with this "change of theme and register," Dioneo "blows the noble frame of the tenth day stories wide open." See Potter, *Five Frames for the Decameron*, p. 151.

137. John of Salisbury, *Policraticus*, trans. Markland, p. 35; ed. Webb 3.4.481a.

138. Rosalind Field astutely notes, however, that in Chaucer's Lombard *fabliau*—the *Merchant's Tale*—fear of death weighs heavier on the protagonists than it does on native soil; "none of Chaucer's English adulterers risk more than a bloody nose or a scalded *towte*" ("Reading Pavia: Civic Reputation and Critical Response").

139. The death of a third Lombard tyrant—Galeazzo, Petrarch's principal patron—makes it likely that Chaucer visited Pavia in the summer of 1378: see Chap. 1 above.

140. See *Eulogium historiarum*, ed. L. S. Haydon, vol. 3, p. 378; see also Gransden, *Historical Writing*, vol. 2, p. 183; Steel, *Richard II*, p. 278; McKisack, *Fourteenth Century*, p. 490.

141. See Royal Commission, *Westminster Abbey*, p. 25; Tancred Borenius and E. W. Tristram, *English Medieval Painting*, p. 26. A large altarpiece at Rome in the

seventeenth century, now lost, depicted Richard and Anne of Bohemia kneeling before the Virgin: see Gordon, *Wilton Diptych*, p. 58.

142. See *De laudibus legum Anglie*, ed. Chrimes, p. 45.

143. *Rotuli Parliamentorum*, vol. 3, p. 416 (part of article 33) as translated in *English Historical Documents 1327–1485*, ed. A. R. Myers, p. 410. For a detailed analysis of article 33 and the deposition process, see Larry Scanlon, "The King's Two Voices: Narrative and Power in Hoccleve's *Regement of Princes*," pp. 216–26; Strohm, *Hochon's Arrow*, pp. 75–82.

144. Myers, *English Historical Documents*, p. 410. Richard is perhaps appealing to an English royal tradition that held that the king's government proceeds from mere will ("mera et spontanea voluntate," a phrase that was expunged from the reissue of Magna Carta in 1216). See Wilks, *Mystical Marriage*, p. 509.

145. For the concept of *sponsus regni*, see Wilks, *Mystical Marriage*, pp. 500–501; E. H. Kantorowicz, *The King's Two Bodies: A Study in Medieval Political Theology*, pp. 221–26.

146. This statement appears in Trinity College, Cambridge, MS R.3.20. The envoy in this manuscript is headed "Lenvoye to kyng Richard": see Laila Z. Gross, notes to *Riverside Chaucer*, p. 1085. See also Wilks, "Mystical Marriage," pp. 500–504. Paul Strohm argues that *Lak of Stedfastnesse* was probably written "in support of the king's attempt to broaden his popular base by opposing livery and maintenance in 1388–89" (*Social Chaucer*, p. 204, n. 14). For information on the scribe, compiler, translator, and literary salesman John Shirley (c. 1366–1456), see A. I. Doyle, "More Light on John Shirley"; R. J. Lyall, "Materials: The Paper Revolution," pp. 16–21; Julia Boffey and John J. Thompson, "Anthologies and Miscellanies: Production and Choice of Texts," pp. 284–88 (with a helpful bibliographical note at p. 305, n. 26). On Shirley and *Lak of Steadfastnesse*, see Seth Lerer, *Chaucer and His Readers*, pp. 122–29.

Chapter 11

1. *De casibus* is hence of interest in reversing the usual necrophiliac thrust of English literary genres: rather than feeding on the death of women, usually young and beautiful women, the genre sustains and extends itself through the serial killing of powerful men.

2. See Stephen Greenblatt, Introduction to *The Power of Forms in the English Renaissance*, p. 4; Jonathan Dollimore, Introduction to *Political Shakespeare*, pp. 8–9.

3. *The Works of Geoffrey Chaucer*, 2d ed. by F. N. Robinson, p. 709; *Riverside Chaucer*, ed. Benson, p. 879. Both editions recognize their indebtedness here to A. S. Cook, "Chauceriana, II: 'Nayled in his cheste.'"

4. *Riverside Chaucer*, p. 879.

5. See Wilkins, *Later Years*, p. 271. For a brief overview of the long history of humanist and literary pilgrimages to Petrarch's tomb, see Umberto Bosco, "Realtà e mito di Arquà," pp. 1–5.

6. *Petrarch and His World*, p. 375.

7. Petrarch makes this clarification in the course of his *Invective contra medicum*: "Here one speaks not of doctors nor of poets and philosophers, but only of those who distinguished themselves through military prowess or by great service to the state" (*Opere latine*, ed. Bufano, vol. 2, p. 862). Were the *De viris illustribus* to be devoted

to a doctor, Petrarch argues, it would need to be retitled *De insigni fatuo* (*Notable Nitwit*) (vol. 2, p. 862).

8. On this tradition, see Piero Boitani, *Chaucer and the Imaginary World of Fame*; Wallace, *Early Writings*, pp. 5–22.

9. See Theodor M. Mommsen, "Petrarch and the Decoration of the Sala Virorum Illustrium in Padua," p. 113; Galvano Fiamma, *Opusculum*, ed. C. Castaglioni, p. 17. I am not suggesting these portraits conform to a Petrarchan model, but rather that their existence at Milan suggests a receptive environment for Petrarch's interest in *viri illustres*.

10. See Mommsen, "Sala Vivorum," p. 106; Giuseppe Billanovich, *Petrarca letterato. I. Lo scrittoio del Petrarca*, pp. 318–20; Wilkins, *Later Years*, pp. 295–302. Mommsen points out that the name "Sala Virorum Illustrium" appears in Paduan documents of the years 1382 and 1390 (p. 100). He also notes that Francesco da Carrara only commissioned the frescoes after Petrarch had dedicated the *De viris* to him (p. 96).

11. This full-length portrait, much repainted, corresponds closely to the frontispiece of an Italian translation of Petrarch's *De viris* dating from the early fifteenth century: see Diana Norman, " 'Splendid Models and Examples from the Past': Carrara Patronage of Art," vol. 1, pp. 165–66.

12. See Foster, *Petrarch*, p. 5; Natalino Sapegno, *Il Trecento*, pp. 215–16; Roberto Weiss, *The Spread of Italian Humanism*, pp. 25–26.

13. See Petrarch, *Secretum*, ed. Carrara, pp. 204–14. For fine analyses of the third and final book of the *Secretum*, see Foster, *Petrarch*, 174–85; F. Rico, *Vida u Obra de Petrarca: I, Lectura del "Secretum."*

14. My translation here is from the edition of Guido Martellotti in *Prose*, ed. Martellotti et al., pp. 218–20. This edition offers the 1351–53 *prohemium* and the life of Adam complete, plus extracts from three Roman lives and chap. 20 of the *De gestis Cesaris*. The complete *De viris* edited by Martellotti for the Edizione Nazionale delle Opere di Francesco Petrarca features a later *prohemium*, intended for the eyes of Francesco da Carrara; "naturally enough," Martellotti observes laconically, "the recriminations against modern princes . . . have disappeared" (p. cxxx).

15. See *Prose*, ed. Martellotti et al., p. 219, n. 4.

16. For a succinct account of the complex history of Petrarch's lifelong revising of the *De viris*, see *Prose*, ed. Martellotti et al., pp. 1163–66. The first sequence, according to Martellotti, was completed c. 1341–43. The second sequence (1351–53) features figures familiar from medieval encyclopaedic tradition, such as Adam, Nimrod, Semiramis, and Hercules. Following some intermittent tinkering, Petrarch worked on a final sequence in his last years that returns to the preponderantly Roman emphasis of the 1341–43 version. This repeats the 23 lives of the first version (from Romulus to Cato) and adds the *De gestis Cesaris*. Following Petrarch's death, the sequence was extended to 36 (as far as Trajan) by Lombardo della Seta.

17. See Mommsen, "Sala Virorum Illustrium," pp. 98–99.

18. See *De viris*, pp. 220–22.

19. See ibid., p. 222: "Quis Gothorum et Unnorum et Vandalorum atque aliarum gentium reges ab ultimis repetitos in orderem digerat . . . ?"

20. *Servus* may be translated either as "slave," "serf," or "servant."

21. *De viris*, p. 224.

22. Ibid.: "Accessit et statura corporis et origo et genus mortis."

23. In the course of a single lengthy period, Petrarch applies the terms "dulce," "delectabilem," and "dulcedinem" to the fruits and process of recalling the lives of great men (ibid.).

24. See *De casibus virorum illustrium*, ed. Pier Giorgio Ricci and Vittorio Zaccaria, in Boccaccio, *Tutte le opere*, ed. Branca, vol. 9, 1.1–2. This volume, published in 1983, is difficult to find, particularly in England. See also Boccaccio, *Opere in versi*, ed. P. G. Ricci, p. 794. This edition of the second (1373) version of the *De casibus* includes only the dedication to Mainardo Cavalcanti, the opening of Book 1 and the whole of Book 9. For discussion of Boccaccio's *De casibus* in relation to *Fürstenspiegel* traditions, see Scanlon, *Narrative, Authority, and Power*, pp. 119–34.

25. See *De casibus* 3.9. The lineaments of this story may be gleaned from Boccaccio, *The Fates of Illustrious Men*, trans. L. B. Hall, pp. 89–94. Hall's translation, which includes about half of Boccaccio's text, is from the 1520 Paris edition of Jean Gourmont and Jean Petit. Ricci points out that the text presented by the printed editions of the fifteenth and sixteenth centuries is "incredibly disfigured by changes of every kind" (*Opere in versi*, p. 1280).

26. Between 1495 and 1602, translations of the *De casibus* appeared in fourteen French, five Italian, four English, three Spanish, and two German editions. See Vittore Branca, *Tradizione delle opere di Giovanni Boccaccio*, vol. 1, pp. 84–89, *Opere in versi*, ed. Ricci, p. 1278. See also *De casibus*, ed. Ricci and Zaccaria, p. LII.

27. Ricci bases his edition on these two manuscripts: see *Opere in versi*, p. 1279.

28. It is worth noting that even Petrarch's "Augustinus" offers qualified approval of Petrarch's understanding of *gloria*: "Ut inglorius degas nunquam consulam, at ne glorie studium virtuti preferas identidem admonebo" (*Secretum*, in *Prose*, ed. Martellotti et al., p. 204: "I will never counsel you to live without fame; but at the same time, I will continue to warn you not to prefer the quest for fame to the pursuit of virtue.")

29. On the association of tyrants with plague, which makes Griselde's resistance to the tyranny of Walter such a fitting end to the *Decameron*, see above, p. 281.

30. This protestation of earth-bound consciousness, with its Boethian and Dantean subtexts, finds its Chaucerian counterpart at the opening of Book 2 of the *House of Fame*.

31. See Franco Simone, "La présence de Boccace dans la culture français du XVe siècle," pp. 24–25.

32. See esp. *De viris*, pp. 224–26.

33. See *Decameron* 8.7 and discussion in Wallace, *Decameron*, pp. 87–91.

34. On "the representation of various literary acts—reading, translating, glossing, creating a literary tradition—as masculine acts performed on [a] feminine body," see Dinshaw, *Sexual Poetics* (p. 17).

35. See Cooper, *Canterbury Tales*, pp. 325–30; *Riverside Chaucer*, pp. 929–30.

36. See Piero Boitani, "The *Monk's Tale*: Dante and Boccaccio," p. 67; Peter Godman, "Chaucer and Boccaccio's Latin Works," p. 272–80.

37. Michel Foucault, "What Is an Author?" in *Language, Counter-Memory, Practice*, p. 123.

38. Ibid., p. 121. Jerome wrote 135 lives (of men as writers), beginning with the

apostle Peter and ending with himself; the sequence was continued by Gennadius. See Gerolamo, *Gli uomini illustri (De viris illustribus)*, ed. Aldo Ceresa-Gastoldo.

39. For an illuminating account of Chaucer's reactions to "the revived interest in tragedy, in particular Senecan tragedy," see Renate Haas, "Chaucer's *Monk's Tale*: An Ingenious Criticism of Early Humanist Conceptions of Tragedy," p. 44. Haas, "Chaucer's Tragödienkonzept im Europäischen Rahmen," represents an earlier version of the first part of the "Ingenious Criticism" article. Although her interest in tragedy induces her to confine discussion of Petrarchan texts almost exclusively to the *De remediis*, Haas does acknowledge that Boccaccio "received a decisive impulse for his *De casibus virorum illustrium* from Petrarch's *De viris illustribus*" ("Ingenious Criticism," p. 67).

40. On the Host's disenchantment with the *Monk's Tale* for its failure to provide "a practical 'remedie' (7.2784–5) for Fortune's havoc," see Lisa Kiser, *Truth and Textuality in Chaucer's Poetry*, p. 124. For a translation of and extensive commentary upon the *De remediis*, see Conrad H. Rawski, *Petrarch's Remedies for Fortune Foul and Fair*.

41. Foster, *Petrarch*, p. 18.

42. Cambridge University Library, MS Ii.VI.39, contains a Middle English translation of the first eleven dialogues of the *De remediis* (ff. 177r.–188r.). The translation, dated to the first quarter of the fifteenth century, has been edited by F. N. M. Diekstra as *A Dialogue Between Reason and Adversity: A Late Middle English Version of Petrarch's "De Remediis."* The ten sections of the manuscript are of different dates, but its contents indicate that part of it "formed quite a typical collection for religious with contemplative interests" (p. 9). The *Dialogue* appears in the sixth section of the manuscript; it is immediately preceded by Albertano of Brescia's "Liber de doctrina dicendi et tacendi" (*explicit*, f. 177r.). This is a complete text of the *De doctrina dicendi et tacendi* (ff. 166r.–177r.) and not, as Diekstra suggests, "only the first book" (p. 7). The first of the "later scribbles in English" that Diekstra reports at the end of the *Dialogue* section of this manuscript (f. 189v.; p. 7) is in fact a four-line religious verse rhyming *abcb*.

43. *Dialogue*, ed. Diekstra, Introduction, p. 16.

44. In the opening essay of the most recent book on Chaucer's religious tales, Derek Pearsall situates the *Monk's Tale* at "the core of the genre, what I have called the narratives of faith." But it is instructive to note that none of the twelve contributors who follow have anything at all to say about the *Monk's Tale* (except R. W. Frank, Jr., who denies it religious status in a footnote). See *Chaucer's Religious Tales*, ed. C. David Benson and Elizabeth Robertson, p. 16; p. 42, n. 6.

45. *Riverside Chaucer*, gloss to 7.1945, p. 240.

46. This proposition confirms Herry in the "distaff" position to which Goodelief has assigned him. Barbara Spackman, in her analysis of the gender politics of Italian fascism, argues thus: "If other men desire to be the man women desire, they also desire the man and hence . . . have been similarly seduced and are therefore, metaphorically, women" ("The Fascist Rhetoric of Virility," p. 84).

47. See Donald Fry, "The Ending of the *Monk's Tale*," pp. 361–64.

48. On the phenomenon of "male homosexual panic," see Eve Kosofsky Sedgwick, *Between Men: English Literature and Male Homosocial Desire*, pp. 83–96.

49. *Oxford Guide*, p. 334.

50. The offer is made by the Host: "sey somwhat of huntyng" (7.2805).

51. See Haas, "Ingenious Criticism," p. 65; D. E. Berndt, "Monastic *Acedia* and Chaucer's Characterization of Daun Piers."

52. Haas, "Ingenious Criticism," pp. 62, 63, 67, 68.

53. Winthrop Wetherbee argues that "with astonishing regularity the Monk's versions of the lives of his tragic heroes attenuate their tragic force and rob them of the moral and historical complexity inherent in their biblical and classical sources" ("The Context of the *Monk's Tale*," p. 167).

54. See Boitani, "The *Monk's Tale*: Dante and Boccaccio."

55. N. F. Blake does place the "modern instances" at the end of the *Monk's Tale*: see his Chaucer, *The Canterbury Tales: Edited from the Hengwrt Manuscript.*

56. The fullest case for placing the "modern instances" at the end of the series of tragedies in future editions of Chaucer has been made by Fry, "The Ending of the *Monk's Tale*." Fry offers some cogent arguments and a helpful survey of a complex manuscript situation. One of the stronger arguments adduced to support a medial position for the "modern instances" concerns the Host's echoing of the last line of "Cresus": "And covere hire brighte face with a clowde" (2766); "He spak how Fortune covered with a clowde . . ." (2782). If the "modern instances" are placed last, some 88 lines separate these two *clowdes*. Fry, repeating Tyrwhitt, suggests that the Host nods off in the interim (pp. 358–59): not an entirely convincing argument.

57. The Ugolino episode has been translated into English more frequently than any other Dantean passage; Paolo and Francesca run a poor second. See Wallace, "Dante in English," pp. 237–38.

58. See Michael Packe, ed. L. C. B. Seaman, *King Edward III*, p. 269. See also Richard Barber, *Edward, Prince of Wales and Aquitaine: A Biography of the Black Prince*, pp. 198–205.

59. My citation of line 2378 here follows that of the manuscript groups associated with Harley 7334, Corpus Christi College, Oxford 198, and Petworth House MS 7. See *The Text of the Canterbury Tales*, ed. John M. Manly and Edith Rickert, vol. 2, pp. 406–9; vol. 4, p. 236. See also Ralph Hanna III's comments in *Riverside Chaucer*, p. 1132.

60. See Packe, *Edward III*, p. 262. It was further claimed that Pedro burned a friar to death for prophesying that he would be murdered by Don Enrique of Trastamara. (Don Enrique was the eldest of three sons born to Leonora de Guzmán, mistress of Pedro's father Alfonso XI.) Such claims were, of course, made in the writings of Pedro's political enemies: see Packe, p. 262; Russell, *English Intervention*, pp. 16–22, 95–96.

61. See Pearsall, *Chaucer*, p. 52; George Lyman Kittredge, *The Date of Chaucer's "Troilus" and Other Chaucer Matters*, p. 45.

62. See McKisack, *Fourteenth Century*, pp. 441–42; Russell, *English Intervention*, pp. 509–10.

63. Catalina became an important diplomatic contact for the English court, especially after the accession of her Lancastrian half-brother, Henry IV. She became even more powerful in 1406 when, following the death of her husband, she became co-regent of Castile during the minority of her son, Juan II. See Russell, *English Intervention*, pp. 551–52.

64. Arguments affirming that the "bastard brother" line was subsequently re-vised by Chaucer are advanced by Manly and Rickert (*Text*, vol. 2, pp. 406–9); see

also Fry, "Ending," pp. 360–61. Manly and Rickert's argument is strengthened by the fact that putative later revision also explains the improvement of line 2426 from "Ugolino": "He herde it wel" (the shutting of the tower door) "but he spak right noght"(Ellesmere and Hengwrt) makes much better sense and is closer to Dante than "He herd it wel but he saugh it noght."

65. See Pearsall, *Life of Chaucer*, pp. 51–53, 141–42.

66. The prince's health seems to have gone into rapid decline "from the moment of his triumph of Nájera" (Packe, *Edward III*, p. 274); see also W. M. Ormrod, *The Reign of Edward III: Crown and Political Society in England, 1327–1377*, p. 29.

67. See Barber, *Black Prince*, pp. 182–206; Russell, *English Intervention*, pp. 553–54. Russell argues that the events of 1369 led directly to a "lamentable seventy-five years of civil strife" (p. 553).

68. See Russell, *English Intervention*, pp. 16–22, 554.

69. See Jean Froissart, *Chroniques*, ed. Siméon Luce et al., vol. 6, pp. 89–92.

70. See, respectively, *Seniles* 8.8, dated July 20, 1367 (addressed to Boccaccio; see also *Seniles* 13.2, dated Nov. 4, 1369, addressed to Philippe de Mézières, lamenting Peter's death); *Chaucer's Knight*, p. 44. Jones is hardly guilty of hyperbole here: the massacres at Alexandria, according to Steven Runciman, "were only equalled by those of Jerusalem in 1099 and Constantinople in 1204"; some five thousand prisoners, "Christians and Jews as well as Moslems," were sold into slavery. See Runciman, *A History of the Crusades*, vol. 3, p. 448 (cited by Jones, p. 44).

71. See Peter W. Edbury, *The Kingdom of Cyprus and the Crusades, 1191–1374*, pp. 173–79.

72. Ibid., p. 174.

73. See Thomas J. Hatton, "Chaucer's Crusading Knight, a Slanted Ideal," pp. 84–86; Fry, "Ending," p. 357.

74. As transcribed and translated in Hatton, "Crusading Knight," pp. 86–87.

75. *A Commentary on the General Prologue*, pp. 55–69 (Bowden becomes as besotted with Peter of Cyprus as any medieval devotee).

76. Fry, "Ending," p. 366.

77. See *An Edition and Study of Guillaume de Machaut's "Prise d'Alixandre,"* Angela Doreen Dzelzainis, p. 32; Costas P. Kyrris, *History of Cyprus*, p. 230. Cyprus, in the mid-fourteenth century, was a place of refuge for scholars, poets, and astronomers from Byzantium and neighboring countries (Costas, pp. 229–30).

78. Jean Froissart, *Le joli Buisson de Jonece*, ed. Anthime Fourier, lines 348–50.

79. See Wimsatt, *The Marguerite Poetry of Guillaume de Machaut*, pp. 40–65.

80. Ibid., pp. 60–62. The "wonderful mule" is described by the chronicler Leontios Makhairas; the queen made good her escape on it after Pierre's death.

81. Ibid., pp. 40–41. Wimsatt further demonstrates that Machaut's *Dit de la Marguerite*—a poem that was to influence Froissart, Deschamps, and Chaucer—imagines Pierre as the lover, thinking of his *Marguerite* when he is "en Chipre ou en Egypte" ("in Cyprus or in Egypt," i.e., Alexandria: see Wimsatt, pp. 47–49).

82. Dzelzainis argues that the poem appeared "sometime between late 1369 and 1371" (*Prise*, p. 44).

83. The anagram occurs three times in the text, at lines 244–45, 1388–89, 8975–76. I follow Dzelzainis's edition; see also her comments on p. 28.

84. Three stanzas are given over to Seneca's fruitless attempts at cultivating "let-

terure and curteisye" (and moral restraint) in Nero (7.2495–2518); Phanye, Croesus's daughter, supposedly respected for her "heigh sentence," has no luck at all in getting her dream interpretation taken seriously (2747–58). See Wetherbee, "Context," pp. 166–67; see further, Scanlon, *Narrative, Authority, and Power*, p. 226; Richard Neuse, *Chaucer's Dante: Allegory and Epic Theater in "The Canterbury Tales,"* pp. 176–78.

85. See Machaut, *Prise*, ed. Dzelzainis, p. 62 and lines 8597–8616. Machaut criticizes Pierre for despotic behavior; his cruelty to women violates standards set by the *Roman de la Rose*.

86. See Wimsatt, "Chaucer and French Poetry," p. 119.

87. Machaut, *Prise*, pp. 52–53.

88. Dzelzainis suggests that Chaucer, in citing Pierre de Lusignan, is "apparently basing his exemplum on Christine's text" (Machaut, *Prise*, p. 50).

89. See Christine de Pisan, *Le Livre de la Mutacion de Fortune*, ed. Suzanne Solente, p. xi and lines 1395–1400. The work was begun after Aug. 24, 1400, and was completed (so we are told at the beginning of "la table des rebriches," p. 4) on Nov. 18, 1403.

90. On Christine's familiarity with Boccaccio's *De casibus*, see Simone, "La présence de Boccace," p. 18; Maureen Quilligan, *The Allegory of Female Authority: Christine de Pizan's "Cité des Dames,"* pp. 162–64. Boccaccio's *De mulieribus claris* is an important source for Christine's *Cité des Dames*.

91. See Fry, "Ending," p. 362.

92. See Hanna's note to 7.2375–2462 in *Riverside Chaucer*, p. 1132.

93. Fry divides the manuscripts into six groups, each presenting a distinctive combination of interruption (Host or Knight), length (long or short), and placement of the "modern instances" ("Ending," pp. 361–64).

94. Braddy, *Geoffrey Chaucer: Literary and Historical Studies*, p. 23; Kittredge, *Date of "Troilus,"* p. 50.

95. Kittredge, *Date of "Troilus,"* p. 49.

96. Ibid. Kittredge draws attention to an entry written in the margin of Malverne's account of Anglo-Lombard affairs that bears striking comparison with the last two lines of Chaucer's "Bernabò" stanza: "Quo in tempore dominus Barnabos moriebatur in carcere, qua morte an gladio aut fame seu veneno ignoratur" (p. 49, but corrected following the text of Malverne's continuation of Higden in *Polychronicon Ranulphi Higden monachi Cestrensis*, ed. Churchill Babington and J. R. Lumby, vol. 9, p. 78).

97. In preparing to fight Norfolk in the famous (aborted) joust of September 1398, Henry reportedly dressed himself in coat and mail sent by Gian Galeazzo Visconti and prepared himself with the aid of four of the best armorers in Lombardy: see *Chronicque de la Traïson et Mort de Richart Deux Roy Dengleterre*, ed. and trans. Benjamin Williams, p. 151, n. 1.

98. See *Chaucer Life-Records*, p. 58; and see Chap. 1 above.

99. Hawkwood was one of the many mercenary captains whom Bernabò attempted to bind to the Visconti state through marriage to an illegitimate daughter.

100. See E. R. Chamberlin, *The Count of Virtue: Giangaleazzo Visconti, Duke of Milan*, pp. 62–63. Chamberlin argues that at the moment of Gian Galeazzo's accession to power at Pavia, "two military humiliations and a piece of political trickery were his sole claim to notice" (p. 63).

101. See *Storia di Milano*, vol. 6, p. 537.

102. Translated from the Latin of ibid.

103. Sacchetti, *Il Trecentonovelle*, ed. Antonio Lanza, IV, 4. Sacchetti was born sometime between 1332 and 1334 and died in Aug. 1400, probably from the plague.

104. *Storia di Milano*, vol. 6, pp. 535–36.

105. See ibid., vol. 5, pp. 538, 808–12; John White, *Art and Architecture in Italy 1250–1400*, 2d ed., pp. 610–12; *Chaucer and the Italian Trecento*, ed. Boitani, pp. xi–xii and back jacket; W. R. Valentiner, "Notes on Giovanni Balducci and Trecento Sculpture in Northern Italy," pp. 53–54.

106. See the edition by Francesco Cognasso in the series *Rerum italicarum scriptores*, vol. 16, part 4, pp. 133–34. Azario is anxious to emphasize that the statue is actually standing on the altar: "super quo altari, dico in superficie ipsius altaris."

107. See *Storia di Milano*, vol. 6, p. 537.

108. See Spackman, "Fascist Rhetoric of Virility."

109. See Trease, *Condottieri*, p. 76; Michael Mallett, *Mercenaries and Their Masters*, p. 49; *Storia di Milano*, vol. 5, p. 494.

110. See *Storia di Milano*, vol. 5, p. 429.

111. In a letter written to Gian Galeazzo in 1383, Bernabò embellishes his own legend by claiming to have killed one of his uncle's doctors when he was a schoolboy of 17. He was, in fact, 23 years old in 1346, the year of his exile. See *Storia di Milano*, vol. 5, pp. 324–25.

112. See *Novelle inedite intorno a Bernabò Visconti*, ed. Piero Ginori Conti, pp. 39–40. These nine *novelle* appear in a fifteenth-century manuscript owned by Ginori Conti that opens with Goro Dati's *Istoria di Firenze* and contains other political material, including a piece in *terza rima* by a Florentine merchant that lists history's greatest traitors. This runs from the beginning of the world to Iacopo da Piano's murder of the *signore* of Pisa under the tutelage of Gian Galeazzo Visconti. The eighth of the Bernabò *novelle* is a much longer version of the miller and the abbot story told by Sacchetti.

113. On this process, see *Storia di Milano*, vol. 6, p. 475.

114. See Gianluigi Barni, "La formazione interna dello Stato Visconteo," p. 38, referring to a document dated Sept. 21, 1382.

115. Translated from text in *Storia di Milano*, vol. 6, p. 537; see also *Storia di Milano*, vol. 5, p. 361. For more on the life and works of Gabrio de' Zamorei, see Marco Vattasso, *Del Petrarca e alcuni suoi amici*, pp. 35–63.

116. See Brucker, *Florentine Politics*, p. 271; *Storia di Milano*, vol. 5, pp. 467–73.

117. See *Storia di Milano*, vol. 6, p. 523.

118. Foucault, *Discipline and Punish*, p. 47.

119. See *Liber gestorum*, p. 161, in which Azario quotes from and comments upon the document sent by Galeazzo "rectoribus suis."

120. In the public execution of traitors as described by William Blackstone, *Commentaries on the Laws of England* (1766), it is specified that the belly of the condemned man is to be ripped open fast enough for him to see, with his own eyes, his own entrails being thrown onto the fire (see Foucault, *Discipline and Punish*, p. 12). See also the account of the public torture and execution of the regicide Damiens on Mar. 2, 1757, as reported by the *Gazette d'Amsterdam*, which twice emphasizes how Damiens raised his head to observe the state of his own body (Foucault, p. 4).

121. Cognasso's edition of the Latin text reads "Executio quorum facta fuit in personas multorum MCCCLXII et MCCCLXII"; I take the second MCCCLXII to be an editor's error for MCCCLXIII.

122. See Azario, *Liber gestorum in Lombardia*, ed. Cognasso, pp. 161–62, n. 3.

123. See *Storia di Milano*, vol. 6, p. 521, which refers to a document dated May 3, 1369.

124. Ibid., vol. 6, p. 475.

125. Howard, *Chaucer*, p. 229.

126. See the photographic essay of John Baldessari, "Crowds with the Shape of Reason Missing," pp. 32–39.

127. See Chamberlin, *Count of Virtue*, pp. 75–83.

128. See *Storia di Milano*, vol. 5, pp. 620–24.

129. See Chamberlin, *Count of Virtue*, pp. 81–82.

130. See Louis Green, *Chronicle into History*, pp. 112, 123–24; Goro Dati, *L'istoria di Firenze dal 1380 al 1405*, ed. Luigi Pratesi, pp. 7–16.

131. See Dati, *Istoria*, ed. Pratesi, p. 9. In Dati's account, Bernabò comes to sound Christ-like in his championing of the poor and of women who seek his help: "'Come to me and be not afraid . . . for just as the rich and the great have their advocates (who are paid by them) so will I be your advocate . . .'" (12). Even the old stories of Bernabò's atrocities are now enveloped in a glow of sentimental affection. A monk has his penis cut off by a barber because Bernabò (en route to visit one of his concubines) believes that he is too young and good-looking to uphold his vow of chastity and obedience. The monk, after convalescing, thanks Bernabò warmly: "Lord, I am in good health [sto bene] thanks to your mercy and grace, for you have saved me from great stimulation [grande stimolo]" (15).

132. Howard, *Chaucer*, p. 230.

133. See Chap. 10 above.

134. Howard, *Chaucer*, p. 230.

135. Franco Sacchetti, *La battaglia delle donne, le lettere, le sposizioni di Vangeli*, ed. Alberto Chiari, p. 84. Sacchetti is writing an *epistola consolatoria* to the recently widowed Franceschina degli Ubertini. He puts aside ancient examples of the adversity of Fortune in order to cite the recent wave of murders, arson attacks, and executions in Florence, the deposition and death of Queen Giovanna of Naples, and the fall of Bernabò. He then turns to the murder of Abel, remarking that "nothing . . . on earth is or was ever new."

136. Braddy, *Literary and Historical Studies*, p. 23. Braddy is more circumspect than Kittredge, who claims that "the Visconti section in the *Tragedies* is peculiar in that it consists of but a single stanza and has no mention of Fortune" (*Date of "Troilus,"* p. 46).

137. See Chamberlin, *Count of Virtue*, p. 81.

138. See "Annales Ricardi Secundi, Regis Angliae (Corpus Christi College, Cambridge, MS VII)", in John de Trokelowe and Henry de Blaneford, *Chronica et Annales*, ed. H. T. Riley, pp. 330–31; *Chronicque de la Traïson et Mort*, ed. Williams, pp. 94–95; Gransden, *Historical Writing II*, pp. 142–43, 190–91. The Lancastrian version of Richard's death proposes that Richard was so griefstricken by the death of his brother, John de Holland, Earl of Huntingdon, that he refused to eat; when he tried to break his fast his throat was too constricted to swallow. The French *Chronicque*

de la Traïson et Mort claims that Richard was cut down by Sir Peter Exton. Another group of chroniclers attributes Richard's death to starvation by his prison keepers; a fourth group either pleads ignorance of the cause or records two or more versions for posterity to choose from: see Duls, *Richard II in the Early Chronicles*, pp. 169–82.

139. See Chap. 10 above.

140. See Steel, *Richard II*, p. 287, n. 3; Steel gives a reference to *Calendar of Patent Rolls*, 1401–5, p. 126.

141. See Steel, *Richard II*, p. 287.

142. See *Rotuli Parliamentorum*, ed. John Strachey et al.: England "avoit estee par longe temps mesnez, reulez, & governez par Enfantz, & conseil des Vefves"; it will now be governed by "un Homme sachant & discret" (vol. 3, p. 415).

143. My understanding of Richard II's ghostly afterlife is comprehensively indebted to Paul Strohm.

144. See Steel, *Richard II*, pp. 120–40, 217–59.

145. In 1395 Richard sent Pope Boniface IX a book of Edward's "miracles" to support his case for Edward's canonization. This request may first have been made as early as 1387: see Steel, *Richard II*, p. 122.

146. Higden's *Polychronicon* is tersely dismissive of claims for Edward's sanctity: "kepynge in prison, vilenes and obprobrious dethe cause not a martir, but if the holynesse of lyfe afore be correspondent" (ed. Babington and Lumby, vol. 8, pp. 325–27). I follow the translation of Harleian MS 2261 (rather than Trevisa) at this point. For a recent application of the term "tyranny" to this monarch, see Natalie Fryde, *The Tyranny and Fall of Edward II, 1321–1326*.

147. See *Die Kultur der Renaissance in Italien: Ein Versuch*, ed. Horst Günther, pp. 15–23, 137–43 (and Chap. 1 above); *Legend of Good Women*, F 374 (and see G 354).

148. "We must distinguish between the two principal meanings of a strong regime: power over civil society, that is, *despotism*; and the power to coordinate civil society, that is, *infrastructural* strength" (Michael Mann, *The Sources of Social Power*, vol. 1, p. 477; see also John A. Hall and G. John Ikenberry, *The State*, pp. 12–14).

149. Derek Pearsall, *John Lydgate*, p. 247.

150. John Lydgate, *Fall of Princes*, ed. Henry Bergen, vol. 1, p. 1. Incipits and headings in this edition are taken from the Rylands-Jersey manuscript, which Bergen dates to the middle of the fifteenth century and lists among the nine manuscripts that comprise the earliest (c. 1450) group. See *Fall of Princes*, ed. Bergen, vol. 4, pp. 3–4, 21–23.

151. Roberto Weiss notes that the Italian humanists Duke Humphrey came in contact with "had sedulously fostered a belief that their art and it alone could confer immediate honor and an undying reputation on the patrons in whose service it was employed" (*Humanism in England During the Fifteenth Century*, p. 40).

152. See Derek Pearsall, "Hoccleve's *Regement of Princes*: The Poetics of Royal Self-Representation"; John H. Fisher, "A Language Policy for Lancastrian England."

153. See Pearsall, *Lydgate*, p. 226.

154. See Weiss, *Humanism in England*, pp. 39–53.

155. See Weiss, *Spread of Humanism*, pp. 90–91; Weiss, *Humanism in England*, pp. 15, 182; Lois A. Ebin, *John Lydgate* pp. 62–64; Pearsall, *Lydgate*, pp. 227–29.

156. See Lydgate, *Fall of Princes*, ed. Bergen, 2.806–1463 and (for Premierfait's text) vol. 4, pp. 172–75; Pearsall, *Lydgate*, p. 249; Ebin, *Lydgate*, p. 63.

157. Lydgate, *Fall of Princes*, ed. Bergen, p. xv.

158. See Ebin, *Lydgate*, p. 67; Pearsall, *Lydgate*, p. 249.

159. Text as translated in *Peasants' Revolt*, ed. Dobson, p. 236. Shortly before this, the man of law Sir John Cavendish was beheaded at the town pillory of Bury St. Edmund's.

160. Pearsall, *Lydgate*, p. 250. Lydgate's willingness to experiment with "modern instances" is attested to outside the framework of the *Fall of Princes* by his seven-stanza poem *Of the Sodein Fal of Princes in oure dayes*. Surviving in just three manuscripts, this curious production has been variously described as a tapestry, mumming, or processional poem. Clearly inspired by Chaucer's *Monk's Tale*, it acclaims ("Behold," line 1) the death of three Frenchmen (all in the fifteenth century) and four Englishmen (all fourteenth century; no Lancastrians). The sequence runs as follows: Edward II ("murdred with a broche in his foundament"); Richard II (who "feyne was to resigne and in prysone dye"); Charles VI of France (died 1422); Louis, duke of Orleans ("in Parys . . . murdred and foule slayne," 1407); Thomas of Woodstock (friend of the "comvne profit"; murdered "at Caleys," 1397); John, duke of Burgundy (murderer of Louis, duke of Orleans; murdered 1419); Robert de Vere, duke of Ireland (died "in meschef"—boar hunting—in 1392). See *Historical Poems of the XIVth and XV Centuries*, ed. Rossell Hope Robbins, pp. 174–75; Pearsall, *Lydgate*, p. 180.

161. On the *Knight's Tale*, see Chap. 4 above.

162. *Petrarca letterato*, p. 321. My final paragraph is much indebted to the third and final section, entitled "Da Padova all'Europa" (pp. 295–419), of Billanovich's brilliant book. See also *Testament*, ed. Mommsen, pp. 27–28, 43–50 (on the Venetian library project); Wilkins, *Later Years*, pp. 34–37.

163. References follow the edition and translation of E. M. Thompson. Usk was born about 1352 at Usk, Monmouthshire. He studied law at Oxford (and participated in the riots of 1388–89, which pitted Welsh and Southern students against Northerners). He practiced law at the Archbishop's Court, Canterbury, between 1392–97 and enjoyed the patronage of Arundel. He was one of the scholars appointed by Henry in 1399 to find legal grounds for deposing Richard II. Convicted of horse theft in 1402, he went to Rome and practiced law at the papal court. Having sailed home to Wales in 1408, he served or pretended to serve Owen Glendower but then deserted him for Henry IV; he was pardoned and lived as a parish priest until 1430. See Duls, *Richard II in the Early Chronicles*, pp. 215–16; Gransden, *Historical Writing in England, II*, pp. 175–77. Anthony Steel characterizes Usk as a "pushing, vulgar attorney without principle or scruple" (*Richard II*, p. 298); Duls characterizes the style of the *Chronicon* as "long-winded, rhetorical, and conceited" (p. 216). Gransden notes that Adam of Usk was an insatiable reader of chronicles in England, Wales, and Italy, always keen "to draw typological parallels between the great men of his own day and those of the past" (p. 177).

164. Žižek's accounts of "bringing about the past" offer further promising lines of enquiry into the repetitive and violent cycles of *de casibus*. See especially his meditation on the death of Caesar (*Sublime Object of Ideology*, pp. 58–62).

Chapter 12

1. On Boccaccio's advice to Petrarch, newly arrived in Milan, see Chap. 10 above.

2. Cod. Pluteo XC sup., 98.1 (Gadd. 593), Biblioteca Laurenziana, Florence. This

well-known manuscript is conclusively proved to be an autograph by Pier Giorgio Ricci, "Studi sulle opere latine e volgari del Boccaccio," pp. 1–12. It forms the basis of Vittorio Zaccaria's edition of the *De mulieribus claris* in *Tutte le opere*, ed. Branca, vol. 10. Guido A. Guarino's useful translation of the *De mulieribus* is based on the edition of Mathias Apiarius: see Giovanni Boccaccio, *Concerning Famous Women*, p. xxxi.

3. See *De mulieribus*, ed. Zaccaria, pp. 458–59; Ricci, "Studi sulle opere," pp. 12–21. Andrea was the sister of Niccolò Acciaiuoli, a Florentine who had risen to become Queen Giovanna of Naples's *gran siniscalco*. Boccaccio, having suffered a severe and mysterious fall in his economic fortunes in Florence during the winter of 1361–62, moved to Naples (not, it was to transpire, permanently) in November 1362. See Ricci, "Studi sulle opere," p. 17; Branca, "Profilo biografico," pp. 128–33; Wallace, *Early Writings*, p. 24.

4. See *De mulieribus* 2.8; *Legend of Good Women* (henceforth *LGW*), pp. 706–9 (the beginning of the Thisbe legend).

5. See Chap. 11 above.

6. Boccaccio actually begins his "modern instances" by commenting on the sexual ambiguity that may hide behind names: "Iohannes, esto vir nomine videatur, sexu tamen femina fuit" (101.1).

7. See *De mulieribus*, chap. 64 (and *Decameron* 1.1); see also *Famous Women*, trans. Guarino, pp. xxiii–v.

8. See Wallace, "*Decameron* 2.3."

9. See Chap. 10 above.

10. See *Familiares* 22.12.7: "quod ego illis vere pater fueram, quanquam illi michi non filii sed insidiatores essent ac sicarii furesque domestici" (to Albertino da Cannobio, physician: Padua, Sept. 6, 1360).

11. See *Familiares* 22.12.7; 21.14.1–2; Wilkins, *Eight Years in Milan*, p. 198.

12. See Wilkins, *Petrarch's Later Years*, p. 137; *Seniles* 3.8, in *F. Petrarchae . . . Opera que extant omnia*, ed. Johannes Herold, p. 861. Although some of the *Seniles* have been edited for the anthologies, the great majority (and almost all of the *Epistolae variae*) are available only in early editions. But for a recent translation, see Francis Petrarch, *Letters of Old Age: Rerum senilium libri I–XVIII*, trans. Aldo S. Bernardo, Saul Levin, and Reta A. Bernardo. This translation has adopted as its base text the *Librorum Francisci Petrarche annotatio impressorum* (Venice, 1501); questionable readings were checked against four fifteenth-century manuscripts.

13. See Wilkins, *Petrarch's Later Years*, p. 203; *Seniles* 15.14 and 13.9.

14. See *Familiares* 21.10 (to Neri Morando of Forlì: Pagazzano, Oct. 15, 1359).

15. "Ita dilectus meus Cicero cuius olim cor, nunc tibiam vulneravit" (*Familiares* 21.10.26).

16. Petrarch describes his lifelong devotion to Cicero and his searches for Cicero manuscripts in *Seniles* 16.1 (to Luca da Penna: c. Mar. 28, 1374; the 1554 Basel edition denotes this, erroneously, as 15.1).

17. See Wilkins, *Later Years*, pp. 56–57; *Seniles* 3.6, 5.3, 6.1.

18. Petrarch loaned this manuscript to Convenevole da Prato, his poverty-stricken old teacher, who subsequently pawned it. Since the manuscript was never recovered, it is impossible to know whether or not it did contain the Ciceronian *De*

gloria (of which no copy now exists). See *Seniles* 16.1; Wilkins, *Petrarch's Later Years*, pp. 263–64.

19. *Familiares* 18.5.4–5 (to his brother Gherardo, a Carthusian monk: Milan, Apr. 25, 1354); my translation here departs from that of Bernardo at several points.

20. Text and translation follow *Testament*, ed. Mommsen, pp. 92–93. Petrarch is typically scrupulous in thinking of each and every member of his household ("de familiaribus autem domesticis"). Named attendants receive twenty ducats (not to be used for gambling); other attendants receive ten ducats and his servants and cook two each (pp. 84–85).

21. *Familiares* 18.6.4–5 (to Forese, a parish priest and member of the Florentine circle of Petrarch's admirers: Milan, Mar. 15, 1354 or 1355).

22. See esp. *Familiares* 20.12.4: "Erat tamen adhuc michi et curis meis gratum familiare solatium." This letter is addressed to "Lelius," Lello di Pietro Stefano dei Tosetti, a dedicated Roman supporter of the Colonna family (Milan, May 1, 1358).

23. *Familiares* 20.12.7: " 'Hic, hic,' dicebat, 'et scientiam et libros habeo.' " The old man goes on to argue for the superiority of the habit of memory to the habitual use of books: " 'libri enim humane fragilitatis emendicata suffragia, nonnisi propter defectum memorie sunt inventi.' "

24. See *Familiares* 21.11 (to Neri Morando of Forlì: Pagazzano, Oct. 15, 1359). Petrarch visited Capra at Bergamo on Oct. 11, 1359, and elected to stay at the gold-smith's house rather than at the *palazzo pubblico*. Capra was so overjoyed at hosting such a celebrity, Petrarch tells us, that "his friends were alarmed for fear that he might fall ill or become mad or, as happened to many in times past, even die" (21.11.12).

25. *Variae* 44, in Franciscus Petrarca, *Epistolae de rebus familiaribus et variae*, ed. Giuseppe Fracasetti, vol. 3, pp. 415–20.

26. "Solitudinem hanc fori instar turbidi suo fecit adventu": *Familiares* 22.8.1, written to "Socrates" from Milan in Jan. 1360. "Socrates" was the Fleming Ludwig van Kempen, chanter in the chapel of Cardinal Giovanni Colonna.

27. Petrarch's adventures in gardening may be followed through the pages of Wilkins, *Eight Years in Milan*, esp. pp. 38–39, 42, 137–38, 205–6.

28. *Familiares* 22.12.4.

29. For a study of Machaut and the concepts of *poète*, poet-narrator, lover-protagonist, and witness-participant, see Kevin Brownlee, *Poetic Identity in Guillaume de Machaut*.

30. On the importance of *tidynges* in the *House of Fame*, see Chap. 7 above.

31. This episode is recounted years after the fact in *Seniles* 3.1 (to Boccaccio, late summer 1363): see Wilkins, *Eight Years in Milan*, pp. 75–76; *Later Years*, p. 56. The heading for this epistle in the 1554 Basel edition is "De astrologorum nugis." Elsewhere Petrarch relates how the same astrologer got himself into a similar muddle when trying to compute the exact hour at which a siege attack should be mounted.

32. *The Westminster Chronicle, 1381–1394*, ed. and trans. L. C. Hector and Barbara F. Harvey. The Monk of Westminster, author of this *Chronicle*, was plainly disturbed by the political implications of this incident: "The truth is that with due regard always to the paths of righteousness and justice he [the archbishop] would never have bent the knee in that fashion to anybody, when according to the canonical rule it is rather the necks of kings and princes which should be bowed in submission at the feet of pontiffs" (p. 139).

33. *Seniles* 8.3 (Nov. 9, 1367: to Tommaso del Garbo, a physician who sometimes treated Galeazzo Visconti).

34. See Wilkins, *Later Years*, p. 87.

35. *Familiares* 21.13 (to Francesco Nelli, Milan, Dec. 7, 1359): "ad comunem et modestum, ne dicam philosophicum, vestis modum" (12). It is interesting to note that Petrarch has to negotiate in earnest with himself in order to give up courtier's clothes; gluttony, laziness, and lust were much easier to renounce.

36. See *Variae* 56 in *Epistolae*, ed. Fracasetti, vol. 3, pp. 458–64. This letter was written to Francesco Nelli on Sept. 18, 1353.

37. It is not known with certainty which of Giovanni Visconti's three nephews (Matteo, Galeazzo, Bernabò) is involved here: Fracasetti assumes it was Galeazzo; Wilkins, with some reservations (and with dubious reference to "later events") tends to agree with him (*Epistolae*, vol. 3, p. 452; *Eight Years in Milan*, pp. 32–33). Visconti territory, we have noted, was divided into three on the death of Giovanni in 1354. Since Matteo Visconti was the eldest nephew, it seems quite possible that Petrarch (perhaps as yet unaware of the plan for territorial division) is referring to Matteo (who died in 1355 of excesses alluded to in Petrarch's *Variae* 61).

38. *Variae* 56, vol. 3, p. 461: "Ipse non modo vocis obsequium mihi praebuerat, sed dexterae."

39. Discussed in Chap. 10 above.

40. "We may take it," Pearsall argues, "that the *Legend* was written in 1386–7, at the height of Chaucer's career as a 'poet of the court'" (*Life of Chaucer*, p. 191). Pearsall surmises that during the autumn of 1386, Chaucer, in walking from the refectory of Westminster Abbey (where he gave evidence at the Scrope-Grosvenor trial) to the chapter house (where he sat in the parliamentary Commons as M.P. for Kent), "could think himself, for a moment, at the centre of his country's affairs" (p. 203).

41. There is no hard and fast evidence for specific dating of the first version of the *Legend*. Paul Strohm, in private correspondence, suggests that it may well be read "as a meditation on the problematics of court life and princepleasing, begun either in 1389–90 (as part of a bid for return) or 1390–92 (dealing with the experience of return)." Such a dating makes the *Legend* seem a braver poem, since Richard's autocratic habits were more fully established by the early 1390s. Whatever the precise moment of its initial composition and circulation, the poem would come to mean *differently*, from week to week, as the 1390s advanced.

42. On the courtly cult of the flower and the leaf, see *"The Floure and the Leafe" and "The Assembly of Ladies,"* ed. Derek Pearsall, esp. pp. 22–52.

43. Compare F 84–85 ("She is the clernesse and the verray lyght / That in this derke world me wynt and ledeth") with *Filostrato*, ed. Branca, 1.2.1–3 ("Tu, donna, se' la luce chiara e bella / per cui nel tenebroso mondo accorto / vivo . . .").

44. Compare F 89–94 with the concluding couplet of *Filostrato* 1.4: "Guida la nostra man, reggi lo 'ngegno, / nell'opera la quale a scriver vegno."

45. The distinction often drawn by critics between Chaucer as poetic *auctor* and as persona represented within the poem—a distinction that Alceste attempts to maintain in her defense of Chaucer—is clearly inadequate to the complexities of the F-*Prologue*; as "Chaucer" discovers, strange things happen once texts leave the minds of their authors.

46. See, for example, Thomas Wyatt, *Collected Poems*, ed. Daalder, 37.19 ("And she also to use newfangleness").

47. See *Paradiso* 26.137–38.

48. "Court Politics and the Invention of Literature: The Case of Sir John Clanvowe," p. 10. Patterson discusses the implications of a line from Clanvowe's *The Boke of Cupide* ("Terme of lyve, love hath withholde me," p. 289), a poem that draws explicitly from the *Prologue* to the *Legend of Good Women*. The term "withholde" is also used by Chaucer to denote the relationship of a chaplain to a fraternity (*CT*, *General Prologue*, 1.511).

49. See G 71–80. Having argued that he sides neither with the leaf against the flower nor with the flower against the leaf, Chaucer insists that "I am witholde yit with never nother" (G 76), adding that he is ignorant even of *knowing* who serves one party or the other.

50. The fact that Absalom and Jonathon are accorded such prominence is just the first indication that this song, supposedly in praise of women, is very odd indeed. The words of the song actually reiterate a denial or negation of female beauty ("Thy faire body, lat yt nat appere, / Lavyne," F 256–57) and assume an attitude of scorn, contempt, and derision ("disdeyne") on the part of an unnamed lady toward her fellow women.

51. Compare *Man of Law's Tale*, 2.372–78, where the "Sowdanesse" promises, falsely, to "reneye hir lay" (376).

52. On the term *cruel* as a standard epithet for tyranny, see Chap. 10 above.

53. See Gordon, *Wilton Diptych*, p. 52.

54. See Seibt, *Karl IV: Ein Kaiser in Europa 1346–1378*, pp. 339–42.

55. See Dante Alighieri, *The Divine Comedy*, trans. Charles S. Singleton, *Inferno*, Part 2, pp. 209–10.

56. Howard H. Schless considers four putative borrowings from *Inferno* 13 in his *Chaucer and Dante: A Reevaluation*, pp. 133, 154, 174, 176. In considering *LGW* F 358–60, Schless quotes only the Dantean tercet from which Chaucer derived his wording: "La meretrice che mai da l'ospizio / di Cesare non torse li occhi putti, / morte comune e de le corti vizio" (13.64–66). But it is not evident from this exactly who, or what, "la meretrice" represents (flattery? barratry?); some wider knowledge of the canto would seem to be necessary for Chaucer's accurate translation, or interpretation, of "la meretrice" as "Envie."

57. See Agnes Strickland, *Lives of the Queens of England*, vol. 1, p. 597. This eight-volume history by the two Strickland sisters (the entry on Anne of Bohemia was actually written by Elizabeth) has been vastly influential. First printed in 1848, it ran through four editions by 1854 and was reprinted as recently as 1972 (with a "New Introduction" by Antonia Fraser under the auspices of the Library Association, London and Home Counties Branch). The headgear supposedly worn by Anne consisted of a cap "at least two feet in height, and as many in width; its fabric was built of wire and pasteboard, like a very wide-spreading mitre, and over these horns was extended some glittering tissue or gauze. Monstrous and outrageous were the horned caps that reared their head in England directly the royal bride appeared in one" (vol. 1, p. 597, n. 1).

58. For basic information on this area, with useful maps, see Roberta Bromley Etter, *Prague*, pp. 112–26; Michael Jacobs, *Czechoslovakia*, pp. 132–46.

59. See Seibt, *Karl IV*, p. 401; Kamil Krofta, "Bohemia in the Fourteenth Century," in *The Cambridge Medieval History*, ed. J. B. Bury et al., vol. 7, p. 174.

60. The richness and intellectual sophistication of this culture may readily be gauged from *Lebensbilder zur Geschichte der Böhmischen Länder*, a series begun in 1974 under the editorship of Karl Bosl. See especially Ernst Schwarz, "Johann von Neumarkt," in *Lebensbilder*, ed. Bosl (vol. 1 of this series) and all thirteen chapters of vol. 3, published as Ferdinand Seibt, *Karl IV und sein Kreis*. See also S. Harrison Thomson, "Learning at the Court of Charles IV." Ferdinand Seibt, ed., *Kaiser Karl IV. Staatsmann und Mäzen*, an extraordinarily rich collection of essays by some 49 scholars, is particularly good on domestic and European politics, culture, and affairs at court. Pierre Grégoire, *Kaiser Karl IV: Eine mediävale Kulturpotenz aus dem Hause Luxemburg* is quite good on manuscript illumination and book production; Alfred Thomas, *Czech Chivalric Romances* offers a succinct overview of the expansion of genres in Czech during the reign of Charles IV (1346–78) and a detailed study of the relationship of Czech to German romance. On Czech drama, see *A Sacred Farce of Medieval Bohemia: Mastičkář*, ed. Jarmila F. Veltruský, pp. 3–117. *Mastičkář* (which survives in two fourteenth-century manuscripts) is a bawdy, scatological farce starring a spice merchant and his manservant Rubin, suppliers of the unguents taken by the women to Christ's tomb on the first Easter Sunday.

61. See Klassen, "Bohemia Moravia," in *Dictionary of the Middle Ages*, ed. Strayer, vol. 2, p. 301. Charles and Wenceslaus IV after him appointed nonnobles to high office. Charles's attempt to impose his *Majestas carolina*, which would have undermined the nobility as a law-interpreting body, was not successful.

62. See Jaroslav Krejčí, *Czechoslovakia at the Crossroads of European History*, p. 26; John Klassen, "Bohemia Moravia," p. 303; Etter, *Prague*, pp. 48, 80, 94; Jacobs, *Czechoslovakia*, pp. 88–89, 94, 119. Terminology as employed in various histories can be confusing; Malá Strana was known as the New Town until the early fourteenth century.

63. A banner presented by Charles IV to the Jews of Prague still hangs in the Staronova ("Old-New") Synagogue: see Jiři Všetečka and Jiři Kuděla, *Osudy Židovské Prahy* (*The Fate of Jewish Prague*), pp. 28–41. The reign of Charles IV is characterized by Milada Vilímková as a period of exceptional peace and prosperity for Jews in Bohemia; matters deteriorated under the rule of Charles's son, Wenceslaus IV (*Die Prager Judenstadt*, p. 18). On medieval Jewish Prague, see further Ctibor Rybár, *Jewish Prague*, pp. 8–25. On the pogrom of 1389, commemorated by the famous *seliha* (elegy) of Rabbi Abigdor Kara, see Rybár, pp. 20–23, Vilímková, pp. 82–83.

64. See Krofta, "Bohemia," p. 160.

65. See Thomson, "Learning," pp. 14–15. *Das Buch der Liebkosung* is a translation of the pseudo-Augustinian *Liber soliloquiorum anime ad Deum*. The Silesian Johann von Neumarkt (Jan ze Středy), like his master Charles, had studied in Italy. He conducted a vigorous exchange of letters with Petrarch and knew some of Dante's Latin texts (and perhaps more): see Seibt, *Karl IV*, p. 370.

66. Thomson, "Learning," p. 9. For the text of this *vita* (followed by Czech and German versions), see *Život Císaře Karla IV*, in *Fontes rerum bohemicarum*, vol. 3, pp. 323–417.

67. See *Familiares* 19.2; *Fontes rerum bohemicarum*, vol. 3, p. 330. Charles spent two years of his youth in Italy (first at Brescia, then at Parma), attempting to uphold

his father's dynastic claims to Italian territory. His Italian experiences are recounted in his autobiographical *vita*. See Count Lützow, *Lectures on the Historians of Bohemia*, pp. 21–26.

68. Characterizing this exchange as "eine merkwürdige Brieffreundschaft" (Seibt, *Karl IV*, p. 218) seems something of an understatement. For discussion of "feminized men," see Hansen, *Fictions of Gender*, *passim* and p. 3, where they are defined as "those who sometimes act as women are said to act and who are treated as women are often treated." For reflections on the applicability of the term "Frühhumanismus" (early humanism) to the culture of Charles IV's Prague, see Seibt, "Kirche und Kultur im 14. Jahrhundert."

69. The Visconti were enraged in June 1355 when Charles granted the imperial vicariate of Pavia to their bitter enemy, the marquis of Montferrato (who happened to be Charles's cousin). Petrarch's sharply reproachful *Familiares* 19.12 (discussed below) was written several weeks later. See Wilkins, *Eight Years in Milan*, pp. 97–98.

70. *Familiares* 19.1.2 (Oct. 1354); 19.12.7 (June 1355). For a detailed account of Charles's first trip to Rome, see Emil Werunsky, *Der Erste Römerzug Kaiser Karl IV (1354–1355)*.

71. *Familiares* 21.1 (to Arnošt ze Pardubic, archbishop of Prague: late Feb., 1357).

72. "Audaces et timidos amor facit" (*Familiares* 21.7.1, dated Mar. 25, 1358).

73. *Familiares* 19.3, a long and detailed account of Petrarch's meeting with the Emperor at Mantua in December of 1354, written to "Lelius" in February 1355). Petrarch also remarks on the emperor's ability to fill the gaps in his autobiographical account, "often knowing my affairs better than I."

74. *Familiares* 19.3.13. It should be emphasized that Petrarch is not addressing the emperor in this letter, but is rather recounting his meeting, or performance, with the emperor to a friend.

75. This letter may have been written anytime between Petrarch's 1356 departure from Prague and 1364: see Wilkins, *Eight Years in Milan*, pp. 242–43.

76. Petrarch himself comments on the heightened importance to be accorded to matter placed first or last in *Seniles* 17.3, his famous response to the Boccaccian Griselde story (see Chap. 10 above).

77. Seibt, *Karl IV*, p. 215.

78. See (for the philology) *Seniles* 16.5 (dated Mar. 21, 1361); Wilkins, *Eight Years in Milan*, pp. 226–30. On Petrarch as a Count Palatine (which gave him various rights, including the power to legitimize persons of illegitimate birth) see Wilkins, *Later Years*, p. 245.

79. See Crosby, Bishko, and Kellogg, *Medieval Studies: A Bibliographical Guide*, pp. 198–207.

80. For a succinct account of Charles IV's rather distant view of England, see Schnith, "England."

81. See Jiří Spěváček, trans. Alfred Dressler, *Karl IV: Sein Leben und seine staatsmännische Leistung*, p. 109.

82. *Historia anglicana*, vol. 2, p. 96 (commenting on events of 1383). On the particular vulnerabilities of foreign queens, see Fradenburg, *City, Marriage, Tournament*, p. 79.

83. *Historia anglicana*, vol. 2, p. 119 (on 1385).

84. Pearsall, *Life of Chaucer*, p. 66.

85. See Margaret Deanesly, *The Lollard Bible and Other Medieval Biblical Versions*, pp. 248, 278–79; Anne Hudson, *The Premature Reformation: Wycliffite Texts and Lollard History*, pp. 248–49. John Purvey's claim that Archbishop Arundel commended Anne at her funeral in 1394 for having obtained his approval to use "the foure gospeleris with the docturis vpon hem" is entertained by Deanesly but dismissed by Hudson as a Lollard concoction dating from no earlier than 1401.

86. See Guillaume de Machaut, *"Le Jugement du roy de Behaigne" and "Remede de Fortune"*, ed. James I. Wimsatt and William W. Kibler, pp. 8, 26–32.

87. See Joseph Bujnoch, "Johann von Neumarkt—Johann von Jenstein—Guillaume de Machaut"; Jitka Snížková, "Les traces de Guillaume de Machaut dans les sources musicales de Prague," and M. Ladislav Vachulka, "Guillaume de Machaut et la vie musicale de Prague." Vachulka states that Machaut "revint de Reims à Prague pour y demeurer presque jusqu'à fin de sa vie" (p. 326).

88. See Bujnoch, "Johann von Neumarkt," p. 97. R. Barton Palmer's suggestion that Machaut dedicated the *Prise d'Alixandre* to Charles, c. 1370, is erroneous. See Guillaume de Machaut, *The Judgment of the King of Bohemia*, ed. Palmer, p. xv.

89. *Chroniques*, ed. Luce, vol. 6, p. 85.

90. See Chap. 11 above.

91. Born on Feb. 26, 1361, Wenceslaus, like his English counterpart, was accused of being proud, irascible, and tyrannical. In 1393 he reportedly had John of Pomuk, vicar-general to the archbishop, burnt with torches and lighted candles. When the tortured man was unable to sign a document swearing him to secrecy, he was bound hand and foot and thrown in the Vltava. Wenceslaus was imprisoned in the castle at Prague in 1393 and again in 1402; in 1400 he was deposed by the German Electors. See Spěváček, *Karl IV*, p. 109; Krofta, "Bohemia," pp. 175–78.

92. See *Riverside Chaucer*, p. 1020. The notion that 1.171 compliments Queen Anne was first advanced by John L. Lowes in 1908.

93. See Machaut, *Jugement*, ed. Wimsatt and Kibler, p. 10.

94. See Spěváček, *Karl IV*, p. 109.

95. See *Život Císaře Karla IV*, *capitulum* 13 (*Fontes*, vol. 3, pp. 356–57). In making the (commonplace) comment that the *margarita* is "sine . . . macula," the *Život* draws our attention to the term "makeles" as employed in the compliment to Anne in *Troilus* 1.172. In the description of the young maiden of *Pearl*, there is considerable interplay (for some sixty lines) between the terms *mascellez* ("spotless") and *makellez* ("matchless"): see *Pearl*, 721–80 (and note) in *The Poems of the Pearl Manuscript*, ed. Malcolm Andrew and Ronald Waldron. The Pearl Maiden finally brings the similar but distinct meanings of these terms together in lines 781–84, maintaining that she is "maskelles," but not a "makelez quene." It is possible, then, for Chaucer's courtly readers to have imagined some symbolic continuity between the "makeles" beauty described in *Troilus* 1.172 and the "noble quene" of the *Legend* who derives her iconography from French *marguerite* tradition. On the etymological history of medieval French daisies, *flors des margerites*, see Alain Rey, ed., *Dictionnaire historique de la langue française*, vol. 2, p. 1192.

96. On Chaucer's "internationalism," see Elizabeth Salter's short but seminal article, "Chaucer and Internationalism." Salter notes that Jean le Bon was followed to England, after his defeat at Poitiers in 1356, by one of his painters, Girard d'Orleans. Girard stayed in England for at least two years and is thought to have worked on a

polyptych during this period depicting Jean, the Dauphin Charles, Edward III, and the Emperor Charles IV. Only the portrait of Jean has survived; see Salter, p. 74; Millard Meiss, *French Painting in the Time of Jean de Berry: The Late Fourteenth Century and the Patronage of the Duke*, p. 62 and fig. 507.

97. I prefer the term "style" to "poetics" because medieval discussion and deployment of the term, especially in rhetorical theory, invariably comes freighted with both literary and political suggestion.

98. A. G. Rigg has argued that because of ties with England through Anne of Bohemia, and political links between Lollards and Hussites, the English satirical tradition "took on a new life, and many Latin anthologies of Bohemian provenance can be related textually to English ones" ("Anthologies," vol. 1, pp. 319–20; Rigg grounds his claims in work conducted for a series of four articles for *Mediaeval Studies* entitled "Medieval Latin Poetic Anthologies"). For connections between English Lollards and Bohemians, see K. B. McFarlane, *Lancastrian Kings and Lollard Knights*, pp. 195–96; Margaret Aston, *Lollards and Reformers*, pp. 263–64; Anne Hudson, *Lollards and Their Books*, pp. 31–42, 45; Hudson, *Premature Reformation*, pp. 100–102, 126–27, 372, and 514 (where she observes that the precise chronology of the transmission of Wyclif's works to Bohemia requires further scrutiny). One of the two surviving medieval manuscripts of William Thorpe's *Testimony* in Latin was written in a variety of Bohemian hands in the 1430s (now Prague Metropolitan Chapter Library, MS O.29); another manuscript at Prague (University Library, IV.H.17) once contained a Latin copy of the *Testimony* (in a section of the manuscript now missing). See *Two Wycliffite Texts*, ed. Anne Hudson, pp. xxvi–xxx.

99. The marriage plans between Anne and Richard were worked out within the complex context of the recent papal schism in which Prague and Westminster both sided with the pope at Rome: see Jörg K. Hoensch, *Geschichte Böhmens*, pp. 135–37.

100. See Pearsall, *Life of Chaucer*, p. 105.

101. See Jones, *Royal Policy*, pp. 12–13, 20–21; McKisack, *Fourteenth Century*, pp. 426–27; Pearsall, *Life of Chaucer*, p. 153. Burley left England for Prague on May 15, 1381: see T. F. Tout, *Chapters in the Administrative History of Mediaeval England*, vol. 3, p. 368; vol. 4, p. 340. Tout also suggests that Burley made long trips to Prague in 1380 and 1381 (vol. 3, p. 382, n. 3, read in conjunction with vol. 4, p. 340, n. 2).

102. See Tout, *Chapters*, vol. 3, p. 331, n. 3.

103. *Rotuli Parliamentorum*, vol. 3, p. 104, as translated by McKisack, *Fourteenth Century*, p. 426.

104. See Antony Steel, *Richard II*, pp. 90, 110. In 1382 Anne supposedly interceded for the rebel and disappointed heir Thomas Farndon, who sought to buttonhole Richard in the street: see Strohm, *Hochon's Arrow*, p. 106.

105. For an excellent account of this role, see "Queens as Intercessors," the fifth chapter of Strohm's *Hochon's Arrow* (pp. 95–119).

106. See Tuck, *Richard II and the English Nobility*, p. 140; Strohm, *Hochon's Arrow*, pp. 105–11.

107. May McKisack argues that "Anne soon won Richard's passionate devotion and he would seldom allow her to leave his side; but there is no evidence that she sought to restrain his excesses and it is likely to have been her docility which charmed him" (*Fourteenth Century*, p. 426).

108. De Bado presses his claims to a personal commission from Anne in intro-

ducing his work: "ad instantiam igitur quarundam personarum & specialiter Domine Anne quondam Regine Anglie compilavi" (Evan J. Jones, *Medieval Heraldry: Tractatus de armis*, p. 1). For an edition of two different texts of this work, see *Medieval Heraldry: Some Fourteenth-Century Heraldic Works*, ed. Evan J. Jones, pp. 95–212. On the Scrope-Grosvenor controversy, see Jones, *Tractatus de armis*, pp. 3–4; on the controversy and Chaucer's part in it, see Patterson, *Subject of History*, pp. 180–98.

109. In 1381, rebels in the south of England employed the organizational structure of commissions of array (designed to organize resistance to French invaders) to march on London: see A. F. Butcher, "English Urban Society and the Revolt of 1381," p. 101; *The Peasants' Revolt of 1381*, ed. R. B. Dobson, p. xxxvi. See also the *Shipman's Tale, passim* (and especially 7.416–19).

110. On Mary and Esther as queenly intermediaries associated primarily and respectively with mercy and sage counsel, see Strohm, *Hochon's Arrow*, pp. 96–98. Strohm discusses Chaucer's references to Esther in the *Melibee* (7.1100), the *Merchant's Tale* (7.1370–74, 1744–46, both subversive), and the *Legend* (F 250, where Esther comes second only to Absolom in the fateful *balade*).

111. Richard Maidstone, *Concordia*, line 442 (as cited by Strohm, *Hochon's Arrow*, p. 110). Maidstone, a Carmelite friar, wrote his poem (which runs to 548 lines) to celebrate Richard's reconciliation with London and his procession through the city with Anne on August 21, 1392.

112. The question of the precise "referential relation between Alceste and Anne" is addressed with considerable subtlety by Strohm, *Hochon's Arrow*, p. 116.

113. *Fall of Princes*, ed. Bergen, 1.330 (*Prologue*).

114. See, for example, "They flee from me, that sometime did me seek," a poem in which Wyatt's metaphors of semidomesticated, half-wild animals, coupled with meditations upon "newfangleness," recall the uneasy courtly rhetoric of Chaucer's *Squire* (*Collected Poems*, ed. Daalder, 37; *Squire's Tale*, esp. 5.604–29).

115. On this terminology, see Janet Coleman, "Property and Poverty," pp. 611–16. For discussion of the Foucauldian "author function," see Chap. 11 above.

116. Steel writes that in March 1379, an English embassy, headed by Michael de la Pole, traveled to Milan "in order to negotiate a marriage between Richard and Catherine Visconti, which had rather surprisingly ended as a marriage between Richard and Anne of Bohemia" (*Richard II*, p. 96). Chaucer had been in Milan for six weeks less than nine months earlier.

117. See *Paradiso* 13.104, 112–20.

118. See *MED, arguing; pleten*, 1(a).

119. See Goodman, *Loyal Conspiracy*, pp. 45–46; McKisack, *Fourteenth Century*, p. 458.

120. See *Chronicque de la Traïson et Mort*, ed. B. Williams, p. 10. Beheading (rather than hanging) was apparently the only concession that Gloucester, Arundel, and Warwick were willing to make; see McKitterick, *Fourteenth Century*, p. 458.

121. *Traïson et Mort*, ed. Williams, p. 10.

122. See McKitterick, *Fourteenth Century*, p. 458.

123. See, for example, Goodman, *Loyal Conspiracy*, p. 47; McKitterick, *Fourteenth Century*, p. 459.

124. See the excellent account of Strohm, "Politics and Poetics: Usk and Chaucer in the 1380s," pp. 92–97; Pearsall, *Life of Chaucer*, pp. 208–9.

125. See Steel, *Richard II*, p. 174.

126. Richard and Anne "were almost exactly the same age," Barron writes, "and it would appear that they were happy together" ("Richard II: Image and Reality," p. 15).

127. See *Chronicon Adæ de Usk*, ed. Thompson, pp. 8, 9; see also Given Wilson, *Royal Household*, p. 31.

128. The fullest account of this episode is interpellated into Walsingham's *Historia Anglicana* in MS Cotton. Faustina B.9 (fol. 198): see H. T. Riley, ed., Trokelowe and Blaneforde, *Chronica et Annales*, ed. Riley, p. 424 (and pp. 168–69). There is a record of Richard's committing Arundel to the Tower on August 3, 1394, and of his ordering his release one week later; see Thomas Rymer, *Foedera*, 3rd ed., vol. 4, p. 101.

129. See McKitterick, *Fourteenth Century*, p. 481.

130. See *Eulogium historiarum*, ed. Haydon, vol. 3, pp. 72–73. According to the continuator of the *Eulogium*, Richard—on cornering Gloucester at his manor of Pleshy, Essex—replied to his uncle's pleas for mercy as follows: "Illam gratiam habebis quam praestitisti Symoni de Burley, cum Regina pro eo coram te genuflecteret" (vol. 3, p. 372).

131. See Chap. 5 above.

132. See Thomas of Burton (and others), *Chronica monasterii de Melsa*, ed. E. A. Bond, vol. 3, pp. 219–20.

133. Thomas of Burton, *Chronica de Melsa*, vol. 3, p. 257; my italics.

134. See John H. Harvey, "The Wilton Diptych—A Re-examination," p. 10, n. 5. Harvey's source here is Oriel College, Oxford, MS 46, ff. 104–6.

135. See Harvey, "Wilton Diptych": "un coler des perles et autres preciouses perres de la liveree de la roigne que derrein murrust, pres de V.m. marcz" (p. 10, n. 5).

136. Chaucer, as Susan Crane suggests, clearly possessed a sense of *generic* obsolescence (as part of a wider historical consciousness): "Romance," Crane argues, "is not only feminine but outmoded in Chaucer's milieu. The pastness that earlier conferred dignity on the genre . . . becomes a mark of obsolescence in the later fourteenth century" (*Gender and Romance*, p. 11).

137. In the copy of Iohannes de Bado Aureo's *Tractatus de armis* copied by the scribe Baddesworth in 1456 (BL Add. MS 30946), Richard II is explicitly associated with the lion ("quod Ricardus secundus leones non leopardos portavit"). The lion is then associated with the king, and the eagle with the queen ("ut leo velut rex, ita aquila velut regina"). The linkage of the eagle with Roman emperors is then (nonetheless) affirmed: "Imperatores Romani aquilam portaverunt." See Jones, *Tractatus de armis*, pp. 6–8.

138. See Édouard Perroy, *L'Angleterre et le Grand Schisme d'Occident*, p. 342; D. M. Bueno de Mesquita, "The Foreign Policy of Richard II in 1397: Some Italian Letters," p. 632.

139. See Gordon, *Wilton Diptych*, pp. 30, 49, and p. 63, n. 13; John H. Harvey, "Richard II and York," p. 214 (and plate opposite 207). One of the painted soffit panels of Richard's tomb depicts "a shield of France and England impaling *the eagle* of the Empire quartering *the crowned lion* of Bohemia" (Royal Commission, vol. 1, *Westminster Abbey*, p. 31).

140. *Rotuli Parliamentorum*, vol. 3, p. 343 ("Legitimation pur Beaufort"). Rich-

ard's grasping after imperial status might be contrasted with the humorously self-assured behavior of Anne's father, the Emperor Charles IV, who had himself crowned King of Arles before that city's cathedral chapter in a parodistic service; see *Sacred Farce*, ed. Veltruský, p. 307.

141. See Bueno de Mesquita, "Foreign Policy," pp. 628–31, 634–37. The epithet "tyrant of Lombardy" is used of Gian Galeazzo by a Florentine observer, writing from London to a Florentine citizen on Jan. 2, 1397 (pp. 628–29). Sienese envoys, writing from Pavia on Mar. 6, 1397/8, write of having heard that the "conte derbi figliuolo del duca del lencaustro, che è nipote carnale del detto Re d'inghilterra, dé venire qui a primavera e credesi farà parentado col Signore di prendere per sua donna madonna Lucia figliuola dimisser Barnabò" (p. 637).

142. For *voluntas arbitrium*, see Chap. 10 above.

143. *Convivio*, ed. Simonelli, 1.1.17 ("for it is appropriate both to speak and behave differently at different stages of life").

144. In the opening sonnet of the *Canzoniere*, earlier texts (now prefaced by present wisdom) are seen to represent "giovenile errore," written "quand'era in parte altr'uom da quel ch'i' sono" ("when I was in part a different man from that which I am"; note the crucial equivocation of "in parte"). See *Canzoniere*, ed. Alberto Chiari, 1.3, 4.

145. See E. F. Jacob, *The Fifteenth Century, 1399–1485*, p. 480; G. L. Harriss, "The King and his Magnates," pp. 49–50; Christopher Allmand, *Henry V*, p. 397, n. 52; A. R. Myers, "The Captivity of a Royal Witch: The Household Accounts of Queen Joan of Navarre, 1419–21."

146. See *Lenvoy de Chaucer a Bukton*, lines 29–30.

147. For a different account of court poetry and its relations to *makyng* beyond the court, see Patterson, "Court Politics and the Invention of Literature," esp. pp. 8–9.

148. See Given-Wilson, *Royal Household*, p. 51.

149. Whether we think as historicists, psychologists, or gender critics, it is important to remember that the long sequence of women in Chaucer who speak to save men from the block is not matched by men who speak to save women; the Virginia story continues to haunt each episode of this dominant Chaucerian paradigm.

Conclusion

1. See Corrigan and Sayer, *The Great Arch*, pp. 43–71; Mann, *Sources of Social Power*, vol. 1, pp. 456–58.

2. And the actors themselves, of course, form but part of the greater "percipient" group involved in a theatrical event (that would include its audience). See John O'Toole, *The Process of Drama: Negotiating Art and Drama*, esp. pp. 185–87.

3. For an account of how "in indirect but important ways the tavern [in *1* and *2 Henry IV*] resembles the contemporary London theater," see Jean E. Howard, *The Stage and Social Struggle in Early Modern England*, pp. 139–44 (p. 142).

4. See Chap. 3 above.

5. See *London and Middlesex Chantry Certificate, 1548*, ed. C. J. Kitling, pp. ix–xvii; Duffy, *Stripping of the Altars*, pp. 454–64.

6. See Chap. 2 above.

7. Chantries share the ideological power of guilds to the extent that they, like guilds, imagine continuous association between the living and the dead. See Chap. 3 above.

8. More, *Utopia*, trans. Robynson, ed. J. Churton Collins, p. 16. Ralph Robynson's translation of *Utopia* was first published at the sign of the "Lambe" in St. Paul's Churchyard in 1551. For More's Latin text, see *Utopia*, ed. Edward Surtz and J. H. Hexter, vol. 1, p. 66.

9. More, *Utopia*, trans. Robynson, ed. Collins, p. 16; ed. Surtz and Hexter, vol. 1, p. 66.

10. More, *Utopia*, trans. Robynson, ed. Collins, p. 74; ed. Surtz and Hexter, vol. 1, p. 146.

11. "Sir John," originally named "Oldcastle" by Shakespeare, was changed to "Falstaff" (presumably following protests from the Cobham family); the 1598 quarto retains traces of the original name. Shakespeare's treatment of Oldcastle prompted the writing of John Weever's *The Mirror of Martyrs* (1601) and the performing of a new play, *Sir John Oldcastle, Part I*, by the Admiral's Men in 1599. For a useful collection of the relevant texts, see *The Oldcastle Controversy*, ed. Peter Corbin and Douglas Sedge. The name "Oldcastle" has been restored in the edition of *1 Henry IV* that forms part of *The Complete Oxford Shakespeare*, ed. Stanley Wells and Gary Taylor; grounds for this decision are established by Taylor, "The Fortunes of Oldcastle." See further Helgerson, *Forms of Nationhood*, pp. 236–37, 249–53.

12. See Chap. 5 above; *2 Henry IV*, III.ii.

13. See Rita Copeland, "Rhetoric and the Literal Sense in Medieval Literary Theory: Aquinas, Wyclif, and the Lollards," pp. 14–23.

14. *2 Henry IV*, 2.iv.33–34.

15. E. Talbot Donaldson, in discussing kinship between Falstaff and the Wife of Bath, does not think to address the intermediate linkage of Lollardy and literalism; he does, however, note that "in dealing with St. Paul, the wife uses a literalist approach worthy of a puritan reformer" (*The Swan at the Well*, p. 136). On relations between fleshly reading and the female body, see Copeland, "Why Women Can't Read"; Lochrie, *Translations of the Flesh*; Dinshaw, *Sexual Poetics*, pp. 18–20.

16. See C. L. Barber, *Shakespeare's Festive Comedy*, pp. 213–21; *Henry IV, Part I*, ed. David Bevington, pp. 24–26.

17. *1 Henry IV*, III.iii.52.

18. *Henry V*, IV.iii.60. It has been noted that this attempt to articulate associational bonds uniting monarch with common soldier actually succeeds in exposing deeper antagonisms: see Anne Barton, "The King Disguised: Shakespeare's *Henry V* and the Comical History," pp. 207–22; Richard Helgerson, *Forms of Nationhood*, p. 231; Peter Womack, "Imagining Communities: Theatres and the English Nation in the Sixteenth Century," pp. 94–96.

19. "By yoking together diverse peoples," Stephen Greenblatt argues, "Hal symbolically tames the last wild areas in the British Isles, areas that in the sixteenth century represented, far more powerfully than any New World people, the doomed outposts of a vanishing tribalism" (*Shakespearean Negotiations*, p. 56).

20. Historical experience suggests that under the pressure of imminent battle, tribal and local loyalties return to displace nationalist sentiment (which is attributed only to the enemy). The British trench soldier of 1914–18, according to Robert Graves,

"thought of Germany as a nation in arms, a unified nation inspired with the sort of patriotism that he himself despised" (*Good-bye to All That*, p. 188).

21. *Imagined Communities*, p. 7. It may seem gratuitously paradoxical to speak of "deep, horizontal comradeship." As Shakespeare intuits, however, it is the historical longevity of companionable structures (deriving from the medieval world) that brings suggestions of *depth* to contemporary political usage.

22. See Chap. 4 above. See also Womack, "Imagining Communities," pp. 98–107.

23. Corrigan and Sayer see this with exemplary clarity, from beginning to end of their *Great Arch*: see, for example, pp. 5, 202.

24. *Chronicon Adæ de Usk*, ed. E. M. Thompson, p. 3.

25. See Ives, *Anne Boleyn*, pp. 343, 386. The imperial ambassador Eustace Chapuys estimated the crowd attending the execution at two thousand; the special stands erected to accommodate them were reported as still standing in 1778 (Ives, p. 386). Retha M. Warnicke, who urges skepticism concerning information stemming from Chapuys, envisions a more modest crowd (*The Rise and Fall of Anne Boleyn*, pp. 1–3, 232).

26. See Chap. 9 above.

27. See Ives, *Anne Boleyn*, pp. 371, 387, 401, 402; J. J. Scarisbrick, *Henry VIII*, pp. 348–50. For an account of Anne's downfall more sympathetic to Henry, see the eccentric and sometimes offensive account of Warnicke, *Rise and Fall*, pp. 191–242.

28. See Chap. 12 above.

29. Ives, *Anne Boleyn*, p. 358.

30. See ibid., p. 366. On the problematic relation of the mature Elizabeth to her parents, see Susan Frye, *Elizabeth I: The Competition for Representation*, pp. 33–34; Marc Shell, *Elizabeth's Glass*, pp. 108–9.

31. Indispensable orientation is offered by Leah S. Marcus, *Puzzling Shakespeare*, pp. 51–105. Elizabeth, Leah Marcus argues, "was the divine Astraea returned or a secularized Virgin Mother to the nation. She was a Queen of Shepherds, a new Deborah, a Cynthia or Diana"; she was also possessed "of a set of symbolic male identities which are much less familiar to us" (p. 53).

32. See *Two Noble Kinsmen*, I.iii, esp. lines 55–97.

33. One of these countrymen claims Bottom's profession: "Ha, boys, heigh for the weavers!" (II.iii.49).

34. An essential Baedeker here, albeit directed to the Elizabethan period, is Frank Whigham, *Ambition and Privilege*.

Bibliography

The following abbreviations are used:

ASL	*Archivio Storico Lombardo*
BIHR	*Bulletin of the Institute of Historical Research*
BJRL	*Bulletin of the John Rylands Library*
BL	British Library
CHMPT	*The Cambridge History of Medieval Political Thought*, ed. J. H. Burns
CR	*The Chaucer Review*
EETS	Early English Text Society
ELH	*English Literary History*
HMSO	Her/His Majesty's Stationery Office
JEGP	*Journal of English and Germanic Philology*
JMRS	*Journal of Medieval and Renaissance Studies*
MED	*Middle English Dictionary*
OED	*Oxford English Dictionary*
PL	*Patrologia Latina*
PRO	Public Record Office
REED	*Records of Early English Drama*
RIS	*Rerum Italicarum Scriptores*
SAC	*Studies in the Age of Chaucer*
UTET	Unione Tipografico-Editrice Torinese

*Indicates the edition or translation normally followed in the text when two or more versions are listed.

Calendars, Catalogues, and Records

Calendar of the Close Rolls Preserved in the Public Record Office: Richard II. Prepared under the Superintendance of the Deputy Keeper of the Records. 6 vols. Vol. 3, 1385–89. Vol. 5, 1392–96. London: HMSO, 1914–27.

Calendar of Early Mayor's Court Rolls of the City of London at the Guildhall, 1298–1307. Ed. A. H. Thomas. Cambridge: Cambridge University Press, 1924.

Calendar of Letter-Books Preserved among the Archives of the Corporation of the City of London at the Guild Hall. Letter-Book H. Circa A.D. 1375–1399. Ed. Reginald R. Sharpe. London: Corporation of the City of London, 1907.

Cambridge Gild Records. Ed. Mary Bateson. Cambridge: Cambridge Antiquarian Society, 1903.

A Catalogue of the Manuscripts Preserved in the Library of the University of Cambridge. 6 vols. Cambridge: Cambridge University Press, 1856–67. Reprint, Munich: Kraus, 1980.

Chaucer Life-Records. Ed. Martin M. Crow and Clair C. Olson. Austin: University of Texas Press, 1966.

Church Wardens' Accounts of Croscombe, Pilton, Yatton, Tintinhull, Morebath, and St. Michael's, Bath. Ed. Bishop Edmund Hobhouse. Somerset Record Society, vol. 4. London: Somerset Record Society, 1890.

A Descriptive Catalogue of the Manuscripts in the Library of Corpus Christi College, Cambridge. By M. R. James. 2 vols. Cambridge: Cambridge University Press, 1912.

A Descriptive Catalogue of the Manuscripts in the Library of Gonville and Caius College, Cambridge. By M. R. James. 2 vols. Cambridge: Cambridge University Press, 1907–8.

English Gilds. Ed. Toulmin Smith and Lucy Toulmin Smith, with an essay by Lujo Brentano. EETS o.s. 40. London: EETS, 1870.

English Historical Documents, 1327–1485. Ed. and trans. A. R. Myers. New York: Oxford University Press, 1969.

The Friars' Libraries. Ed. K. W. Humphreys. Corpus of British Library Catalogues. London: British Library, 1990.

Letter Books A–L (1275–1498). Corporation of London Records Office.

London and Middlesex Chantry Certificate, 1548. Ed. C. J. Kitching. London Record Society Publications, vol. 16. London: LRS, 1980.

London Assize of Nuisance 1301–1431: A Calendar. Ed. H. M. Chew and W. Kellaway. LRS Publications, vol. 10. London: LRS, 1984.

Memorials of London and London Life in the Thirteenth, Fourteenth, and Fifteenth Centuries, A.D. 1276–1419. Ed. Henry Thomas Riley. London: Longmans, Green, and Co., 1868.

The Parish Gilds of Mediaeval England. Ed. H. F. Westlake. London: Society for Promoting Christian Knowledge, 1919.

Public Record Office, Chancery Miscellanea, C.47/38–46 (1389 guild returns).

REED. Cambridge. Ed. Alan H. Nelson. 2 vols. Toronto: University of Toronto Press, 1989.

REED. Coventry. Ed. R. W. Ingram. Toronto: University of Toronto Press, 1981.

REED. York. Ed. Alexandra F. Johnston and Margaret Rogerson. 2 vols. Toronto: University of Toronto Press, 1979.

Records of the Gild of St. George in Norwich, 1389–1547. A Transcript with an Introduction. Ed. Mary Grace. Norfolk Record Society, vol. 9 (1937).

Records of the Guild of the Holy Trinity, St. Mary, St. John the Baptist, and St. Katherine of Coventry. Ed. Geoffrey Templeman, Publications of the Dugdale Society, vol. 19. London: Oxford University Press, 1944.

Register of the Guild of the Holy Trinity, St. Mary, St. John the Baptist and St. Katherine of Coventry. Ed. Mary Dormer Harris, Publications of the Dugdale Society, vol. 13. London: Oxford University Press, 1935.

Rotuli Parliamentorum: Ut et petitiones, et placita in Parliamento 1278–1503. Ed. John Strachey et al. 6 vols. London, 1783. See also translations in *English Historical Documents, 1327–1485,* ed. and trans. A. R. Myers.

Royal Commission on Historical Monuments (England). *An Inventory of the Historical Monuments in London.* Vol. 1, *Westminster Abbey.* London: HMSO, 1924.

Rymer, Thomas. *Foedera.* 3d ed. 10 vols. The Hague: J. Neaulme, 1745.

The Statutes of the Realm, 1235–1713. Ed. Alexander Luders, T. E. Tomlins, John France, W. E. Tarnton, and John Raithby. 11 vols. London: Dawsons, 1963 (reprinting ed. of 1810–22).

Yorkshire Sessions of the Peace, 1361–64. Ed. Bertha H. Putnam. Yorkshire Archaeological Society, Record Series, 100 (1939). Wakefield: YAS, 1939.

Primary Sources

Adam of Usk. See *Chronicon Adæ de Usk.*

Aegidius Romanus. See Egidio Colonna.

Albertano of Brescia. *De amore et dilectione Dei et proximi et aliarum rerum et de forma vitae. An Edition.* Ed. Sharon Hiltz. Ph.D. diss., University of Pennsylvania, 1980.

———. *De doctrina dicendi et tacendi.* Ed. Thor Sundby in his *Brunetto Latinos levnet og skrifter* (Copenhagen: Jacob Lunds Boghandel, 1869), pp. lxxxv–cxix. (Edition also included as part of Sundby, *Della vita e delle opere di Brunetto Latini,* pp. 475–506.)

———. *Liber consolationis et consilii.* Ed. Thor Sundby, Chaucer Society, 2d series, vol. 8. London: Trübner, 1873.

———. *Sermones quattuor: edizione curate sui codici bresciani.* Ed. Marta Ferrari. Lonato: Fondazione Ugo da Como, 1955.

———. *Dei trattati morali di Albertano da Brescia. Volgarizzamento inedito fatto nel 1268 da Andrea da Grosseto.* Ed. Francesco Selmi. Bologna: Gaetano Romagnoli, 1873.

Aquinas, St. Thomas. *Opuscula philosophica.* Ed. R. M. Spiazzi. Turin: Marietti, 1954.

———. *The Political Ideas of Thomas Aquinas.* Ed. Dino Bigongiari. New York: Hafner, 1953.

———. *De regimine principum ad regem Cypri.* In *Opuscula philosophica,* ed. Spiazzi, pp. 257–80.

———. *Selected Political Writings.* Ed. A. P. d'Entrèves, trans. J. G. Dawson. Oxford: Basil Blackwell, 1959.

———. *Summa theologiae.* Ed. Dominicans from the English-speaking Provinces. 61 vols. London: Blackfriars, in association with Eyre and Spottiswoode, 1963–76.

Augustine of Hippo, St. *On Christian Doctrine.* Trans. D. W. Robertson. Indianapolis: Bobbs-Merrill, 1958.

Ayenbite of Inwyt by Dan Michel of Northgate. Ed. Richard Morris. 2 vols. EETS o.s. 23. London: Trübner, 1866.

Azario, Pietro. *Liber gestorum in Lombardia.* Ed. Francesco Cognasso. *RIS,* vol. 16, part 4. Bologna: Nicola Zanichelli, 1939.

The Babees Book. Ed. Frederick J. Furnivall. EETS o.s. 32. London: Trübner, 1868.

Benvenuto da Imola, *Comentum super Dantis Aldigherii Comoediam.* Ed. J. P. Lacaita. 5 vols. Florence: G. Barbèra, 1887.

Biblia sacra iuxta vulgatam versionem. Ed. B. Fischer, OSB, et al. 2d ed. 2 vols. Stuttgart: Württembergische Bibelanstalt, 1975.

Boccaccio, Giovanni. *Boccaccio in Defence of Poetry: Genealogiae deorum gentilium liber XIV.* Ed. Jeremiah Reedy. Toronto: Pontifical Institute for Medieval Studies, 1978.

———. *Chaucer's Boccaccio.* Trans. and ed. N. R. Havely. Cambridge: D. S. Brewer, 1980.

———. *Concerning Famous Women.* Trans. Guido A. Guarino. London: Unwin, 1964.

———. *The Corbaccio.* Trans. and ed. Anthony K. Cassell. Urbana: University of Illinois Press, 1975.

———. *The Decameron.* Trans. G. H. McWilliam. Harmondsworth: Penguin, 1972.

———. *The Fates of Illustrious Men.* Trans. Louis Brewer Hall. New York: Ungar, 1965.

———. *Opere in versi: Corbaccio, Trattatello in laude di Dante, Prose Latine, Epistole.* Ed. Pier Giorgio Ricci. Milan: Ricciardi, 1965.

———. *Opere latine minori.* Ed. A. F. Massèra. Scrittori d'Italia 111. Bari: Laterza, 1928.

———. **Tutte le opere di Giovanni Boccaccio.* Ed. Vittorio Branca. 12 vols. Milan: Mondadori, 1964– .

Bonvesin de la Riva. *De magnalibus Mediolani.* Ed. and trans. Angelo Paredi. Milan: Pizzi, 1967.

———. *Volgari scelti.* Ed. and trans. Patrick S. Diehl and Ruggero Stefanini. American University Series, series 2, vol. 58. New York: Lang, 1987.

A Book of London English 1384–1425. Ed. R. W. Chambers and Marjorie Daunt. Oxford: Clarendon, 1931.

Botticelli, Sandro. *The Complete Paintings of Botticelli.* Introduction by Michael Levey, notes and catalogue by Gabriele Mandel. Harmondsworth: Penguin, 1985.

Cantari del Trecento. Ed. Armando Balduino. Milan: Marzorati, 1970.

Caxton, William. *Ordre of Chyvalry.* Ed. A. T. P. Byles. EETS o.s. 168. London: EETS, 1926.

Charles IV, Emperor. "Život Císaře Karla IV." In *Fontes rerum bohemicarum,* vol. 3, pp. 323–417. Prague: Palackého, 1882.

Chaucer, Geoffrey. *Canterbury Tales.* Ed. William Thynne. 1532. Facsimile, Oxford: Henry Frowde, Oxford University Press, 1905.

———. *The Canterbury Tales by Geoffrey Chaucer. Edited from the Hengwrt Manuscript.* Ed. N. F. Blake. London: Arnold, 1980.

———. *The Canterbury Tales: Nine Tales and the General Prologue.* Ed. V. A. Kolve and Glending Olson. New York: Norton, 1989.

———. *The Complete Poetry and Prose of Geoffrey Chaucer.* Ed. John H. Fisher. 2d ed. New York: Holt, Rinehart and Winston, 1989.

———. *The Complete Works of Geoffrey Chaucer.* Ed. William W. Skeat. 7 vols. Oxford: Clarendon, 1894–97.

———. *The Manciple's Tale.* Ed. Donald C. Baker. Variorum Chaucer, vol. 2, part 10. Norman: University of Oklahoma Press, 1982.

———. *The Minor Poems.* Ed. George B. Pace and Alfred David. Variorum Chaucer, vol. 5, part 1.

————. *The Riverside Chaucer. Ed. Larry D. Benson. Boston: Houghton Mifflin, 1987.

————. The Text of the Canterbury Tales. Ed. John M. Manly and Edith Rickert. 8 vols. Chicago: University of Chicago Press, 1940.

————. Troilus and Criseyde: A New Edition of "The Book of Troilus." Ed. B. A. Windeatt. Longmans: London, 1984.

————. The Works, 1532, with Supplementary Material from the Editions of 1542, 1561, 1598, and 1602. Ed. D. S. Brewer. Menston: Scholar Press, 1969.

————. Works of Geoffrey Chaucer. Ed. F. N. Robinson. 2d ed. London: Oxford University Press, 1957.

Chaucer: Sources and Backgrounds. Ed. Robert P. Miller. New York: Oxford University Press, 1977.

Christine de Pisan. Le Livre de la Mutacion de Fortune. Ed. Suzanne Solente. 4 vols. Paris: Picard, 1959–66.

Chronica et annales. See Trokelowe, John de.

Chronicles of London. Ed. C. L. Kingsford. Oxford: Oxford University Press, 1905.

Chronicon Adæ de Usk. A.D. 1377–1421. Ed. Sir Edward Maunde Thompson. 2d ed. London: Henry Frowde, 1904.

Chronicque de la Traïson et Mort de Richart Deux Roy Dengleterre. Ed. and trans. Benjamin Williams. London: English Historical Society, 1846.

Cicero, Marcus Tullius. De inventione. Trans. H. M. Hubbell. Loeb Classical Library, vol. 386. Cambridge, Mass.: Harvard University Press, 1968.

Damian, Peter, St. L'opera poetica di S. Pier Damiani. Ed. Margareta Lokrantz. Studia Latina Stockholmiensia, vol. 12. Stockholm: Almquist and Wiksell, 1964.

Dante Alighieri. *Il Convivio. Ed. Maria Simonelli. Bologna, 1966.

————. Convivio. Ed. G. Busnelli and G. Vandelli. 2 vols. Florence: Le Monnier, 1934–54.

————. De vulgari eloquentia. Ed. P. V. Mengaldo. In Opere minori, ed. Mengaldo et al.

————. *The Divine Comedy. Trans. with a commentary by Charles S. Singleton. 6 parts in 3 vols. Second printing, with corrections. Princeton: Princeton University Press, 1977.

————. The Divine Comedy of Dante Alighieri. Trans. Allen Mandelbaum. 3 vols. New York: Bantam, 1982–86.

————. Epistolae. Ed. Paget Toynbee. 2d. ed., C. G. Hardie. Oxford: Clarendon, 1966.

————. Monarchia. Ed. Bruno Nardi. In Opere minori, ed. Mengaldo et al., vol. 2, pp. 241–503.

————. On World-Government (De Monarchia). Trans. Herbert W. Schneider. Indianapolis: Bobbs Merrill, 1957.

————. Opere minori, vol. 2. Ed. Pier Vincenzo Mengaldo et al. Milan and Naples: Ricciardi, 1979.

————. Opere minori di Dante Alighieri, vol. 1. Ed. G. B. Squarotti et al. Turin: UTET, 1983.

————. Vita nuova. Ed. G. B. Squarotti. In Opere minori, ed. Squarotti, vol. 1.

————. Vita nuova. Trans. Barbara Reynolds. Harmondsworth: Penguin, 1969.

Dati, Gregorio. *L'istoria di Firenze dal 1380 al 1405*. Ed. Luigi Pratesi. Norcia: Tonti Cesare, 1905.

De Man, Paul. *Wartime Journalism, 1939–1943: Paul de Man*. Ed. Werner Hamacher, Neil Hertz, and Thomas Keenan. Lincoln: University of Nebraska Press, 1988.

Egidio Colonna. *De regimine principum libri III*. Ed. H. Samaritanius. Rome: B. Zannettus, 1607.

Eliot, T. S. *Collected Poems, 1909–1962*. London: Faber and Faber, 1974.

Engels, Friedrich. *The Peasant War in Germany*. Trans. and ed. Vic Schneierson. 2d ed. Moscow: Progress Publishers, 1965.

Eulogium historiarum temporibus: Chronicon ab orbe condito usque ad Annum Domini MCCCLXVI. Ed. Frank Scott Haydon. 3 vols. Rolls Series, 9. London: Longmans et al., 1858–63.

Fiamma, Galvano. *Chronicon extravagans et chronicon maius*. Ed. Antonio Ceruti. Turin: Royal Printers, 1869.

———. *Opusculum de rebus gestis ab Azone, Luchino et Johanne Vicecomitibus ab anno MCCCXXVIII usque ad annum MCCCXLII*. Ed. Carlo Castiglioni. *RIS*, vol. 12, part 4. Bologna: Zanichelli, 1938.

Five Illuminated Manuscripts of Giangaleazzo Visconti. Ed. Edith W. Kirsch. University Park: Pennsylvania State University Press, 1991.

"The Floure and the Leafe" and "The Assembly of Ladies." Ed. Derek Pearsall. London: Nelson, 1962.

Fontes rerum bohemicarum. See Charles IV, Emperor.

Fortescue, Sir John. *The Governance of England, otherwise called The Difference between an Absolute and a Limited Monarchy, by Sir John Fortescue*. Ed. Charles Plummer. Oxford: Clarendon, 1885.

———. *De laudibus legum Angliae*. Ed. S. B. Chrimes. Cambridge: Cambridge University Press, 1942.

Foxe, John. *The Acts and Monuments of John Foxe*. Ed. Josiah Pratt. 4th ed. 8 vols. London: The Religious Tract Society, 1877.

Froissart, Jean. *Chroniques*. Ed. Siméon Luce et al. 15 vols. Paris: Société de l'Histoire de France, 1869–1975.

———. *Le joli Buisson de Jonece*. Ed. Anthime Fourier. Geneva: Librairie Droz, 1975.

Gower, John. *The Complete Works of John Gower*. Ed. G. C. Macaulay. 4 vols. Oxford: Clarendon, 1899.

Graves, Robert. *Goodbye to All That*. Rev. ed. New York: Anchor Books, 1989.

Higden, Ranulph. *Polychronicon Ranulphi Higden monachi Cestrensis, together with the English translations of John Trevisa and of an unknown writer of the fifteenth century*. Ed. Churchill Babington and J. R. Lumby. 9 vols. Rolls Series, 41. London: Longmans, 1865–86.

Historical Poems of the Fourteenth and Fifteenth Centuries. Ed. Rossell Hope Robbins. New York: Columbia University Press, 1959.

Hoccleve, Thomas. *Hoccleve's Works*. Ed. F. J. Furnivall. 3 vols. EETS e.s. 61, 72, 73. London: EETS, 1892–95.

———. *Selections from Hoccleve*. Ed. M. C. Seymour. Oxford: Oxford University Press, 1981.

Jerome, St. *Gli uomini illustri (De viris illustribus)*. Ed. Aldo Ceresa-Gastoldo. Florence: Nardini, 1988.

Johannes de Bado Aureo. *Tractatus de armis*. In *Medieval Heraldry*, ed. Evan J. Jones, pp. 95–212.

John of Salisbury. *Policraticus*. Ed. C. C. I. Webb. 2 vols. Oxford: Clarendon, 1909.

———. *Policraticus*. Trans. M. F. Markland. New York: Ungar, 1979.

Julian of Norwich. *Revelations of Divine Love*. Trans. Clifton Wolters. Harmondsworth: Penguin, 1966.

Langland, William. **Piers Plowman. An Edition of the C-text*. Ed. Derek Pearsall. York Medieval Texts, 2d series. London: Edward Arnold, 1978.

———. *Piers Plowman: The B Version. Will's Visions of Piers Plowman, Do-Well, Do-Better and Do-Best. An Edition in the form of Trinity College Cambridge MS B.15.17, corrected and restored from the known evidence, with variant readings*. Ed. George Kane and E. Talbot Donaldson. London: Athlone Press, 1975.

———. **The Vision of Piers Plowman. A Critical Edition of the B-Text based on Trinity College Cambridge MS B.15.17 with selected variant readings, an Introduction, Glosses, and a Textual and Literary Commentary*. Ed. A. V. C. Schmidt. London: J. M. Dent and Sons, 1978.

Latini, Brunetto. *Li livres dou Trésor*. Ed. Francis J. Carmody. Berkeley: University of California Press, 1948.

Leland, John. *Commentarii de scriptoribus brittanicis*. Oxford: Sheldonian Theater, 1709.

La lirica toscana del Rinascimento anteriore ai tempi del Magnifico. Ed. F. Flamini. Pisa: Tip. T. Nistri, 1891.

Lotario dei Segni (Pope Innocent III). *De miseria condicionis humane*. Ed. Robert E. Lewis. The Chaucer Library. Athens: University of Georgia Press, 1978.

Lydgate, John. *Fall of Princes*. Ed. Henry Bergen. 4 vols. EETS e.s. 121–4. London: Oxford University Press, 1924–27.

Machaut, Guillaume de. *An Edition and Study of Guillaume de Machaut's "La Prise d'Alixandre."* By Angela Doreen Dzelzainis. Ph.D. diss., University of Cambridge, 1985.

———. *The Judgment of the King of Bohemia*. Ed. R. Barton Palmer. New York: Garland, 1984.

———. *"Le Jugement du roy de Behaigne" and "Remede de Fortune."* Ed. James I. Wimsatt and William W. Kibler. The Chaucer Library. Athens: University of Georgia Press, 1988.

Marx, Karl. *Capital*. 3 vols. Trans. Ben Fowkes. New York: Vintage Books, 1977.

———. *Karl Marx: A Reader*. Cambridge: Cambridge University Press, 1986.

———. *Preface to "A Critique of Political Economy."* In *Karl Marx: A Reader*, ed. Elster, pp. 187–88.

———. *Theories of Surplus Value*. Trans. Emile Burns. Moscow: Foreign Language Publishing House.

Mastičkář. See *A Sacred Farce*, ed. Jarmila F. Veltruský.

Medieval Heraldry: Some Fourteenth-Century Heraldic Works. Ed. Evan J. Jones. Cardiff: William Lewis (Printers) Ltd., 1943.

Medieval Literary Theory and Criticism, c. 1100–1375: The Commentary Tradition. Ed. A. J. Minnis and A. B. Scott, with the assistance of David Wallace. Oxford: Clarendon, 1988.

Le Menagier de Paris. Ed. Georgine E. Brereton and Janet M. Ferrier. Oxford: Clarendon, 1981.

Michel of Northgate, Dan. See *Ayenbite of Inwyt.*

More, Thomas, St. *The Complete Works.* Ed. Louis L. Martz et al. 15 vols. New Haven: Yale University Press, 1963–86.

———. *Utopia.* Ed. Edward Surtz and J. H. Hexter. Vol. 4 of *Complete Works.*

———. *Utopia.* Trans. Ralph Robynson, ed. J. Churton Collins. Oxford: Clarendon, 1904.

Morison, Richard. *Humanist Scholarship and Public Order: Two Tracts Against the Pilgrimage of Grace by Sir Richard Morison.* Ed. David Sandler Berkowitz. Washington, D.C.: Folger Books, 1984.

Morrison, Toni. *Beloved.* London: Chatto and Windus, 1987.

Narrative and Dramatic Sources of Shakespeare. Ed. Geoffrey Bullough. 8 vols. London: Routledge and Kegan Paul, 1957–75.

Nelli, Francesco. *Lettres de Francesco Nelli a Pétrarque.* Ed. Henry Cochin. Paris: Champion, 1892.

The New Jerusalem Bible. Gen. ed. Henry Wansbrough. London: Darton, Longman and Todd, 1985.

Nicholas of Lynn. *The Kalendarium of Nicholas of Lynne.* Ed. Sigmund Eisner. The Chaucer Library. Athens: University of Georgia Press, 1980.

Novelle inedite intorno a Bernabò Visconti. Ed. Piero Ginori Conti. Florence: Fondazione Ginori Conti, 1940.

The Oldcastle Controversy. Ed. Peter Corbin and Douglas Sedge. Manchester: Manchester University Press, 1991.

Oresme, Nicole. *Le Livre de Politiques d'Aristote.* Ed. A. D. Menut. Transactions of the American Philosophical Society, n.s., vol. 60, part 6. Philadelphia: American Philosophical Society, 1970.

Ovid. *Heroides and Amores.* Trans. Grant Showerman. Rvd. G. P. Goold. Loeb Classical Library, 41. Cambridge, Mass.: Harvard University Press, 1977.

———. *Metamorphoses.* Ed. F. J. Miller. Rvd. G. P. Goold. Loeb Classical Library, 42–43. Cambridge, Mass.: Harvard University Press, 1976–77.

The Peasants' Revolt of 1381. Ed. R. B. Dobson. 2d ed. London: MacMillan, 1983.

Petrarca, Francesco (Petrarch). *Canzoniere.* Ed. Alberto Chiari. Milan: Mondadori, 1985.

———. *De sui ipsius et multorum ignorantia.* See *Opere latine,* ed. Bufano, vol. 2, pp. 1025–151.

———. **De viris illustribus.* Extracts and 1351–53 *prohemium.* Ed. Guido Martellotti. In *Prose,* ed. Martellotti et al., pp. 218–67.

———. *De viris illustribus.* Ed. Guido Martellotti. Edizione Nazionale delle Opere di Francesco Petrarca. Florence: Sansoni, 1964.

———. *De vita solitaria.* Ed. Guido Martellotti. In *Prose,* ed. Martellotti et al. See also *The Life of Solitude,* trans. J. Zeitlin.

———. *A Dialogue Between Reason and Adversity: A Late Middle English Version of Petrarch's "De Remediis."* Ed. F. N. M. Diekstra. Assen: Van Gorcum, 1968.

———. *Epistolae de rebus familiaribus et variae.* Ed. Giuseppe Fracasetti. 3 vols. Florence: Le Monnier, 1859–63.

————. *Le familiari.* Vols. 1–3 ed. Vittorio Rossi, vol. 4 ed. Umberto Bosco. Sansoni: Florence, 1933–42.

————. *F. Petrarchae . . . Opera que extant omnia.* Ed. Johannes Herold. Basel: Henrichus Petri, 1554.

————. *Invectiva contra eum qui maledixit Italie.* Ed. P. G. Ricci. In *Prose,* ed. Martellotti et al.

————. *Invective contra medicum.* See *Opere latine,* ed. Bufano.

————. *Letters from Petrarch.* Trans. Morris Bishop. Bloomington: Indiana University Press, 1966.

————. *Letters of Old Age: Rerum senilium libri I–XVIII.* 2 vols. Trans. Aldo S. Bernardo, Saul Levin, and Reta A. Bernardo. Baltimore: Johns Hopkins University Press, 1992.

————. *The Life of Solitude.* Trans. Jacob Zeitlin. Urbana: University of Illinois Press, 1924.

————. *Opere latine di Francesco Petrarca.* Ed. Antonietta Bufano. 2 vols. Turin: UTET, 1975.

————. *Prose.* Ed. G. Martellotti et al. Milan-Naples: Ricciardi Editore: Milan, 1955.

————. *Remedies for Fortune Fair and Foul: A Modern English Translation of "De remediis utriusque Fortune," with a Commentary.* By Conrad H. Rawski. 5 vols. Bloomington: Indiana University Press, 1991.

————. **Rerum familiarum libri.* Trans. Aldo S. Bernado. Vol. 1, Albany: State University of New York Press, 1975. Vols. 2 and 3, Baltimore: Johns Hopkins University Press, 1982–85.

————. *Rime sparse.* Ed. Giovanni Ponte. Milan: Mursia, 1979.

————. *Secretum.* Ed. Enrico Carrara in *Prose,* ed. Martellotti et al.

————. *Seniles.* See *F. Petrarchae . . . Opera,* ed. Herold; *Letters of Old Age,* trans. Bernardo et al.

————. *Testament.* Ed. and trans. Theodor Mommsen. Ithaca: Cornell University Press, 1957.

Phillipe de Mézières. *Le Songe du Vieil Pèlerin.* Ed. G. W. Coopland. 2 vols. Cambridge: Cambridge University Press, 1969.

The Poems of the Pearl Manuscript. Ed. Malcolm Andrew and Ronald Waldron. Berkeley: University of California Press, 1978.

Poeti minori del Trecento. Ed. Natalino Sapegno. Milan and Naples: Garzanti, 1978.

Political Poems and Songs Relating to English History, From the Accession of Edward III to that of Richard III. Ed. Thomas Wright. 2 vols. Rolls Series, 14. London: Longmans et al., 1859–61.

Proverbs, Sentences, and Proverbial Phrases: From English Writings Mainly Before 1500. By Bartlett Jere Whiting, with the collaboration of Helen Westcott Whiting. Cambridge, Mass.: Belknap Press, 1968.

Pucci, Antonio. *Le bellezze di Firenze.* In Giovanni Villani, *Cronica,* ed. Dragomanni, vol. 4, pp. 292–300.

Puttenham, George. *The Arte of English Poesie.* Ed. Gladys D. Willcock and Alice Walker. Cambridge: Cambridge University Press, 1936.

The Renaissance Philosophy of Man: Petrarca, Valla, Ficino, Pico, Pomponazzi, Vives. Ed. Ernst Cassirer, Paul Oskar Kristeller, and John Herman Randall, Jr. Chicago: University of Chicago Press, 1948.

Renaud de Louens. *Le Livre de Mellibee et Prudence*. Ed. J. Burke Severs in *Sources and Analogues of Chaucer's Canterbury Tales*, ed. W. F. Bryan and G. Dempster, pp. 568–614.

Robynson, Ralph. See More, Thomas, St.

Russell, John. *The Boke of Nurture*. In *The Babees Book*, ed. Frederick J. Furnivall, pp. 63–259.

Sacchetti, Franco. *La battaglia delle donne, le lettere, le sposizioni di Vangeli*. Ed. Alberto Chiari. Scrittori d'Italia 166. Bari: Laterza, 1938.

———. *Il Trecentonovelle*. Ed. Antonio Lanza. Florence: Sansoni, 1984.

A Sacred Farce from Medieval Bohemia. Mastičkář. Ed. Jarmila F. Veltruský. Michigan Studies in the Humanities, vol. 6. Ann Arbor: Horace H. Rackham School of Graduate Studies, 1985.

Scriptores rerum mythicarum latini tres Romae nuper reperti. Ed. G. H. Bode. Celle: E. H. C. Schulze, 1834.

Secular Lyrics of the Fourteenth and Fifteenth Centuries. Ed. R. H. Robbins. 2d ed. Oxford: Clarendon, 1955.

Shakespeare, William. *The Complete Oxford Shakespeare*. Ed. Stanley Wells and Gary Taylor. 3 vols. Oxford: Oxford University Press, 1987.

———. *The Complete Signet Classic Shakespeare*. Ed. Sylvan Barnet. New York: Harcourt Brace Jovanovich, 1972.

———. *Henry IV, Part I*. Ed. David Bevington. Oxford: Clarendon, 1987.

———. *A Midsummer Night's Dream*. Ed. Harold F. Brooks. Arden Edition. London: Methuen, 1979.

———. *The Riverside Shakespeare*. Ed. G. Blakemore Evans. Boston: Houghton Mifflin, 1974.

Sidney, Sir Philip. *The Defence of Poesie*. London: William Ponsonby, 1595.

Sidney, Sir Philip. Ed. Katherine Duncan-Jones. The Oxford Authors. Oxford: Oxford University Press, 1989.

Skelton, John. *The Complete English Poems*. Ed. John Scattergood. New Haven: Yale University Press, 1983.

Sources and Analogues of Chaucer's Canterbury Tales. Ed. W. F. Bryan and Germaine Dempster. New York: Humanities Press, 1958.

Spenser, Edmund. *The Faerie Queen*. Ed. Thomas P. Roche, Jr., with the assistance of C. Patrick O'Donnell, Jr. New Haven: Yale University Press, 1981.

———. *Poetical Works*. Ed. J. C. Smith and E. de Selincourt. Oxford: Oxford University Press, 1970.

Stans puer ad mensam (Lambeth MS 853). In *The Babees Book*, ed. Frederick J. Furnivall, pp. 27–33.

Taylor, William. See *Two Wycliffite Texts*, ed. Hudson.

Tennyson, Alfred, Lord. *The Works of Tennyson*. Ed. Hallam, Lord Tennyson, annotated by Alfred, Lord Tennyson. 9 vols. London: Macmillan, 1907–8.

Thomas of Burton. *Chronica monasterii de Melsa, 1150–1506*. Ed. Edward A. Bond. 3 vols. Rolls Series, 43. London: Longman et al., 1866–68.

Thorpe, William. See *Two Wycliffite Texts*, ed. Hudson.

Trevisa, John. See Higden, Ranulph.

Trivet, Nicholas. *Chronique*. "Life of Constance" extract, ed. Margaret Schlauch. In *Sources and Analogues*, ed. W. F. Bryan and G. Dempster, pp. 165–81.

Trokelowe, John de, and Henry de Blaneforde. *Chronica et annales*. Ed. H. T. Riley. Rolls Series 28.3. London: Longman et al., 1866.

Two Wycliffite Texts: The Sermon of William Taylor 1406; The Testimony of William Thorpe 1407. Ed. Anne Hudson. EETS o.s. 301. Oxford: Oxford University Press for EETS, 1993.

Vasari, Giorgio. *Le vite de' più eccellenti architetti, pittori, et scultori italiani, da Cimabue insino a' tempi nostri*. Ed. Luciano Bellosi and Aldo Rossi. Turin: Einaudi, 1986.

Villani, Giovanni. *Cronica*. Ed. F. G. Dragomanni. 4 vols. Florence: Sansone, 1844–45.

———. *Nuova cronica*. Ed. Giuseppe Porta. Parma: University of Guarda, 1991.

Villani, Matteo. *Cronica*. Ed. F. G. Dragomanni. 2 vols. Florence: Sansone, 1846.

The Visconti Hours. Ed. Millard Meiss and Edith W. Kirsch. New York: George Braziller, 1972.

Walsingham, Thomas. *Gesta abbatum monasterii Sancti Albani*. Ed. Henry T. Riley. 3 vols. Rolls Series, 28.4. London: Longmans et al., 1867–69.

———. *Historia anglicana*. Ed. Henry T. Riley. 2 vols. Rolls Series, 28.1. London: Longmans et al., 1863–64.

Weber, Max. *Economy and Society*. Ed. Guenther Roth and Claus Wittich. 2 vols. Berkeley: University of California Press, 1978.

The Westminster Chronicle, 1381–1394. Ed. and trans. L. C. Hector and Barbara F. Harvey. Oxford: Clarendon, 1982.

Whiting, Bartlett Jere. See *Proverbs*.

Wyatt, Sir Thomas. *Collected Poems*. Ed. Joost Daalder. London: Oxford University Press, 1975.

Secondary Sources (Including Dictionaries)

Abel, Elizabeth, ed. *Writing and Sexual Difference*. Chicago: University of Chicago Press, 1982.

D'Adda, G. *Indagini storiche, artistiche e bibliografiche sulla Libreria Visconteo-Sforzesco del Castello di Pavia*. Milan: G. Brigola, 1875.

Aers, David. *Community, Gender, and Individual Identity: English Writing 1360–1430*. London: Routledge, 1988.

———. "A Whisper in the Ear of Early Modernists; or, Reflections on Literary Critics Writing the 'History of the Subject.'" In D. Aers, ed., *Culture and History*, pp. 177–202.

———, ed. *Culture and History, 1350–1600: Essays on English Communities, Identities, and Writing*. New York: Harvester Wheatsheaf, 1992.

Alford, John A. *Piers Plowman: A Glossary of Legal Diction*. Cambridge: D. S. Brewer, 1988.

———. "The Wife of Bath Versus the Clerk of Oxford: What Their Rivalry Means." *CR* 21 (1986): 108–32.

Allen, Mark, and John H. Fisher. *The Essential Chaucer: An Annotated Bibliography of Major Modern Studies*. London: Mansell, 1987.

Allison, K. J. *The East Riding of Yorkshire Landscape*. London: Hodder and Stoughton, 1976.

Allmand, Christopher. *Henry V*. Berkeley: University of California Press, 1992.

Amodio, Mark C., ed. *Oral Poetics in Middle English Poetry*. New York: Garland, 1994.

Anderson, Benedict. *Imagined Communities: Reflections on the Origin and Spread of Nationalism*. 2d ed. London: Verso, 1991.

Anderson, David. *Before the Knight's Tale: Imitation of Classical Epic in Boccaccio's "Teseida."* Philadelphia: University of Pennsylvania Press, 1988.

Anderson, Perry. *In the Tracks of Historical Materialism*. New York: Verso, 1983.

———. *Lineages of the Absolutist State*. London: Verso, 1979.

———. *Passages from Antiquity to Feudalism*. London: Verso, 1978.

Argegni, Corrado. "Dal Verme, Jacopo." In *Condottieri, capitani e tribuni*. 3 vols. Rome: Tosi, 1936–37.

Armitage-Smith, Sidney. *John of Gaunt*. London: Constable, 1904.

Arnold, Morris S., et al., eds. *On the Laws and Customs of England: Essays in Memory of Samuel E. Thorne*. Chapel Hill: University of North Carolina Press, 1981.

Askins, William. "The Anxiety of Affluence: Chaucer's Man of Law and His Colleagues in Late Fourteenth-Century England." Unpublished paper read at the New Chaucer Society Congress, Dublin, 1994.

———. "Chaucer and the Latin Works of Albertano of Brescia." Unpublished paper read at the New Chaucer Society Congress, Canterbury, 1990.

———. "*The Tale of Melibee* and the Crisis at Westminster, November, 1387." *SAC Proceedings*, vol. 2. Knoxville: New Chaucer Society, 1987, pp. 103–12.

Aston, Margaret. *Lollards and Reformers: Images and Literacy in Late Medieval Religion*. London: Hambledon Press, 1984.

Aston, T. H., and C. H. E. Philpin, eds. *The Brenner Debate: Agrarian Class Structure and Economic Development in Pre-Industrial Europe*. Cambridge: Cambridge University Press, 1985.

Attridge, Derek, Geoff Bennington, and Robert Young, eds. *Post-Structuralism and the Question of History*. Cambridge: Cambridge University Press, 1987.

Attwater, Donald. *A Dictionary of Saints*. Harmondsworth: Penguin, 1965.

Babbitt, Susan M. *Oresme's "Livre de Politiques" and the France of Charles V*. Philadelphia: American Philosophical Society, 1985.

Baechler, Jean. *The Origins of Capitalism*. Trans. Barry Cooper. Oxford: Basil Blackwell, 1975.

Bainbridge, Virginia R. *Guild and Parish in Late Medieval Cambridgeshire, c. 1350–1558*. Ph.D. diss., University of London, 1994.

Baker, J. H. *The Legal Profession and Common Law: Historical Essays*. London: Hambledon Press, 1986.

———. *The Order of Serjeants at Law*. London: Selden Society, 1984.

———, and S. F. C. Milsom. *Sources of English Legal History: Private Law to 1750*. London: Butterworth, 1986.

Baldass, Ludwig von. *Hieronymous Bosch*. New York: Abrams, 1960.

Baldessari, John. "Crowds with the Shape of Reason Missing." Photographic essay. *Zone* 1/2 (1986): 32–39.

Baldini, Umberto, ed. *Santa Maria Novella*. Florence: Nardini, 1981.

Baldwin, Anna P. *The Theme of Government in Piers Plowman*. Cambridge: D. S. Brewer, 1981.

Baldwin, John W. *Masters, Princes, and Merchants: The Social Views of Peter the Chanter and His Circle.* 2 vols. Princeton: Princeton University Press, 1970.

Barber, C. L. *Shakespeare's Festive Comedy: A Study of Dramatic Form and its Relation to Social Custom.* Princeton: Princeton University Press, 1959.

Barber, Richard. *Edward, Prince of Wales and Aquitaine: A Biography of the Black Prince.* London: Allen Lane, 1978.

Barker, Juliet R. V. *The Tournament in England, 1100–1400.* Woodbridge: Boydell, 1986.

Barni, Gianluigi. "La formazione interna dello Stato Visconteo." *ASL* n.s. 6 (1941): 3–66.

Baron, Hans. "Articulation and Unity in the Italian Renaissance and in the Modern West." In S. Pargellis, ed., *The Quest for Political Unity*, pp. 123–38.

———. "Cicero and the Roman Civic Spirit in the Middle Ages and Early Renaissance." *BJRL* 22 (1938): 72–97.

———. *The Crisis of the Early Italian Renaissance: Civic Humanism and Republican Liberty in an Age of Classicism and Tyranny.* Princeton: Princeton University Press, 1966.

———. "Moot Problems of Renaissance Interpretation: An Answer to Wallace K. Ferguson." *Journal of the History of Ideas* 19 (1958): 26–34.

———. *In Search of Civic Humanism.* 2 vols. Princeton: Princeton University Press, 1988.

———. "A Sociological Interpretation of the Early Renaissance in Florence." *South Atlantic Quarterly* 38 (1939): 427–48.

Barron, Caroline M. "The Deposition of Richard II." In J. Taylor and W. Childs, eds., *Politics and Crisis*, pp. 132–49.

———. "The London Middle English Guild Certificates of 1388–9." *Nottingham Medieval Studies* 38 (1995): 1–13.

———. "The Parish Fraternities of Medieval London." In Barron and Harper-Bill, eds., *Essays in Honour of F. R. H. Du Boulay*, pp. 13–37.

———. "The Quarrel of Richard II with London 1392–7." In Du Boulay and Barron, ed., *Essays in Honour of May McKisack*, pp. 173–201.

———. "Richard II: Image and Reality." In D. Gordon, *Wilton Diptych*, pp. 13–19.

———. "The Tyranny of Richard II." *BJHR* 41 (May 1968): 1–18.

———, and Christopher Harper-Bill, eds. *Essays in Honour of F. R. H. Du Boulay.* Woodbridge: The Boydell Press, 1985.

Barton, Anne. "The King Disguised: Shakespeare's *Henry V* and the Comical History." An essay of 1975, now published as part of *Essays, Mainly Shakespearean.* Cambridge: Cambridge University Press, 1994, pp. 207–33.

Bataille, Georges. *The Accursed Share: An Essay on General Economy.* 3 vols. published as 2 books. New York: Zone Books, 1988, 1991.

Bec, Christian. "Il mito di Firenze da Dante al Ghiberti." In P. Ragionieri, ed., *Lorenzo Ghiberti*, pp. 3–26.

Becker, Marvin B. *Florence in Transition.* Baltimore: Johns Hopkins University Press, 1967–68.

———. "The Florentine Territorial State and Civic Humanism in the Early Renaissance." In N. Rubinstein, ed., *Florentine Studies*, pp. 109–39.

————. *Medieval Italy: Constraints and Creativity.* Bloomington: Indiana University Press, 1981.

Beckwith, Sarah. *Christ's Body: Identity, Culture, and Society in Late Medieval Writings.* London: Routledge, 1993.

Beichner, Paul. "Chaucer's Man of Law and *disparitas cultus.*" *Speculum* 23 (1948): 70–75.

Bell, Dora M. *Etude sur "Le Songe du Vieil Pèlerin" de Philippe de Mézières.* Geneva: Librairie E. Droz, 1955.

Bellamy, J. G. *Bastard Feudalism and the Law.* London: Routledge, 1989.

————. *The Law of Treason in England in the Middle Ages.* Cambridge: Cambridge University Press, 1970.

Belting, Hans. "Wandmalerei und Literatur im Zeitalter Dantes—Zwei öffentliche Medien an einer Epochenschwelle." In R. Herzog and R. Koselleck, eds., *Epochenschwelle,* pp. 53–79.

Benjamin, Walter. *Illuminations.* Ed. Hannah Arendt, trans. Harry Zohn. London: Fontana Press, 1992.

Bennett, J. A. W. "Chaucer, Dante, and Boccaccio." In P. Boitani, ed., *Trecento,* pp. 89–139.

————. *Chaucer at Oxford and Cambridge.* Oxford: Clarendon, 1974.

Bennett, Judith. "Medieval Women, Modern Women: Across the Great Divide." In D. Aers, ed., *Culture and History, 1350–1600,* pp. 147–75.

————. *Women in the Medieval English Countryside: Gender and Household in Brigstock before the Plague.* Oxford: Oxford University Press, 1987.

Bennington, Geoff. "Demanding History." In D. Attridge, G. Bennington, and R. Young, eds., *Post-Structuralism and the Question of History,* pp. 15–29.

Benson, C. David, and Elizabeth Robertson, eds. *Chaucer's Religious Tales.* Cambridge: D. S. Brewer, 1990.

Benson, Larry D., ed. *The Learned and the Lewed: Studies in Chaucer and Medieval Literature.* Cambridge: Harvard University Press, 1974.

Bernado, Aldo S., ed. *Francesco Petrarca: Citizen of the World.* Albany: State University of New York Press, 1980.

Berndt, D. E. "Monastic *Acedia* and Chaucer's Characterization of Daun Piers." *Studies in Philology* 68 (1971): 435–50.

Biasin, Gian-Paolo, A. Mancini, and N. Perella, eds. *Studies in the Italian Renaissance: Essays in Memory of Arnolfo B. Ferruolo.* Naples: Società Editrice Napoletana, 1984.

Billanovich, Giuseppe. *Petrarca letterato. I. Lo scrittoio del Petrarca.* Rome: Edizioni di "Storia e Letteratura," 1947.

————, and Giuseppe Frasso, eds. *Il Petrarca ad Arquà.* Padua: Antenore, 1975.

Bird, Ruth. *The Turbulent London of Richard II.* London: Longmans, 1949.

Bishop, Morris. *Petrarch and His World.* Bloomington: Indiana University Press, 1963.

Black, Antony. *Guilds and Civil Society in European Political Thought from the Twelfth Century to the Present.* Ithaca: Cornell University Press, 1984.

————. *Political Thought in Europe, 1250–1450.* Cambridge: Cambridge University Press, 1992.

————. "St. Thomas Aquinas: The State and Morality." In B. Redhead, ed., *Political Thought,* pp. 61–72.

Black, H. C., ed. *Black's Law Dictionary*, 5th ed. St. Paul, Minn.: West Publishing, 1979.

Bloch, R. Howard. "Medieval Misogyny." *Representations* 20 (Fall 1987): 1–24.

———. *Medieval Misogyny and the Invention of Western Romantic Love*. Chicago: University of Chicago Press, 1991.

Block, Edward A. "Originality, Controlling Purpose, and Craftsmanship in Chaucer's *Man of Law's Tale*." *PMLA* 68 (1953): 572–616.

Bloom, Harold, ed. *Modern Critical Views: Dante*. New York: Chelsea House Publishers, 1986.

———, ed. *Modern Critical Views: Geoffrey Chaucer*. New York: Chelsea House Publishers, 1985.

Boffey, Julia, and John J. Thompson. "Anthologies and Miscellanies: Production and Choice of Texts." In J. Griffiths and D. Pearsall, eds., *Book Production*, pp. 279–315.

Boitani, Piero. *Chaucer and Boccaccio*. Medium Aevum Monographs, n.s. 8. Oxford: Society for the Study of Mediaeval Languages and Literature, 1977.

———. *Chaucer and the Imaginary World of Fame*. Cambridge: D. S. Brewer, 1984.

———. "*The Monk's Tale*: Dante and Boccaccio." *Medium Aevum* 45 (1976): 50–69.

———. "Petrarch's *Dilectoso Male* and Its European Context." In J. Fichte, ed., *Zusammenhänge, Einflüsse, Wirkungen*, pp. 299–314.

———. "Style, Iconography and Narrative: the Lesson of the *Teseida*." In P. Boitani, ed., *Trecento*, pp. 185–99.

———. "What Dante Meant to Chaucer." In P. Boitani, ed., *Trecento*, pp. 115–39.

———, ed. *Chaucer and the Italian Trecento*. Cambridge: Cambridge University Press, 1983.

———, and Jill Mann, eds. *The Cambridge Chaucer Companion*. Cambridge: Cambridge University Press, 1986.

———, and Anna Torti, eds. *Interpretation: Medieval and Modern*. Cambridge: D. S. Brewer, 1993.

Bolton, J. L. *The Medieval English Economy 1150–1500*. London: Dent, 1980.

Bolton, W. F. "Pinchbeck and the Chaucer Circle in the Law Reports and Records of 11–13 Richard II." *Modern Philology* 84 (1987): 401–7.

Borenius, Tancred, and E. W. Tristram. *English Medieval Painting*. First published 1927; reissued New York: Hacker, 1976.

Borsook, Eve. *The Mural Painters of Tuscany*. London: Phaidon, 1960.

Bosco, Umberto. "Realtà e mito di Arquà." In G. Billanovich and G. Frasso, eds., *Il Petrarca ad Arquà*, pp. 1–5.

Boskovits, Miklòs. *Pittura fiorentina alla vigilia del Rinascimento 1370–1400*. Florence: Edam, 1975.

Bosl, Karl, ed. *Handbuch der Geschichte der Böhmischen Länder*, vol. 1, *Die Böhmischen Länder von der Archaischen Zeit bis zum Ausgang der Hussitischen Revolution*. Stuttgart: Anton Hiersemann, 1967.

———. *Lebensbilder zur Geschichte der Böhmischen Länder*, vol. 1. Munich: Oldenbourg, 1974.

Boswell, John. *The Kindness of Strangers: The Abandonment of Children in Western Europe from Late Antiquity to the Renaissance*. New York: Vintage, 1988.

Bourdieu, Pierre. *Distinction: A Social Critique of the Judgment of Taste*. Trans. Richard Nice. Cambridge, Mass.: Harvard University Press, 1984.

———. *The Field of Cultural Production: Essays on Art and Literature*. Ed. and intr. Randal Johnson. New York: Columbia University Press, 1993.

Bowden, Muriel A. *A Commentary on the General Prologue to the Canterbury Tales*. 2d ed. London: Souvenir Press, 1973.

Bowen, William R., ed. *Confraternities in the Renaissance*. A special issue of *Renaissance and Reformation* n.s. 13, no. 1 (1989).

Braddy, Haldeen. *Geoffrey Chaucer: Literary and Historical Studies*. Port Washington, N.Y.: Kennicat Press, 1971.

Braden, Gordon. "It's Not the Years, It's the Mileage." *New Literary History* 14 (Spring 1983): 665–76.

Branca, Vittore. *Boccaccio medievale*. 3d ed. Florence: Sansoni, 1970.

———. *Boccaccio: The Man and His Works*. Trans. Richard Monges. New York: New York University Press, 1976.

———. "Giovanni Boccaccio: Profilo biografico." In Giovanni Boccaccio, *Tutte le opere*, ed. V. Branca, vol. 1.

———. *Tradizione delle opere di Giovanni Boccaccio*. 2 vols. Rome: Edizioni di Storia e Letteratura, 1958–91.

Brand, Paul. "Courtroom and Schoolroom: The Education of Lawyers in England prior to 1400." *Historical Research* 60, no. 142 (June 1987): 147–65. Now collected as part of *The Making of the Common Law*, pp. 57–75.

———. *The Making of the Common Law*. London: Hambledon Press, 1992.

Braswell, Mary Flowers. "Chaucer's 'Court Baron': Law and *The Canterbury Tales*." *SAC* 16 (1994): 29–44.

Brenner, Robert. "The Agrarian Roots of European Capitalism." *Past and Present* 97 (1982): 16–113.

Brewer, Derek S., ed. *Chaucer: The Critical Heritage*. 2 vols. London: Routledge and Kegan Paul, 1978.

Brewer's Dictionary of Phrase and Fable. 14th ed. Ed. Ivor H. Evans. London: Cassell, 1989.

———, ed. *Writers and Their Background: Geoffrey Chaucer*. London: G. Bell & Sons, 1974.

Bridenthal, Renate, and Claudia Koonz, eds. *Becoming Visible: Women in European History*. Boston: Houghton Mifflin, 1977.

Brose, Margaret. "Petrarch's Beloved Body: 'Italia mia.'" In L. Lomperis and S. Stanbury, eds., *Feminist Approaches to the Body in Medieval Literature*, pp. 1–20.

Brown, Alison. "Jacob Burckhardt's Renaissance." *History Today* 38 (Oct. 1988): 20–26.

Brown, James Wood. *The Dominican Church of Santa Maria Novella at Florence*. Edinburgh: Otto Schulze, 1902.

Brownlee, Kevin. *Poetic Identity in Guillaume de Machaut*. Madison: University of Wisconsin Press, 1984.

Brucker, Gene A. *The Civic World of Early Renaissance Florence*. Princeton: Princeton University Press, 1977.

———. *Florentine Politics and Society 1343–1378*. Princeton: Princeton University Press, 1962.

———. "The Florentine *popolo minuto* and its political role, 1340–1450." In L. Martines., ed., *Violence and Disorder*, pp. 155–83.

———. "The Medici in the Fourteenth Century." *Speculum* 32 (1957): 1–26.

———. *Renaissance Florence*. New York: John Wiley, 1969.

Buck, August. "Hans Baron's Contribution to the Literary History of the Renaissance." In A. Molho and J. A. Tedeschi, eds., *Renaissance Studies in Honor of Hans Baron*, pp. xxxi–lviii.

Bueno de Mesquita, Daniel Meredith. "The Foreign Policy of Richard II in 1397: Some Italian Letters." *English Historical Review* 56 (1941): 628–37.

———. *Giangaleazzo Visconti, Duke of Milan, 1351–1402: A Study in the Political Career of an Italian Despot*. Cambridge: Cambridge University Press, 1941.

Bujnoch, Joseph. "Johann von Neumarkt—Johann von Jenstein—Guillaume de Machaut." In F. Seibt, ed., *Karl IV und sein Kreis*, pp. 67–98.

Burckhardt, Jacob. *The Civilization of the Renaissance in Italy*. Trans. S. G. C. Middlemore. 2 vols. New York: Harper and Row, 1958.

———. *Die Cultur der Renaissance: Ein Versuch*. Basel: Schweighausersche Verlagsbuchhandlung, 1860.

———. **Die Kultur der Renaissance in Italien: Ein Versuch*. Ed. Horst Günther. Frankfurt am Main: Deutscher Klassiker Verlag, 1989.

Burford, E. J. *Bawds and Lodgings: A History of the London Bankside Brothels c. 100–1675*. London: Peter Owen, 1976.

Burgess, Glyn S., ed. *Court and Poet: Selected Proceedings of the Third Congress of the International Courtly Literature Society (Liverpool 1980)*. Liverpool: Francis Cairns, 1981.

Burnley, David. *Chaucer's Language and the Philosophers' Tradition*. Cambridge: D. S. Brewer, 1979.

Burns, J. H., ed. *The Cambridge History of Medieval Political Thought*. Cambridge: Cambridge University Press, 1988.

Burrow, John. *Essays on Medieval Literature*. Oxford: Clarendon, 1984.

———. *Ricardian Poetry: Chaucer, Gower, Langland, and the Gawain Poet*. London: Routledge and Kegan Paul, 1971.

Bury, J. B., and J. M. Hussey, eds. *The Cambridge Medieval History*. 8 vols. Cambridge: Cambridge University Press, 1911–36.

Butcher, A. F. "English Urban Society and the Revolt of 1381." In R. Hilton and T. H. Aston, eds., *The English Rising*, pp. 84–111.

Butler, Judith. *Gender Trouble: Feminism and the Subversion of Identity*. New York: Routledge, 1990.

Butler, W. F. *The Lombard Communes: A History of the Republics of North Italy*. London: T. Fisher Unwin, 1906.

Cadei, Antonio. *Studi di miniatura lombarda: Giovanni de' Grassi, Belbello da Pavia*. Rome: Viella, 1984.

The Cambridge History of Medieval Political Thought. Ed. J. H. Burns. Cambridge: Cambridge University Press, 1988.

Carlin, Martha. *The Urban Development of Southwark, c. 1200–1550*. Ph.D. diss., University of Toronto, 1983.

Carlyle, A. J. and R. W. Carlyle. *A History of Medieval Political Theory in the West*. 6 vols. New York: Barnes & Noble, 1903–36.

Carruthers, Mary J. *The Book of Memory: A Study of Memory in Medieval Culture.* Cambridge: Cambridge University Press, 1990.

———. "Seeing Things: Locational Memory in Chaucer's *Knight's Tale.*" In *Art and Context*, ed. R. R. Edwards, pp. 93–106.

———. "The Wife of Bath and the Painting of Lions." *PMLA* 94 (1979): 209–22.

Carus-Wilson, Eleonora. "The Woollen Industry." In M. M. Postan and E. Miller, eds., *Cambridge Economic History of Europe*, pp. 614–90.

Cassell, Anthony K. *Dante's Fearful Art of Justice.* Toronto: University of Toronto Press, 1984.

Castellano, Aldo. "Il postgotico lombardo e le origini del Duomo di Milano." In A. A. Villa et al. eds., *La Lombardia*, pp. 155–90.

Cazelles, Raymond. "The Jacquerie." In R. H. Hilton and T. H. Aston, eds., *English Rising*, pp. 74–83.

Celant, Germano. *Unexpressionism: Art Beyond the Contemporary.* New York: Rizzoli International, 1988.

Certeau, Michel de. *The Writing of History.* Trans. Tom Conley. New York: Columbia University Press, 1988.

Chadwick, Henry. "Christian Doctrine." In *CHMPT*, pp. 11–20.

Chamberlin, E. R. *The Count of Virtue: Giangaleazzo Visconti, Duke of Milan.* London: Eyre and Spottiswoode, 1965.

A Chaucer Glossary. Ed. Norman Davis, Douglas Gray, Patricia Ingham, and Anne Wallace-Hadrill. Oxford: Clarendon, 1979.

Childs, Wendy. "Anglo-Italian Contacts in the Fourteenth Century." In P. Boitani, ed., *Trecento*, pp. 65–87.

Chojnacki, Stanley, ed. "Recent Trends in Renaissance Studies: The Family, Marriage, and Sex." *Renaissance Quarterly* 40 (1987): 660–761.

Christianson, C. Paul. "Evidence for the Study of London's Late Medieval Manuscript-Book Trade." In J. Griffiths and D. Pearsall, eds., *Book Production and Publishing in Britain*, pp. 87–108.

Clark, Alice. *Working Life of Women in the Seventeenth Century.* London: Routledge, 1919.

Clément, Catherine. *The Lives and Legends of Jacques Lacan.* Trans. A. Goldhammer. New York: Columbia University Press, 1983.

Clough, Cecil H., ed. *Profession, Vocation, and Culture in Later Medieval England: Essays Dedicated to the Memory of A. R. Myers.* Liverpool: Liverpool University Press, 1982.

Cohen, Jeremy. *The Friars and the Jews: The Evolution of Medieval Anti-Judaism.* Ithaca: Cornell University Press, 1982.

Cohen, Walter. *Drama of a Nation: Public Theater in England and Spain.* Ithaca: Cornell University Press, 1985.

Cohn, Samuel. "Florentine Insurrections, 1343–1385." In R. H. Hilton and T. H. Aston, eds., *English Rising*, pp. 143–64.

Coleman, Janet. "English Culture in the Fourteenth Century." In P. Boitani, ed., *Trecento*, pp. 33–63.

———. "Property and Poverty." In *CHMPT*, pp. 607–48.

———. "St. Augustine: Christian Political Thought at the End of the Roman Empire." In B. Redhead, ed., *Political Thought*, pp. 45–60.

Coleman, William E. "Chaucer, the *Teseida*, and the Visconti Library at Pavia." *Medium Aevum* 51 (1982): 92–101.

Coletti, Teresa. "Reading REED: History and the Records of Early English Drama." In L. Patterson, ed., *Literary Practice*, pp. 248–84.

Collins, Randall. *Weberian Sociological Theory*. Cambridge: Cambridge University Press, 1986.

Cook, A. S. "Chauceriana II: 'Nayled in his cheste.'" *Romanic Review* 8 (1917): 222–24.

Cooper, Helen. *The Canterbury Tales*. Oxford Guides to Chaucer. Updated paperback edition. London: Oxford University Press, 1991.

———. *Pastoral: Mediaeval into Renaissance*. Ipswich: D. S. Brewer, 1977.

———. *The Structure of the Canterbury Tales*. London: Duckworth, 1983.

Copeland, Rita. "The Pardoner's Body and the Disciplining of Rhetoric." In S. Kay and M. Rubin, eds., *Framing Medieval Bodies*, pp. 138–59.

———. "Rhetoric and the Politics of the Literal Sense in Medieval Literary Theory: Aquinas, Wyclif, and the Lollards." In P. Boitani and A. Torti, eds., *Interpretation: Medieval and Modern*, pp. 1–23.

———. *Rhetoric, Hermeneutics, and Translation in the Middle Ages: Academic Traditions and Vernacular Texts*. Cambridge: Cambridge University Press, 1991.

———. "Why Women Can't Read: Medieval Hermeneutics, Statutory Law, and the Lollard Heresy Trials." In S. S. Heinzelman and Z. B. Wiseman, eds., *Representing Women*, pp. 253–86.

Correale, Robert M. "Chaucer's Manuscript of Nicholas Trevet's *Les Cronicles*." *CR* 25 (1991): 238–65.

Corrigan, Philip, and Derek Sayer. *The Great Arch: English State Formation as Cultural Revolution*. Oxford: Basil Blackwell, 1985.

Crane, Susan. *Gender and Romance in Chaucer's "Canterbury Tales."* Princeton: Princeton University Press, 1994.

Crosby, Everett U., C. Julian Bishko, and Robert L. Kellogg. *Medieval Studies: A Bibliographical Guide*. New York: Garland, 1983.

Culler, Jonathan. "Criticism and Institutions: The American University." In D. Attridge et al., eds., *Post-Structuralism and the Question of History*, pp. 82–98.

David, Alfred. "How Marcia Lost Her Skin: A Note on Chaucer's Mythology." In L. D. Benson, ed., *The Learned and the Lewed*, pp. 19–29.

Davidsohn, Robert. *Storia di Firenze*. 4 parts published as 8 vols. Florence: Sansoni, 1956–68.

Davies, R. H. C. "An Oxford Charter of 1191 and the Beginnings of Municipal Freedom." *Oxoniensia* 33 (1968): 53–65.

Davis, Charles T. "Il Buon Tempo Antico." In N. Rubenstein, ed., *Florentine Studies*, pp. 45–69.

Deanesly, Margaret. *The Lollard Bible and Other Medieval Biblical Versions*. Cambridge: Cambridge University Press, 1920.

Deiss, Joseph Jay. *Captains of Fortune: Profiles of Six Italian Condottieri*. London: Victor Gollancz, 1966.

Delasanta, Rodney K. "Chaucer, Pavia, and the Ciel d'Oro." *Medium Aevum* 54 (1985): 117–21.

Derrida, Jacques. "Like the Sound of the Sea Deep Within a Shell: Paul de Man's War." In W. Hamacher et al., eds., *Responses*, pp. 126–64.

Dictionary of the Middle Ages. Ed. Joseph R. Strayer. 13 vols. New York: Scribner, 1982–89.

Dictionary of National Biography. Ed. Sir Leslie Stephen and Sir Sidney Lee. 63 vols. London: Smith, Elder, 1885–1900.

Dictionary of National Biography Supplement: Jan. 1901–Dec. 1911. Ed. Sir Sidney Lee. 3 vols. Oxford: Oxford University Press, 1912.

Dictionnaire Historique de la Langue Française. Ed. Alain Rey. 2 vols. Paris: Dictionnaires Le Robert, 1992.

Dinshaw, Carolyn. *Chaucer's Sexual Poetics*. Madison: University of Wisconsin Press, 1989.

———. "The Law of Man and Its 'Abhomynacions.'" *Exemplaria* 1 (1989): 117–48.

———, ed., with David M. Halperin. *GLQ: A Journal of Gay and Lesbian Studies*.

Dizionario biografico degli italiani. Ed. A. M. Ghisalberti. Incomplete. Rome: Istituto della Enciclopedia Italiana, 1960–.

Dollimore, Jonathan, and Alan Sinfield, eds. *Political Shakespeare: New Essays in Cultural Materialism*. Ithaca: Cornell University Press, 1985.

Donaldson, E. Talbot. *The Swan at the Well: Shakespeare Reading Chaucer*. New Haven: Yale University Press, 1985.

Douglas, Mary. *Purity and Danger: An Analysis of Concepts of Pollution and Taboo*. New York: Praeger, 1966.

Doyle, A. I. "More Light on John Shirley." *Medium Aevum* 30 (1961): 93–101.

Dreyfus, H. L., and Paul Rabinow, eds. *Michel Foucault: Beyond Structuralism and Hermeneutics*. 2d ed. Chicago: University of Chicago Press, 1983.

Du Boulay, F. R. H., and Caroline M. Barron, eds. *The Reign of Richard II*. London: Athlone Press, 1971.

Duby, Georges. *The Chivalrous Society*. Trans. C. Postan. London: Arnold, 1977.

"Due secoli di architettura lombarda." In A. A. Villa et al., eds., *La Lombardia*, pp. 191–218.

Duffy, Eamon. *The Stripping of the Altars: Traditional Religion in England, c. 1400–c. 1580*. New Haven: Yale University Press, 1992.

Duls, Louisa D. *Richard II in the Early Chronicles*. The Hague: Mouton, 1975.

Dunbabin, Jean. "Government." In *CHMPT*, pp. 477–519.

Durkheim, Emile. *The Division of Labor in Society*. Trans. W. D. Halls. Introduction by Lewis Coser. London: Macmillan, 1984.

———. *Durkheim on Politics and the State*. Ed. and intr. Anthony Giddens. Trans. W. D. Halls. Cambridge: Polity Press, 1986.

———. *Textes*. Ed. Victor Karady. 3 vols. Paris: Les Editions de Minuit, 1975.

Dyer, C. C. "Power and Conflict in the Medieval English Village." In D. Hooke, ed., *Medieval Villages*, pp. 27–32.

Ebin, Lois. *John Lydgate*. Boston: Twayne, 1985.

Eckhardt, Caroline D. *Chaucer's General Prologue to the "Canterbury Tales": An Annotated Bibliography 1900 to 1982*. Toronto: University of Toronto Press, 1990.

Edbury, Peter W. *The Kingdom of Cyprus and the Crusades, 1191–1374*. Cambridge: Cambridge University Press, 1991.

Edwards, A. S. G. "Critical Approaches to the *Man of Law's Tale*." In C. D. Benson and E. Robertson, eds., *Chaucer's Religious Tales*, pp. 85–94.

Edwards, Robert R., ed. *Art and Context in Late Medieval English Narrative: Essays in Honor of Robert Worth Frank, Jr.* Cambridge: D. S. Brewer, 1994.

Ellis, Roger. *Patterns of Religious Narrative in the Canterbury Tales*. London: Croom Helm, 1986.

Emerton, Ephraim. *Humanism and Tyranny: Studies in the Italian Trecento*. Cambridge, Mass.: Harvard University Press, 1925.

Esmein, A. *A History of Continental Criminal Procedure with Special Reference to France*. Trans. John Simpson. Boston: Little, 1913.

Etter, Roberta Bromley. *Prague*. Hong Kong: Guidebook Company, 1994.

Evans, Ivor H., ed. See *Brewer's Dictionary*.

Farmer, Sharon. "Persuasive Voices: Clerical Images of Medieval Wives." *Speculum* 61 (1986): 517–43.

Fein, Susanna Grier, David Raybin, and Peter C. Braeger, eds. *Rebels and Rivals: The Contestive Spirit in "The Canterbury Tales."* Kalamazoo: Medieval Institute Publications, 1991.

Ferguson, Margaret W., Maureen Quilligan, and Nancy J. Vickers, eds. *Rewriting the Renaissance: The Discourses of Sexual Difference in Early Modern Europe*. Chicago: University of Chicago Press, 1986.

Ferguson, Wallace K. "The Interpretation of Italian Humanism: The Contribution of Hans Baron." *Journal of the History of Ideas* 19 (1958): 14–25.

Ferrante, Joan M. *The Political Vision of the Divine Comedy*. Princeton: Princeton University Press, 1984.

Ferrari, Giuliana. "Gli spettacoli all'epoca dei Visconti e degli Sforza: dalla festa cittadina alla festa celebrativa." In A. A. Villa et al., eds., *La Lombardia*, pp. 219–43.

Fichte, Joerg, ed. *Zusammenhänge, Einflüsse, Wirkungen: Kongressakten zum ersten Symposium des Mediävistenverbandes in Tübingen, 1984*. Berlin: Walter de Gruyter, 1986.

Field, Rosalind. "Reading Pavia: Civic Reputation and Critical Response." Paper read at the New Chaucer Society Conference, Dublin, July 1994.

Fisher, John Hurt. "A Language Policy for Lancastrian England." *PMLA* 107 (1992): 1168–80.

Fleckenstein, Josef, ed. *Investiturstreit und Reichsverfassung*. Sigmaringen: Jan Thorbeke, 1973.

Fleming, John V. "The Antifraternalism of the *Summoner's Tale*." *JEGP* 65 (1966): 688–700.

———. "The Summoner's Prologue: An Iconographic Adjustment." *CR* 2 (1967–68): 95–107.

Foligno, Cesare. "Di alcuni documenti viscontei in biblioteche inglesi." *ASL* series 4, vol. 4, anno 32 (1905): 239–45.

Foss, Edward. *The Judges of England*. Vol. 1. London: Longman, Brown, Green, and Longmans, 1848.

Foster, Kenelm. *Petrarch: Poet and Humanist*. Edinburgh: Edinburgh University Press, 1984.

———. *The Two Dantes and Other Studies.* London: Darton, Longman and Todd, 1977.

Foucault, Michel. *Discipline and Punish: The Birth of the Prison.* Trans. Alan Sheridan. New York: Vintage Books, 1979.

———. *Language, Counter-Memory, Practice.* Trans. Donald B. Bouchard and Sherry Simon. Ithaca: Cornell University Press, 1977.

Fowler, Alastair. *Kinds of Literature: An Introduction to the Theory of Genres and Modes.* Oxford: Clarendon, 1982.

Fradenburg, Louise. "Chaucer and the Politics of Salvation." Paper delivered at the New Chaucer Society Congress, Dublin, July 25, 1994.

———. *City, Marriage, Tournament: Arts of Rule in Late Medieval Scotland.* Madison: University of Wisconsin Press, 1991.

———. "The Manciple's Servant Tongue: Politics and Poetry in *The Canterbury Tales.*" *ELH* 52 (1985): 85–118.

———. " 'Voice Memorial': Loss and Reparation in Chaucer's Poetry." *Exemplaria* 2 (1990): 169–202.

Frantzen, Allen J. *Desire for Origins: New Language, Old English, and Teaching the Tradition.* New Brunswick: Rutgers University Press, 1990.

Frati, Vasco, ed. *Brescia nell'età delle signorie.* Brescia: Grafo, 1980.

Frederick James Furnivall: A Volume of Personal Record. Ed. anon. London: Oxford University Press, 1911.

Fry, Donald. "The Ending of the Monk's Tale." *JEGP* 71 (1972): 355–68.

Fryde, Natalie. *The Tyranny and Fall of Edward II, 1321–1326.* Cambridge: Cambridge University Press, 1979.

Frye, Susan. *Elizabeth I: The Competition for Representation.* New York: Oxford University Press, 1993.

Gallagher, Catherine. "Blindness and Hindsight." In W. Hamacher et al., eds., *Responses,* pp. 204–7.

Galloway, James. *Historical Sketches of Old Charing. The Hospital and Chapel of Saint Mary Roncevall. Eleanor of Castile, Queen of England, and the Monuments Erected in Her Memory.* London: Bale and Danielsson, 1914.

Gennep, Arnold van. *The Rites of Passage.* Trans. Monika B. Vizedom and Gabrielle L. Caffee. London: Routledge and Kegan Paul, 1960.

Georgianna, Linda. "Lords, Churls, and Friars: The Return to Social Order in the *Summoner's Tale.*" In S. G. Fein, D. Raybin, and P. C. Braeger, eds., *Rebels and Rivals,* pp. 149–72.

Gerchow, Jan. "Memoria als Norm: Aspekte englischer Gildestatuten des 14. Jahrhunderts." In *Memoria in der Gesellschaft des Mittelalters,* ed. D. Geuenich and O. G. Oexle, pp. 207–66.

Geuenich, Dieter, and Otto Gerhard Oexle, eds. *Memoria in der Gesellschaft des Mittlealters.* Göttingen: Vandenhoeck and Ruprecht, 1994.

Gibson, Michael. *Peter Bruegel.* Secaucus, N.J.: Wellfleet Press, 1989.

Giddens, Anthony. *Durkheim.* Hassocks: Harvester Press, 1978.

Gierke, Otto von. *Community in Historical Perspective. A Translation of Selections from "Das Deutsche Genossenschaftsrecht" ("The German Law of Fellowship") by Otto von Gierke, principally from volume 1.* Ed. Antony Black. Trans. Mary Fischer. Cambridge: Cambridge University Press, 1990.

——. *Das Deutsche Genossenschaftsrecht*. 4 vols. Berlin: Weidmannsche Buchhandlung, 1868–1913.

Gilby, Thomas. "Prudence." In *New Catholic Encyclopedia*, vol. 11, pp. 925–28.

Giulini, Giorgio. *Memorie spettanti alla storia di Milano*. 12 vols. Milan: B. Bianchi, 1760–71.

Given-Wilson, Chris. *The Royal Household and the King's Affinity: Service, Politics, and Finance in England 1360–1413*. New Haven: Yale University Press, 1986.

Goad, Harold. "The Suggested Portrait of an Englishman in the Frescoes of the Spanish Chapel." *Bollettino degli studi inglesi in Italia* 2.2 (April 1933): 10–14.

Godman, Peter. "Chaucer and Boccaccio's Latin Works." In P. Boitani, ed., *Italian Trecento*, pp. 269–95.

Goodman, Anthony. *John of Gaunt: The Exercise of Princely Power in Fourteenth-Century Europe*. Harlow: Longman, 1992.

——. *The Loyal Conspiracy: The Lords Appellant under Richard II*. London: Routledge and Kegan Paul, 1971.

Gordon, Dillian. With an essay by Caroline M. Barron and contributions by Ashok Roy and Martin Wyld. *Making and Meaning: The Wilton Diptych*. London: National Gallery Publications, 1993.

Gottfried, Robert S. *The Black Death: Natural and Human Disaster in Medieval Europe*. New York: The Free Press, 1983.

——. *Bury St. Edmunds and the Urban Crisis: 1290–1539*. Princeton: Princeton University Press, 1982.

Grafton, Anthony, and Lisa Jardine. *From Humanism to the Humanities: Education and the Liberal Arts in Fifteenth- and Sixteenth-Century Europe*. London: Duckworth, 1986.

Gransden, Antonia. *Historical Writing in England, Volume 2, c. 1307 to the Early Sixteenth Century*. Ithaca: Cornell University Press, 1982.

Green, Louis. *Chronicle into History: An Essay on the Interpretation of History in Florentine Fourteenth-Century Chronicles*. Cambridge: Cambridge University Press, 1972.

Greenblatt, Stephen. *Marvelous Possessions: The Wonder of the New World*. Chicago: University of Chicago Press, 1991.

——. *Renaissance Self-Fashioning*. Berkeley: University of California Press, 1980.

——, ed. *The Power of Forms in the English Renaissance*. Norman: Pilgrim Books, 1982.

——, ed. *Representing the Renaissance*. Berkeley: University of California Press, 1988.

——, and Giles Gunn, eds. *Redrawing the Boundaries: The Transformation of English and American Literary Studies*. New York: MLA, 1992.

Grégoire, Pierre. *Kaiser Karl IV: Eine mediävale Kulturpotenz aus dem Hause Luxemburg*. Luxemburg: Verlag "De Frëndeskrees," 1984.

Griffiths, Jeremy, and Derek Pearsall, eds. *Book Production and Publishing in Britain 1375–1475*. Cambridge: Cambridge University Press, 1989.

Gubar, Susan. " 'The Blank Page' and the Issues of Female Creativity." In E. Abel, ed., *Writing and Sexual Difference*, pp. 100–122.

Guenée, Bernard. *States and Rulers in Later Medieval Europe*. Oxford: Basil Blackwell, 1985.

Guerrini, P. "Albertano da Brescia." In *Dizionario biografico degli italiani*, vol. 1, p. 669.

Guidoni, Enrico. "Appunti per una storia dell'urbanistica nella Lombardia tardo-medievale." In C. Pirovani, ed., *Lombardia*, vol. 1, pp. 109–62.

Guillaume de Machaut: Poète et Compositeur. Organized by L'Université de Reims, Actes et Colloques 23. Paris: Klincksieck, 1982.

Haas, Renate. "Chaucer's *Monk's Tale*: An Ingenious Criticism of Early Humanist Conceptions of Tragedy." *Humanistica Lovaniensia* 36 (1987): 44–70.

———. "Chaucers Tragödienkonzept im Europäischen Rahmen." In J. Fichte, ed., *Zusammenhänge*, pp. 451–65.

Hahn, Thomas. "Indians East and West: Primitivism and Savagery in English Discovery Narratives of the Sixteenth Century." *JMRS* 8 (1978): 77–114.

———. "The Indian Tradition in Western Medieval Intellectual History." *Viator* 9 (1978): 213–34.

Hall, John A., and G. John Ikenberry. *The State.* Minneapolis: University of Minnesota Press, 1989.

Halpern, Richard. *The Poetics of Primitive Accumulation: English Renaissance Culture and the Genealogy of Capital.* Ithaca: Cornell University Press, 1991.

Hamacher, Werner, Neil Hertz, and Thomas Keenan, eds. *Responses: On Paul de Man's Wartime Journalism.* Lincoln: University of Nebraska Press, 1989.

Hanawalt, Barbara A. *Crime and Conflict in English Communities, 1300–1348.* Cambridge, Mass.: Harvard University Press, 1979.

———. *Growing Up in Medieval London: The Experience of Childhood in the Middle Ages.* Oxford: Oxford University Press, 1993.

———. "Keepers of the Lights: Late Medieval English Parish Guilds." *JMRS* 14 (1984): 21–37.

———. *The Ties That Bound: Peasant Families in Medieval England.* Oxford: Oxford University Press, 1986.

———, ed. *Women and Work in Preindustrial Europe.* Bloomington: Indiana University Press, 1986.

———, and David Wallace, eds. *Bodies and Disciplines: Intersections of Literature and History in Fifteenth-Century England.* Minneapolis: University of Minnesota Press, 1996.

Hanna, Ralph, III. "Brewing Trouble: On Literature and History; and Alewives." In B. A. Hanawalt and David Wallace, eds., *Intersections*, pp. 1–17.

———. "Textual Notes to *The Canterbury Tales*." In *The Riverside Chaucer*, ed. L. Benson, pp. 1118–35.

Hansen, Elaine Tuttle. *Chaucer and the Fictions of Gender.* Berkeley: University of California Press, 1992.

Harding, Alan. "The Revolt Against the Justices." In R. H. Hilton and T. H. Aston, eds., *The English Rising of 1381*, pp. 165–93.

Harris, Elizabeth Kay. *The Case of Lancelot and Guinevere in Malory's "Morte Darthur": Proving Treason and Attainting Traitors in Fifteenth-Century England.* Ph.D. diss., University of Texas at Austin, 1993.

Harrison, Robert Pogue. *The Body of Beatrice.* Baltimore: Johns Hopkins University Press, 1988.

Harriss, G. L. "The King and His Magnates." In G. L. Harriss, ed., *Henry V: The Practice of Kingship*, pp. 31–51.

———, ed. *Henry V: The Practice of Kingship*. Oxford: Oxford University Press, 1985.

Harvey, John H. "Richard II and York." In F. R. H. Du Boulay and C. M. Barron, eds., *Reign of Richard II*, pp. 202–15.

———. "The Wilton Diptych—A Re-examination." In *Archaeologia* 98 (1961): 1–28.

Harwood, Britton J. "The 'Fraternitee' of Chaucer's Guildsmen." *Review of English Studies* n.s. 39 (1988): 413–17.

Hatton, Thomas J. "Chaucer's Crusading Knight, a Slanted Ideal." *CR* 3 (1968): 77–87.

Havely, Nicholas R. "Chaucer, Boccaccio, and the Friars." In P. Boitani, ed., *Trecento*, pp. 249–68.

———. "The Self-Consuming City: Florence as Body Politic." *Deutsches Dante-Jahrbuch* 61 (1986): 99–113.

Hay, Denys. *Renaissance Essays*. London: Hambledon Press, 1988.

Heffernan, Carol Falvo. "Tyranny and *Commune Profit* in the *Clerk's Tale*." *CR* 17 (1983): 332–40.

Heinzelman, Susan Sage, and Zipporah Batshaw Wiseman, eds. *Representing Women: Law, Literature, and Feminism*. Durham: Duke University Press, 1994.

Helgerson, Richard. *Forms of Nationhood: The Elizabethan Writing of England*. Chicago: University of Chicago Press, 1992.

Henderson, John S. "Confraternities and Politics in Fifteenth-Century Florence." *Collegium Medievale* 2 (1989): 53–72.

———. *Piety and Charity in Late Medieval Florence*. Oxford: Clarendon, 1994.

Henshall, Nicholas. *The Myth of Absolutism: Change and Continuity in Early Modern European Monarchy*. London: Longman, 1992.

Herlihy, David. *Medieval Households*. Cambridge: Harvard University Press, 1985.

Herman, Peter C. *Rethinking the Henrician Era: Essays on Early Tudor Texts and Contexts*. Urbana: University of Illinois Press, 1994.

Herzog, Reinhart, and Reinhart Koselleck, eds. *Epochenschwelle und Epochenbewusstsein*. Munich: Wilhelm Fink, 1987.

Hills, Paul. *The Light of Early Italian Painting*. New Haven: Yale University Press, 1987.

Hilton, Rodney H., and T. H. Aston, eds. *The English Rising of 1381*. Cambridge: Cambridge University Press, 1984.

Hinnebusch, W. A. *The History of the Dominican Order: Origins and Growth to 1500*. Vol. 1. Staten Island: Alba House, 1966.

Hoensch, Jörg K. *Geschichte Böhmens: Von der slavischen Landnahme bis ins 20. Jahrhundert*. Munich: C. H. Beck, 1987.

Holmes, George. *The Good Parliament*. Oxford: Clarendon, 1975.

Holt, Richard, and Gervase Rosser, eds. *The Medieval Town: A Reader in English Urban History 1200–1540*. London: Longman, 1990.

Hooke, Della, ed. *Medieval Villages: A Review of Current Work*. Oxford: Oxford University Committee for Archaeology, 1985.

Hornsby, Joseph Allen. *Chaucer and the Law*. Norman: Pilgrim Books, 1988.

Hoskins, W. G. *The Age of Plunder: King Henry's England 1500–1547*. London: Longman, 1976.

Hotson, Leslie J. "The Tale of Melibeus and John of Gaunt." *Studies in Philology* 18 (1921): 429–52.

Howard, Donald. *Chaucer: His Life, His Works, His World.* New York: Dutton, 1987.

Howard, Jean E. *The Stage and Social Struggle in Early Modern England.* London: Routledge, 1994.

Howell, Martha C. *Women, Production, and Patriarchy in Late Medieval Cities.* Chicago: University of Chicago Press, 1986.

————. "Women, the Family Economy, and the Structures of Market Production in Cities of Northern Europe during the Late Middle Ages." In B. A. Hanawalt, ed., *Women and Work in Preindustrial Europe,* pp. 198–222.

Hudson, Anne. *The Premature Reformation: Wycliffite Texts and Lollard History.* Oxford: Clarendon, 1988.

Irigaray, Luce. *Speculum of the Other Woman.* Trans. Gillian C. Gill. Ithaca: Cornell University Press, 1985.

Ives, Eric W. *Anne Boleyn.* Oxford: Basil Blackwell, 1986.

————. "The Common Lawyers." In C. H. Clough, ed., *Profession, Vocation and Culture,* pp. 181–217.

Jacob, E. F. *The Fifteenth Century, 1399–1485.* Oxford: Clarendon, 1961.

Jacobs, Michael. *Czechoslovakia.* Blue Guide. New York: Norton, 1992.

Jacoff, Rachel. *The Cambridge Companion to Dante.* Cambridge: Cambridge University Press, 1993.

Jameson, Fredric. *The Political Unconscious: Narrative as a Socially Symbolic Act.* Ithaca: Cornell University Press, 1983.

Jarratt, Susan C. *Rereading the Sophists: Classical Rhetoric Refigured.* Carbondale: Southern Illinois University Press, 1991.

Jewell, Helen. "*Piers Plowman*—A Poem of Crisis: An Analysis of Political Instability in Langland's England." In J. Taylor and W. Childs, eds., *Politics and Crisis,* pp. 59–80.

Johnson, Harold J., ed. *The Medieval Tradition of Natural Law.* Kalamazoo, Mich.: Medieval Institute Publications, 1987.

Johnston, Alexandra F. "English Guilds and Municipal Authority." In W. R. Bowen, ed., *Confraternities in the Renaissance,* pp. 69–88.

Jones, Evan J. *Medieval Heraldry: Tractatus de Armis by Johannes de Bado Aureo: An Enquiry into the Authorship of a Fourteenth-Century Treatise.* Cardiff: Privately printed by Western Mail & Echo Ltd., 1936.

Jones, P. J. "Communes and Despots: The City State in Late-Medieval Italy." *Transactions of the Royal Historical Society,* series 5, vol. 15 (1965): 71–96.

Jones, Richard H. *The Royal Policy of Richard II: Absolutism in the Later Middle Ages.* Oxford: Basil Blackwell, 1968.

Jones, Terry. *Chaucer's Knight: The Portrait of a Medieval Mercenary.* Baton Rouge: Louisiana State University Press, 1980.

Jones, William R. "English Religious Brotherhoods and Medieval Lay Piety: The Inquiry of 1388–89." *The Historian* 36 (1974): 646–59.

Justice, Steven. *Writing and Rebellion: England in 1381.* Berkeley: University of California Press, 1994.

Kaeuper, Richard W. *War, Justice, and Public Order: England and France in the Later Middle Ages.* Oxford: Clarendon, 1988.

Kahn, Victoria. *Rhetoric, Prudence, and Skepticism in the Renaissance*. Ithaca: Cornell University Press, 1985.

Kantorowicz, E. H. *The King's Two Bodies: A Study in Medieval Political Theology*. Princeton: Princeton University Press, 1957.

Kawai, Michio, ed. *Language and Style in English Literature: Essays in Honor of Michio Masui*. Tokyo: English Research Association of Hiroshima, 1991.

Kay, F. George. *Lady of the Sun: The Life and Times of Alice Perrers*. New York: Barnes and Noble, 1966.

Kay, Sarah, and Miri Rubi, eds. *Framing Medieval Bodies*. Manchester: Manchester University Press, 1994.

Kearney, Milo. *The Role of Swine Symbolism in Medieval Culture*. Lewiston, New York: Edwin Mellen Press, 1991.

Keen, M. H. *The Laws of War in the Middle Ages*. London: Routledge and Kegan Paul, 1965.

Kellogg, Alfred J., and Louis A. Haselmayer. "Chaucer's Satire of the Pardoner." *PMLA* 66 (1951): 251–77.

Kelly-Gadol, Joan. "Did Women Have a Renaissance?" In R. Bridenthal and C. Koonz, eds., *Becoming Visible*, pp. 137–64.

Kempton, Daniel. "Chaucer's Tale of Melibee: 'A Litel Thyng in Prose.'" *Genre* 21 (1988): 263–78.

Kerrigan, William, and Gordon Braden. *The Idea of the Renaissance*. Baltimore: Johns Hopkins University Press, 1989.

King, John N. "Henry VIII as David: The King's Image and Reformation Politics." In P. C. Herman, ed., *Rethinking the Henrician Era*, pp. 78–92.

King, Margaret L. "Book-Lined Cells: Women and Humanism in the Early Italian Renaissance." In A. Rabil, ed., *Renaissance Humanism*, vol. 2, pp. 434–53.

Kinneavy, James L. "*Kairos*: A Neglected Concept in Classical Rhetoric." In J. D. Moss, ed., *Rhetoric and Praxis*, pp. 79–105.

Kirkham, Victoria, ed. *Lecturae Boccaccii II*. Philadelphia: University of Pennsylvania Press, forthcoming.

Kirkpatrick, Robin. *Dante's "Inferno": Difficulty and Dead Poetry*. Cambridge: Cambridge University Press, 1987.

———. *English and Italian Literature from Dante to Shakespeare: A Study of Source, Analogue, and Divergence*. London: Longman, 1995.

———. "The Griselda Story in Boccaccio, Petrarch and Chaucer." In P. Boitani, ed., *Trecento*, pp. 231–48.

Kiser, Lisa J. *Truth and Textuality in Chaucer's Poetry*. Hanover: University Press of New England, 1991.

Kittredge, George Lyman. *The Date of Chaucer's "Troilus" and Other Chaucer Matters*. London: Chaucer Society, 1909.

Klapisch-Zuber, Christiane. *Women, Family, and Ritual in Renaissance Italy*. Trans. Lydia Cochrane. Chicago: University of Chicago Press, 1985.

———. "Women Servants in Florence During the Fourteenth and Fifteenth Centuries." In B. Hanawalt, ed., *Women and Work*, pp. 56–80.

Klassen, John. "Bohemia Moravia." In Strayer, ed., *Dictionary of the Middle Ages*, vol. 2, pp. 297–305.

Knapp, Peggy. *Chaucer and the Social Contest*. New York: Routledge, 1990.

Knowles, David. *The Religious Orders in England.* 3 vols. Cambridge: Cambridge University Press, 1948–59.

Kolve, V. A. *Chaucer and the Imagery of Narrative: The First Five Canterbury Tales.* Stanford: Stanford University Press, 1984.

———. "'Man in the Middle': Art and Religion in Chaucer's *Friar's Tale.*" *SAC* 12 (1990): 5–46.

Krejčí, Jaroslav. *Czechoslovakia at the Crossroads of European History.* London: Tauris, 1990.

Kristeller, P. O. *Studies in Renaissance Thought and Letters.* Rome: Edizioni di storia e letteratura, 1956.

Kristeva, Julia. *Strangers to Ourselves.* Trans. Leon S. Roudiez. New York: Columbia University Press, 1991.

Krofta, Kamil. "Bohemia in the Fourteenth Century." In J. B. Bury et al., eds., *Cambridge Medieval History,* vol. 7, pp. 155–82.

Kruger, Steven F. *Dreaming in the Middle Ages.* Cambridge: Cambridge University Press, 1992.

Kyrris, Costas P. *History of Cyprus.* Nicosia: Nicocles, 1985.

Lacan, Jacques. *Four Fundamental Concepts of Psycho-Analysis.* Ed. J.-A. Miller. Trans. Alan Sheridan. New York: Norton, 1978.

Laclau, Ernesto. "Metaphor and Social Antagonisms." In C. Newton and L. Grossberg, eds., *Marxism and the Interpretation of Culture,* pp. 249–57.

Lagarde, Georges de. *La naissance de l'esprit laïque au déclin du moyen âge.* 5 vols. Louvain: Editions E. Nauwelaerts, 1956–70.

Lansing, Carol. *The Florentine Magnates: Lineage and Faction in a Medieval Commune.* Princeton: Princeton University Press, 1991.

Larner, John. *Italy in the Age of Dante and Petrarch, 1216–1380.* London: Longman, 1980.

Lawler, Traugott. *The One and the Many in the Canterbury Tales.* Hamden: Archon Books, 1980.

Leff, Gordon. *The Dissolution of the Medieval Outlook: An Essay on Intellectual and Spiritual Change in the Fourteenth Century.* New York: Harper, 1976.

Le Goff, Jacques. *Time, Work, and Culture in the Middle Ages.* Trans. A. Goldhammer. Chicago: University of Chicago Press, 1980.

———. *Your Money or Your Life: Economy and Religion in the Middle Ages.* New York: Zone Books, 1988.

Leicester, Henry Marshall. *The Disenchanted Self: Representing the Subject in the Canterbury Tales.* Berkeley: University of California Press, 1990.

Lentricchia, Frank. *Criticism and Social Change.* Chicago: Chicago University Press, 1984.

Lerer, Seth. *Chaucer and His Readers: Imagining the Author in Late-Medieval England.* Princeton: Princeton University Press, 1993.

———. "'Now holde youre mouth': The Romance of Orality in the *Thopas-Melibee* Section of the *Canterbury Tales.*" In M. C. Amodio, ed., *Oral Poetics,* pp. 181–205.

Lewis, C. S. "What Chaucer Really Did to *Il Filostrato.*" *Essays and Studies by Members of the English Association* 17 (1932): 56–75.

Leyerle, John, and Anne Quick. *Chaucer: A Bibliographical Introduction.* Toronto: University of Toronto Press, 1986.

Lindahl, Charles. *Earnest Games: Folkloric Patterns in the Canterbury Tales*. Bloomington: Indiana University Press, 1987.

Little, Lester K. *Religious Poverty and the Profit Economy in Medieval Europe*. Ithaca: Cornell University Press, 1978.

Loach, Jennifer, and Robert Tittler, eds. *The Mid-Tudor Polity c. 1540–1560*. London: Macmillan, 1980.

Lochrie, Karma. *Margery Kempe and Translations of the Flesh*. Philadelphia: University of Pennsylvania Press, 1991.

Lomperis, Linda, and Sarah Stanbury, eds. *Feminist Approaches to the Body in Medieval Literature*. Philadelphia: University of Pennsylvania Press, 1993.

Lowes, John Livingston. "The Prologue to the *Legend of Good Women* Considered in Its Chronological Relations." *PMLA* 20 (1905): 749–864.

Lukács, Georg. *History and Class Consciousness: Studies in Marxist Dialectics*. Trans. Rodney Livingstone. London: Merlin Press, 1971.

Luscombe, D. E. "Introduction: The Formation of Political Thought in the West." In *CHMPT*, pp. 157–73.

———, and G. R. Evans. "The Twelfth-Century Renaissance." In *CHMPT*, pp. 306–38.

Lützow, Count. *Lectures on the Historians of Bohemia: Being the Ilchester Lectures for the Year 1904*. First published 1905. New York: Benjamin Blom, 1971.

Lyall, R. J. "Materials: The Paper Revolution." In J. Griffiths and D. Pearsall, eds., *Book Production*, pp. 11–29.

Lyotard, Jean-François. *The Postmodern Condition: A Report on Knowledge*. Trans. Geoff Bennington and Brian Massumi; foreword by Fredric Jameson. Minneapolis: University of Minnesota Press, 1989.

Maddicott, J. R. *Law and Lordship: Royal Justices as Retainers in Thirteenth- and Fourteenth-Century England*. Past and Present Supplement 4. Oxford: Past and Present Society, 1978.

Magoun, Francis F., Jr. *A Chaucer Gazetteer*. Chicago: University of Chicago Press, 1961.

Mainoni, Patrizia. "I mercanti milanesi in Europa." In A. A. Villa et al., eds., *Lombardia*, pp. 77–96.

Mallett, Michael. *Mercenaries and Their Masters*. London: Bodley Head, 1974.

Manly, J. M. *Some New Light on Chaucer: Lectures Delivered at the Lowell Institute*. New York: Henry Holt, 1926.

Mann, Jill. "Chance and Destiny in *Troilus and Criseyde* and the *Knight's Tale*." In P. Boitani and J. Mann, eds., *Chaucer Companion*, pp. 75–92.

———. *Chaucer and Medieval Estates Satire: The Literature of Social Classes and the General Prologue to the Canterbury Tales*. Cambridge: Cambridge University Press, 1973.

———. *Geoffrey Chaucer*. Feminist Readings series. Hemel Hempstead: Harvester Wheatsheaf, 1991.

Mann, Michael. *The Sources of Social Power, Volume 1: A History of Power From the Beginning to A.D. 1760*. Cambridge: Cambridge University Press, 1985.

Mann, Nicholas. "Petrarch and Humanism: The Paradox of Posterity." In A. S. Bernardo, ed., *Francesco Petrarca*, pp. 287–99.

Manning, Roger B. *Village Revolts: Social Protest and Popular Disturbances in England, 1509–1640*. Oxford: Clarendon, 1988.

Marcus, Leah S. *Puzzling Shakespeare: Local Reading and Its Discontents*. Berkeley: University of California Press, 1988.

———. "Renaissance / Early Modern Studies." In *Redrawing the Boundaries*, ed. S. Greenblatt and G. Gunn, pp. 41–63.

Markus, R. A. "The Latin Fathers." In *CHMPT*, pp. 92–122.

Martin, John E. *Feudalism to Capitalism: Peasant and Landlord in English Agrarian Development*. Basingstoke: Macmillan, 1983.

Martines, Lauro. *Power and Imagination: City States in Renaissance Italy*. Harmondsworth: Peregrine, 1983.

———. *The Social World of the Florentine Humanists*. Princeton: Princeton University Press, 1963.

———, ed. *Violence and Disorder in Italian Cities, 1220–1500*. Berkeley: University of California Press, 1972.

Matsuda, Takami. "Death, Prudence, and Chaucer's *Pardoner's Tale*." *JEGP* 91 (1992): 313–24.

Matthew, Gervase. *The Court of Richard II*. London: John Murray, 1968.

Mauri, Luisa Chiappa. "Aspetti del mondo rurale lombardo nel Trecento e nel Quattrocento." In A. A. Villa et al., eds., *La Lombardia*, pp. 101–16.

Mazzotta, Giuseppe. *The World at Play in Boccaccio's Decameron*. Princeton: Princeton University Press, 1986.

McAlpine, Monica, ed. *Chaucer's "Knight's Tale": An Annotated Bibliography, 1900 to 1985*. Toronto: University of Toronto Press, 1991.

McFarlane, K. B. "Bastard Feudalism." *BIHR* 20 (1943–45): 161–80.

———. *Lancastrian Kings and Lollard Knights*. Oxford: Clarendon, 1972.

McHardy, A. K. The *Church in London, 1375–1392*. London: London Record Society, 1977.

McKenna, Isobel. "The Making of a Fourteenth Century Sergeant of the Lawe." *Revue de l'Université d'Ottawa* 45 (1975): 244–62.

McKisack, May. *The Fourteenth Century, 1307–1399*. Oxford: Clarendon, 1959.

McRee, Ben R. "Religious Gilds and Regulation of Behavior in Late Medieval Towns." In J. Rosenthal and C. Richmond, eds., *People, Politics, and Community in the Later Middle Ages*, pp. 108–22.

Meale, Carol M., ed. *Women and Literature in Britain, 1150–1500*. Cambridge: Cambridge University Press, 1993.

Medin, Antonio. "I Visconti nella poesia contemporanea." *ASL*, series 2, vol. 8, anno 18 (1891): 733–95.

Mehling, Franz N., ed. *Italy*. Oxford: Phaidon, 1985.

Meiss, Millard. *French Painting in the Time of Jean de Berry: The Late Fourteenth Century and the Patronage of the Duke*. 2 vols: vol. 1, text; vol. 2, plates. London: Phaidon, 1967.

Michaud-Quantin, Pierre. *Universitas: Expressions du mouvement communautaire dans le moyen âge latin*. Paris: Librairie Philosophique J. Vrin, 1970.

Middle English Dictionary. Ed. Hans Kurath, Sherman M. Kuhn, John Reidy, and Robert E. Lewis. Ann Arbor: University of Michigan Press, 1952– .

Middleton, Anne. "Chaucer's 'New Men' and the Good of Literature." In E. Said., ed., *Literature and Society*, pp. 15–56.

———. "The Clerk and His Tale: Some Literary Contexts." *SAC* 2 (1980): 121–50.

———. "The Idea of Public Poetry in the Reign of Richard II." *Speculum* 53 (1978): 94–114.

———. "William Langland's 'Kynde Name': Authorial Signature and Social Identity in Late Fourteenth-Century England." In L. Patterson, ed., *Literary Practice*, pp. 15–82.

Minnis, A. J. *Chaucer and Pagan Antiquity*. Cambridge: D. S. Brewer, 1982.

———. *Medieval Discussions of the Role of Author*. Ph.D. diss., Queen's University, Belfast, 1976.

———. *Medieval Theory of Authorship: Scholastic Literary Attitudes in the Later Middle Ages*. 2d ed. Aldershot: Wildwood House, 1988.

Mitchell, R. J. *John Tiptoft, 1427–1470*. London: Longman, 1938.

Molho, Anthony, and John A. Tedeschi, eds. *Renaissance Studies in Honor of Hans Baron*. De Kalb: Northern Illinois University Press, 1971.

Mollat, Michel, and Philippe Wolff, eds. *The Popular Revolutions of the Later Middle Ages*. Trans. A. L. Lytton-Sells. London: George Allen and Unwin, 1973.

Mommertz, Paul. *Wannsee Conference*. Screenplay. Film directed by Heinz Schirk. U.S. distribution of English subtitled version by Films Incorporated. German, 85 min., 1987.

Mommsen, Theodor M. "Petrarch and the Decoration of the Sala Virorum Illustrium in Padua." *The Art Bulletin* 34 (1952): 95–116.

Montrose, Louis Adrian. "Shaping Fantasies: Figurations of Gender and Power in Elizabethan Culture." In S. Greenblatt, ed., *Representing the Renaissance*, pp. 31–64.

———. "The Work of Gender in the Discourse of Discovery." *Representations* 33 (Winter 1991): 1–41.

Moore, Samuel. "Chaucer's Pardoner of Rouncival." *Modern Philology* 25 (1927): 59–66.

Morse, Charlotte. "The Exemplary Griselde." *SAC* 7 (1985): 51–86.

Moss, Jean Dietz, ed. *Rhetoric and Praxis: The Contribution of Classical Rhetoric to Practical Reasoning*. Washington, D.C.: Catholic University of America Press, 1986.

Muir, Kenneth. *The Sources of Shakespeare's Plays*. London: Methuen, 1977.

Murphy, James J. *Rhetoric in the Middle Ages: A History of Rhetorical Theory from St. Augustine to the Renaissance*. Berkeley: University of California Press, 1974.

Muscatine, Charles. *Chaucer and the French Tradition*. Berkeley: University of California Press, 1957.

———. *Poetry and Crisis in the Age of Chaucer*. Notre Dame: University of Notre Dame Press, 1972.

Myers, A. R. "The Captivity of a Royal Witch: The Household Accounts of Queen Joan of Navarre, 1419–21." *BJRL* 24 (1940): 263–84.

Nelson, Janet. "Kingship and Empire." In *CHMPT*, pp. 211–51.

Nerlich, Michael. *Ideology of Adventure: Studies in Modern Consciousness, 1110–1750*. 2 vols. Minneapolis: University of Minnesota Press, 1987.

Neuse, Richard. *Chaucer's Dante: Allegory and Epic Theater in "The Canterbury Tales."* Berkeley: University of California Press, 1991.

New Catholic Encyclopedia. 17 vols. New York: McGraw-Hill, 1967–79.

Newton, C., and L. Grossberg, eds. *Marxism and the Interpretation of Culture.* Urbana: University of Illinois Press, 1988.

Nicholls, Jonathan W. *The Matter of Courtesy: Medieval Courtesy Books and the Gawain-Poet.* Cambridge: D. S. Brewer, 1985.

Nicholson, Peter. "The *Man of Law's Tale*: What Chaucer Really Owed to Gower." *CR* 26 (1991): 153–74.

Nolan, Barbara. *Chaucer and the Tradition of the "Roman Antique."* Cambridge: Cambridge University Press, 1992.

———. "Chaucer's Tales of Transcendence: Rhyme Royal and Christian Prayer in the *Canterbury Tales*." In C. D. Benson and E. Robertson, eds., *Chaucer's Religious Tales*, pp. 21–38.

Norman, Diana. "The Art of Knowledge: Two Artistic Schemes in Florence." In D. Norman, ed., *Siena, Florence, and Padua*, vol. 2, pp. 217–41.

———. "'Splendid Models and Examples from the Past'": Carrara Patronage of Art." In D. Norman, ed., *Siena, Florence, and Padua*, vol. 1, pp. 155–75.

———, ed. *Siena, Florence, and Padua: Art, Society, and Religion 1280–1400.* 2 vols. New Haven: Yale University Press, 1995.

North, J. D. *Chaucer's Universe.* Oxford: Clarendon, 1988.

Olson, Glending. "Geoffrey Chaucer." In D. Wallace, ed., *The Cambridge History of Medieval English Literature*, forthcoming.

———. *Literature as Recreation in the Later Middle Ages.* Ithaca: Cornell University Press, 1982.

Olson, Paul A. The *"Canterbury Tales" and the Good Society.* Princeton: Princeton University Press, 1986.

Origo, Iris. "The Domestic Enemy: The Eastern Slaves in Tuscany in the Fourteenth and Fifteenth Centuries." *Speculum* 30 (1955): 321–66.

———. *The Merchant of Prato: Francesco di Marco Datini, 1335–1410.* Boston: Nonpareil, 1986.

Ormrod, W. M. *The Reign of Edward III: Crown and Political Society in England 1327–1377.* New Haven: Yale University Press, 1990.

O'Toole, John. *The Process of Drama: Negotiating Art and Meaning.* London: Routledge, 1992.

The Oxford English Dictionary. Ed. Sir James A. H. Murray. 13 vols. Oxford: Clarendon, 1961.

Oxford Latin Dictionary. Ed. P. G. W. Glare. 2 vols. Oxford: Clarendon, 1968–82.

Packe, Michael, ed. *King Edward III.* London: Routledge and Kegan Paul, 1983.

Panzarasa, Maria Pia Andreolli. "Il Petrarca e Pavia viscontea." *ASL* series 9, anno 100 (1974): 42–65.

Pargellis, Stanley, ed. *The Quest for Political Unity in World History.* Washington: U.S. Government Printing Office, 1944.

Paris, Paulin. *Les Manuscrits françois de la Bibliothèque du roi, et celles des textes allemands, anglois, hollandois, italiens, espagnols de la même collection.* 7 vols. Paris: Techener, 1836.

Parker, Patricia. *Literary Fat Ladies: Rhetoric, Gender, Property*. London, Methuen, 1987.

Patterson, Lee. *Chaucer and the Subject of History*. Madison: University of Wisconsin Press, 1991.

———. "Court Politics and the Invention of Literature: The Case of Sir John Clanvowe." In D. Aers., ed., *Culture and History, 1350–1600*, pp. 7–41.

———. "'For the Wyves love of Bathe': Feminine Rhetoric and Poetic Resolution in the *Roman de la Rose* and the *Canterbury Tales*." *Speculum* 58 (1983): 656–95.

———. *Negotiating the Past*. Madison: University of Wisconsin Press, 1987.

———. "On the Margin: Postmodernism, Ironic History, and Medieval Studies." *Speculum* 65 (1990): 87–108.

———. "'What Man Artow?': Authorial Self-Definition in the *Tale of Sir Thopas* and the *Tale of Melibee*." *SAC* 13 (1991): 117–75.

———, ed. *Literary Practice and Social Change in Britain, 1380–1530*. Berkeley: University of California Press, 1990.

Pearsall, Derek A. *The Canterbury Tales*. London: George Allen and Unwin, 1985.

———. "Chaucer's Religious Tales: A Question of Genre." In C. D. Benson and E. Robertson, eds., *Chaucer's Religious Tales*, pp. 1–19.

———. "Hoccleve's *Regement of Princes*: The Poetics of Royal Self-Representation." *Speculum* 69 (1994): 386–410.

———. *John Lydgate*. London: Routledge and Kegan Paul, 1970.

———. *The Life of Geoffrey Chaucer: A Critical Biography*. Oxford: Blackwell, 1992.

———. *Old English and Middle English Poetry*. London: Routledge, 1977.

Pennington, Kenneth. "Law, Legislative Authority and Theories of Government, 1150–1300." In *CHMPT*, pp. 424–53.

Perroy, Édouard. *L'Angleterre et le Grand Schisme d'Occident*. Paris: Monnier, 1933.

Petit-Dutaillis, C. *Les communes françaises, caractère et évolution des origines au XVIIIe siècle*. Paris: Albin Michel, 1947.

Peyronnet, Georges. "François Sforza: De condottiere à Duc de Milan." In G. Peyronnet et al., eds., *Gli Sforza a Milano*, pp. 7–25.

——— et al., eds. *Gli Sforza a Milano e in Lombardia e i loro rapporti con gli stati italiani ed europei (1450–1535)*. Milan: Cisalpino-Goliardica, 1982.

Phillips, J. R. S. *The Medieval Expansion of Europe*. Oxford: Oxford University Press, 1988.

Phillips, William D., Jr. *Slavery from Roman Times to the Early Transatlantic Trade*. Minneapolis: University of Minnesota Press, 1985.

Phythian-Adams, Charles. *Desolation of a City: Coventry and the Urban Crisis of the Late Middle Ages*. Cambridge: Cambridge University Press, 1979.

Pirovano, Carlo, ed. *Lombardia: il territorio, l'ambiente, il paesaggio*. 5 vols. Milan: Electa, 1981–85.

Plucknett, Theodore. *A Concise History of the Common Law*. 5th ed. London: Butterworth, 1956.

Pocock, J. G. A. *The Machiavellian Moment: Florentine Political Thought and the Atlantic Republican Tradition*. Princeton: Princeton University Press, 1975.

Postan, M. M., and Edward Miller, eds., assisted by Cynthia Postan. *The Cambridge Economic History of Europe*, vol. 2. *Trade and Industry in the Middle Ages*. Cambridge: Cambridge University Press, 1987.

Potter, Joy Hambuechen. *Five Frames for the "Decameron": Communication and Social Systems in the "Cornice."* Princeton: Princeton University Press, 1982.

———. "Woman in the Decameron." In Gian-Paolo Biasin et al., eds., *Studies in the Italian Renaissance*, pp. 87–103.

Powell, James M. *Albertanus of Brescia: The Pursuit of Happiness in the Early Thirteenth Century*. Philadelphia: University of Pennsylvania Press, 1992.

Pratt, Robert A., "Chaucer and the Visconti Libraries." *ELH* 6 (1939): 191–99.

Prescott, Andrew. "London in the Peasants' Revolt: A Portrait Gallery." *London Journal* 7 (1981): 125–43.

Preston, Raymond. *Chaucer*. London: Sheed and Ward, 1952.

Proctor, Robert E. *Education's Great Amnesia*. Bloomington: University of Indiana Press, 1988.

Pullan, Brian. *Rich and Poor in Renaissance Venice. The Social Institutions of a Catholic State, to 1620*. Oxford: Basil Blackwell, 1971.

Pulling, Alexander. *The Order of the Coif*. London: William Clowes and Sons, 1884.

Quillet, Jeannine. "Community, Counsel and Representation." In *CHMPT*, pp. 520–72.

Quilligan, Maureen. *The Allegory of Female Authority: Christine de Pizan's "Cité des Dames."* Ithaca: Cornell University Press, 1991.

Rabil, Albert, Jr. "Humanism in Milan." In Rabil, ed., *Renaissance Humanism*, vol. 1, pp. 235–63.

———. "The Significance of Civic Humanism in the Interpretation of the Italian Renaissance." In Rabil, ed., *Renaissance Humanism*, vol. 1, pp. 141–74.

———, ed. *Renaissance Humanism: Foundations, Forms, and Legacy*. 3 vols. Philadelphia: University of Pennsylvania Press, 1988.

Ragionieri, Pina, ed. *Lorenzo Ghiberti nel suo tempo. Atti del Convegno Internazionale di Studi*. Istituto Nazionale di Studi sul Rinascimento. Florence: Olschki, 1980.

Razi, Zvi. *Life, Marriage, and Death in a Medieval Parish: Economy, Society, and Demography in Halesowen, 1270–1400*. Cambridge: Cambridge University Press, 1980.

Redhead, Brian, ed. *Political Thought from Plato to NATO*. London: Ariel, BBC, 1984.

Réville, André. *Le Soulèvement des travailleurs d'Angleterre en 1381*. Ecole des Chartres, Mémoires et Documents, 2. Paris: A. Picard, 1898.

Reynolds, Susan. *Fiefs and Vassals: The Medieval Evidence Reinterpreted*. Oxford: Oxford University Press, 1994.

———. *An Introduction to the History of English Medieval Towns*. Oxford: Clarendon, 1977.

Ricci, Pier Giorgio. "Studi sulle opere latine e volgari del Boccaccio." *Rinascimento* 10 (1959): 3–32.

Rico, Francisco. *Vida u Obra de Petrarca, 1, Lectura del "Secretum."* Padua: Antenore, 1974.

Riddy, Felicity. " 'Women Talking About the Things of God': A Late Medieval Sub-culture." In C. Meale, ed., *Women and Literature*, pp. 104–27.

Rigg, A. G. "Anthologies." In *Dictionary of the Middle Ages*, ed. J. Strayer, vol. 1, pp. 317–20.

———. "Medieval Latin Poetic Anthologies." *Mediaeval Studies* 39 (1977): 281–30; 40 (1978): 387–407; 41 (1979): 468–505; 43 (1981): 472–97.

Robertson, D. W. " 'And for My Land Thus Hastow Mordred Me?' Land Tenure, the Cloth Industry, and the Wife of Bath." *CR* 14 (1979–80): 403–20.

———. *Chaucer's London*. New York: John Wiley, 1968.

———. *A Preface to Chaucer: Studies in Medieval Perspectives*. Princeton: Princeton University Press, 1962.

Rodolico, N. *I Ciompi: Una pagina di storia del proletariato operaio*. Florence: Sansoni, 1971.

Rogers, Nicholas, ed. *England in the Fourteenth Century: Proceedings of the 1991 Harlaxton Symposium*. Stamford: Paul Watkins, 1993.

Romano, G. "Un matrimonio alla corte de' Visconti." *ASL* series 3, vol. 8 (1891): 601–28.

———. "Regesto degli atti notarili di C. Cristiani dal 1391 al 1399." *ASL* series 3, vol. 11 (1894): 5–86, 281–330.

Rondinini, Gigliola Soldi. "Visconti e Sforza nelle terre padane: origine e sviluppo di uno stato regionale." In A. A. Villa et al., eds., *La Lombardia*, pp. 7–26.

Roques, Mario. "Traductions françaises des traités moraux d'Albertano de Brescia." *Histoire littéraire de la France* 37 (1938): 488–506.

Rose, Mary Beth, ed. *Women in the Middle Ages and the Renaissance*. Syracuse: Syracuse University Press, 1986.

Rosenthal, Joel, and Colin Richmond, eds. *People, Politics, and Community in the Later Middle Ages*. Gloucester: Alan Sutton, 1987.

Rosser, Gervase. "Communities of Parish and Guild in the Late Middle Ages." In S. J. Wright, ed., *Parish, Church and People*, pp. 29–55.

Rubin, Miri. *Charity and Community in Medieval Cambridge*. Cambridge: Cambridge University Press, 1987.

Rubinstein, Nicolai. "The Beginnings of Political Thought in Florence: A Study in Mediaeval Historiography." *Journal of the Warburg and Courtauld Institutes* 5 (1942): 198–227.

———. "Florence and the Despots: Some Aspects of Florentine Diplomacy in the Fourteenth Century." *Transactions of the Royal Historical Society*, 5th series, vol. 2 (1952): 21–45.

———, ed. *Florentine Studies: Politics and Society in Renaissance Florence*. Evanston, Ill.: Northwestern University Press, 1968.

Runciman, Steven. *A History of the Crusades*. 3 vols. Cambridge: Cambridge University Press, 1951.

Ruskin, John. *Mornings in Florence: Being Simple Studies of Christian Art for English Travellers*. 6 pamphlets. Orpington: George Allen, 1875–77.

Russell, P. E. *English Intervention in Spain and Portugal in the Time of Edward III and Richard II*. Oxford: Clarendon, 1955.

Rybár, Ctibor. *Jewish Prague*. Prague: TV Spektrum, 1991.

Sabine, Ernest L. "City Cleaning in Mediaeval London." *Speculum* 12 (1937): 19–43.

Said, Edward. *The World, the Text, and the Critic*. Cambridge, Mass.: Harvard University Press, 1983.

———, ed. *Literature and Society*. Baltimore: Johns Hopkins University Press, 1980.

Sale, Kirkpatrick. *The Conquest of Paradise: Christopher Columbus and the Columbian Legacy*. New York: Knopf, 1990.

———. "How Paradise Was Lost: What Columbus Discovered." *The Nation* 251.13 (Oct. 22, 1990): 444–46.

Salmi, Mario. *La miniatura italiana*. Milan: Electa, no date.

Salter, Elizabeth. "Chaucer and Internationalism." *SAC* 2 (1980): 71–79.

Salusinszky, Imre. *Criticism in Society*. New York: Methuen, 1987.

Salvini, Roberto. "Il Cappellone degli Spagnoli." In U. Baldini, ed., *Santa Maria Novella*, pp. 88–125.

Sapegno, Natalino. *Il Trecento: Storia letteraria d'Italia*. Padua: Nuova Libraria Editrice, 1982.

Sapori, Armando. *The Italian Merchant in the Middle Ages*. Trans. Patricia Kennen. New York: Norton, 1970.

Sartre, Jean-Paul. *Being and Nothingness*. Trans. Hazel E. Barnes. New York: Washington Square Press, 1966.

Scaglione, Aldo D. *Nature and Love in the Middle Ages*. Berkeley: University of California Press, 1963.

Scanlon, Larry. "The King's Two Voices: Narrative and Power in Hoccleve's *Regiment of Princes*." In L. Patterson, ed., *Literary Practice and Social Change*, pp. 216–47.

———. *Narrative, Authority, and Power: The Medieval Exemplum and the Chaucerian Tradition*. Cambridge: Cambridge University Press, 1994.

Scarisbrick, J. J. *Henry VIII*. Berkeley: University of California Press, 1968.

———. *The Reformation and the English People*. Oxford: Basil Blackwell, 1984.

Scarry, Elaine. *The Body in Pain: The Making and Unmaking of the World*. Oxford: Oxford University Press, 1985.

Scattergood, V. J. "Chaucer and the French War: *Sir Thopas* and *Melibee*." In G. S. Burgess, ed., *Court and Poet*, pp. 287–96.

Scheps, Walter. "Chaucer's Theseus and the *Knight's Tale*." *Leeds Studies in English* n.s. 8 (1975): 19–34.

Schevill, Ferdinand. *History of Florence: From the Founding of the City Through the Renaissance*. First published 1936. New York: Ungar, 1961.

Schlauch, Margaret. "Chaucer's Doctrine of Kings and Tyrants." *Speculum* 20 (1945): 133–56.

Schless, Howard H. *Chaucer and Dante: A Reevaluation*. Norman: Pilgrim Books, 1984.

Schlucter, Wolfgang. *The Rise of Western Rationalism: Max Weber's Developmental History*. Trans. Guenther Roth. Berkeley: University of California Press, 1981.

Schnapp, Jeffrey, and Barbara Spackman, eds. *Fascism and Culture*. *Stanford Italian Review* 8, 1–2 (1988).

Schnith, Karl. "England." In F. Seibt, ed., *Kaiser Karl IV: Staatsmann und Mäzen*, pp. 161–64.

Schoenbaum, S. *William Shakespeare: A Compact Documentary Life*. Oxford: Oxford University Press, 1977.

Schwarz, Ernst. "Johann von Neumarkt." In K. Bosl, ed., *Lebensbilder*, pp. 27–47.

Sebregondi, Ludovica. "A Confraternity of Florentine Noble Women." *Confraternitas* 4.2 (Fall 1993): 3–6.

Sedgwick, Eve Kosofsky. *Between Men: English Literature and Male Homosocial Desire.* New York: Columbia University Press, 1985.

———. *Tendencies.* Durham, N.C.: Duke University Press, 1993.

Seibt, Ferdinand. *Karl IV: Ein Kaiser in Europa 1346–1378.* Munich: Süddeutscher Verlag, 1978.

———. "Kirche und Kultur im 14. Jahrhundert." In K. Bosl, ed., *Handbuch*, vol. 1, pp. 434–73.

———, ed. *Kaiser Karl IV: Staatsmann und Mäzen.* Munich: Prestel, 1987.

———, ed. *Karl IV und sein Kreis.* Vol. 3 of K. Bosl, gen. ed., *Lebensbilder zur Geschichte der Böhmischen Länder.* Munich: Oldenbourg, 1978.

Severs, J. Burke. *The Literary Relationships of Chaucer's "Clerk's Tale."* New Haven: Yale University Press, 1942.

Shannon, Edgar F. "Mediaeval Law in *The Tale of Gamelyn.*" *Speculum* 26 (1951): 458–64.

Shell, Marc. *Elizabeth's Glass: With "The Glass of the Sinful Soul" (1544) by Elizabeth I and "Epistle Dedicatory" and "Conclusion" by John Bale.* Lincoln: University of Nebraska Press, 1993.

Shohat, Ella, and Robert Stam, eds. *Unthinking Europeanism: Multiculturalism and the Media.* London: Routledge, 1994.

Simon, Eckehard, ed. *The Theatre of Medieval Europe: New Research in Early Drama.* Cambridge: Cambridge University Press, 1991.

Simone, Franco. "La présence de Boccace dans la culture français du XVe siècle." *IMRS* 1 (1971): 17–32.

Simpson, James. "'After Craftes Conseil Clotheth Yow and Fede': Langland and London City Politics." In *England in the Fourteenth Century*, ed. N. Rogers, pp. 109–27.

Skinner, Quentin. "Ambrogio Lorenzetti: The Artist as Political Philosopher." *Proceedings of the British Academy* 72 (1986): 1–56.

———. *The Foundations of Modern Political Thought.* Vol. 1. *The Renaissance.* Cambridge: Cambridge University Press, 1978.

Smart, Alastair. *The Dawn of Italian Painting, 1250–1400.* Ithaca: Cornell University Press, 1978.

Smith, Alan G. R. *The Emergence of a Nation State: The Commonwealth of England, 1529–1660.* London: Longman, 1984.

Snížková, Jitka. "Les traces de Guillaume de Machaut dans les sources musicales de Prague." In *Guillaume de Machaut*, organized by l'Université de Reims, pp. 69–74.

Southern, R. W. *Western Society and the Church in the Middle Ages.* Harmondsworth: Penguin, 1970.

Spackman, Barbara. "The Fascist Rhetoric of Virility." In *Fascism and Culture*, ed. J. Schnapp and B. Spackman, pp. 81–101.

Spearing, A. C. *The Medieval Poet as Voyeur: Looking and Listening in Medieval Love-Narratives.* Cambridge: Cambridge University Press, 1993.

———. *Medieval to Renaissance in English Poetry.* Cambridge: Cambridge University Press, 1986.

Spěváček, Jiří. Trans. Alfred Dressler. *Karl IV: Sein Leben und seine Staatsmännische Leistung.* Prague: Academia, 1978.

Spiegel, Gabrielle M. "History, Historicism, and the Social Logic of the Text in the Middle Ages." *Speculum* 65 (1990): 59–86.

Spruyt, Hendrik. *The Sovereign State and Its Competitors*. Princeton: Princeton University Press, 1994.

Spurgeon, Caroline F. E. *Five Hundred Years of Chaucer Criticism and Allusion, 1357–1900*. 3 vols. Cambridge: Cambridge University Press, 1925.

Staines, David. "The English Mystery Cycles." In E. Simon, ed., *Theatre of Medieval Europe*, pp. 80–96.

Stanbury, Sarah. "Feminist Masterplots: The Gaze on the Body of *Pearl*'s Dead Girl." In L. Lomperis and S. Stanbury, eds., *Feminist Approaches*, pp. 96–115.

Starn, Randolf. "Florentine Renaissance Studies." *Bibliothèque d'humanisme et Renaissance* 32 (1970): 677–84.

———. "Historians and 'Crisis.' " *Past and Present* 52 (Aug. 1971): 3–22.

Steel, Antony. *Richard II*. Cambridge: Cambridge University Press, 1962.

Stillinger, Thomas C. *The Song of Troilus: Lyric Authority in the Medieval Book*. Philadelphia: University of Pennsylvania Press, 1992.

Stone, Lawrence. *The Family, Sex, and Marriage in England, 1500–1800*. New York: Harper and Row, 1977.

Storia di Milano. Directed by Sen. Conte Dr. Giovanni Treccani degli Alfieri. 17 vols. Milan: Fondazione degli Alfieri, 1953–66.

Strickland, Agnes (and Elizabeth). *Lives of the Queens of England: A New Edition, Revised and Greatly Augmented with Portraits of Every Queen*. 8 vols. London: Colburn, 1852. Facsimile in 8 vols. Introduction by Antonia Fraser. Bath: Cedric Chivers, 1972.

Strohm, Paul. *Hochon's Arrow: The Social Imagination of Fourteenth-Century Texts*. Princeton: Princeton University Press, 1992.

———. " 'Lad with Revel to Newegate': Chaucerian Narrative and Historical Meta-Narrative." In R. R. Edwards, ed., *Art and Context*, pp. 163–76.

———. "Politics and Poetics: Usk and Chaucer in the 1380s." In *Literary Practice*, ed. L. Patterson, pp. 83–112.

———. "The Social and Literary Scene in England." In P. Boitani and J. Mann, eds., *Chaucer Companion*, pp. 1–18.

———. *Social Chaucer*. Cambridge, Mass.: Harvard University Press, 1989.

———, and Thomas J. Heffernan, eds. *Reconstructing Chaucer*. SAC, Proceedings no. 1, 1984. Knoxville: New Chaucer Society, 1985.

Stuard, Susan Mosher. "To Town to Serve: Urban Domestic Slavery in Medieval Ragusa." In B. Hanawalt, ed., *Women and Work*, pp. 39–55.

Sullivan, Margaret A. *Bruegel's Peasants: Art and Audience in the Northern Renaissance*. Cambridge: Cambridge University Press, 1994.

Sundby, Thor. *Della vita e delle opere di Brunetto Latini*. Trans. Rodolfo Renier. Florence: Le Monnier, 1884.

Sutherland, Donald. "Legal Reasoning in the Fourteenth Century: The Invention of 'Color' in Pleading." In M. S. Arnold, ed., *On the Laws and Customs of England*, pp. 182–94.

Swanson, Heather. "The Illusion of Economic Structure: Craft Guilds in Late Medieval English Towns." *Past and Present* 121 (November 1988): 29–48.

Szittya, Penn R. *The Antifraternal Tradition in Medieval Literature*. Princeton: Princeton University Press, 1986.

Taylor, Gary. "The Fortunes of Oldcastle." *Shakespeare Survey* 38 (1985): 85–100.

Taylor, John. *English Historical Literature in the Fourteenth Century*. Oxford: Clarendon, 1987.

———, and Wendy Childs, eds. *Politics and Crisis in Fourteenth-Century England*. Gloucester: Alan Sutton, 1990.

Taylor, Karla. *Chaucer Reads "The Divine Comedy."* Stanford: Stanford University Press, 1989.

Tedeschi, John A., and Andrew W. Lewis. "Bibliography of the Writings of Hans Baron 1924–1969." In A. Molho and J. A. Tedeschi, eds., *Renaissance Studies*, pp. lxxi–lxxxviii.

Tenenti, Alberto. "Etudes anglo-saxonnes sur la renaissance florentine." *Annales* 25 (1970): 1394–99.

Thomas, Alfred. *The Czech Chivalric Romances "Vévoda Arnošt" and "Lavryn" in Their Literary Context*. Göppinger Arbeiten zur Germanistik, no. 504. Göppingen: Kümmerle, 1989.

Thompson, E. P. *The Making of the English Working Class*. Revised, with new preface. Harmondsworth: Penguin, 1980.

Thomson, John A. F. *The Transformations of Medieval England, 1370–1529*. London: Longman, 1983.

Thomson, S. Harrison. "Learning at the Court of Charles IV." *Speculum* 25 (1950): 1–20.

Thorne, S. E. "The Early History of the Inns of Court with Special Reference to Gray's Inn." *Graya* 1 (1959): 79–96.

———. *Essays in Legal History*. London: Hambledon Press, 1985.

Thrupp, Sylvia. *The Merchant Class of Medieval London, 1300–1500*. Chicago: University of Chicago Press, 1948.

Tittler, Robert. "The Emergence of Urban Policy, 1536–58." In J. Loach and R. Tittler, eds., *The Mid-Tudor Policy*, pp. 74–93.

Todorov, Tzvetan. *The Conquest of America*. Trans. Richard Howard. New York: Harper and Row, 1985.

———. *Theories of the Symbol*. Trans. Catherine Porter. Ithaca: Cornell University Press, 1982.

Toesca, Pietro. *La pittura e la miniatura nella Lombardia*. Turin: Einaudi, 1966.

Tout, T. F. *Chapters in the Administrative History of Mediaeval England*. 6 vols. Manchester: Manchester University Press, 1920–33.

Trasselli, C. Sicilia. *Levante e Tunisia nei secoli XIV e XV*. Trapani, 1952.

Trease, Geoffrey. *The Condottieri: Soldiers of Fortune*. New York: Holt, Rinehart and Winston, 1971.

Treccani degli Alfieri. See *Storia di Milano*.

Trevor-Roper, Hugh. "Jacob Burckhardt." Master-mind Lecture. *Proceedings of the British Academy* 70 (1984): 359–78.

Trexler, Richard C. *Public Life in Renaissance Florence*. New York: Academic Press, 1980.

———. *The Spiritual Power: Republican Florence under Interdict*. Leiden: E. J. Brill, 1974.

Trimpi, Wesley. *Muses of One Mind*. Princeton: Princeton University Press, 1983.

Trinh, T. Minh-ha. *Woman, Native, Other: Writing Postcoloniality and Feminism*. Bloomington: Indiana University Press, 1989.

Trinkhaus, Charles. *The Scope of Renaissance Humanism*. Ann Arbor: University of Michigan Press, 1983.

Tuck, Anthony. *Crown and Nobility, 1272–1461*. Oxford: Basil Blackwell, 1986.

———. *Richard II and the English Nobility*. London: Edward Arnold, 1973.

Tuck, J. A. "The Cambridge Parliament of 1388." *English Historical Review* 84 (1969): 225–43.

Turchini. "La Lombardia centro artistico internazionale." In A. A. Villa et al., eds., *La Lombardia*, pp. 117–43.

Turner, Victor W., and Edith Turner. *Image and Pilgrimage in Christian Culture: Anthropological Perspectives*. Oxford: Basil Blackwell, 1978.

Tuve, Rosamund. *Allegorical Imagery: Some Mediaeval Books and Their Posterity*. Princeton: Princeton University Press, 1966.

Tyrwhitt, Thomas. *Observations and Conjectures upon some Passages of Shakespeare*. Oxford: Clarendon, 1766.

Ullmann, Berthold L. *The Humanism of Coluccio Salutati*. Padua: Editrice Antenore, 1963.

Ullmann, Walter. *Law and Politics in the Middle Ages: An Introduction to the Sources of Medieval Political Ideas*. Ithaca: Cornell University Press, 1975.

Vachulka, M. Ladislav. "Guillaume de Machaut et la vie musicale de Prague." In *Guillaume de Machaut*, organized by l'Université de Reims, pp. 321–27.

Valentiner, W. R. "Notes on Giovanni Balducci and Trecento Sculpture in Northern Italy." *The Art Quarterly* 10 (1947): 40–60.

Van Caenegem, R. C. "Government, Law and Society." In *CHMPT*, pp. 174–210.

Vance, Eugene. *Mervelous Signals: Poetics and Sign Theory in the Middle Ages*. Lincoln: University of Nebraska Press, 1986.

Van D'Elden, Karl H. "The Development of the Insurance Concept and Insurance Law in the Middle Ages." In H. J. Johnson, ed., *Medieval Tradition of Natural Law*, pp. 191–99.

Van Marle, Raimond. *The Development of the Italian Schools of Painting*. 19 vols. The Hague: Martinus Nijhoff, 1923–38.

Vattasso, Marco. *Del Petrarca e alcuni suoi amici*. Studi e Testi 14. Rome: Tipografia Vaticana, 1904.

Verga, Ettore. *Storia della vita milanese*. 2d ed. Milan: Nicola Moneta, 1931.

Vickers, Nancy J. "Diana Described: Scattered Woman and Scattered Rhyme." In E. Abel, ed., *Writing and Sexual Difference*, pp. 95–109.

Vilímková, Milada. *Die Prager Judenstadt*. Trans. from the Czech by Helena Tomanová-Weisová. Brno: Aventinum, 1990.

Villa, Anna Antoniazzi. "Dinamismo economico dello stato visconteo-sforzesco: Aspetti del ruolo commerciale-finanziario e culturale della communità ebraica." In A. A. Villa et al., eds., *La Lombardia*, pp. 31–38.

———, et al., eds. *La Lombardia delle Signorie*. Milan: Electa, 1986.

Villa, Claudia. "La tradizione delle 'Ad Lucilium' e la cultura di Brescia dall' età carolingia ad Albertano." *Italia medioevale e umanistica* 12 (1969): 9–51.

Viviano, Bruno. "Ospedali e organizzazione della beneficenza a Milano dal 1277 al 1535." In A. A. Villa et al., eds., *La Lombardia*, pp. 57–76.

Völger, Gisela, and Karin V. Welck, eds. *Männerbande—Männerbünde: Zur Rolle des Mannes im Kulturvergleich*. 2 vols. Cologne: Ethnologica, 1990.

Všetčka, Jiří (photography), and Jiří Kuděla. *Osudy židovské Prahy (The Fate of Jewish Prague)*. Prague: Grafoprint-Neubert, 1993.

Wack, Mary F. *Lovesickness in the Middle Ages: The "Viaticum" and Its Commentaries*. Philadelphia: University of Pennsylvania Press, 1990.

Waley, Daniel. *The Italian City-Republics*. 2d ed. London: Longman, 1978.

Walker, David M. *The Oxford Companion to Law*. Oxford: Clarendon, 1980.

Wallace, David. *Giovanni Boccaccio: Decameron*. Cambridge: Cambridge University Press, 1991.

———. "Carving Up Time and the World: Medieval-Renaissance Turf Wars; Historiography and Personal History." Center for Twentieth-Century Studies, University of Wisconsin, Milwaukee, working paper no. 11 (1990–91).

———. "Chaucer and Boccaccio's Early Writings." In P. Boitani, ed. *Trecento*, pp. 141–62.

———. *Chaucer and the Early Writings of Boccaccio*. Cambridge: D. S. Brewer, 1985.

———. "Chaucer and the European *Rose*." In P. Strohm and T. J. Heffernan, eds., *SAC*, Proceedings no. 1, pp. 61–67.

———. "Chaucer's Body Politic: Social and Narrative Self-Regulation." *Exemplaria* 2.1 (1990): 221–40.

———. "Chaucer's Continental Inheritance: The Early Poems and *Troilus and Criseyde*." In P. Boitani and J. Mann, eds., *Chaucer Companion*, pp. 19–37.

———. "Dante in English." In R. Jacoff, ed., *Cambridge Companion to Dante*, pp. 237–58.

———. "*Decameron* 2.3." In V. Kirkham, ed., *Lecturae Boccaccii II* (forthcoming).

———. "Mystics and Followers in Siena and East Anglia." In *The Medieval Mystical Tradition in England: Dartington, 1984*. Cambridge: D. S. Brewer, 1984, pp. 169–91.

———. "Pilgrim Signs and the Ellesmere Chaucer." *The Chaucer Newsletter* 11.2 (Fall 1989): 1–3.

———. Review of *CHMPT*. *SAC* 11 (1989): 194–202.

———, ed. *Beatrice Dolce Memoria, 1290–1990: Essays on the "Vita Nuova" and the Beatrice-Dante Relationship*. Special issue of *Texas Studies in Literature and Language* 32 (Spring 1990).

———, ed. *The Cambridge History of Medieval English Literature: Writing in Britain, 1066–1547*. Cambridge: Cambridge University Press, forthcoming.

Wallace, W. A., and J. A. Weisheipl. "Thomas Aquinas, St." In *New Catholic Encyclopedia*, vol. 14, pp. 102–15.

Warnicke, Retha M. *The Rise and Fall of Anne Boleyn: Family Politics at the Court of Henry VIII*. Cambridge: Cambridge University Press, 1989.

Warren, Edward H. "Serjeants-at-Law: The Order of the Coif." *Virginia Law Review* 28 (1942): 911–50.

Waters, Lindsay, and Wlad Godzich, eds. *Reading de Man Reading*. Minneapolis: University of Minnesota Press, 1989.

Webster's Ninth New Collegiate Dictionary. Springfield: Meriam-Webster, 1984.

Weinstein, Donald. "The Myth of Florence." In N. Rubenstein, ed., *Florentine Studies*, pp. 15–44.

Weiss, Roberto. *The Dawn of Humanism in Italy.* London: H. K. Lewis, 1947.

———. *Humanism in England During the Fifteenth Century.* Oxford: Blackwell, 1967.

———. *The Spread of Italian Humanism.* London: Hutchinson, 1964.

Wells, Stanley. *Shakespeare: A Dramatic Life.* London: Sinclair-Stevenson, 1994.

Werunsky, Emil. *Der Erste Römerzug Kaiser Karl IV (1354–1355).* Innsbruck: Wagner'sche Universitäts-Buchhandlung, 1878.

Wetherbee, Winthrop. "The Context of the *Monk's Tale.*" In M. Kawai, ed., *Language and Style in English Literature*, pp. 159–77.

———. *Platonism and Poetry in the Twelfth Century.* Princeton: Princeton University Press, 1972.

Whigham, Frank. *Ambition and Privilege: The Social Tropes of Elizabethan Courtesy Theory.* Berkeley: University of California Press, 1984.

White, Eileen. *The St. Christopher and St. George Guild of York.* Borthwick Papers, no. 72. York: Borthwick Institute, 1987.

White, John. *Art and Architecture in Italy, 1250–1400.* 2d ed. Harmondsworth: Penguin, 1987.

Whiting, Bartlett Jere. *Chaucer's Use of Proverbs.* Harvard Studies in Comparative Literature, vol. 11. Cambridge: Harvard University Press, 1934.

Wiesner, Merry E. "Women's Defence of Their Public Role." In M. B. Rose, ed., *Women in the Middle Ages and the Renaissance*, pp. 1–27.

———. *Working Women in Renaissance Germany.* New Brunswick: Rutgers University Press, 1986.

Wilkins, E. H. "Cantus Troili." *ELH* 16 (1949): 167–73.

———. *Petrarch's Eight Years in Milan.* Cambridge, Mass.: Medieval Academy of America, 1958.

———. *Petrarch's Later Years.* Cambridge, Mass.: Medieval Academy of America, 1959.

Wilks, Michael. "Chaucer and the Mystical Marriage in Medieval Political Thought." *BJRL* 44 (1962): 489–530.

———. *The Problem of Sovereignty in the Later Middle Ages: The Papal Monarchy with Augustinus Triumphus and the Publicists.* Cambridge: Cambridge University Press, 1963.

Williams, John Bryan. *From the Commercial Revolution to the Slave Revolution: The Development of Slavery in Medieval Genoa.* 2 vols. Ph.D. diss., University of Chicago, 1995.

Williams, Raymond. *The Country and the City.* St. Albans: Paladin, 1975.

———. *Keywords: A Vocabulary of Culture and Society.* Rev. ed. London: Fontana, 1983.

Wilson, Blake. "Music and Merchants: The *Laudesi* Companies in Early Renaissance Florence." In W. R. Bowen, ed., *Confraternities*, pp. 151–71.

Wimsatt, James I. "The Blessed Virgin and the Two Coronations of Griselde." *Mediaevalia* 6 (1980): 187–207.

———. "Chaucer and French Poetry." In D. Brewer, ed., *Writers and Their Background*, pp. 109–36.

———. *Chaucer and His French Contemporaries: Natural Music in the Fourteenth Century*. Toronto: University of Toronto Press, 1991.

———. *The Marguerite Poetry of Guillaume de Machaut*. Chapel Hill: University of North Carolina Press, 1970.

Witt, Ronald G. *Hercules at the Crossroads: The Life, Works, and Thought of Coluccio Salutati*. Durham, N.C.: Duke University Press, 1983.

Wittig, Susan. *Stylistic and Narrative Structures in the Middle English Romance*. Austin: University of Texas Press, 1978.

Womack, Peter. "Imagining Communities: Theatres and the English Nation in the Sixteenth Century." In D. Aers, ed., *Culture and History*, pp. 91–145.

Wood, Ellen Meiksins, and Neal Wood. *Class Ideology and Ancient Political Theory: Socrates, Plato, and Aristotle in Social Context*. Oxford: Basil Blackwell, 1978.

Wright, Herbert G. *Boccaccio in England from Chaucer to Tennyson*. London: Athlone Press, 1957.

Wright, Laura. "*OED*'s Tabard, 4.(?)." *Notes and Queries* 237 (1992): 155–57.

Wright, S. J., ed. *Parish, Church and People: Local Studies in Lay Religion, 1350–1750*. London: Hutchinson, 1988.

Žižek, Slavoj. *The Sublime Object of Ideology*. London: Verso, 1989.

Index

In this index "f" after a number indicates a separate reference on the next page, and "ff" indicates separate references on the next two pages. A continuous discussion over two or more pages is indicated by a span of page numbers. *Passim* is used for a cluster of references in close but not consecutive sequence. Subentries, other than lists, are arranged in order of ascending page number.

Library of Congress Cataloging-in-Publication Data

Wallace, David
  Chaucerian polity : absolutist lineages and associational forms in
England and Italy / David Wallace.
      p.   cm. — (Figurae)
  Includes bibliographical references (p.   ) and index.
  ISBN 0-8047-2724-4 (cloth : alk. paper)
    1. Chaucer, Geoffrey, d. 1400—Political and social views.
2. Political poetry, English—History and criticism.   3. Chaucer,
Geoffrey, d. 1400. Canterbury tales.   4. Chaucer, Geoffrey, d.
1400—Knowledge—Italy.   5. Politics and literature—England—
History.   6. Civilization, Medieval, in literature.   7. English
poetry—Italian influences.   8. Constitutional history, Medieval.
9. Despotism in literature.   10. Italy—In literature.   I. Title.
II. Series: Figurae (Stanford, Calif.)
PR1933.P64W35   1997
821'.1—dc20   96-21911
                                                                      CIP

Original printing 1996
Last figure below indicates year of this printing:
05   04   03   02   01   00   99   98   97   96